Distributed COM
Application Development
Using Visual Basic 6.0

ISBN 0-13-021343-8

90000

9 780130 213433

PRENTICE HALL SERIES ON MICROSOFT TECHNOLOGIES

JIM MALONEY

Distributed COM
Application Development
Using Visual Basic 6.0

A UCI Series Book

Prentice Hall PTR
Upper Saddle River, NJ 07458
www.phptr.com

Library of Congress Cataloging-in-Publication Data

Maloney, Jim, 1957-
   Distributed COM application development using Visual Basic 6 / by Jim Maloney.
      p. cm.
  ISBN 0-13-021343-8
  1. DCOM (Computer architecture)   2. Electronic data processing—Distributed processing.
  3. Application software—Development.   4. Microsoft Visual BASIC. I. Title.
  QA76.9.D5 M35 1999
  004'.36–dc21   99-24599
                                           CIP

Editorial/Production Supervision: *Kathleen M. Caren*
Acquisitions Editor: *Michael Meehan*
Marketing Manager: *Brian Gambrel*
Manufacturing Manager: *Pat Brown*
Cover Design: *Scott Weiss*
Cover Design Direction: *Jerry Votta*
Series Design: *Gail Cocker-Bogusz*

Prentice Hall books are widely used by corporations and government agencies for training, marketing, and resale.

The publisher offers discounts on this book when ordered in bulk quantities. For more information, contact Corporate Sales Department, Phone: 800-382-3419; fax: 201-236-7141; email: corpsales@prenhall.com
Or write Corporate Sales Department, Prentice Hall PTR, One Lake Street, Upper Saddle River, NJ 07458.

Product and company names mentioned herein are the trademarks or registered trademarks of their respective owners.

Printed in the United States of America

10 9 8 7 6 5 4 3 2 1

ISBN 0-13-021343-8

Prentice-Hall International (UK) Limited, *London*
Prentice-Hall of Australia Pty. Limited, *Sydney*
Prentice-Hall Canada Inc., *Toronto*
Prentice-Hall Hispanoamericana, S.A., *Mexico*
Prentice-Hall of India Private Limited, *New Delhi*
Prentice-Hall of Japan, Inc., *Tokyo*
Prentice-Hall (Singapore) Pte. Ltd., *Singapore*
Editora Prentice-Hall do Brasil, Ltda., *Rio de Janeiro*

For Patty

CONTENTS

PREFACE

The day C. J. "Buck" Trayser of Digital Equipment Corporation suggested that I become certified to teach Microsoft's Visual Basic course was a major turning point in my career. The last time I had used the BASIC programming language was when I was working on an extra-credit project while pursuing a degree in Computer Science in 1976. The program was to run on a DEC PDP-8 and had to be saved on paper tape. I was trying to write a program that played backgammon, but ran out of memory after creating routines to make an opening move from an openings book and drawing the board on a character cell terminal. Now, nearly fifteen years later, I had considered myself a seasoned C and C++ programmer, and was on a contract assigned to teach VMS programmers how to call System Services using the C programming language. If Buck had not been such a good friend and respected colleague, I may have laughed at his suggestion. But he convinced me that becoming certified to teach Visual Basic 3.0 would be a good business decision – the demand for such training was skyrocketing.

I have since taken quite a liking to Visual Basic, and have used the language in developing corporate applications for many of my customers, often combining it with Visual C++. Its appeal stems from its many interesting attributes. For one, Visual Basic is amazingly easy to use, and is probably responsible for making many new programmers out of folks who were once "just" users. It is quite non-intimidating to approach, yet can end up challenging the most experienced programmer due to its rich feature content. It reminds me of what is printed on the box of *MasterMind*, a game in which one attempts to guess a color code created by an opponent – *"A minute to learn, a lifetime to master."*

I thought of Buck again when Andrew Scoppa suggested that I write a book on developing distributed applications with Visual Basic. My affiliation with Andrew's company, UCI Software Training Centers, goes back over 16 years, and my respect for him is immense. As a quality provider of developer training, I take any suggestions Andrew makes quite seriously. Of course, at the time Buck suggested I look into Visual Basic, its features were not quite rich enough to develop distributed applications. But that has changed.

The Evolution of Visual Basic

As a language for developing Windows dialog-based user interfaces, Visual Basic is in its original element. As a teaching language, Visual Basic is ideal for illustrating not only Windows user interface programming concepts, but topics related to modular software development, code reuse, data scope, and even object-oriented design and programming techniques. For testing COM objects developed in C++ and ATL, Visual Basic offers the quickest solution.

The popularity of Visual Basic is no doubt responsible for its evolution from a graphical user interface development tool to an advanced, high-performance application development environment. Its ease of use, data access capabilities, multi-threading conformance, COM compliance, and native code generation capabilities now make it an excellent choice for the rapid development of the server-hosted business components of a distributed application. Having taught Visual Basic to developers for a number of years, I am beginning to see the language finally receive the respect it deserves. With over 20 years of software development experience and a degree in Computer Science, I feel qualified to author a book that treats Visual Basic with the same kind of respect.

About This Book

This is a book for serious developers of distributed applications. While it is, strictly speaking, an intermediate-level book, I expect the reader to be an experienced programmer. The main theme of this book is to get you started with the development of distributed applications using Visual Basic in the quickest way possible. I have provided complete examples of both 2-tier and 3-tier applications – these applications have thousands of lines of Visual Basic code. Complementing these complete applications are dozens of small demos that illustrate one or two important concepts. While instructions for running these demos are included in the chapters that follow, you should check the *README.TXT* file on the enclosed CD-ROM for additional and last-minute information regarding the use of the demos.

Probably the most unusual thing about this book is that I start with a chapter on *deploying* multi-tiered distributed applications. This approach has worked well in the classroom when I teach my courseware, and I expect the same results in this book. Since many of the demos used in later chapters depend on the sample applications being installed, it is essential that you read the first chapter and go through the installation procedures.

In Chapter 2, I discuss how to use objects from a Visual Basic application, using the sample video store objects provided with this book. Even if you are familiar with using COM objects in a Visual Basic application, you should read this chapter. The chapter may seem like a "show-and-tell" for an existing application, but it provides good examples of object design and documentation.

In Chapter 3, I cover how to develop Win32 user interface applications that use COM objects. In addition to providing more examples of object use, the chapter is an excuse for me to introduce some advanced user interface techniques. In this chapter, you will learn how to use the Windows registry, display a splash screen, use OLE drag-and-drop, and use advanced user interface controls such as the tree view, list view, tab strip, and toolbar controls. My advanced Visual Basic students often ask to see how to use these controls and techniques in their programs.

I consider Chapter 4 to be the "paying your dues" chapter. In earlier days, programmers had to use APIs such as the TCP/IP socket *API* to develop distributed applications. The Windows platform SDKs and developer tools such as Visual Basic have made the creation of distributed applications much easier. If you are pressed for time, you can skip Chapter 4.

As an essential and fundamental introduction to developing the middle tiers of a distributed application, Chapter 5 is required reading. This chapter introduces ActiveX Data Objects (ADO), showing both their programmatic use and their use through the new ADO Data Control. Additionally, the chapter explains *Data Environments* and how to create programs that generate reports from a database.

Chapters 6, 7, and 8 are all about objects. First, I cover the use of class modules in Visual Basic, then move to their use in creating ActiveX Components. Finally, the internals of COM, the Component Object Model, are revealed in more detail than the typical Visual Basic developer would probably want – but more is better than less! If you are familiar with using class modules in Visual Basic, you can skip Chapter 6, but since some of the examples in Chapter 7 extend concepts presented in Chapter 6, it may be better to skim it rather than skip it.

In Chapter 9, I provide all you will need to know, and then some, about creating ActiveX Controls in Visual Basic. Although their development and use is, strictly speaking, not required in a distributed application, it is one of the most popular and requested topics of my students. If you wish, you can skip this chapter.

Interesting uses of COM are presented in Chapter 10, which covers automation fundamentals. In this chapter, you'll learn how to develop Visual Basic applications that launch and control other applications. You'll also learn how to add an automation interface to your own applications so that other programs can control yours. It's a short chapter, and one of my favorite topics, so I suggest you read this one.

A fundamental and hands-on introduction to DCOM, the Distributed Component Object Model, is presented in Chapter 11. Reading this chapter and performing the walkthroughs will give you a solid introduction to DCOM, as well as an appreciation for the features provided by Microsoft

Transaction Server (MTS). The serious distributed application developer will want to read and understand this chapter.

Based on my experience, I am quite certain that many of you purchased this book for the topic covered in Chapters 12 and 13 – using MTS. For over a year now, I have often entertained myself by seeing the reaction of students when I ask, "How many of you are interested in learning about MTS?" Even people who have never raised their hands in public since the third grade eagerly raise one, if not both arms, often adding a vigorous circular motion. It goes without saying that you'll want to read both of these chapters.

One of the strongest objections to using a distributed approach to software development is the inherent difficulty in maintenance and troubleshooting – "How would you debug that thing?" In Chapter 14, I attempt to show you that it is not that hard to maintain a distributed application. Additionally, I provide information about the often-dreaded binary compatibility features of Visual Basic. This chapter is essential reading for the serious developer.

Entire books have been written on the topic covered in Chapter 15 – creating Internet interfaces using Active Server Pages (ASP). I have purposely kept this chapter light, because I never really bought into the concept of mixing a program (e.g., "script") with graphic content (e.g., HTML). Certainly there are thousands of developers who love this sort of thing, and are capable of creating interesting Web pages while also providing the programming behind them. The chapter goes a bit beyond getting you started, and I would consider it to be required reading, if only because chances are the existing Web applications you now have were implemented as ASP pages.

A far better approach to developing Web applications was introduced in Visual Basic 6.0, and is the subject of Chapter 16 – creating Internet IIS applications. This new approach allows an applications programmer to program applications and a graphics designer to design graphics. I highly recommend reading this chapter thoroughly.

In Chapter 17, I introduce ActiveX Documents, which many Visual Basic developers are likely to find as appealing solutions for intranet development. While their reach is limited, due to browser compatibility, if you don't need broad reach capabilities for your intranet application, ActiveX Documents are at least worth a look.

Wrapping up the book is Chapter 18, in which you will learn how to use the *Internet Transfer* and *Web Browser* controls. In this chapter, you will see how to embed browser capabilities directly in your Visual Basic application, and automate file transfers via FTP.

Acknowledgements

I have quite a list of people to thank for assistance in writing this book. First, I want to thank Buck Trayser of Digital Equipment Corporation for persuading me that learning Visual Basic would be a good thing. I must also thank Cheryl Jacobs and Tony Todd of M&M/Mars, great customers of mine, for asking that I do a course on Visual Basic 3.0. That course turned out to be the start of a total of eight courses I developed covering Visual Basic from its fundamentals to its advanced features.

Certainly this book would not have been possible without the help of Andrew Scoppa and Donna Thayer of UCI Software Training Centers in Stoneham, Massachusetts. As a senior consulting partner with UCI, I have enjoyed working with Andrew and Donna for nearly 16 years. In my opinion, they offer the best developer training anywhere.

Thanks to Dave Libertone, also of UCI, for his help on this book – as a published author himself, he was a great pathfinder for me. Dave provided me with a terrific opportunity to get my feet wet as an author when I wrote a short chapter for his excellent book *Windows NT Cluster Server Guidebook,* also published by Prentice Hall. In addition to being a great friend, Dave's technical advice is always as good as gold.

Claudio Ghisolfi and Kay Connolly, also of UCI, deserve a great deal of credit for this book as well. I want to especially thank Claudio for his patience and determination in examining the demos and walkthroughs presented in this book.

Thanks to the excellent instructors who have used my courseware and provided feedback on errors, omissions, and suggestions, especially Karen Gallagher and Andy Macentee.

Thanks also to Art Kane and Olivia Kane of Ameriteach/UCI, Chip Hillman, Ed Stepian, and Debby Stepian of the Orange County Sheriff's Office; Mary Anne Vaughn of Microsoft Corporation; Melody Glover at the Kennedy Space Center; Michael Gorman and Dominic Vergata of Avon Corporation; Rick Wallace and Vicki Kyle-Flowers of Digital Equipment Corporation; Mike Meehan of Prentice Hall; Bob Barnes of Allen-Bradley; and Jim Slate, Bruce Kepley, and Ken Kelly. Also, I want to give a very big thank you to Robin at Sir Speedy.

Thanks to everyone at the Clearwater Research Group for providing the fresh academic and research environment that one needs to experiment with new technologies such as those discussed in this book.

The many students I have had the pleasure of teaching have helped a great deal with their comments and suggestions. In particular, I want to thank Connie Patton and everyone at Liberty Mutual; Rich Lagasse at Mathworks; Michael Joy at Sensitech; and Daniel Bagley.

Kasey, Tracy, Mary, and James, my children, deserve credit for their support. I wish to mention James in particular, a freshman at the University of Florida, for his fantastic job of data entry for the Mom-n-Pop Video Store database, and for providing me with the excellent opening paragraph of Chapter 16.

Lastly, and most of all, I cannot begin to thank Patty, my wife, for her support, encouragement, faith, and companionship during the development of this book and the courses that preceded it, and for all the errands, big and small, she ran for me, and for the excellent job she has done keeping the household running while I wrote this book. Without Patty, this book would literally have not been possible, especially since she helped me through a scare in which I thought the entire book was lost on my laptop – Patty found the hidden reset button on my ThinkPad!

Jim Maloney, MCSD, MCT
Honorary Research Fellow, Clearwater Research Group
St Petersburg, FL, November 1998

Deploying a Multi-Tiered Client/Server Application

My favorite *Seinfeld* episode is the one that goes backwards. If you're a *Seinfeld* fan, you know which episode I'm talking about. It did not literally go backwards—it's not as though they reversed the videotape, resulting in people talking and walking backwards. Instead, the episode showed little snippets of different events, then showed the event before that one, and so on. The interesting thing about this episode was that you knew how the episode was going to end. Knowing this information got your attention, and you became curious to see how it was going to start! I wonder just how well the episode could have kept your attention if had been played out in the traditional fashion—from beginning to end?

This book will begin with an overview of what multi-tiered applications are, and how to deploy them. Naturally, deploying a multi-tiered client/server application would be the final step in development. So, why start here? The reason is that the methodology used to develop multi-tiered applications is quite foreign to most developers, so I'll present the development process backwards, using a completed application in both 2-tier and 3-tier versions. This will help you see the benefits and challenges of developing applications using this methodology. Like my favorite *Seinfeld* episode, I hope I can keep your interest by illustrating the ending, so that you become curious about the start.

A word of warning before getting started: You'll need to follow the instructions presented in this chapter very carefully to be successful. Since these steps will have you modifying your registry, as well as creating new SQL Server databases, it is imperative that you perform these steps on a

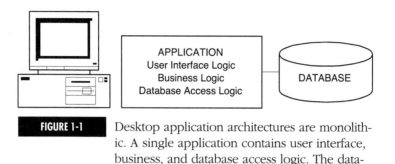

FIGURE 1-1   Desktop application architectures are monolith-ic. A single application contains user interface, business, and database access logic. The data-base is local.

development machine that does not perform a critical function. You should back up your system(s) before proceeding with these steps.

Application Architectures

The industry now recognizes three distinct architectures for application development. What the industry fails to agree upon, however, is exactly what constitutes each type of architecture. In Microsoft circles, there are generally considered to be three types of architectures: desktop, 2-tier, and 3-tier.

Desktop Application Architecture Overview

The term "***desktop architecture***" is applied to most legacy applications, which are completely self-contained and therefore monolithic. In a desktop architecture, all layers exist on the client machine, including the database itself, as shown in Figure 1-1. When the database is remote, the application is no longer considered to be a desktop architecture, and is probably considered a 2-tier architecture.

Many, if not most, of the applications that use the desktop architecture do not have a clean separation between the traditional layers of an applica-tion. These layers include the user interface, business logic, and database access logic layers. The less distinction between these layers, the more diffi-cult it is to convert the desktop application to any type of distributed applica-tion architecture.

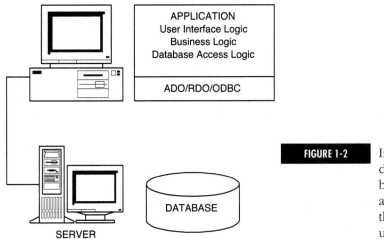

FIGURE 1-2   In a 2-tier architecture, the database is remote, but the business and database access logic still reside on the client, along with the user interface code.

2-Tier Application Architecture Overview

An application that accesses a remote database is, at a minimum, a ***2-tier*** architecture. The database can be accessed by any client/server database API, such as ActiveX Data Objects (ADO), Remote Data Objects (RDO), the ODBC API, and others (see Figure 1-2).

Converting a desktop application to a 2-tier architecture can be easy. In fact, with all mentioned database access APIs (ADO, RDO, ODBC), the conversion may be as simple as modifying the attributes of a data source to enable the application to access a remote, instead of local, database. This fact contributes to one source of confusion regarding the classification of distributed applications—is a 2-tier-"capable" application considered to be a desktop architecture when the database is deployed locally? In other words, does the term "N-tier" apply to a logical model or to a physical (deployment) model? Experts disagree on this issue. However, as distributed architectures become more commonplace, a growing number of developers are beginning to consider the term "N-tier" to apply to the logical model, and that is the working definition for this book. For example, all components, including the database, of a 3-tier application can be deployed on a single machine. Implementing such a deployment plan does not make your application a desktop architecture, since it is capable of being deployed in a distributed environment.

3-Tier Application Architecture Overview

An additional layer between the user interface and database will make an application a *3-tier* architecture (see Figure 1-3). This middle layer is often referred to as the business rules or business logic, and this layer is typically deployed on the server, along with the database. Since the Visual Basic development environment makes it easy to develop event procedures that are invoked as a side effect of user interaction with controls, many existing Visual Basic applications can be difficult to move to a 3-tier model.

The business and database access logic software is contained in a separate entity from the user interface logic in a 3-tier architecture. Although any type of remote communication may be used between the client and server, including TCP/IP sockets, named pipes, network DDE, and others, the best approach is to use *DCOM, the Distributed Component Object Model.*

Clearly, in the 3-tier architecture, an additional potential bottleneck is introduced between the user interface logic and business logic—the network. In effect, one bottleneck has been traded off for another. The 3-tier model gains performance from processing data where it resides. That is, by moving the business logic over to the database server, less data must be moved from the client to the server. However, communication between the user interface and business logic has now gone remote. Depending on how much communication is required between the user interface logic and the business logic, the performance gain from processing the data locally may be washed away by the resulting increase in network round-trips.

The latest proposed solution to this problem is to design objects in the middle layer to be stateless. Unlike traditional objects, stateless objects cannot have persistent properties. Typically, such objects have only methods (procedures), which must declare sufficient parameters to accomplish a given task in one procedure call. In this scenario, state is held on the client machine until sufficient information has been gathered from the user, at which time a method is invoked on an object in the middle layer. While the use of this technique can result in a more scalable application, invoking methods with numerous parameters is undesirable to many programmers, especially those schooled in good object-oriented design techniques. This dilemma, along with a solution, is discussed in further detail in the following section.

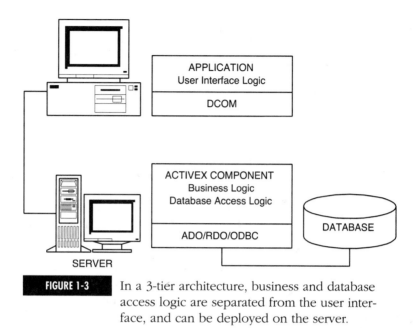

FIGURE 1-3 In a 3-tier architecture, business and database access logic are separated from the user interface, and can be deployed on the server.

N-Tier Application Architecture Overview

If yet another layer is inserted between the presentation layer and the database, would one then have a 4-tier client/server architecture? Such a question is perfectly valid and illustrates how the terminology has gotten out of hand. In general, the industry has adopted the term "***N-tier***" to refer to a new architecture in which layers of an application are cleanly separated and accessed via well-defined interfaces. Therefore, you are not likely to encounter the term "4-tier" in much of the technical literature describing distributed applications.

I bring up the issue of 4-tier architectures because there is a tremendous amount of controversy surrounding the 3-tier architecture, mainly concerning the stateless nature of the objects in a 3-tier architecture's middleware. The concept and importance of stateless objects is discussed throughout this book, beginning with this chapter. I will mention at this point that ***stateless*** objects are objects with no properties (attributes). Stateless objects have only ***methods*** (functions), and these functions often have a far greater number of parameters than properly schooled object-oriented programmers are comfortable with. Stateless objects are designed primarily for Internet- or intranet-based client applications, in which the presentation layer runs within a Web browser

In this book, I present a new approach to distributed application development, which considers both Internet/intranet clients and Win32 clients (see Figure 1-4). In using this approach, I suggest that Internet/intranet presentation

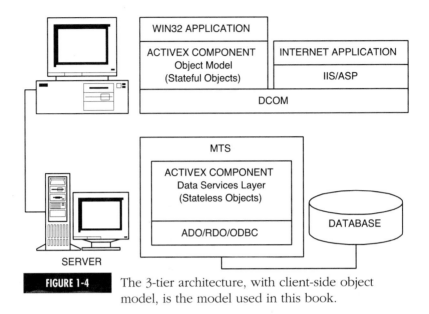

FIGURE 1-4   The 3-tier architecture, with client-side object model, is the model used in this book.

layer clients use the stateless objects of the data services layer and that in-house Win32 presentation layer clients use an object model, which consists of stateful objects and acts as a thin layer of object-oriented code over the stateless objects in the data services layer. Since I have introduced yet another layer between the presentation layer and the database, one may suggest that this book presents a 4-tier architecture. However, I prefer to think of the object model as an extension to a Win32 client application's presentation layer.

About 2-Tier Client/Server Applications

In a ***2-tier client/server application***, database access is from the client side, either directly from the presentation layer (user interface), or via an object model, if present (see Figure 1-5). Code in the object model is typically distributed on the *client side* since the objects in the object model must hold state. In general, code that exists between the presentation layer and the database is referred to as ***middleware***, although many client/server developers apply this term only to 3-tier client/server applications (discussed next). For the purposes of this book, we will consider middleware to be any layer of custom software that exists between the presentation layer and the database.

To access the database, the presentation layer or client-side middleware typically uses a remote database API or set of objects that encapsulate a remote database API, as in ActiveX Data Objects (ADO). In the logical model of 2-tier client/server applications, there are the presentation and database layers. Business logic is deployed on the client side in a 2-tier architecture.

As Figure 1-5 suggests, code in the presentation layer does not have to access an object model. Instead, code to carry out business logic can be contained in one application, which implements both the user interface logic and business logic. However, this is not recommended, as the key to a successful distributed application lies in the separation between the layers of logic: user interface, business logic, and database access. The role of the object model in a 2-tier client/server architecture is both to implement the business rules and to provide database access to the presentation layer.

In a 2-tier architecture, client applications are somewhat monolithic, although not entirely so. Since the database is remote, but the business logic is contained on the client side, such applications are considered 2-tier. When the database is located on the same machine as the code implementing the presentation and business logic layers, the application is considered a desktop architecture.

Applications developed according to the 2-tier model may use stored procedures defined in the database. Such stored procedures may be simple or complex; in fact, many database designers come close to implementing business logic in stored procedures. Strictly speaking, however, applications that access remote databases via stored procedures are still considered to be a 2-tier architecture.

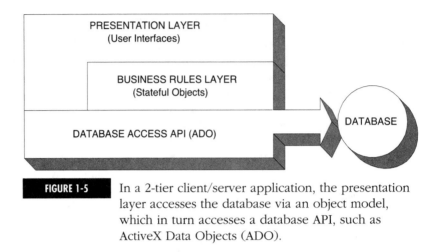

FIGURE 1-5 In a 2-tier client/server application, the presentation layer accesses the database via an object model, which in turn accesses a database API, such as ActiveX Data Objects (ADO).

Physical Deployment of 2-Tier Client/Server Applications

In the physical model, which specifies how the components of the client/server application are deployed, you have the option of deploying both the presentation layer (or user interface) and the business rules (or object model) on the client side. Alternatively, you can deploy the presentation layer on the client side while deploying the business rules on the server side, preferably on the same machine as the database(s). Since, in general, the business rules layer consists of stateful objects, it is recommended that it be deployed on the client machine, along with the presentation layer. This will minimize the number of network round-trips.

Deploying stateful business objects on a remote machine has advantages in the way of maintenance. As for performance, it is generally acceptable for modest (under 100 clients) workloads, although this of course depends on the nature of the objects.

Experts disagree on what is considered a 2-tier model. Many experts suggest that the tiers refer to physical deployment. If you accept this definition, the model discussed here would be considered 2-tier when the presentation layer and business rules layer are on the same machine (with a remote database). The same logical model would be considered 3-tier (according to this interpretation) when the business rules layer is moved to another machine. For the purposes of this book, we will consider the tiers to refer to the logical model. According to the most commonly-used definition, an application is a 3-tier client/server model if you separate the presentation layer from the business rules.

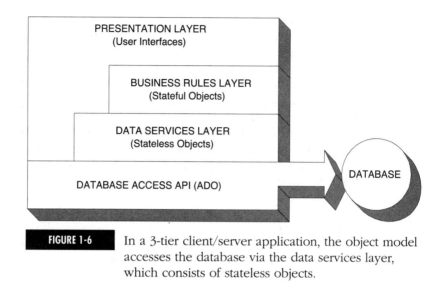

FIGURE 1-6   In a 3-tier client/server application, the object model accesses the database via the data services layer, which consists of stateless objects.

About 3-Tier Client/Server Applications

In a 3-tier client/server application, the business rules access the database via a second tier, known as the ***data services layer*** (see Figure 1-6). Objects in the data services layer are generally transactional and stateless, and are designed according to the required transactions of the business. Examples from the Video Store case study presented in this book include renting videos, returning videos, signing in new members, and so on. While it is certainly possible (and generally recommended) that the objects in the data services layer use stored procedures defined in the database, in many ways the methods of these objects are advanced stored procedures. Creating transactional code in a language such as Visual Basic provides you with a much richer set of features than the SQL language can provide. Additionally, data services layer objects, when deployed with Microsoft Transaction Server, can take advantage of just-in-time activation and connection pooling, two features that considerably improve the scalability of a multi-tiered client/server application.

Since methods of objects in the data services layer must be stateless to ensure scalability, it is not unusual for their methods to contain an unusually large number of parameters. This is why it is an excellent idea to wrap access to the data services layer with a thin layer of object-oriented code known as the object model. This object model is to be used only by Win32 clients and not by Internet/intranet clients, which, for scalability purposes, must use only the stateless objects of the data services layer.

The 3-tier model provides the greatest amount of flexibility in deployment. Applications (actually presentation layer "front-ends") can be written that either directly access the database, directly access the data services layer, or directly access the object model layer. With proper design, all types of front-ends can co-exist without interference.

Note that for intranet or Web-based (browser-hosted) applications, using the object model layer is generally inappropriate. Browser-based applications should use the data services layer, while "in-house" applications (written as Win32 clients in, for example, Visual Basic or Visual C++) should use the object model layer. The reason for this is that objects in the business rules layer hold state and must therefore be deployed on the client side. This is clearly inappropriate for Internet applications.

Physical Deployment of 3-Tier Client/Server Applications

To physically deploy a 3-tier client/server application, the data services layer is installed on the same machine as the database(s), while the object model is installed client-side, along with the Win32 application(s) in the presentation layer.

For proper scalability, objects in the data services layer must be stateless. This means that they can contain virtually no properties, and that literally all their methods must be able to run to completion without retaining state. Objects in the data services layer are typically deployed using Microsoft Transaction Server (MTS). In addition to providing utilities to deploy and monitor objects, MTS provides an excellent runtime environment that developers use to create scalable objects that use just-in-time activation and database connection pooling. *Microsoft Transaction Server* is introduced in Chapter 14, and an in-depth case study of MTS components is presented in Chapter 15.

The Forgotten Tier: The Object Model

The problem with much of the literature and courseware covering multi-tiered application development is that the focus is almost entirely on Internet clients with user interfaces hosted in a Web browser. Such literature proposes the development of N-tier client/server applications using only a presentation layer and a data services layer. Typically, the data services layer is referred to in such documents as the business rules or business layer. I certainly don't want to start a controversy over the terminology used in N-tier client/server applications, but a growing number of developers are beginning to realize that many of us have forgotten a tier: the object model.

Examine any reference to 3-tier client/server applications and you'll see countless examples of objects that have methods with well over a dozen parameters. Any good programmer will recognize this as a bad idea and will suggest breaking such methods into smaller methods that can be sequentially invoked by the caller, or by adding properties that have convenient default values that can be referenced by the called methods. However, when an object is hosted remotely, calling methods involves network round-trips. Furthermore, data structures for holding properties of objects always reside with the object, which means that objects with properties must hold their state on the server if they are remote. Such an implementation will not scale to a large number of clients. This situation has given rise to a new type of object, the stateless object.

Can an object be stateless and still be an object? If you've been through the traditional schooling of object-oriented design, you'll agree that it cannot. You have no doubt been taught that objects have both attributes and behavior, which translate to properties and methods, which translate to data and code. All objects in real life have both state and behavior. For example, my dog Pepper has a weight, which is one of his properties (or states), and can speak on command, which is like a method. Pepper is an object, specifically an instance of a dog class object.

If you approach many experts on scalable multi-tiered applications and complain about the use of stateless objects, you may be branded an "object-oriented purist." You may additionally be told that object-oriented programming does not scale. However, there is a common ground, and it is an excellent approach to client/server application development. The approach is to use an object model that consists of stateful objects whenever possible, and when scalability is a concern, use stateless objects in the data services layer. Code in the object model is primarily just a thin layer of object-oriented code over the stateless objects in the data services layer. This is the approach presented in this book.

Another point of objection for many developers in using an object model is that it will complicate the distribution of applications, since the object model must be distributed on the client side. To counter this objection, let me first state that it is not essential to distribute the object model on the client machine. You can deploy a single copy of the object model on a server and use DCOM to deploy it. For a small (i.e., departmental) workload, this deployment technique works well. However, this point is moot since using an object model does not really complicate the distribution of an application. While it is true that you must create a single setup program that distributes both a Win32 presentation layer client (Standard EXE in Visual Basic) and the object model (a Visual Basic ActiveX DLL), this is easily done with the *Package and Deployment Wizard* included with Visual Basic. Let me also counter this objection with another point. If your Win32 clients use the stateless objects of the data services layer, what are you going to do when you must change one of those methods that require over a dozen parameters (and you will have to)? If you use an object model to "wrap" the methods of the data services layer, you'll generally have far fewer places in your code that you'll have to change. So, using an object model that consists of stateful objects can actually make it easier for you to maintain your software.

Building a Suite of Applications

Application development today consists of the development of several programs, really a suite of programs that, taken together, define an application. We are past the days of creating monolithic applications that do everything. Today, using a modular, N-tiered approach to application development, we can create Win32 clients with rich user interface features, while we also develop broad-reach, browser-based front-ends for globally distributed applications. Not all of these applications need to be scalable, but they can, and should, share common code whenever possible (see Figure 1-7). For example, there is no need for the *Mom-n-Pop Video Store* application (presented later in this chapter and throughout this book) to be able to support thousands of users of the *Point-of-Sale* application, which is used in-house by a clerk when videos are rented by members of the video store. However, the *Mom-n-Pop Video Store* application also has several Internet-based front-ends so that members (and potential members) can browse the database of available videos. If, in the future, the *Mom-n-Pop Video Store* application needs an Internet-based front-end for renting videos, that user interface will need to use the scalable objects in the data services layer.

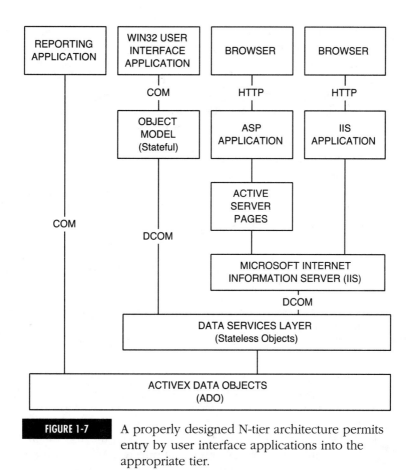

FIGURE 1-7   A properly designed N-tier architecture permits entry by user interface applications into the appropriate tier.

The *Mom-n-Pop Video Store* application presented in this book is actually a suite of applications. The most visible application in the suite is the *Point-of-Sale* application, which is used in-house at the video store. As a Win32 client application, it uses the object model to carry out actions entered by the user. Technically, the *Point-of-Sale* application is a presentation layer application, and is a client of the object model, which, in turn, is a client of the data services layer. Creating a Win32 presentation layer client that uses an object model is the subject of Chapter 3. In Chapter 6, I will show you how to create the object model.

Another pair of *Mom-n-Pop Video Store* applications presented in this book implement Internet presentation layer clients. The first such application I'll present to you is an Active Server Page *(ASP)* application, discussed in Chapter 15. Another Internet front-end is presented in Chapter 16, which discusses using new features of Visual Basic to create Internet IIS applications. Again referring to Figure 1-7, you'll notice that both these applications use the objects in the data services layer, instead of accessing the object model.

As you can see, presentation layer clients can use either the object model interface or the data services layer interface. But these are not the only options. Some client applications will continue to access the remote database directly through a remote database API, such as ActiveX Data Objects (ADO). In the *Mom-n-Pop Video Store* suite of applications, for example, there is a *Reporting* application that creates a report of rented videos. Database reporting and maintenance applications do not need to use either the object model or data services interfaces. Using ADO and creating report-generating programs is covered in Chapter 5.

As you can see, separating the traditional components of an application—user interface, business logic, and database access—has a number of advantages. Code is reused to its maximum potential, and the application can scale to a large number of users.

WIN32 PRESENTATION LAYER APPLICATIONS

A Win32 presentation layer application is a client application written specifically to run on a Windows platform. Such applications can use the rich user interface features of Windows, including common controls such as the *ListView* and *TreeView* controls. A Win32 presentation layer client's entry point into a distributed application should be via the object model, which is often deployed client-side to keep state management away from the server.

In the *Mom-n-Pop Video Store* suite of applications, the *Point-of-Sale* application is the most visible Win32 client. Additionally, there are several other demonstration programs included with this book, including a *MemberLister* application that demonstrates the use of OLE drag-and-drop. These and other Win32 presentation layer clients presented in this book enter into the distributed architecture via the object model (see Figure 1-8). In Chapter 3, I will explain how to develop Win32 presentation layer clients such as these.

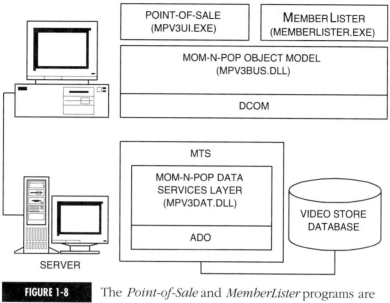

FIGURE 1-8 The *Point-of-Sale* and *MemberLister* programs are Win32 presentation layer clients, which enter into the distributed application via the object model.

BROWSER-BASED PRESENTATION LAYER APPLICATIONS

Since presentation layers hosted in Internet browsers may reach a much larger number of users, and since such clients may run on many different platforms, this type of application enters into the distributed application via the stateless objects in the data services layer. A presentation layer client written for a browser may use ASP, or it can be developed to take advantage of a new feature of Visual Basic—an Internet IIS application. In Chapter 15, I will explain how to develop ASP applications. In Chapter 16, I will illustrate the creation of Internet IIS applications. The architecture of these types of applications is illustrated in Figure 1-9.

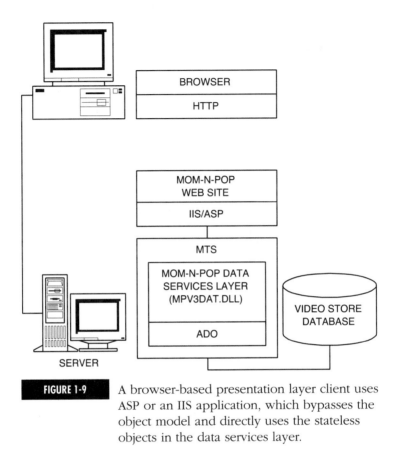

FIGURE 1-9 A browser-based presentation layer client uses ASP or an IIS application, which bypasses the object model and directly uses the stateless objects in the data services layer.

DATABASE REPORTING AND MAINTENANCE APPLICATIONS

There is little motivation for encapsulating tasks related to database maintenance and reporting into objects in either the object model or data services layer. Such applications can be written according to the 2-tier architecture, co-existing with Win32 and browser-based clients.

The *Mom-n-Pop Video Store* suite of applications includes an application that produces a daily report of rented videos (see Figure 1-10). Creating reporting applications is a subject of Chapter 5.

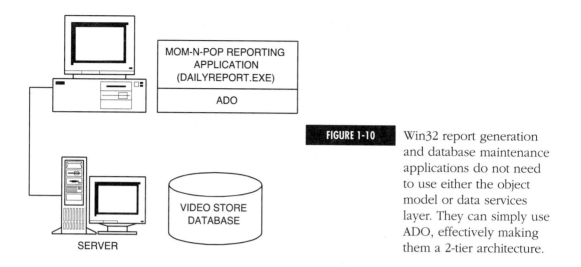

FIGURE 1-10 Win32 report generation and database maintenance applications do not need to use either the object model or data services layer. They can simply use ADO, effectively making them a 2-tier architecture.

The Legacy Systems of Tomorrow

As a *Microsoft Certified Trainer* and *Solution Developer*, I often joke with my students that they are creating the legacy systems of tomorrow. It seems that it is only in our industry that "legacy" is a bad word. If your career were in sports, you would be honored to be called a legacy. If you think about it, a legacy system has stood the test of time, and clearly must have provided immeasurable value to a company to survive long enough to be called a legacy system. Although today's software must be designed to withstand change, I certainly hope that you don't plan to discard the systems you are developing today anytime soon.

I conclude from my own analysis and experience that the best model of client/server application development is the one I present in this book. You must design a normalized and efficient database that contains efficient stored procedures that can be accessed directly with ADO for database maintenance and reporting programs. On top of this tier, you must design a stateless and scalable set of objects with methods that can be accessed by browser-based applications driven by HTML and scripting languages, using ASP and/or other server-side technologies. On top of this tier, you must design a set of stateful objects that provide an elegant abstraction of your business model and that simplify the interface to the data services layer. Finally, for your in-house Win32 clients, you must use a language such as Visual Basic to easily access the rich, native user interface features provided by the Windows operating system. This approach to software development scales from small, to medium, to large applications, and provides a growth path for future development. Such systems will be the legacy systems of tomorrow, only we will perhaps by then have learned that that is, after all, a compliment to the original designers of the system.

Deploying the Sample N-Tier Applications

In the following sections, I will guide you through the installation of the sample N-tier applications included with this book. I have provided both 2-tier and 3-tier versions, and will be analyzing them in the chapters that follow. The application was designed and developed for a fictitious company, the *Mom-n-Pop Video Store*. It is written completely in Visual Basic and is moderate in size—large and complete enough to include examples of virtually every aspect of an N-tier architecture application. The steps that follow will be similar, if not identical, to the steps that you will follow once you have completed your N-tier application.

Deploying a 2-Tier Client/Server Application

Deploying any type of client/server application is complex, regardless of the number of tiers. Clearly, the more tiers, the more difficult it is. You should take steps to automate the installation and updating process as much as possible. Using the *Visual Basic Package and Deployment Wizard* or third-party setup generation tools such as *InstallShield*, this is quite possible. However, you can't create a setup program if you can't deploy the application manually! In addition, knowing how to manually deploy a multi-tiered client/server application will help you to troubleshoot it if necessary.

In this book, we will learn how to manually deploy a client/server application. The steps presented have some flexibility. Once you get the hang of it, you can take whatever shortcuts you desire. The steps listed assume the object model will be installed client-side:

1. Install the database on the server using whatever approach is appropriate for the type of database used.
2. If necessary, create any DSNs required on client machines. Alternatively, you can use file DSNs or, if using ADO, DSNs are not specifically required. Test database access from the client machine.
3. Install and register the object model on the client machine. Make sure that any components the object model requires are also installed and registered on the client machine.
4. Install the presentation layer application(s) on the client machine.

Deploying the 2-Tier Mom-n-Pop Video Store Application

Included with this book is a 2-tier version of the *Mom-n-Pop Video Store*, which uses a *Microsoft Access* database. Once you've followed the instructions to install the 2-tier version, each client will have a copy of a database. Although it is certainly possible to access a remote database in a 2-tier client/server application, we won't do that until we use the 3-tier model, which uses a SQL Server database.

You actually have two versions of the 2-tier model of the *Mom-n-Pop Video Store* software. One version, located in the demos folder under *Mom-n-Pop\2Tier\MPVserver,* is a development version that you may experiment with. The second version is located in the demos folder under *Mom-n-Pop\Release\2Tier\MPVserver.* This is a release version built with binary compatibility. If you modify this version, many of the other demos may fail to work properly.

Before proceeding with the following instructions, please check the latest setup guidelines by viewing the *README.TXT* file on the CD-ROM accompanying this book.

INSTALLING THE DATABASE FOR THE 2-TIER MODEL

The database for the 2-tier version is in the file *VideoStore.MDB*, and will already be located in the folder *VB6Adv\Database* after you install the files included with this book. The object model for the 2-tier *Mom-n-Pop Video Store* demo requires a DSN. You can create middleware that does not require a DSN, but for this demo, you need one.

To create the DSN for the 2-tier version of the *Mom-n-Pop Video Store* application:

1. Access the *OBDC Data Source Administrator* by double-clicking *ODBC* in the *Control Panel.*

2. On the *User DSN* tab, select the *Add* button.

3. In the resulting *Create New Data Source* dialog, choose *Microsoft Access* and click *Finish.*

4. In the resulting dialog, enter *AccessVideoStore* in the *Data Source Name* text box (see Figure 1-11).

5. Click the *Select* button, then navigate to and select *VB6Adv\Database-\VideoStore.MDB.*

6. Click *OK* to dismiss the dialogs and exit the *ODBC Data Source Administrator.*

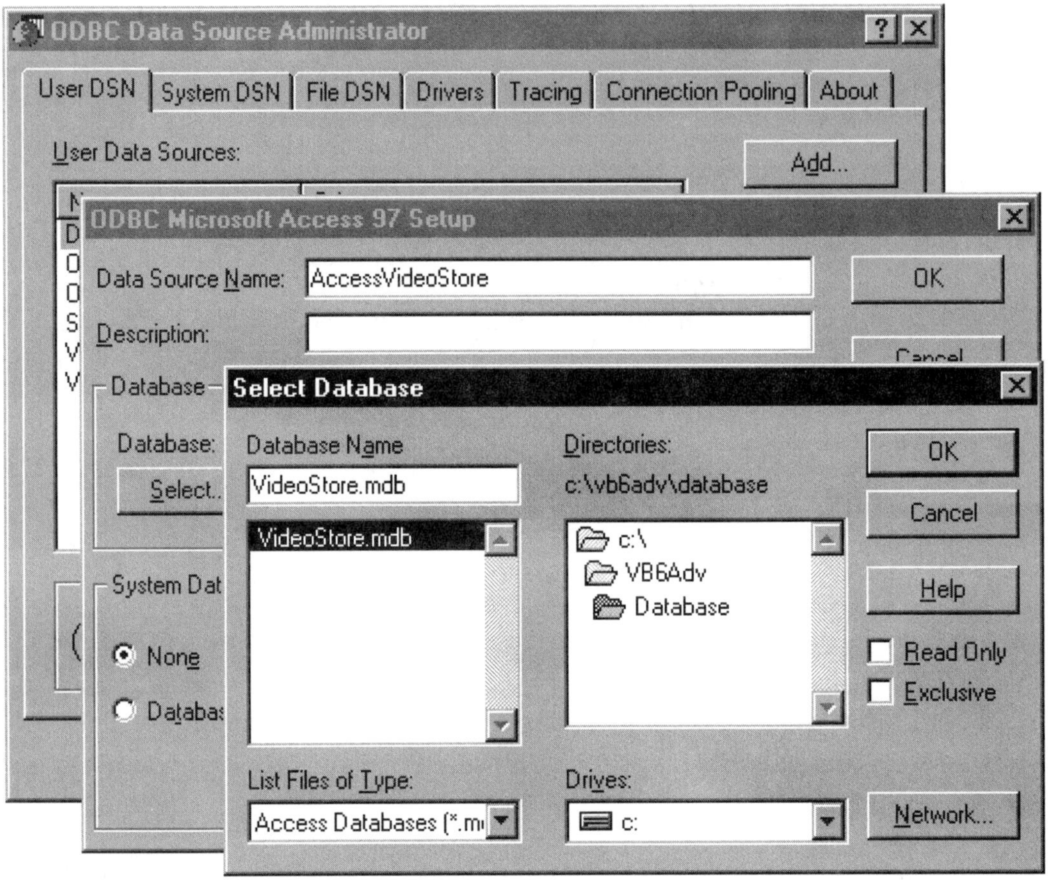

FIGURE 1-11 The 2-tier version of the Mom-n-Pop Video Store requires a DSN on the client machine.

INSTALLING THE MIDDLEWARE FOR THE 2-TIER MODEL

The middleware for the 2-tier version of the *Mom-n-Pop Video Store* is already built and located in the file *MPV2BUS.DLL* in folder *VB6Adv\Demos\ MomPop\Release\2Tier\MPVServer.* You need to register the server by issuing the following command from the *Run* dialog:

```
regsvr32 \VB6Adv\Demos\MomPop\Release\2Tier\MPVServer\MPV2BUS.DLL
```

The most common error is to incorrectly specify the pathname or file-name, in which case, you'll receive an error message about *LoadLibrary* returning error *7E*. Use the *Error Lookup* utility for other errors. To make it easier to register COM servers, use the following instructions:

1. In *Windows Explorer*, double-click on the DLL you wish to register. This will cause the *Open With* dialog to appear.
2. In the *Open With* dialog, click *Other*.
3. Navigate to and select *Winnt\System32\Regsvr32.EXE*.
4. Back in the *Open With* dialog, check *"Always use this program to open this file"*.
5. The DLL you selected in Step 1 above will be registered. To register other DLLs, simply double-click on them.

RUNNING THE 2-TIER APPLICATION

Once you've followed the previous steps, run the program *MPV2UI.EXE* from folder *VB6Adv\Demos\MomPop\Release\2Tier\MPVui*. When the application is started for the first time, it displays a dialog to confirm the DSN (see Figure 1-12). On this dialog, you can check the box *Do not display this dialog in the future* to prevent the DSN dialog from appearing again. This dialog illustrates the use of saving and restoring application settings in the registry. I'll show you exactly how this is done in Chapter 3. Once you choose not to display the *DSN* dialog, the *VideoStore* program will instead display a splash screen as it starts up. This is another technique discussed in Chapter 3.

Some tips on using the application:

1. You can search by a member's last name or member ID. The "mem-bers" of *Mom-n-Pop Video* are actually taken from the employees of the *NorthWind Traders* database (i.e., *Davolio, Leverling, etc.*).
2. Member IDs range from 12000 to 12009.
3. To search by last name, enter any part of a last name that matches. You can also enter a percent sign as a wildcard.
4. You can search by a video's title or video ID. Videos include such (once) popular titles as *Airplane, Forrest Gump*, and *Maverick*.
5. Video IDs range from 52000 to 52028. There are initially 20 copies of each video available for rental.
6. All videos can be rented for three nights at a price of $2.00. The late fee is $1.00 per night.
7. A feature is provided for "advancing" the date ahead to test late charges, etc. When you use this feature of the program (discussed shortly), you are not changing your system clock.

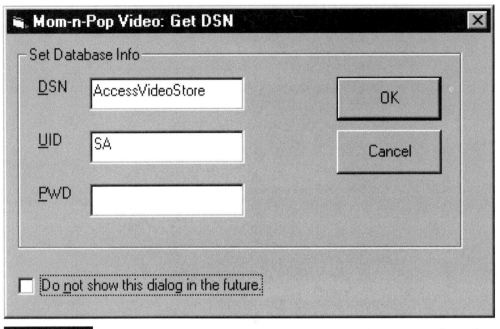

FIGURE 1-12   The first time you run the 2-tier video store application, you'll get this dialog. Confirm the DSN and click *OK*. You may also wish to check *Do not show this dialog in the future.*

RENTING VIDEOS

Next, rent three videos to member *Nancy Davolio*, using the following instructions:

1. Click the **Rent Videos** button.
2. For *Member ID*, enter **12001**, then click the **Find Member** button (or press *Enter*).
3. For *Video ID*, enter **52000** and enter **1** for *Copy No*. Click the **Rent Video** button.
4. Repeat the previous step twice, renting **52001** and **52002**. Select Copy *No 1* for both videos.
5. Click the **Finish** button. Click **OK** to dismiss the *Point of Sale* dialog (see Figure 1-13).

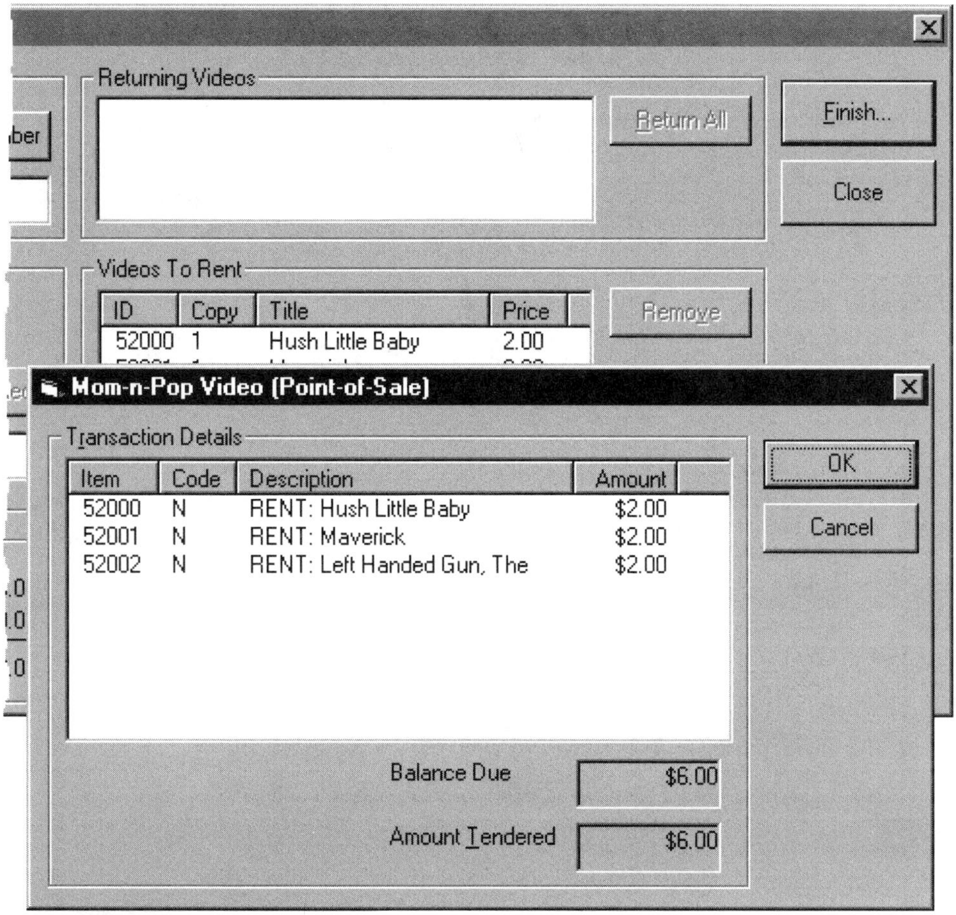

FIGURE 1-13   Follow the instructions to rent three videos to member Nancy Davolio.

ADVANCING THE SIMULATION DATE

The *Mom-n-Pop Video Store* program has a feature to advance the date for simulation purposes. When this feature is used, it does not actually advance your system's date. When the application starts, it sets "today's" date to the latest of either the latest due date in the *Rentals* table **or** the latest returned date in the *LateCharges* table. If no records exist in either table, "today's" date is set to the actual date.

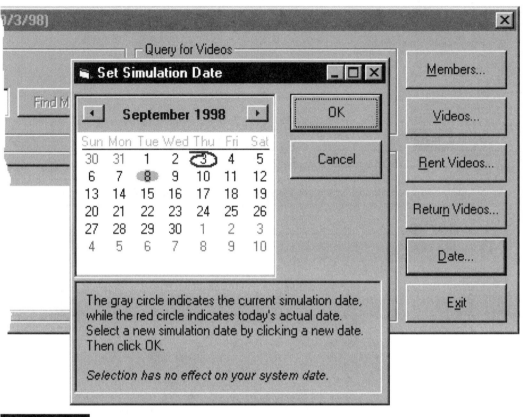

FIGURE 1-14   The *Mom-n-Pop Video Store* program has a feature that allows you to advance the date to test late charges.

At this point, you should advance the simulation date by five days to experiment with late charges handling. This is done as follows:

1. From the main window, select the **Date** button.
2. Select a date that is five days ahead of the simulation date (see Figure 1-14).
3. The caption of the main window should indicate the new date.

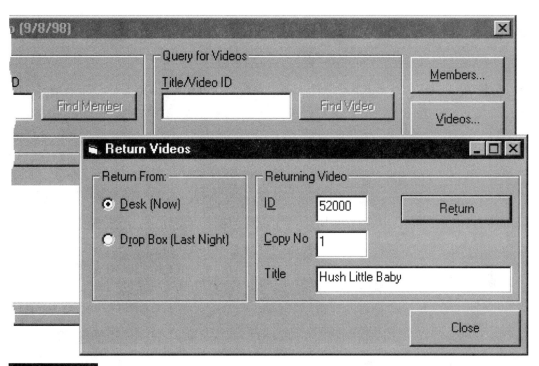

FIGURE 1-15 Customers can deposit returned videos in the drop box or at the desk when they rent new videos.

RETURNING VIDEOS FROM THE DROP BOX

Assume *Nancy Davolio* returns her videos (now several days late) by dropping them off at the desk as she shops for some new videos to rent. Process the returns as follows:

1. From the main window, select the ***Return Videos*** button.
2. Make sure that the *Return From* option is set to ***Desk*** (see Figure 1-15).
3. Enter each video ID and copy number, selecting the ***Return*** button for each. Recall that *Nancy Davolio* rented videos *52000, 52001,* and *52002*, all of which were copy number 1.
4. Select the ***Close*** button when finished.

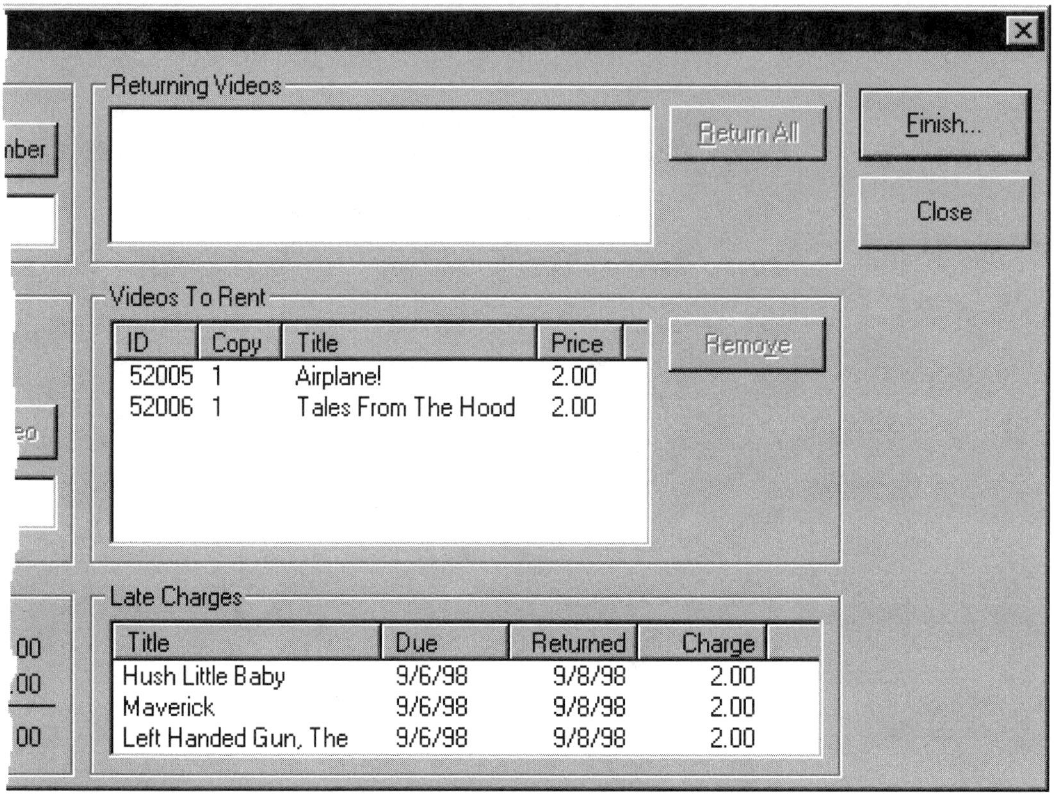
Returning Videos
Return All
Finish...
Close
Videos To Rent
ID Copy Title Price
52005 1 Airplane! 2.00
52006 1 Tales From The Hood 2.00
Remove
Late Charges
Title Due Returned Charge
Hush Little Baby 9/6/98 9/8/98 2.00
Maverick 9/6/98 9/8/98 2.00
Left Handed Gun, The 9/6/98 9/8/98 2.00

FIGURE 1-16 When *Nancy Davolio* appears back at the point-of-sale to rent new videos, she will also be assessed some late charges.

COLLECTING LATE CHARGES

Now, perform the following steps to make member *Nancy Davolio* rent two new videos:

1. Select the ***Rent*** button from the main window.

1. Enter *12001* for *Member ID* and click the ***Find Member*** button. The late charges should appear in the *Late Charges* frame (see Figure 1-16).
2. Enter two new videos for rental, using copy number *1* for both *52005* and *52006*.
3. Select the ***Finish*** button and click ***OK*** in the resulting message box.

To continue the demos for this book, it is recommended that you keep these two videos rented to *Nancy Davolio*.

Deploying a 3-Tier Client/Server Application

For the first part of this book, you will be working with and analyzing the 2-tier version of the *Mom-n-Pop Video Store* application. Therefore, it is not essential that you deploy the 3-tier version immediately. The 3-tier version requires MTS, IIS, and *SQL Server,* so its setup is more involved than the 2-tier version. If you wish, you may return to this section when you are ready to analyze 3-tier applications.

Deploying a 3-tier client/server application involves more steps. The following steps assume you will install the data services layer and database on one machine, and the presentation layer and object model on another. As an overview, you will first install the server-side components:

1. Restore the *SQL Server* database on the server machine.
2. Create a DSN on the server machine if the data services layer requires one.
3. Using the *MTS Explorer Utility,* create a package for the data services layer.
4. Install the data services layer components into the package created in the previous step.
5. Export the package to create a client setup program. Make sure the client setup executable is located on a shared directory, accessible from the client machines.

Next, you'll deploy the client-side components. Following is an overview of the steps involved:

1. Install and register the object model.
2. Run the client setup program you created in Step 5 above.
3. Install the presentation layer application(s)

DEPLOYING THE 3-TIER MOM-N-POP VIDEO STORE APPLICATION

Included with this book is a 3-tier version of the *Mom-n-Pop Video Store,* which uses a *SQL Server* database. The instructions that follow assume that you will be installing the database and data services layer (using MTS) on the server. The object model and presentation layer will each be installed client-side. You must copy the data services layer component DLL and *SQL Server VideoStore* backup to the server machine. These files can be copied to a folder on the server that you create. You'll find the data services layer component in the file *MPV3DAT.DLL,* located in folder *VB6Adv\Demos\ MomPop\Release\3Tier\MPVdata.*

You'll find the *VideoStore* backup in *VB6Adv\Database\VSBack up.DAT.*

Before proceeding with the following instructions, please check the latest setup guidelines by viewing the *README.TXT* file on the CD-ROM accompanying this book.

RESTORING THE SQL SERVER VIDEO STORE DATABASE

The following instructions are for *SQL Server 6.5*. You must execute these instructions on the server:

1. Run the *SQL Enterprise Manager.*
2. In the *Server Manager* window, expand the node indicating the server that will host your database.
3. Right-click on *Databases* and select *New Database.*
4. In the resulting *New Database* dialog, enter *VideoStore* for the name. Give the database a size of *11 MB,* then click *Create Now.*
5. Back in the *Server Manager* window, under *Databases,* right-click on *VideoStore* and select *Backup/Restore.*
6. In the resulting *Database Backup/Restore* dialog, choose the *Restore* tab.
7. Select *VideoStore* as the database, then click the *From Device* button.
8. In the resulting *Restore From Device on Server* dialog, click the *Add File* button.
9. In the resulting *Add Backup Disk File* dialog, click the browse button (…) and navigate to and select the *VSBackup.DAT* file (originally distributed in *VB6Adv\Database).*
10. Back in the *Restore From Device on Sever* dialog, click the *Restore Now* button.
11. Click *Close* to dismiss the *Restore from Device on Server* dialog.
12. Click *Close* to dismiss the *Database Backup/Restore* dialog.
13. Before exiting the *SQL Enterprise Manager,* you may wish to run the *SQL Query Tool* and do a simple query on the *VideoStore* database. Try *Select * From Members.*

CREATING THE DSN ON THE SERVER FOR THE 3-TIER VERSION

The *Mom-n-Pop Video Store data services layer* uses a hard-coded DSN of *SQLVideoStore,* which must be created on the server machine, using the following instructions:

1. Start the *ODBC Data Source Administrator* from the *Control Panel.*
2. Select the *User DSN* tab. Select *SQL Server* and click the *Add* button.
3. In the resulting *Create a New Data Source* dialog, enter *SQLVideoStore*

for the name. Select the proper server (local), then click *Next*.

4. Click *Next* (use defaults for authentication).

5. Check *Change the default database* and choose *VideoStore*. Then click *Next*.

6. Click *Next* (use defaults for translation and regional settings).

7. Click *Finish* (use defaults for the final screen).

8. It is recommended that you click the *Test Data Source* button in the last screen.

9. Exit the *ODBC Data Source Administrator*.

CREATING THE MTS PACKAGE

Data services layer objects are typically deployed in an MTS package. I'll discuss exactly what these are and what they do in Chapter 12. The following steps take place on the server. Once accomplished, you'll have installed the data services layer components on the server. The next step will be to generate a setup program that can be run from the clients.

To create the MTS package used by the *Mom-n-Pop Video Store* data services layer components:

1. Start the *MTS Explorer* utility from the *NT Option Pack* program group and expand *Microsoft Transaction Server*, *Computers*, *My Computer*, and then *Packages Installed*.

2. Select *Packages Installed* by clicking it with the left mouse button. Then, right-click on *Packages Installed* and select *New*, then *Package*.

3. Click the *Create an Empty Package* button. Enter *Mom-n-Pop* as the name of the package, then click *Next*.

4. Click *Finish* (use defaults for package identity).

5. Under *Packages Installed*, expand *Mom-n-Pop*.

6. Under *Mom-n-Pop*, select *Components* by clicking it with the left mouse button. Then, right-click on *Components* and select *New*, then *Component*.

7. Click the *Install new Components* button.

8. Click the *Add Files* button, then navigate to and select *MPV3DAT.DLL* (originally distributed in *\VB6Adv\Demos\MomPop\Release\3Tier\ MPVdata*).

9. Click *Finish*.

GENERATING A CLIENT INSTALL PROGRAM

MTS makes it easy to perform the required client-side setup. Using the *Export* feature of MTS, you can create an EXE that clients can run to set up server access. The following steps take place on the server:

1. Back in the *MTS Explorer* utility, select the *Mom-n-Pop* package by clicking it with the left mouse button, then right-click *on Mom-n-Pop* and select *Export*.

2. In the resulting *Export Package* dialog, enter (or browse to) a file specification for the exported package. Be sure it is in a shared folder so clients can get to it. Call the package *VSPackage*.

3. Click the *Export* button.

CLIENT-SIDE SETUP FOR A 3-TIER APPLICATION

You will be installing both the presentation layer and object model on the client. The object model for the 3-tier version of the *Mom-n-Pop Video Store* is already built and located in the file *MPV3BUS.DLL* in folder *VB6Adv\Demos\MomPop\Release\3Tier\MPVServer*. You need to register the server by issuing the following command from the *Run* dialog:

```
regsvr32 \VB6Adv\Demos\MomPop\Release\3Tier\MPVServer\MPV3BUS.DLL
```

To help ease the installation of the data services layer components, see the tip under the topic *Installing the Middleware for the 2-Tier Model* in this chapter. To set up remote access to the data services layer components, you must run *VSPackage.EXE,* located under the *Clients* subfolder in the folder into which you placed the exported package during the previous step.

1. Register the object model component. It is located in *MPV3BUS.DLL*, in folder *VB6Adv\Demos\MomPop\Release\3Tier\MPVServer*.

2. Run the *VSPackage.EXE* program, located in the *Clients* subfolder in the folder into which you placed the exported package.

RUNNING THE 3-TIER APPLICATION

Run *\VB6Adv\Demos\MomPop\Release\3Tier\MPVui\MPV3UI.EXE.* The first time you run the application, it takes considerably longer to start up than the 2-tier version does. Be patient (no news is good news).

Once you've started the application, you'll see a front-end that is identical to the 2-tier version. Remember, however, that the 3-tier version uses a different database (a SQL Server version instead of the Access version). Thus, the two videos you rented earlier to *Nancy Davolio* will not appear in her list of rented videos. For much of this book, we'll work with the 2-tier version since it is somewhat easier to install.

Using Objects in a Visual Basic Application

Informally, everyone is familiar with objects. Anything and everything can be considered an object, since an object is the most generic description of any item. For example, the book you are currently reading is an object. Everything around you is an object. In fact, even abstract items can be considered objects. Such items may exist only in our heads, or as concepts.

About Objects

As human beings, we have a natural intellectual tendency to categorize, or classify things. An object's category is considered its ***class***. Formally, an ***object*** is an ***instance*** of a certain class of object. For example, I have a dog by the name of Pepper, who could be considered to be an object that is an instance of a dog class. More specifically, Pepper is a Dalmatian, which is a kind of dog. Put another way, Pepper's class is Dalmatian, which is a subclass of dog. Organizing objects and classes of objects is one of the most powerful intellectual tools possessed by human beings.

Although there are countless objects in our world and in our minds, and even though any two given objects may be vastly different from each other, all objects have two things in common: All objects appear a certain way and act a certain way. In fact, how an object appears and behaves helps us to classify that object. In addition, by stating an object's class, one would have certain expectations about that object. For example, if I were to tell you that I was about to bring Pepper, a dog, into this room, you would have a certain picture in your mind about what Pepper looks like and, being a dog, how he might act when he enters the room.

Objects and Programming

Thinking in terms of objects is a natural thing; everyone does this. This is obviously true of both programmers and non-programmers. Yet, until recently, a programmer was forced to think in an unnatural way while designing and implementing an application. It used to be that all programmers assumed that, to develop a program, one had to think like a computer. Computers, of course, cannot think. Computers can only process instructions, and most computers have a limited set of instructions. So a programmer would take a complex problem and break it down into smaller, easier to solve problems, resulting in a set of primitive functions that, when put together, would become an application. When dealing with data, a programmer was forced to construct complex relationships between pieces of information using primitive data types that the computer understood; in other words, bits and bytes. After all, a computer does not understand videos, for example. But a computer does understand numbers and strings. So, a programmer would define records and structures that created relationships between the data components of the items the application would deal with. A structure describing a video would use an integer for the video ID, a string for the title, and so on. These structures and records would be passed as parameters to the functions created by the functional decomposition of the problem. For example, a *RentVideo* function might be used to rent a video to a customer. A programmer would pass structures describing the video to be rented, and the member renting the video, to this function.

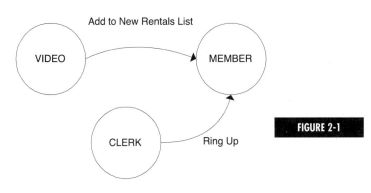

FIGURE 2-1 An informal diagram indicating the relationships between objects in the video store application.

Many excellent methodologies emerged during the years programmers were using functional decomposition. Structured programming techniques were introduced which encouraged standardizing the parameters of procedures in an application. Programmers were taught to put a lot of thought in designing functions, because changing a function's parameters could have serious rippling effects throughout an application. This early emphasis on parameter standardization is the forerunner of today's concept of interfaces and remains an important concept of object-oriented programming. If you have good structured programming skills, don't worry—you'll still make use of these skills in object-oriented programming.

For example, imagine that you are meeting with the owner of a video store to discuss the requirements for an application. The owner may explain that a member will come into her store and select a list of videos to rent. The clerk then "rings up" the member and collects the balance due for the transaction.

To clarify your understanding of the process of renting a video, you may draw a diagram using circles and arrows to represent the process. Such an informal diagram (see Figure 2-1) is a powerful way to communicate an idea, and, best of all, can be understood by both you and the video store owner, regardless of how much computer knowledge she may have. You may say to the video store owner, "Let's say this is a video, and this is a member," indicating the circles. Believe me, this is something your client will be able to do. In other words, you will both be able to use your imaginations and pretend like the circles you're drawing on a cocktail napkin really are, in actual fact, videos and members. Of course, they are nothing but symbolic representations of real-world objects, but the natural ability of humans to think abstractly enables the two of you to communicate a high-level concept in a concise and unambiguous way. I'm sure you've sat in many a design meeting with other programmers and drawn lots of circles and arrows. You were performing the fundamental steps of what object-oriented programmers call ***abstraction***, which is the process of discovering the essential objects that make up your problem domain and how these objects interact with each other and with the system user.

This brings me to an important feature of object-oriented programming. If communicating ideas abstractly is so powerful and universal, why lose track of it? Wouldn't it be fantastic if we could maintain this level of abstraction as we program? In fact, we can do this using object-oriented programming, but it requires a bit more formality than drawing circles and arrows. For example, the concept of renting videos as presented in the preceding diagram may be expressed more formally as follows:

- *Let **V** represent a video, specifically video number 52001.*
- *Let **M** represent a member of the video store, specifically member number 12001.*
- ***Add** copy number **3** to member **M**'s list of **New Rentals**.*
- ***Ring Up** member **M**.*

Expressing the operation formally may lose some of its appeal; most people will understand the diagram more quickly than the formal, almost mathematical, description that appears above. However, we cannot compile the diagram and use it as the source code of the program.

The most formal way to express an operation is to use a high-level language that can be compiled into an executable component. Using the *Mom-n-Pop Video Store* object model, which is discussed in detail later in this chapter, this operation can be expressed as follows:

```
Dim V As Video
Dim M As Member
Set V = FindVideoByID(52001)
Set M = FindMemberByID(12001)
M.NewRentals.Add V, 3
M.RingUp 2
```

The code shown above finds a video given its ID, then finds a member given a member ID. Copy number *3* of the video is added to the member's *New Rentals* list. Then, the code "rings up" the member, collecting a balance due of two dollars.

As another example, the following Visual Basic code will, for *Member 12001*, list all rented videos and their due dates:

```
Dim M As Member
Dim RV As RentedVideos
Dim V As RentedVideo
Set M = FindMemberByID(12001)
For Each V In M.RentedVideos
    MsgBox V.Title & "Due: " & V.DateDue
Next
```

The following Visual Basic code will return all videos rented by *Member 12001:*

```
Dim M As Member
Dim v As RentedVideo
Set M = FindMemberByID(12001)
For Each v In M.RentedVideos
    M.Returns.Add v, v.CopyNo
Next
M.RingUp 0
```

Most developers are impressed when they see something like this for the first time. Hopefully you can already see the benefits of designing and developing applications in tiers. In using an object model that encapsulates the business rules, the programmer of a Win32 user interface can focus primarily on user interface details, and does not need to actually implement business rules. For example, notice how the *Rent* method of the *Video* object took care of all the details of renting a video, including calculating the due date. In other words, the middleware implements the business rules.

At this point, you may be wondering how this all works. Many developers that see examples like this for the first time express their confusion in the following way: "I know what that code *does*, I just don't know *how* it does it." But that is exactly the way a middleware developer expects the presentation (or user interface) layer developer to feel. It's the job of the middleware developer to create object models that are easy to use and which naturally reflect the ways of the business—remember that another name for middleware is business rules. Middleware developers "sweat the details" and provide programmers of the presentation layer with a rich, robust set of objects. In other words, at this point, you're not supposed to know how the objects work internally. By going through the steps in this chapter, you'll appreciate what presentation layer programmers go through when developing the user interface. Many of these programmers will feel uncomfortable trusting the middleware to do so much.

Programmers have, historically speaking, often been the ones who had to sweat all the details. It was often necessary for a programmer to fully understand all the internal workings of a program before undertaking a modification or enhancement. It's interesting to note that this is not the case in everyday life. For example, the fact that you, as a developer of user interface code, will not be aware of how the *Video* object is implemented should not discourage you from using it. You don't need to know how a video works in real life to view it. Did you ever take apart a video cassette tape? Internally, real video cassette tapes are more complicated than you may have thought. The VCR itself is, of course, even more complicated. Fortunately, you don't need to understand the internal workings of either the VCR or the videotape to play a video on your VCR. This is also the case when working with objects at the presentation layer; programmers don't need to know how the *Video* object is implemented internally.

Many programmers are nervous about using object-oriented programming techniques because they tend to "hide" details. Such programmers, as previously mentioned, often feel it necessary to fully understand the inner workings of an application's supporting functions before they can use them. This is no longer possible, since the software developed today is often too large and complex for a single programmer, or at least for all programmers, to be able to be completely familiar with all parts of an application. Using object-oriented programming techniques, it's much easier for a project manager to delegate development among the programming staff.

Objects and Visual Basic

Moving back into the technical world of Visual Basic, let me return to the concept of an object. By technical definition, an ***object*** is an encapsulation of code and data that can be treated as a unit. Examples of objects used in Visual Basic include forms and controls; you have certainly used these objects before. Objects have properties and methods and can also raise events, which are really methods implemented on the client side and invoked from the server side (more about that later in this book). Applications written as ActiveX components expose their objects to external applications, which can then control them. In Visual Basic, programmers can implement objects using class modules. I'll show you how to design and create class modules in Chapters 6 and 7. For now, I'm going to focus on using existing classes of objects.

About Object Variables

An ***object variable*** is a variable that refers to, or references, an object. In other words, the object variable is not the object; rather, it provides the programmer with the means to access and control the underlying, or referenced, object. In this respect, Visual Basic is like the Java programming language, but different than the C++ programming language. Java programmers are accustomed to considering an object and its referencing variable as two different things. In both Visual Basic and Java, using an object is typically a two-step process: an object variable is declared, and then an object is created. The object variable is then used to reference the underlying object.

Note, however, that this discussion assumes you are comfortable (or will soon become comfortable) programming abstractly. This is because, in Visual Basic programming terms, the object is not a real object either, but an abstract representation of a real object. Like the circle used to represent a video in the diagram you used to clarify your understanding of the application, the object variable simply represents an actual, real-life video. Consider the following Visual Basic statement:

```
Dim V As Video
```

In this case, the object variable *V* can represent a real video, but is not, of course, a real video. A real video can be placed inside a VCR, viewed, paused, and rewound. This so-called "video object" cannot do that; if you want to watch a video, you'll have to get a real one. The variable *V* in this case is a representation, or an abstract model, of a real video. However, you can rent this video object as well as return it and calculate late charges on it. These operations were implemented because they fall within the scope of the so-called problem domain. Put another way, an object models a real-world object. Using an object-oriented approach to software design and development enables us to maintain a level of abstraction close to that which we used when we drew circles and arrows in a diagram, even while writing code.

Creating Objects in Visual Basic

When you declare an object variable in Visual Basic, it initially refers to no object. The object variable must be set to an instance of an object, either to an existing object or to a newly created one. The **Set** keyword is required when modifying the object reference, which is another point of confusion among Visual Basic programmers: When and why do I use **Set?** I'll return to this question shortly.

Visual Basic programmers can use the keyword *Nothing* to test for empty object variables. Actual instances of an object are created using the **New** keyword, the **CreateObject** function, or, if running the object as an MTS component, the **CreateInstance** method of the **ObjectContext** object. There is a great deal of misunderstanding regarding which technique is appropriate and most efficient. Using **New** requires that the application have a reference to the object's type library, unless the class being instantiated is defined inside the project. If the class is defined within the project and you use the **New** keyword to create the object, Visual Basic uses an internal mechanism to create the object—it does not use COM. This approach is unacceptable for creating an object from within an MTS component. An MTS component must use the *CreateInstance* method of the *ObjectContext* object to create objects that are either passed back from the application or which use the same transaction context as the creating object. Even if neither of these conditions are true, most MTS developers always use the *CreateInstance* method to create objects; doing so is always safe. Creating and managing MTS components is discussed in Chapters 12 and 13.

USING *NEW* TO CREATE AN OBJECT

In general, client-side code can use either the **New** keyword or the **Create-Object** function to create an object, so I'll focus on the distinction between these approaches. When you use the **New** keyword to create an object, Visual Basic uses COM to create the object if the class is not declared inside the project. If the class is declared inside the project, Visual Basic uses an internal mechanism to create the object, which is generally more efficient than COM. If the class is not declared within your project, you must insert a reference to the server's type library (this is done by selecting *References* from the *Project* menu). If the type library is not registered, you can use the *browse* button to browse to the type library, which is contained in a TLB, DLL, or EXE file.

If an object variable is declared **As Class-Name**, Visual Basic uses **early binding**, or what C++ programmers refer to as **vtable binding**, which is a direct function call binding. For example,

```
' Early (vtable) binding with the New keyword:
Dim objVideo As Video
Set objVideo = New Video
```

If an object variable is declared **As Object**, Visual Basic uses **late binding**. This translates to using the **dispatch interface,** which looks up properties and methods by name, which is slower. For example,

```
' Late (dispatch) binding with the New keyword:
Dim objVideo as Object
Set objVideo = New Video
```

Now I'll return to a question posed earlier. Why is it necessary to use the **Set** keyword? The reason is because an object reference on its own as an expression implicitly references the default property of an object. If an object has no default property, Visual Basic will display an error indicating that the *Object doesn't support this property or method.* If an object has a default property, without the keyword *Set*, you are attempting to set the default property to a new instance of the object. In this case, Visual Basic will probably indicate that there is a type mismatch on the property.

If you reference a property or method through an object variable for which no object reference has been given, Visual Basic gives you a runtime error indicating *Object variable or with block variable not set.*

USING THE *CREATEOBJECT* FUNCTION TO CREATE AN OBJECT

When you use the **CreateObject** function to create an object, Visual Basic always uses COM to create the object, even if the class is defined inside the project. A common misconception is that the *CreateObject* function always uses late, or dispatch binding, but this is not the case. It is possible for Visual Basic to use either late or early binding with either the *New* keyword or the *CreateObject* function. It is a matter of how the object is declared, and whether or not the object supports vtable binding (via a custom or dual interface). This is discussed in more detail in Chapter 8.

The syntax for *CreateObject* is as follows:

```
Set objVariable = CreateObject ( "server.class" , _
                                  "server-name"
```

The first parameter to the *CreateObject* function, which is required, specifies the programmatic ID, or ProgID, of the object to be created. By convention, this is *server.class*. However, it can really be any string desired by the component developer. A COM object created with Visual Basic will be assigned a ProgID of *project-name.class-name*, but C++ programmers using ATL often specify a version number as well. Thus, it is not unusual to see ProgIDs in the format *server.class.version*. The Visual Basic format, which uses no version number, is known by COM developers as a version-independent ProgID.

The *CreateObject* function has an optional parameter that specifies the server on which the object should be created. This information cannot be expressed with the *New* keyword, which uses the registry to locate the remote server hosting the object. The use of this parameter is discussed in more detail in Chapter 11.

It is not necessary to insert a reference to the server's type library to use *CreateObject*, unless you want to declare the object variable *As Class-Name*. If an object variable is declared *As Class-Name*, Visual Basic uses early binding, or what C++ programmers refer to as vtable binding, which is a direct function call binding. For example,

```
' Late (vtable) binding with CreateObject:
Dim objVideo As Video
Set objVideo = CreateObject ("MPV2BUS.Video")
```

If an object variable is declared *As Object*, Visual Basic uses late binding. This translates to using the dispatch interface, which looks up properties and methods by name, which is slower. For example:

```
' Early (dispatch) binding with CreateObject:
Dim objVideo as Object
Set objVideo = CreateObject ("MPV2BUS.Video")
```

Object Models

Prior to implementing the middle tier of an N-tier client/server application, it is often necessary to design an object model. An object model provides an idealized, abstract representation of the objects discovered in the problem domain. It also defines the relationships, particularly containment, between objects. An object model is an excellent tool for visualizing the objects provided by the middleware; it can be used as a design document for middleware developers, and as a reference for developers of the presentation layer. Visual Studio 6.0 provides a new graphical tool, the *Visual Modeler,* to create graphical representations of object models and other components. *Visual Modeler* can also generate stubbed Visual Basic code from the model.

Note that many enterprise applications exist without an object model, using instead only stateless objects in the data services layer. Such applications are driven primarily by Internet-based clients using a Web browser in the presentation layer. In fact, many developers consider this model to be a 3-tier client/server application, since code in the presentation layer does not directly access the database. Stateless objects are more difficult to use than object models, since they cannot provide properties, and typically have an above average number of parameters. If any of your presentation layer applications will be Win32 clients (running on Windows), you should definitely consider using an object model as a thin layer of object-oriented code over the stateless data services layer components running under MTS. Browser-based user interface clients, which typically cannot hold state, must use the stateless components in the data services layer, driving them with a scripting language and using, for example, ASP. Using MTS as an environment for hosting objects is covered in Chapters 12 and 13. In Chapter 15, I will introduce ASP and scripting.

Understanding an Object Model

Developers of the presentation layer will spend a great deal of time studying and using the objects represented in the object model. For this reason, it is essential to provide good documentation on the objects contained in an application's middleware. In the next section, I'll list and describe the objects provided in the *Mom-n-Pop Video Store* object model. But before I get into that, you should know that an object model, and the diagram that represents it, is a purposely over-simplified, logical view of the middleware. If you are not careful, you can easily make incorrect deductions about an object model, so I'll point out a few of these misconceptions.

First of all, object models do not have to reflect the actual implementation of the objects they model—this is particularly true for containment. While it may appear that one object contains another, this is often not the case. Containment is often accomplished by implementing a property, named after the contained object, in the container object. For example, the object model diagram for the *Mom-n-Pop Video Store* (see Figure 2-2) indicates that the *Member* object contains a *RentedVideos* collection, which contains zero or more *RentedVideo* objects. In actual fact, the *Member* object has a *RentedVideos* property, which, when invoked, creates a *RentedVideos* collection object, which is returned as the return value of the method. Thus, a presentation layer programmer can use an expression such as *M.RentedVideos.Count*, where *M* is an instance of a member, to return the number of videos rented by that member.

A second point to make about object models is that their diagrams do not necessarily list all the objects (that is, classes) that are implemented by the middleware. Several so-called utility classes may exist that do not fit into the hierarchy.

The final point to make is that, like much of the public side of middleware, object models do not necessarily reflect the design or implementation of the underlying database or databases. One can make no assumptions about the design of a database from the design of the object model. For example, there is not a one-to-one correspondence between objects in an object model and tables in a database. Nor is there necessarily a one-to-one correspondence between the properties of an object and the columns of a table in the database. In fact, middleware developers can and should have a completely different set of design goals than database developers. A database developer concentrates on normalizing the database design, making certain that data can be referenced uniquely and unambiguously, and that there is no duplication of data. Designers of object models, on the other hand, use an ideal representation of the data. To do a good job designing an object model, a middleware designer must imagine what a presentation layer programmer will want to do. For example, the *Mom-n-Pop Video Store* object model has a *RentedVideo* class, which provides properties to obtain the ID and title of a rented video. The *Video* class has these same properties. A database designer would correctly point out that the title of a rented video could be obtained from the *Videos* table, which can be relationally joined with the *RentedVideos* table. In fact, this is exactly how the video store middleware is implemented; it simply hides this detail from the presentation layer. The *Title* property of a *RentedVideo* object is available because it's likely that a presentation layer programmer will need to access the title of a rented video. It would become quite tedious for a programmer to have to look up the title of each rented video by using the video ID.

In summary, you can break all the database designer's normalization rules when designing middleware. Besides, there would be little need for a layer between the user interface and the database if all the middleware did was reflect the database design. Middleware should be optimized for usability and programmability at the user interface programmer's level.

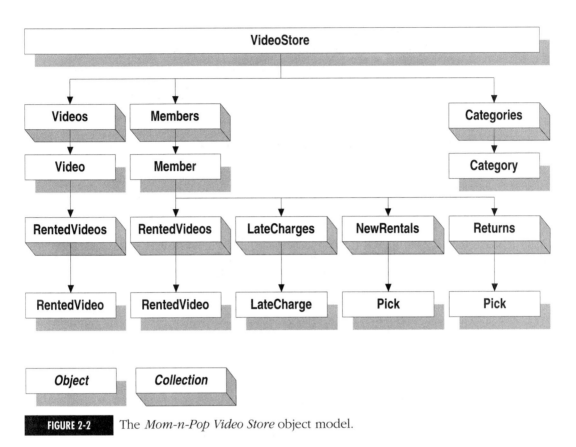

FIGURE 2-2   The *Mom-n-Pop Video Store* object model.

The Mom-n-Pop Video Store Object Model

I know from twenty years of experience as a developer how boring it can be to look at someone else's application. This is true whether or not you're looking at code or at a design document. I have to admit that whenever a student approaches me during a break to discuss his or her own application, I cringe when they grab a marker and start drawing circles and arrows on the board. However, if I were you, I wouldn't start developing a multi-tiered application until you've seen how a successful one was designed and implemented. The following sections describe the *Mom-n-Pop Video Store* object model. The sections also provide me with a convenient place to discuss a number of topics, including important design issues. I encourage you to study this object model carefully; be assured that the good stuff is forthcoming.

The *Mom-n-Pop Video Store* object model (see Figure 2-2) is an abstraction of the objects discovered in the problem domain (the techniques used to design and create this object model will be discussed in Chapter 7). The model defines a top-level object called **VideoStore**. This top-level, or root object, serves as a convenient container object for the other objects in the object model. Because of the way the *VideoStore* object is implemented, it is neither explicitly created nor referenced by programmers using the object model.

Under the *VideoStore* top-level object is a collection called **Categories**, which in turn contains **Category** objects that describe the categories of videos at the video store. The **Members** collection contains **Member** objects. Each *Member* object has four collections, **LateCharges**, **RentedVideos, NewRentals,** and **Returns**. The **Videos** collection, which contains the list of videos at the video store, also contains a *RentedVideos* collection, which is a list of the copies of a particular video rented, and to which member. The **Details** collection contains **Detail** objects, which are used to return a receipt detailing a transaction. Brief descriptions of each object are listed in Table 2-1.

Using this object model, it is easy for an application to iterate through all the members and all the videos in the video store. It is also easy to list, for a particular member, the videos rented to that member—this would be done by iterating though the *RentedVideos* collection of a particular *Member* object. Likewise, it is easy to list, for a particular video, which copies of the video are rented and to which member.

TABLE 2-1	Objects in the Mom-n-Pop Object Model
Object	**Description**
VideoStore	Top-level, or root object. Contains the *Categories* collection and methods that are used to locate member and video objects. This is implemented as a global object, which means it does not have to be referenced in your Visual Basic application.
Categories	An enumerable collection of *Category* objects. By enumerable, I mean that a VB programmer can use a *For Each* loop to iterate through the items in the collection.
Category	Describes a video category, such as Family, Drama, Horror, and so on. Each category has a maximum nights rental, price, etc.
Members	A collection of *Member* objects, returned by the *FindMemberByName* method of the *VideoStore* object.
Member	Represents a member of the video store. This object has properties such as first name, last name, and so on. It also has two collections, *LateCharges* and *RentedVideos*, and an *Update* method to make changes to the member's database record.
LateCharges	An enumerable collection of *LateCharge* objects.
LateCharge	Represents a late charge assessed to a member. This object has properties indicating which video was rented, when it was due, when it was returned, and the total late fee.
RentedVideos	An enumerable collection of *RentedVideo* objects.
RentedVideo	Represents a rented video. Describes which copy of the video was rented, when it was rented, when it is due, and which member rented the video. Has a method, *ReturnVideo*, which is used to return a video to the shelf.
NewRentals	Actually a property of class **Picks,** this collection is contained in a *Member* object. New videos to be rented are added to this collection before invoking the *RingUp* method on a *Member*.
Returns	Actually a property of class **Picks,** this collection is contained in a *Member* object. Videos to be returned are added to this collection before invoking the *RingUp* method on a *Member*.
Pick	A simplified *Video* class that basically consists of a *video ID* and a *copy number*. This class makes up the collection class **Picks**, of which a *Member* object has two - one for renting and one for returning videos.
Videos	A collection of *Video* objects, returned by the *FindVideoByName* method of the *VideoStore* object.
Video	Represents a video in the inventory. Has properties describing the video, such as its title, cast, director, number of copies, and so on. Also has methods to update its record in the database and check if the video is rented.

OBJECT MODEL REFERENCE: VIDEOSTORE

The *VideoStore* object is the top-level, or root object, in the *Mom-n-Pop Video Store* object model. As a global object, there is no need for the developer to explicitly reference the *VideoStore* object. In other words, methods such as *ReturnVideo* can be invoked as though they were global functions. Properties and methods of the *VideoStore* object are listed in Tables 2-2 and 2-3. As an example of using this object, the following code returns a rented video, specifically copy number *1* of video number *52000*:

```
' Invoke ReturnVideo method on VideoStore object:
ReturnVideo 52000, 1, False
```

There are two things to note from this simple example. First, the *ReturnVideo* function is invoked as though it were a global function. In actual fact, *ReturnVideo* is a method of the *VideoStore* object. Since *VideoStore* is a global (or top-level) object, there is no need for the programmer to explicitly invoke the method through an instance of a *VideoStore* object. This is being done implicitly. In Chapter 7, I'll show you how to implement an object model that includes a top-level object.

The second thing to note is just how simple this example is. A great deal of complexity may be hidden behind the implementation of the business tasks related to returning a video. Clearly, the function must ultimately update the database. But it's not that simple. Returning a video may trigger the calculation of late charges for a member—how these late charges are calculated, if indeed any are calculated, is not the concern of a user interface programmer. Additionally, the application logic behind the *ReturnVideo* function may end up executing on a remote computer if the application has been deployed across multiple hosts. In Chapter 7, I'll show you how the object model can hide database access logic from the presentation layer in a 2-tier application architecture. In Chapters 12 and 13, I'll show you how to take this concept to a 3-tier application architecture, which uses stateless objects and connection pooling to increase the scalability of an application. It is interesting to note that, in either architecture, the statements required to return a video are the same—the presentation layer developer is not concerned with the details.

TABLE 2-2	Properties of the VideoStore Object		
Property	**Type**	**Description**	
LateFee	Currency	Returns the per-night late fee.	
Categories	Categories	Returns the *Categories* collection.	

TABLE 2-3	Methods of the VideoStore Object

Method	Description
MoveAheadDate (nDays as Integer)	Advances the simulation date.
ReturnVideo (*nVideoID* as Long, *nCopyNo* as Integer, *fYesterday* as Boolean)	Used to return a video from the return box. May cause a late charge to be added to the database.
TodaysDate () As Date	Returns the current simulation date.
FindMemberByID (*nMemberID* As Long) As Member	Returns the Member object with a member ID of nMemberID.
FindMemberByName (*strLastName* as String) As Members	Returns a *Members* collection of *Member* objects with last names containing *strLastName*
FindVideoByID (*nVideoID* As Long) As Video	Returns the Video object with a video ID of *nVideoID*.
FindVideoByTitle (*strTitle* As String) As Videos	Returns a *Videos* collection of *Video* objects with titles containing *strTitle*.

OBJECT MODEL REFERENCE: CATEGORIES

The **Categories** object is an enumerable collection of *Category* objects. The methods of the *Categories* object are listed in Table 2-4. As an enumerable collection, a Visual Basic developer can use the *For Each* loop to iterate through the collection. In Chapters 6 and 7, I will illustrate how to create collections, make them enumerable, and use them to hide access to the database queries used to generate them. For now, I'd like to focus on how easy it is for a user interface developer to use the *For Each* loop to iterate through the *Categories* collection:

```
' Display names of each video category:
Dim C As Category
For Each C in Categories
  MsgBox C.Name
Next
```

A developer may also use the *Count* and *Item* methods to iterate through the collection. For example,

```
' Display names of each video category using the
' Count and Item methods:
Dim C As Category
Dim I As Integer
For I = 1 To Categories.Count
  Set C = Categories.Item(I)
  MsgBox C.Name
Next
```

| TABLE 2-4 | Methods of the Categories Object |

Method	Description
Count () As Integer	Returns number of categories.
ID (*strCategoryName* as String) As Category	Returns the *Category* object with this category name.
Item (*nIndex* as Integer) As Category	Returns the *Category* object with this category ID.

OBJECT MODEL REFERENCE: CATEGORY

The **Category** object represents a video category, such as Family, Horror, etc. Each category has its own rules for maximum number of nights rented, price, and so on. Properties of the *Category* object are listed in Table 2-5.

| TABLE 2-5 | Properties of the Category Object |

Property	Type	Description
ID	Integer	Returns the category ID number.
Name	String	Returns the category name.
Nights	Integer	Returns the maximum number of nights videos in this category can be rented.
Price	Currency	Returns the price for rental (total, *not per night*).

OBJECT MODEL REFERENCE: LATECHARGES

The **LateCharges** object is an enumerable collection of *LateCharge* objects. Properties and methods of the *LateCharges* object are listed in Tables 2-6 and 2-7. Although the *LateCharges* object has a *Total* method, which returns the total amount of late charges for a member, it is interesting to look at an example that calculates this total:

```
' Calculate total late charges:
Dim TotalLateCharges As Currency
Dim LC As LateCharge
Dim M As Member

Set M = FindMemberByID (12001)
For Each LC In M.LateCharges
   TotalLateCharges = TotalLateCharges + LC.Charge
Next
```

Note that late charges for a member appear to be contained in a *Member* object, as seen by the expression *M.LateCharges*. However, the *Member* object actually has a *LateCharges* property. The type of this property is *LateCharges*. In other words, the property's name is the same as its type. While this may seem confusing, it is illustrative of the proper way to "embed" one object into another. This technique is introduced in Chapter 6, with a complete example of the technique presented in Chapter 7.

TABLE 2-6	Properties of the LateCharges Object	
Property	**Type**	**Description**
Total	Currency	Total late charges for this customer

TABLE 2-7	Methods of the LateCharges Object
Method	**Description**
Item (*nIndex* As Integer) As LateCharge	Returns the *LateCharge* object in position *nIndex* in the collection (1 – based).

OBJECT MODEL REFERENCE: LATECHARGE

The **_LateCharge_** object represents a late charge assessed to a member (properties are listed in Table 2-8). The rules of late charges at the video store are more complex than you may at first realize:

- If a video is returned past its due date, the middleware creates a record in a _Late Charge_ table. The member must pay this fee the next time he or she rents videos.
- If a video has not been returned but is past its due date and the member rents new videos, the member must pay late charges to date before renting new videos. The middleware will not create a late charge record, but will instead adjust the due date so that the video is due "this evening."

There are no reasons for creating a late charge other than those mentioned above. Therefore, presentation layer programmers have no methods for creating late charges or adding them to a member's _LateCharges_ collection. The _LateCharge_ object is defined in such a way as to prevent its creation at the presentation layer level. You can verify this by inserting a reference to the _Mom-n-Pop Video Store_ object model (which you will do later in this chapter) and typing the following statement into your form's declarations section:

```
Dim L As New LateCharge
```

Such a statement won't compile in Visual Basic because the object model prevents the creation of _LateCharge_ objects outside the middleware. You can use _LateCharge_ objects in the presentation layer (see previous example in the section documenting the _LateCharges_ collection), but you cannot create them.

The fact that a late charge is only created when a rented video is late comes from discovering a rule in the business model. That is, in "real life," the rule of the Mom-n-Pop Video Store is that "Late charges are assessed when a video has not been returned prior to its due date." Using an object model, business rules such as this one can be enforced. This is the reason that the middleware layer is often referred to as the **_business rules_**. Implementing late charges in this manner comes from discovering a rule in the business model. Using an object model, business rules such as these can be enforced.

TABLE 2-8	Properties of the LateCharge Object	
Property	**Type**	**Description**
Charge	Currency	Returns the total late fee for a single video returned late.
CopyNo	Integer	Returns the copy number of the late video.
DateDue	Date	Returns the original due date of the late video.
DateRented	Date	Returns the original date the late video was rented.
WasReturned	Boolean	Returns **TRUE** if the video has been returned. If FALSE, the video is past due but has not yet been returned.
DateReturned	Date	Returns date video was returned. This property is only valid if the *WasReturned* property is **TRUE**. If *WasReturned* is **FALSE** and this property is referenced, the middleware will generate an error.
DaysLate	Integer	Returns the total number of days this video was late.
MemberID	Long	Returns the ID of the member who returned the video past its due date.
Title	String	Returns the title of the late video.
VideoID	Long	Returns the ID of the late video.

OBJECT MODEL REFERENCE: MEMBERS

The **Members** object is an enumerable collection of *Member* objects. It is returned from the **FindMemberByName** method of the *VideoStore* object. For example,

```
' List count of videos rented by all members with
' a last name containing "Davolio"
Dim MR As Members
Dim M As Member
Set MR = FindMemberByName("Davolio")
For Each M In MR
  MsgBox M.LastName & _
          " has rented " & _
          M.RentedVideos.Count & " videos."
Next
```

The object contains a collection of *Member* objects with last names containing the string specified as the parameter to the *VideoStore.FindMemberByName* method. Note that, since *VideoStore* is a top-level object, it does not need to be specified in the call to *FindMemberByName*. Instead, the *FindMemberByName* method appears to the presentation layer programmer as a global function.

OBJECT MODEL REFERENCE: MEMBER

The **Member** object represents a member of the video store. See Tables 2-9 and 2-10 for a list of its properties and methods. The object has a **ComputeBalance** method, which returns a **Details** collection, indicating the items (each a *Detail* object) of a transaction in progress. The *Member* object also has a **RingUp** method, which actually performs the transaction consisting of returning videos, renting new videos, and paying late charges. The object also has an **Update** method for updating the member's database record. For example,

```
Dim M As Member
Set M = FindMemberByID (12001)
M.Phone = "555-1234"
M.Address1 = "2020 Hugh Downs Lane"
M.Update
```

TABLE 2-9	Properties of the Member Object

Property	Type	Description
Address1	String	Returns/sets member's address line 1.
Address2	String	Returns/sets member's address line 2.
City	String	Returns/sets member's city.
FirstName	String	Returns/sets member's first name.
ID	Long	Returns member's ID number.
LastName	String	Returns/sets member's last name.
LateCharges	LateCharges	Returns late charges collection for this member.
NewRentals	Picks	Returns/sets list of new videos to be rented.
Phone	String	Returns/sets member's phone number.
RentedVideos	RentedVideos	Returns list of videos rented by this member.
Returns	Picks	Returns/sets list of videos being returned by this member.
State	String	Returns/sets member's state.
Zip	String	Returns/sets member's zip code.

TABLE 2-10	Methods of the Member Object

Method	Description
ComputeBalance (*objDetails* As Details) As Currency	Computes balance due for a transaction, using the *NewRentals* and *Returns* collection, and any late charges contained in the database. Returns a detailed list of charges and the total amount that will be due.
RingUp(*nTotalCollected* As Currency)	Actually performs transaction of renting and returning videos, and paying late charges. Raises an error if the balance collected does not match the balance due.
Update ()	Updates this member's record in the database.

OBJECT MODEL REFERENCE: VIDEOS

The **Videos** object is an enumerable collection of *Video* objects. It is returned from the **FindVideoByTitle** method of the *VideoStore* object. The role of the *Videos* object is comparable to that of the *Members* object. For example, to display a list of videos with the word "the" in their titles, use the following:

```
Dim VR As Videos
Dim V As Video
Set VR = FindVideoByTitle ("the")
For Each V in VR
  MsgBox V.Title
Next
```

OBJECT MODEL REFERENCE: VIDEO

The **Video** object represents a video in the database. The object has properties describing the video, such as title, copies, and so on. The *RentedTo* property (see Table 2-11) returns a *RentedVideos* collection, which is a list of the copies of this video rented to members. There are methods (see Table 2-12) to update its record in the database, and to see if the video is already rented (*IsRented*). There are also convenient properties to obtain the number of copies available and get the next date a copy of this video is due to be returned.

Note there is not a method to rent a video. To rent videos, code in the presentation layer must add each video to the *NewRentals* collection of a *Member* object, and then invoke the *RingUp* method on the *Member* object. More about this shortly.

There will be one *Video* object for each video, but not for each copy of a video. Even if, for example, the video store has forty copies of *Citizen Kane*, there will be only one *Video* object representing it. To indicate the number of copies of a particular video in the store's inventory, the *Video* object has a *Copies* property that indicates the total number of copies of a particular video.

The *RentedTo* property returns a *RentedVideos* collection, which is a list of the copies of the video rented to members. As I've indicated, the *Member* object also has a *RentedVideos* collection (available via the *RentedVideos* property). There is no difference in the structure of these objects; the *RentedVideos* object in the *Video* object is the same kind of object as *RentedVideos* in the *Video* object. With this implementation, a presentation layer programmer can, for a given member, list the videos rented by the member. The programmer can also, for a given video, list which copies of the video are rented and to which member.

Convenient properties are provided for checking the availability of a video. The *CopiesAvailable* property indicates the number of copies of a video that are available for renting. The *NextDue* property returns the earliest due date of the video (if all copies are available, the property returns today's date). Using these properties, it should be no problem for a programmer to provide a feature for an operator to respond to a member's inquiry regarding when a desired video will be available for rental.

| **TABLE 2-11** | Properties of the Video Object |

Property	Type	Description
Cast	String	Returns/sets a CR/LF-delimited string of actors in this movie.
CategoryID	Integer	Returns/sets the video's category ID.
CategoryName	String	Returns the name of the video's category.
Copies	Integer	Returns/sets the total number of copies of this video.
CopiesAvailable	Integer	Returns the number of non-rented copies.
Description	String	Returns/sets a description of this movie.
Director	String	Returns/sets the name of this movie's director.
ID	Long	Returns this video's ID number.
NextDue	Date	Returns the first date a rented copy of this video is scheduled to be returned.
Price	Currency	Returns the rental price of this video.
Rating	VideoRatingConstants	Returns/sets the rating of this video (G, PG, etc.).
RentedTo	RentedVideos	Returns a list of copies of this video that are rented.
Stars	Integer	Returns/sets the number of "stars" given this video by movie reviewers.
Title	String	Returns/sets the video's title.
Year	Integer	Returns/sets the year this video was released.

TABLE 2-12	Methods of the Video Object

Method	Description
IsRented (*nCopyNo* As Integer) As Boolean	Returns **TRUE** if the copy of this video is rented.
Update ()	Updates this video's record in the database.

OBJECT MODEL REFERENCE: RENTEDVIDEOS

The **RentedVideos** object is an enumerable collection of **RentedVideo** objects. Instances of this type of object exist in both *Video* and *Member* objects. When used from a *Video* object, the collection lists which copies, if any, of this video are rented and to which member. When used from a *Member* object, the collection lists which videos, if any, are rented to the member.

The following example illustrates how a simple function can be written to display all videos rented to a particular member:

```
' *** Display all videos rented to a member
Dim M As Member
Dim RV As RentedVideo

Set M = Members.Member (12001)
For Each RV In M.RentedVideos
  MsgBox RV.Title
Next
```

The **RentedVideos** object contains no methods for adding or removing rented videos to the collection. In this application's middleware, a rented video can only be added to the *RentedVideos* collection as a side effect of invoking the **RingUp** method on a **Member** object. The same method may also remove videos from a member's *RentedVideos* collection, since members often return videos as they check out new ones (note that videos can also be returned from a drop box, in which case the *ReturnVideo* method of the *VideoStore* object is used).

OBJECT MODEL REFERENCE: RENTEDVIDEO

The **RentedVideo** object represents a copy of a video that has been rented to a member. Properties of the *RentedVideo* object are listed in Table 2-13. At first, you may disagree with the design decision to use a different object than *Video* to represent a video that is rented. In fact, the *Video* object could have been written to maintain a state as to the video's availability (rented or not), but it is not that simple. For reasons stated in the following paragraphs, the *Mom-n-Pop Video Store* object model forces a distinction between a video and a rented video.

First of all, in this object model, a *Video* object can represent one or more copies of a video. The store may have, for example, ten copies of *The Wizard of Oz* in the video store. When a member rents a video, it must be one of these ten copies. While the *Video* object has a *Copies* property, which indicates the total number of copies of the video in the inventory, the *RentedVideo* object has a *Copy* property, which indicates which copy of the video is rented.

There are other considerations as well. For example, a *RentedVideo* has a due date, while a *Video* does not. Since there appears to be a different set of properties and methods for a video that is rented, I decided to create two different types of objects.

Now, if you've done any object-oriented design and/or programming, you may point out that a rented video is a *kind of* video. That is, a rented video has the same properties as a video (title, cast, and so forth), in addition to other properties and methods (copy number, return, and so on). Object-oriented designers look for this is-a-kind-of relationship between classes, as it suggests using derivation. A C++ or Java programmer may use inheritance to derive the *RentedVideo* class from the *Video* class. While this can also be done in Visual Basic, it would have to be done using interface inheritance. A C++ or Java programmer has the advantage of having the availability of implementation inheritance. All a C++ or Java programmer has to do is derive a class from a base class, and a fully implemented "clone" of the base class is available in the derived class. With interface inheritance, which is the only type of inheritance provided by Visual Basic (C++ and Java have both), implementation inheritance can be accomplished only by implementing all the properties and methods of the base class, delegating each property/method call to a so-called "inner object," created when the derived class is instantiated. This is a tedious process and is just as susceptible to the "fragile base class" problem familiar to C++ and Java programmers, making such casual use of inheritance in Visual Basic impractical. Interface inheritance is useful in Visual Basic – a primary use occurs when developing MTS components, which may be called back by the *MTS Executive*. Examples of interface inheritance are presented in Chapters 6 and 12.

TABLE 2-13		Properties of the RentedVideo Object

Property	Type	Description
CopyNo	Integer	Returns the copy number of the video that is rented.
DateDue	Date	Returns the date the video is scheduled to be returned.
DateRented	Date	Returns the original date the video was rented.
FirstName	String	Returns the first name of the member who rented this copy of the video.
IsPastDue	Boolean	Returns **TRUE** if the video is still rented and it is past the due date.
LastName	String	Returns the last name of the member who rented this copy of the video.
MemberID	Long	Returns the renter's member ID.
Title	String	Returns the video's title.
VideoID	Long	Returns the video's ID.

OBJECT MODEL REFERENCE: THE PICKS COLLECTION

The *Picks* collection is a class that implements a list of *Pick* objects. Properties and methods of the *Picks* collection are listed in Tables 2-14 and 2-15. A *Pick* object is a simplified version of a *Video* object. There are two *Picks* collections for each *Member* object. The *NewRentals* property of a *Member* object returns a *Picks* collection that consists of new videos to be rented by that member. The *Returns* property of a *Member* object returns a *Picks* collection that consists of videos that the member is returning.

To rent new videos, presentation layer code must add a *Video* object to the *Picks* collection accessed via the *NewRentals* property of the *Member* object. To return videos, the presentation layer code must add a *RentedVideo* object to the *Picks* collection accessed via the *Returns* property of the *Member* object.

Since the *Add* method of the *Picks* collection can accept either a *Video* or *RentedVideo*, the *Add* method declares the parameter as an *Object*. This is somewhat similar to the polymorphism features of languages such as C++.

TABLE 2-14		Methods of the Picks Object

Property	Type	Description
Count	Long	Returns the count of *Video/RentedVideo* objects in the collection.

TABLE 2-15	Methods of the Member Object
Method	**Description**
Add (*PickObject* As Object, *CopyNo* As Integer)	Adds a *Video* or *RentedVideo* object to the collection.
Clear	Clears the collection of all objects.
Remove (*nIndex* As Integer)	Removes a *Video* or *RentedVideo* object from the collection.

OBJECT MODEL REFERENCE: PICK

A **Pick** object is a simplified *Video* object that consists entirely of read-only properties (see Table 2-16). The *Pick* object implements the items of a *Picks* collection, which is a list of new videos to be rented by a member, or videos to be returned by a member.

Code in the presentation layer cannot directly create *Pick* objects; it can only create *Pick* objects as a side effect of invoking the *Add* method on a *Picks* collection. Presentation layer code can, however, iterate through a list of existing *Pick* objects by accessing a *Picks* collection, through either the *NewRentals* or *Returns* properties of a *Member* object. I'll illustrate how *Pick* objects and *Picks* collections are used shortly, and explain why it was necessary to use these objects in the object model.

TABLE 2-16	Properties of the Pick Object	
Property	**Type**	**Description**
CopyNo	Integer	Returns copy number of video to be rented or returned.
Price	Currency	Returns rental price of video.
Title	String	Returns title of video to be rented or returned.
VideoID	Long	Returns ID of video to be rented or returned.

OBJECT MODEL REFERENCE: DETAILS

The **Details** object is an enumerable collection of **Detail** objects (see Table 2-17 for a list of its properties). A *Details* object lists the details of a transaction to be performed. It is returned by the *ComputeBalance* method of the *Member* object.

TABLE 2-17	Properties of the Details Object	
Property	**Type**	**Description**
Count	Long	Returns number of *Detail* objects in the collection.
Total	Currency	Returns total amount that will be due if this transaction is actually carried out.

OBJECT MODEL REFERENCE: DETAIL

The **Detail** object implements the items in the **Details** collection. Each *Detail* object has a set of read-only properties (listed in Table 2-18) that describe the particulars of a transaction that is to be carried out.

TABLE 2-18	Properties of the Detail Object	
Property	**Type**	**Description**
Amount	Currency	Returns the amount due for this particular item.
Code	String	Returns a code indicating what this item is. Code **N** indicates a new rental, while code **L** indicates a late charge.
Description	String	Returns a description of the item.
ItemID	Long	Returns an item ID (the video ID is used).

OBJECT MODEL REFERENCE: CONSTANTS

The *Mom-n-Pop Video Store* object model exports several constants to the developer. These constants provide meaningful symbols that can be used in place of numbers for such items as error codes and movie ratings. For example, in the database, the rating number of 2 indicates that the movie is rated PG. If a programmer uses the symbol *vrPG* instead of the number 2, it is likely that the code will be more readable.

Constants are defined using Visual Basic enumerations, and are often prefixed with a code to avoid name collisions. The video rating constants, for example, are all prefixed by the letters "*vr*," for video rating, while the video store error code constants are all prefixed by the letters "*vse*," which stands for video store error.

The *VideoRatingConstants* enumeration defines code numbers for the motion picture industry's rating system (G, PG, etc.). The *VideoStoreErrors* enumeration defines code numbers representing errors that may be raised from the ActiveX component that implements the *Video Store* object model. A Visual Basic programmer can trap errors raised by ActiveX Components using the *On Error* statement and, in the error handler, use the expression

Err.Number, to determine the error number. Note that all errors are offset by the constant *vbObjectError*. The reason for having to use this constant for user-defined error codes is discussed in Chapter 6.

The enumerations that define the constants in the *Mom-n-Pop Video Store* application are defined in the *VideoStore* object, and appear as follows:

```
Public Enum VideoRatingConstants
    vrNR = 0
    vrG = 1
    vrPG = 2
    vrPG13 = 3
    vrR = 4
    vrNC17 = 5
End Enum


Public Enum VideoStoreErrors
    vseNoSuchMember = vbObjectError + 100
    vseNoSuchVideo = vbObjectError + 110
    vseTxnAlreadyStarted = vbObjectError + 120
    vseNoTxnStarted = vbObjectError + 130
    vseInvalidCopyNumber = vbObjectError + 140
    vseAlreadyRented = vbObjectError + 150
    vseNoDSN = vbObjectError + 160
End Enum
```

Stateful Objects and Transactions

Using the **Picks** collection and **Pick** objects deserve an explanation. In short, these objects are necessary because it is a bad idea to expect the server to hold state across a database transaction. If you ignore this advice, you will have trouble moving to three tiers and building scalable, stateless objects in the data services layer.

Business-Focused Design

Many object-oriented designers would have used a *Rent* method of the *Video* object (or perhaps the method would have been assigned to the *Member* object). Having a *Rent* method on the *Video* object would have perhaps been an elegant abstraction. But it does not reflect how the video store works! You must be very careful to design your object models close to the real world, especially when database transactions will be involved. Videos do not rent themselves. Therefore, we would not use a *Rent* method on the *Video* object.

Also, members do not just rent a video—they may rent a list of videos! And, as members rent videos, they can return videos and pay late charges.

In other words, the dynamics of the point-of-sale transaction are more complex than renting an individual video.

Object-oriented designers must walk a thin line between using elegant abstractions and implementing concrete business tasks. Conversely, many developers with several years of experience dating back to the days before object-oriented programming focus only on the procedures or tasks involved in a transaction. The appropriate paradigm, especially when designing a scalable, multi-tiered application is to arrive at a middle ground. Important details of the business rules should not be casually abstracted away. Many object-oriented designers need to take more of a business attitude when designing an object model. In short, to design a successful object model, you must model the business and not just the objects in the business.

Candidate Solutions for State and Transactions

At this point, I'll compare two candidate solutions for renting videos to a member. In the first candidate solution, I'll provide a *Rent* method for the *Video* object. The second candidate solution (which is used in the released version of the *Mom-n-Pop Video Store*) uses a *Picks* collection to "batch up" a list of new rentals, then rents all the videos at once.

CANDIDATE SOLUTION: USING A RENT METHOD ON A VIDEO

If I had used a **Rent** method on the **Video** object, I would have needed another method in the middleware to indicate the start of a list of videos to rent (see Figure 2-3). The server (or ActiveX Component) would have to keep track of these videos. In other words, it would have to *hold state* across the transaction.

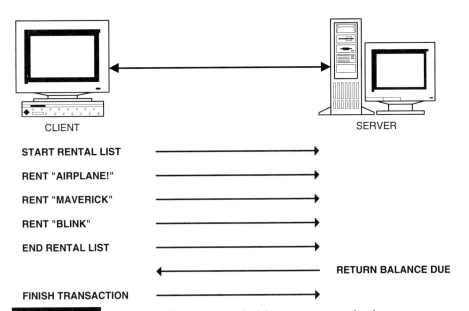

CLIENT   SERVER

START RENTAL LIST

RENT "AIRPLANE!"

RENT "MAVERICK"

RENT "BLINK"

END RENTAL LIST

RETURN BALANCE DUE

FINISH TRANSACTION

FIGURE 2-3 Expecting the server to hold state across a database transaction will result in a non-scalable solution.

The presentation layer would then need to tell the middleware that the list is complete, at which time the middleware would compute the balance. I would not want the presentation layer to compute the balance, as this requires database access and is governed by the business rules.

Holding state in the middleware is fine in a 2-tier client/server application, but not when it's being done across a database transaction. Holding state in the data services layer of a 3-tier client/server application is never okay if you expect it to scale to a large number of users.

ALTERNATIVE SOLUTION: USING A LIST OF VIDEOS TO BE RENTED

Using a collection of videos to rent is better, and is closer to the way business is actually done at the video store (see Figure 2-4). In a 2-tier client/server application, methods can be provided to add new rentals to a collection. This can be done independently of any database transaction. A method can be provided to compute the balance due of all rentals at once. Another method can be used to actually perform the transaction. The latter method would require a transaction on the database; its lifetime would be no longer than the method itself.

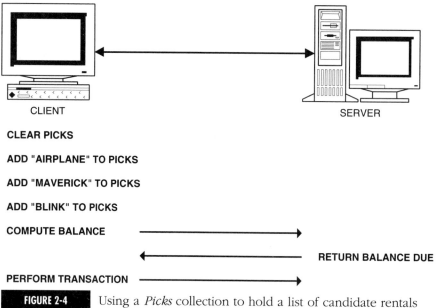

CLIENT　　　　　　　　　　　　　　　　　**SERVER**

CLEAR PICKS

ADD "AIRPLANE" TO PICKS

ADD "MAVERICK" TO PICKS

ADD "BLINK" TO PICKS

COMPUTE BALANCE

RETURN BALANCE DUE

PERFORM TRANSACTION

FIGURE 2-4 Using a *Picks* collection to hold a list of candidate rentals on the client is a better approach. The entire list can be sent as an array to the sever.

In a 3-tier client/server application, an object model layer can hold the state, since this component is typically distributed on the client. It can then convert the *Picks* collection to an array and send it at once to an object in the data services layer, which would not need to hold state.

Using an Object Model in a Visual Basic Application

To use an object model from a Visual Basic program, you will need to insert a reference to its type library. While this step is not absolutely necessary, it does enable early object binding. Early object binding is generally preferable to a Visual Basic programmer because it provides a number of features.

First of all, inserting a reference to the middleware's type library enables the Visual Basic compiler to recognize all the objects in the library as types. For example, you can declare a variable to be of type **Video**. If you don't insert a reference to the middleware's type library, you will need to declare all object variables as **Object**. This may make it more difficult for you or some other programmer to understand your code at a later time. You can also use the Visual Basic keyword **New** to create instances of objects, instead of having to use the **CreateObject** function, which requires the object's programmatic ID (or ProgID) as a parameter.

Early object binding also enables the compiler to perform type checking and syntax validation on the properties and methods of the objects in the object model. In fact, if you use late binding (declaring your objects as *Object*), the Visual Basic compiler will not verify any of the properties or methods invoked on the objects. If, for example, you accidentally misspelled the *RingUp* method as *RangUp*, the compiler would still generate code, and you would not discover the mistake until runtime, when you would receive an error indicating that the "object does not support this property or method." This is because, lacking knowledge of the underlying type of object, Visual Basic must literally look up the property or method by name at runtime. This brings me to the next advantage of using early binding.

When a Visual Basic programmer uses late binding, implying that objects are declared as *Object* and no type library reference has been inserted, Visual Basic is forced to use the object's dispatch interface, or dispinterface. A dispinterface is a standard COM interface, officially known as *IDispatch*. This interface contains functions for dynamically invoking an ActiveX Component's properties and methods at runtime. Typically, *IDispatch* interfaces exist inside automation servers, but any ActiveX Component can have them. This interface contains, among other functions, a function for looking up an ID number for a property or method by name (*GetIDsOfNames*), and a function for indirectly invoking a property or method by returned ID number (*Invoke*). The interface is intended primarily for scripted or interpreted languages, which lack the benefit of a compiler to perform early binding.

Clearly, invoking properties and methods from a dispinterface is slower than invoking a function directly. Just how much slower is a matter of controversy and can be somewhat of a moot point. For one thing, dispinterfaces are the only type of interface that can be used by scripting languages such as *VBScript*. Supporting scripting languages through the availability of a dispinterface is highly recommended, as it provides programmers with more deployment options for the middleware. For this reason, as a middleware developer, you will want to provide a dispinterface. So, how much slower is a dispinterface? Well, that's not a valid question, since it depends on whose dispinterface you're referring to. Each and every ActiveX Component developer must implement a dispinterface to support automation controllers, which means there are potentially as many implementations of *GetIDsOfNames* and *Invoke* as there are automation components. Therefore, the speeds of dispinterfaces vary from component to component. It should be noted, however, that "canned" dispinterfaces, such as those provided by Visual Basic and the Active Template Library (ATL) of Microsoft Visual C++, are pretty fast.

The fastest and most direct means of property and method invocation is to use what is known as **vtable** binding. The name "vtable" comes from the C++ virtual table, a compiler-generated structure consisting of a table of pointers to the functions that implement properties and methods. C++ clients of COM components have always used vtable binding. To use vtable binding, a compiler is required, and the language (or runtime environment) must be capable of invoking functions through pointers.

To support both vtable binding and dispinterface binding on the same interface, Microsoft introduced a third type of interface. This "hybrid" interface is known as a dual interface, which is capable of supporting both vtable (fast) and dispinterface (slow) interface binding. Visual Basic is capable of vtable binding to a dual interface; in addition, when Visual Basic creates a COM object, it provides it with a dual interface. This enables Visual Basic to bind to a COM object using the most efficient means, as well as allowing VB, C++, and Java clients to bind to COM objects created with Visual Basic using vtable binding, the most efficient binding mechanism.

In summary, you'll get the best results in your user interface programs by inserting references to the middleware's type library. The code will be more readable, the compiler will catch silly mistakes, and you'll use the most efficient binding mechanism.

USING THE MOM-N-POP OBJECT MODEL

At this point, you may wish to invoke Visual Basic and create a new Standard EXE project, since I'll be walking you through using the *Mom-n-Pop Video Store* object model in a simple application. First, it will be necessary to insert a reference to the object model as follows:

1. Start a new *Standard EXE* project in Visual Basic.

2. From the *Project* menu, select *References*. From the list of type libraries, select *Mom-n-Pop 2-Tier Business (Release)*, then click the *OK* button to dismiss the *References* dialog.

If the *Mom-n-Pop* reference does not appear in the list of references, check that you have deployed the 2-tier version of the application included with this book, as outlined in the first chapter.

USING THE VISUAL BASIC OBJECT BROWSER

The Visual Basic *Object Browser* tool can be used to explore the objects, properties, methods, events, and constants exported by an ActiveX Control. There are a number of ways to invoke *Object Browser.*

- Choose **Object Browser** from the **View** menu.
- Press the **Object Browser** button in the Visual Basic toolbar.
- Press *F2.*

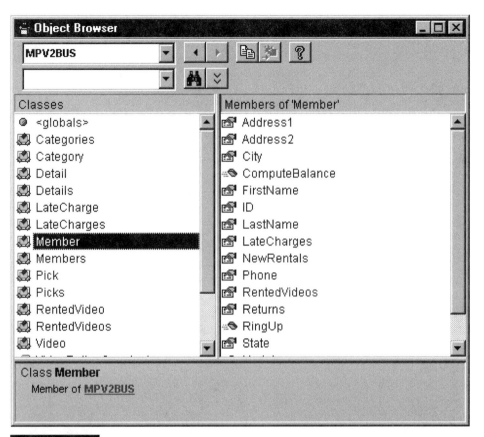

FIGURE 2-5 Use the Visual Basic *Object Browser* to browse the objects of the *Mom-n-Pop Video Store* object model, and their properties and methods.

BROWSING THE MOM-N-POP OBJECT MODEL

After inserting a reference to the *Mom-n-Pop Video Store* object model, you can use the *Object Browser* to explore the objects in the library, and their properties and methods. Invoke the *Object Browser* as indicated in the previous section (see Figure 2-5), then select *MPV2BUS* from the *Library* dropdown list (the topmost drop-down list in the *Object Browser's* window).

LISTING THE MEMBERS OF THE VIDEO STORE

You can now add a list box and command button to your application. When clicked, the list box will show the last names of all the members of the video store. Code behind your command button's click event should appear as follows:

```
Private Sub Command1_Click ()
    Dim MS As Members
    Dim M As Member
    List1.Clear
    Set MS = FindMemberByName ("%")
  For Each M In MS
        List1.AddItem M.LastName
    Next
End Sub
```

To create this application (see Figure 2-6) and supply the above code, use the following instructions:

1. Add a list box control to your form.
2. Add a command button control to your form.
3. In the command button's click event, enter the code shown above.
4. Run your program and click the command button.

In the next chapter, which discusses the presentation layer, you will get even more practice using the objects in the *Mom-n-Pop Video Store* object model.

FIGURE 2-6   A sample user interface application.

Implementing Win32 User Interface Clients

Developing an N-tier client/server application requires splitting the traditional components of a Windows application—user interface, business rules, and database access logic—into individual parts. There are many benefits to this approach, as you'll see throughout this book. Before looking at the most interesting part of an N-tier client/server application (the middleware), I will focus on some advanced aspects of the user interface, or presentation layer. In this chapter, I'll use some advanced controls such as the list and tree view controls, and focus on improving an application's interoperability with other Windows applications using *OLE drag-and-drop* and clipboard data transfer. Throughout this chapter, we'll use an existing object model, the *Mom-n-Pop Video Store* objects. Later in this book, I'll show you how to design and deploy an object model.

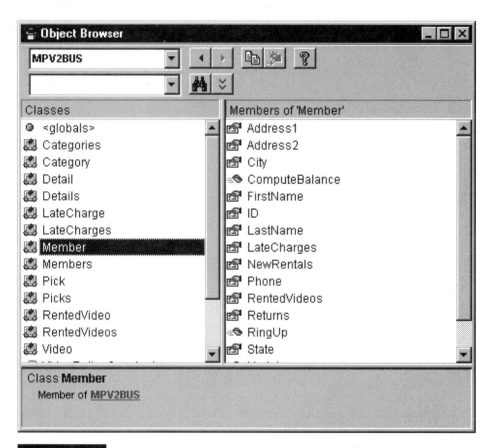

FIGURE 3-1 You can use the Visual Basic *Object Browser* to explore the objects provided by an ActiveX Component such as the Video Store object model.

Using the Mom-n-Pop Video Store Object Model

To experiment with some of the techniques discussed in this chapter, and create additional user interfaces for the *Mom-n-Pop Video Store*, you must insert a reference to the object model's type library. You can use the following steps to insert a reference to this type library:

1. Start a new *Standard EXE* project in Visual Basic.
2. From the *Project* menu, select *References*.
3. Find the entry *Mom-n-Pop Video 2-Tier Business (Release)* and check the box next to it.
4. Click *OK* to dismiss the *References* dialog.

To browse the objects in the ActiveX Component that implements the object model, after inserting a reference,

1. Invoke the *Object Browser* by selecting *Object Browser* from the *View* menu (see Figure 3-1).

2. In the *Object Browser's Project/Library* drop-down list, select *MPV2BUS*. This is the name of the ActiveX Component implementing the object model.

3. You can now examine objects, properties, and methods of the *Mom-n-Pop Video Store* object model.

Example: Using the Mom-n-Pop Video Store Objects

You can create a simple program (see Figure 3-2) that lists titles of videos rented by a member. The source code appears below. After placing a text box, list box, and command button on your form, add the following code (note the naming I used on my controls):

```
Private Sub cmdList_Click()

    Dim M As Member
    Dim RV As RentedVideo
    Dim nID As Long

    nID = txtMemberID.Text

    Set M = FindMemberByID(nID)

    lstRented.Clear

    If M.RentedVideos.Count = 0 Then
        MsgBox "No rentals"
        Exit Sub
    End If

    For Each RV In M.RentedVideos
        lstRented.AddItem RV.Title
    Next


End Sub
```

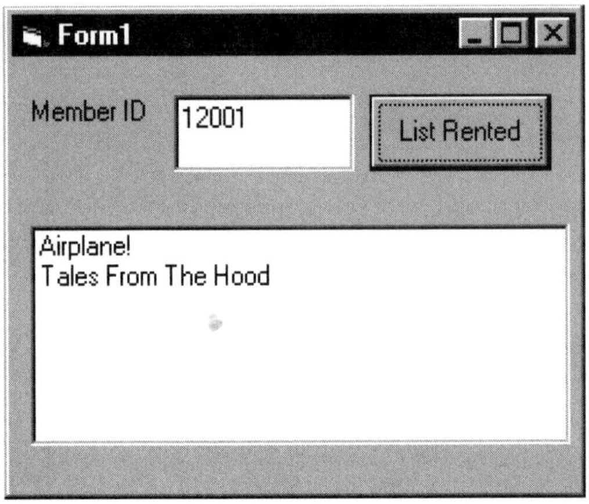

FIGURE 3-2 You can easily create a simple program that lists videos rented to a member.

Saving Application Settings in the Registry

When your application provides mechanisms for customizing the user interface, it is essential that the application remember these settings the next time it is invoked. Otherwise, users will become frustrated with having to constantly reset their preferred settings each time the application is used.

For example, the *Mom-n-Pop Video Store* application (2-tier version) allows you to enter the data source name for the database the first time the application is started, using the dialog shown in Figure 3-3. Once you check *"Do not show this dialog in the future"*, the program remembers never to show the dialog again. It uses the Windows registry to save this setting. Formerly, application settings were saved in an INI file—this is now discouraged. Application settings should be saved in the Windows registry. Visual Basic provides an easy way of doing this with the GetSetting and SaveSetting functions.

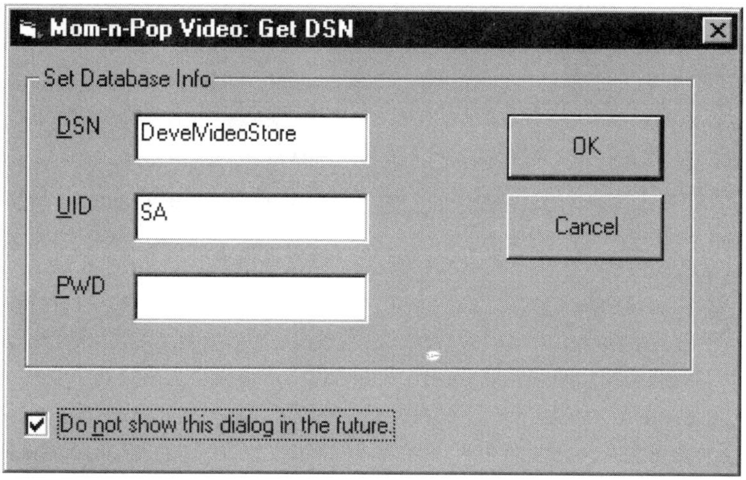

FIGURE 3-3   The first time you run the *Mom-n-Pop Video Store* application, it displays the dialog shown above.

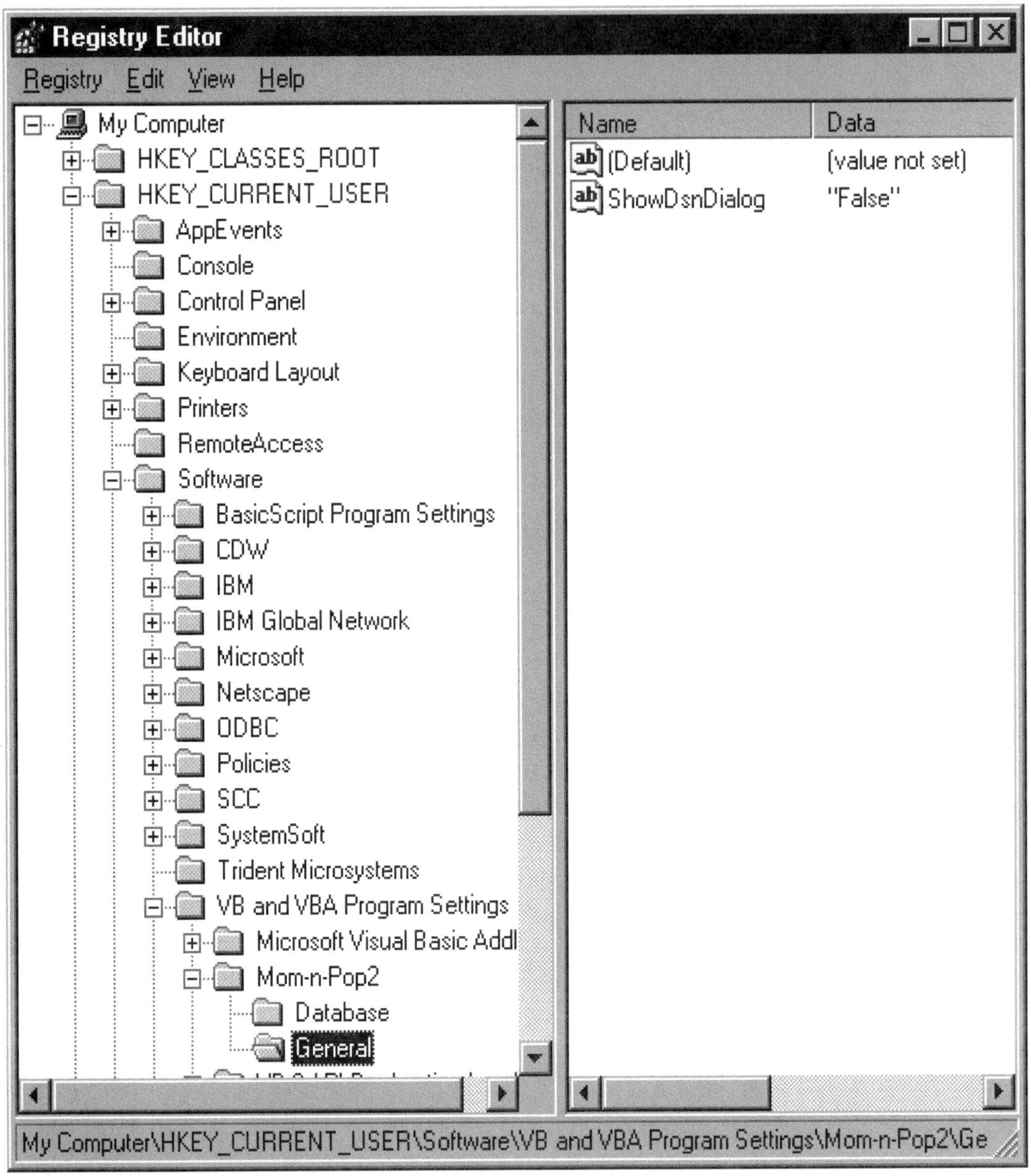

FIGURE 3-4 Visual Basic program settings are found in the Windows registry.

Settings saved for Visual Basic applications appear in the registry under a key named after your application (see Figure 3-4). This key, in turn, is located under the key *VB and VBA Program Settings*, located under the *Software* key, which is located under the key *HKEY_CURRENT_USER*. You can find your application's settings using *regedit*.

For example, to locate the settings for the *Mom-n-Pop Video Store* application:

1. Run ***regedit***.

2. Expand the key *HKEY_CURRENT_USER*, then *Software*, then *VB and VBA Program Settings*.

3. You will see the application name *Mom-n-Pop2* as a subkey. Expand this.

4. Select the subkey General, where you will find the key ShowDsnDialog and its value (either TRUE or FALSE).

Modify the setting by right-clicking on the key and selecting *Modify*.

How to Save and Restore Application Settings

The *GetSetting* function returns the current setting of a key in the registry. It will return a specified default value if the key does not exist. The *SaveSetting* function sets a key to a specified value. Both functions require an application name as a parameter. You should use something meaningful and unique for this parameter. Parameters for these functions are listed in Table 3-1. The syntax used for the functions is

```
value = GetSetting(appname, section, key, default)
SaveSetting appname, section, key, value
```

Your settings go under a subkey by the name of your application, which in turn is under the subkey *HKEY_CURRENT_USER/Software/VB and VBA Program Settings*. The *section* parameter specifies the name of a section, under which keys are stored. This value has the same classic use as it did when you used INI files.

TABLE 3-1	Parameters for GetSetting and SaveSetting
Parameter	**Description**
appname	String expression containing the name of the application or project to which the setting applies.
section	String expression containing the name of the section where the key setting is being saved.
key	String expression containing the name of the key setting being saved.
default	String expression containing the default value. Returned if the key cannot be found in the registry.
setting	Expression containing the value that key is being set to.
value	Value of key or default (*GetSetting*), or value to set for the key (*SaveSetting*).

Example: Saving Application Settings in Mom-n-Pop

Following are two examples from the *Mom-n-Pop Video Store* application, which illustrate use of the registry. To explore code in *Mom-n-Pop*, load project group *VS2Group*, located in folder *VB6Adv\Demos\MomPop\2Tier\ MPVui*. The first example reads application settings from the registry.

```
Dim strDSN As String
Dim strUID As String
Dim strPWD As String

strDSN = GetSetting("Mom-n-Pop2", "Database", _
                    "DSN", "<none>")
strUID = GetSetting("Mom-n-Pop2", "Database", _
                    "UID", "<none>")
strPWD = GetSetting("Mom-n-Pop2", "Database", _
                    "PWD", "<none>")
```

The second example saves application settings to the registry.

```
Private Sub Form_Unload(Cancel As Integer)
    Dim fShowDsnDialog As Boolean

    fShowDsnDialog = (chkDoNotShow.Value <> 1)

    If Not fCancel Then

        SaveSetting "Mom-n-Pop", "General", _
                    "ShowDsnDialog", fShowDsnDialog
        SaveSetting "Mom-n-Pop2", "Database", _
                    "DSN", txtDSN.Text
        SaveSetting "Mom-n-Pop2", "Database", _
                    "UID", txtUID.Text
        SaveSetting "Mom-n-Pop2", "Database", _
                    "PWD", txtPWD.Text

    End If

    Me.Hide

End Sub
```

Displaying a Splash Screen

While you may consider a splash screen to fall into the bells and whistles category, consider that enterprise applications are typically larger than the average Visual Basic program, and may need to attach to databases and start ActiveX Components. In other words, they may take longer than a typical desktop application to start. A user is likely to start a program twice if the program does not display its user interface quickly. A splash screen provides the user with positive visual feedback that the application is initializing—this makes the user less likely to become impatient and try to start the application again.

If you're going to display a splash screen, make sure that it is a "true" splash screen—one that displays while the application performs as much up-front initialization as it needs to get started. Few users would claim to actually enjoy looking at a splash screen. Users are much more interested in gaining access to your application. Don't be concerned if the splash screen displays too quickly for the user to examine closely. In fact, the 2-tier version of the *Mom-n-Pop Video Store* application may do just that—compare the time its splash screen is displayed with that of the 3-tier version, which starts MTS components and attaches to a remote database. Once the splash screen is removed from view, you have positive confirmation that your application has initialized. I do not recommend introducing timers to cause your splash screen to display any longer than necessary.

A splash screen should have a *BorderStyle* of *1* (fixed single), with no caption (clear the *Caption* property). To display the splash screen while your program initializes, use the following steps:

1. First of all, use *Sub Main* as your startup object, and not the initial form!

2. In your *Sub Main*, declare an object variable, using your main form class as its data type.

3. Set your mouse pointer to an hourglass.

4. Invoke the *Show* method on your splash screen form. Omit all parameters, allowing the form to be displayed modeless.

5. Invoke the *Refresh* method on your splash screen form. If you don't do this, you won't see the splash screen.

6. Create a new instance of your main form, using *Set* and the *New* keyword, storing the result the variable you declared in Step 2.

7. Invoke the *Load* statement, loading the form by specifying the same variable from the previous step.

8. Unload the splash screen and set the mouse pointer back to normal.

9. Invoke the *Show* method on the main form (using the object variable declared in Step 2). Omit parameters, loading it modeless.

Following is the code from the *Mom-n-Pop Video Store* application related to displaying a splash screen. The code is located in *Sub Main* of the module *UIGlobals* in both the 2-tier and 3-tier versions.

```
Dim frmMainForm As frmMain

Screen.MousePointer = vbHourglass
frmSplash.Show
frmSplash.Refresh
Set frmMainForm = New frmMain
Load frmMainForm
Unload frmSplash

Screen.MousePointer = 0
frmMainForm.Show
```

Using Drag-and-Drop in an Application

Adding drag-and-drop to an application provides your user with direct manipulation user interface capabilities. Drag-and-drop features can add a powerful and abstract flavor to an application, making the user feel directly involved in the operation of the application. For example, instead of entering a command to delete a file, a user can drag an icon representing the file to an icon that represents the recycle bin. This means of direct manipulation makes the user interface abstractly behave as though the user were, in real life, picking up a printed document and dropping it into a real recycle bin.

Drag-and-drop is, of course, simply a user interface gesture. During drag-and-drop, nothing at all is actually moved other than a picture that represents something—it's all an illusion. Your application responds to drag-and-drop the same way it responds to any other user interface gesture, whether or not a button is clicked, a menu item is chosen, and so on.

Since drag-and-drop features provided by an application are not easily discoverable, they should never be the only means by which an application carries out a given command. Advanced users will appreciate the shortcuts provided by a drag-and-drop interface, but the same action should be possible with menu choices or command button selections—actions that the user is more likely to discover by examining your user interface.

There are two ways to implement drag-and-drop in a Visual Basic application. The first of these methods is ***intra-application drag-and-drop***, which provides a way for the user to drag and drop items within an application. Programs that use only intra-application drag-and-drop do not participate with other applications—you can neither drag items from such applications to another application, nor can you drop items that originated in another application onto such a program.

To allow your application to participate in drag-and-drop with other applications, your program must use ***OLE drag-and-drop***. With OLE drag-and-drop, your application places data, in multiple formats, into a data object. When an item from your application is dragged over the user interface of another application, the target application examines the format(s) of the data contained in the data object. By calling a Win32 API function, the target application indicates whether or not the data is in a recognized format—if it is, the mouse pointer is changed to indicate positive feedback to the user. Dropping data on the target application causes the application to extract the data and perform some action.

Implementing Intra-Application Drag-and-Drop

Visual Basic includes features that make it easy to implement intra-application drag-and-drop. Inter-application drag-and-drop, or OLE drag-and-drop, in which multiple applications drag and drop data (rather than controls), was introduced in Visual Basic 5.0, and is covered later in this chapter.

It is important to realize that drag and drop are two different things. **Drag** is a method that is initiated on a control. **Drop** is an event that occurs to the control being "dropped-upon." To initiate dragging on a control, you can use either automatic or manual drag mode. With automatic drag mode, dragging is initiated when the user presses the mouse button down on a control, and is completed when the user releases the mouse button. You can enable a control (typically a picture box) for automatic drag mode by setting the *DragMode* property to *1—Automatic*. If a control's *DragMode* property is set to *0 -Manual*, the default, you can initiate dragging by invoking the *Drag* method on the control. This is typically done in the control's *MouseDown* event.

While a control is being dragged, the user sees some sort of image that moves along with the mouse pointer. You control what image is displayed by setting the control's *DragIcon* property; by default, the user simply sees a black box. As the control is dragged over a form or control, the form or control being dragged over receives a *DragOver* event. In the *DragOver* event, code can be written to change the appearance of the mouse pointer, by changing the *DragIcon* property of the control being dragged. Such an action is recommended, since you will want to change the image to provide visual hints to the user as to where it is meaningful to drop the control.

Releasing the mouse button indicates that the control should be dropped, at which time a *DragDrop* event is sent to the control or form that was dropped on. In the *DragDrop* event procedure, the program can take whatever action is appropriate. Typically, this means carrying out some action represented by the user interface gesture of dragging and dropping. Note that this does not typically mean actually moving the control.

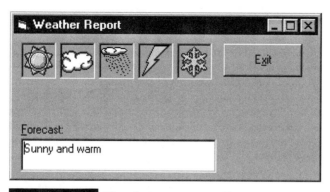

FIGURE 3-5   The demo program allows you to drop weather symbols on a text box, resulting in a description of the predicted weather condition.

A practical use of drag-and-drop is to take action when something is dropped on something else. The *Weather Report* demo program (see Figure 3-5) uses this to generate a weather report. This demo is located in project *AppDrag.VBP*, in folder *VB6Adv\Demos\AppDrag*. To run the application, drag one of the weather symbols down to the text box, and drop it there. A weather forecast description will appear in the text box.

As a further test, try dragging one of the weather symbols off the application, and attempt to drop it into a *WordPad* document. If you try this, you will see that *WordPad* does not accept the data. This is because the *Weather Report* demo program is using intra-application drag-and-drop. Later, you'll see a different version of the same program that uses *OLE drag-and-drop*— this version does allow you to drop a weather symbol onto *WordPad*, which supports OLE drag-and-drop.

Source code for the intra-application drag-and-drop version follows. Note that the program uses automatic dragging to initiate the drag operation. You can verify this by examining the *DragMode* property of any one of the weather symbols, which are implemented as picture boxes. The program itself contains no code to initiate the drag operation.

```
Private Sub cmdExit_DragOver(Source As Control, _
                             X As Single, _
                             Y As Single, _
                             State As Integer)
    If State = vbEnter Then
        Source.DragIcon = picDontDrop.Picture
    ElseIf State = vbLeave Then
        Source.DragIcon = Source.Picture
    End If
End Sub

Private Sub txtWeather_DragDrop(Source As Control, _
                                X As Single, Y As Single)
    Select Case Source.Index
        Case 0
            txtWeather.Text = "Sunny and warm"
        Case 1
            txtWeather.Text = "Partly cloudy"
        Case 2
            txtWeather.Text = "Chance of rain"
        Case 3
            txtWeather.Text = "Thunderstorms likely today"
        Case 4
            txtWeather.Text = "Snow is in the forecast"
    End Select
    Source.DragIcon = Source.Picture
End Sub

Private Sub txtWeather_DragOver(Source As Control, _
                                As Single, Y As Single, _
                                State As Integer)
    If State = vbEnter Then
        Source.DragIcon = picDropHere(Source.Index).Picture
    ElseIf State = vbLeave Then
        Source.DragIcon = Source.Picture
    End If
End Sub
```

Using OLE Drag-and-Drop

OLE drag-and-drop allows you to drag data instead of controls, often without writing any code whatsoever. Several controls in Visual Basic have two or more drag-and-drop-related properties: *OLEDropMode* and/or *OLEDragMode*. When *OLEDragMode* is set to automatic, dragging starts without program

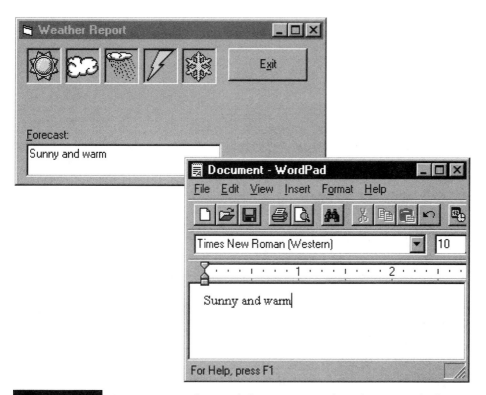

FIGURE 3-6 By using OLE drag-and-drop, you can drag data instead of controls, and you can do so between applications.

code. But, the control initiates the dragging of data instead of dragging the control. Each control drags data differently; for example, list boxes drag the selected text. When *OLEDropMode* is set to automatic, the control handles the dropped data in a control-specific way, as long as it recognizes the data. Prompts via mouse cursor changing are automatic—if a target does not recognize the data being dragged, a not sign is displayed for the mouse cursor. If, however, the target recognizes the data, the standard Windows OLE drop cursor is displayed. This cursor may also show a plus sign, indicating that the data will be copied instead of moved to the target application. As you will see, this cursor can be customized by the source application.

An OLE drag-and-drop version of the *Weather Report* program (see Figure 3-6) is located in the project *OLEDrag.VBP*, located in folder *VB6Adv\Demos\OLEDrag*. Run this program and try dragging a weather symbol to a *WordPad* document (*Notepad* will not participate in OLE drag-and-drop). Note also that the program still supports dropping a weather symbol onto its own text box control.

MANUAL AND AUTOMATIC OLE DRAG-AND-DROP

Almost all Visual Basic controls support OLE drag-and-drop to some degree. For those controls that support OLE drag-and/or-drop, there is always a choice to use manual drag-and/or-drop. When you implement OLE drag in manual mode, it means that you will invoke methods in your code to initiate the drag. In addition, you will have to write event-handling code. When you implement OLE drop in manual mode, it means that you will write event-handling code to respond to the OLE drop event(s).

Some controls support fully automatic OLE drag-and-drop. For these controls, no code needs to be written to either drag from or drop to the control. You simply set the *OLEDragMode* and *OLEDropMode* properties to *Automatic*.

There are some controls that implement fully automatic OLE drop, but only provide manual OLE drag. When a control supports manual or automatic drag-and/or-drop, it indicates that you can either use automatic drag/drop, or write your own code to customize the OLE drag/drop behavior. The availability of manual and/or automatic support for OLE drag-and-drop for each standard control is listed in Table 3-2.

TABLE 3-2	OLE Drag-and-Drop Support for Standard Controls	
Type of Control	**OLE Drag**	**OLE Drop**
Check Box	Manual Only	Manual Only
Combo Box	Manual or Automatic	Manual Only
Command Button	Manual Only	Manual Only
Data Control	Manual Only	Manual Only
DB Combo Box	Manual or Automatic	Manual Only
DB Grid	Manual or Automatic	Manual or Automatic
DB List Box	Manual or Automatic	Manual Only
Directory List Box	Manual or Automatic	Manual Only
Drive List Box	Manual Only	Manual Only
File List Box	Manual or Automatic	Manual Only
Frame	Manual Only	Manual Only
Image	Manual or Automatic	Manual or Automatic
Label	Manual Only	Manual Only
List Box	Manual or Automatic	Manual Only
List View	Manual or Automatic	Manual Only
Mask Edit	Manual or Automatic	Manual or Automatic
Option Button	Manual Only	Manual Only
Picture Box	Manual or Automatic	Manual or Automatic
Rich Text Box	Manual or Automatic	Manual or Automatic
Text Box	Manual or Automatic	Manual or Automatic

PROPERTIES, EVENTS, AND METHODS
RELATED TO OLE DRAG-AND-DROP

There are only a few properties, events, and methods related to OLE drag-and-drop. These are listed in Tables 3-3, 3-4, and 3-5, and will be discussed in the sections that follow.

TABLE 3-3	Properties Related to OLE Drag and Drop
Property	**Description**
OLEDragMode	Enables automatic or manual dragging of a control (if the control supports manual but not automatic OLE drag, it will not have this property but it will support the *OLEDrag* method and OLE drag-and-drop events).
OLEDropMode	Specifies how the control will respond to a drop.

TABLE 3-4	Events Related to OLE Drag-and-Drop
Event	**Description**
OLEDragDrop	Recognizes when a source object is dropped onto a control.
OLEDragOver	Recognizes when a source object is dragged over a control.
OLEGiveFeedback	Provides customized drag icon feedback to the user, based on the source object.
OLEStartDrag	Specifies which data formats and drop effects (copy, move, or refuse data) the source supports when dragging is initiated.
OLESetData	Provides data when the source object is dropped.
OLECompleteDrag	Informs the source of the action that was performed when the object was dropped into the target.

TABLE 3-5	Methods Related to OLE Drag-and-Drop
Method	**Description**
OLEDrag	Starts manual dragging.

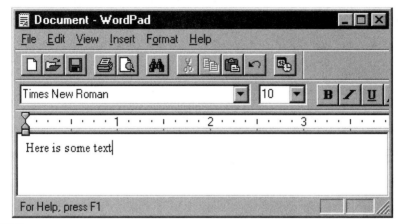

FIGURE 3-7   You can discover how automatic OLE drag-and-drop works without writing any code.

Using Automatic OLE Drag-and-Drop

As an introduction to OLE drag-and-drop, you can try the following walk-through, in which you will create an application that participates in inter-application drag-and-drop (see Figure 3-7):

1. Place a text box control on a form and set both the *OLEDropMode* and *OLEDragMode* properties to *Automatic*.

2. Run the program, then also start *WordPad* (this won't work with *Notepad*).

3. Enter some text into the text box, select it, then drag the selected text over to *WordPad* and drop it.

4. Enter some text into *WordPad* and drag it over to the text box.

5. Note that the text is erased from the text box and from *WordPad*. This is the behavior for a text box's OLE drag-and-drop in automatic mode.

6. You can hold the control key down while dragging to force a copy instead of a move.

7. Try this with other applications, such as *Microsoft Word* and *Microsoft Excel.*

Manual OLE Drag-and-Drop

You may choose to use manual OLE drag-and/or-drop for one of two reasons: either the control does not support automatic OLE drag-and-drop, or you don't like the default behavior implemented by the control's automatic OLE drag-and-drop. With manual OLE drag-and-drop, you have greater control over each step of the process. You can provide the user with customized visual feedback, create your own data format, or override the automatic OLE drag-and-drop behavior. For example, you may not like the text box's default behavior of moving the text from the destination or to the source (although this is the default behavior, supposedly, for all applications that implement OLE drag-and-drop).

To implement manual OLE drag-and-drop, you'll need to understand the overall model of the OLE drag-and-drop operation. The object from which data is dragged is referred to as the **source**. The object into which data is dropped is referred to as the **target**. The data being dragged is represented by a *DataObject* object. The source places data (in multiple formats) into a *DataObject* object, then initiates the drag. The target, when being dragged over, provides visual feedback during the drag to indicate its willingness to accept the data contained in the *DataObject* object. As you'll see, it does this by querying the *DataObject* object for what type of format(s) it contains. The target, when being dropped upon, copies the data from the *DataObject* object and communicates the drop completion back to the source. The source, upon receiving notification of drop completion, either deletes its data (in the case of a move), or does nothing (in the case of a copy). All of these actions are accomplished using the properties, events, and methods of the controls supporting manual drag-and-drop, as well as interacting with a *DataObject* object.

ABOUT THE DATAOBJECT OBJECT

Recall that in OLE drag-and-drop, you're dragging and dropping data, not a control. The object that contains the data being dragged is a *DataObject* object. The *DataObject* object has methods that must be invoked appropriately to implement OLE drag-and-drop.

On the source side, an important method is the *SetData* method. The syntax of the *SetData* method is shown below; other methods will be discussed shortly. Parameters of the *SetData* method are listed in Table 3-6; important format constants are listed in Table 3-7.

```
DataObject.SetData data, format
```

It is not only possible, but also typical, to put multiple formats of your data into a *DataObject*. The more formats you place in a *DataObject*, the more applications that will accept your data. Note the distinction. You place one data item into a *DataObject*, but you do it multiple times, in different formats. Some formats are listed in Table 3-7; see *Help* for more information. Next, you'll see how the *DataObject* is used on the source side to implement a complete manual OLE drag operation.

TABLE 3-6	Parameters for the SetData Method
Parameter	**Description**
data	A variant containing the data to be passed to the *DataObject* object.
format	A constant that specifies the format of the data being passed.

TABLE 3-7	Format Constants		
Format Constant	**Value**	**Description**	
vbCFText	1	Text	
vbCFDIB	8	Device-independent bitmap	
vbCFFiles	15	List of files	

THE SOURCE SIDE OF OLE DRAG-AND-DROP

To implement the source side of an OLE drag-and-drop operation:

1. Invoke the *OLEDrag* method on the source control. This results in the *OLEStartDrag* event being sent to your control.

2. In the control's *OLEStartDrag* event, which is passed a *DataObject* (*Data*) and a long parameter (*AllowedEffects*), invoke the *SetData* method on the *DataObject*, specifying the data and its format.

3. Repeat the above step for as many different formats as you wish to include.

4. Set the *AllowedEffects* parameter to a combination of one or more drop effect constants to indicate what your control is willing to do, that is, copy and/or move the data (see Table 3-8).

5. Upon exiting the *OLEStartDrag* event, actual dragging occurs. When the data is dropped, your control will receive an *OLECompleteDrag* event. In this event, you are passed a drop effect constant.

6. In your *OLECompleteDrag* event handler, check the effect parameter. If it is equal to the constant *vbDropEffectMove,* remove the data from your application.

TABLE 3-8	Drop Effect Constants		
Constant	**Value**	**Description**	
vbDropEffectNone	0	Drop target cannot accept the data.	
vbDropEffectCopy	1	Drop results in a copy of data from the source to the target. The original data is unaltered by the drag operation.	
vbDropEffectMove	2	Drop results in data being moved from drag source to drop source. The drag source should remove the data from itself after the move.	

THE DESTINATION SIDE OF OLE DRAG-AND-DROP

You can manually control what happens on the destination side of OLE drag-and-drop by appropriately responding to the *OLEDragOver* and *OLEDragDrop* events. To receive the events, the control's *OLEDropMode* property must be set to *Manual*. You will not receive these events if the property is set to either *Automatic* or *None*.

As mentioned previously, some controls support only manual drop mode. To implement OLE drag-and-drop with such controls, you must code the event procedures. You may also want to implement manual OLE drop for controls that support automatic OLE drop, to override the automatic behavior. This will be shown in my first example.

When a *DataObject* is dragged over a destination control, the first event it receives is the *OLEDragOver* event. In this event, you must indicate your willingness to accept the data. The *OLEDragOver* event is passed a *DataObject* as a parameter. You can invoke the *GetFormat* method to see if the *DataObject* contains data in a format that you recognize.

If the *DataObject* contains a format that your destination control recognizes, set the *Effect* parameter to either *vbDropEffectCopy* (if the control key is down) or *vbDropEffectMove*. If the *DataObject* does not contain a format that your destination control recognizes, set the *Effect* parameter to *vbDropEffectNone*.

When a *DataObject* is dropped on your destination control, it will receive an *OLEDragDrop* event. In the destination control's *OLEDragDrop* event, you invoke the *GetData* method on the *Data* parameter to retrieve the data. You then set the *Effect* parameter to either *vbDropEffectCopy* (if the control key is pressed) or *vbDropEffectMove*.

As an example of manual OLE drag-and-drop, I'll modify the drop behavior of a text box control. While this is somewhat unorthodox, it is still perfectly "legal" in Windows. The default behavior (in automatic OLE drop) of a text box is to add the text to the text box, and move the text from the source application. Using manual OLE drag-and-drop, it's easy to modify this drop behavior to completely replace the contents of the text box with the data in the *DataObject*, and copy the text from the source application. Following is the code to accomplish this (don't forget to set the *OLEDrop-Mode* property of the text box to *manual*).

```
Private Sub Text1_OLEDragOver(Data As DataObject, _
                              Effect As Long, _
                              Button As Integer, _
                              Shift As Integer, _
                              X As Single, _
                              Y As Single, _
                              State As Integer)

    If Data.GetFormat(vbCFText) Then
        Effect = vbDropEffectCopy
    Else
        Effect = vbDropEffectNone
    End If

End Sub

Private Sub Text1_OLEDragDrop(Data As DataObject, _
                              Effect As Long, _
                              Button As Integer, _
                              Shift As Integer, _
                              X As Single, _
                              Y As Single)

    Text1.Text = Data.GetData(vbCFText)
    Effect = vbDropEffectCopy

End Sub
```

Customizing Automatic OLE Drag

Unlike OLE drop, with OLE drag in automatic mode, you still receive related events while OLE dragging. Namely, the *OLEStartDrag* and *OLECompleteDrag* events are still sent to the source control, even with *OLEDragMode* set to *Automatic*. But with *OLEDropMode* set to *Automatic*, the related events (*OLEDragOver* and *OLEDragDrop*) are not sent to the destination control.

If, in automatic *OLEDragMode*, you do not handle the *OLEStartDrag* and *OLECompleteDrag* events, you get completely automatic (and default) drag behavior. If you provide an *OLEStartDrag* event handler for a source control with an *OLEDragMode* property set to automatic, you should know that the source control places its data in the *DataObject* before it invokes the

OLEStartDrag event. If you want to add additional formats, do so in the *OLEStartDrag* event. If you want to remove the standard format (automatically placed in the *DataObject* by the source control), invoke the *Clear* method on the *DataObject* passed to the event handler.

The example event handler that follows, implemented for a text box with its *OLEDragMode* property set to *Automatic*, modifies the drag behavior of the text box so that it always copies (never moves) the selected text to the destination.

```
Private Sub Text1_OLEStartDrag(Data As DataObject, _
                               AllowedEffects As Long)
   AllowedEffects = vbDropEffectCopy
End Sub
```

Using a Custom Data Format with OLE Drag-and-Drop

You can define and use your own custom data format with OLE drag-and-drop. By using a custom data format, you can drag and drop your own custom data objects. For example, you can drag and drop a *Video* object from one application to another, perhaps causing the video to be rented to a member. In a moment, I'll show you a pair of demo programs that do just that.

To define your own custom data format, you must use the Win32 function *RegisterClipboardFormat*. The *Declare Function* statement to import this function is as follows:

```
Private Declare Function RegisterClipboardFormat Lib _
        "user32.dll" Alias "RegisterClipboardFormatA" _
        (ByVal lpszFormat$) As Integer
```

Additionally, all applications (whether source or destination) that participate in using the custom data format must use the following procedure:

1. Include a *Declare Function* statement in one of your modules to import the *RegisterClipboardFormat* function.

2. When your application starts up, invoke *RegisterClipboardFormat*, passing as the parameter a unique string that describes your format.

3. Save the return value from *RegisterClipboardFormat* in a module-level or global variable. You will need this return value, as it is a unique integer code that identifies your format.

4. On the source side, use the return value from *RegisterClipboardFormat* as the *Format* argument to the *SetData* method of the *DataObject*. Your data must be packed into a byte array.

5. On the destination side, you use the return value from *Register-ClipboardFormat* as the *Format* parameter to the *GetFormat* and *GetData* methods. Your data must be returned into a byte array, from where it can be unpacked.

Since the *GetData* and *SetData* methods of the *DataObject* require a byte array, you must pack your data into a byte array. You can use the *CopyMemory* procedure in the Windows API to do this. The required *Declare* statement is as follows:

```
Private Declare Sub CopyMemory Lib "kernel32" _
       Alias "RtlMoveMemory" _
       (Destination As Any, Source As Any, _
        ByVal Length As Long)
```

EXAMPLE: USING A CUSTOM DATA FORMAT

There are two demo programs that illustrate the technique of using a custom data format for OLE drag-and-drop. The *VideosLister* program acts as the source and is located in folder *VB6Adv\Demos\Mom-n-PopListers\VideosLister*. The *MemberLister* program acts as the destination and is located in folder *VB6Adv\Demos\Mom-n-PopListers\MemberLister*. Run both programs (the EXE files are already built) and select a member from the *MemberLister* program (enter a *Member ID* and click the *Find* button). The *MemberLister* program will list all rented videos for the selected member.

You can drag a video from the list in the *VideosLister* program and drop it in the *Rentals* list in the *MemberLister* program (see Figure 3-8). This action causes the *MemberLister* program to locate the first available copy of the selected video and rent it to the selected member. You should also try dragging a video to a *WordPad* document. When you do this, *WordPad* inserts the title of the selected video into the document.

Whenever I show this demonstration to students, I am often asked whether or not the *MemberLister* program will accept the title of a video that was typed into *WordPad*, selected, and dragged to the *MemberLister* program. The answer is that it will not, but you should try this to convince yourself. When data is dragged from the *VideosLister* application, it is placed in the data object in two formats—one format is text, which *WordPad* will accept, and the other format is my custom format that is only recognized by the *MemberLister* and *VideosLister* applications. The *MemberLister* application will only recognize this custom format—it will not take text that was simply typed into *WordPad* and dragged over to its window.

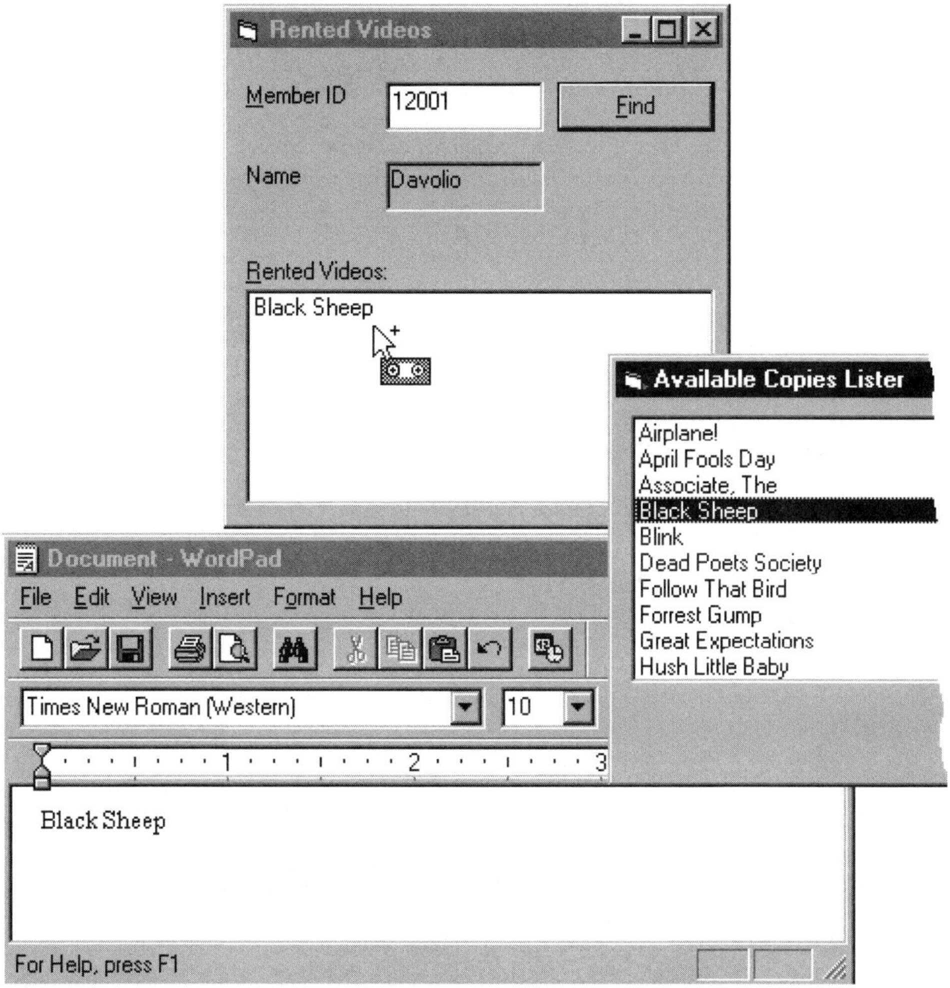

FIGURE 3-8 You can create your own custom data formats with OLE drag-and-drop.

Both the *MemberLister* and *VideosLister* applications use the *Register-ClipboardFormat* function to create and register the custom data format. It does not matter which application runs first. The first application to run creates and registers the custom format, at which time a unique number representing the format is generated. The second application to run does not create a new format. The same generated format number returned to the first application is returned to the second and any subsequent applications that register the clipboard format. Note that "registering" a clipboard format does not involve the Windows registry and is not permanent on your system. An internal in-memory table, managed by the Windows operating system, is used to keep track of custom clipboard formats. When your system is rebooted and the applications are run again, a new number may be generated. Thus, you should never save a custom clipboard format number in persistent storage.

The code shown below, which is used to register the custom clipboard format, appears in both demo applications, specifically in the *Form Load* events of each application:

```
'- Declarations section:

Private Declare Function RegisterClipboardFormat Lib _
       "user32.dll" Alias "RegisterClipboardFormatA" _
       (ByVal lpszFormat$) As Integer

Private MyFormat As Integer

'- Form Load event:

Private Sub Form_Load()

    ' Register our clipboard format

    MyFormat = RegisterClipboardFormat("Mom-n-Pop")

End Sub
```

Related code to store data in multiple formats follows. Note that the program stores data in both a custom format and text format. This enables you to drop a video on applications such as *WordPad*, in which case the title of the video is passed as text.

```
Private Sub lstAvailable_OLEStartDrag _
        (Data As DataObject, _
         AllowedEffects As Long)

    Dim nID As Long
    ReDim arID(1 To 4) As Byte

    ' Get ID from Item Data

    nID = lstAvailable.ItemData(lstAvailable.ListIndex)

    ' Pack ID into a byte array

    CopyMemory arID(1), nID, 4
```

```
' Add to data object

Data.SetData arID, MyFormat
Data.SetData lstAvailable.Text, vbCFText

AllowedEffects = vbDropEffectCopy

End Sub
```

On the destination side, the application rents the first available copy of the video that was dropped on the rentals list box to the selected member. Related code for the destination application follows.

```
Private Sub lstRented_OLEDragDrop
            (Data As DataObject, Effect As Long, _
             Button As Integer, Shift As Integer, _
             X As Single, Y As Single)

    Dim nID As Long
    Dim arID() As Byte

    ' Get the data in a byte array

    arID = Data.GetData(MyFormat)

    ' Convert to long

    CopyMemory nID, arID(LBound(arID)), 4

    ' Find video with this ID

    Dim V As Video
    Dim nCopies As Integer
    Dim i As Integer
    Dim objMember As Member

    Set V = FindVideoByID(nID)
    Set objMember = FindMemberByID(nMemberID)

    ' Find first available copy and rent it to me

    Dim nTotal As Currency
    Dim objDetails As Details

    For i = 1 To V.Copies
```

```
            If Not V.IsRented(i) Then
                objMember.NewRentals.Add V, i
                nTotal = objMember.ComputeBalance(objDetails)
                objMember.RingUp nTotal
                Exit For
            End If
    Next

    ShowRentedVideos

    Effect = vbDropEffectCopy
End Sub
```

Providing Drag-and-Drop Feedback with a Custom Cursor

You can create and use your own custom cursor with OLE drag-and-drop. The event *OLEGiveFeedback* is used on the source side to set a custom cursor. The procedure is as follows:

1. Check the *Effect* parameter passed to your *OLEGiveFeedback* event procedure. If it is *vbDropEffectNone*, do nothing.
2. Otherwise, set the *MousePointer* property of the *Screen* object to *vbCustom*, and set the *MouseIcon* property of the *Screen* object to the *Picture* property of a non-visible picture box that has been loaded with an appropriate cursor or icon.

You must set the cursor back to the default in your *OLECompletedDrag* event procedure. For example,

```
Private Sub lstAvailable_OLEGiveFeedback _
         (Effect As Long, _
          DefaultCursors As Boolean)

    If Effect = vbDropEffectCopy Then
        DefaultCursors = False
        Screen.MousePointer = vbCustom
        Screen.MouseIcon = picDragIcon.Picture
    End If

End Sub


Private Sub lstAvailable_OLECompleteDrag(Effect As Long)
    Screen.MousePointer = 0
End Sub
```

Clipboard Interoperability

To complete your application's interoperability features, you should support **clipboard** data transfer in addition to OLE drag-and-drop. More applications support data transfer through the clipboard than through OLE drag-and-drop. Inter-operating with the clipboard is easier than OLE drag-and-drop, so it's a quick topic.

The Visual Basic Clipboard Object

In Visual Basic, you use the *Clipboard* object to manipulate text and graphics on the clipboard. With the *Clipboard* object, you can enable a user to copy, cut, and paste text or graphics to or from your application. The *Clipboard* object has no properties, only methods to get, set, and clear its contents.

To see a demonstration of a Visual Basic application that interacts with the clipboard, run program *Order.EXE* (see Figure 3-9) from folder *VB6Adv\Demos\Clipboard* (source code for the program can be examined by opening project *Order.VBP* from the same folder). The application, which also presents a whimsical example of inter-application drag-and-drop, allows you to order a hamburger by dragging the hamburger icon and dropping it on a picture box. Once a hamburger is ordered, you can drag lettuce, cheese, and/or ketchup icons, and drop them on the hamburger. Once you've customized the hamburger, right-click on it and select either *Cut* or *Copy*. You can then paste into either *WordPad* or *NotePad*, which will copy a text description of the hamburger. You can also paste into *Paint*, which will copy a picture of the hamburger.

It's important to realize that the clipboard must be under user control. Never place anything into the clipboard unless it's a direct result of user interaction. In addition, do not clear the contents of the clipboard when your application exits. It's perfectly normal and typical for a user to copy/cut from an application, exit the application, and then paste the clipboard contents into another application. (Note that some applications ask if you want the clipboard contents cleared on exit, in particular if a large amount of data was placed there).

Using the clipboard is almost like using OLE drag-and-drop. You place data in the clipboard in multiple formats using the *Clipboard* object's *SetData* method. However, the *SetData* method is used only for graphics. To place text into the clipboard, you use the *SetText* method of the clipboard object. Likewise, the *GetData* method of the *Clipboard* object is only used to get graphics data out of the clipboard. Use the *GetText* method to retrieve text from the clipboard. Before placing anything into the clipboard, invoke the *Clear* method on the *Clipboard* object to erase the clipboard's previous contents. Finally, the *GetFormat* method can be used to test the available format(s) in the clipboard. It is exactly the same as the *DataObject's GetFormat* method; even the constants are the same.

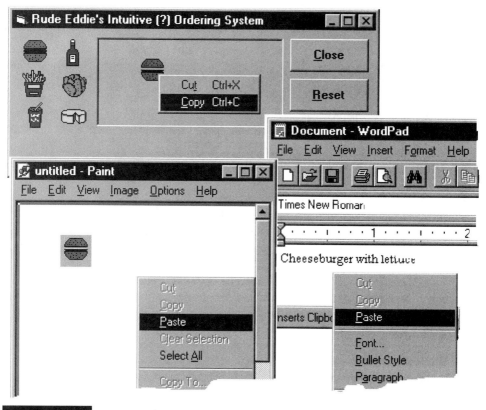

FIGURE 3-9 More applications support clipboard data transfer than OLE drag-and-drop.

Example: Implementing Clipboard Interoperability

The following code, taken from the *Order* demo, illustrates clipboard interoperability:

```
Private Sub picOrderBurger_MouseUp(Button As Integer, _
                              Shift As Integer, _
                              X As Single, _
                              Y As Single)
    If Button = vbRightButton Then
        Me.PopupMenu mnuPopup, vbRightButton
    End If
End Sub


Private Sub mnuCopy_Click()
    Clipboard.Clear
```

```
        Clipboard.SetText strDesc
        Clipboard.SetData picOrderBurger.Image
End Sub

Private Sub mnuCut_Click()
        mnuCopy_Click
        cmdReset_Click
End Sub
```

The ListView Control

The *ListView* control displays items using one of four different views. You can arrange items into columns with or without column headings, as well as display accompanying icons and text. The *ListView* control is added to a project by inserting the component *Microsoft Windows Common Controls 6.0*. Using the *ListView* control, you can organize list entries, called *ListItem* objects, into one of four different views. The type of view displayed is indicated by setting the *View* property of the *ListView* control. The types of views are:

1. Large (standard) icons.
2. Small icons.
3. List.
4. Report.

The *ListView* control contains *ListItem* and *ColumnHeader* objects. A *ListItem* object defines the various characteristics of items in the *ListView* control, such as

- A brief description of the item.
- Icons that may appear with the item, supplied by an *ImageList* control.
- Additional pieces of text, called subitems, associated with a *ListItem* object that you can display in *Report* view.

Column headings can be added to a *ListView* control at either design time or runtime. To set column headings at design time, use the *Column Headers* tab of the *ListView Control Properties* dialog box. To set column headings at runtime, use the *Add* method to add a *ColumnHeader* object to the *ColumnHeaders* collection.

Creating Column Headings at Runtime

Add column headers at runtime using the *Add* method on the *ColumnHeaders* collection of the *ListView* control. The syntax of the *Add* method is as follows (parameters are listed in Table 3-9):

```
ListView.ColumnHeaders.Add index, key, text, _
                           width, alignment
```

The *Clear* method of the *ColumnHeaders* collection removes all columns. The *Mom-n-Pop Video Store* user interface dynamically creates column headers for the *List View* control that appears on the main form.

| **TABLE 3-9** | Parameters for the ColumnHeader's Add Method |

Parameter	Description
index	Optional integer that uniquely identifies a member of an object collection.
key	Optional unique string expression that can be used to access a member of the collection.
text	Optional string that appears in the *ColumnHeader* object.
width	Optional numeric expression specifying the width of the object using the scale units of the control's container.
alignment	Optional integer that determines the alignment of text in the *ColumnHeader* object.

The following code, from the *Mom-n-Pop Video Store* user interface, adds column headers to a *ListView* control dynamically at runtime:

```
Private Sub MemberQueryUISetup()
    MemberUIActive = True
    VideoUIActive = False
    cmdDetails.Enabled = False
    txtVideoTitle.Text = ""
    lvListView.ColumnHeaders.Clear
    lvListView.ListItems.Clear
    lvListView.ColumnHeaders.Add , , "ID", 320
    lvListView.ColumnHeaders.Add , , "Name", 1200
    lvListView.ColumnHeaders.Add , , "Address", 2000
    lvListView.ColumnHeaders.Add , , "Rentals", 450
End Sub
```

Entering Subitems into a ListView Control

In *Report* view, the *ListView* control considers rows to be items. You add items to a *ListView* control by invoking the *Add* method of the *ListItems* collection of the *ListView* control. The *Add* method creates and returns a *ListItem* object, which will have subitems for each of columns 2—n. The syntax of the *Add* method follows; parameters are listed in Table 3-10.

```
Dim LI As ListItem
Set LI = ListView.ListItems.Add(index, key, text, _
                                icon, smallIcon)
LI.SubItems(2) = "column 2 text"
```

TABLE 3-10	Parameters for the Add Method of ListItems

Parameter	Description
index	Optional integer specifying the position where you want to insert the *ListItem*. If no index is specified, the *ListItem* is added to the end of the *ListItems* collection.
key	Optional unique string expression that can be used to access a member of the collection.
text	Optional string that is associated with the *ListItem* object control.
icon	Optional integer that sets the icon to be displayed from an *ImageList* control, when the *ListView* control is set to *Icon* view.
smallIcon	Optional integer that sets the icon to be displayed from an *ImageList* control, when the *ListView* control is set to *SmallIcon* view.

The following code adds an entry to a *ListView* control in *Report* view. After adding the entry, three subitems, representing columns 2 – 4, are entered:

```
Private Sub AddMemberToListView(ByVal M As Member)
    Dim L As ListItem

    Set L = lvListView.ListItems.Add(, , M.ID)
    L.SubItems(1) = M.LastName & ", " & M.FirstName
    L.SubItems(2) = M.Address1
    L.SubItems(3) = Str(M.RentedVideos.Count)
End Sub
```

The TreeView Control

A *TreeView* control displays a hierarchical list of *Node* objects, each of which consists of a label and an optional bitmap. After creating a *TreeView* control, you can add, remove, arrange, and otherwise manipulate *Node* objects by setting properties and invoking methods. You can programmatically expand and collapse *Node* objects to display or hide all child nodes. *Nodes* are added to the tree using the *Add* method of the *Nodes* collection of the *ListView* control. Parameters of the *Add* method are listed in Table 3-11. Constants for the *relation* parameter, which indicates the relative placement of the *Node* object, are listed in Table 3-12. The syntax of the *Add* method is

```
Dim N As Node
Set N = TreeView.Nodes.Add (relative, relation, key, _
                            text, image, sel)
```

TABLE 3-11	Parameters for the Add Method of Nodes

Parameter	Description
relative	Optional index number or key of a pre-existing *Node* object. The relationship between the new node and this pre-existing node is found in the next argument, *relation*.
relation	Specifies the relative placement of the *Node* object, as described below.
key	Optional unique string that can be used to retrieve the *Node* with the *Item* method.
text	Required string that appears in the *Node*.
image	Optional index of an image in an associated *ImageList* control.
sel	Optional index of an image in an associated *ImageList* control that is shown when the *Node* is selected.

TABLE 3-12	Relation Constants	

Relation Constant	Value	Description
tvwFirst	0	First. The *Node* is placed before all other nodes at the same level of the node named in *relative*.
tvwLast	1	Last. The node is placed after all other nodes at the same level of the *Node* named in relative. Any node added subsequently may be placed after one added as *Last*.
tvwNext	2	Next (default). The *Node* is placed after the node named *relative*.
tvwPrevious	3	Previous. The *Node* is placed before the node named in *relative*.
tvwChild	4	Child. The *Node* becomes a child node of the node named in *relative*.

The demo program, *MomPopTree*, located in folder *VB6Adv**Demos*\
Mom-n-PopListers, illustrates how you can use the *TreeView* control (see
Figure 3-10). Run the program and expand nodes. The program shows
videos rented by member. Code from the demo follows:

```
Private Sub Form_Load()
    Dim MR As Members
    Dim M As Member
    Dim RV As RentedVideo
    Dim objRootNode As Node
    Dim objMemberNode As Node
    Dim objVideoNode As Node
    Dim strCopy As String
    Dim strDateRented As String
    Dim strDateDue As String

  ' Create root node

Set objRootNode = tvMembers.Nodes.Add(,,,"Members",2,3)
Set MR = FindMemberByName("%")

For Each M In MR

    Set objMemberNode = tvMembers.Nodes.Add _
                (objRootNode, _
                 tvwChild, , _
                 M.LastName, 2, 3)
```

```
For Each RV In M.RentedVideos
    strCopy = "Copy: " & Format(RV.CopyNo)
    strDateRented = "Rented: " & _
                    Format(RV.DateRented, _
                        "Short Date")
    strDateDue = "Due: " & Format(RV.DateDue, _
                                "Short Date")

    Set objVideoNode = tvMembers.Nodes.Add _
                        (objMemberNode, _
                        tvwChild, , RV.Title, 1)

    tvMembers.Nodes.Add objVideoNode, _
                tvwChild, , strCopy

    tvMembers.Nodes.Add objVideoNode, _
                tvwChild, , strDateRented

    tvMembers.Nodes.Add objVideoNode, _
                tvwChild, , strDateDue
    Next

Next

End Sub
```

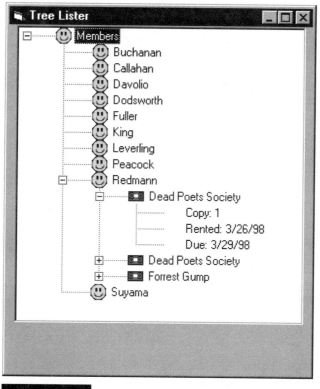

FIGURE 3-10 The demo program illustrates how to use a *TreeView* control.

The TabStrip Control

A ***TabStrip*** control acts like the dividers in a notebook, or the labels on a group of file folders. By using a *TabStrip* control, you can define multiple pages for the same area of a window or dialog box in your application. The control consists of one or more *Tab* objects in a *Tabs* collection. At both design time and runtime, you can affect the *Tab* object's appearance by setting properties, and at runtime, by invoking methods to add and remove *Tab* objects. The demo program, *MomPopTabStrip* (see Figure 3-11), located in folder *\VB6Adv\Demos\Mom-n-PopListers\TabStripLister*, illustrates the use of the *TabStrip* control.

Controls must be positioned on the *TabStrip* control at runtime, so you'll have a lot of work to do in your *Form Load* event procedure. Basically, all controls are moved to the client area of the *TabStrip* control, all on top of each other.

To make things easier for you to manage, you should create a picture box control for each tab of your *TabStrip* control. Place appropriate controls

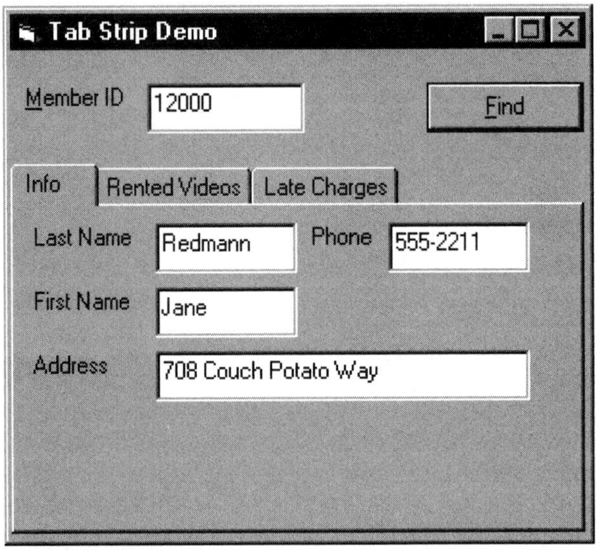

FIGURE 3-11 The *TabStrip* control makes great use of screen real estate, but takes a lot of programming effort.

inside each picture box. Making all the picture boxes part of a control array will make programming easier.

Use the *ZOrder* method to bring the picture box associated with a tab to the front when the *TabStrip* control receives a *Click* event. The best way to understand the mechanics involved is to examine the demo project in design mode.

Following is an example of a *Form Load* event that arranges three picture box controls, part of the control array *picTab*, into a *TabStrip* control:

```
Private Sub Form_Load()
    Dim i As Integer

    lvRented.Move 0, 0, _
                picTab(1).Width, picTab(1).Height

    lvLateCharges.Move 0, 0, _
                picTab(2).Width, picTab(2).Height

    For i = 0 To picTab.Count - 1
        picTab(i).BorderStyle = 0
        picTab(i).Move TabStrip1.ClientLeft, _
            TabStrip1.ClientTop, _
```

```
            TabStrip1.ClientWidth, _
            TabStrip1.ClientHeight
    Next i

    picTab(0).ZOrder 0
    Me.Height = 4050
    Me.Width = 4590

End Sub
```

The following code illustrates how to bring a picture box associated with the just-selected tab to the front of the *TabStrip* control:

```
Private Sub TabStrip1_Click()
    picTab(TabStrip1.SelectedItem.Index - 1).ZOrder 0
End Sub
```

Toolbars and Status Bars

A **toolbar** enhances an application's user interface by providing a collection of buttons and other controls, usually ones that correspond to items in the application's menu. Using the *Toolbar* control, part of the *Microsoft Windows Common Controls*, you can create professional toolbars with many of the features you've seen in other applications.

A **status bar** provides an additional window at the bottom of the parent form, and gives the user visual feedback concerning an application's state and what it is doing. Using the *StatusBar* control, also part of the *Microsoft Windows Common Controls*, you can create professional status bars, which will also enhance your application.

The *VbFunEdit* demo program (see Figure 3-12), located in folder *VB6Adv\Demos\Toolbar*, is analyzed in the following sections. The program illustrates the use of both toolbars and status bars.

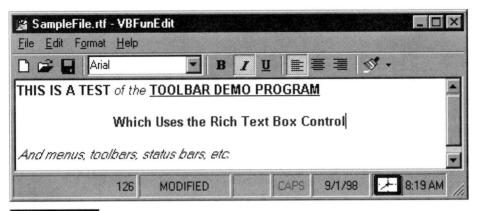

FIGURE 3-12 Toolbars enhance your application by providing a collection of buttons that correspond to items in your menu. A status bar contains panels that display text and/or graphics for the purpose of displaying status and feedback to the user.

Planning for a Toolbar

It is essential that you do not underestimate the amount of planning required for toolbars. The Visual Basic development environment does not provide a graphical editor for creating toolbars. The design environment provided by Visual Basic for creating both toolbars and status bars does not lend itself well to ad-hoc design. Plan your toolbars carefully. Consider all styles of buttons that you'll require and how you want them to behave. Consider also separation between groups of buttons and placeholders for controls other than *Button* objects. Separators and placeholders, as you'll see, count as "buttons." You'll need at least one *ImageList* control (two or more are required for additional graphical features) for your toolbar. The diagram shown in Figure 3-13 should help you identify these elements.

For proper Windows application design, you must have a menu in addition to your toolbar. You'll need to keep both menu items and toolbar buttons synchronized. For example, if you have a *Bold* button and a *Bold* menu item, you need to place a checkmark next to the *Bold* menu item when the user selects the *Bold* button, and viceversa. Synchronizing toolbar buttons and menu options may require a significant amount of extra code.

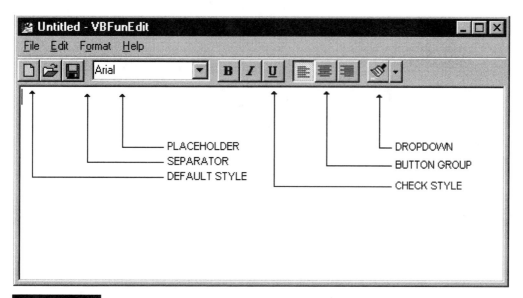

FIGURE 3-13 You may spend a significant amount of time in design mode when designing your toolbar. Buttons need to be grouped logically, and you need to plan for separation and space for other controls, such as combo boxes.

The ImageList Control

The ***ImageList*** control acts as a repository of images. It may be used to hold images for any purpose required by your application. An *ImageList* is required for the *Toolbar* control and certain other *Windows Common Controls*. It is used to hold pictures of buttons.

Using the *ImageList* control may seem difficult at first, but using a single repository for images actually saves development time. You don't need to load pictures from files at runtime, nor do you need a Picture Box control for each image on your toolbar. Images can be loaded into an *ImageList* control at design time; this is typically where you start when creating a toolbar.

The *Toolbar* control can require up to three separate *ImageList* controls, depending on the features you want in the toolbar. The demonstration program uses two image lists, one with "hot" pictures and one with "cold" pictures.

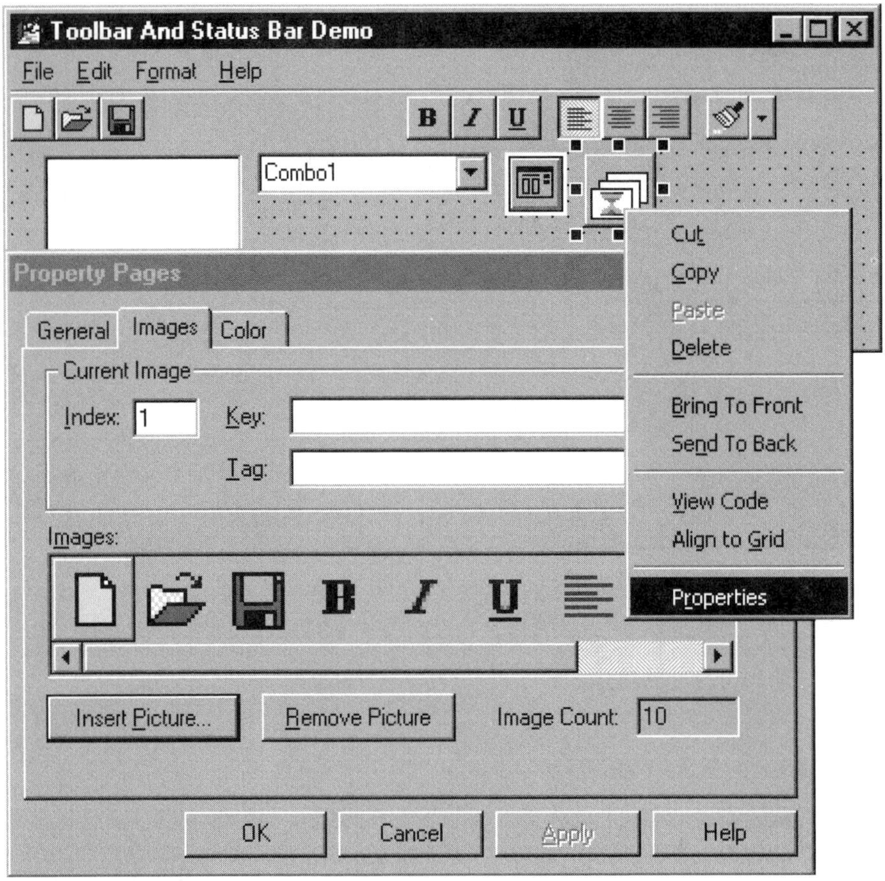

FIGURE 3-14 The *ImageList* control acts as a repository of images, and is required for toolbars.

SETTING UP AN IMAGELIST CONTROL

Pictures can be added to the *ImageList* control at design time (see Figure 3-14). This is typically the approach taken when designing an image list to be used by a toolbar. You must load pictures into the *ImageList* control before associating it with a toolbar. Once associated with a toolbar, the *ImageList* control cannot be modified. Later, if you want to add or replace pictures, you'll have to disassociate the *ImageList* from the toolbar, update the image list, and reassign pictures in the toolbar. This is another reason why planning for toolbars is essential.

Images in an *ImageList* must be given a unique index number. They may optionally be given a unique key string. Either the index or the key may be used at runtime to refer to a particular picture in an image list. To add images to an *ImageList* control at design time:

1. Right-click the *ImageList* control and choose *Properties*.
2. On the resulting *Property Pages* dialog, choose the *Images* tab.
3. Click the *Insert Picture* button and navigate to the desired bitmap or icon file.
4. Optionally, assign a unique string to the *Key* field.
5. Repeat these steps until all pictures are assigned.

Setting Up a Toolbar at Design Time

The *Toolbar* control is an ActiveX Control—not a built-in standard control. It must be added to your toolbox by selecting *Components* from the *Project* menu. Select the component *Windows Common Controls 6.0*. This brings in a number of additional controls, including the *StatusBar* control. After adding this component to your project, you can place a *Toolbar* control on your form by double-clicking its icon in the toolbox. The toolbar will snap to the top of the form and will initially have no border.

To start setting up the toolbar, right-click on the toolbar control and choose *Properties* (see Figure 3-15). You should start by setting options from the *General* tab, including the assignment of an *ImageList* control. The height of the toolbar will be set automatically, depending on the height of the pictures assigned.

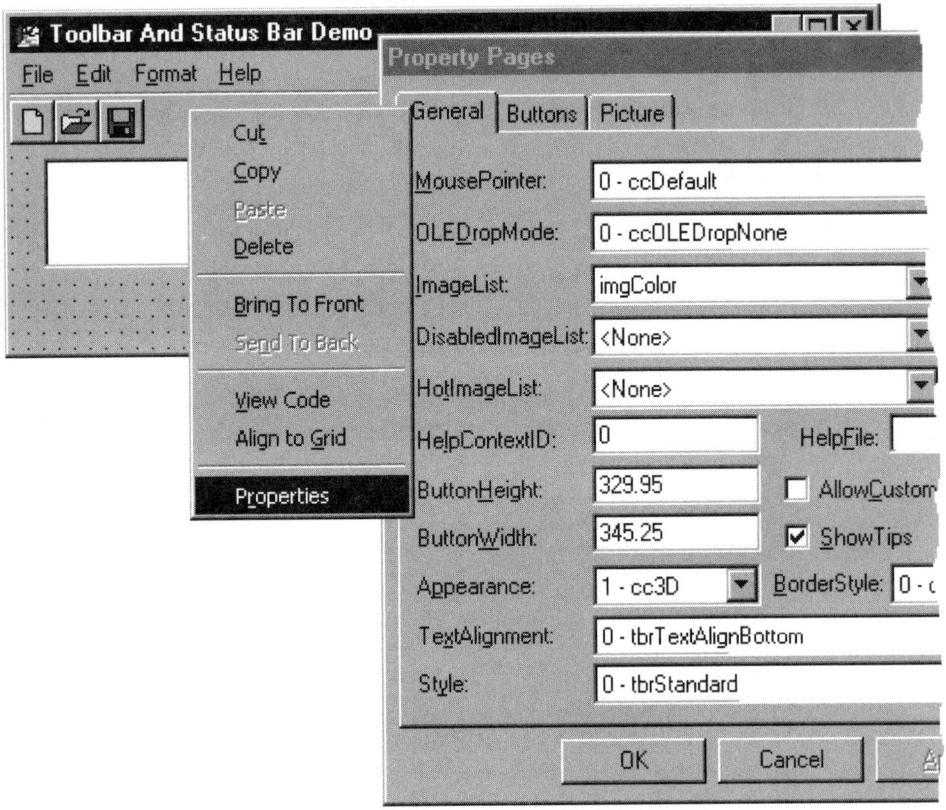

FIGURE 3-15 Plan to spend a lot of time setting up the toolbar at design time.

ASSOCIATING AN IMAGELIST WITH A TOOLBAR CONTROL

Up to three *ImageList* controls can be associated with a toolbar control, depending on what features you want. If you are not using "hot" images or "disabled" images, use only one image list, which is assigned to the *ImageList* property of the toolbar. This can be set at design time from the *General* tab of the toolbar's *Property Pages* dialog.

The *DisabledImageList* property indicates an alternate list of images to display when toolbar buttons are disabled. If you leave this property as *none*, the toolbar will generate disabled images automatically. Unless you are particularly fussy, these images are generally acceptable. The *HotImageList* property indicates an image list that contains an alternate list of images to display when a button becomes hot; that is, when the mouse hovers over it. This feature is demonstrated later in this chapter.

It is recommended that you disable the *AllowCustomize* feature (found under the *General* tab in the *Property Pages* dialog), unless you are willing to allow users to customize your toolbar, and you add required additional code (more about this later).

Toolbar Button Styles

Buttons can be added to a toolbar at design time using the *Toolbar* control's *Property Pages*. However, you must be familiar with each of the different styles before proceeding. Each toolbar button can be one of six different styles (see Table 3-13). A button's style is set as it is created, from the *Buttons* tab on the *Property Pages* dialog. Each of the button styles is discussed briefly below, and in more detail in the sections that follow.

The *default* style is used for buttons that, when clicked, cause your program to execute a command. The *separator* style is used to insert standard 8-pixel separation between related groups of toolbar buttons. Although it cannot be clicked by the user, a button with a separator style stills counts as a button and must be given a unique index number (and optional key). The *check* and *button group* styles are used for check-box and option-button-style toolbar buttons. The *placeholder* style is used to consume space in the toolbar. This space can be replaced at runtime by a control other than a button, such as a combo box or text box. The *drop-down* style indicates a button that has two parts: a "normal" button that can be clicked to cause an action, and a "drop-down" button that can display a menu of choices.

TABLE 3-13 Toolbar Button Styles

Style Constant	Value	Description
tbrDefault	0	Acts like a regular command button.
tbrCheck	1	Toggles between checked and unchecked state.
tbrButtonGroup	2	Remains pressed until another button in the group is pressed.
tbrSeparator	3	Acts as a standard 8-pixel separator.
tbrPlaceholder	4	Looks and acts like a separator, but has an adjustable width. Other controls can be placed over the placeholder.
tbrDropDown	5	Drops down a list of *MenuButton* objects.

DEFAULT- AND SEPARATOR-STYLE TOOLBAR BUTTONS

Buttons with a style of *tbrDefault* (0) act similar to command buttons. Use this style for buttons that cause your application to carry out a command. Examples of buttons that should have the *tbrDefault* style include *New File, Open File, Save File, Select Color*, and so on. Unlike check or group styles, buttons with the default style have no state and stay pressed only temporarily. Like all other styles, buttons with the default style must have a unique index, and optionally, can be given a unique key string.

Buttons with a style of *tbrSeparator* (3) act as visual separators between semantically related groups of buttons. On a standard-style toolbar, buttons with a separator style have no visual appearance other than a standard 8-pixel blank area on the toolbar. On a flat-style toolbar (discussed later in this chapter), a separator appears as a line. A separator must appear both before and after buttons that are grouped as option buttons using the button group style (discussed next).

CHECK- AND BUTTON GROUP-STYLE TOOLBAR BUTTONS

Toolbar buttons with a style of *tbrCheck* (1) are used for checkbox-style behavior. Such buttons have a state, remaining pressed until clicked again by the user. The check style should be used for buttons that can be toggled on or off by the user. In the demo program, the *Bold, Italic,* and *Underline* buttons have this style. At design time, a button can be initially toggled on by setting its *Value* property to *tbrPressed*. This can be done from the *Buttons* tab of the toolbar's *Property Pages* dialog.

Toolbar buttons with a style of *tbrButtonGroup* (2) are used for option-button-style behavior. Such buttons also have a state. One of the buttons in the group is pressed until another button in the group is pressed. They have automatic radio button behavior. Each button in the group must be visually contiguous and must have contiguous indexes. They must also be both preceded and followed by buttons with the separator style. One of the buttons in the group should be selected as initially chosen—this button's *Value* property should be set to *tbrPressed*. In the demo program, the *Left Justify, Center,* and *Right Justify* buttons have this style. At runtime, both check- and button group-style toolbar buttons have a *Value* property of *tbrPressed* when chosen or *tbrUnpressed* when not chosen.

PLACING OTHER CONTROLS IN A TOOLBAR USING PLACEHOLDERS

The *Toolbar* control is a container control, which allows you to place virtually any other type of control in it. To place a control other than a toolbar button in a toolbar, you can draw it in the toolbar in the same way you place option buttons inside a frame. However, this is not the best approach. Since toolbars can be dynamically resized when the user resizes your form, it is

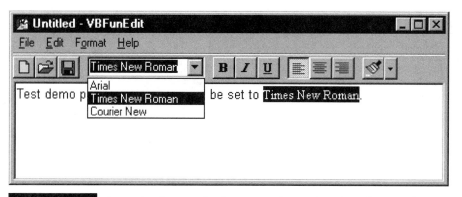

FIGURE 3-16 A combo box and other controls can be placed over a button with the separator style.

better to write code to place a control in the proper place when the form is resized. To do this, you'll start by reserving space in the toolbar using the *tbrPlaceholder* (4) style.

The recommended approach is to place the control (combo box, text box, etc) directly on the form (and not in the toolbar). At design time, set the width of the control to its desired width, and note the width. Create a place-holder- style toolbar button, setting its *Width* property to the width desired for the target control. Both the *Style* and *Width* properties are set from the *Buttons* tab of the *Property Pages* dialog for the toolbar. The *Width* property is used only for buttons with the placeholder style. At runtime, you must move the control (combo box, text box etc) to the area reserved for the placeholder. I'll show you the code required for doing this later in this chapter. The demo program places a combo box, used for selecting a font, in the toolbar (see Figure 3-16).

DROPDOWN- STYLE TOOLBAR BUTTONS

A toolbar button with the style of *tbrDropdown* (5) is used for toolbar buttons that have two visual parts (see Figure 3-17). The part of the button containing the image can be clicked, and acts like a button with the default style; that is, it can be clicked by the user to enter a command or display a dialog. Next to the image in a drop-down- style button is a drop-down arrow. When clicked, the button displays a list of *ButtonMenus*. The *ButtonMenus* are also entered from the *Buttons* tab of the toolbar's *Property Pages* dialog. This section of the dialog is ignored unless the current button has a style of *tbrDropdown*.

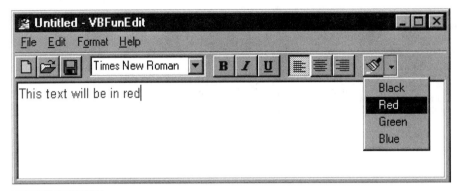

FIGURE 3-17   Toolbar buttons with a style of *tbrDropdown* drop down a
list of *ButtonMenu* items.

Creating Toolbar Buttons at Design Time

Before creating buttons for your toolbar, you must have already created an
ImageList control and loaded it with images. You must also associate the
ImageList control with the toolbar by selecting the *ImageList* control from the
list of image lists on the *General* tab of the toolbar's *Property Pages* dialog.
Once these tasks have been completed, create toolbar buttons. To create
each button, select the *Buttons* tab on the *Property Pages* dialog and click
Insert Button (see Figure 3-18).

You may assign a caption to a button and/or image. To assign an
image to a button, enter a number in the *Image* text box. This number must
correspond to an index used in the associated *ImageList* control. Optionally,
you may assign a string to be used as a key for the button. In code, you can
refer to this button using either the index or the key.

At this time, you must also select a style for the button. For placeholders, you should also enter a width. A tool tip can be assigned by entering
the desired string in the *ToolTipText* text box.

Buttons are created by clicking *Insert Button* on the toolbar's *Property Pages* dialog.

Creating ButtonMenus at Design Time

Toolbar buttons with a style of *tbrDropdown* (5) are capable of dropping down a list of *ButtonMenu* objects. To create *ButtonMenu* objects, first create the toolbar button itself, using the procedure discussed in the previous section. Then, create *ButtonMenu* objects by clicking *Insert Button Menu* in the *ButtonMenus* frame (see Figure 3-19). You must do this while the dropdown button is selected. You may only enter text for a button menu. A *button menu* also has an index that your program will refer to at runtime. Optionally, you may create a unique key string for a button menu.

Drop-down-style buttons have a list of *ButtonMenus* objects, which can be added by clicking *Insert Button Menu* in the *ButtonMenus* frame of the toolbar's *Pages* property dialog.

Referring to Buttons in a Toolbar at Runtime

A *Toolbar* control consists of a collection of **Button** objects. These *Button* objects should not be confused with standard command button controls, which have a class of *CommandButton* (note the distinction). Referencing a button in a toolbar requires a bit of advanced Visual Basic syntax, since you're using an object contained in a collection, which is inside another object.

The easiest way to reference a toolbar button is to declare a *Button* object in your program, and set it to refer to a particular button in the toolbar. To refer to a particular button in the toolbar, use the toolbar's **Buttons** property, passing either an index or key as a parameter. Assuming, for example, that the *Bold* button has an index of *7*, the following code checks to see if the *Bold* button was the selected button:

```
Dim B As Button
Set B = Toolbar1.Buttons("btnBold")

If B.Value = tbrPressed Then
    .
    .
End If
```

As another example, assuming the *Bold* button has a key of *btnBold,* the following code checks to see if the *Bold* button was the selected button:

```
Dim B As Button
Set B = Toolbar1.Buttons(7)

If B.Value = tbrPressed Then
    .
    .

End If
```

USING CONSTANTS TO REFERENCE TOOLBAR BUTTONS

If you decide to use indexes instead of keys to address your toolbar buttons, you should use constants instead of hard-coded numbers. For example, the following constants appear in the declarations section of the demo program:

```
'- Constants for buttons in the toolbar. If the
'- buttons are rearranged, these constants will
'- have to be changed to reflect new indexes.

Private Const nButtonNew = 1
Private Const nButtonOpen = 2
Private Const nButtonSave = 3
Private Const nButtonBold = 7
Private Const nButtonItalic = 8
Private Const nButtonUnderline = 9
Private Const nButtonLeft = 11
Private Const nButtonCenter = 12
Private Const nButtonRight = 13
Private Const nButtonFontColor = 15
```

This permits code to use a constant as the index parameter, which is more readable.

```
Dim B As Button
Set B = Toolbar1.Buttons(nButtonBold)

If B.Value = tbrPressed Then
    .
    .
End If
```

IDENTIFYING WHICH BUTTON WAS CLICKED AT RUNTIME

When *any* clickable button is chosen by the user at runtime, the *Toolbar* control sends a single event to the program, ***ButtonClick***, regardless of which button was selected:

```
Private Sub ToolBarName_ButtonClick(ByVal Button As Button)
```

You are passed a *Button* object as a parameter to the *ButtonClick* event. You can find out which button was pressed by reading either the index or key of the *Button* object passed to this event procedure. A *Select Case* statement is typically used for this purpose. In the following sample code, note that the program avoids duplicate code by passing control to the menu event procedures, rather than carrying out the action in the *ButtonClick* event procedure:

```
Private Sub Toolbar1_ButtonClick(ByVal Button As Button)

    '- Expression 'Button.Index' gives us the button
    '- number.  Remember, separators and placeholders
    '- use an index also!

    Dim nButtonIndex As Integer
    nButtonIndex = Button.Index

    Select Case nButtonIndex
        Case nButtonNew
            mnuFileNew_Click

        Case nButtonOpen
            mnuFileOpen_Click

        Case nButtonSave
```

```
            mnuFileSave_Click

        Case nButtonBold
            mnuBold_Click

        Case nButtonItalic
            mnuItalic_Click

        Case nButtonUnderline
            mnuUnderline_Click

        Case nButtonLeft, nButtonCenter, nButtonRight
            mnuAlign_Click nButtonIndex - nButtonLeft

        Case nButtonFontColor
            mnuFontColor_Click

        Case Else
            MsgBox "Error!  Unknown button clicked!"

    End Select

End Sub
```

Recalculating Form Layout Using a Toolbar

If you are resizing and moving controls when your user resizes a form, you must consider the toolbar. You must also move any controls, such as combo boxes, that you want to appear inside the toolbar.

In the demo program, a *Rich Text* control takes up all available space on the form, and a combo box is moved to a predefined placeholder. The following example illustrates how the demo program resizes the *Rich Text* control when the form is resized. Note that the *ZOrder* method is used to bring the combo box in front of the toolbar. You must check that the form is not being minimized, or the code will fail when it attempts to move and resize the controls – check for this by testing the form's *WindowState* property to see if it equals *vbMinimized.*

The following example illustrates resizing a *Rich Text* control to fit a form when it is resized:

```
Private Sub Form_Resize()

    '- Ignore if being minimized

    If Me.WindowState = vbMinimized Then Exit Sub

    '- Move combo box to designated placeholder in
    '- the toolbar, then use ZOrder method to bring
    '- it to the top

    Dim b As Button
    Set b = Toolbar1.Buttons("btnCombo")
    cmbFonts.Move b.Left, b.Top + 32, b.Width
    cmbFonts.ZOrder 0

    '- Resize Rich Text Control to fit between
    '- the toolbar and the bottom of the form

    Dim nTop As Integer
    Dim nHt As Integer

    nTop = Toolbar1.Height
    nHt = Me.ScaleHeight - Toolbar1.Height
    rtfText.Move 0, nTop, Me.ScaleWidth, nHt


End Sub
```

Using Flat-Style Toolbar Buttons

The trend today seems to be towards the use of flat toolbars, which display buttons that become hot when the user moves the mouse over them. To get your toolbar to behave this way, set the toolbar's **Style** property to ***tbrFlat*** (1). This can be done at design time from the *General* tab on the toolbar's *Property Pages* dialog. The *Toolbar* control will automatically draw a three-dimensional frame over a toolbar button when it becomes hot, as shown in Figure 3-20.

FIGURE 3-20 A flat-style toolbar displays a 3D border around a button when it becomes "hot." If you use a hot image list, you can also display an alternate image when the button becomes hot.

Using a Hot Image List in a Toolbar

You may display an alternate image for a toolbar button when it becomes hot. To do this, you start by creating another *ImageList* control, into which you place an alternate set of images to be displayed when the toolbar button becomes hot. The hot image list must contain the same number of pictures as the "cold" image list, and these images must be in the same order.

To assign a hot image list to a toolbar, set the ***HotImageList*** property of the toolbar to the image list containing your hot images (see Figure 3-21). The demo program uses black-and-white images for the "cold" image list, and color images for the hot image list.

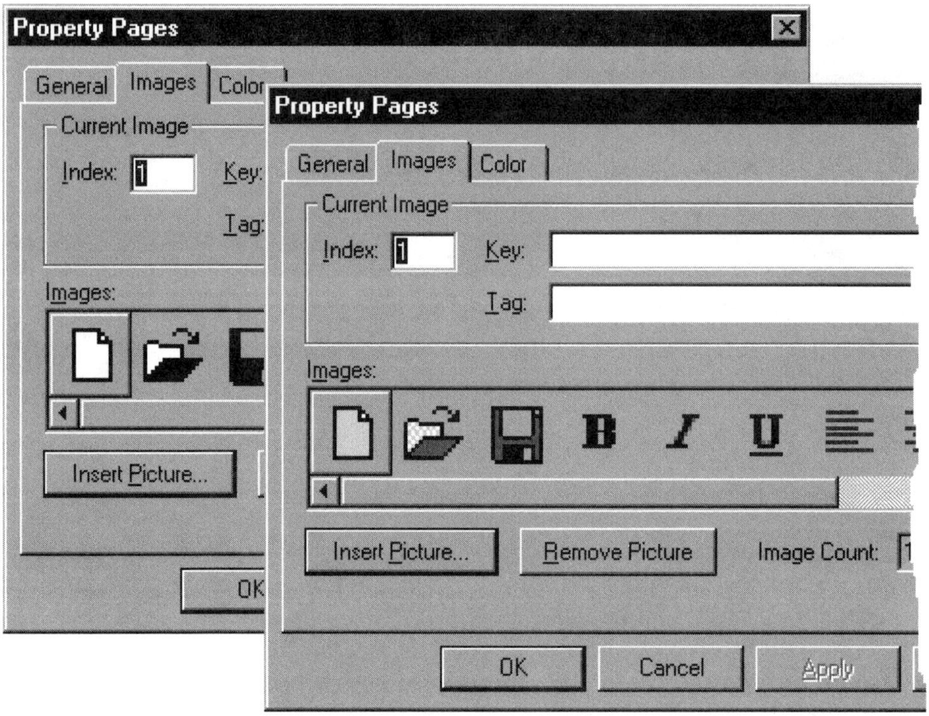

FIGURE 3-21   A hot image list can be used with the "normal" image list. In the demo program, an image list with color buttons is used as the hot image list.

Synchronizing Menu Selections with Toolbar Buttons

It can be challenging to keep menu selections synchronized with toolbar buttons (see Figure 3-22). The recommended approach is to create the menu first, writing code for each menu item. You can then invoke the appropriate menu *Click* event procedure from the *ButtonClick* event procedure. This will eliminate duplicate code, as well as keep the buttons and menu items in synch with each other.

As an example, the following code handles the *Bold* menu item:

```
Private Sub mnuBold_Click()

    '- Toggle bold on or off, keeping the
    '- toolbar toggle button in synch.

    Dim b As Button
```

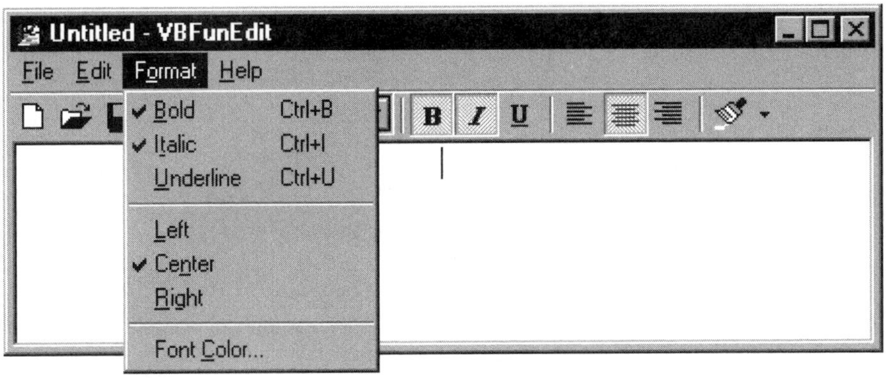

FIGURE 3-22 When the user presses the *Bold* and/or *Italic* buttons in the toolbar, check-marks should appear in the corresponding menu items. Likewise, selecting the menu item should press the button.

```
Set b = Toolbar1.Buttons("btnBold")

If mnuBold.Checked = True Then
    b.Value = tbrUnpressed
    mnuBold.Checked = False
Else
    b.Value = tbrPressed
    mnuBold.Checked = True
End If

rtfText.SelBold = mnuBold.Checked
```

End Sub

The next example is a bit more complicated, since it keeps a group of "radio-button" behavior buttons synchronized with a control array of menu items (the alignment options (left, center, right) are mutually exclusive):

```
Private Sub mnuAlign_Click(Index As Integer)

    '- Uncheck all the menu items, then check the
    '- one that was clicked.

    mnuAlign(0).Checked = False
    mnuAlign(1).Checked = False
    mnuAlign(2).Checked = False
```

```
        mnuAlign(Index).Checked = True

        '- Turn on selected alignment for the Rich Text
        '- Control.

        Select Case Index
            Case 0
                rtfText.SelAlignment = rtfLeft
            Case 1
                rtfText.SelAlignment = rtfCenter
            Case 2
                rtfText.SelAlignment = rtfRight
        End Select

        '- Update the appropriate toolbar button.

        Toolbar1.Buttons(nButtonLeft + Index).Value = tbrPressed


    End Sub
```

About Customizable Toolbars

If you set a toolbar's **AllowCustomize** property to *TRUE*, your user can customize your toolbar by double-clicking on it (see Figure 3-23). This property is set to *TRUE* by default, which allows customization. There are additional responsibilities for the programmer that enable this option. For one, users will expect the toolbar to remain in its customized state, even when they restart the program at a later time, so you must arrange to save the toolbar's last customized state in the registry. Secondly, if you are using placeholders to hold controls such as combo boxes, you may have to recalculate the layout of the toolbar each time it is customized by the user. The *Toolbar* control's **SaveToolbar** and **RestoreToolbar** methods can be used to save the toolbar's state in the Windows registry. Additionally, if you need to recalculate the layout of a customized toolbar, you can add the required code in the toolbar's *Change* event.

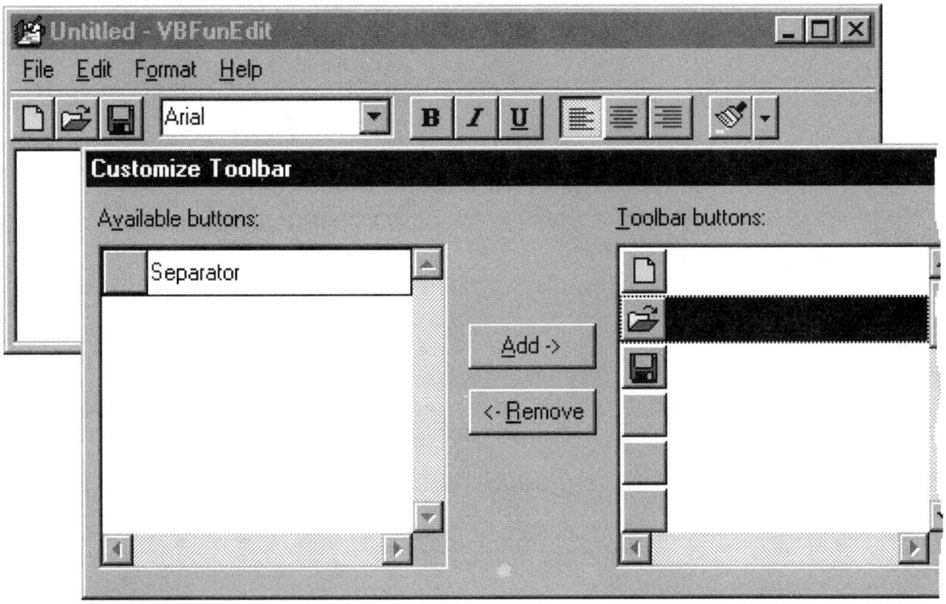

FIGURE 3-23 When the user double-clicks on your toolbar, they will see the above *Customize Toolbar* dialog.

Status Bars

A ***status bar*** is a window that appears at the bottom of a parent form. It is normally used only to display status information and give feedback to the user. A status bar consists of panels that can display text and/or graphics.

The ***StatusBar*** control can be used in a Visual Basic application to implement a status bar for your application. First, you must bring the status bar into your toolbox. Then, select the component *Microsoft Windows Common Control 6.0* to get the *StatusBar* control. Note that both the *Toolbar* and *StatusBar* controls are contained in the same OCX.

Creating Status Bar Panels

Once you've added the *StatusBar* control to your toolbox, you can add it to your form by double-clicking the control in the toolbox. The *StatusBar* control automatically snaps to the bottom of the form. When the *StatusBar* control is added to your form, you automatically get one panel. Additional panels can be added by clicking ***Insert Panel***, which is available on the *Panels* tab of the status bar's *Property Pages* dialog (see Figure 3-24). Like toolbar buttons, panels in a status bar reside in a collection held by the *StatusBar* control. You can identify a panel by its index or by an optional key string.

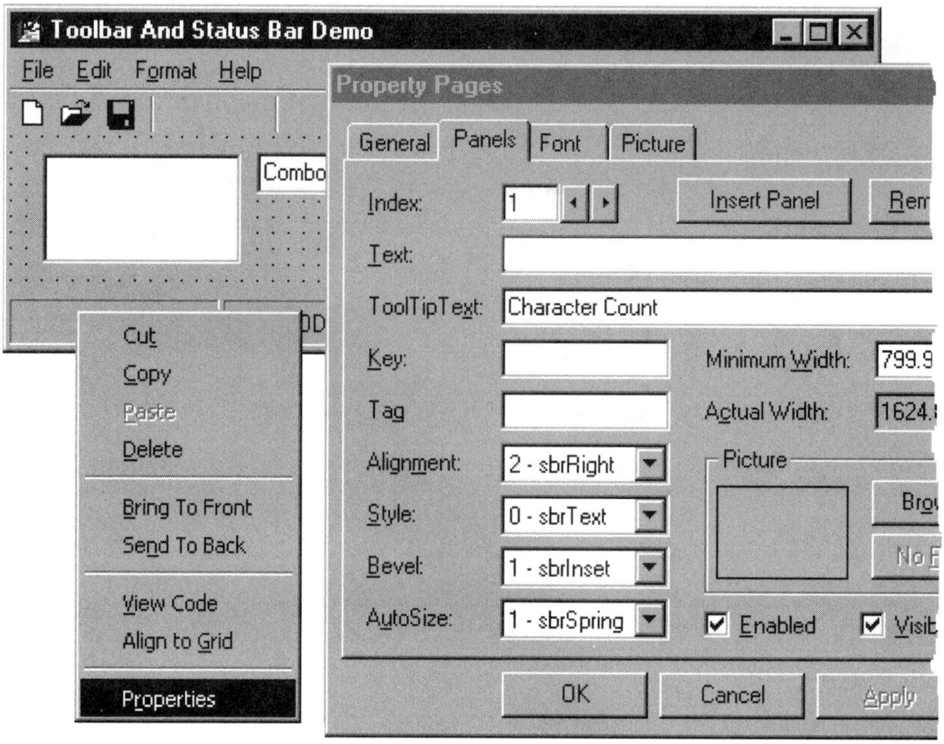

FIGURE 3-24 Panels for a status bar are added by clicking *Insert Panel* from the *Panels* tab, located on the *Property Pages* dialog for the status bar.

STATUS BAR PANEL STYLES

There are several styles available for status bar panels:

- For displaying your own text and/or graphics, use the ***sbrText*** (0) style.
- The ***sbrCaps*** (1) style causes the panel to display CAPS in bold when the *Caps Lock* key is pressed; otherwise CAPS appears in a lighter font.
- The ***sbrNum*** (2) style causes the panel to display NUM in bold when the *Num Lock* key is pressed; otherwise NUM appears in a lighter font.
- The ***sbrIns*** (3) style causes the panel to display INS in bold when the *Insert* key is enabled; otherwise INS appears in a lighter font.
- The ***sbrScrl*** (4) style causes the panel to display SCRL in bold when *Scroll Lock* is enabled; otherwise SCRL appears in a lighter font.
- The ***sbrTime*** (5) style causes the panel to display the current time.
- The ***sbrDate*** (6) style causes the panel to display the current date.

STATUS BAR PANEL AUTO-SIZE FEATURES

Panels have an auto-sizing feature that behaves according to how you set their *AutoSize* property. If a panel's *AutoSize* property is set to *sbrNoAutoSize* (0), the panel's size does not change from its *Width* property. If a panel's *AutoSize* property is set to *sbrContents* (2), the panel's size changes to fit its contents. The panel's size will not be shortened below its *MinWidth* property. If a panel's *AutoSize* property is set to *sbrSpring* (1), it indicates that the panel should "spring" to fit the space left over from the other panels. All panels with this setting divide the leftover space between them. The panel's size will not be shortened below its *MinWidth* property.

You can have as many panels as you want with the *sbrSpring* auto-sizing feature; however, Windows user interface design guidelines suggest that only one panel have this attribute, and furthermore, it should be the first panel.

UPDATING PANEL TEXT AT RUNTIME

Updating a panel's text at runtime uses a bit of advanced Visual Basic syntax. This is because the panels of a status bar are contained in the *Panels* collection. The following example shows how the demo program updates panels when the user changes the text in the *Rich Text* control:

```
Private Sub rtfText_Change()
    StatusBar1.Panels(1).Text = Len(rtfText.Text)
    StatusBar1.Panels(2).Text = "MODIFIED"
    fFileDirty = True
End Sub
```

USING A PICTURE IN A STATUS BAR PANEL

You can add a picture to a status bar panel at runtime from the *Panels* tab of the status bar's *Property Pages* dialog. The picture will appear in addition to any text you put in the panel. A panel's picture can be changed at runtime by referencing the **Picture** property of a *Panel* object. You can also add or clear a picture at runtime.

The demo program uses an invisible Picture Box control as the source for a picture of a mouse. When the mouse button is pressed, a panel displays the picture of a mouse. When the mouse button is released, it clears the picture using the LoadPicture function with no parameter. Related code is as follows:

```
Private Sub rtfText_MouseDown(Button As Integer, _
                         Shift As Integer, _
                         X As Single, _
                         Y As Single)
    StatusBar1.Panels(3).Picture = picMouse.Picture
End Sub


Private Sub rtfText_MouseUp(Button As Integer, _
                         Shift As Integer, _
                         X As Single, _
                         Y As Single)
    StatusBar1.Panels(3).Picture = LoadPicture()
End Sub
```

Recalculating Form Layout with a Status Bar

If you are resizing a control to fit an entire form, as the demo program illustrates, you must place the correct code in the form's ***Resize*** event. The example below shows how you can place a control between the bottom of a toolbar and the top of a status bar. Do not execute the code if the user is minimizing the form, or the code will fail. Check for this condition by comparing the form's ***WindowState*** property to ***vbMinimized*** (1).

```
Private Sub Form_Resize()

    '- Ignore if being minimized.

    If Me.WindowState = vbMinimized Then Exit Sub

    '- Move combo box to designated placeholder in
    '- the toolbar, then use ZOrder method to bring
    '- it to the top.

    Dim b As ComctlLib.Button
    Set b = Toolbar1.Buttons("btnCombo")
    cmbFonts.Move b.Left, b.Top + 32, b.Width
    cmbFonts.ZOrder 0

    '- Resize Rich Text Control to fit between
    '- the toolbar and the status bar.

    Dim nTop As Integer
    Dim nHt As Integer

    nTop = Toolbar1.Height
    nHt = Me.ScaleHeight - (Toolbar1.Height + _
                        StatusBar1.Height)
    rtfText.Move 0, nTop, Me.ScaleWidth, nHt

End Sub
```

About Input Validation in the Presentation Layer

Students and clients frequently ask me whether or not it is necessary to perform input validation in the presentation layer, and if so, how much validation is necessary. This is a good question, since databases often contain constraints and referential integrity checks to make sure that only valid data gets into the database. If input is validated when it is entered, the question goes, won't revalidating it cause performance problems?

Clearly, you must perform the minimum amount of input validation required to keep your presentation layer application from aborting. For example, if an integer is expected, your code must either check the input or declare an error handler to trap invalid input. However, I believe it is a good idea to do as much input validation as possible, within reason of course, in all tiers.

For an explanation of my reasoning behind this opinion, let me tell you a story. I once spent time during my career in the automation and manufacturing industry, specializing in machine vision systems that inspected products on an assembly line. In such industries, it is not unusual to inspect a product during many phases of its production. Inspecting products is costly, and one may at first think that only a final inspection is necessary, in order to reduce costs. However, as a product moves though an assembly line, it becomes more and more expensive, each process adding value to the product. This makes the product more expensive to discard or fix when deficiencies are discovered.

The same concept holds true for N-tier distributed applications. In a 3-tier application, input is often moved from the user, to the presentation layer, to the object model, to the data services layer, and finally to the database. By the time data reaches the database, processor time, network traffic, transaction locks, and other expensive resources may have been consumed. It would be a shame to have wasted all those resources due to invalid data.

In addition to using resources more effectively, when each tier performs reasonable, albeit redundant, validation, the tiers become more robust and can often be used in more general applications than the original developer anticipated.

Using the WinSock Control

When Senator John Glenn made his famous return to space at age 77, there was a humorous editorial cartoon that showed Astronaut Glenn nagging at his fellow crewmembers. "In my day," he is saying, "we had to walk to the launch pad, in the snow, uphill—both ways... and we liked it!" In reality, of course, Senator Glenn played a critical role in an important mission and acted as professionally as any astronaut on any shuttle mission. But I wonder how much restraint Senator Glenn required himself to muster to avoid letting his fellow astronauts know just how different things were in the old days.

With over twenty years of experience as a developer, I often find myself practicing the same restraint, especially when I am teaching. So, in writing this book, I made the decision that it would be essential to require the serious distributed application developer to experience at least a taste of what client/server computing was like in the old days—call it "paying your dues." Any serious developer of distributed applications should have at least an appreciation for how involved it is to establish a communications link between remote processes, define an application protocol, send and receive messages, and handle the inevitable communications errors. I won't take you back to the really old days—in fact I'll illustrate client/server communications using the Visual Basic *WinSock* control. But in my day, you didn't have a *WinSock* control—oops.

The TCP/IP Protocol

Usually, you'll want to use DCOM (probably via MTS) to communicate between components of your enterprise application. This includes components that are not running under Windows, as there are now versions of DCOM for VMS, Solaris, and other systems. However, you may have existing applications that use TCP/IP that you wish to communicate with, or you may simply need a simple, lightweight way of doing it. In this chapter, you'll see how to use the *WinSock* control to communicate using TCP.

TCP/IP actually refers to a large suite of communications protocols. TCP/IP was developed in the mid-1970's as part of the creation of the Internet's predecessor, ARPANET. The *TCP* part stands for Transmission Control Protocol, which is the process-to-process communication part of the protocol. The **IP** part stands for Internet Protocol, which is the routing part of the protocol. This is why we often call Internet addresses IP addresses. The role of *IP* is to look at destination addresses and decide how and where to send a packet.

TCP/IP routing depends on each computer in the network having a unique address. An IP address consists of a 32-bit value, divided into four eight-bit numbers. Addresses are assigned by the Internet Network Information Center (InterNIC). IP addresses can also have a "friendly" name. For example, Microsoft's Web server has an IP address of *207.68.137.60*, and a friendly name of *www.microsoft.com*.

TCP/IP cannot directly use the friendly name, and must translate the friendly name by using the Domain Name System (DNS). This system is basically a distributed database on the Internet that contains the friendly name and corresponding IP address of every registered Internet host. For intranet systems (local "Internets"), you can set up your own private DNS, or simply place the translation in the hosts table. On Windows NT, the hosts table is located in the file *\Winnt\System32\Drivers\etc\HOSTS*. On Windows 95, the hosts table is located in the file *\Windows\HOSTS*. The format of each entry is straightforward. Each line contains an IP address and a host name, separated by at least one space.

For process-to-process communication over TCP/IP, the IP address is not enough, since each host is capable of providing more than one server. To indicate what service (or server/application) a remote client wants to connect to, the client and server must agree on what is known as a port number.

Ports

While an IP address will get a client to the server's host machine, the *port* is used to identify a particular server (or service, or application) on that host. This additional information is required because one server machine may provide several different services. The port number identifies the server the client wants to connect to and use. Therefore, for clients and servers to get "connected," these two pieces of information are required; in other words, you must have both the *IP address* and a *port number*. Internet and Web architects have agreed upon a number of standard port numbers—some are listed in Table 4-1. You can use any port numbers not currently used by your system. However, whatever port you use must be the same in the client and the server.

Having explained IP addresses and port numbers, I can now explain that a **socket** is a network endpoint that consists of a combination of an IP address and a port number.

TABLE 4-1	Well-Known Port Numbers

Port Number	Used by
80	HTTP
20 and 21	FTP
70	Gopher
25	SMTP E-Mail
110	POP3 E-Mail
23	Telnet
79	Finger

About the Microsoft WinSock ActiveX Control

Sockets present you with the lowest level possible for Internet programming. As you may have guessed, programming sockets is quite complex. However, the Microsoft **WinSock** ActiveX Control gives your application easy and direct access to the Windows Sockets API.

The Windows Sockets API, also known simply as **WinSock**, is based on the original University of California's Berkeley Sockets Distribution (or BSD sockets), which is also widely used on UNIX platforms. A **socket** is used to communicate between two application programs. The *WinSock* control is like a "wrapper" around the WinSock API, handling low-level control while giving Visual Basic programmers high-level control over a Windows socket.

Using the *WinSock* control, you can connect to a remote machine and exchange data with another application using either the User Datagram Protocol (UDP) or the Transmission Control Protocol (TCP). The **UDP** and **TCP** protocols are the fundamental protocols used on the Internet. For example, the **HTTP** (Hypertext Transfer Protocol), the fundamental "language" of the Web, actually relies on TCP for low-level data transfer.

With the *WinSock* control, you can create applications that collect information and send it to a central server, or that collect data from several clients. You can also develop applications that participate in an existing distributed application that uses BSD sockets, even those that are not based on

Windows (for example, UNIX and/or VMS). Using the *WinSock* control, you can use a programmer-defined protocol to create custom distributed applications. These are just a few examples of the useful applications that can be created using the *WinSock* control.

Comparing the TCP and UDP Protocols

One of the first decisions you'll have to make in using the *WinSock* control is whether to use the TCP or UDP protocol. The TCP protocol has the following characteristics:

1. It is a connection-based protocol. This means that the client must establish a connection to the server before communication can take place.
2. There is no limit to the size of a message. The protocol will (transparently) break a message up into smaller packets if necessary.
3. However, it is stream-based (as opposed to record-based), which means that it may take several reads from the socket to get a complete message.
4. It guarantees delivery of a message to/from client/server. That is, if a message cannot be delivered from one application to another, an error will be raised.

The UDP protocol has the following characteristics:

1. It is a connectionless protocol; no connection from client to server is required. In fact, it is also a peerless protocol, meaning that there really is not a client and a server. Both applications are "peers."
2. There is no guarantee of message delivery. When a peer application sends a message to another peer application, the socket attempts to deliver the message; if it cannot, no error is returned.
3. There is no guarantee of the order of messages.
4. The maximum size of a message is limited by the network configurations of the involved computers.

The classic analogy for the TCP protocol is the telephone. A call is made, someone answers (possibly switching the caller to another line), and a conversation occurs. When the conversation ends, both parties politely say goodbye and hang up. The classic analogy for the UDP protocol is the radio. A station may be broadcasting a message, but there is no way to know if anyone is receiving the message.

Choosing Between TCP and UDP Protocols

If an application requires acknowledgment from the server or client when data is sent or received, you should use TCP protocol. Note that your application does not have to actually do the acknowledgement; this is handled by the TCP protocol. If the amount of data to be transferred is large (for example, image or sound files), consider using the TCP protocol. If you are sending small amounts of data intermittently, consider using the UDP protocol.

Using the WinSock Control

The *WinSock* control won't work unless you have TCP/IP installed as one of the protocols on your system. To verify that TCP/IP is installed on your system, double-click the *Network* icon in the *Control Panel* and select the *Configuration* tab. If TCP/IP does not appear in the list of network components, you'll have to install it. Once you've installed TCP/IP, you can use the *PING.EXE* utility to test TCP/IP.

The *WinSock* control must be added to your project using the *Components* dialog (from the *Project* menu, select *Components*). You'll then need to place a *WinSock* control on your form. It has no visual appearance at runtime. A list of some noteworthy properties, events, and methods appear in Tables 4-2, 4-3, and 4-4.

TABLE 4-2	Properties of the WinSock Control
Property	**Description**
BytesReceived	Number of bytes received.
LocalHostName	Local machine name.
LocalIP	Local IP address.
LocalPort	Returns or sets local port number.
Protocol	Returns or sets protocol (TCP or UDP).
RemoteHost	Remote host name.
RemoteHostIP	Returns or sets the remote host IP address.
RemotePort	Returns or sets the remote port number.
State	Socket state.

TABLE 4-3	Methods of the WinSock Control
Method	**Description**
Accept	Accepts an incoming client connection.
Close	Closes the connection.
Connect	Connects to a remote socket.
GetData	Retrieves data sent by remote host.
Listen	Listens for incoming connect requests.
SendData	Sends data to a remote socket.

TABLE 4-4	Events of the WinSock Control
Event	**Occurs When...**
Close	The connection is closed.
Connect	The connection request completes.
ConnectionRequest	A remote client attempts to connect.
DataArrival	Data is received from a remote socket.
Error	An error occurs in the background.
SendComplete	A send operation completes.

ABOUT THE TCPIP1 DEMO PROGRAMS

In folder *VB6Adv\Demos\Tcp\TCPIP1*, you'll find a pair of folders, *Client* and *Server*. In these folders are the Visual Basic projects for the first TCP/IP demo discussed in this chapter. Executable files are already built for these applications. To run the demo (see Figure 4-1):

1. Start the *Server.EXE* program, located in folder *VB6Adv\Demos\Tcp\ TCPIP\Server*.

2. In the server program, click the *Listen* button

3. Start the *Client.EXE* program, located in folder *VB6Adv\Demos\Tcp\ TCPIP1\Client*. If you prefer, you may run this program from another machine on your network.

4. In the client program, click the *Connect* button.

5. Both applications display information in a log fashion. Note the log entries on both sides when the client connects to the server.

6. In the client program, enter a string into the *Send Data* text box and click the *Send* button.

7. Exit both programs.

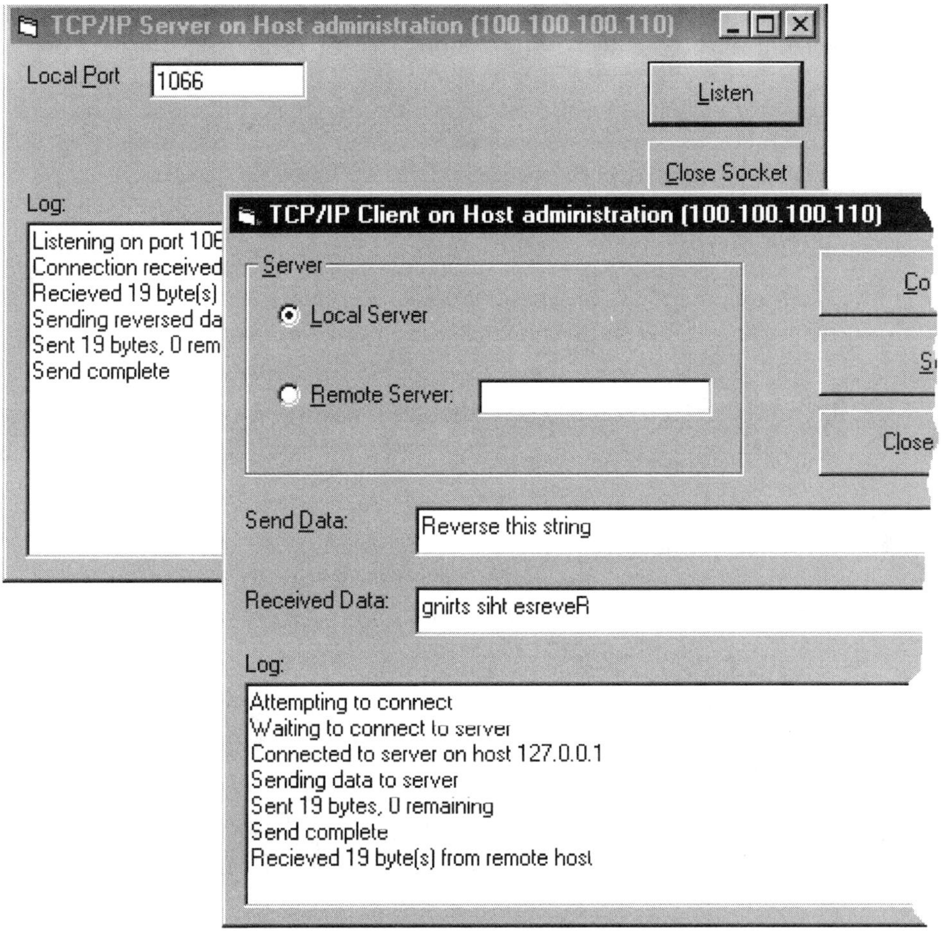

FIGURE 4-1 In the first demo, a server receives a string from a client, reverses it, and sends it back.

Creating a Server Application

Servers (or server-side applications) accept incoming client connection requests. Once a client is connected to a server, communication over the socket can begin. Both client and server can send data over the socket. Typically, a server starts by setting the **LocalPort** property of the *WinSock* control to the agreed-upon *port number*. Then, the server invokes the **Listen** method on the *WinSock* control to start "listening" for incoming connect requests.

The server listens in the background; that is, code following the *Listen* method executes immediately. Your program does not stall waiting for clients to connect. When an incoming client connects to the port and IP address of the server's socket, the *WinSock* control sends a *Connection-Request* event to the server application. The server must accept the connection request by invoking the *Accept* method on an available socket. For servers that will accept only one client at a time, this can be the same socket as the one the server was listening on, but it must be closed first. The *ConnectionRequest* event sends a parameter, *resquestID*, to the event procedure. This ID must be used as a parameter to the *Accept* method.

The following code illustrates how to listen for client connections. The demo starts listening when the *cmdListen* button is clicked. Note the use of error handling. This is good practice when using the *WinSock* control. Also note that the server *closes* the socket if an error occurs. This is also a good idea, and closing a socket that was not opened does not result in an error.

```
Private Sub cmdListen_Click()
    Dim LocalPort As Long
    On Error GoTo ListenError

    ' Start listening

    LocalPort = txtLocalPort.Text

    Winsock1.LocalPort = LocalPort
    Winsock1.Listen

    ' Show status

    LocalPort = Winsock1.LocalPort
    AddStatus "Listening on port " & LocalPort

    Exit Sub

ListenError:
    AddStatus "WinSock Error: " & Err.Description
    Winsock1.Close
End Sub
```

Incoming connection requests are signaled by the firing of the *ConnectionRequest* event. The event procedure receives a parameter, *requestID*. This value must be passed as a parameter to the *Accept* method. Single-client servers can use the same socket as the listening socket to accept the client connection request; however, the socket must be closed first by invoking the *Close* method. Once the connection is accepted, the *RemoteHostIP* property will contain the IP address of the connecting client. However, the *RemoteHost* property is not set to the remote host's name.

Clients only use the *RemoteHost* property when connecting to a remote host. The related code from the demo program follows:

```
Private Sub Winsock1_ConnectionRequest _
                        (ByVal requestID As Long)
    Dim RemIPAddr As String

    ' Close the listening socket and reuse it to
    ' accept the connection from the remote host

    Winsock1.Close
    Winsock1.Accept requestID

    ' Get remote host information and show it
    ' in the status log

    RemIPAddr = Winsock1.RemoteHostIP

    AddStatus "Connection received from " & RemIPAddr

End Sub
```

Receiving Data from the Client

When data is sent from a client to the server, the *WinSock* control fires a **DataArrival** event. The *DataArrival* event procedure is passed a parameter, **bytesTotal**, which indicates the number of bytes received. Remember that the TCP protocol is stream-oriented. This means that you may or may not receive the same number of bytes sent by the client in one shot. You may receive two or more *DataArrival* events to get a whole message. You may also receive one *DataArrival* event for two or more chunks of data sent by a client. Normally, a private protocol is used to flag where a message starts and ends.

In the *DataArrival* event procedure, you can access the data sent by the client by invoking the **GetData** method. The *GetData* method takes two parameters, the variable in which to receive the data, and a constant indicating the type of data. An optional third parameter indicates the maximum number of bytes you want to receive with this call (unused bytes stay in a buffer until requested with a subsequent invocation of *GetData*). The same approach is used in the client-side application to receive data from the server.

Sending Data to the Client

Data is sent from the server to a client by invoking the **SendData** method of the *WinSock* control. The method takes a single parameter, the data to send to the client. If you are sending binary data, use a byte array.

The same approach is used for sending data from a client to the server. Shown below is code from the demo program, which receives data from a client, reverses the string, and sends it back to the client.

```
Private Sub Winsock1_DataArrival(ByVal bytesTotal As Long)
    Dim vtData As String

    ' Get the data

    Winsock1.GetData vtData, vbString

    ' Reverse and send back

    vtData = strReverse (vtData)
    Winsock1.SendData vtData

End Sub
```

THE SENDCOMPLETE AND SENDPROGRESS EVENTS

When a send operation completes, the *WinSock* control fires a **Send-Complete** event. You will also get one or more **SendProgress** events. The *SendProgress* event indicates how many bytes have been sent, and how many are remaining. If you wish, you can use the information in the *SendProgress* event to update a *ProgressBar* control to graphically show the transmission progress to the user. The same approach can be taken on the client-side application. The following demo program simply displays the status in a text box when these events occur.

```
Private Sub Winsock1_SendComplete()
    AddStatus "Send complete"
End Sub

Private Sub Winsock1_SendProgress _
            (ByVal bytesSent As Long, _
             ByVal bytesRemaining As Long)
    AddStatus "Sent " & bytesSent & " bytes, " & _
            bytesRemaining & " remaining"
End Sub
```

Handling a Closed Socket

When a client closes a socket, the server is notified. Notification comes by way of the ***Close*** event of the *WinSock* control. When your server receives a *Close* event, it should close its own socket as well. The server can then go back and listen on the socket for another client. Likewise, if the server closes the socket, the client receives a ***Close*** event. The client should then close its own socket. As an example, the *Close* event procedure from the server is shown below. Similar code appears in the client application.

```
Private Sub Winsock1_Close()
    ' Socket has been closed by remote client.
    ' We need to close it also.

    AddStatus "Socket closed by remote client"
    Winsock1.Close
    AddStatus "Socket closed by server"

End Sub
```

Handling "Background" Errors

Errors can occur in the "background" when using the *WinSock* control. For example, while your server is waiting for connection requests, an error could occur. Or, an error could occur during the transmission of a message, or while receiving a message.

If you want your application to be robust, you should handle the ***Error*** event of the *WinSock* control. This event fires when background errors occur. Both the client and the server should have *Error* event handlers. The event procedure is passed quite a few parameters; the first two are an error code and a description of the error. A minimal error handler will display or log an error message and close the socket. An example, taken from the server, appears below.

```
Private Sub Winsock1_Error(ByVal Number As Integer, _
                        Description As String, _
                ByVal Scode As Long, _
                ByVal Source As String, _
                ByVal HelpFile As String, _
                ByVal HelpContext As Long, _
                        CancelDisplay As Boolean)

    AddStatus "WinSock background error: " & Description
    Winsock1.Close
    AddStatus "Socket closed by server"

End Sub
```

Creating a Client Application

Client applications typically start by setting the ***RemoteHost*** property of the *WinSock* control to either the host name or IP address. Then, the client application sets the ***RemotePort*** property of the *WinSock* control to the agreed-upon port number. Finally, it invokes the ***Connect*** method of the *WinSock* control. Note that if you want to use the host name for the *RemoteHost* property, that host must appear in the *hosts* table (or you must have a DNS server configured). Also, you can use the address 127.0.0.1 for the local host (the server can be running on the local machine). This address is known as the loopback address.

The ***Connect*** method returns control to your program immediately. Your client application does not stall waiting to be connected to the server. When the server accepts the client's connection request, the client's *WinSock* control fires a ***Connect*** event. Any errors that occur while waiting for connection are signaled in the ***Error*** event. You should have error-handling code in the client.

Connecting to a Server from the Client

The following code illustrates how a client can connect to a server. Note the use of error handling, and note that the client closes the socket when an error occurs.

```
Private Sub cmdConnect_Click()
    On Error GoTo ConnectError
    ' If local server is selected, use loopback address;
    ' otherwise read local server name/address from text box

    Winsock1.Close
    If optLocalServer.Value Then
        Winsock1.RemoteHost = "127.0.0.1"
    Else
        Winsock1.RemoteHost = txtRemoteServer.Text
    End If

    AddStatus "Attempting to connect"

    Winsock1.RemotePort = txtPort.Text
    Winsock1.Connect

    AddStatus "Waiting to connect to server"

    Exit Sub

ConnectError:
```

```
        AddStatus "WinSock Error: " & Err.Description
        Winsock1.Close
End Sub
```

Handling the Connect Event in the Client

The **Connect** event of the *WinSock* control is fired when the server accepts the client's connection request. Once the *Connect* event is fired, you can send and receive data. The code shown below is taken from the client demo program.

```
Private Sub Winsock1_Connect()
        Dim RemIP As String

        RemIP = Winsock1.RemoteHostIP
        AddStatus "Connected to server on host " & RemIP
End Sub
```

Transferring Data Between the Client and the Server

Code on the client side is basically the same as the code on the server side when it comes to sending and receiving data. Data is sent using the **SendData** method. Once the data has been transmitted, the client's *WinSock* control fires a **SendComplete** event. Data is received by invoking the **GetData** method, which is done when the client's *WinSock* control fires a **DataArrival** event. For example,

```
Private Sub cmdSend_Click()
        On Error GoTo SendError
        AddStatus "Sending data to server"
        Winsock1.SendData txtSend.Text

        txtSend.Text = ""

        Exit Sub

SendError:
        AddStatus "WinSock Error: " & Err.Description
        Winsock1.Close
End Sub

Private Sub Winsock1_DataArrival(ByVal bytesTotal As Long)
        Dim vtData As Variant
        Dim msg As String
```

```
' Get data

Winsock1.GetData vtData, vbString
txtReceive.Text = vtData

' Show status

msg = "Received " & bytesTotal & _
    " byte(s) from remote host"
AddStatus msg

End Sub
```

Using the UDP Protocol

The UDP protocol is a bit easier to use than TCP, but is less reliable. UDP is a connectionless protocol. There is not a "server" that listens for incoming client requests—both applications are said to be "peers." With UDP, each peer binds to a local port and specifies the remote port of its peer. In other words, two ports are used, one for each peer (that is, one on each host).

For example, if one peer binds to local port 1066, and uses remote port 1067 for transmission, the other peer would bind to local port 1067, and use remote port 1066 for transmission. Whenever either peer wants to send data to the other, it simply invokes the **SendData** method of the *WinSock* control. When data is received, the peer receiving the data receives a **DataArrival** event.

Since **TCP** is the default protocol, to use UDP, you must set the **Protocol** property of the *WinSock* control to *1 - sckUDPProtocol*. Typically, a UDP peer performs the following steps to get ready to send and receive data:

1. Set the **RemoteHost** property of the *WinSock* control to the host name or IP address of the remote peer.

2. Set the **RemotePort** property of the *WinSock* control to the port that the remote peer has bound to.

3. Invoke the **Bind** method of the *WinSock* control, passing as a parameter the local port number of this peer.

The remote peer performs the same steps, but swaps the ports used, so that the remote peer's local port is the same port as the local peer's remote port.

ABOUT THE TCPIP2 DEMO—THE UDP PROTOCOL

The demo program that illustrates the use of the UDP protocol is called *Peer.EXE*, and is located in folder *VB6Adv\Demos\TCP\TCPIP2\Peer*. To experiment with the demo program, refer to Figure 4-2 and the following instructions:

1. Run the *Peer.EXE* program.
2. Run a second copy of the *Peer.EXE* program. In this instance, swap the numbers shown in the *Remote Port* and *Local Port* text boxes. If you wish, you can run this second instance on another machine.
3. Click the *Bind* buttons of both running programs.
4. Enter text into either of the program's *Send Data* text boxes, and click the *Send* button. Sent text should appear in the *Receive Data* text box of the send program.

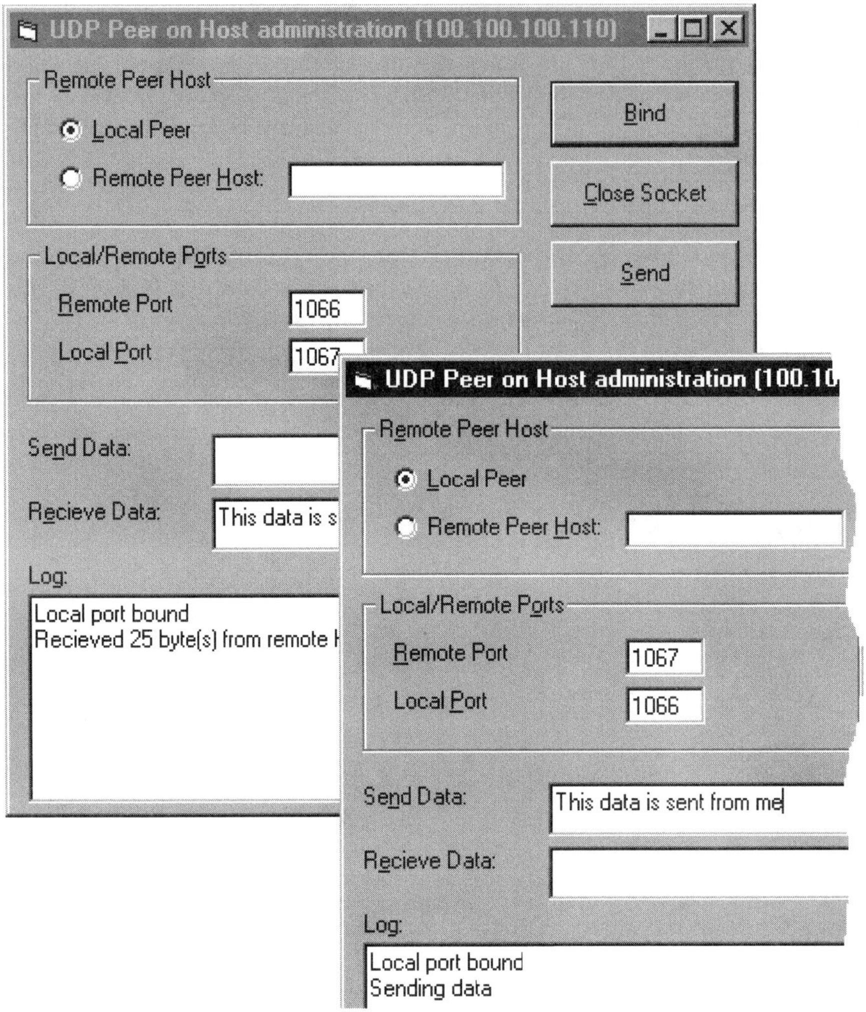

UDP Peer on Host administration (100.100.100.110)

FIGURE 4-2   Run two copies of *Peer.EXE*, swapping the remote and local port numbers in one of them.

Example: Using the UDP Protocol

There is only one application to demonstrate the UDP protocol. You can start the same program on the same system twice to experiment with it (or start one on one system, and one on another). Be sure to swap local and remote ports. The second peer's remote and local ports should be the opposite of the first peer's remote and local ports.

The following code illustrates how a socket is bound to an IP address and port number when the UDP protocol is used. Binding is necessary since we no longer have a client that connects to a server, as in the TCP protocol.

```
Private Sub cmdBind_Click()
    Dim RemHost As String
    Dim RemPort As Long
    Dim LocPort As Long

    On Error GoTo BindError

    If optLocalPeer.Value Then
        RemHost = "127.0.0.1"
    Else
        RemHost = txtRemotePeerHost.Text
    End If

    RemPort = txtRemotePort.Text
    LocPort = txtLocalPort.Text

    ' Bind

    Winsock1.Protocol = sckUDPProtocol

    Winsock1.RemoteHost = RemHost
    Winsock1.RemotePort = RemPort
    Winsock1.Bind LocPort

    AddStatus "Local port bound"

    Exit Sub

BindError:
    AddStatus "Bind Error: " & Err.Description
    Winsock1.Close
End Sub
```

Sending and Receiving Data with the UDP Protocol

When a peer wants to send data to a remote peer using UDP, it simply invokes the **SendData** method of the *WinSock* control. When data is sent to a peer, the *WinSock* control fires the **DataArrival** event. Code in the event procedure invokes the **GetData** method to retrieve the data. For example,

```
Private Sub cmdSend_Click()
    On Error GoTo SendError

    AddStatus "Sending data"
    Winsock1.SendData txtSendData.Text

    txtSendData.Text = ""

    Exit Sub

SendError:
    AddStatus "Send Error: " & Err.Description
    Winsock1.Close
    AddStatus "Socket closed (by me)"
End Sub

Private Sub Winsock1_DataArrival(ByVal bytesTotal As Long)
    Dim vtData As Variant
    Dim msg As String

    ' Show status

    msg = "Received " & bytesTotal & _
          " byte(s) from remote host"
    AddStatus msg

    ' Get the data

    Winsock1.GetData vtData, vbString
    txtReceiveData.Text = vtData

End Sub
```

TCP Servers that Handle Multiple Clients

To handle multiple clients in the server, you'll have to continue listening on a socket. This means that you cannot close and reuse the socket you're using for listening. Instead, you'll have to dynamically create a new *WinSock* control for each client that connects. You can dynamically create a *WinSock* control the same way you dynamically create any type of control—by using the *Load* statement to load another instance of a *WinSock* control that starts off as a control array at design time.

To create a server that can handle multiple clients, first create *one* *WinSock* control at design time, and set its **Index** property to 0. This creates a control array of a single *WinSock* control, indexed by zero. When you receive a **ConnectionRequest** event, increment a global variable that keeps track of the number of clients connected. Then, use the **Load** statement to create a new instance of a *WinSock* control. Do not close the listening socket. In the *ConnectionRequest* event, *accept* the connect request on the newly created *WinSock* control.

ABOUT THE TCPIP3 DEMO—THE MULTI-CLIENT SERVER

This chapter includes a demo program that is a chat program. Once the chat server is started, clients can connect to it and type in messages. A client sends a message to the server, which then sends the message back to each connected client. The code for the chat server and client applications is discussed in the following sections.

To run the demo, start the server application *Server.EXE* from folder *VB6Adv\Demos\Tcp\TCPIP3\ChatServer* and click the *Listen* button. Then, run the client application *Client.EXE* from folder *VB6Adv\Demos-\Tcp\TCPIP3\ChatClient*. This can be done on a different computer, but if so, you will need to enter the server's IP address in the provided text box. Once you've started and configured the client application, click its *Connect* button. You can run as many copies of the client application as you wish, either on the same machine or on different machines. When you enter text into the *Send Chat* text box (see Figure 4-3), the text makes a trip to the server, which then replicates the text back to your client application as well as any other client applications connected to the server.

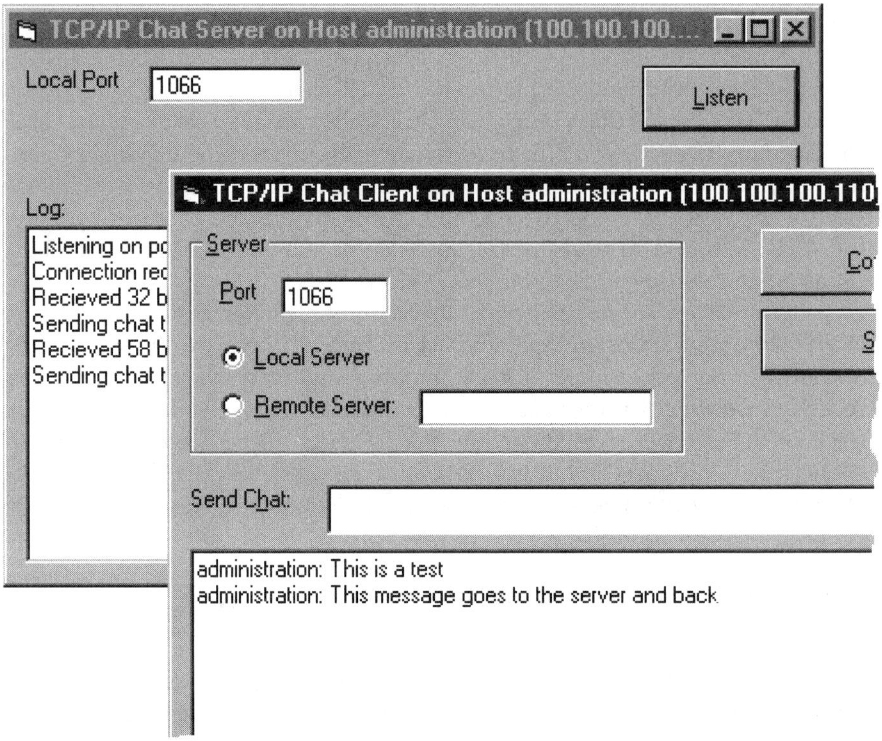

FIGURE 4-3 The multi-client *chat* program.

The Chat Server's Initialization Code

The *Chat Server* application has a single *WinSock* control created at design time, just like the first TCP. However, the *WinSock's* **Index** property is set (at design time) to 0. This makes it a control array with one *WinSock* control. The only change in the listening code is to index the *WinSock* control with 0. The server's initialization code is as follows:

```
Private Sub cmdListen_Click()
    Dim LocalPort As Long
    On Error GoTo ListenError

    ' Start listening

    LocalPort = txtLocalPort.Text

    Winsock1(0).LocalPort = LocalPort
    Winsock1(0).Listen
```

```
' Show status

LocalPort = Winsock1(0).LocalPort
AddStatus "Listening on port " & LocalPort

Exit Sub

ListenError:
    AddStatus "WinSock Error: " & Err.Description
    Winsock1(0).Close
End Sub
```

The Chat Server's ConnectionRequest Event Handler

When the chat server receives a *ConnectionRequest* event, it increments a form-level variable, *nSockets*. It then uses the Visual Basic *Load* statement to create a new instance of a *WinSock* control. The *Accept* method is invoked on the new *WinSock* control. For example,

```
Option Explicit
Private nSockets As Integer

Private Sub Winsock1_ConnectionRequest _
            (       Index As Integer, _
             ByVal requestID As Long)

    Dim RemIPAddr As String

    ' Create a new socket and accept the connection

    If Index = 0 Then
        nSockets = nSockets + 1
        Load Winsock1(nSockets)

        Winsock1(nSockets).LocalPort = 0
        Winsock1(nSockets).Accept requestID

        ' Get remote host information and show it
        ' in the status log

        RemIPAddr = Winsock1(nSockets).RemoteHostIP
        AddStatus "Connection received from " & RemIPAddr
    End If

End Sub
```

Handling Received Data in the Chat Server

When the chat server receives data from a chat client, it receives a *DataArrival* event. The *Index* parameter of the event procedure identifies the client's socket. The server simply loops through each socket (starting with *Index* 1, since 0 is the listening socket), using **SendData** to send the message to each connected client. The **On Error Resume Next** statement keeps the server from aborting when it tries to send the message to a socket that no longer exists. Related code follows:

```
Private Sub Winsock1_DataArrival(Index As Integer, _
                                 ByVal bytesTotal As Long)
    Dim vtData As String
    Dim msg As String
    Dim i As Integer

    ' Show status

    msg = "Received " & bytesTotal & _
          " byte(s) from socket " & Index
    AddStatus msg

    ' Get the data

    Winsock1(Index).GetData vtData, vbString

    ' Send data to all clients

    On Error Resume Next

    For i = 1 To nSockets
        AddStatus "Sending chat to client " & i
        Winsock1(i).SendData vtData
        DoEvents
    Next

End Sub
```

Handling the Close Event in the Chat Server

The chat server receives a *Close* event when a chat client closes its socket. The *Index* parameter of the *Close* event identifies which socket was closed. The chat server responds by invoking the *Close* method on the socket, using the Visual Basic *Unload* statement to delete the socket. For example,

```
Private Sub Winsock1_Close(Index As Integer)
    ' Socket has been closed by remote client
    ' We need to close it also

    AddStatus "Socket closed by remote client"

    Winsock1(Index).Close
    Unload Winsock1(Index)

    AddStatus "Socket closed by server"

End Sub
```

The Chat Client Application

Clients that connect to multi-client servers don't have to know that they are talking to multi-client servers. Like the first TCP application provided in this chapter, the *Chat Client* application uses one socket. It uses that socket to *Connect* and *SendData* to the server. When the chat client receives data from the server, it receives a *DataArrival* event. It simply adds the message to the end of a text box. For example,

```
Private Sub cmdConnect_Click()
    On Error GoTo ConnectError
    ' If Local Server is selected, use loopback address;
    ' otherwise read local server name/address from text box

    Winsock1.Close
    If optLocalServer.Value Then
        Winsock1.RemoteHost = "127.0.0.1"
    Else
        Winsock1.RemoteHost = txtRemoteServer.Text
    End If

    Screen.MousePointer = vbHourglass

    Winsock1.RemotePort = txtPort.Text
    Winsock1.Connect
```

```
      Exit Sub

ConnectError:
      Screen.MousePointer = 0
      MsgBox "WinSock Error: " & Err.Description
      Winsock1.Close
End Sub
```

Sending a Message from the Chat Client

The chat client puts the local host name in front of the message, and adds a carriage return/line feed to the end of the message. The message is then sent to the chat server using *SendData*.

```
Private Sub cmdSend_Click()
      Dim chatMsg As String
      On Error GoTo SendError

      chatMsg = Winsock1.LocalHostName & ": " & _
            txtSend.Text & vbCrLf

      Winsock1.SendData chatMsg

      txtSend.Text = ""
      txtSend.SetFocus

      Exit Sub

SendError:
      MsgBox "WinSock Error: " & Err.Description
      Winsock1.Close
End Sub
```

Receiving Data in the Chat Client

When the chat client receives a message from the chat server, it gets a **DataArrival** event. The chat client uses **GetData** to retrieve the message, then adds the message to the end of a multi-line text box.

```
Private Sub Winsock1_DataArrival(ByVal bytesTotal As Long)
    Dim vtData As String
    Dim msg As String

    ' Get data

    Winsock1.GetData vtData, vbString

    ' Add to Chat text box

    txtChat.SelStart = Len(txtChat.Text)
    txtChat.SelText = vtData

End Sub
```

Database Access with ADO

The latest installment of database access tools includes ADO and OLE DB. ADO, or ActiveX Data Objects, provides the API to an OLE database (OLE DB). The solution provides the best of both DAO and RDO—lightweight, client-side, remote database access (as in RDO), and access to data not traditionally stored in relational databases (as in DAO). Any new applications you develop in VB should definitely use ADO.

ADO and OLE DB

The terms "ADO" and "OLE DB" are not interchangeable. While they are certainly related, they are two different things. Strictly speaking, **OLE DB** is a set of COM interfaces that provides applications with uniform access to data stored in diverse information sources. These interfaces support the amount of DBMS functionality appropriate to the data source, enabling it to share its data. **ADO** is the object model that encapsulates the interface to an OLE DB data source. Put another way, ADO is the object-oriented interface. In this respect, it is similar in functionality to DAO or RDO.

Why the need for yet another specification for database access? Because ADO provides the best of both worlds provided by DAO and RDO. DAO evolved to provide relational access to information found outside databases, such as data in worksheets, text files, etc. But, its desktop origins make it cumbersome to use for client/server database access. Its object model is also cumbersome to navigate; too much emphasis is placed on hierarchy and containment. RDO was designed exclusively to provide fast client/server database access using as few client-side resources as possible, and it has a simplified object model. It was not designed to provide relational access to data other than that contained inside databases.

Problems Solved by ADO and OLE DB

Much of the information used by businesses today is not inside a "traditional" database. Often such information is contained in "flat" files, in ISAM files (*Access, Btrieve*, etc.), in spreadsheets, email, etc. If a company wishes to access such data, it has two options. First, applications can be developed that use whatever interfaces to the information are available and appropriate. This results in inconsistent interfaces and makes software support more challenging. The second option is to convert the information from its original containing system into a DBMS. This process is time-consuming, tedious, expensive, and redundant. The proposed solution is to develop applications that use the same interface to data stored in diverse information sources. This is OLE DB.

The ADO Object Model

The ADO object model (see Figure 5-1) does not emphasize hierarchy. All objects can be created and used independently. Each of these objects are described briefly in Table 5-1, and in further detail in the following sections.

TABLE 5-1	The ADO Objects	
Object	**Containing Collection**	**Description**
Connection	NA	A connection to a data source.
Recordset	NA	A set of records returned by executing a command.
Field	Fields	A column that is part of a recordset.
Command	NA	A command definition, such as an SQL statement.
Parameter	Parameters	A parameter for a command.
Error	Errors	Information about errors resulting from provider operations.
Property	Properties	A provider-defined ("dynamic") property.

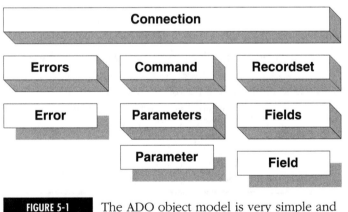

FIGURE 5-1 The ADO object model is very simple and places little emphasis on hierarchy. All of ADO's objects can be used independently.

The ADO Connection Object

An ADO **Connection** object encapsulates an open connection to an OLE DB data source, representing a unique session with a data source. The *Connection* object provides **Open** and **Close** methods for establishing and closing the physical connection to a data source. It also provides properties to configure a connection before opening it. Examples of such properties include the **ConnectionTimeout** and **Mode** properties. In addition, the *Connection* object provides properties and methods to manage transactions and isolation levels. Examples include the **BeginTrans, CommitTrans**, and **RollbackTrans** methods. SQL statements can be directly executed on the database using the *Connection* object's **Execute** method.

Important properties of the *Connection* object are summarized in Table 5-2.

TABLE 5-2	Important Properties of the Connection Object

Property	Description
ConnectionString	Specifies a data source name (DSN) or a detailed connection string containing a series of argument = value statements separated by semicolons.
ConnectionTimeout	Indicates how long, in seconds, to wait while establishing a connection before terminating the attempt and generating an error. Default value is 15 seconds.
Mode	Indicates the intended access (read, write) and allowed shared access (deny read, deny write). Must be set before opening the connection.
IsolationLevel	Indicates the desired transaction isolation level. Examples include repeatable reads, browsing, etc. See help for additional information.
Attributes	Indicates whether a new transaction should be started automatically upon the invocation of either the *CommitTrans* method, the *RollbackTrans* method, or both.
Version	Returns a string describing the ADO version number.

The ConnectionString Property

The **ConnectionString** property of the ADO *Connection* object specifies the information required to connect to a database. The *ConnectionString* property can be either a Data Source Name (DSN) or a detailed connection string containing a series of *argument = value* statements separated by semicolons. To connect to a database, you can use any of the following approaches:

- Set the *ConnectionString* property to a DSN, then invoke the **Open** method of the *Connection* object.
- Set the *ConnectionString* property to a detailed *ConnectionString*, then invoke the **Open** method of the *Connection* object.
- Specify a DSN as the first argument to the **Open** method of the *Connection* object.
- Specify a detailed *ConnectionString* as the first argument to the **Open** method of the *Connection* object.

Regardless of which approach is used, the OLE DB provider typically modifies the ConnectionString property upon opening the database, filling in provider-specific values.

SETTING UP A DATA SOURCE FOR THE DEMO PROGRAMS

To run the demonstrations for this chapter, you'll need to set up a data source. All the demo programs expect a *DSN* of *OLE_DB_NWIND_JET*. To set up this data source,

1. From the *Control Panel*, start the *ODBC Data Source Administrator*.
2. Select the *User DSN* tab and click the *Add* button.
3. In the *Create New Data Source* dialog, select *Microsoft Access Driver* and click the *Finish* button.
4. Enter *OLE_DB_NWIND_JET* for the *Data Source Name*.
5. Click the *Select* button and navigate to the *Northwind Traders Database*. You'll find it in folder *Program Files\Microsoft Visual Studio\Vb98*.
6. Click *OK* to dismiss this dialog, then click *OK* to dismiss the *ODBC Data Source Administrator*.

Connecting to a Database Using ADO

The easiest way to connect to a database is to set up and use a DSN. The DSN can be specified as the first parameter to the *Open* method of the *Connection* object, or you can set the *ConnectionString* property and invoke the *Open* method without any parameters. Parameters of the *Open* method are listed in Table 5-3. The syntax is as follows:

```
Dim connection as ADODB.Connection
Set connection = new ADODB.Connection
connection.Open ConnectionString, UserID, Password
```

Before connecting to a database, you must create a **Connection** object. This can be done by using the **New** keyword in Visual Basic. The first demo program (*ADO1*) uses the the following approach to connect to the database:

1. Declares a variable to refer to the *Connection* object.

2. Sets the *Connection* object variable to a new instance of a *Connection* object.

3. Invokes the *Open* method of the *Connection* object, specifying the DSN or *ConnectionString* specified by the user in a text box.

TABLE 5-3	Parameters of the Connection Object's Open Method

Parameter	Description
ConnectionString	An optional string containing connection information. See the *ConnectionString* property for details on valid settings.
UserID	An optional string containing a user name to use when establishing the connection.
Password	An optional string containing a password to use when establishing the connection.

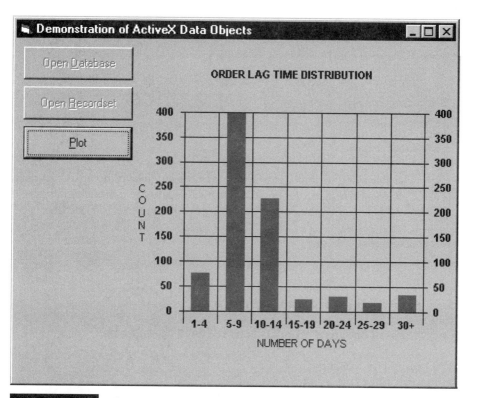

FIGURE 5-2 The *ADOPlot* demo does not use a DSN, so its connection string is a DSN-less connection.

ABOUT DSN-LESS CONNECTIONS

You do not have to use a DSN for the *ConnectionString* property of the *Connection* object. You can use what is known as a **DSN-less** connection. However, the string must specify, at a minimum, the **driver name** and **database name**. Formats of the connection string vary according to which OLE DB Provider you are using. The *ADOPlot* demo (see Figure 5-2) uses a DSN-less connection.

For ***Microsoft Access* databases**, you must specify the *Microsoft Jet OLE DB* driver and the location of the database for the *ConnectionString* as follows:

```
Provider=Microsoft.Jet.OLEDB.3.51;
Data Source=path-to-database
```

For ***Microsoft SQL Server* databases**, you must specify the *SQL Server* driver and the names of the server and database. You must typically also supply a user ID and password, as follows:

```
Driver={SQL Server};
Server=server;
UID=uid;
PWD=pwd;
Database=dbname
```

The following example is from the ***ADOPlot*** demo, using an *Access* database (*NWIND.MDB*). Line continuation characters and the concatenation operator are used for clarity; the connection string is too long to fit on one line:

```
Private Sub cmdOpenDatabase_Click()
    Dim strCon As String

    strCon = _
     "Provider= Microsoft.Jet.OLEDB.3.51;" & _
     "Data Source=" & _
     "\Program Files\Microsoft Visual Studio\VB98\Nwind.MDB"

    Screen.MousePointer = vbHourglass
    objCon.ConnectionString = strCon
    objCon.Open

    cmdOpenDatabase.Enabled = False
    cmdOpenRecordset.Enabled = True

    Screen.MousePointer = 0
End Sub
```

The Errors Collection and Error Objects

Since connecting to a database is an operation that can potentially fail, it is important to understand how ADO reports error conditions back to your program. First, you should know that ADO raises errors in the way Visual Basic programmers have come to expect. You can use traditional Visual Basic error handling—using the *On Error* statement and obtaining properties of the *Err* object, such as *Err.Description*. However, using the **Errors** collection and **Error** objects may be preferable to some programmers. Using the *Errors* collection, it is often possible to display and/or log a list of error messages that describe the problem in greater detail. This can be very useful in troubleshooting.

The *Connection* object contains a collection called *Errors*, which contains a collection of *Error* objects. The set of *Error* objects in the *Errors* collection describes exactly one error. When another ADO operation generates an error, the *Errors* collection is cleared, and the new set of *Error* objects may be placed in the *Errors* collection. ADO operations that don't generate an error have no effect on the *Errors* collection. Use the **Clear** method to manually clear the *Errors* collection. Properties of the *Error* object are summarized in Table 5-4.

Some error conditions are considered warnings. If you perform an operation that results in a warning, no error is raised. Instead, you would test for this condition by checking the **Count** property of the *Errors* collection. If you intend to check the *Count* property of the *Errors* collection, your code must invoke the *Clear* method of the *Errors* collection prior to invoking the operation that may generate the error(s).

TABLE 5-4   Properties of the Error Object

Property	Description
Description	Text of the error alert.
Number	Integer value of the error constant.
Source	String that identifies the object that raised the error.
HelpFile	Indicates the appropriate Microsoft Windows *Help* file and *Help* topic,
HelpContext	respectively, (if any exist) for the error.
SQLState	Provides information from ODBC data sources.
NativeError	

ERROR CODES RETURNED FROM ADO

Table 5-5 lists error codes defined at the time of this writing. These errors can be returned by ADO itself; the provider defines additional error codes. Check *Help* for the latest error codes.

| **TABLE 5-5** | Error Codes Returned from ADO |

Constant	Error Number	Description
adErrInvalidArgument	3001	You are using arguments that are of the wrong type, are out of acceptable range, or are in conflict with one another.
adErrNoCurrentRecord	3021	Either BOF or EOF is True, or the current record has been deleted; the operation you requested requires a current record.
adErrIllegalOperation	3219	The operation you requested is not allowed in this context.
adErrInTransaction	3246	You may not explicitly close a Connection object while in the middle of a transaction.
adErrFeatureNotAvailable	3251	The provider does not support the operation you requested.
adErrItemNotFound	3265	ADO could not find the object in the collection corresponding to the requested name or ordinal reference.
adErrObjectNotSet	3420	The object reference you are using no longer points to a valid object.
adErrDataConversion	3421	You are using a value of the wrong type for the current operation.
adErrObjectClosed	3704	The operation you requested is not allowed if the object is closed.
adErrObjectOpen	3705	The operation you requested is not allowed if the object is open.
adErrProviderNotFound	3706	ADO could not find the specified provider.
adErrBoundToCommand	3707	You cannot change the *ActiveConnection* property of a *Recordset* object with a *Command* object as its source.
adErrInvalidParamInfo	3708	You have improperly defined a *Parameter* object.
adErrInvalidConnection	3709	You requested an operation on an object with a reference to a closed or invalid *Connection* object.

EXAMPLE: CONNECTING TO A DATABASE USING ADO

The following code, taken from the demo (*ADO1*), illustrates connecting to a database using ADO:

```
Option Explicit
Private MyCN As New Connection

Private Sub cmdConnect_Click()
    Screen.MousePointer = vbHourglass
    MyCN.Open txtConnect.Text
    cmdConnect.Enabled = False
    OpenRS
End Sub
```

The Connection Object's Mode Property

The **Mode** property indicates the available permissions for modifying data in a *Connection* object. It must be set prior to opening the connection. Constants for the *Mode* property are listed in Table 5-6.

TABLE 5-6	Connection Mode Property Constants	
Constant	**Value**	**Description**
adModeUnknown	0	The permissions have not yet been set or cannot be determined (default).
adModeRead	1	Read-only permissions.
adModeWrite	2	Write-only permissions.
adModeReadWrite	3	Read/write permissions.
adModeShareDenyRead	4	Prevents others from opening connection with read permissions.
adModeShareDenyWrite	8	Prevents others from opening connection with write permissions.
adModeShareExclusive	12	Prevents others from opening connection with read/write permissions.
adModeShareDenyNone	16	Prevents others from opening connection with any permissions.

Working with Transactions Using ADO

The ADO *Connection* object provides the **BeginTrans**, **CommitTrans**, and **RollbackTrans** methods for managing transactions on a database. A related property is the **Attributes** property, which can be set to indicate that you want a new transaction to be automatically started upon executing either the *CommitTrans* method, the *RollbackTrans* method, or either.

- To automatically start a new transaction when you execute the *CommitTrans* method, set the *Attributes* property to the constant *adXactCommitRetaining*.
- To automatically start a new transaction when you execute the *RollbackTrans* method, set the *Attributes* property to the constant *adXactAbortRetaining*.
- To automatically start a new transaction when you either commit or roll back, set the *Attributes* property to the sum of the two constants mentioned above.

Depending upon the provider, nested transactions may or may not be allowed. If nested transactions are allowed, the *BeginTrans* method returns the nesting level (starting with one, indicating a "top-level" transaction). In general, providers instantaneously commit any changes as you make them, unless you are within a transaction.

The ADO Recordset Object

The ADO **Recordset** object represents the entire set of records from a table or from the results of an executed command. At any time, the *Recordset* object only refers to a single record within the set. This is known as the current record.

Recordset objects are used to manipulate data from a provider at the record level. Note that data in a database can also be manipulated with the **Execute** method of the *Connection* object. *Recordset* objects can be created independently of any other object simply by using the keyword *New* in Visual Basic. However, to populate the recordset with rows, you must use the *Open* method of the *Recordset* object.

Important properties of the *Recordset* object appear in Table 5-7. Important methods appear in Table 5-8.

TABLE 5-7	Important Properties of the Recordset Object

Property	Description
ActiveConnection	Indicates to which *Connection* object the specified *Command* or *Recordset* object currently belongs.
BOF EOF	Indicates if the current record position is before the first record in a Recordset object (BOF) or after the last record (EOF). If both are true, the Recordset contains no records (empty recordset).
Bookmark	Returns a bookmark that uniquely identifies the current record in a *Recordset* object, or sets the current record in a *Recordset* object to the record identified by a valid bookmark.
CursorType	Indicates the type of cursor used in a *Recordset* object.
EditMode	Indicates the editing status of the current record (no edit, edit in progress, add in progress).
LockType	Indicates the type of locks placed on records during editing. This will be covered in greater detail shortly.
MaxRecords	Indicates the maximum number of records to return to a *Recordset* object from a query.
AbsolutePage PageCount PageSize	Used to implement "page-by-page" scrolling through a recordset. More on these properties shortly.
RecordCount	Returns number of records in the recordset. As using this property indiscriminately may cause significant performance drain, it is discussed in greater detail shortly.
Source	Indicates the source of records. This can be an SQL command, table name, query name, or a *Command* object (covered shortly). Can be set prior to opening the recordset, or can be specified as a parameter to the *Open* method (covered shortly). The property is read-only once the recordset is opened.

TABLE 5-8	Important Methods of the Recordset Object

Method	Description
Open Close	Used to open and close *Recordset* objects.
GetRows	Retrieves multiple records of a recordset into an array. This method is covered in greater detail later in this chapter.
AddNew	Creates a new record for an updatable *Recordset* object.
Delete	Deletes the current record in an open *Recordset* object.
Requery	Refreshes a recordset by re-issuing the query. Equivalent to closing, then opening the recordset with the same query source.
Resynch	Refreshes a data in the current *Recordset* object from the underlying database. More on this method later in the chapter.
Update	Saves any changes you make to the current record of a *Recordset* object. More on this method shortly.

About ADO Recordset Cursors

When a *Recordset* object is opened, you must indicate the type of cursor desired. There are four types of cursors, each of which is described in Table 5-9.

TABLE 5-9	Recordset Cursor Types		
Cursor Type	**Constant**	**Value**	**Description**
Dynamic	adOpenDynamic	2	Allows you to view additions, changes, and deletions by other users, and allows all types of movement through the recordset (fully scrollable).
Keyset	adOpenKeyset	1	Behaves like a dynamic cursor, except that it prevents you from seeing records that other users add to your request, and prevents access to records that other users delete from your recordset. Allows all types of movement through the recordset (fully scrollable).
Static	adOpenStatic	3	Provides a static copy of a set of records for you to use to find data or generate reports. Allows all types of movement through the recordset (fully scrollable). Additions, changes, or deletions by other users will not be visible.
Forward-Only	adOpenForwardOnly	0	Behaves identically to a static cursor except that it allows you to only scroll forward through records. This can significantly improve performance in situations where you need to make only a single pass through a recordset. Note that **MoveLast** is not allowed (even though, strictly speaking, it's moving forward!)

Opening a Recordset Using ADO

A recordset is opened by invoking the *Open* method on the *Recordset* object, which must first be created using the Visual Basic *New* statement. All of the parameters to the *Open* method are optional and have defaults. The exception is the *Source* parameter, which, while optional to the *Open* method, would have to be set using the *Source* property of the *Recordset* object before invoking the *Open* method. Parameters of the *Open* method are summarized in Table 5-10. The syntax is as follows:

```
Dim recordset As New Recordset

recordset.Open Source, ActiveConnection, CursorType, _
               LockType, Options
```

After invoking the *Open* method, the current record is positioned to the first record (if any) and the *BOF* and *EOF* properties are set to FALSE. If the recordset contains no records, the *BOF* and *EOF* properties are both TRUE.

The **Source** parameter is used to determine how to query the database to fetch the records. This is covered in the following section. The **LockType** parameter will be discussed shortly.

TABLE 5-10	Parameters of the Recordset Open Method

Parameter	Description
Source	Indicates source of records. May be a *Command* object variable name, an SQL statement, a table name, or a stored procedure call.
CursorType	Determines the type of cursor that the provider should use when opening the recordset.
LockType	Determines what type of locking (concurrency) the provider should use when opening the recordset.
Options	Indicates how the provider should evaluate the *Source* argument if it represents something other than a *Command* object.

THE SOURCE PARAMETER OF THE OPEN METHOD

The **Source** parameter of the *Recordset's* **Open** method specifies a data source for a *Recordset* object. This parameter can be any of the following:

- **Command** object variable (covered later in this chapter).
- String containing an SQL statement.
- String containing the name of a stored procedure.
- String containing a table name.

Alternatively, you may set the *Source* property of the *Recordset* object, then invoke the *Open* method, omitting the *Source* parameter. The effect is identical. The *Source* property is read/write for closed *Recordset* objects and read-only for open *Recordset* objects. You can improve the performance of the *Open* method by indicating, via the **Options** parameter of the *Open* method, how the *Source* parameter should be evaluated. If used, this parameter must be set to one of the constants shown in Table 5-11. The *Options* parameter is ignored if the *Source* parameter is a **Command** object.

TABLE 5-11	Options Parameter Constants	

Constant	Value	Description
adCmdText	1	Evaluates source as a textual definition of an SQL command.
adCmdTable	2	Evaluates source as a table name.
adCmdStoredProc	4	Evaluates source as a stored procedure.
adCmdUnknown	8	The type of command in the source argument is not known.

EXAMPLE: OPENING A RECORDSET

The following example opens a recordset. Note the use of the *Errors* collection to report errors. This process is identical to the process demonstrated in connecting to a database. Also note the type of cursor requested. The choice of **adOpenForwardOnly** results in a recordset that can only be scrolled forward. This is the most efficient type of recordset. Note also that the **LockType** parameter has been set to **adLockReadOnly**. This is strongly recommended for operations that will only read from the recordset. Other lock options will be discussed shortly. Finally, also note the use of the constant **adCmdText** for the **Options** parameter. While not required, this improves performance because the *Open* method does not have to "figure out" what the *Source* parameter is. The following example reads in all the rows using the **GetRows** method, to be discussed shortly:

```
Private Sub OpenRS()
    Dim strsql As String
    Dim vRows As Variant
    Dim lstItem As ListItem
    Dim nRowNum As Integer

    strsql = "Select ProductID, ProductName, " & _
             " CompanyName, UnitsInStock, ReorderLevel " & _
             " from Products inner join Suppliers on" & _
             " products.supplierid = suppliers.supplierid"

    MyRS.Open strsql, MyCN, adOpenForwardOnly, _
             adLockReadOnly, adCmdText

    vRows = MyRS.GetRows
    lvResults.ListItems.Clear

    For nRowNum = 0 To UBound(vRows, 2)

        Set lstItem = lvResults.ListItems.Add
        lstItem.Text = vRows(0, nRowNum)

        lstItem.SubItems(1) = vRows(1, nRowNum)
        lstItem.SubItems(2) = vRows(2, nRowNum)
        lstItem.SubItems(3) = vRows(3, nRowNum)

    Next

    Screen.MousePointer = 0

End Sub
```

Accessing Fields in a Recordset

Fields in a recordset are accessed from the **Fields** collection of the *Recordset* object. If you're already familiar with DAO and/or RDO, you'll be happy to know that the syntax is the same. All of the following expressions can be used to access a field in a recordset:

```
recordset!field_name
recordset.Fields(field_number).Value
recordset.Fields(field_number)
recordset.Fields("field_name").Value
recordset.Fields("field_name")
```

The value of a field called *"LastName,"* for example, can be retrieved using any of the following expressions (assuming *LastName* is the first field in the recordset):

```
myrs!LastName
myrs.Fields(0).Value
myrs.Fields(0)
myrs.Fields(LastName).Value
myrs.Fields(LastName)
```

The **Fields** collection contains one **Field** object for each field in the recordset. *Field* object properties include **Name** and **Value**. Using these properties, you can display both a field name and a value, allowing you to develop extremely general programs.

The following example shows a general procedure from the demo, which loads values of fields into text boxes. The procedure is invoked after each operation that moves the current record. Moving through a recordset is the next topic.

```
Private Sub ShowRecord()
    On Error GoTo CannotShow
    txtFirstName.Text = myrs!FirstName
    txtLastName.Text = myrs.Fields("LastName").Value
    Exit Sub
CannotShow:
    txtFirstName.Text = ""
    txtLastName.Text = ""
End Sub
```

Scrolling Through a Recordset Using Move Methods

Assuming the type of the selected cursor supports it, you can use the **MoveFirst**, **MoveLast**, **MoveNext**, and **MovePrevious** methods, as well as the **Move** method to reposition the current record. Use the *BOF* and *EOF* properties to determine if you've moved forward past the end (*EOF*) or backwards past the start (*BOF*) of the recordset. Forward-only *Recordset* objects support only the *MoveNext* method. For example,

```
Private Sub cmdNext_Click()
    myrs.MoveNext
    If myrs.EOF Then
        cmdNext.Enabled = False
        myrs.MoveLast
    Else
        cmdPrev.Enabled = True
    End If
    ShowRecord
End Sub

Private Sub cmdPrev_Click()
    myrs.MovePrevious
    If myrs.BOF Then
        myrs.MoveFirst
        cmdPrev.Enabled = False
    Else
        cmdNext.Enabled = True
    End If
    ShowRecord
End Sub
```

ADO recordsets support "page-by-page" scrolling, allowing you to specify how many records constitute a "page." Setting a recordset's **PageSize** property establishes the number of records per page. The *PageSize* property can be set at any time, even after opening the recordset.

To move to the first record of a page, set the **AbsolutePage** property. This property is one-based; that is, page 1 contains the first page and the first record. The **PageCount** property, which is read-only, indicates the number of logical pages in the recordset. This value depends on your setting for *PageSize* and the number of records are in the recordset. Expect the last page to contain fewer records than *PageCount*, unless you have an exact multiple of that many records. Not all providers will support this feature. Properties related to scrolling by page are summarized in Table 5-12.

TABLE 5-12	Recordset Properties Related to Scrolling by Page

Property	Description
PageCount	Indicates how many "pages" of data the *Recordset* object contains. This may not be supported by a provider; if so, the property returns -1.
PageSize	Indicates how many records constitute one "page" in the recordset. This property can be set; the default is 10. Used in conjunction with the *AbsolutePage* property, you can implement *Next Page* and *Previous Page* buttons to implement advanced scrolling features in your application.
AbsolutePage	Specifies to which "page" to move for a new current record.

Requerying and Resynching Recordsets

Some cursor types, notably static cursors, result in recordsets that may contain data that is not reflected in the database. For example, records may have changed in the database since being added to your recordset. If your application needs access to the most up-to-date data, there are several approaches. One approach is to use a dynamic cursor; however, not all OLE DB providers will support this. In addition, dynamic cursors are expensive in terms of performance. Another approach is to use a static cursor and requery or resynch the recordset when necessary.

The ***Requery*** method rebuilds a recordset. It is equivalent to closing a recordset and opening it again. The resulting recordset will have both the latest updates to records in your recordset, as well as any new records added since your recordset was created. The ***Resynch*** method, on the other hand, does not rebuild a recordset. It causes the *Recordset* object to check for the latest updates to the current record (or all records) in your recordset. Records added by other users since your recordset was created will not be added to your recordset. Constants for the parameter of the *Resynch* method are listed in Table 5-13. The syntax of the *Resynch* method is:

```
' Syntax of the Resynch Method:
recordset.Resynch AffectedRecordsConstant
```

If you must use one or the other, use *Resynch* if possible, as it is more efficient. It will also result in a recordset that is the same size (in row count) as the original. The *Resynch* method gives you a choice of just resynching the current record, just those records meeting the criteria of the *Filter* property, or all records in the recordset (the default). Another approach is to use the ***Field*** object's ***UnderlyingValue*** property. Retrieving this property for a *Field* object gives you the current value (visible to your transaction) of only that particular field of the current row.

TABLE 5-13	Affected Records Constants	
Constant	**Value**	**Description**
adAffectCurrent	1	Refreshes only the current record.
adAffectGroup	2	Refreshes the records that satisfy the current *Filter* property setting.
adAffectAll	3	Default. Refreshes all the records in the *Recordset* object, including any hidden by the current *Filter* property setting.

Retrieving Multiple Rows with the GetRows Method

Retrieving multiple rows at once with the *Recordset* object's **GetRows** method can result in very high performance, especially in forward-only cursor result sets. The *GetRows* method copies records from a recordset into a two-dimensional dynamic array or variant. The array variable is automatically dimensioned to the correct size when the data is returned. The first subscript identifies the field and the second identifies the record number.

If you do not specify a value for the *Rows* argument, the *GetRows* method automatically retrieves all the records in the *Recordset* object. If you request more records than are available, *GetRows* returns only the number of available records. To restrict the fields that *GetRows* returns, you can pass either a single field name (or number) or an array of field names (or numbers) for the *Fields* argument of the *GetRows* method. After your call to *GetRows*, the current record is the next unread record. The *EOF* property is set to *TRUE* if there are no more records. Parameters for the *GetRows* method are listed in Table 5-14. The syntax of the *GetRows* method is:

```
'  Syntax of the GetRows Method:
Set array = recordset.GetRows(Rows, Start, Fields)
```

TABLE 5-14	Parameters of the GetRows Method
Parameter	**Description**
Array	A variant in which to store the returned data.
recordset	An object variable representing a *Recordset* object.
Rows	An optional long expression indicating the number of records to retrieve. Default is *adGetRowsRest* (-1).
Start	An optional string or variant that evaluates to the bookmark for the record from which the *GetRows* operation should begin.
Fields	An optional variant representing a single field name, ordinal position, or an array of field names or ordinal position numbers. ADO returns only the data in these fields.

The following code illustrates how all rows and fields can be retrieved into a dynamic array (declared as a variant). The code is taken from the demo (*ADO1*), and also illustrates the use of the *ListView* control. For more information on the *ListView* control, refer to Chapter 3.

```
Private Sub OpenRS()
    Dim strsql As String
    Dim vRows As Variant
    Dim lstItem As ListItem
    Dim nRowNum As Integer

    strsql = "Select ProductID, ProductName, " & _
            " CompanyName, UnitsInStock, ReorderLevel " & _
            " from Products inner join Suppliers on" & _
            " products.supplierid = suppliers.supplierid"

    MyRS.Open strsql, MyCN, adOpenForwardOnly, _
            adLockReadOnly, adCmdText

    vRows = MyRS.GetRows
    lvResults.ListItems.Clear


    For nRowNum = 0 To UBound(vRows, 2)

        Set lstItem = lvResults.ListItems.Add
        lstItem.Text = vRows(0, nRowNum)

        lstItem.SubItems(1) = vRows(1, nRowNum)
        lstItem.SubItems(2) = vRows(2, nRowNum)
        lstItem.SubItems(3) = vRows(3, nRowNum)


    Next

End Sub
```

About Parameterized Queries

A *parameterized query* is simply a query that has parameters which may be replaced with actual values prior to opening a recordset. Imagine a scenario in which you wish to execute a query on the *North Wind Traders* database. Your query will return products from a selected category that have units in stock greater than a selected number. The following query has hard-coded selection criteria, returning beverages (*CategoryID = 1*) that have units in stock greater than or equal to 10:

```
Dim StrSQL as String

StrSQL = "Select ProductID, ProductName, CompanyName, " & _
         " UnitsInStock, ReorderLevel " & _
   "From    Products Inner Join Suppliers" & _
   "On      Products.SupplierId = Suppliers.SupplierId " & _
   "Where   CategoryID = 1 " & _
   "And     UnitsInStock >= 10 "
```

The hard-coded query is obviously unacceptable. The following query uses a dynamically-created SQL string that is built by obtaining values from controls.

```
Dim StrSQL as String
Dim nCatID as Integer
DIm nUnits as Integer

StrSQL = "Select ProductID, ProductName, CompanyName, " & _
         " UnitsInStock, ReorderLevel " & _
   "From    Products Inner Join Suppliers" & _
   "On      Products.SupplierId = Suppliers.SupplierId " & _
   "Where   CategoryID =  " & Str(nCatID) & _
   "And     UnitsInStock >= " & Str(nUnits)
```

The second query may meet your needs, but will be an inefficient solution if the query is executed several times. The overhead is in constantly recompiling the query. A better solution is to use ADO **Command** and **Parameter** objects, discussed in the following section.

ADO Command Objects

An ADO *Command* object is a definition of a specific command that you intend to execute against a data source. With *Command* objects, you can prepare an SQL statement (with or without parameters) in advance, and use the *Execute* method of the *Command* object to create a recordset. To use an ADO *Command* object, you will typically perform the following steps:

1. Create the *Command* object with the Visual Basic *New* keyword.
2. Associate the *Command* object with your connection by setting the **ActiveConnection** property of the *Command* object to your *Connection* object.
3. Set the **CommandText** property of the *Command* object to an SQL string. Use question marks for parameter placeholders.
4. Set the **Prepared** property of the *Command* object to **FALSE**.
5. Create a **Parameter** object for each parameter in the SQL string and, using the **Append** method, add the *Parameter* object to the *Parameters* collection of the *Command* object.

Sample code for the first few steps is shown below. A complete example will be presented shortly.

```
Dim MyCommand As New Command
MyCommand.ActiveConnection = MyConnection
MyCommand.CommandText = strSql
MyCommand.Prepared = False
```

The SQL statement, as mentioned, must have question marks for parameter placeholders. For example,

```
Dim strSql As String

strSql = "Select ProductID, ProductName, CompanyName, " & _
         " UnitsInStock, ReorderLevel " & _
   " From  Products Inner Join Suppliers" & _
   " On    Products.SupplierId = Suppliers.SupplierId " & _
   " Where CategoryID = ? " & _
   " And   UnitsInStock >= ? "
```

ADO Parameter Objects

ADO **Parameter** objects are used in conjunction with *Command* objects that represent parameterized queries. Each parameter of a *Command* object must have a *Parameter* object. As you create these *Parameter* objects, you add them to the *Command* object's **Parameters** collection, using the **Append** method.

A *Parameter* object is created by invoking the **CreateParameter** method of the *Command* object. The method is supplied arguments to give the parameter a name, and to indicate its type and direction. As each *Parameter* object is created, it must be added to the *Parameters* collection of the *Command* object. This is done by invoking the *Append* method. Constants related to the *CreateParameter* method are listed in Tables 5-15 and 5-16. The syntax of the *CreateParameter* method is

```
Dim P As Parameter
Set P = command.CreateParameter (name, type, direction)
```

TABLE 5-15	Parameter Type Constants

Type Constant	Value	Indicates
adBigInt	20	An 8-byte signed integer.
adBinary	128	A binary value.
adBoolean	11	A Boolean value.
adBSTR	8	A null-terminated character string (Unicode).
adChar	129	A string value.
adCurrency	6	A currency value (8-byte signed integer, scaled by 10,000).
adDate	7	A date value.
adDBDate	133	A date value (yyyymmdd).
adDBTime	134	A time value (hhmmss).
adDBTimeStamp	135	A date-time stamp (yyyymmddhhmmss, plus a fraction in billionths).
adDecimal	14	An exact numeric value with a fixed precision and scale.
adDouble	5	A double-precision floating point value.
adEmpty	0	No value was specified.
adError	10	A 32-bit error code.
adGUID	72	A globally unique identifier (GUID).
adIDispatch	9	A pointer to an *IDispatch* interface on an OLE object.
adInteger	3	A 4-byte signed integer.
adIUnknown	13	A pointer to an *IUnknown* interface on an OLE object.
adLongVarBinary	205	A long binary value (*Parameter* object only).
adLongVarChar	201	A long string value (*Parameter* object only).
adLongVarWChar	203	A long null-terminated string value (*Parameter* object only).
adNumeric	131	An exact numeric value with a fixed precision and scale.
adSingle	4	A single-precision floating point value.
adSmallInt	2	A 2-byte signed integer.
adTinyInt	16	A 1-byte signed integer.
adUnsignedBigInt	21	An 8-byte unsigned integer.
adUnsignedInt	19	A 4-byte unsigned integer.
adUnsignedSmallInt	18	A 2-byte unsigned integer
adUnsignedTinyInt	17	A 1-byte unsigned integer.
adUserDefined	132	A user-defined variable.
adVarBinary	204	A binary value (*Parameter* object only).
adVarChar	200	A string value (*Parameter* object only).
adVariant	12	An OLE automation variant.
adVarWChar	202	A null-terminated Unicode character string (*Parameter* object only).
adWChar	130	A null-terminated Unicode character string.

TABLE 5-16	Parameter Direction Constants	
Direction Constant	**Value**	**Description**
adParamInput	1	Input parameter (default).
adParamOutput	2	Output parameter.
adParamInputOutput	3	Input and output parameter.
adParamReturnValue	4	Return value.

EXAMPLE: SETTING UP A COMMAND OBJECT AND PARAMETERS

The following code is taken from the second demo (*ADO2*). Note that the code returns no records – it simply sets up a query that can later be used to return records. To create a recordset from the *Command* and *Parameter* objects, you must invoke the **_Execute_** method on the *Command* object. This is the next topic.

```
Private MyCommand As New Command

Private Sub MakeCommand()
    Dim P As Parameter

    Dim strSql As String

    strSql = "Select ProductID, ProductName, ", _
      " CompanyName, UnitsInStock, ReorderLevel " & _
      " From Products Inner Join Suppliers" & _
      " on Products.SupplierId = Suppliers.SupplierId " & _
      " where CategoryID = ? " & _
      " and   UnitsInStock >= ? "

    MyCommand.CommandText = strSql

    Set P = MyCommand.CreateParameter("CatID", adInteger, _
                                    adParamInput)
    MyCommand.Parameters.Append P

    Set P = MyCommand.CreateParameter("Units", adInteger, _
                                    adParamInput)
    MyCommand.Parameters.Append P

    MyCommand.Prepared = False
    MyCommand.ActiveConnection = MyCN

End Sub
```

Using the Command Object to Create a Recordset

Each time you wish to create a new recordset from your *Command* object, you must supply values for each parameter and invoke the **Execute** method on the *Command* object. The **Execute** method returns a *Recordset* object, which you can then traverse in the usual manner. For example,

```
Private Sub OpenRS()
    Dim vRows As Variant
    Dim lstItem As ListItem
    Dim nRowNum As Integer
    Dim nUnits As Integer
    Dim nCatID As Integer
    Dim n As Integer

    Screen.MousePointer = vbHourglass

    lvResults.ListItems.Clear

    n = cboCategory.ListIndex

    nCatID = cboCategory.ItemData(n)
    nUnits = txtUnits.Text

    MyCommand.Parameters(0).Value = nCatID
    MyCommand.Parameters(1).Value = nUnits

    Set MyRS = MyCommand.Execute

    If MyRS.EOF And MyRS.BOF Then
        Screen.MousePointer = 0
        Exit Sub
    End If

    vRows = MyRS.GetRows

    For nRowNum = 0 To UBound(vRows, 2)

        Set lstItem = lvResults.ListItems.Add
        lstItem.Text = vRows(0, nRowNum)

        lstItem.SubItems(1) = vRows(1, nRowNum)
        lstItem.SubItems(2) = vRows(2, nRowNum)
        lstItem.SubItems(3) = vRows(3, nRowNum)

    Next
```

```
Screen.MousePointer = 0

End Sub
```

Updating Records in a Recordset

Updating data using ADO is similar to updating data using DAO (or RDO). However, there are some differences. For one, there is no **Edit** method for the *Recordset* object, unlike in both DAO and RDO. With ADO, modifying a field's value is like making an implicit "call" to *Edit* (note the wording here; it's not as though calling *Edit* is optional—there's no *Edit* to call); you use the **Update** method.

Adding new records is the same as in DAO and RDO; the **AddNew** method is used, followed by the *Update* method. Canceling an edit or new record is accomplished by using the **CancelUpdate** method of the Recordset object. Deleting data at the record level is the same as in DAO and RDO – use the **Delete** method of the *Recordset* object.

By default, your recordset is read-only. Use the **LockType** property (or *LockType* parameter of *Open*) to specify a lock that allows updating (this is the next topic).

Before looking at operations that update data in a database using a *Recordset* object, consider that, in general, the **Execute** method of the **Connection** and **Command** objects is usually more efficient. Consider updating data by creating an SQL statement and executing it with the *Execute* method of the *Connection* or *Command* object.

Locking and the LockType Property

To update data in a recordset, the *Recordset* object must be created with the appropriate lock type. The lock type can be specified by either of the following methods:

- By setting the **LockType** property of the **Recordset** object before invoking the **Open** method, in which the *LockType* parameter is omitted.
- By specifying the lock type as the **LockType** parameter of the **Recordset** object's Open method, in which case the *LockType* property is inherited from the *LockType* parameter.

The *LockType* parameter/property can be set to the constant ***adLockReadOnly*** to indicate a read-only recordset. The remaining lock types indicate an updateable recordset. Lock type constants are shown in Table 5-17. The constant ***adLockBatchOptimistic*** requests optimistic batch updates. The remaining constants, ***adLockPessimistic*** and ***adLockOptimistic***, indicate a traditional updateable recordset.

The difference between pessimistic and optimistic locking is defined by the underlying OLE DB provider. Not all providers support all lock types, in which case the provider will substitute another type of locking. Use the ***Supports*** method to determine what types of lock(s) a provider supports.

In general (and if supported by a provider), **optimistic locking** indicates that the provider will lock records only when you call the ***Update*** method. If the record cannot be locked, the *Update* operation will fail. In general, **pessimistic locking** indicates that the provider will do what is necessary to ensure successful editing of the records, usually by locking records at the data source immediately upon editing. Note that some providers have a more severe treatment for pessimistic locking than others, perhaps locking a record as soon as it is touched.

TABLE 5-17	LockType Property Constants	
Constant	**Value**	**Description**
adLockReadOnly	1	Read-only—you cannot alter the data.
adLockPessimistic	2	Pessimistic locking, record by record—the provider does what is necessary to ensure successful editing of the records, usually by locking records at the data source immediately upon editing
adLockOptimistic	3	Optimistic locking, record by record—the provider uses optimistic locking, locking records only when you call the *Update* method.
adLockBatchOptimistic	4	Optimistic batch updates—required for batch update mode as opposed to immediate update mode.

The AddNew, Update, and CancelUpdate Methods

The **AddNew** method prepares your *Recordset* object to act as a buffer to receive field values for a new record. After invoking the *AddNew* method, move new values into the fields of the recordset. Complete the insert operation by invoking the *Update* method. The *Update* method is also used to save any changes you make to the current record of a *Recordset* object. Unlike DAO and RDO, there is no Edit method. Simply moving a new value into a field is like performing an *Edit* method in DAO and RDO. To cancel updates (both modifications and new records), invoke the **CancelUpdate** method.

The *Update* and *CancelUpdate* methods cannot be invoked unless you are modifying or adding a record. If necessary, your program can use the **EditMode** property of the *Recordset* object to determine what the edit mode is – see Table 5-18.

In contrast to RDO and DAO, if you move from the record you are adding or editing before calling the *Update* method, ADO will automatically call *Update* to save the changes. You must call the *CancelUpdate* method if you want to cancel any changes made to the current record or to discard a newly added record. The demo program *ADO3* illustrates the use of the *AddNew, Update,* and *CancelUpdate* methods.

TABLE 5-18	EditMode Constants	
EditMode Constant	**Value**	**Description**
adEditNone	0	No editing operation is in progress.
adEditInProgress	1	Data in the current record has been modified but not yet saved.
adEditAdd	2	The *AddNew* method has been invoked, and the current record in the copy buffer is a new record that hasn't been saved in the database.

The ADO *Recordset* object's *Update* and *AddNew* methods have an alternate syntax that many Visual Basic programmers may find useful:

```
recordset.Update Fields, Values
recordset.AddNew Fields, Values
```

Using the *Update* or *AddNew* method, you can pass two parameters. The first can be a field name as a string, in which case the second parameter is the new value. Another syntax for the *Update* and *AddNew* methods is to pass two variant arrays. The first array contains a list of field names or ordinal field positions. The second array contains a list of values that correspond to the first array. Parameters are shown in Table 5-19.

TABLE 5-19	Update and AddNew Parameters
Parameter	**Description**
Fields	An optional variant representing a single name, or a variant array representing names or ordinal positions of the field(s) you wish to modify.
Values	An optional variant representing a single value, or a variant array representing value(s) for the field(s) in the new record.

Following is an example of using the *Update* method to update one field of the current record:

```
Private Sub cmdUpdate_Click()
    MyRs.Update "ContactTitle", "President"
End Sub
```

Following is an example of using the *Update* method to update several fields of the current record:

```
Private Sub cmdUpdate_Click()
    ReDim f(1 To 2) As Variant
    ReDim v(1 To 2) As Variant

    f(1) = "ContactTitle"
    f(2) = "City"
    v(1) = "President"
    v(2) = "Tinytown"

    MyRs.Update f, v

End Sub
```

The Execute Method of the Connection Object

An alternative to creating *Recordset* objects for queries that return no records (action queries) is to use the **Execute** method of the *Connection* object. The method can be passed an SQL string, and will return an integer indicating the number of rows affected by the query.

You can also use the **Execute** method to create a recordset. If the query returns rows, the *Execute* method will return a *Recordset* object as a return value. If the query does not return rows, the *Execute* method returns a closed recordset. Parameters of the *Execute* method are listed in Table 5-20. The syntax of the *Execute* method is

```
' Syntax 1 — Returns records
Set recordset = cn.Execute(CommandText, _
                            RecordsAffected, _
                            Options)


' Syntax 2 — Does not return records
cn.Execute CommandText, RecordsAffected, Options
```

TABLE 5-20	Parameters of the Execute Method
Parameter	**Description**
connection	An object variable representing a *Connection* object on which the query is executed.
RecordsAffected	An optional long variable to which the provider returns the number of records that the operation affected.
Parameters	An optional variant array of parameter values passed with an SQL statement. (Output parameters will not return correct values when passed in this argument.)
CommandText	A string containing the SQL statement, table name, or stored procedure to execute.
Options	An optional *CommandTypeEnum* value that indicates how the provider should evaluate the *CommandText* argument. Valid constants are *adCmdText*, *adCmdTable*, *adCmdStoredProc*, and *adCmdUnknown*.

The following example shows the use of the *Execute* method of the *Connection* object:

```
Dim strSQL As String
Dim nRecs As Long

strSQL = "Update Categories " & _
    "   Set CategoryName = 'Drinks'" & _
    " Where CategoryID = 1"
MyCn.Execute strSQL, nRecs, adCmdText
```

ABOUT THE CONNECTION EXECUTE DEMO

The demo in the *ADO4* folder allows you to enter SQL strings and execute them. If you enter an SQL string that returns records, the program dynamically lists the columns and their values in a *ListView* control. Try some of the following queries, but be sure to enter them one at a time, and do not press *Enter* until the entire command is entered:

```
Insert Into Categories Values (100, 'Books',
        'Things You Read', NULL)

Select * From Categories

Delete From Categories Where CategoryID = 100
```

Mom-n-Pop Video Store Case Studies

The *Mom-n-Pop Video Store* application included with this book uses ADO in both the 2-tier and 3-tier versions. Since it is a complete implementation of a small business, it is useful as a case study of database access with ADO. As mentioned, both versions use ADO. However, the 3-tier version uses ADO from its MTS components. It is probably easier for you to examine the code in the 2-tier version, which includes both the business logic and database access code in the same tier. You can look at the code by opening project *MPV2Devel.VBP,* which is located in folder *VB6Ent\Demos\MomPop\ 2Tier\MPVServer.*

Loading the Categories Collection

The following code fragment reads in all the categories in the *Categories* table and stores them in the *Categories* collection. The code appears in the *Class_Initialize* method of the *VideoStore* class module. Creating and using class modules is covered in Chapters 6 and 7.

```
Set gConnect = New Connection
gConnect.Open strDSN, strUID, strPWD

' Get list of categories from the database
' and store in Categories collection

Dim R As New Recordset
Dim C As Category

R.Open "Select * From Categories Order By CatID", _
        gConnect, adOpenStatic, adLockReadOnly

Do While Not R.EOF
    Set C = New Category
    C.ID = R.Fields("CatID").Value
    C.Name = R.Fields("CategoryName").Value
    C.Nights = R.Fields("Nights").Value
    C.Price = R.Fields("Price").Value
    gobjCategories.Add C
    R.MoveNext
Loop

R.Close
```

Setting Up a Parameterized Query

The *Mom-n-Pop Video Store* application uses parameterized queries for virtually all its queries. In fact, the only reason for not using them in certain places is for illustration only. Using a parameterized query is preferred because of performance. Shown below is code that sets up a parameterized query to get a video with a given video ID. The code is located in the procedure *PrepareQueries*, located in module *DBGlobals*.

```
Dim strSQL As String
Dim P As ADODB.Parameter

' Prepare the Video Results By ID query, which selects all
' fields from the Videos table with an indicated ID
```

```
strSQL = "Select * From Videos Where VideoID = ?"

Set gqryVideoResultsByID = New ADODB.Command
Set P = gqryVideoResultsByID.CreateParameter("ID", _
                                         adInteger, _
                                         adParamInput)

gqryVideoResultsByID.Parameters.Append P
gqryVideoResultsByID.CommandText = strSQL
gqryVideoResultsByID.CommandType = adCmdText
gqryVideoResultsByID.Prepared = False
gqryVideoResultsByID.ActiveConnection = gConnect
```

Using a Parameterized Query

The code fragment shown below is used to find a video given its video ID. It uses the parameterized query shown in the previous section. The code is located in the *FindVideoByID* method of the *VideoStore* class module.

```
Public Function FindVideoByID(nVideoID As Long) As Video

    ' Find and return video with this video ID

    Dim RS As Recordset

    ' Use parameterized query (defined in DBGlobals) to
    ' find the video with this ID

    gqryVideoResultsByID.Parameters(0) = nVideoID
    Set RS = gqryVideoResultsByID.Execute

    If RS.EOF And RS.BOF Then
        Set FindVideoByID = Nothing
        Err.Raise vseNoSuchVideo, "Videos", _
                "Video does not exist"
    End If

    ' Copy video's information into object and return

    Dim V As New Video

    CopyVideoRsToVideoObj V, RS
    RS.Close

    Set Video = V

End Function
```

Setting Up for Invoking a Stored Procedure

There are several stored procedures in the *Mom-n-Pop Video* database. For example, the **RentedVideos** query returns a list of videos that a particular member has rented. The code shown below prepares a query that will be used to execute the stored procedure. It is located in the procedure *PrepareQueries*, located in module *DBGlobals*.

```
' Prepare the Rented Videos query, which selects rows
' from the Rentals table with matching Member ID
'
' This query uses a stored procedure (RentedVideos)

Set gqryRentedVideos = New ADODB.Command
Set P = gqryRentedVideos.CreateParameter("nMemberID", _
                                         adInteger, _
                                         adParamInput)

gqryRentedVideos.Parameters.Append P
gqryRentedVideos.CommandText = "RentedVideos"
gqryRentedVideos.CommandType = adCmdStoredProc
gqryRentedVideos.Prepared = False
gqryRentedVideos.ActiveConnection = gConnect
```

Using a Stored Procedure

The following code uses the *Command* object that executes the stored procedure prepared in the previous section. The code is located in the *Property Get* procedure for the property *RentedVideos*, located in the *Member* class module.

```
Public Property Get RentedVideos() As RentedVideos

    '- Build this list by "procrastination"
    '- That is, don't build it until it's asked for.
    '- However, once built, it "stays" built.

    If Not mvarRentedVideos Is Nothing Then
        Set RentedVideos = mvarRentedVideos
        Exit Property
    End If

    '- First time it's asked for, build query.

    Set mvarRentedVideos = New RentedVideos
```

```
'- Build a recordset containing list of rented
'- videos for this customer.  We use a parameterized
'- query defined in DBGlobals.

Dim RS As Recordset

gqryRentedVideos.Parameters("nMemberID").Value = Me.ID
Set RS = gqryRentedVideos.Execute

' For each video rented to customer, add to
' the just created collection.

Dim V As RentedVideo

Do While Not RS.EOF
    Set V = New RentedVideo
    CopyRentedVideoRsToRentedVideoObj V, RS
    mvarRentedVideos.Add V
    RS.MoveNext
Loop

' Close recordset and return RentedVideos collection.

RS.Close
Set RentedVideos = mvarRentedVideos

End Property
```

Finding the Next Due Date of a Video

The code to find the next due date of a video is interesting because it must deal with the possibility of using a null value returned from an SQL query. It also illustrates using the *Execute* method of a *Connection* object to create a recordset. The code, which follows, is located in the *PropertyGet* procedure for the property *NextDue*, which is located in the *Video* class module.

```
Public Property Get NextDue() As Date
    ' Create a query that returns the earliest date
    ' from the Rentals table with this Video ID.

    Dim strSQL As String
    Dim RS As Recordset

    strSQL = "Select Min(DateDue) From Rentals" & _
            " Where VideoID = " & Me.ID

    Set RS = gConnect.Execute(strSQL, , adCmdText)

    ' If the one and only field returned by the
    ' above query is NULL, it indicates nobody has
    ' currently rented this video, in which case,
    ' we return "Today".

    Dim NextDueDate As Date

    If IsNull(RS.Fields(0).Value) Then
        NextDueDate = GetTodaysDate()
    Else
        NextDueDate = RS.Fields(0).Value
    End If

    ' Close recordset and return computed date.

    RS.Close
    NextDue = NextDueDate

End Property
```

Inserting a Record into the LateCharges Table

The *Mom-n-Pop Video Store* application creates an SQL ***Insert*** statement to add entries to the *LateCharges* table. The code is located in the procedure *ProcessReturn*, in module *DBGlobals*.

```
If dtReturnDate > RV.DateDue Then

    ' Calculate and assess late charge

    Dim nDaysLate As Integer
    Dim nLateCharge As Currency

    nDaysLate = dtReturnDate - RV.DateDue
    nLateCharge = nDaysLate * gLateFee

    strSQL = "Insert Into LateCharges (" & _
        "    MemberID, VideoID, CopyNo, " & _
        "    DateRented, DateDue, DateReturned, " & _
        "    DaysLate, Charge) " & _
        " Values (" & _
        Str(RV.MemberID) & ", " & _
        Str(RV.VideoID) & ", " & _
        Str(RV.CopyNo) & ", " & _
        "'" & Format(RV.DateRented, "Short Date") & "', " & _
        "'" & Format(RV.DateDue, "Short Date") & "', " & _
        "'" & Format(dtReturnDate, "Short Date") & "', " & _
        Str(nDaysLate) & ", " & _
        Str(nLateCharge) & ")"

    gConnect.Execute strSQL, , adCmdText

End If
```

Deleting Entries from the LateCharges Table

The *Mom-n-Pop* application removes late charges by creating and executing an SQL *Delete* statement. The code is located in the *RemoveLateCharges* procedure of the module *DBGlobals*.

```
Public Sub RemoveLateCharges(nMemberID as Long)

    ' Remove all late charges for customer

    Dim strSQL As String

    strSQL = "Delete From LateCharges" & _
             " Where MemberID = " & Me.ID

    gConnect.Execute strSQL, , adCmdText

End Sub
```

Using ADO Data Sources

An ***ADO data source*** provides data for a control or for variables in your program. Examples of ADO data sources include the ADO Data Control and *Data Environment* objects. The ADO Data Control is the next subject I'll cover. The ADO Data Control provides the same and better functionality than the old Data Control, now know as the Intrinsic Data Control. The concepts are the same; you place an ADO Data Control on your form and bind controls to it. However, the properties, methods, and events of the ADO Data Control are different.

Using a *DataEnvironment* object, you can drag and drop database fields to your form, saving time in development. You can also easily get data into variables in your program from an *Environment* object. An *Environment* object, like the ADO Data Control, is considered a data source.

Using the ADO Data Control

With the ADO Data Control, you can create simple database applications without writing code. With a few statements, your application can become quite sophisticated. The ADO Data Control uses bound controls to display selected columns of the current row of a table. It provides controls to move forward and backward in the table. You can also program the ADO Data Control with code statements.

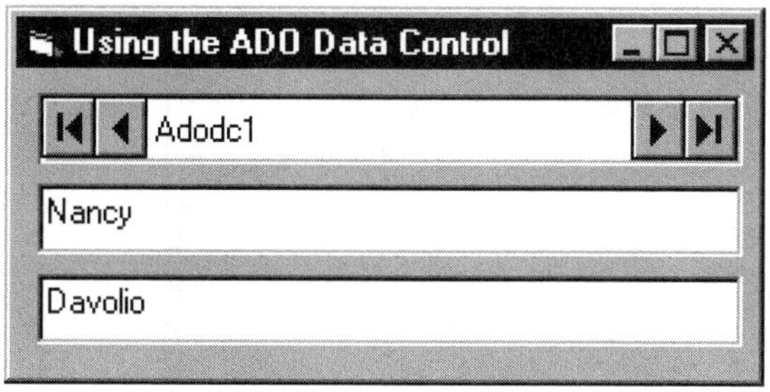

FIGURE 5-3 You can use the ADO Data Control to create simple database applications without writing any code. With just a few statements, the program can become very sophisticated.

In the following sections, I will guide you through a demo in which you will create a simple program that allows a user to browse through, and modify, the records of the *Employees* table in the *NorthWind Traders* database. Your resulting application will appear as shown in Figure 5-3. To do this walkthrough and run the demos presented in the remainder of this chapter, you must have set up the *OLE_DB_NWIND_JET* data source, as described at the beginning of this chapter.

INSERTING THE ADO DATA CONTROL COMPONENT

The ADO Data Control is not an intrinsic control. Do not confuse it with the Intrinsic Data Control, which is still supported for old applications. New applications should use the ADO Data Control. The ADO Data Control is an ActiveX Control, which must be added to your program. The following instructions indicate how to get started with this walkthrough, beginning with adding the ADO Data Control to a new Standard EXE project:

1. Start a new *Standard EXE* project.
2. From the *Project* menu, select *Components*.
3. Scroll down to and select the component *Microsoft ADO Data Control*.
4. Double-click on the *ADO Data Control* in your toolbox to place one on your form.
5. Size the control as desired, using Figure 5-3 as a guide.

SETTING THE CONNECTIONSTRING PROPERTY

The **ConnectionString** property indicates how to connect to the database. In this walkthrough, you'll use the DSN you set up previously (*OLE_DB_NWIND_JET*). To set the *ConnectionString* property,

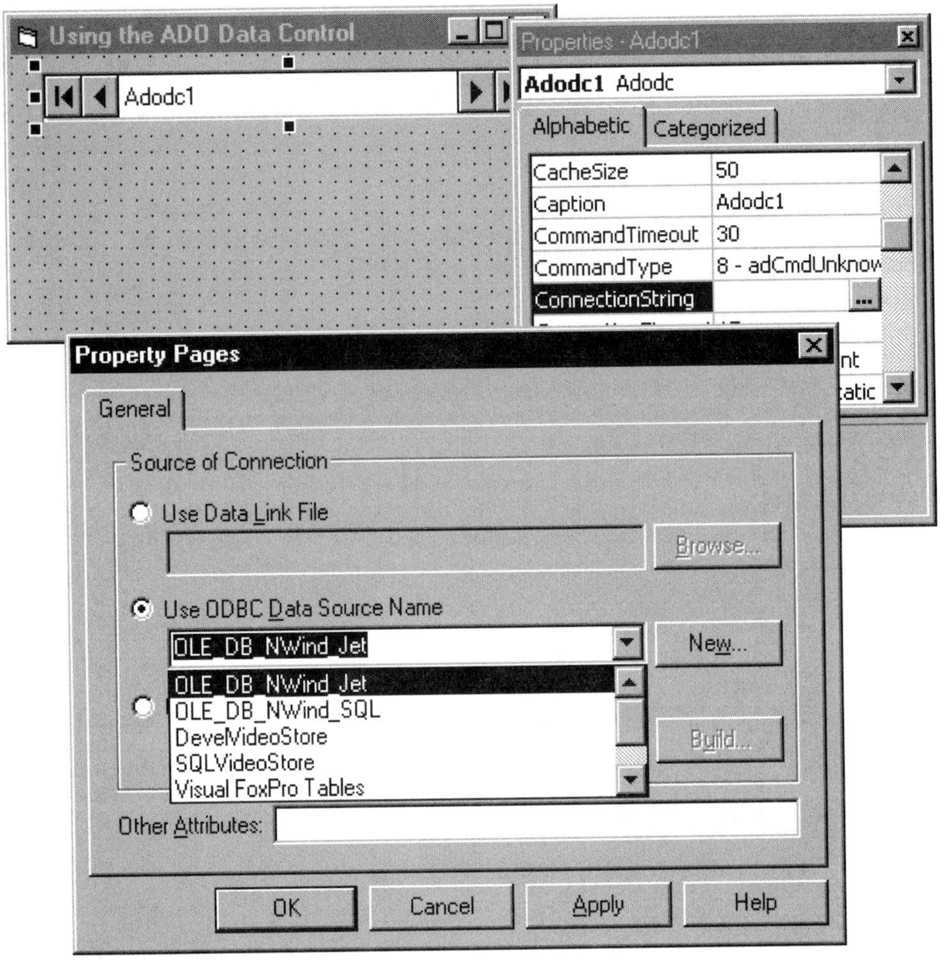

FIGURE 5-4   Once you have added the ADO Data Control to your form, set the *ConnectionString* property.

1. Select the *ADO Data Control* on your form.

2. In the *Properties Window*, select the *ConnectionString* property and click the *browser* button (the … button).

3. In the resulting *Property Pages* dialog, select the option *Use ODBC Data Source Name*.

4. In the dropdown list, select *OLE_DB_NWIND_JET*.

An example of the dialog shown when the *ConnectionString* property is selected appears in Figure 5-4.

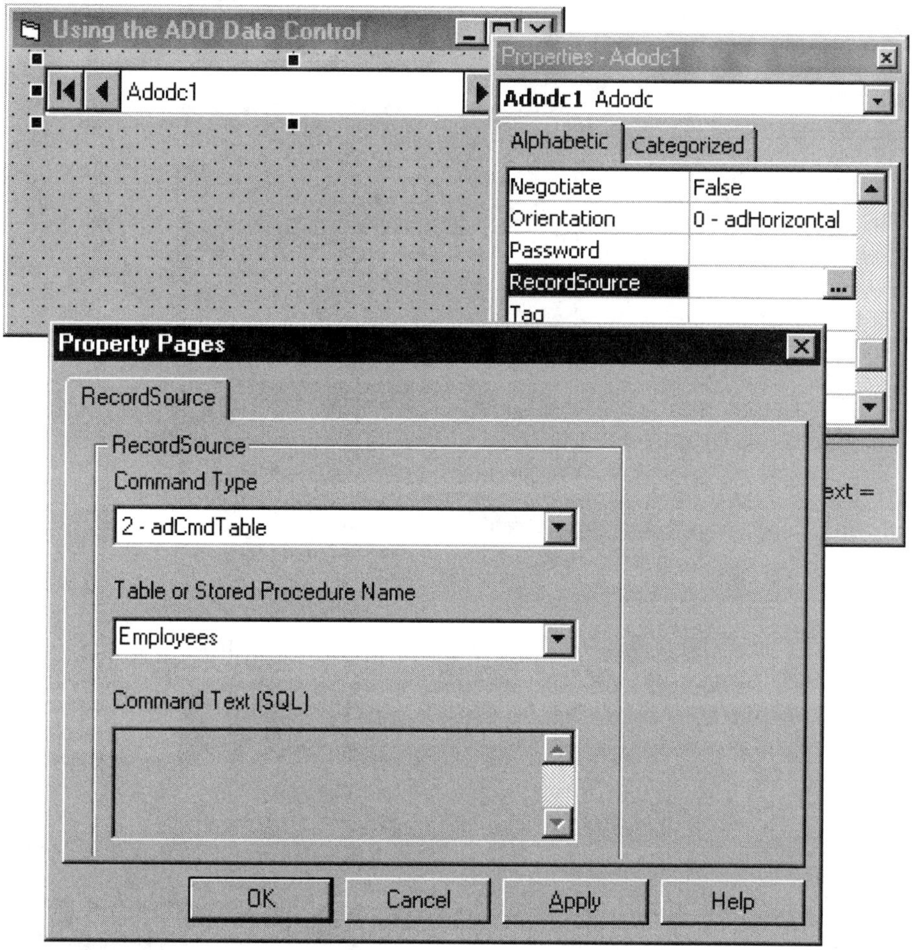

FIGURE 5-5 Set the **RecordSource** property to indicate you want to access the *Employees* table.

SETTING THE RECORDSOURCE PROPERTY

Next, the **RecordSource** property is set. This can be a table, a stored procedure, or an SQL statement that you enter. In this walkthrough, you'll reference the *Employees* table. Refer to Figure 5-5 and the following instructions:

1. Select the *RecordSource* property in the *Properties* window and click the *browse* button.

2. For *Command Type*, select *2 – adCmdTable.*

3. Select *Employees* from the *Table or Stored Procedure Name* dropdown list.

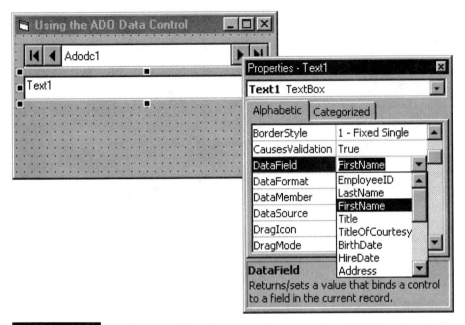

FIGURE 5-6   Finally, you'll bind two text boxes to the ADO Data Control. One will display an employee's first name, while the other displays the last name.

BINDING CONTROLS TO THE ADO DATA CONTROL

Next, controls are bound to the ADO Data Control. In the walkthrough, you'll bind two text box controls to the ADO Data Control – one displays the employee's first name while the other displays the employee's last name. Once you've accomplished these steps, you can run your program. Refer to Figure 5-6 and the following instructions:

1. Place two text box controls on your form.
2. Select the first text box and set its *DataSource* property to *Adodc1*.
3. For the same text box, set its *DataField* property to *FirstName*.
4. Repeat the above two steps for the second text box, but set its *DataField* property to *LastName*.
5. Run the program.

Important ADO Data Control Properties and Methods

The **ConnectionString** property provides information for connecting to a database. There are other options besides a DSN – in fact, the property has the same usage and options discussed earlier in this chapter. The *RecordSource* property is set to the table you wish to access. It can also be an SQL *Select* statement or the name of a stored procedure. The **CommandType** property gives the control a "hint" as to what is contained in the *RecordSource* property. When the *RecordSource* property indicates a table name, it should be set to the constant *adCmdTable*. This property was examined earlier in this chapter.

The *RecordSource* and *CommandType* properties can be set at design time or runtime. If one is changed at runtime, you must execute the **Refresh** method on the data control. I'll illustrate this in the next section.

The **UserName** and **Password** properties provide necessary authentication information to the database, if required. This information can also be supplied in the *ConnectionString* property.

USING AN SQL SELECT STATEMENT

The *RecordSource* property can also be an SQL *Select* statement. In this case, the *CommandType* property should be set to *2 – adCmdText*. The *Select* statement can be entered manually, but you may also use the *SQL Statement Builder* feature of *Data Environment* objects to build an SQL statement. *Data Environment* objects are discussed in detail later in this chapter.

The demo program, *SQLString.VBP*, located in folder *VB6Adv\Demos\ AdoDataCtl\AdoDataCtl2*, illustrates how to use an SQL *Select* statement for a record source. In Figure 5-7, you can see how the SQL *Select* statement was entered as the *RecordSource* property. The demo program's user interface is shown in Figure 5-8.

| FIGURE 5-7 | The *RecordSource* property can be set to an SQL *Select* statement, either at runtime or design time. The *CommandType* should be set to *adCmdText* in this case. |

CHANGING THE SQL STATEMENT AT RUNTIME

You can dynamically create an SQL *Select* statement using string concatenation at runtime. You must execute the **Refresh** method to get the ADO Data Control to rebuild the recordset. Note that this approach is not as efficient as using an ADO *Command* object with parameters, although the procedure is simple and will work fine for small workloads. Later in this chapter, I'll show you how you can use *Data Environments* to set up parameterized queries using ADO *Command* objects; earlier in this chapter you were shown how to do this using ADO directly.

The following code, from the project *SQLString*, illustrates how you can generate a new SQL *Select* statement for the *RecordSource* property:

```
Private Sub cmdGO_Click()
    Dim strSQL As String

    strSQL = "Select LastName From Employees" & _
        " Where LastName >= '" & _
            txtCharacter.Text & "'" & _
```

| FIGURE 5-8 | You can change the *RecordSource* property to a new SQL *Select* statement at runtime, but you must execute the *Refresh* method to get the ADO Data Control to create a new recordset. |

```
                "
Order By LastName"

    Adodc1.RecordSource = strSQL
    Adodc1.Refresh

End Sub
```

Using the ADO Data Control's Recordset Object

The ADO Data Control has a property called **Recordset** that provides access to its underlying *Recordset* object. The *Recordset* object represents a set of rows in the table, and supports several methods (see Table 5-21). These methods are discussed in the following sections. The methods are performed on the *Recordset* object, not the data control. For example, to advance the recordset under program control, use

```
' Advance data control to next record
ADODC1.Recordset.MoveNext
```

The demo program, *ADODataCtl3* (see Figure 5-9), illustrates how adding a small amount of code to an ADO Data Control project can result in a program with significantly more features than the data control itself provides. In the following sections, I will use this demo for examples on how to use the properties of the data control's *Recordset* object.

TABLE 5-21	Important Properties of the Recordset Object

Method(s)	Description
AddNew	Prepares the recordset as a buffer for adding a new record.
Update	Saves changed or new records.
Delete	Deletes a record.
MoveFirst	Moves between records.
MoveLast	
MovePrevious	
MoveNext	
Find	Finds first/next record in the recordset that meets a given search criteria.

FIGURE 5-9	The demo in the folder *ADOData-Ctl3* demonstrates some advanced features that are possible by using the *Recordset* object of the ADO Data Control.

THE MOVE METHODS

In addition to the user accessing the ADO Data Control buttons to navigate around the data control's recordset, your application can use **MoveNext**, **MovePrevious, MoveFirst,** and **MoveLast** to move the current record. You must be careful not to move past the last row with *MoveNext* and not to move past the first row with *MovePrevious.* A runtime error will occur otherwise. Use the **BOF** and **EOF** properties of the *Recordset* object to determine where you are (see Table 5-22).

TABLE 5-22	Using the EOF and BOF Properties	
If EOF is	**...and BOF is**	**... then**
FALSE	FALSE	The current row is valid.
TRUE	FALSE	You are positioned past the last row.
FALSE	TRUE	You are positioned ahead of the first row.
TRUE	TRUE	There are no rows.

For example,

```
Private Sub cmdNext_Click()
    Adodc1.Recordset.MoveNext
    If Adodc1.Recordset.EOF Then
        Adodc1.Recordset.MoveLast
    End If
End Sub

Private Sub cmdPrev_Click()
    Adodc1.Recordset.MovePrevious
    If Adodc1.Recordset.BOF Then
        Adodc1.Recordset.MoveFirst
    End If
End Sub
```

The Find Method

The **Find** method can be used to locate a record using search criteria. Used appropriately, it can also be used to find the next and subsequent records matching the criteria. You must understand that the method does not result in a requerying of records; using the *Find* method, you are actually searching the already-built recordset. Thus, the *Find* method is useful for searching a subset of database records to allow the user to refine a search. Do not use the *Find* method to locate your primary list of records. It is tempting to use a simple table name as the *RecordSource* property, then use the *Find* method to locate the records required by your application. A far more efficient approach is to use a *Select* statement or a stored procedure to access your primary set of records. Again, think of the *Find* method as providing a convenient way for your user to refine a search.

The *Find* method requires the criteria to be specified as a string. The format of the string is the same as the SQL *where* clause, without the word "where". If the record cannot be found, the current row moves past the last row and the **EOF** property is set to *true*. Prior to executing the *Find* method, you should save your place using the **Bookmark** property of the *Recordset* object. This is also required if you wish to keep a context for finding the next record that meets the search criteria.

The demo *ADODataCtl3* illustrates the use of the *Find* method, as seen in Figure 5-10. The next few sections will analyze the code from this demo.

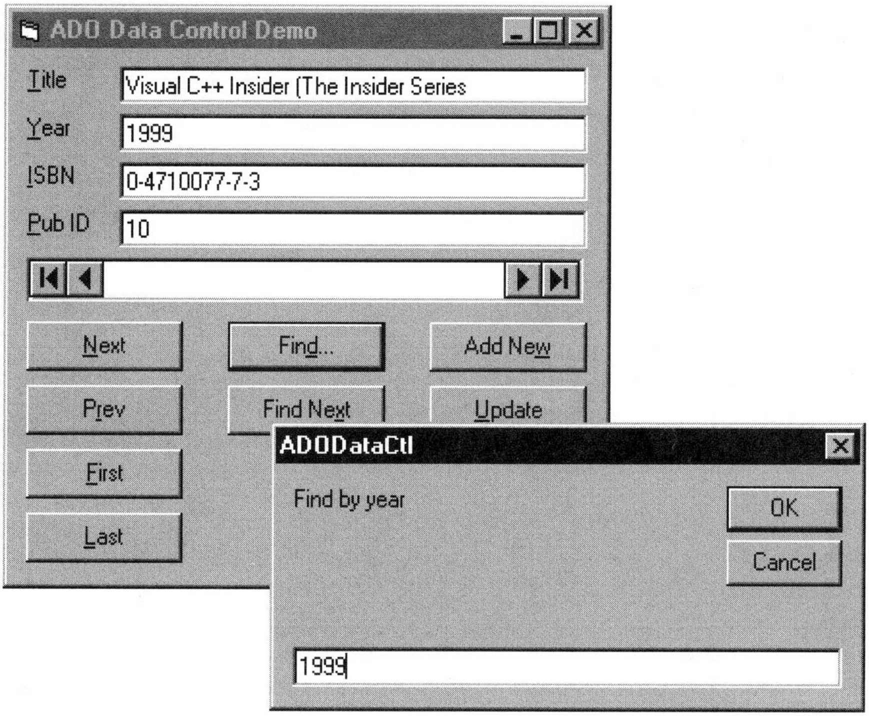

FIGURE 5-10 You can use the *Find* method to locate a specific record by search criteria.

FINDING THE FIRST RECORD MEETING A CRITERIA

The ***Find*** method can be used to find the first, next, and subsequent records matching a search criteria, but you must understand the parameters of the method. Parameters of the method are shown in Table 5-23. The syntax of the method is

```
ADODataControl.Recordset.Find criteria, skip, _
                    dir, start-bookmark
```

You may use the comparison operators >, <, =, and **like** (pattern-matching). String values are delimited with single quotes. Date values are delimited with "**#**" (number sign). If the comparison operator is "*like*", the string value may contain an asterisk, which matches one or more occurrences of any character. You may also use the underscore to match exactly one occurrence of any character.

TABLE 5-23	Parameters of the Find Method
Parameter	**Description**
criteria	A string containing a statement that specifies the column name, comparison operator, and value to use in the search.
skip	An optional value that specifies the offset from the current row or starting bookmark position to begin the search. Default is zero. Omit this parameter to find the first record.
dir	An optional value that specifies whether the search should begin on the current row or the next available row in the direction of the search. Its value can be *adSearchForward* or *adSearchBackward*.
start-bookmark	An optional *Variant* bookmark to use as the starting position for the search. Omit this parameter to find the first record.

Since the *Find* method will move to the end of the recordset if it does not find a record, you should save your position using the **Bookmark** property, and restore the *Bookmark* if no record is found. If you wish to implement a *Find Next* feature, you should save the *Bookmark* in a module-level variable after the record is found. You'll need this position to carry on with the search. For example,

```
Option Explicit
Private vLastFind As Variant
Private strFindCrit As String

Private Sub cmdFind_Click()
    Dim strYear As String
    Dim vTempBookmark As Variant

    strYear = InputBox("Find by year")
    If strYear = "" Then Exit Sub

    If Not IsNumeric(strYear) Then
        MsgBox "Enter a year!"
        Exit Sub
    End If

    vTempBookmark = Adodc1.Recordset.Bookmark

    strFindCrit = "[Year Published] = " & strYear
    Adodc1.Recordset.Find strFindCrit
```

```
If Adodc1.Recordset.EOF Then
    Adodc1.Recordset.Bookmark = vTempBookmark
    MsgBox "No records meet that criteria"
    Exit Sub
End If

cmdFindNext.Enabled = True
vLastFind = Adodc1.Recordset.Bookmark

End Sub
```

FINDING THE NEXT RECORD MEETING A CRITERIA

To find the next and subsequent records that meet a criteria, use the *Find* method to start one record past the last record found. To do this, you need to use the *Bookmark* that was saved from the first find. You also need to continue to save the *Bookmark* to allow searching from the next record. For example,

```
Private Sub cmdFindNext_Click()
    Dim vTempBookmark As Variant

    vTempBookmark = Adodc1.Recordset.Bookmark
    Adodc1.Recordset.Find strFindCrit, 1, , vLastFind

    If Adodc1.Recordset.EOF Then
        Adodc1.Recordset.Bookmark = vTempBookmark
        MsgBox "No more records meet that criteria"
        cmdFindNext.Enabled = False
        Exit Sub
    End If

    vLastFind = Adodc1.Recordset.Bookmark

End Sub
```

Modifying Data with the ADO Data Control

The ADO Data Control's underlying recordset can be the source of methods that modify the database. Such methods include *AddNew*, *Update*, and *Delete*. Each of these methods is discussed in the following sections.

THE ADDNEW METHOD

To add a new record, use the **AddNew** method. The *AddNew* method prepares the recordset for adding a new record, and clears the bound controls. The user can enter new data into the controls. When the user moves off the new record, the record is added to the database. Your program can also execute the **Update** method on the ADO Data Control to add the record right away. This method is discussed shortly.

To make it easy on your user, you may want to *SetFocus* to the first bound control on the form. This enables the user to begin entering data for the new record. For example,

```
Private Sub cmdAddNew_Click()
    Adodc1.Recordset.AddNew
    Text1.SetFocus
End Sub
```

THE DELETE METHOD

The **Delete** method deletes the current record without changing the recordset position. To provide visual feedback to your user that a record has been deleted, you should move to the next record. Note that some databases have integrity constraints that prevent records from being deleted. If this is the case, an error may occur when your code attempts to delete a record.

The following code leverages off of existing code to advance the recordset upon deleting the current record, by invoking the same code used when the user clicks the *Next* button:

```
Private Sub cmdDelete_Click()
    Adodc1.Recordset.Delete
    cmdNext_Click
End Sub
```

THE UPDATE METHOD

Modified records are updated when the user moves off the current record. You can have the record updated immediately with the *Update* method on the *recordset*. To require the user to click an *Update* button before moving

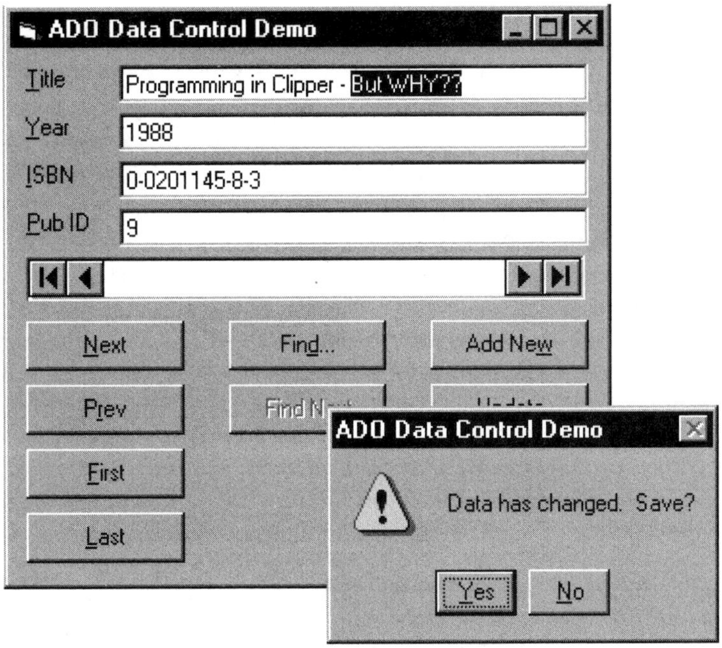

FIGURE 5-11 You can use the *WillMove* event to detect when the user changes the database and attempts to move off the record without clicking the *Update* button.

off a record being modified, you can use the **WillMove** event to determine if the record has been modified. In this event procedure, you can force the user to click this button before moving to the next record. The *WillMove* method is discussed in the following section.

Invoking the *Update* method on the ADO Data Control's recordset is straightforward, as shown in the following:

```
Private Sub cmdUpdate_Click()
    Adodc1.Recordset.Update
End Sub
```

The WillMove Event

The **WillMove** event is sent to the ADO Data Control whenever either the user or your code does something that will result in moving to a new current record. In the event procedure, you have an opportunity to see if an *Edit* or *AddNew* is in progress. If so, you can ask if the user wishes to save changes. The demo *ADODataCtl3* illustrates this, as shown in Figure 5-11.

The parameters sent to the ***WillMove*** event indicate the reason for moving. This is expressed as a constant that indicates a *MoveNext, MovePrevious,* or whatever was performed. In the *WillMove* event, you can check the ***EditMode*** parameter of the *Recordset* object. If it does not equal the constant ***adEditNone***, it indicates that the user has changed and moved off the current record without clicking the *Update* button. To cancel an update, invoke the ***CancelUpdate*** method on the recordset.

The event procedure is passed the *Recordset* object as parameter ***pRecordset***. It is recommended that, in this event procedure, you use this parameter to perform operations on the recordset. If you are using the *WillMove* event for the reasons discussed in this section, there is no need to use the other parameters passed into the event procedure. Refer to Help for information on these parameters. Following is an example of using the *WillMove* event to determine if it is necessary to prompt the user to save a modified record:

```
Private Sub Adodc1_WillMove _
  (ByVal adReason As EventReasonEnum, _
        adStatus As EventStatusEnum, _
  ByVal pRecordset As Recordset)

    Dim nResponse As Integer

    If pRecordset.EditMode = adEditNone Then Exit Sub

    nResponse = MsgBox("Data has changed.  Save?", _
                    vbExclamation + vbYesNo, _
                    "ADO Data Control Demo")

    If nResponse = vbNo Then pRecordset.CancelUpdate

End Sub
```

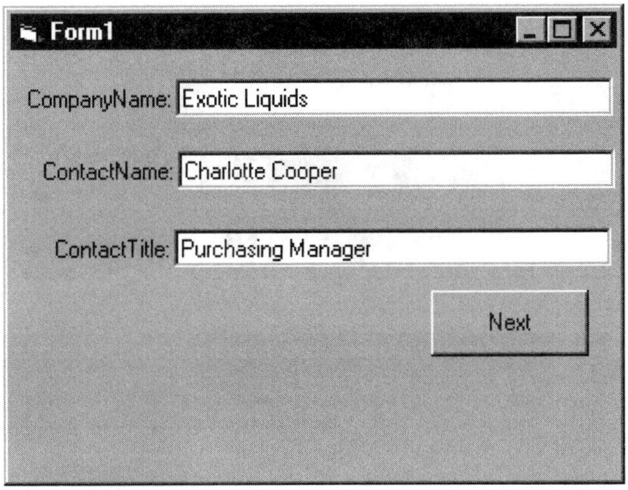

FIGURE 5-12   The user interface for a simple program that illustrates the use of *Data Environments*.

Data Environments

In addition to the ADO Data Control, a **Data Environment** can be used as a data source. A **Data Environment** is all the tables, views, and relationships that are to be opened when you run or modify a form or report. The *Data Environment* is saved with the form or report and can be modified in the *Data Environment Designer.* Many Visual Basic programmers may find using *Data Environments* to be much easier than programmatically creating sources for data. In addition, using a *Data Environment* will reduce your dependency on the ADO Data Control, and will enable you to use simple drag-and-drop features to build a form that acts as the user interface for a database browsing or reporting application.

In the next few sections, I'll present a walkthrough that you can follow to see how easy it is to create and use *Data Environments*. Once you've completed the walkthrough, your user interface will look similar to that shown in Figure 5-12.

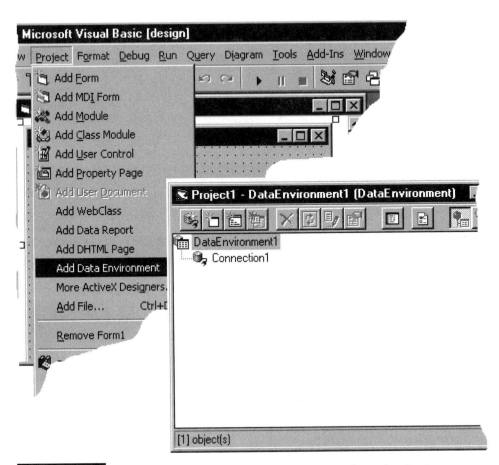

FIGURE 5-13 After starting a new Standard EXE project, from the *Project* menu, select *Add Data Environment*.

Creating a Data Environment

In this part of the walkthrough, you'll add a *Data Environment* to a new Standard EXE project. Refer to Figure 5-13 and the following instructions:

1. Start a new *Standard EXE* project.
2. From the *Project* menu, select *Add Data Environment*. This will bring up the *Data Environment Designer* for *DataEnvironment1*. You can change the name if you wish.

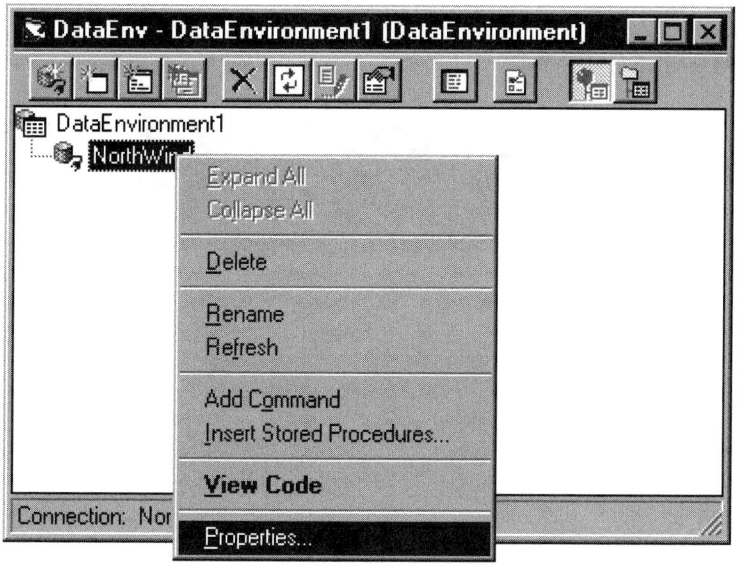

FIGURE 5-14   Change the name of *Connection1* to
NorthWind. Then, right-click on the connection
and select *Properties* to prepare for setting up
data link properties.

SETTING CONNECTION PROPERTIES

Under the *DataEnvironment* object is a *Connection* object, called
Connection1 by default. A *Connection* object contains information for connecting to the database. It is recommended that you give a meaningful name
to the *Connection* object as follows (refer to Figure 5-14):

1. Click, then click again on the *Connection* object (*Connection1*) under
   DataEnvironment1. Do not double-click, as you want to open the bor-
   derless edit box.
2. Enter the name *NorthWind* to replace the name *Connection1.*

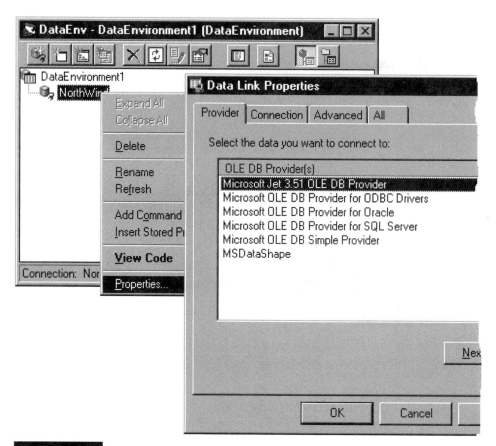

FIGURE 5-15   On the *Provider* tab, select *Microsoft Jet.*

Next, you'll set the provider for the *Connection* object to indicate *Microsoft Access.* Use the following instructions and refer to Figure 5-15:

1. Right-click on the *NorthWind Connection* object and select *Properties.*
2. On the *Provider* tab, select *Microsoft Jet 3.51 OLE DB Provider.*
3. Click the *Next* button.

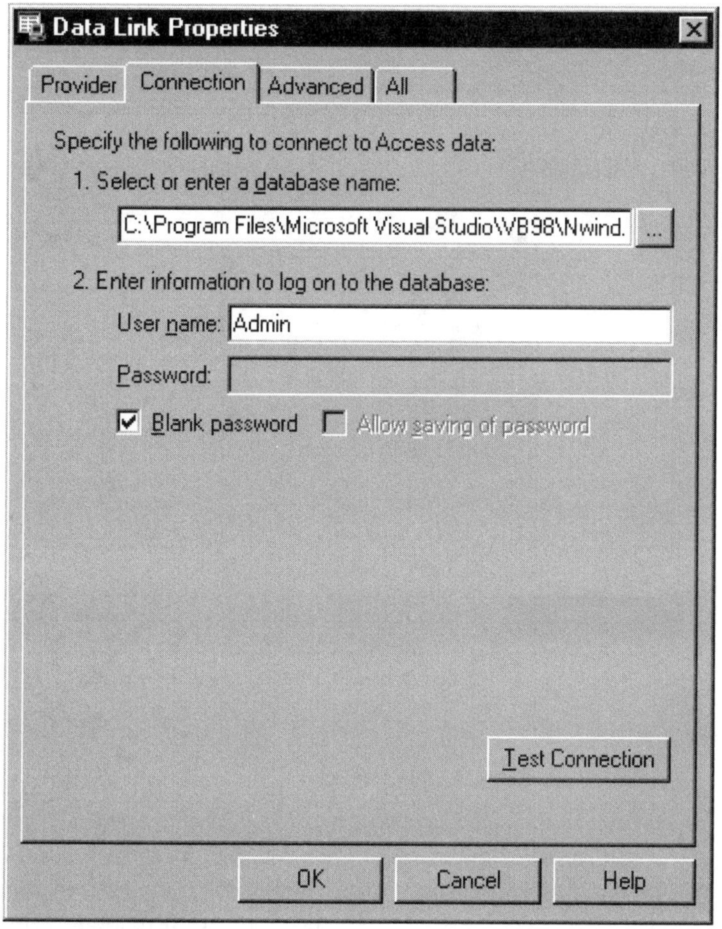

FIGURE 5-16   After clicking *Next*, you're advanced to the *Connection* tab. Select the *NorthWind Traders* database.

Next, you will select the *NorthWind Traders* database. Refer to Figure 5-16 and the following instructions:

1. On the *Connection* tab, click the *browse (...)* button.
2. Navigate to and select the *NorthWind Traders Database*.
3. Click the *OK* button to dismiss the *Data Link Properties Dialog*.

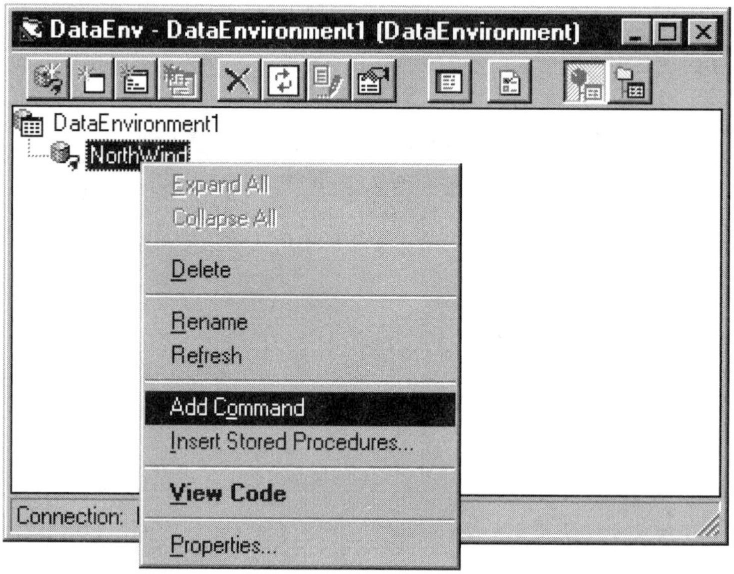

FIGURE 5-17   You can have multiple *Command* objects under your *Connection* objects. Use one for each table or query your program requires.

ADDING A COMMAND OBJECT

Next, you'll add a ***Command*** object under the *NorthWind Connection* object. A *Data Environment* can have multiple *Command* objects – use one for each table or query your application requires. A *Command* object can also have ***child commands***; these are used to build a hierarchy of record-sets. This technique will be illustrated later in this chapter, in the section *Child Commands and the Hierarchical Flex Grid Control*, and again in the section *Adding Reporting Capabilities*. For this walkthrough, you will create a simple *Command* object that uses a table as its source of data. Refer to Figure 5-17 and the following instructions to add a *Command* object:

1.   Right-click on the *NorthWind Connection* object and select *Add Command*.

2.   A *Command* object with a default name of *Command1* appears under the *Connection* object. Rename this command object to *Suppliers*.

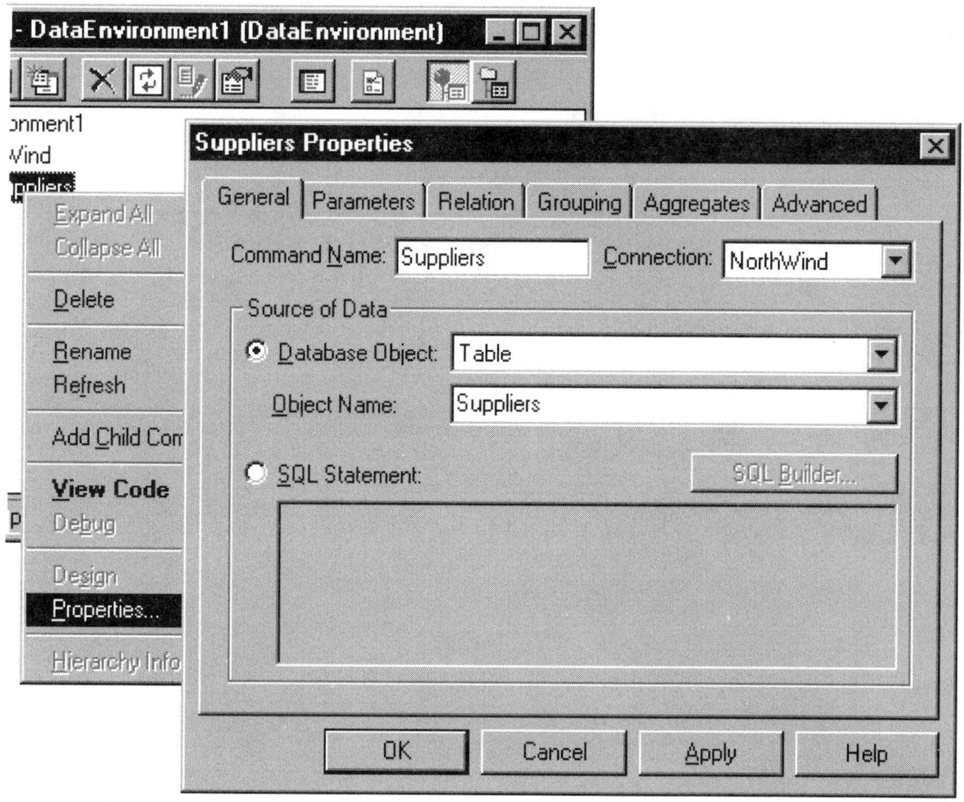

FIGURE 5-18 You set properties of the *Command* object to establish how a query is to be performed.

Next, set properties of the **Command** object to indicate the table to retrieve or query to perform, referring to Figure 5-18 and the following instructions:

1. Right-click on the *Suppliers* command object and select *Properties*.

2. On the *General* tab, select *Database Object*.

3. In the *Database Object* dropdown list, select *Table*.

4. In the *Object Name* dropdown list, select the *Suppliers* table.

5. Click *OK* to dismiss the *Properties* dialog.

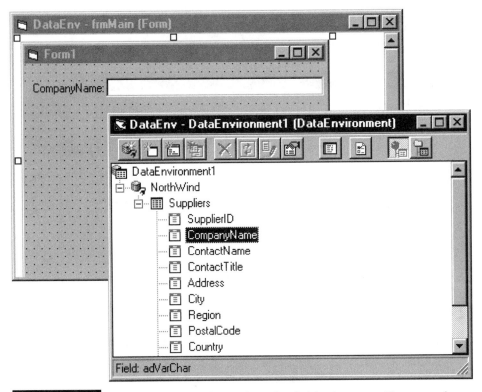

FIGURE 5-19 When you expand *Suppliers,* the fields show up. These can be dragged and dropped to the form to create bound controls.

DRAGGING FIELDS TO THE FORM

Next, you'll drag and drop fields from the *Data Environment Designer* window to your form. After completing this step, you can run your program, but you'll only see the first record. In the following step, you'll add a button that moves to the next record.

Refer to Figure 5-19 and the following instructions to drag fields to your form:

1. Arrange your workspace to see both the *Data Environment Designer* and *Form Designer* windows.

2. Expand *Suppliers.*

3. Drag and drop fields as desired from the *Data Environment Designer* window to your form.

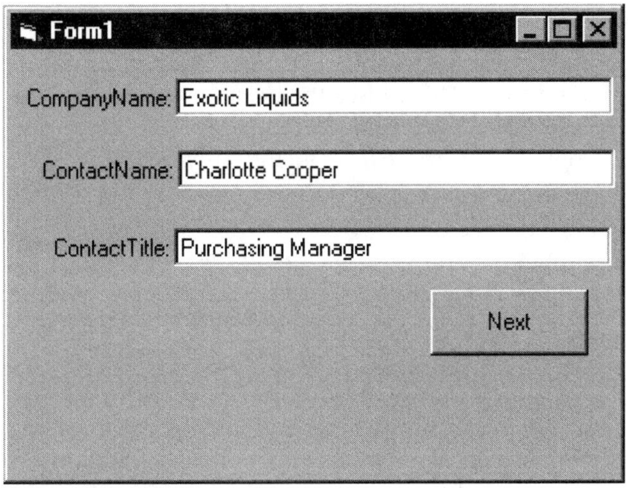

FIGURE 5-20 Add a *Next* button. In the button's click event, invoke the *MoveNext* method on the recordset under the *DataEnvironment* object.

ADDING A MOVENEXT BUTTON

Each *Command* object has an associated recordset available as a property of the *DataEnvironment* object. The property is named after the *Command* name, prefixed with *rs*. Code for moving to the next record is shown below. Note that it is not robust, as it does not check for **EOF**.

```
Private Sub Command1_Click()
    DataEnvironment1.rsSuppliers.MoveNext
End Sub
```

This code should be added to a command button's click event. To do this, refer to Figure 5-20 and the following instructions:

1. Add a command button to the form, giving it a caption of *Next*. Retain the default name of *Command1* for this button.

2. Add the code shown above to the button's click event.

3. Run and test your program.

DRAGGING AND DROPPING A COMMAND OBJECT TO A FORM

In addition to dragging and dropping fields, you can drag a *Command* object to the form. This causes the creation of a control for every field in the *Command* object. For example, dragging *Suppliers* to the form will create bound controls for every field in the *Suppliers* table – I would encourage you to try this with the program you created in the previous walkthrough. If you right-drag (drag and drop with the right mouse button), you'll get a pop-up menu when you drop the *Command* object on your form. From this menu, you can select *Grid, FlexGrid,* or *Bound Controls.* In the next section, I will discuss the use of the *Microsoft Hierarchical Flex Grid* control.

Child Commands and the Hierarchical Flex Grid Control

In a *Data Environment,* you can add child commands to *Command* objects to create hierarchical relationship queries. In addition to providing your application with advanced query capabilities, this technique allows you to use the **Microsoft Hierarchical Flex Grid** control. The *Microsoft Hierarchical Flex Grid* control is like the *DBGrid* control, but some of the columns are bound to one command, while the remaining ones are bound to a related child command. The user can expand data on the "one" side to see related data on the "many" side.

A completed demo can be found in project *FlexGrid.VBP,* located in folder *VB6Adv\Demos\DataEnv.* You can run that program and examine its code, but I would recommend that you perform the following walkthrough to generate the program. The resulting user interface of the program you will create in this walkthrough is shown in Figure 5-21.

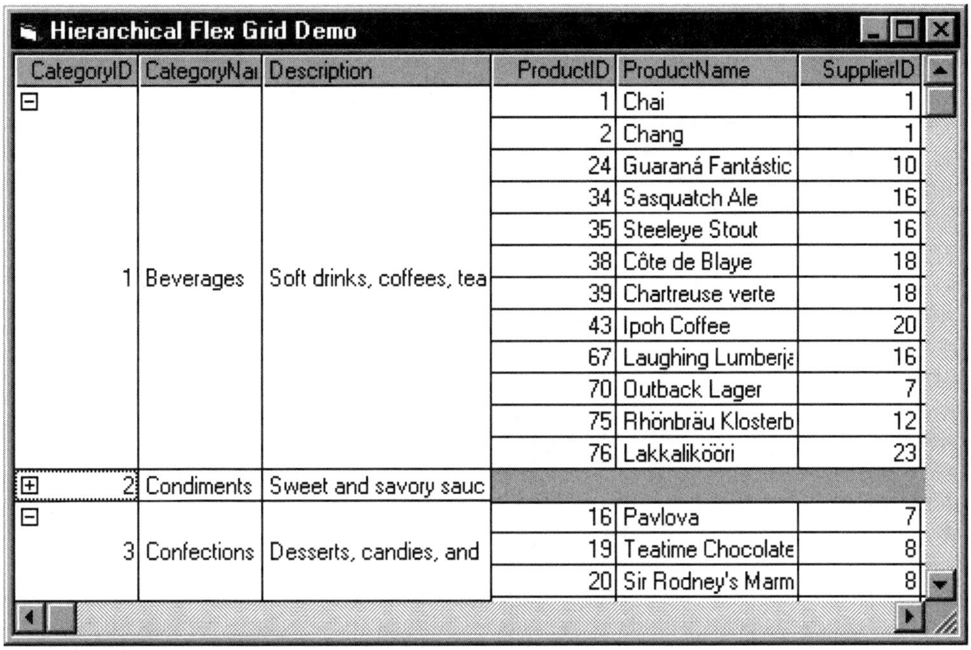

⌐ Hierarchical Flex Grid Demo					_ □ ☒

CategoryID	CategoryNam	Description	ProductID	ProductName	SupplierID
⊟			1	Chai	1
			2	Chang	1
			24	Guaraná Fantástic	10
			34	Sasquatch Ale	16
			35	Steeleye Stout	16
			38	Côte de Blaye	18
1	Beverages	Soft drinks, coffees, tea	39	Chartreuse verte	18
			43	Ipoh Coffee	20
			67	Laughing Lumberja	16
			70	Outback Lager	7
			75	Rhönbräu Klosterb	12
			76	Lakkalikööri	23
⊞	2	Condiments	Sweet and savory sauc		
⊟			16	Pavlova	7
	3	Confections	Desserts, candies, and	19	Teatime Chocolate	8
			20	Sir Rodney's Marm	8

FIGURE 5-21 The *Microsoft Hierarchical Flex Grid Control* is like the *DBGrid Control*, but it can display related data in a hierarchical fashion.

CREATING PARENT AND CHILD COMMANDS

A parent command is created using the same technique illustrated in the previous walkthrough. In this walkthrough, you'll create a grid that shows products by category. This requires you to start by creating a *Command* object for the *Categories* table. Refer to Figure 5-22 and the following instructions:

1. Start a new *Standard EXE* project and add a *Data Environment*.

2. Set up the properties of the *Connection* object so that it references *NorthWind*.

3. Add a *Command* object called *Categories* that references the *Categories* table.

4. Right-click on the *Command* object and select *Add Child Command*. This adds a command called *Command1*, which you should rename to *Products*.

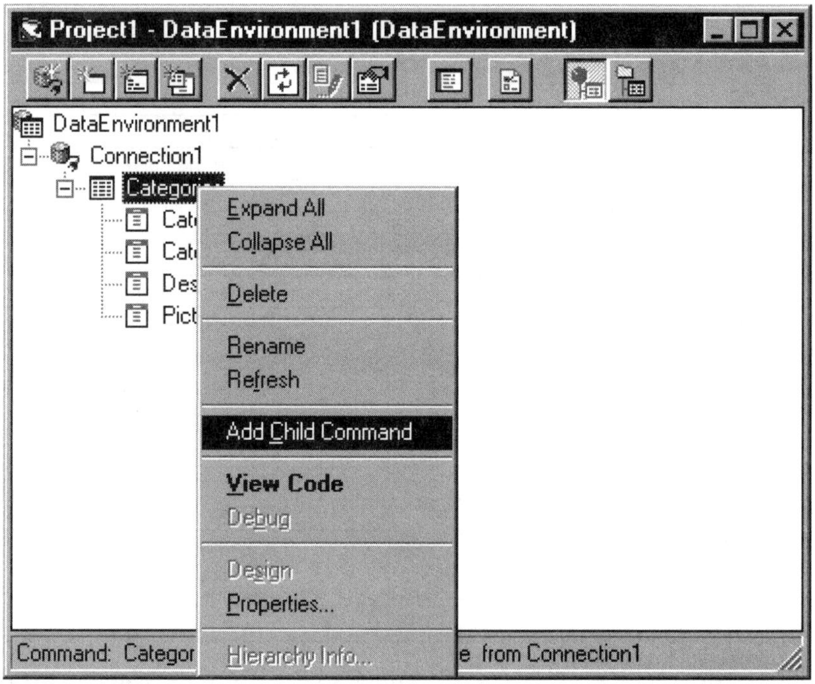

FIGURE 5-22 Using the procedure discussed earlier, create a *Command* object that references the *Categories* table. Then, right-click on the *Command* object and select *Add Child Command.*

SETTING PROPERTIES FOR THE CHILD COMMAND

Next, you'll set the properties of the child command so that it references the *Products* table. When you've set these properties, do not dismiss the *Properties* dialog. You'll need to select the *Relation* tab to set up the related column. Refer to Figures 5-23 and 5-24 and the following instructions:

1. Right-click on the *Products* command object and select *Properties.*
2. Under the *General* tab, set up the command for referencing the *Products* table. Proceed to the next step without dismissing the *Properties* dialog.
3. On the *Command* object's *Property Page*, select the *Relation* tab.
4. The proposed relation definition is to relate the two tables by the common field *CategoryID.* Click the *Add* button to accept the proposed relation definition.
5. Click *OK* to dismiss the *Properties* dialog.

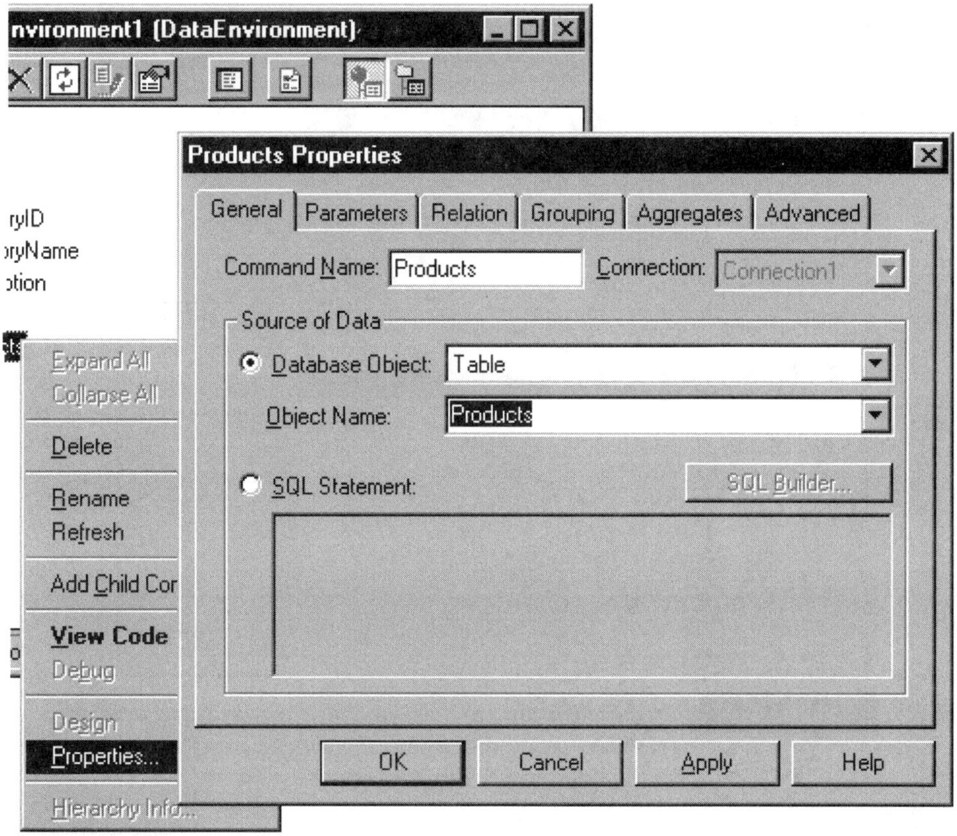

nvironment1 (DataEnvironment)

ryID
ryName
tion

Products Properties

General | Parameters | Relation | Grouping | Aggregates | Advanced

Command Name: Products   Connection: Connection1

Source of Data

- Database Object: Table
  - Object Name: Products

- SQL Statement: SQL Builder...

Expand All
Collapse All

Delete

Rename
Refresh

Add Child Cor

View Code
Debug

Design
Properties...
Hierarchy Info...

OK   Cancel   Apply   Help

FIGURE 5-23   Set the child command's properties to reference the *Products* table.

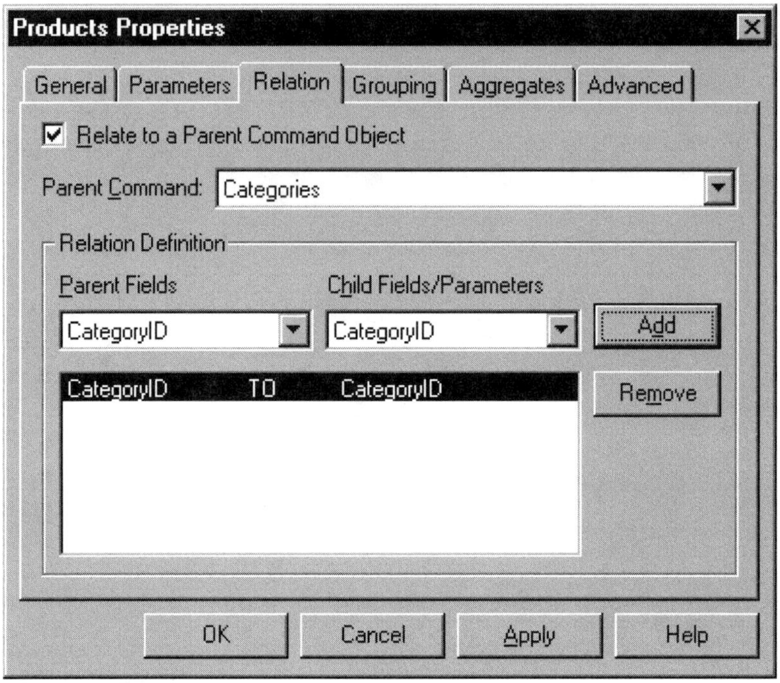

FIGURE 5-24   On the *Relation* tab, click the *Add* button to accept the proposed relation definition, which relates the tables by the common field *CategoryID*.

COMPLETING THE APPLICATION

Next, you'll add the *Hierarchical Flex Grid* control to the form by right-dragging the *Categories* command to the form. For the best effect, add code to the form's *Resize* event to resize the *Flex Grid* control to fit the form:

```
Private Sub Form_Resize()
    MSHFlexGrid1.Move 0, 0, Me.ScaleWidth, Me.ScaleHeight
End Sub
```

Before entering this code, you must create a *Hierarchical Flex Grid* on your form. The easiest way to do this is to use drag-and-drop from the *Data Environment* window. This can be done using the following instructions:

1. Arrange your workspace so that you can see both the *Form* and *Data Environment Designer* windows.

2. Drag the *Categories* command with the right mouse button (right-drag) from the *Data Environment Designer* window to the *Form Designer* window.

3. Select *Flex Grid* from the pop-up menu.

4. Add code to the form's *Resize* event to resize the *Flex Grid* to fit the form (see above).

Once you've completed these steps, you can run the program and experiment with the *Hierarchical Flex Grid* control.

Adding Reporting Capability

Working with **Data Environments**, the **Microsoft Report Designer** included with Visual Basic 6.0 allows you to create sophisticated reports that may be displayed in a preview window and/or printed. They may also be exported in many different formats, including HTML. In the following sections, I'll cover just about anything you would want to do with the *Report Designer*, including grouping data and providing a selection criteria.

The program *DailyReport.EXE*, located in folder *VB6Adv\Demos\ MomPop\Reports*, produces a daily report of rented videos (see Figure 5-25). As a reporting program, it uses neither the object model nor the data services layer; instead it uses ADO to access the database directly. I should note that this program uses the *Access* database, but you can easily modify the program to use the *SQL Server* version of the *Mom-n-Pop* database instead.

In the following sections, you will create a similar type of report using the *North Wind Traders* database.

| FIGURE 5-25 | The *DailyReport* program provided with this book is part of the *Mom-n-Pop Video Store* suite of applications. |

About the Microsoft Report Designer

Your first reaction to creating reports with the new *Microsoft Report Designer* may be that it is tedious and complicated. However, it gets easier the more you use it, and you certainly wouldn't want to create a report without it. You need to have the proper expectations. Do not underestimate the time it takes to set up the *Data Environment* for a report, and the time you'll need to spend designing the report.

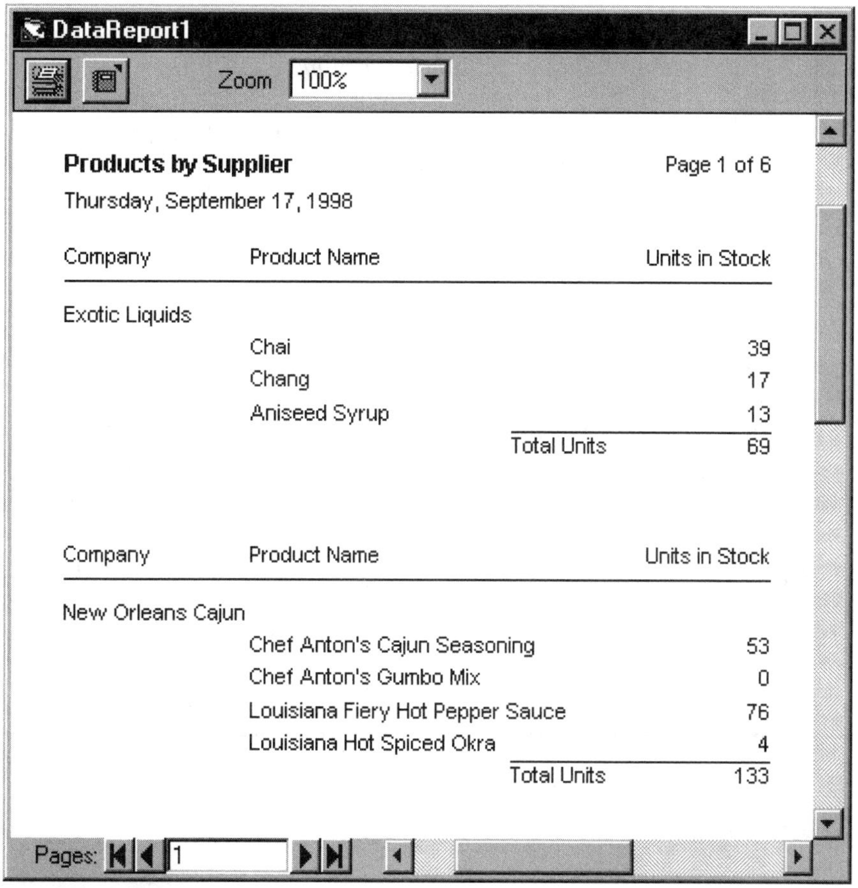

Products by Supplier — Page 1 of 6

Thursday, September 17, 1998

Company	Product Name	Units in Stock
Exotic Liquids		
	Chai	39
	Chang	17
	Aniseed Syrup	13
	Total Units	69

Company	Product Name	Units in Stock
New Orleans Cajun		
	Chef Anton's Cajun Seasoning	53
	Chef Anton's Gumbo Mix	0
	Louisiana Fiery Hot Pepper Sauce	76
	Louisiana Hot Spiced Okra	4
	Total Units	133

FIGURE 5-26   You'll generate a Visual Basic program that produces a report that lists products by suppliers.

In the following sections, I will provide a walkthrough that will illustrate how to use just about every feature of the *Report Designer*. If you prefer, you can load the completed project *ReportDemo.VBP*, located in folder *VB6Adv\Demos\Report*. To perform the walkthrough, you first need to set up a **Data Environment** that provides the report with the necessary data. To demonstrate as many features as possible, the *Data Environment* uses a hierarchy of *Command* objects to illustrate grouping. The *Data Environment* also uses parameters to provide selection criteria capabilities to the user. When completed, the generated report will appear as shown in Figure 5-26.

Report Sections

After setting up a *Data Environment*, you drag and drop fields to sections in the report. By default, a report consists of **Report Header, Page Header, Detail, Page Footer,** and **Report Footer** sections. If you bind the report to a *Data Environment* that consists of a hierarchy of commands, you will also get **Group Header** and **Group Footer** sections. These sections are described in Table 5-24. At design time, sections have a different appearance than at runtime. In Figure 5-27, you can see what the sample report looks like in design mode.

TABLE 5-24	Report Sections

Section(s)	Description
Report Header Report Footer	Text that appears at the very beginning/end of a report, such as the report title.
Page Header	Information that goes at the top of every page, such as the report's title.
Group Header Group Footer	Repeating section of the data report. Each group header is matched with a group footer. Associated with a single *Command* object in the *Data Environment Designer.*
Details	Innermost repeating part of the report. Associated with the lowest-level *Command* object in a *Data Environment* hierarchy.
Page Footer	Information that goes at the bottom of every page, such as the page number.

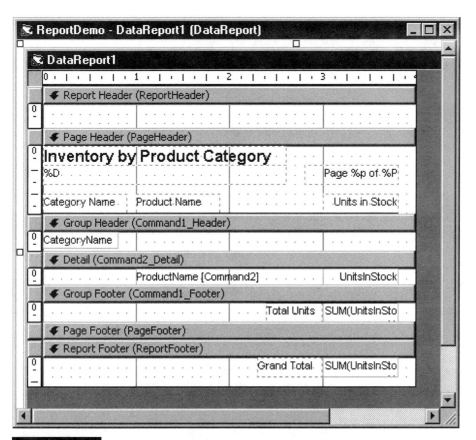

FIGURE 5-27 In design mode, a report looks very different. It consists of sections for headers, groups, details, and footers.

Setting up a Data Environment for a Report

You will need to set up a rather complex **Data Environment** for this report, but it starts simple. First, you will set up a connection to the *NorthWind Traders* database, and add a *Command* object called *Suppliers*. In the next step, you'll set properties of the *Suppliers* command so that it accepts a parameter that can be passed to a child command. To get started, refer to Figure 5-28 and the following instructions:

1. Start a new *Standard EXE* project and select *Add Data Environment* from the *Project* menu.

2. Rename the *Data Environment* object to *deNWind*, and rename the *Connection* object to *cnNorthWind*.

3. Set up the *cnNorthWind* connection to access the *NorthWind* database.

4. Add a *Command* object and rename it to *Suppliers*.

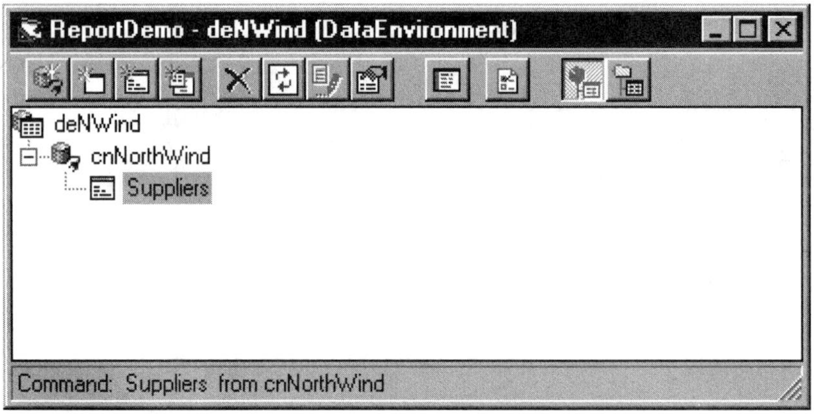

FIGURE 5-28　After creating a new Standard EXE project, begin the walkthrough by setting up a *Data Environment*.

CREATING AN SQL QUERY WITH A PARAMETER

The final version of the application generated by this walkthrough will permit your user to provide a minimum ***UnitsInStock*** as selection criteria, but this field is not in the *Suppliers* table. However, all required parameters must be passed from the outermost *Command* object down to the inner (child) *Command* objects. The solution to the dilemma is to declare a parameter in the outermost command, and select it as a computed field. You must provide an alias column name when you do this; in our example, the alias column name is the same as the parameter name. The SQL statements that you will use for this *Command* object are as follows:

```
Parameters pInStock Integer;
Select Suppliers.*, pInStock As pInStock From Suppliers;
```

Refer to Figure 5-29 and the following instructions to set up the parameterized SQL query that will be used as the parent command for this program:

1. Right-click on *Suppliers* and select *Properties*.
2. On the *General* tab, select *SQL Statement* as the *Source of Data*.
3. Enter the SQL statements shown above.
4. Do not dismiss the dialog; proceed to the next section to establish a default value for the parameter.

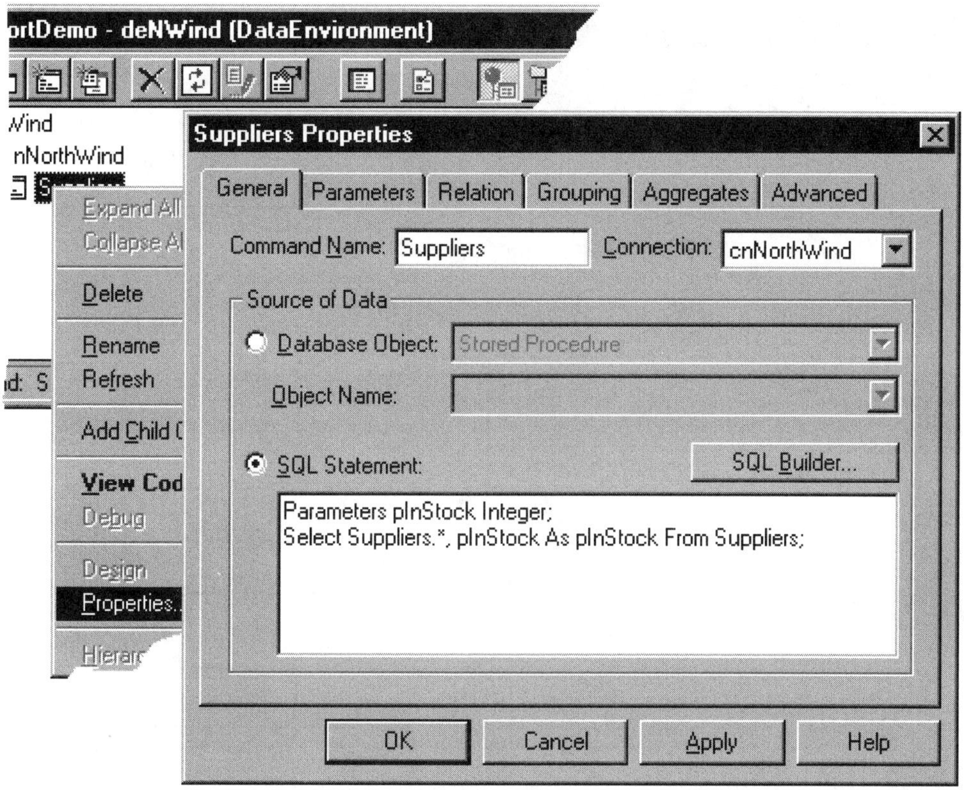

ortDemo - deNWind (DataEnvironment)

Suppliers Properties

General | Parameters | Relation | Grouping | Aggregates | Advanced

Command Name: Suppliers   Connection: cnNorthWind

Source of Data

◯ Database Object: Stored Procedure

Object Name:

◉ SQL Statement: SQL Builder...

```
Parameters pInStock Integer;
Select Suppliers.*, pInStock As pInStock From Suppliers;
```

OK   Cancel   Apply   Help

FIGURE 5-29 The source of data for the *Suppliers* command will be an SQL statement that declares a parameter.

PROVIDING A DEFAULT PARAMETER VALUE

You can provide a default value for your parameter. In this example, you will provide a default value of *1000* for the *pInStock* parameter. Use the following instructions, referring to Figure 5-30:

1. Select the *Parameters* tab.
2. In the *Value* text box, enter *1000*. This will be the default value for the *pInStock* parameter.
3. Click *OK* to dismiss the dialog.

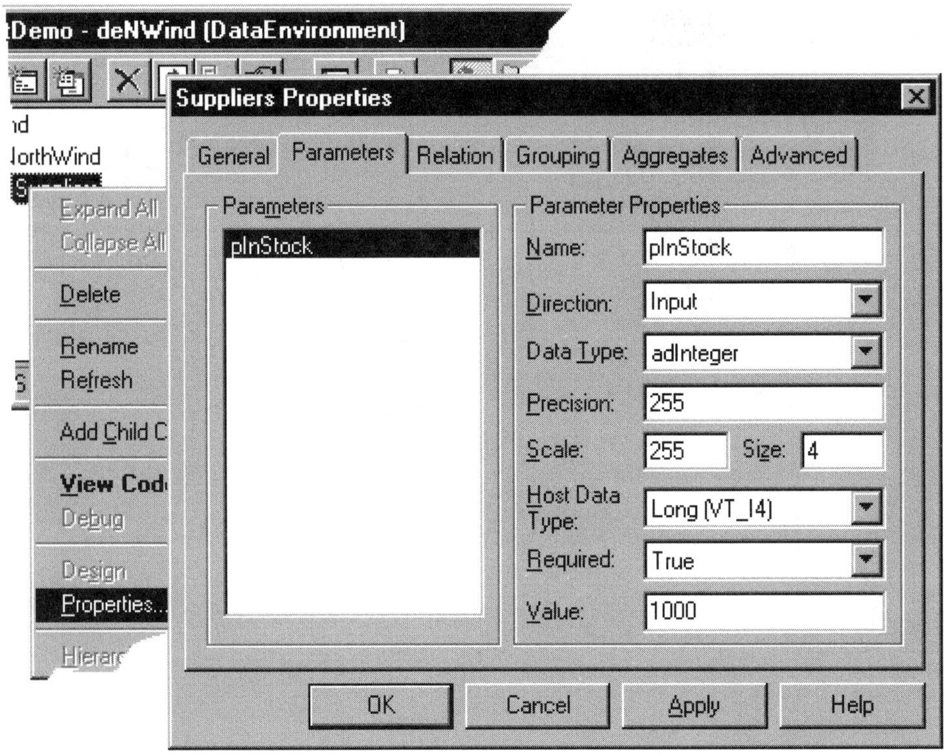

FIGURE 5-30 On the *Parameters* tab, set the *Value* property to *1000* to give it a default value.

ADDING A CHILD COMMAND FOR THE PRODUCTS TABLE

Next, you'll add a child command that will select the products for a supplier. The required SQL statements are

```
Parameters pInStock Integer;
Select * From Products Where UnitsInStock <= pInStock;
```

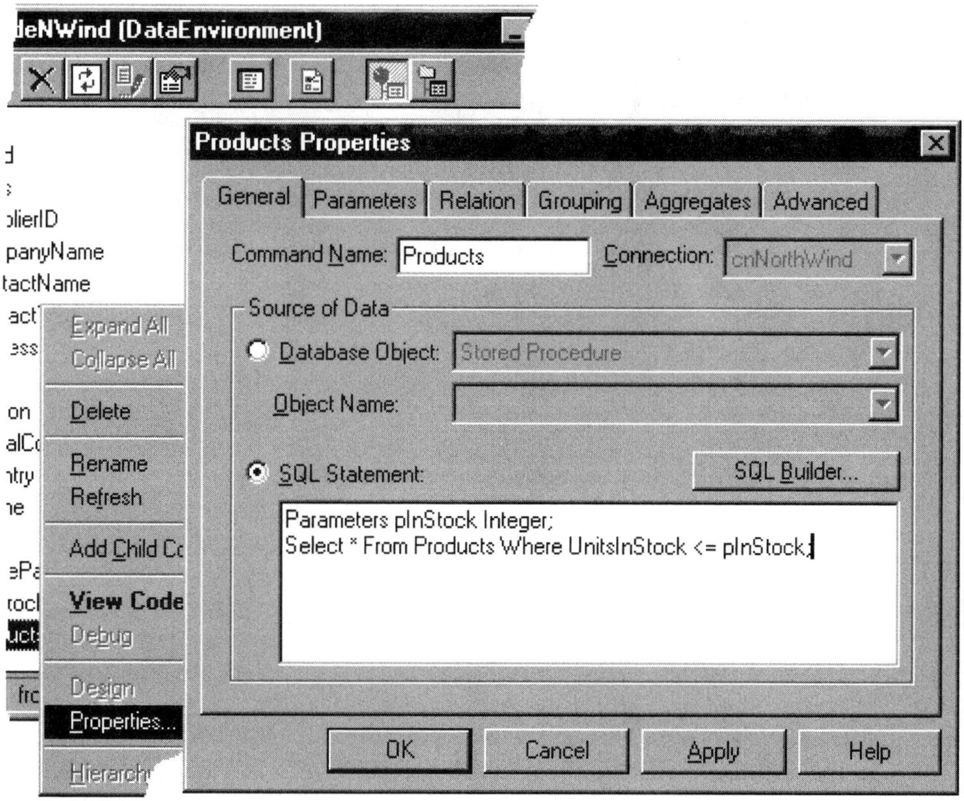

JeNWind (DataEnvironment)

d
;
olierID
panyName
tactName
act
ess

on
alCc
ltry
le

eP₂
tock
uct

fro

Products Properties

General | Parameters | Relation | Grouping | Aggregates | Advanced

Command Name: Products   Connection: cnNorthWind

Source of Data
○ Database Object: Stored Procedure
   Object Name:

⊙ SQL Statement: SQL Builder...

Parameters pInStock Integer;
Select * From Products Where UnitsInStock <= pInStock.

OK   Cancel   Apply   Help

Expand All
Collapse All

Delete

Rename
Refresh

Add Child Cc

View Code
Debug

Design
Properties...

Hierarch⁣

FIGURE 5-31   Add a child command called *Products* under the *Suppliers* command.

Note that this is where the parameter *pInStock* is actually used. However, it must also appear in the parent command, from where it is passed to the child command. To establish these SQL statements as the source for the child command, refer to Figure 5-31 and the following instructions:

1. Right-click on the *Suppliers* command and select *Add Child Command*. Rename the command to *Products*.

2. Right-click on *Products* and select *Properties*.

3. On the *General* tab, select *SQL Statement* for the source of data. Enter the SQL statements shown above.

4. Do not dismiss the dialog; go on to the next section to establish the relationship between the parent and child commands.

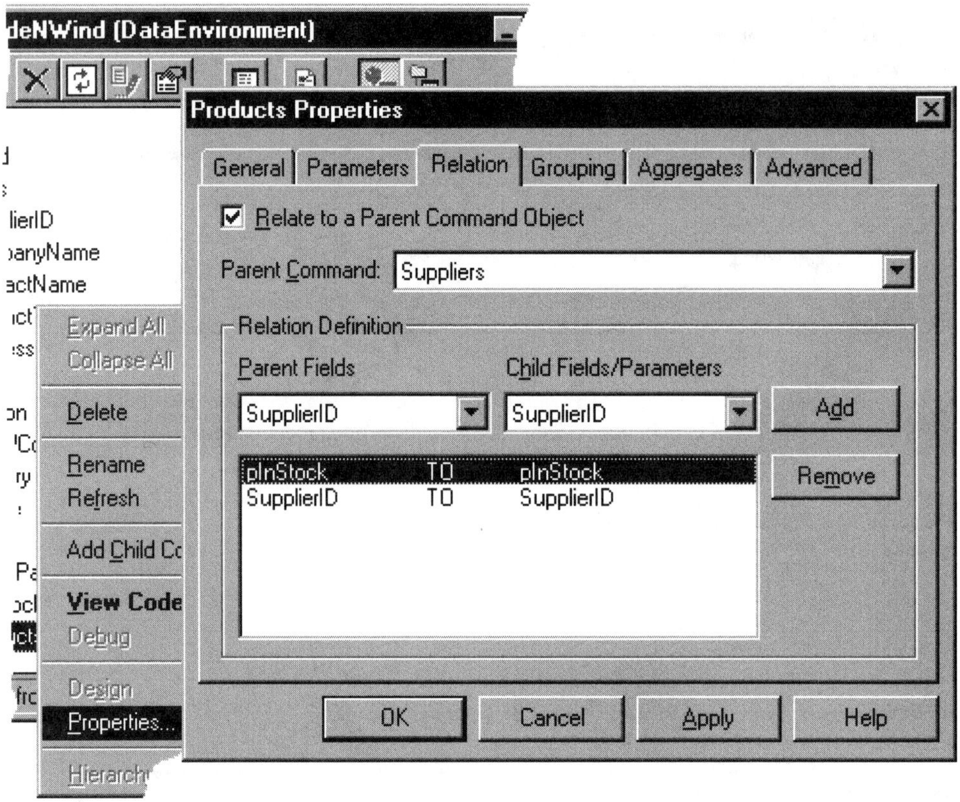

FIGURE 5-32
Next, establish the relationship between the parent and child commands.

ESTABLISHING THE RELATIONSHIP BETWEEN COMMANDS

Next, you'll establish the related field and parameter. Once this step is accomplished, the *Data Environment* is established and you are ready to start designing the report. Refer to Figure 5-32 and the following instructions to establish the relationship between the parent and child commands:

1. Select the *Relations* tab.

2. In the *Parent Fields* drop-down list, select *pInStock*. Select the same entry in the *Child Fields/Parameters* drop-down list, then click *Add*.

3. In the *Parent Fields* drop-down list, select *SupplierID*. Select the same entry in the *Child Fields/Parameters* drop-down list, then click *Add*.

4. Click *OK* to dismiss the dialog.

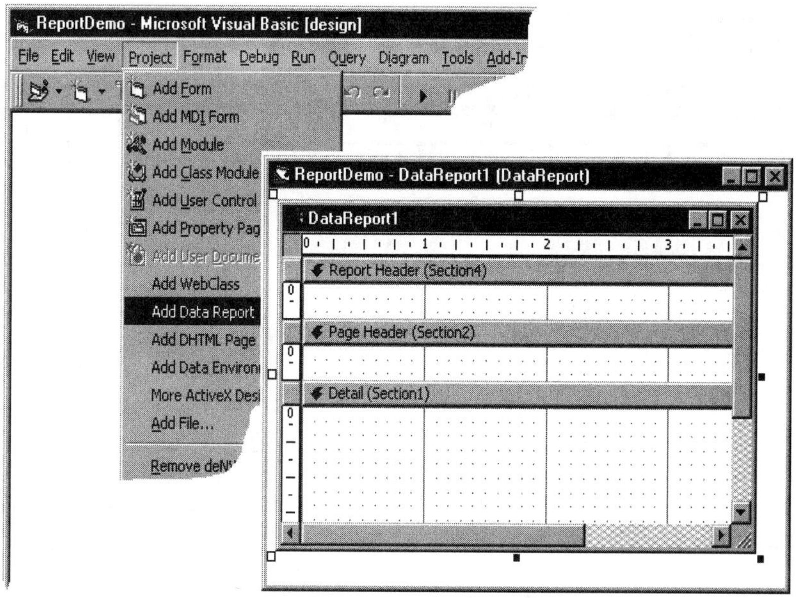

FIGURE 5-33   Select *Add Data Report* from the *Project* menu to add the data report to your project.

Adding a Data Report to Your Project

Next, you'll add a **Data Report** to your project. A *Data Report* is just a form at runtime. Once designed, you invoke the *Show* method at runtime to display the report, just as you do a form—it even has the same parameters (mode and parent form).

When a D*ata Report* is first added to a project, it will not yet have group sections. In a later step, you will cause the *Data Report* to retrieve the structure of the source command, in which it will discover the hierarchy of commands. At that time, the *Data Report* will have group sections.

After adding a *Data Report* to a project, you need to associate the report with a command. To add a *Data Report* and associate it with a command, refer to Figures 5-33 and 5-34 and the following instructions:

1. From the *Project* menu, select *Add Data Report*.

2. Select *DataReport1* from the *Properties* window.

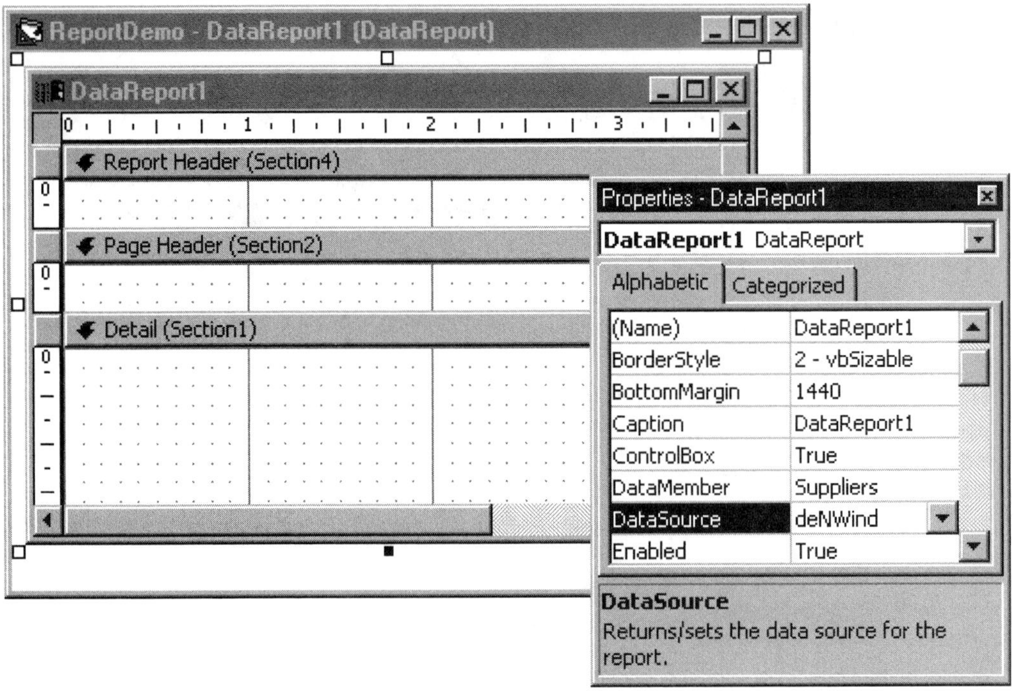

FIGURE 5-34 Set the *DataSource* property of the *Data Report* to *deNWind*, and set the *DataMember* property to *Suppliers*.

3. Set the *DataSource* property to *deNWind*.

4. Set the *DataMember* property to *Suppliers*.

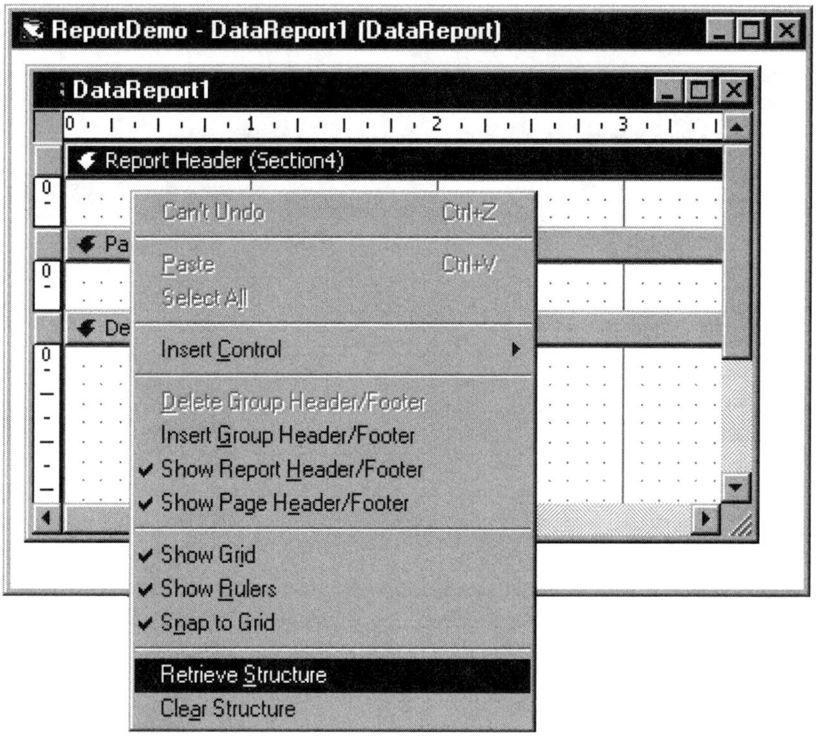

FIGURE 5-35   Right-click on the *Data Report's* designer window and select *Retrieve Structure.*

RETRIEVING THE STRUCTURE OF THE DATA ENVIRONMENT

Next, you'll use the *Retrieve Structure* command on the *Data Report* to retrieve the structure of the *Data Environment*. Once you've done this step, the *Data Report* will understand that there is a hierarchy of *Command* objects, and will create as many group sections as there are child commands.

To retrieve the structure of your *Data Environment*, refer to Figure 5-35 and the following instructions:

1. Right-click on the *Data Report's* design window and select *Retrieve Structure.*

2. Click *OK* on the resulting dialog.

3. Verify that you have group header and group footer sections.

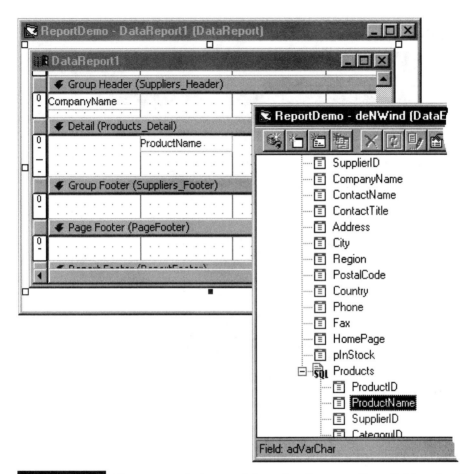

FIGURE 5-36 To get started, drag and drop the *CompanyName* field to the *GroupHeader* section, and the *ProductName* and *UnitsInStock* fields to the *Detail* section.

Dragging and Dropping Fields to the Report

You can now drag and drop fields from the *Data Environment Designer* window to the *Report Designer* window. Before dragging fields to the report, you should turn off *"caption dragging"* or you'll get captions along with the fields. While you usually want captions when setting up forms, you generally don't want them on reports—you use column headers instead. Refer to Figure 5-36 and the following instructions to drag and drop fields to the report:

1. In the *Data Environment Designer* window, right-click on the *deNWind* data environment and select *Options*.

FIGURE 5-37 Add a button to the form that will create the report when clicked.

2. On the *Field Mapping* tab, uncheck the option *Drag and Drop Field Captions*. Then, click *OK* to dismiss the *Options* dialog.

3. Arrange your workspace so that you can see both the *Data Environment Designer* and *Report Designer* windows.

4. Drag and drop the *CompanyName* field to the *GroupHeader* section.

5. Drag and drop the *ProductName* and *UnitsInStock* fields to the *Detail* section.

ADDING CODE TO GENERATE THE REPORT

You can now add code to the form to generate the report (you'll add other report elements later). For a report that uses a *Data Environment* with no parameters, all you need to do is invoke the **Show** method on the *DataReport* object. You can show the report as either a modal or modeless dialog. In this walkthrough, you'll add code to display the report using only the default value for the parameter. However, I will illustrate the required code to permit selection criteria to be entered at runtime by the user.

Since a *Data Report* is actually a kind of form, all that is required to produce the report is to invoke the *Show* method on the *Data Report* object:

```
Private Sub cmdPreviewReport_Click ()
     DataReport1.Show vbModal, Me
End Sub
```

Enter the above code into the *Click* event procedure for a command button that you add to your form (see Figure 5-37). You can then run and test the program.

1. Add a command button to your form.

2. In the command button's *Click* event, enter code to show the data report in modal format (see above).

3. Run and test your program.

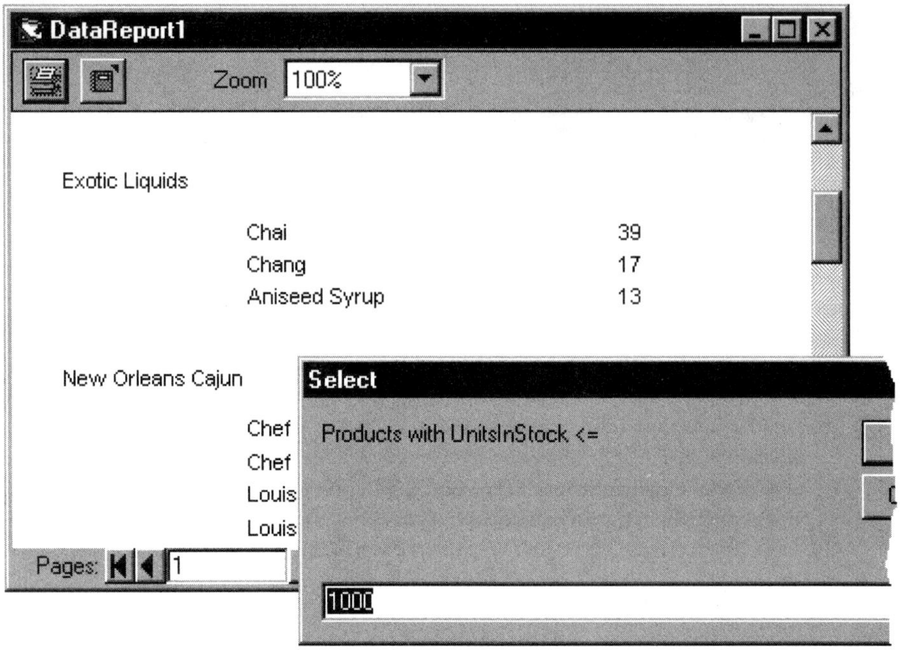

FIGURE 5-38 The final version of the demo allows the user to enter the parameter value at runtime.

Providing a Report Parameter Value at Runtime

To access a parameter at runtime, you must write code that accesses the *Suppliers* command object at runtime. All command objects are available as custom methods of the *Data Environment* object. They will be given the same name as you gave them in the *Data Environment Designer*. Using the *Command* object, you can access the *Parameters* collection to get to the parameter by name. You can then set the *Value* property of the parameter.

To improve performance, by default the recordset is persisted between displaying the report. Therefore, if you are passing parameters to a query that is the source of the report, you must close the recordset after displaying the report. Otherwise, the parameter is not refreshed.

The completed demo program, *ReportDemo,* displays an input box to accept the parameter for the *units-in-stock* parameter (see Figure 5-38). Code to accomplish the regeneration of the report when the parameter changes is as follows:

```
Private Sub cmdPreviewReport_Click()
    Dim nNewUnits As Integer
    Dim nOldUnits As Integer
    Dim c As Command

    '- Get current parameter value and use as default
    '- for new parameter value.

    Set c = deNWind.Commands("Suppliers")
    nOldUnits = c.Parameters("pInStock").Value

    nNewUnits = InputBox("Products with UnitsInStock <=", _
                "Select", nOldUnits)

    '- Set new parameter value.  Be sure to close
    '- the recordset after showing the report, or
    '- else the new parameter value is not used.

    c.Parameters("pInStock").Value = nNewUnits
    DataReport1.Show vbModal, Me
    deNWind.rsSuppliers.Close
End Sub
```

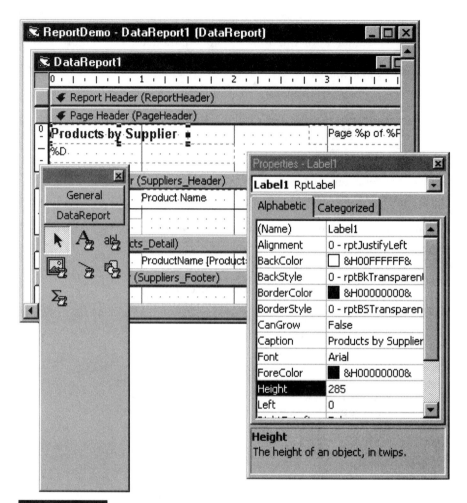

FIGURE 5-39   You can add additional report elements using the special set of *DataReport* controls, which appears in your toolbox after adding a *Data Report* to your project.

Adding Additional Report Elements

Additional report elements can be added using the special **DataReport** controls, which become part of your toolbox when you add a *Data Report* to your project. The most commonly used *DataReport* controls are the **RptLabel,** **RptTextBox,** and **RptLine** controls. These controls appear in your toolbox after you've added a *Data Report* to your project (see Figure 5-39).

The **RptTextBox** control is not at all like the intrinsic text box control; the user does not enter text into it. It's used as the source for data fields. In fact, when you drag and drop a field onto the *Report Designer* window, you're creating an *RptTextBox* control on the report. The **RptLabel** control is used for column headers, titles, dates, and so on. The **RptLine** control simply provides a line – it's used under column headers and for providing visual separation between a column of numbers and the total. The demo also uses the **RptFunction** control to provide a total. More on this control shortly.

SPECIAL CHARACTER CODES USED IN LABELS

Several special character codes can be used in labels (see Table 5-25). These codes are *substituted* with items such as date, time, and page number. The demo program uses several of these character codes in its labels.

TABLE 5-25	Special Character Codes Used in Labels

Item	Special Character Code
Current Page Number	%p
Total Number of Pages	%P
Current Date (Short Format)	%d
Current Date (Long Format)	%D
Current Time (Short Format)	%t
Current Time (Long Format)	%T

USING THE RPTFUNCTION DATAREPORT CONTROL

The **RptFunction** *DataReport* control displays data that is calculated at runtime. A typical function of the *RptFunction* control is to display a subtotal or grand total. The *RptFunction* control can execute a number of aggregate functions (see Table 5-26).

A *RptFunction* control can only be used in a group or report footer section. The function operates on the current group of data if the control is placed in a group footer section, or on all the data if the control is placed in the report footer section. After placing a *RptFunction* control on a report, you need to set its **DataMember** property to the appropriate *Command* object and its **DataField** property to the appropriate field. The default function is to sum the data. You indicate other functions by setting the *RptFunction* control's **FunctionType** property.

TABLE 5-26	RptFunction Control Function Types

FunctionType Value	Constant	Description
0	rptFuncSum	Sums the values of *DataField*.
1	rptFuncAve	Averages the values of *DataField*.
2	rptFuncMin	Returns the minimum value of *DataField*.
3	rptFuncMax	Returns the maximum value of *DataField*.
4	rptFuncRCnt	Counts the rows in the section.
5	rptFuncVCnt	Counts the fields with non-null values.
6	rptFuncSDEV	Calculates the standard deviation.
7	rptFuncSERR	Calculates the standard error.

Introducing
Class Modules

In this chapter, I'll present an introduction to **class modules**, which are the Visual Basic programmer's gateway to distributed applications. To implement ActiveX Components, which host the objects in your data services layer and object model, you will need to know as much as possible about class modules. Each object in your object model and data services layer will be implemented from a Visual Basic class module. This includes your top-level objects, collections, items in the collections, and every other object.

If you are already familiar with using class modules in Visual Basic, you can skip this chapter and go on to the next chapter, in which I'll show you how to package your class modules into ActiveX Components that hide business rules and database access from the presentation layer.

Chapter Six • Distributed COM Application Development Using Visual Basic 6.0

About Class Modules

One of the most powerful features of Visual Basic is the ability to define your own classes using class modules. By using class modules, you can come pretty close to doing object-oriented programming with Visual Basic. In fact, with Visual Basic 5.0, which introduced interface inheritance, the case for Visual Basic being an object-oriented programming language is even stronger. I may debate that somewhat in this chapter, but arguing that point won't get me far. I'll say instead that Visual Basic is object-using or perhaps object-centric. At any rate, Visual Basic allows you to define your own class of object, as well as define its properties and methods.

There is a price to pay in using class modules – a learning curve to traverse! The concepts presented in this chapter are certainly advanced, and it will take a bit of a mind-set adjustment to buy into it. However, by implementing your application using an object model, you will separate your interface from the implementation. This will give you a great deal of flexibility, including the ability to implement your business logic as an ActiveX Component. That will allow you to completely separate the interface from the implementation; they can run as separate processes, on separate hosts. Thus, you'll have a true client/server implementation.

Why Use Class Modules?

If your application will be a standalone, non-distributed application, using class modules is completely optional. However, proper use of class modules will give your application several advantages. The benefits of using class modules include:

1. Class modules allow the programmer to use object-oriented programming techniques, which brings up a whole list of advantages in and of itself!

2. Class modules make it easier to manage multiple instances of "objects" from your problem domain.

3. The use of class modules makes it easier to separate the user interface from the processing of interface commands (also known as "business rules" or "middleware").

4. The use of class modules is required for the implementation of your own ActiveX Component applications.

5. Class modules are also required for the implementation of Visual Basic add-ins.

While a class module in Visual Basic is not exactly the same thing as a class in the C++ and Java programming languages, it provides the programmer with the same fundamental advantages, and allows you to develop elegant and easily maintained programs. Class modules also provide you with an additional kind of "package" to improve modularity and promote code reuse. So, from the point of view of benefits and advantages, Visual Basic class modules are every bit as powerful as classes in C++ and Java.

Object-Oriented Programming in Visual Basic?

The debate over whether Visual Basic is an object-oriented programming language began with the release of Visual Basic 3.0, which introduced *OLE automation* (now simply called automation). With automation, which is introduced in Chapter 10, a Visual Basic programmer could declare an object variable that referenced a running instance of an application instrumented with an automation interface. By setting properties and invoking methods on this object variable, one application could control another in an object-oriented and consistent manner. *OLE automation* provided a solution that was far more elegant than using Dynamic Data Exchange (DDE), which was the predominant method for one application to control another at the time.

The Visual Basic object-oriented debate grew stronger with the release of Visual Basic 4.0, which introduced class modules as a way of defining templates for your own objects. With this release of Visual Basic, a programmer could create classes that defined objects, much like a C++ or Java programmer could. However, few experts were ready to classify Visual Basic as an object-oriented programming language simply because it contained the ability to create class modules.

Inheritance and Polymorphism

Visual Basic 5.0 introduced inheritance and polymorphism, so the debate continued and the case for Visual Basic as an object-oriented programming language grew even stronger. Using **inheritance**, one class is derived from another, which results in a derived class that has the same set of properties and methods as its parent, or base class. With inheritance, it is possible to create a hierarchy of classes, defining common processing in the base class with localized differences in behavior implemented in the derived classes. For example, a *2DShape* base class, which would encapsulate the behavior of two-dimensional shapes, could define properties such as *OriginX* and *OriginY,* along with the methods *Area* and *Perimeter*. From this base class, one could derive *Square* and *Circle* classes, adding necessary properties such as *Width* (in the case of the *Square*) and *Radius* (in the case of the *Circle*). The *Area* and *Perimeter* methods could then be overridden in local implementations of both the *Square* and *Circle* classes.

With **polymorphism,** an object can be declared to be of a given base class, such as a *2DShape*. At runtime, this object can take the form of the base class or any class derived from the base class, such as a *Square* or *Circle*. When a method is invoked on the object, such as *Area* or *Perimeter*, the appropriate implementation is chosen dynamically; either the *Square* version or the *Circle* version (or perhaps a default implementation in the base class). This is exactly what polymorphism is: the ability of an object to respond differently, but appropriately, to a method call. The word polymorphism means many forms. Although polymorphism is implemented in Visual Basic in a different way than in C++, it is still polymorphism in the strictest sense.

Interface Inheritance and Implementation Inheritance

Even with the object-centric enhancements to Visual Basic, to date most pure object-oriented programmers (academics and hard-core C++ users, for example) still do not consider Visual Basic to be an object-oriented programming language. Reasons include the fact that Visual Basic lacks both function and operator overloading, but especially that Visual Basic uses interface inheritance exclusively, and provides no means of implementation inheritance. If a language supports implementation inheritance, as do C++ and Java, a programmer can derive a class from a base class, and the result is a "clone" of the base class. Nothing more needs to be done by the programmer, although he or she will typically override or add functionality to the derived class. However, with interface inheritance, a derived class only inherits the interface of the base class. This means that the programmer using interface inheritance is obligated to provide implementations of the properties and methods of the base class, but an implementation is not provided automatically.

If you have been programming in C++ for a long time, you may not understand the benefits of interface inheritance, although the C++ language supports it as well. (Java also supports interface inheritance, but in a more obvious way—a C++ programmer uses interface inheritance by defining a base class that consists solely of pure virtual functions, while the Java language has native interface support).

The concepts of interface inheritance and interfaces in general are relatively new to the object-oriented programming world. Object-oriented programmers used to focus on only two major concepts: the class and the object. An ***object*** is an instance of a ***class,*** which is implemented with code and data to define the attributes and behavior of an object. Now it has been realized that there is also the ***interface***, which is basically a list of semantically related properties and methods (or member access functions and member functions, as they are called in C++). An interface has no implementation; the class provides the implementation. When a class asserts that it implements a given interface, code can be written to use the class via the well-known interface (set of properties and methods). The same code can be used to drive a different implementation of that interface through a different class that also asserts that it implements the interface.

Thus, there are actually three important concepts in object-oriented programming: the interface, the class, and the object. An ***interface*** is a specification for a set of well-known and semantically related functions. Since it has no implementation, an interface cannot be used directly from code. A ***class*** is an implementation of one or more interfaces. It provides the code and data to implement the interfaces (or it implements only its own private interface). Since a class is like a template or definition, it cannot be used directly by code either. An ***object*** is an instance of a class. Through an object, code can actually invoke properties and methods defined, or implemented by, the class.

Interface Inheritance and Code Reuse

Can interface inheritance be used to reuse code as implementation inheritance can? The answer is yes, but it's tedious. To reuse code in a base class using only interface inheritance, a derived class must declare an instance of the base class object. This object, which is typically referred to as the inner object, is hidden from clients of the derived class. To use an implemented method of the base class, the implementation of the method in the derived class delegates the call to the inner object. In fact, most calls to the derived class must be implemented to also call the base class to keep the inner object synchronized with the derived class. This basically means that every property and method must be implemented in the derived class – that is what is so tedious about it.

While interface inheritance can be employed for code reuse, the most frequent use of interface inheritance in Visual Basic is to enable communication between components. If an already developed component needs to invoke code in your component, the existing component can define an interface to be implemented by your component. This is exactly how MTS is able to invoke code in your component to inform it that it is about to be activated or deactivated – you will be using interface inheritance to enable this communication with MTS. I'll be providing an example of using interface inheritance for communicating with the MTS runtime environment in Chapter 12.

Returning to the debate: Have I settled the question of whether or not Visual Basic is an object-oriented programming language? I'm sure I have not. But, one can certainly perform an object-oriented design and then implement the solution in Visual Basic. For most programmers that need to do Rapid Application Development (RAD), that is sufficient. Let the academics continue to debate the issue.

Using Class Modules

A class module in Visual Basic is used to implement several key concepts of object-oriented programming. It defines (or is a template of) an object's behavior (processing) and attributes (properties). It is a means for instantiating (creating) objects from the class (template). It provides an encapsulation of an object's properties (data) and methods (functions/processing). And, it is a means for controlling the accessibility to an object's data (keeping data private and allowing methods to be public).

Class modules allow Visual Basic programmers to use abstraction, another important concept of object-oriented programming. ***Abstraction*** is a key object-oriented design concept, in which the designer defines the essential details of an object from the problem domain, and brings those details to the front, while hiding the non-essential (or implementation) details from the clients of the object. This allows code that uses the object to focus on a well-defined interface, while only the programmer that implements the object has to know (or care) about low-level implementation details.

There are major benefits of using abstraction (and its implementation through Visual Basic class modules). For one, those parts of the application that need to use an object can do so through a simplified, well-defined interface. For another, those parts of an application that implement the object can be changed without affecting the rest of the application, as long as the interface does not change. The interface to the object very closely matches the real-world object it models. Therefore, object-oriented implementations are usually more flexible.

Class modules are more closely related to standard modules (BAS files) than they are to form modules, in that class modules contain only code and data (no visual appearance, as in forms). However, unlike standard modules, the code and data in a class module are available only through an instance of the class (that is, an object).

Using an Object Model in Your Application

In this chapter, we will see how to create a simple object model in which all the data is hard-coded; there is no database access. In addition, we will be developing a private object model that can be used by a single application. In the next chapter, I will illustrate the use of advanced class module techniques to build a public object model that encapsulates database access. If you are not familiar with creating class modules, you should continue to read this chapter.

To create an object-oriented program, you should design, and then implement, an object model. This involves the following steps:

1. Identifying objects (and collections of objects) in your problem domain (that is, the scope of the problem your application will solve).
2. Identifying the properties (attributes, characteristics) of the objects.
3. Identifying the methods (processing, behavior) of the objects.
4. Implementing the objects using Visual Basic class modules.

Identifying objects starts, quite simply, by searching for nouns (or noun phrases) in the problem statement. Consider the sample problem statement appearing in the box below. Like most problem statements, this one is fuzzy, and may use several words to describe the same objects.

▶ Problem Statement

Training Center

A software training company requires a scheduling system to keep track of course offerings, students that register for a course, and the instructor assigned to teach each particular offering. The training center has a curriculum, which is a list of courses that may be offered in a schedule. Each course has a course number and a title. The schedule is a list of sessions, which is a particular offering of a course. Each session has a code number assigned to it, and is offered at a particular location and at a particular starting date, and has an instructor assigned to teach the course. When a student registers for a session, the student's name must be added to the roster for that offering.

Identifying Candidate Objects in the Problem Statement

There are many excellent methodologies for performing object-oriented design, and especially for a large project, you should select and follow one. However, for small to medium-sized projects, an informal approach can often work just as well.

The first pass at identifying objects in the problem statement involves finding nouns and noun phrases. I have arrived at the following list of nouns (see box) after the first pass at the problem statement. Since the first pass is rarely usable as the final list, we could consider this to be the list of candidate objects (this list is somewhat "gleaned" in the interest of time). The candidate objects identified in this pass are listed in Table 6-1.

▶ Problem Statement

Candidate Objects

A software training company requires a scheduling system to keep track of **course offerings**, **students** that register for a **course**, and the **instructor** assigned to teach each particular **offering**. The training center has a **curriculum**, which is a list of courses that may be offered in a **schedule**. Each course has a **course number** and a **title**. The schedule is a list of **sessions**, which is a particular offering of a course. Each **session** has a **code number** assigned to it, and is offered at a particular **location** and at a particular **starting date**, and has an instructor assigned to teach the course. When a **student** registers for a session, the student's **name** must be added to the **roster** for that offering.

TABLE 6-1	Candidate Objects in the Training Center Domain

Candidate Object	Definition
Course offerings	A list of courses, each offered at a particular location and date.
Students	A list of students.
Course	A possible offering in the schedule. Has a title and description.
Instructor	A person that conducts the course.
Offering	A particular event in which a course runs at a particular location and date.
Curriculum	A list of courses that may be offered in the schedule.
Schedule	A list of courses, each offered at a particular location and date. Appears to be a synonym for *course offerings*.
Course number	A number assigned to a course.
Title	A short description of a course.
Session	A particular event in which a course runs at a particular location and date. Appears to be a synonym for *offering*.
Code number	A number assigned to a session.
Location	A place where a session is held.
Starting date	The beginning date of a session.
Student	Someone who can register for a session. Has a name.
Name	The name of a student.
Roster	A list of students. Appears to be a synonym for *students*.

Refining the List of Objects

In the second pass through the list of candidate objects, duplicates (synonyms) are eliminated and decisions are made (sometimes arbitrary) about what will be objects and what will simply become properties of identified objects. Rarely is a second pass sufficient. In the interest of time and space, consider this second pass to be the final pass (see Table 6-2).

Note that some of the objects appear to be lists. In object-oriented terms, these are referred to as **collections**. For example, a roster could be considered to be a collection of student objects.

In this chapter, I will show how to implement *Schedule, Session, Student,* and *Roster* class objects. There will be no implementation of the course or curriculum object. Instead, the *Course* object will be "folded" into the *Session* object – not the best approach, but the goal here is not to provide a complete implementation, it's to get you started on using class modules.

TABLE 6-2	Final List of Objects in the Training Center Domain
Object	**Definition**
Course	A possible offering in the schedule, as well as an entry in the curriculum. Has a title, description, and course number.
Curriculum	A list of courses that may be offered in the schedule.
Schedule	A list of sessions.
Session	A particular event in which a course runs at a particular location and date. Has an instructor assigned to it, as well as a code number, or session ID. Also has a list of students (or roster) associated with it.
Student	Someone who can register for a session. Has a name.
Roster	A list of students associated with a session.

Object, Class, Instance – A Discussion of Definitions

The terms "object" and "class" are somewhat ambiguous and interchangeable. During design, you may use either word to mean the same thing. However, during implementation, you need to be more precise. A class is like a category (or classification) to which an object belongs. So, in this design, everything identified as objects will actually be considered classes in the implementation. An object, therefore, can be defined as an instance of a class. For example, *Nancy Davolio* is an instance of a *Student* class object.

A class is not directly usable. For example, a *Student* class cannot be added to a roster. However, an object (that is, an instance of a class) is usable. For example, *Nancy Davolio* (an instance of a *Student* class) can be added to a roster. Objects must be created (also called instantiated) before they can be used. The class of an object is used as a template for its creation. All objects of a particular class have the same attributes and behavior. However, instances can vary slightly from one another because they each have their own set of properties, which can have different values. For example, *Nancy Davolio* (an instance of a *Student* class object) differs from *Michael Suyama* (another instance of a *Student* class object), by her *Name* property.

Identifying Properties and Methods of a Class

Once the list of classes has been created, the next step is to identify properties and methods for each class. Recall that properties are the attributes or characteristics of an object. Put another way, it's the list of important data items associated with an object. Recall that methods implement the behavior, or processing, that is internal to an object. Put another way, it's the list of functions associated with an object. The *Session* class will be the first to be implemented, so its properties and methods are identified first. Properties and methods of the *Session* class object are listed in Table 6-3.

TABLE 6-3	Properties and Methods of the Session Class

Property or Method	**Type**	**Description**
SessionID	Property	ID number of the session.
Number	Property	The course number.
Title	Property	The course title.
Location	Property	Where the session is held.
StartDate	Property	When the session starts.
InstructorID	Property	The instructor's ID number. Arbitrarily added, since presumably it will come from a database.
InstructorName	Property	The name of the instructor.
Roster	Property	List of students in the class.

CREATING THE SESSION CLASS MODULE

To create the *Session* class module:

1. Select *Add Class Module* from the *Project* menu. This will open a new *Code Editor* window, and the *Project Explorer* window will be updated to show a new class module.

2. In the *Properties* window, set the *Name* property to *Session*. The *Name* property is the one and only property of the class module.

3. It's a good idea to save the project at this point. If you do so, note that Visual Basic proposes *Session.cls* for the filename of the *Session* class module.

Adding Properties Using Public Variables

The easiest way to add properties to a class is to declare public variables in the declarations section of the class module. Such variables automatically become properties of the class. However, this is usually not the best way, since these properties are directly accessible to outside code. This means that code in the class module will not be notified of changes to properties, and that code using the class can set a property to any value – even an invalid value. In spite of this, the first attempt at implementing the *Session* class will use public variables to implement the properties (note that the *Roster* property implementation is delayed at this time, as it will be a collection). This will serve as a baseline for comparing the technique of using public variables for properties with the other, preferred technique – using *Property Let* and *Get* procedures, which are discussed shortly.

To add a property to a class module using a public variable:

1. In the *Code Editor* window, go to the declarations section of the module.

2. Enter the declaration of a public variable. This will become a property of the class.

For example, the declarations section of the *Session* class module would appear as follows:

```
Option Explicit
Public SessionID As Integer
Public Number As Integer
Public Title As String
Public Location As String
Public StartDate As Date
Public InstructorID As Integer
Public InstructorName As String
```

Creating an Instance of a Class

To create an instance of a class, the code that creates the instance must declare an object variable, using the class name as the type, then set the object variable to a newly created instance of the class, using the *New* keyword. For example,

```
Dim Session1 As Session
Set Session1 = New Session
```

The two steps can be combined into one statement by using **As New** when declaring the object variable. For example,

```
' Declares and creates a Session object:
Dim Session As New Session
```

Once an object is created, you can access its properties and methods. Managing multiple instances of classes becomes easy. In considering multiple instances of classes, remember that each instance has its own set of properties, which is maintained independently of other instances. However, each instance shares a common copy of the code (methods). For example,

```
Dim Session1 As New Session
Dim Session2 As New Session

Session1.Number = 2403
Session1.Title = "Fundamentals of Microsoft Visual Basic"

Session2.Number = 2404
Session2.Title = "Programming in Microsoft Visual Basic"
```

To try any of these code examples, you should place them in a form using, perhaps, a command button's click event procedure. You'll notice that the Visual Basic statement builder, using Microsoft's *Intellisense* technology, has already "learned" about the *Session* object and its properties. You may wish, however, to delay actually entering code for a client test program; a full implementation of a client test program is provided later in this chapter.

Setting a New Instance of an Object to a Known State

New instances of objects can be initialized in the class's **Initialize** method. You can also clean up after an object by placing code in the class's **Terminate** method. These methods can be implemented by accessing the class module's code window. Drop down the object list and select *Class*, then select *Initialize* or *Terminate* from the procedure list. In the following example, new instances of *Session* objects are initialized so that their course number is zero and their title is *Untitled*.

```
Option Explicit
Public SessionID As Integer
Public Number As Integer
Public Title As String
Public Location As String
Public StartDate As Date
Public InstructorID As Integer
Public InstructorName As String

Private Sub Class_Initialize()

    ' Initialize properties to known values

    SessionID = 0
    Number = 0
    Title = "Untitled"
    Location = "Unknown"
    StartDate = Today
    InstructorID = 0
    InstructorName = "Unassigned"


End Sub
```

Implementing Methods

Methods are implemented by adding public procedures to a class module. Public sub-procedures of a class become methods of a class, which do not return values. Public function procedures of a class become methods of a class, which return values. Parameters of public procedures in a class module become parameters of the method. Since no methods were discovered when designing the *Session* class, examples of methods will be delayed until an implementation of the *Schedule* class, which will have an *Add* method.

Implementing Code to Create and Manage a Session

A sample user interface test program.

At this point, you can begin to create the user interface test program for your *Session* class module. In addition to the startup form already provided by Visual Basic for a Standard EXE project, you'll need a form that can be used to display the attributes of a session. Note that a completed demo program for this exercise is provided in folder *VB6Adv\Demos\ClassModules* (see Figure 6-1).

In the first pass at the solution, you can hard-code the creating and showing of a single session. The session is created in the *cmdNewSession* button's click event, using a form-level variable, *Session1*, to hold the *Session* object. This variable is declared in the declarations section of *frmMain*. For example,

```
Private Session1 as Session

Private Sub cmdNewSession_Click()

    Set Session1 = New Session

    Session1.Number = 2404
```

```
    Session1.Title = "Programming in Visual Basic"
    Session1.Location = "Denver"
    Session1.StartDate = #4/11/98#
    Session1.InstructorID = 1
    Session1.InstructorName = "Davolio, Nancy"

    cmdNewSession.Enabled = False
    cmdShowSession.Enabled = True

End Sub
```

Code for displaying the *Session* object is as follows:

```
Private Sub cmdShowSession_Click()
    Dim i As Integer

    Load frmSession
    frmSession.lblCourseNumber = Session1.Number
    frmSession.lblCourseTitle = Session1.Title
    frmSession.lblInstructorID = Session1.InstructorID
    frmSession.lblInstructorName = Session1.InstructorName
    frmSession.lblLocation = Session1.Location
    frmSession.lblStartDate = Session1.StartDate

    frmSession.Caption = "Session ID # " & _
                         Session1.SessionID
    frmSession.Show vbModal, Me

End Sub
```

Object Lifetime Management and Reference Counting

If you closely examine the sample code presented in the previous section, you'll discover that there is only one object variable that references a *Session* object (remember, the object variable and the object are two separate things). When you click the *New Session* button for the first time, a new *Session* object is created, and a reference to it is assigned to the variable *Session1*. The question is: What happens when the button is clicked a second time?

When a second *Session* object is created, its reference is assigned to the *Session1* variable. Now, there is no longer a reference to the initial *Session* object you created. At first, you may think that the initial object is "orphaned." Since there is no longer a reference to the object, the program has lost track of it, yet does it still exist? The answer is no, due to the reference-counting mechanism provided for you automatically by Visual Basic.

When an object variable is set to reference an object, the object's reference count is automatically incremented. The reference count is decremented whenever the reference variable goes out of scope, is set to nothing, or is set to reference a different object (in which case, the new object's reference count is incremented after the first object's reference count is decremented). When an object's reference count reaches zero, the object automatically deletes itself. This reference-counting mechanism is provided automatically by Visual Basic as part of the standard "plumbing" that is required for all well-behaved objects.

You can, if you wish, verify this behavior by placing **Debug.Print** statements in the *Session* object's *Initialize* and *Terminate* methods (results will go to Visual Basic's *Immediate* window). You will see that, when the *New Session* button is clicked for the first time, its *Initialize* method will run. When the button is clicked a second time, the *Initialize* method will run (as a side effect of creating and initializing the new *Session* object), then the *Terminate* method will run (as a side effect of destroying the first *Session* object). This pattern will continue as long as you click the *New Session* button. When you finally exit the program (normally, that is, without clicking the Visual Basic *Stop* button), the form-level object variable, *Session1*, goes out of scope, and the last *Session* object you created is destroyed, as evidenced by the execution of the *Terminate* method.

Using the Object Browser to View the Session Class

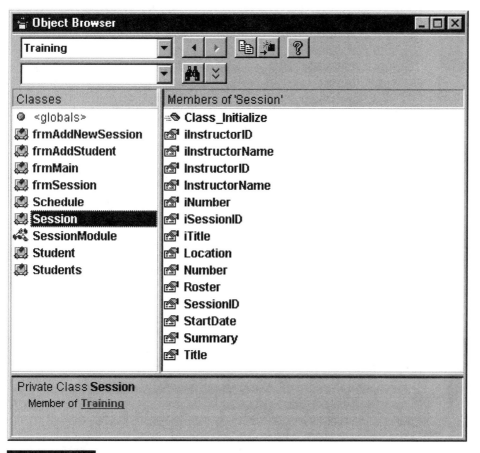

FIGURE 6-2   The *Object Browser* can be used to view the classes defined in a
Visual Basic project.

The ***Object Browser*** is an interactive tool that provides a graphical view of
the objects used by your application (see Figure 6-2). It also provides a
means to navigate around the code in your project. The *Object Browser* is
especially useful when you are not familiar with the objects you will be
using, as it can be used to discover properties and methods of a class. To use
the *Object Browser* to browse the properties and methods of the *Session* class,

1. From the Visual Basic ***View*** menu, select ***Object Browser***.

2. To make it easier to see the objects in your application, select your
   project name from the *Libraries* drop-down list.

3. In the list of classes, select the class you wish to browse (in this case, *Session*).

4. The members (a list of both properties and methods) appear. To view the code or definition of a method or property, double-click on its name in the members list.

A SUMMARY OF THE TRAINING PROJECT SO FAR

So far, I've illustrated how to create class modules, and create instances of classes in code. I have also illustrated how to implement properties by using a simple approach – by adding public variables to the class module. As mentioned earlier, using public variables to implement properties is not the best approach. Consider the *Number* and *Title* properties. The *Number* property should only be set to a valid course number, and the *Title* property should automatically be set as a side effect of setting the course number. Also, the *Title* property should ideally be a read-only property. As it stands, client code using the *Session* class module can set the *Number* property to any integer value – positive or negative. Additionally, the code currently requires that the *Title* property be set in addition to the *Number* property – even though there is no doubt a relationship between a course number and its title. The relationship between the *InstructorID* and *InstructorName* properties poses a similar problem. The next pass at the *Training Center* application will address these problems, and bring up some new concepts as well.

TRAINING CENTER APPLICATION – A SECOND PASS

In the next pass at the *Training Center* application, I will illustrate the use of a feature that allows code in a class module to have more control over how properties are set – by using the **Property Let** and **Property Get** procedures. In addition, I will discuss how to raise errors from a class module.

Using the Property Let and Get Procedures

A better approach to implementing properties is to use the **Property Let** and **Property Get** procedures. The procedures are named after a property. For example, to implement the *InstructorID* property, we would create a *Property Let* procedure called *InstructorID* (and do the same for a *Property Get* procedure).

A *Property Let* procedure is like a sub-*procedure*. When client code using a class assigns a value to a property, its *Property Let* procedure is invoked. The parameter passed to the procedure is the proposed new value for the property. In your *Property Let* procedure, you can check the proposed new value and reject it if it is invalid. You can additionally perform any side effects related to the setting of the property. For example, code in the *Number* property's *Let* procedure can look up the proposed course number in a database, and automatically assign the course name to the *Title* property.

A *Property Get* procedure is like a function procedure. When client code using a class module reads the property, as in an expression, the property's *Get* procedure is invoked. The return value is the current value for the property.

As indicated, using the *Property Let* and *Get* procedures is the best way to implement a property. As a side note, it is, in actual fact, the only way. When you create properties using public variables in a class module, Visual Basic actually generates a hidden pair of *Property Let* and *Get* procedures. The generated *Property Let* procedure unconditionally sets the property to whatever value the client code proposes, as long as it does not generate a type mismatch.

If you create *Property Let* and *Get* procedures, you must, in general, also provide a private module-level variable to hold the value of the property. This technique is the same technique used by a C++ programmer; a private member variable is created, and public member access functions are provided to allow client code to read and set the "property."

Using *Property Let* and/or *Get* procedures does not affect the way a property is referenced by the user. Code using the object still uses dotted notation to reference a property. Thus, it will not be necessary to change the client test program illustrated previously.

It is not necessary to implement both the *Let* and *Get* procedures. Implementing only a *Property Get* procedure creates a read-only property. The *Title* and *InstructorName* properties are ideal candidates for read-only properties. When the *Number* property of a *Session* is assigned a value, the *Property Let* procedure for the *Number* property can assign the appropriate value to the *Title* property, which can be made available to client code only through a *Property Get* procedure. The same technique can be used when assigning the *InstructorID* property.

PROPERTY IMPLEMENTATION PLAN FOR THE SESSION CLASS

Since a course number must be set from a limited list of valid course numbers, the *Number* property should be implemented via *Property Get* and *Property Let* procedures. In addition, when client code sets the *Number* property of the *Session* object, the *Title* property should be set automatically, as a side effect of setting the *Number* property. In reality, the *Property Let* procedure would probably look up the title from a database. However, to keep the demonstration simple, I'll hard-code a limited list of course numbers. In the following chapter, you will see how to implement an object model that actually uses a database, and is implemented as an ActiveX Component that can be reused by several client applications.

Since the *Title* property should not be directly set, it will be implemented using only a *Property Get* procedure. Once this modification is made, the only way that client code will be able to set the *Title* property is by setting the *Number* property. The *Title* property will be a read-only property.

A similar approach will be taken with the *InstructorID* and *InstructorName* properties. Client code will be able to read and write to the *InstructorID* property, but will only able to read from the *InstructorName* property. The *InstructorName* property will be set as a side effect of setting the *InstructorID* property.

Although one can make a case for implementing *Location* and *StartDate* using property procedures, in this implementation, I will not do that. Thus, the user can still directly access these properties. This is not something I would do if creating an actual application. Obviously, the *StartDate* property would require validation. Code would probably need to ensure that the starting date is a valid date and is in the future. Further, it may apply localized business rule validations, for example, ensuring that the start date is on a Monday if the course runs for five days. As for the *Location* property, even if it could be any string value (which is not likely), it may be desired to at least trim leading and trailing blanks from the string, and/or validate that its length does not exceed some maximum.

Providing *Property Let* and *Get* procedures raises another issue – what to do when client code attempts to set a property to an illegal value. The wrong approach is to display an error message in the form of a message box. Middleware should not do anything that requires a response from a user. Following this advice makes it possible to implement the object model (or any other components) for unattended execution. The appropriate response is to raise a custom error. Therefore, the next pass at the *Training Center* application will raise an error if client code attempts to set either the *Number* or *InstructorID* properties to an invalid value.

Adding a Property Let Procedure

A ***Property Let*** procedure is similar to a sub-*procedure*. A *Property Let* procedure is automatically invoked when client code uses a property as the target of an assignment statement, or when client code otherwise sets the property, as when it is used as a parameter to a routine. A parameter is automatically passed to the *Property Let* procedure. This parameter contains the value that client code is attempting to use as the new value for the property, in other words, a proposed new value. The syntax for the *Property Let* procedure is as follows:

```
Private internal-variable As type

Public Property Let property-name (parameter-name As type)
   ' Validate property
   ' Set internal variable, eg:
   internal-variable = parameter-name
   ' Execute side effects
End Property
```

Normally, in a *Property Let* procedure, the new value is stored into some private internal variable that the class module uses to keep track of that property's value. For example, the private variable ***m_Number*** may be used to hold the actual value of the ***Number*** property:

```
Private m_Number As Integer

Public Property Let Number (newNumber As Integer)
   m_Number = newNumber
End Property
```

Note that the way in which a property is referenced in client code does not change. The following client code, for example, will invoke the *Property Let* procedure for *Number,* passing the value *2404* as the parameter *newNumber.*

```
' Set number property to 2404
Session1.Number = 2404
```

It's possible to use more than one parameter in a *Property Let* procedure, to implement parameterized properties. This technique is not used in the implementation of the *Training Center* application.

Adding a Property Get Procedure

A **Property Get** procedure is similar to a function. Its return value is the value of the property. Normally, a *Property Get* procedure returns the value of some private internal variable that the class module uses to keep track of the property's value. For example, the variable **m_Number** may hold the actual value of the **Number** property. To return the value of the property, assign a value to the name of the property. This is the same type of syntax used in a Visual Basic function. The syntax of a *Property Get* procedure is as follows:

```
Private internal-variable As type

Public Property Get property-name () As type
    property-name = internal-variable
End Property
```

For example, to implement a *Property Get* procedure for the *Number* property,

```
Private m_Number As Integer

Public Property Get Number () As Integer
    Number = m_Number
End Property
```

The *Property Get* procedure is invoked whenever client code reads a property. How a property is read does not change from the way it is read when implemented as a public variable. For example,

```
' Read the Number property:
If Session1.Number = 2404 Then MaxStudents = 20
```

CREATING PROPERTY LET AND GET PROCEDURES

To create either a *Property Get* or *Property Let* procedure, you can type the code into the *Code Editor* window (be sure not to start typing it into the middle of an existing procedure). Or, if you prefer, you may select **Add Procedure** from the **Tools** menu, enter the name of the property, and select **Property** as the procedure type. Note that this will "stub" out both a *Property Let* and a *Property Get* procedure. Remember that you do not have to implement both the *Let* and a *Get* procedures. To make a read-only property, implement only a *Property Get* procedure.

Raising Errors in a Class Module

As a general rule, you should not display an error message via a message box (or form) in a class module. There are two reasons for this. First of all, the developer that is using the class may wish to trap an error instead, or display a different error message. The second reason is more compelling: Middleware should not implement any part of a user interface; that is, it should be capable of running unattended. The user interface provides interaction with the user.

How should code in a class module communicate an error back to the client code? The preferred technique is to either raise a user-defined error or return an error code. Returning an error code is possible when implementing a method, but is not possible when setting a property. Thus, I'll concentrate on raising errors from a class module.

ABOUT VBOBJECTERROR AND USER-DEFINED ERROR CODES

The first step in raising a user-defined error is to assign an error code number. User-defined error codes begin with error number 80040000 (hex). That number, in decimal, has the rather startling value of–2,147,221,504 (yes, that's negative two billion or so). I have often been asked by students how the Visual Basic developers came up with this number. The answer is that they didn't; COM specified it. To understand the seemingly outrageous value of this number, first you must realize that the number only makes sense in hex. The first digit (8) makes the number negative. A status code, known as an *HRESULT* to COM programmers, indicates an error if the code is negative. The number 4 in the hex representation of *vbObjectError* is the constant *FACILITY_ITF,* which indicates the generic facility "interface." This is the facility code that is used by the custom interfaces of components developed in COM. In fact, you'll notice the same range of errors being raised from *SQL Server*, ADO, and other components.

The natural questions are: how does a client know which component raised an error and how does it distinguish among the same error code raised by different components? The answer to the first question is easy. When an exception is raised, it is raised to the code using the component. Meanwhile, a thread is executing the code using the component. When an exception is raised to a thread, the thread knows that the error must have come from the last object it used. Thus, the thread can tell which component raised an error.

The answer to the second question is more difficult to answer. To support exceptions from a component, the object must support a COM interface known as **ISupportErrorInfo**. This interface includes methods that the client can invoke to obtain information about the last error raised by the component. Using these methods, client code can obtain a description of the error, the source of the error, and optionally, the name of a *Help* file and a *Help* context ID (the latter information is useful for the end-user of the application). In fact, Visual Basic encapsulates calling the *ISupportErrorInfo* interface with the **Err** object. Fortunately for the Visual Basic COM developer, you do not need to implement or invoke the methods of the *ISupportErrorInfo* interface.

For your convenience, the symbolic constant, **vbObjectError**, can be used for this number. Add your error code number to *vbObjectError* to get the final number. Your error numbers should be in the range (*vbObjectError* + 513) to (*vbObjectError* + 65535). Error numbers in the range 0 to 512 may conflict with other errors.

RAISING AN ERROR FROM VISUAL BASIC COMPONENTS

To raise an error, invoke the **Raise** method of the **Err** object. Parameters for the *Raise* method are listed in Table 6-4. The syntax is as follows:

```
Err.Raise Number, [Source], [Description], _
        [Help-file], [Help-context]
```

Code that uses your class can trap an error. The **Err.Description** property will have your error description in it.

TABLE 6-4	Parameters of the Raise Method
Parameter	**Description**
Number	Identifies the error. Use values in the range (*vbObjectError* + 512) to (*vbObjectError* + 65535).
Source	The optional name of the class raising the error; use the string *project.class*.
Description	An optional string expression describing the error.
Help-file	An optional string specifying the fully-qualified path to the application's *Help* file.
Help-context	An optional *Help* context ID referring to a topic that gives the user additional help on the error.

EXAMPLE: RAISING ERRORS IN A CLASS MODULE

The following examples below assume that any session number is valid as long as it is greater than zero. First, here is an example of raising the error:

```
Private m_Number as Integer

Public Property Let Number (newNumber As Integer)
   If newNumber < 0 Then
      Err.Raise vbObjectError + 600, _
                  "Training.Session", _
                  "Invalid session number"
        Exit Property
   End If
   m_Number = newNumber
End Property
```

And here is an example of trapping the error in client code:

```
On Error Goto BadNumber
Session1.Number = -10
        .
        .
        .
Exit Sub

BadNumber:
   If Err.Number = vbObjectError + 600 Then
        MsgBox "Please enter a valid session number"
   End If
```

USING AN ENUMERATION FOR ERROR CODES

Instead of hard-coding error code numbers (and expecting client code to do the same), you can define error codes using an enumeration in your class module. Doing so will make both server and client code easier to read. Be sure to make the enumeration public. For example, in the server, you can write

```
Public Enum SessionErrors
    errBadSessionNumber = vbObjectError + 600
    errBadStartDate = vbObjectError + 602
    errBadInstructorID = vbObjectError + 604
                     .
                     . (Etc.)
                     .
End Enum

Private m_Number as Integer

Public Property Let Number (newNumber As Integer)
    If newNumber < 0 Then
        Err.Raise errBadSessionNumber, _
                  "Training.Session", _
                  "Invalid session number"
        Exit Property
    End If
    m_Number = newNumber
End Property
```

Then, in the client code trapping the error, you can write

```
On Error Goto BadNumber
Session1.Number = -10
        .
        .
        .
Exit Sub

BadNumber:
    If Err.Number = errBadSessionNumber Then
            MsgBox "Please enter a valid session number"
    End If
```

IS RAISING ERRORS ALWAYS A GOOD IDEA?

When you raise an error in Visual Basic, what actually happens is that the code raises an ***exception.*** Visual Basic clients can handle exceptions fairly easily, simply by using the *On Error* statement. However, it is not always as easy from languages like C++ and Java, but it can be done using *try* and *catch* blocks.

You most definitely do not want to raise exceptions from MTS components, or at least you do not want to allow them to propagate outside the component. MTS does not allow exceptions to propagate outside components; if an exception is raised, the MTS process hosting the component is terminated. This condition will ultimately result in an error in client code using the component. In MTS components, you should return error codes instead. Note that this is less of an issue with MTS components, which generally do not have properties. The typical approach a programmer uses when implementing methods of MTS components is to return an error code rather than to raise an exception.

Sharing Data Among Instances of a Class

Sometimes it is desirable to have all instances of a class reference common data. This cannot be done by declaring data in the class module. Each instance of an object has its own copy of data declared in the class module. To share data among instances of a class, the data must be declared as public in a standard module.

In this pass of the *Training Center* application, I'll add a property called *SessionID*, using only a *Property Get* procedure. This makes the *SessionID* property a read-only property. I'll also add a public variable called **LastSessionID** to a newly added standard module. This variable will keep track of the last ID assigned to a session, and will be incremented each time a *Session* object is created. In the ***Initialize*** event of the *Session* object, I'll increment this variable and assign the result to the *SessionID* property. Note that this variable is not persistent. In reality, you would want to save and restore this value from a database. However, it is useful for illustrating sharing data among instances of a class.

Note that, under certain threading models, public variables are not shared. This will be discussed in Chapter 8. In fact, as a general rule, using the technique I'm about to show you is not recommended. If your component is to run under MTS, using global data is extremely unreliable and unpredictable. Global data in MTS components is implemented using the *Shared Property Manager,* a topic I'll be discussing in detail in Chapter 12.

To share data between instances of objects, declare the shared variables in a public module. For example,

```
Option Explicit

' Public data in a module is SHARED among
' all instances of a class. We'll use the
' following variable to keep track of the
' last session ID we assigned.

Public LastSessionID As Integer
```

Whenever code in a class module refers to the public variable in a standard module, it is using the shared copy, common to all instances of objects. For example,

```
Private Sub Class_Initialize()

    ' Initialize properties to known values

    Location = "Unknown"
    StartDate = Date

    m_Number = 0
    m_Title = "Untitled"
    m_InstructorID = 0
    m_InstructorName = "Unassigned"

    ' Automatically assign the next available session ID
    ' (NOTE) - LastSessionID is declared as public in
    '          module SessionModule

    m_SessionID = LastSessionID + 1
    LastSessionID = m_SessionID

End Sub
```

IMPLEMENTING THE STUDENT CLASS

To create a collection of students, it is necessary to first create a *Student* class. To create the *Student* class, you can simply add a new class, give it a name of *Student*, and provide two properties called **LastName** and **FirstName**. These properties can be implemented simply by using *public* variables in the class module. You can then proceed to create the *Students* collection, which will be used as the *Roster* property of the *Session* object.

Understanding Collections

A **collection** is like an array or list of objects. Just like in real life, a collection is typically composed of identical (or at least similar) objects. A collection is also an object in and of itself, having its own set of properties and methods. For example, a collection could (and usually does) have a **Count** property, which is the number of items in the collection. You may also have an add and a remove method, depending on whether the collection is static or dynamic. In this chapter, I'll get you started with collections. The topic is discussed in much greater detail in Chapter 7.

To implement collections in Visual Basic, you can use the built-in Visual Basic **Collection** class. The *Collection* class has methods to add (*Add*) and remove (*Remove*) items from a collection, and an **Item** method, which is used to access an item in the collection by its index. It also has a **Count** property, which is the number of objects in the collection.

For example, the following code creates a collection and adds a *Student* class object to it:

```
Dim Students As New Collection
Dim Student1 As New Student

Student1.LastName = "Smith"
Student1.FirstName = "Jane"
Students.Add Student1
```

The following code example uses the **Count** and **Item** properties to iterate through the list of students. Note that, although it is possible for code that uses the *Student* class to declare and maintain its own collection of students, it is desirable to create a new class that keeps the collection private and provides properties and methods to access the collection. This is the approach I will illustrate in this chapter.

```
Dim I As Integer

For I = 1 to Students.Count
    MsgBox Students.Item(I).LastName
Next
```

GOALS OF THE STUDENTS COLLECTION CLASS

The best way to implement collections is to encapsulate them in a class. The actual collection should be declared private in the class module. If server code allows direct access to the collection, then client code could put any object into the collection. For example, client code could add a *Session* class object to the *Students* collection, which would no doubt eventually cause the server code to fail.

In this implementation, client code will not be allowed to directly insert *Student* objects into the *Students* collection. Instead, client code must invoke a method, called **Add**, which will require two parameters, the first and last names of the newly added student. Upon completion of this implementation, adding a new student to the *Students* collection can be accomplished by invoking the *Add* method on the *Roster* property, which also creates a new *Student* object. This statement bears repeating: Client code must invoke the *Add* method on the *Roster* property of the *Session* object to add a student to the list of students taking a course. I repeat this because, while it nearly perfectly describes the necessary code required to implement a client application, it also perfectly describes the business rule. In other words, the implementation is modeled after the real-world business rules. For example,

```
Dim newStudent as Student
Set newStudent = Session1.Roster.Add "Smith", "Jerry"
```

To implement a *Students* collection, you must start by inserting a new class module and naming it **Students**. You must then declare a private *Collection* class object in the declarations section. The next step is to add the **Add** method, the **Item** method, and the **Count** property. Later, you can modify the *Session* class, adding the *Roster* property, which will be of type *Students*.

IMPLEMENTING THE ADD METHOD FOR THE STUDENTS CLASS

An implementation of the **Add** method, a public function that returns a *Student*, follows. It requires two parameters, the first and last names of the new student. The *Add* method is responsible for actually creating the new student, and adding it into the private *StudentList* collection (this is similar to the way new workbooks are added to the workbooks collection of Excel). For example,

```
Option Explicit

Private m_StudentList As New Collection

Public Function Add(newLastName As String, _
                    newFirstName As String) As Student
    Dim newStudent As Student
```

```
' First create a new Student and set its properties

Set newStudent = New Student

newStudent.FirstName = newFirstName
newStudent.LastName = newLastName

' Now add it to the collection

m_StudentList.Add newStudent

' Return the newly created student object

Set Add = newStudent

End Function
```

The most common question regarding this code concerns the last line of the *Add* function – why is it necessary to use **Set**? The reason is that you are returning an object from this function (in this case, a method, since it is public and appears in a class module). Since the function returns an object and not an "ordinary" type, it is necessary to use the *Set* keyword.

IMPLEMENTING THE ITEM METHOD FOR THE STUDENTS CLASS

The **Item** method of a collection is used to gain access to a member of a collection. It requires a parameter, the index of the item. In the *Students* implementation of the *Item* method, you can simply use the **Item** method of the private collection to return the student at the given index. In other words, you are delegating the *Item* method to the private collection declared in the declarations section of the *Students* class module.

In addition to providing an *Item* method to allow client code to iterate through the students in the *Students* collection, you may also want to provide an enumerator so that client code can use the *For Each* loop in Visual Basic. This technique is discussed in Chapter 7. If you wish, you can implement the *Item* method as a parameterized property instead, and declare it as the default property of the *Students* collection. If this is done, client code can use the expression *objStudents.Item(n)*, or the equivalent expression *objStudents(n)*. This technique is also discussed in Chapter 7.

The *Item* method can be implemented as follows:

```
Public Function Item(ByVal Index As Long) As Student
    Set Item = m_StudentList.Item(Index)
End Function
```

IMPLEMENTING THE COUNT PROPERTY FOR THE STUDENTS CLASS

The **Count** property of a collection returns the number of objects in the collection. In the *Students* implementation, you can simply use the **Count** property of the *private* collection. Note that this technique is identical to the technique used to implement the *Item* method; you are delegating the *Count* property to the private collection declared in the *Students* class module.

The *Count* property of the *Students* collection is implemented as a *Property Get* procedure. There is no *Let* procedure; thus, it is a read-only property.

```
Public Property Get Count() As Long
    Count = m_StudentList.Count
End Property
```

ADDING THE ROSTER PROPERTY TO THE SESSION OBJECT

To associate a *Roster* (list of students) with a *Session* class object, you can add a public property called *Roster*, which is of type *Students*, to the *Session* class module. Now, to add a new student, client code invokes the **Add** method of the **Students** collection, which it obtains from the **Roster** property of the **Session** object. This method also returns the newly created student object.

Client code can then add a student to a session's roster as follows:

```
Dim newStudent as Student
Set newStudent = Session1.Roster.Add "Smith", "Fred"
```

The *Roster* property of the *Session* object can be implemented as follows:

```
Private m_Roster As New Students

Public Property Get Roster() As Students
    Set Roster = m_Roster
End Property
```

FINAL STEP OF THE TRAINING CENTER APPLICATION

In the final step of the *Training Center* application, the steps that are related to creating collections are repeated to create the **Schedule** class. The *Schedule* class has a private collection used to hold *Session* objects, **Add** and **Item** methods, and a **Count** property. For example,

```
Public Function Add() As Session
    Dim newSession As Session
```

```
' Here, all we need to do is create a new
' session, add it into our private collection,
' and return it back to the caller.

Set newSession = New Session
m_SessionList.Add newSession

Set Add = newSession

End Function

Public Function Item(ByVal Index As Integer) As Session
    Set Item = m_SessionList.Item(Index)
End Function

Public Property Get Count() As Long
    Count = m_SessionList.Count
End Function
```

A Look at the Client Code

Client code for the *Training Center* application primarily consists of the user interface and little else. In the declarations section of **_frmMain_**, a *Schedule* object is declared. When the *New Session* button is clicked, it causes the execution of the code shown below, which creates a new *Session* object and receives its attributes from the user via a form called *frmAddNewSession*. For example,

```
Private Schedule As New Schedule

Private Sub cmdNewSession_Click()
    Dim newSession As Session

    ' Add another session

    Set newSession = Schedule.Add

    ' Invoke form to get properties of new session object

    Load frmAddNewSess
    frmAddNewSess.lblSessionID = newSession.SessionID
    frmAddNewSess.Show 1

    ' Copy settings from controls to properties
    ' of session object

    On Error GoTo errhandler
```

```
newSession.Number = frmAddNewSess.txtCourseNumber
newSession.Location = frmAddNewSess.txtLocation
newSession.StartDate = frmAddNewSess.txtStartDate
newSession.InstructorID = frmAddNewSess.txtInstructorID

Unload frmAddNewSession

' Add value of Summary property to list box

lstRoster.AddItem newSession.Summary

Exit Sub

errhandler:
    MsgBox Err.Description

End Sub
```

The code to add a new student follows (*lstRoster* is the name of the list box control that holds the list of sessions):

```
Private Sub cmdAddStudent_Click()
    Dim s As Session
    Dim LastName As String
    Dim FirstName As String

    ' Get student name

    Load frmAddStudent
    frmAddStudent.Show 1

    LastName = frmAddStudent.txtLastName
    FirstName = frmAddStudent.txtFirstName

    Unload frmAddStudent

    ' Set a reference to selected session
    ' and add the student to the roster


    Set s = Schedule.Item(lstRoster.ListIndex + 1)
    s.Roster.Add LastName, FirstName

End Sub
```

WHY CHOOSE CLASSES FOR THIS IMPLEMENTATION?

The concepts presented in this chapter may seem very difficult to grasp. However, with practice, it will become natural for you to use class modules. Although such an implementation is a bit more complex than a traditional approach, consider the interface, which is now separated from the implementation. In the next chapter, this separation will be taken further, by implementing an object model as an ActiveX Component. This will enable a complete separation of interface from implementation. The interface and implementation will literally run as separate components. It will also enable you to distribute the application, because the interface and implementation can run on separate hosts in your network.

Implementing an Object Model with ActiveX Components

One of the major advantages of using class modules and an object model in your application is that you can create an ActiveX Component. Doing so will provide the highest level of reusability available. For example, you can completely separate the interface from the implementation, having them execute as two separate processes or as a DLL used in-process by the ActiveX Component's client.

In this chapter, advanced concepts related to class modules are presented. If you read the previous chapter, you may experience a bit of deja-vu as you read this one. The duplication of some concepts is necessary because some of these concepts are extremely important and fundamental to creating COM objects in Visual Basic. In the first half of this chapter, I'll walk you through the steps that are generally used to create ActiveX Components, or COM servers. In the last half, I'll walk you through the creation of a partial object model that encapsulates access to a database and is implemented as an ActiveX Component.

Deploying an application using ActiveX Components also makes it possible to distribute your application across a network, resulting in a true, distributed client-server application. To do this, you'll use DCOM and perhaps MTS, but as I'll illustrate, MTS is probably best used for deploying stateless objects, the interface to your data services layer.

About ActiveX Components

The term "*ActiveX*" has little or no meaning to the serious component developer. The C and C++ programmers that have for years been creating component-based software rarely use this term, opting instead for the term "*COM server*". I prefer to think of ActiveX as a layman's term. In Visual Basic, you have a choice of creating ActiveX DLLs and ActiveX EXEs, but you should know that they are both COM servers. A COM server created as either an ActiveX DLL or ActiveX EXE is every bit as much a COM server as one created by a C++ programmer using the Active Template Library (ATL). Visual Basic COM servers match the features provided by a C++ ATL COM server almost one for one. In many cases, depending on the nature of the work performed by the server, Visual Basic COM servers are nearly as efficient as those created in C++ using ATL. But, the Visual Basic developer has far less work to do and a much shorter learning curve as well.

An ActiveX Component is what VB developers call an EXE or DLL that exposes its objects, and their properties and methods, to external code. Note that an ActiveX Component, or server, can potentially host many objects. In fact, this is typical. The *Mom-n-Pop Video Store* ActiveX Component hosts over a dozen objects. A C++ programmer using ATL would say that a COM server hosts many COM objects. It's really all the same thing.

In-Process and Out-of-Process COM Servers

ActiveX Components can be written as executables that execute as a separate process and under a separate thread as the client application. In general, an ActiveX Component written as an executable is not a standalone application. If an executable has a standalone interface and can additionally be controlled from a client application using COM, it is generally referred to as an *automation component*. Clients of automation components are referred to as *automation controllers*. Examples of automation components include *Microsoft Excel, Microsoft Outlook*, and *Microsoft Internet Explorer*. While it is entirely possible to develop both automation components and controllers in Visual Basic, they do not fit into the distributed application development methodology used by this book. The only types of executable ActiveX Components that we're interested in are ones that serve objects to clients and cannot run as standalone applications, in particular because they have no user interface. Such ActiveX Components are also known as *out-of-process servers*.

ActiveX Components can also be written as DLLs that execute under the same process and (in general) under the same thread (or threads) as the client application. Deploying an ActiveX Component as a DLL is rapidly becoming the implementation method of choice, particularly because MTS won't have them any other way. In both the object model and data services layers of the *Mom-n-Pop Video Store*, DLLs are used to implement ActiveX Components. This type of ActiveX Component is also known as an *in-process server*.

While it may seem that there are simply two types of COM servers, in-process and out-of-process, this is over-simplified. Both in-process and out-of-process servers can be written using different approaches. An out-of-process server (ActiveX EXE) can be written as single-threaded or multi-threaded, even in Visual Basic. Multi-threaded out-of-process COM servers can be auto-threaded, automatically starting a new thread for each object, or thread-pooled, assigning object method execution to one of a limited number of available threads. In addition, out-of-process servers can be single-use or multi-use. A single-use COM server serves only one client; each COM object created from a single-use COM server runs a separate copy of the server. A multi-use COM server serves multiple clients with one process running a single copy of the server. So, there are several ways to create an out-of-process server. There is a lot more information about threads later in this chapter and in Chapter 8, which includes a demonstration of the use of threads in Visual Basic COM servers.

If you will be creating an in-process COM server, you must decide if the objects it provides will be deployed under MTS. While most COM objects can run under MTS without modification, it is best if they are written specifically to run under MTS. If you're careful, you can create in-process COM servers that run either with or without MTS.

While you cannot create a multi-threaded in-process server, you must indicate what threading model you support. This is because, in general, an in-process server relies on its clients to create the threads that execute the methods of its objects.

COM servers created with Visual Basic contain all the necessary shell code and are self-registering. If your COM server is an EXE (out-of-process server), running the server will register it. If your server is an in-process server, it can be registered using the *REGSVR32* tool.

Selecting the Appropriate ActiveX Component Type

Given all the ways to create COM servers, how do you know which solution to use? While each approach has its advantages and disadvantages, you really can't go wrong using apartment-model in-process COM servers, known in VB parlance as ActiveX DLLs. This type of COM server can be deployed on the same machine and run under the same process as the client. It can also be deployed remotely, on a different machine than the client, using either a DLL surrogate or MTS. Selecting apartment-model threading ensures that only the thread that created the object can execute properties and methods of that object; this is a simple yet effective solution to synchronization problems such as race conditions. Even though Visual Basic developers do not, in general, directly create threads, threading and synchronization are issues in an in-process server. A C++ developer can use Visual Basic COM objects from a multi-threaded application, and MTS will create threads that execute properties and methods of COM objects hosted by in-process servers.

Out-of-process servers, or ActiveX EXEs, are generally considered more robust than in-process servers, simply because they run as separates processes with a separate address space. Since an in-process server runs in the same address space as the client, errant client software can accidentally overwrite data belonging to the server; this cannot happen with an out-of-process server. Out-of-process servers, as mentioned, also offer more choices on threading, and may be of interest for that reason. If you're not planning on using MTS and you want to run a COM server remotely using DCOM, the best solution is an out-of-process COM server. Although you can run an in-process COM server remotely using DCOM and a DLL surrogate, it's easier to use an out-of-process server for this type of solution, primarily because you can easily generate an installation application using the *Package and Deployment Wizard*. Using a DLL surrogate instead of MTS to remotely connect an in-process server would require a custom setup program, and would not be any more or less efficient than using a remote out-of-process server. Either way, method and property parameters must be marshaled on the client side, sent over the network, and unmarshalled on the server side; the overhead is the same.

Setting up an ActiveX Component Project

As with any Visual Basic application, it is important to set project properties appropriately. This is even more important in a VB project that defines an ActiveX Component (or COM server). Improper project settings for an ActiveX Component can result in major problems during development and maintenance. You want to be certain that the server is installed properly the first time and that revised server versions replace existing ones and do not cause existing clients to lose their references to the COM server.

Since COM servers do not run standalone (except in the case of automation servers), developers typically need a user interface project that tests the server as it is being developed. Usually this is a simple user interface program, created as a Visual Basic Standard EXE project, which is rarely considered part of a software development project's deliverables. The Visual Basic IDE provides an excellent way of setting up such a development environment; this is the project group. It is highly recommended that you set up a COM server project as a project group, containing both a Standard EXE project that contains a simple user interface that tests the COM server, and either an ActiveX DLL or ActiveX EXE project, which contains source for the COM server itself.

Project Directory Structure

To begin an ActiveX Component project, start by creating a folder to contain the user interface test project and the ActiveX Component project. It is recommended that you create two sub-folders in this folder, one for the user interface project and one for the middleware (ActiveX Component) project. I prefer to call these sub-folders *UI* and *Middleware*. For example, if I am creating a COM server called *MyServer*, I create a folder called *MyServer*, and in this folder I create two sub-folders, *MyServer\UI* and *MyServer\Middleware*. The COM server project will be saved in the sub-folder *MyServer\Middleware*, and the testing user interface project will be saved in the sub-folder *MyServer\UI*. I prefer to save the project group in the *UI* sub-folder. If you follow this approach, it will be much easier to keep track of the source code for each project, each of which, by the way, can be opened independently, even though they are also part of a project group. You must, however, pay careful attention to the proposed filenames and folder locations provided by Visual Basic when you save new modules in either project. Visual Basic does not always propose the folder you want; the proposed location for saving a module depends on where you saved the last module. Be careful that you do not save, for example, a class module belonging to the server in the folder you're using for the test user interface project.

The User Interface Test Project

After creating the project's directory structure, you can create the user interface project, the ActiveX Component project, and the project group. You should actually create the test user interface project first, since Visual Basic will, by default, use this as the startup project. You can create the ActiveX Component project first if you prefer, but you will then need to change the startup project to the user interface project after it is created. Visual Basic lets you start an ActiveX Component project even though it will not run as a standalone application; this allows you to run the component in the debugger. If you create the ActiveX Component first, and then create the user interface project, you can set the user interface project as the startup project by right-clicking on the user interface project in the project window and choosing *Set as Start Up* from the context menu.

To create the test user interface project, select *New* from the *File* menu and choose *Standard EXE* as the project type. Project properties for the test user interface project are not really important, but you should, at a minimum, give the project a meaningful name. Of course, Visual Basic provides a startup form for you in a Standard EXE project; this form should also be given a meaningful name. Be sure you're using the *Option Explicit* statement in this form to force yourself to declare variables. Even though the test user interface project is just a scratch-pad, you don't want to waste your time troubleshooting problems that never would have occurred if you had declared a variable. Once you've done all of those tasks, I recommend saving the project in your *UI* sub-folder, to establish the project's directory. Be sure that both the project file and form file are saved in the *UI* sub-folder.

The ActiveX Component Project

Next, you can create the ActiveX Component (COM server) project, which will also result in the creation of a project group. This step is accomplished by choosing *Add Project* from the *File* menu. If you are creating an in-process COM server, choose *ActiveX DLL* as the project type. For an out-of-process COM server, choose *ActiveX EXE* as the project type. When you create either an *ActiveX DLL* or *ActiveX EXE* project, Visual Basic provides an initial class module with a name of *Class1*. You can either use this class module as a starting point for the first class you plan to develop, or you can remove it by right-clicking on it in the *Project Window* and selecting *Remove Class1* (choose *No* when asked if you want to save changes to *Class1*). If you plan on using the *VB Class Builder*, which will save you a great deal of time, it's probably best that you remove the class module initially provided when you start an ActiveX Component project.

At this point, you'll have two projects contained in a project group, so there are really three major entities. There is the Standard EXE project, which will host the code for your test interface project, the ActiveX Component project, which will host the code for your COM server, and the project group, which maintains the relationship between the two projects. From now on, you'll have to be careful to work within the correct project. For example, you must be careful not to add test forms to the ActiveX Component project. You must also be careful to add class modules that define your COM objects to the ActiveX Component project, and not to the user interface project. Even though it may take some time to shift your way of thinking to using a project group, it is the best way to develop, test, and debug a COM server, especially considering the issue of client/server compatibility (discussed later in this chapter). It is not difficult to keep track of which project you're working with; Visual Basic's title bar indicates which project is active. Don't confuse the active project with the startup project; the startup project is shown in boldface type in the project window. To move from project to project within a project group, simply click on the project name in the project window, or open any module from the desired project. Keep an eye on the Visual Basic title bar for an indication of the active project, and watch the proposed folder locations when saving new modules. Mistakes can always be corrected by removing modules from the incorrect project and adding them to the correct one, using the *Windows Explorer* utility to move files to the proper folder if necessary.

ActiveX Component Project Properties

The next step is to set the ActiveX Component project's properties. This step is very important and is one that I take as soon as a start such a project. There are numerous ActiveX Component project properties that are important and must be understood, even though you'll use default responses for many of them. Complicating matters is that some properties are only relevant according to the type of ActiveX Component you create, either EXE or DLL.

ACTIVEX COMPONENT PROJECT PROPERTIES: GENERAL TAB

The *General* tab of the *Project Properties* dialog, includes several important properties. The first of these is the *Project Type*, which, for a COM server, should be *ActiveX DLL* for an in-process server or *ActiveX EXE* for an out-of-process server. This should be set automatically from the choice you indicated when you started the project; however, you can change it here. The *Startup Object* for an ActiveX Component project is, by default, *none*, but you can change it to *Sub Main* if you want to write code that is executed when your component starts up. In fact, *Sub Main* is a good place to do global initialization, but individual objects should be initialized in their *Class_Initialize* procedures. Global initialization can also be done in your top-level, or application object; in fact, this is what I prefer to do (top-level objects are discussed later in this chapter). If you will be performing initialization in the top-level object, as I do, leave the *Startup Object* option setting to *none*.

Next on the list of important project properties found on the *General* tab is the *Project Name*. This setting is especially important for an ActiveX Component project, because it is how clients will know your COM server and its type library. As a rule, COM objects will have a Programmer ID (or ProgID), named by their library name and class name, in the form *library_name.class_name*. For example, a class known as *MyClass* in the ActiveX Component project *MyServer* will have a Prog ID of *MyServer.MyClass*. The value you set for the *Project Name* becomes the root name for the ActiveX Component's project file, EXE or DLL, type library, remote server file (VBR), and others. This is why an ActiveX Component project's name should be established immediately.

Next, you should set the project's description, which also appears on the *General* tab of the *Project Properties* dialog. Whatever you place here becomes the help string associated with the component's type library, and will appear as-is in the Visual Basic references list (available by selecting *References* from the *Project* menu). By convention, COM developers should precede the description with their company name. For example, the *Mom-n-Pop Video Video Store* component uses the description *Mom-n-Pop Video DLL Release*.

Another important item on the *General* tab of the *Project Properties* dialog is the *Unattended Execution* check box. By all means, you should select this option. Once the *Unattended Execution* check box is selected,

Visual Basic will not allow you to add forms or other user interface objects to the ActiveX Component project. It's good to have this option selected so that you do not accidentally add user interface objects; they do not belong in a COM server implementing middleware. Remember that middleware does not do the presentation layer's job, and the presentation layer should not do the middleware's job. Keep the roles of the layers separate. Selecting the *Unattended Execution* option also enables additional threading options for an ActiveX EXE project, specifically the *Thread Per Object* and *Thread Pool* options, each of which are discussed briefly in this section, and in more detail later in this chapter and in Chapter 8.

The last project property on the *General* tab that you should set is the *Threading Model* option, which is available only for ActiveX DLL (in-process server) projects. In virtually every case, this should be set to *Apartment Model*. This is the same threading model used by almost all clients, and will give you the greatest amount of concurrency in addition to enabling the use of MTS to deploy your component. Exactly what this option does will be discussed later in this chapter.

The rest of the options that appear under the *General* tab do not need to concern you when starting a new COM server project, and can be changed later without adversely affecting existing clients. The *Retained In Memory* option, available only for ActiveX DLL projects, indicates that the DLL hosting the COM objects will remain loaded even when serving no objects. Such COM servers unload only when the last process using the COM server terminates. In general, you'll want to select this option, but you can turn it on later and rebuild the server without affecting client/server compatibility.

The *Thread Per Object* and *Thread Pool* options, available only for out-of-process (ActiveX EXE) projects, provide you with multi-threading options. Realistically, it is nearly impossible to predict which choice provides the best concurrency until the project is nearly completed. At that time, you can benchmark different threading options to discover the best multi-threading option to use. Changing the *Thread Per Object* and *Thread Pool* options does not affect client/server compatibility, provided you follow the guidelines presented later in this chapter.

ACTIVEX COMPONENT PROJECT PROPERTIES: MAKE TAB

Of all the properties that appear on the *Make* tab of the *Project Properties* dialog, the most crucial are those that appear in the *Version Number* frame, although they are not as crucial as they were with Visual Basic 5.0. The appropriate approach would be to increment the version number with each build that is to be released. The version number will be automatically incremented with each build if you choose the *Auto Increment* option. Previous versions of the Visual Basic setup wizard demanded that you increment the version number of an already installed application or COM server. If the version number of the application or component being installed was less than or equal to the version already installed, the new version was not copied, even if the file timestamp was later. This was done silently and without warning, although a log file created by the setup wizard would indicate that the file was not copied. Clearly, this was a source of frustration to developers installing new versions of applications and components.

This behavior changes with the new *Package and Deployment Wizard* included with Visual Basic 6.0. Setup programs created with this new utility copy new applications and components to the target system if the version numbers are the same but the file date of the source is newer than the target. If the version number of the source, as set in the *Version Number* frame on the *Make* tab of the project properties dialog, is less than the version number of the target, the setup program asks the user if the older version should replace the existing one.

Even with this new setup behavior, I recommend that you either select the *Auto Increment* option, or manually increase the version number before doing a build that will be released. It's important to keep track of software versions, so take advantage of this feature.

ACTIVEX COMPONENT PROJECT PROPERTIES: COMPONENT TAB

Most of the options that appear on the *Component* tab of the project properties dialog are not initially important, but become extremely important as you approach the time to release your COM server to presentation layer developers.

The *Start Mode* options have no effect on how your COM server is built. This option, which is only available for out-of-process servers (ActiveX EXEs), indicates how your COM server should start when it is run directly from the Visual Basic IDE. Properly written out-of-process COM servers, such as those generated by Visual Basic, shut down when all objects they have been serving are deleted. If you run the EXE of an out-of-process COM server directly, it will register itself and exit. However, when run from the Visual Basic development environment, you can instruct Visual Basic to have your COM server stay loaded while waiting for clients to create objects. This makes it very easy to troubleshoot out-of-process COM servers. You can, for example, set breakpoints in your COM server before running it. To enable this feature, you will not need to do anything, as the option *ActiveX Component* is selected as the default.

Checking the *Remote Server Files* option causes Visual Basic to build, in addition to the EXE or DLL, a separate type library (TLB) file. This file is required by developers who use early (also known as vtable) binding, even if these developers are on a machine other than the one that hosts the COM server. Checking this option also causes Visual Basic to create a registry file (VBR), which is used by the *Package and Deployment Wizard* when creating a setup program for a remote server. It is not important to check this option unless and until you are going to create a setup program to distribute the server using DCOM. If you are creating an in-process server that you will deploy remotely using MTS, the option does not need to be selected. This option is covered in more detail in Chapter 11.

The final option under the *Component* tab on the *Project Properties* dialog is the *Version Compatibility* option, and this is a very important option. During development, if you use the recommended project group approach discussed in this chapter, you should leave this option's setting at *Project Compatibility*. This option allows you to change the interfaces (classes and their properties/methods) in your COM server as much as you like without breaking the link between your COM server and the user interface test project, which is part of the same project group.

When the interfaces, and not necessarily the implementation, of your COM server is complete, you must build your COM server and change the *Version Compatibility* option to *Binary Compatibility*. This option, which uses your already built EXE or DLL as a reference, prevents you from making changes to the already published interface of your COM server.

The *Version Compatibility* option is an important and welcome feature in Visual Basic; it's an option that even C++ developers using ATL do not have. A full discussion of this option must be postponed until I've provided you with more information about how COM servers are located in the registry and how interfaces in COM should be immutable. For now, when starting a new COM server project using the recommended project group approach, you will want to leave this option set to *Project Compatibility*. Version compatibility options are discussed in greater detail later in this chapter, and in Chapter 14.

The Instancing Property of Class Modules

The *Instancing* property is valid only for class modules that appear in ActiveX Component projects, and provides the middleware developer with a powerful means of enforcing object model abstraction. At first glance, it appears to be a complex property, because it controls several attributes of a class as a whole. For one, the *Instancing* property controls the visibility of the class outside the middleware. It also controls whether or not instances of the class can be created outside the middleware. And, in addition to a few other nuances of object creation, the *Instancing* property indicates whether the class indicates an instance of a top-level, or application object, also known as a root object.

Understanding the *Instancing* property is important to a middleware developer. Possible values for this property are *Private, PublicNotCreatable, SingleUse, GlobalSingleUse, MultiUse,* and *GlobalMultiUse*. This may seem to be at lot of choices to consider, but all the choices apply only to out-of-process servers (ActiveX EXEs). For class modules in an in-process server (ActiveX DLL), the *SingleUse* and *GlobalSingleUse* choices are not appropriate. Thus, the *Instancing* property for a class module in an ActiveX DLL must be set to *Private, PublicNotCreatable, MultiUse,* or *GlobalMultiUse*.

In this chapter, I'll explain the effect that each *Instancing* property value has on class modules, but first I'll make deciding upon a selection easy for you. Starting with the assumption that you are creating an in-process server, I'll present three simple questions that you can ask yourself for each class that you are adding to your server. This will make it very simple to choose the *Instancing* property value for each class.

■ *Will this class be visible outside the middleware?* The answer to this question is typically yes, in which case you'll need to go on to the next question. However, it's perfectly valid for a middleware developer to use so-called utility, or support classes that are for the middleware's internal use only. Such class modules should have their *Instancing* property set to *Private*. If this is appropriate for the class module in question, you should set its *Instancing* property to *Private* and move on to the next class module. Otherwise, if the answer to this question is yes, go on to the next question.

■ *Are clients of the middleware allowed to create their own instances of this class?* Remember that this question applies only if you answered yes to the previous question; that is, the class will be visible outside the middleware. This question applies to the unconditional creatability, rather than simply the usability of objects of the class in question. If the answer to this question is no, you should set the *Instancing* property to *PublicNotCreatable* and move on to consider the next class module. Class modules with an *Instancing* property of *PublicNotCreatable* can be seen and used by code outside the middleware, but not created. Instances of such classes must be created by the middleware and handed back to the presentation layer, typically as a side effect of invoking one of the middleware's properties or methods. If you want to allow code outside the middleware to create instances of this class, then the answer to the question is yes, and you should go on to the next question. Note that, for in-process servers, you are down to only two possibilities, *MultiUse* and *GlobalMultiUse*. By answering only one more question, you can make the choice between these two options.

■ *Is this a top-level, or root object?* Again, this question applies only if you answered yes to both of the previous questions. Top-level objects go by many other names. Some developers call them application objects, while other developers call them root objects. Visual Basic developers call them global objects. If the class module in question is visible, creatable, and is a top-level object, you should set the *Instancing* property to *GlobalMultiUse*. Class modules that describe objects that are visible, creatable, but not global should have their *Instancing* property set to *MultiUse* (remember, in this section I'm assume that you are creating an in-process server). Instances of objects described by class modules with their *Instancing* property set to *GlobalMultiUse* are automatically created as global objects by Visual Basic client code when one of their properties is first referenced. Property procedures and methods of global objects can be referenced as though they were global functions. The middleware layer typically will have only one, if any, *GlobalMultiUse* object, especially when the middleware describes a hierarchical object model, as is the case with the *Mom-n-Pop Video Store* object model.

The other two options for the *Instancing* property, *SingleUse* and *GlobalSingleUse*, apply only to out-of-process (ActiveX EXE) COM servers. These choices are presented later in this chapter. For a complete middleware layer implemented as an in-process server, you will typically have cases of at least three of the possibilities of the *Instancing* property: *PublicNotCreatable*, *MultiUse*, and *GlobalMultiUse*. The last of these, *Private*, is not often used as an *Instancing* option, and *GlobalMultiUse* is used only for your top-level object, if you have one. Thus, most class modules in an ActiveX DLL component project will have an *Instancing* property of either *MultiUse* or *PublicNotCreatable*.

Instancing Property Reference

This section formally describes each choice for the *Instancing* property of class modules that appears in ActiveX Component projects.

Setting *Instancing* to *Private* indicates that code outside the middleware cannot access information about the class, and cannot create instances of it. Private objects can only be used within your component, and are typically used as utility classes.

PublicNotCreatable indicates that code outside the middleware can use objects of the class, but code in your component must create the object. Other applications cannot directly create these objects; they must use a property or method in your component to do so. It is perfectly valid for the middleware to pass references to such objects back to the presentation layer, which can then invoke public properties and methods on the object. Setting the *Instancing* property to *PublicNotCreatable* affects the creatability, but not the usability of the class in question.

The *MultiUse* option of the *Instancing* property indicates that the class is both public and creatable. For an in-process COM server (ActiveX DLL), this option simply indicates that the class represents an object that is visible, creatable, and not a top-level object. However, it means more than this for classes contained in an out-of-process (ActiveX EXE) COM server. In an out-of-process server, using this option indicates that only one copy of the server process is started. All applications that use the server will use the same copy of the server process; that is, only one process is started to serve all requests for this object. In out-of-process servers, this option is contraindicated by the *SingleUse* option, discussed later in this section. For in-process servers, this option is the most common one.

The *GlobalMultiUse* option of the *Instancing* property is similar to *MultiUse*, in that classes using this *Instancing* property option describe objects that are both public and creatable. This setting is used for global objects, also known as top-level, application, or root objects. In an in-process (ActiveX DLL) COM server, *GlobalMultiUse* is the only choice available for top-level objects. In out-of-process (ActiveX EXEs) COM servers, a middleware developer has two choices: *GlobalMultiUse* or *GlobalSingleUse,* the latter of which is described later in this section.

If a class module has an *Instancing* property of *GlobalMultiUse*, a global object is automatically created as an instance of the class when Visual Basic client code first references one of its properties. A global object's property procedures and methods can be used by code outside the middleware as though they were global functions. This is contrasted with non-global objects, whose property procedures and methods must be referenced via an explicit object reference.

The *SingleUse* option of the *Instancing* property also indicates that the class is both public and creatable; however, this option is only valid for out-of-process (ActiveX EXEs) COM servers. Classes created in ActiveX DLL component projects cannot use this value because it is inappropriate.

When a class module in an ActiveX EXE component project has an instancing property of *SingleUse*, it indicates that a COM server process can serve only one of these objects. Each time a new instance of such an object is created, even if it is from the same client, a new COM server process is started. Clearly, this option will require greater system resources, but may, in a distributed environment, improve response time, since a server will never be busy while another request is pending. It should be noted, however, that an out-of-process COM server is capable of being *multi-threaded*, which offers an alternative solution to improving a server's response time and concurrency. This option, along with multi-threading alternatives, will be discussed in a later section in this chapter.

The last choice for the *Instancing* property is *GlobalSingleUse.* Like the *SingleUse* option of the *Instancing* property, it is valid only for out-of-process COM servers, and indicates that a separate copy of the server should be started for each instance of the class. And, like the *GlobalMultiUse* option, it indicates that a global object is automatically created. Properties and methods of the class can be invoked as if they were global functions.

Deciding Between Multi-Use or Single-Use

Recall that both the multi-use and single-use options implicitly indicate both public and creatable. The distinction between the two options is that instances of multi-use class objects share the same copy of the ActiveX Component process. Instances of single-use class objects each have their own copy of an ActiveX Component process. This is true regardless of how many clients are creating objects. If a single client application creates multiple objects hosted in an ActiveX EXE, there will be separate copies of the server for each object.

At first, one may assume that multi-use is the only way to go. Why would you ever want multiple copies of the ActiveX Component to be running? Here is what you need to consider. For several, long-living instances of classes, having each instance of a class have its own server may improve performance, provided you have plenty of memory and processor resources. You want such instances to be long-living to avoid the overhead of starting a new process with each new instance of a class.

In general, you will want your ActiveX Components to be multi-use. However, there is a major consideration. You must be very careful in using public data declared in standard modules. Remember that this data is shared among all instances of classes. In the previous chapter, the *Training Center* application's use of global data to keep track of the last session number used is not safe if the component is deployed using MTS, or if it is deployed as a multi-use component using a thread pool. The only way it would be a safe implementation is if the component were either deployed as a mutli-use component with one thread in the thread pool, or as a single-use component. In the latter case, however, there would be a separate copy of the global data for each object, which would defeat the entire purpose. You can see that using global data in an ActiveX Component is a bad idea; you should try coming up with another solution. If the mentioned *Training Center* component is to be deployed with MTS, the last session number should be stored using the *Shared Property Manager.* The *Shared Property Manager* is discussed in Chapter 12.

Adding Event Notification to an ActiveX Component

In addition to providing properties and methods, an ActiveX Component can send notifications of events to its client, in the same way an ActiveX Control does. From the component side, sending event notification is a two-step process. The event must first be declared with the *Event* statement. This is done once, in the declarations section. The event may then be signaled with the *RaiseEvent* statement. This statement can be used anywhere in the code where appropriate. In fact, there may be several places in the code where the same event is raised.

On the container (client) side, there is also a two-step process. When an object is declared, the keyword *WithEvents* is used. The object will then appear in the *Code Window's Object* list, with the declared events appearing in the *Code Window's Proc* list. It is then easy to add event handlers. When the *WithEvents* keyword is used, the *New* keyword cannot be used. An instance of the object must be created in a separate statement. Events can have parameters; these are declared in the *Events* statement, and values are passed for the parameters in the *RaiseEvent* statement.

Using the *Training Center's Session* object presented in the previous chapter as an example, the following modifications cause the server to raise the *SessionAdded* event back to client code when a new session is added:

```
Option Explicit

Event SessionAdded()
Private m_SessionList As New Collection

Public Function Add() As Session
    Dim newSession As Session

    Set newSession = New Session
    m_SessionList.Add newSession

    Set Add = newSession

    RaiseEvent SessionAdded

End Function
```

Client code using this event may be written as follows:

```
Option Explicit

Private WithEvents Schedule As Schedule

Private Sub Schedule_SessionAdded()
    MsgBox "SessionAdded Event: New Session Added"
End Sub
```

About Inheritance and Polymorphism

Object-oriented programmers have long used inheritance and polymorphism as means for code reuse. *Inheritance* implies a derivation of one class (the derived class) from a base class (also known as the parent class). When a class is derived from an existing class, it inherits all the properties, events, and methods of the parent class. Several related classes can be derived from an existing class. This allows programmers to model the is-a-kind-of relationship that so often exists in the problem domain.

Considering the *Training Center* object model presented in the previous chapter, you may find it necessary to define a new type of session to handle customers that wish to have a course conducted at their site. An *OnSite* class object can be considered to be a kind of *Session* object. It is similar to but different from the *Session* object. The *OnSite* class object has the following characteristics: like an ordinary session, it has an instructor, a course number, and so on. Unlike an ordinary session, it is scheduled at a company rather than at a training center location. Thus, the location is a company name rather than a city. The validation rules would be different. Perhaps the billing would be different, and so on. But, for those things that are common, the derived class can reuse existing code.

Polymorphism literally means "many forms." It suggests the ability of an object to exist as one of many classes that are bound by a common base class. Using polymorphism in code, a programmer can declare an object to be of a general type, such as *Session*. At runtime, this object variable can be set to an instance of a *Session* object, or any class derived from *Session*, such as *OnSite*.

When a programmer invokes the *Property Let* procedure for the *Location* property of the *Session* object, the actual procedure that is invoked is either the one for the *Session* class, or the *OnSite* class, depending upon the actual type of the *Session* object. Note that, at the "global" level, the code does not really care about the minor differences between *Session* and *OnSite* objects.

Prior to inheritance and polymorphism, programmers dreaded the "similar but different" problem. Typically, this was handled at the global level by defining a type code in the structure describing an object. Code was dispatched to routines according to the type code. There were several problems with this (still widely used) approach. Any new types of objects required the modification of existing code, raising the possibility (or likelihood) of breaking already tested code. Global dispatching code becomes more and more complex as new types are added. Minor differences between related objects become globalized, instead of being localized, as they should be.

About Implementation and Interface Inheritance

The most widely used object-oriented programming language, C++, gives us one kind of inheritance, known as implementation inheritance. With **implementation inheritance**, a programmer declares a new class as being derived from an existing one. The new class inherits the complete implementation of the base class, and can then select certain members to override. The problem with implementation inheritance is that it is at the source code level. For example, a C++ programmer can only derive classes created with C++.

Another type of inheritance, which provides binary compatibility, is interface inheritance. With *interface inheritance*, a programmer indicates that all of the members of the base class interface will be implemented in the derived class as well. Like implementation inheritance, existing code that uses the base class can seamlessly use any class derived from it (using polymorphism). Which is better? That is subject to opinion. However, it is interesting to note that Java uses both, at the option of the programmer. Interface inheritance is implemented in Windows with COM, the Component Object Model, which is discussed in Chapter 8.

The main advantage to using interface inheritance is its binary compatibility. Using interface inheritance (and the supporting COM framework), Visual Basic programmers can derive new classes from classes created with Visual Basic, C++, Java, and others.

Using Interface Inheritance in Visual Basic

With Visual Basic, interface inheritance is indicated by using the **Implements** keyword. Don't let the keyword confuse you. You use the *Implements* keyword, but you don't get implementation inheritance; you get interface inheritance. In saying "implements," the Visual Basic programmer is really saying, "I will implement the interface of the base class in this derived class." The typical procedure for using interface inheritance in VB is to

1. Create a new class module, naming it for the derived class.
2. In the declarations section of the new class module, use the *Implements* keyword, followed by the base class name.
3. In the declarations section, declare a private object variable of the base class type (sometimes referred to as the "inner object").
4. Implement all functions of the base class. Those that are identical to the base class can be passed along via the inner object. Passing work to an inner object is referred to as "delegating to an implemented object."

Using Interface Inheritance – Step-by-Step

To use interface inheritance to provide implementation inheritance requires the use of an inner object. This object is typically declared as private in the derived class's module. The general code pattern used for interface inheritance is as follows:

```
Option Explicit
Implements base_class_name
Private inner_object_name As base_class_name
```

Using this code pattern, the following procedure is typically used in interface inheritance:

1. Add a new class module to the application. Name the module according to what you want the derived class name to be.
2. In the declarations section, use the *Implements* keyword to indicate that your class will implement the base class's interface. Additionally, declare a private instance of the base class object (the inner object).
3. In the *Class_Initialize* procedure, create an instance of *inner_object_name*.
4. In the *Object* drop-down list of the *Code Window*, select the *base_class_name*.
5. Select the first procedure from the *Proc* list to create a "stub" for that procedure.
6. Repeat the above step for each and every procedure in the *Proc* list.
7. Go back and implement each "stubbed" function. You can either delegate the work to the "inner" object (*inner_object_name*) or write a completely new implementation to replace the base class function.

For example, the following code fragment shows how you might add an *OnSite* class object that implements the *Session* interface:

```
Option Explicit
Implements Session

Private m_obj As Session

Private Sub Session_Show()
    m_obj.Show
End Sub

Private Sub Class_Initialize()
    Set m_obj = New Session
```

```
End Sub

Private Sub Session_Hide()
    m_obj.Hide
End Sub

Private Property Let Session_InstructorID(RHS As Integer)
    m_obj.InstructorID = RHS
End Property

Private Property Get Session_InstructorID() As Integer
    Session_InstructorID = m_obj.InstructorID
End Property

Private Property Get Session_Summary() As String
    Session_Summary = m_obj.Summary
End Property

   … etc …
```

Overriding Base Class Members

To override a base class member, simply provide a new implementation instead of delegating the work to the inner object. For example, we may want to change the *Summary* property of the *OnSite* class so that it differs slightly from the *Summary* property of the *Session* class (the base class). In the following example, the *Summary* property for *OnSite* adds the string *"Onsite @ "* to the front of the *Location* property to create a summary string for the *OnSite* session.

```
Private Property Get Session_Summary() As String
    Dim s As String

    ' Create a "summary" string of this Onsite session

    s = Format(m_obj.SessionID, "##: ")
    s = s & Format(m_obj.StartDate, "Short Date")
    s = s & " " & Format(m_obj.Number, "(####) ")
    s = s & m_obj.Title & " " & _
            "(Onsite @ " & m_obj.Location & ")"

    Session_Summary = s

End Property
```

An ActiveX Component Object Model

In this half of the chapter, I'll use the steps presented earlier to illustrate how to create a partial object model that encapsulates the *NorthWind Traders* business, using the *NorthWind Traders* database that is distributed with Visual Basic.

To build an object model that can be reused between multiple applications, you must create an ActiveX Component. This can be either an ActiveX DLL or an ActiveX EXE. Of the two, ActiveX DLLs are preferred for their performance advantages, size, and deployment options. The only type of ActiveX Component you can deploy in MTS is an ActiveX DLL. The terminology is confusing at first. An ActiveX Component is not an object. Rather, it is either an EXE or a DLL that hosts one or more objects. Each object in an ActiveX Component is implemented by a class module.

About User Interface Test Programs

Since ActiveX Components that implement object models do not run standalone, testing them is problematic. You must have some sort of user interface project, preferably one that is grouped with the ActiveX Component, that is used to test the object model. The temptation is for a middleware developer to create "scratch" user interface test programs that often test only one or two new features, and then discard the test program. This is discouraged.

It is strongly recommended that the middleware development team create and maintain a simple, yet elegant, user interface that fully tests the middleware. This test program can serve as a permanent test program, and can be used to discover deficiencies in the middleware. If the middleware development team cannot create a simple interface, the presentation layer development team cannot create a complex, fancy one. The user interface test program can also serve as a check for compatibility with previous releases of the middleware. When a new feature is added, or a bug is corrected, the user interface test program can be used to validate the middleware, before a new version is released to the presentation layer development team. The user interface test program can also help to discover where the bugs are. If a problem discovered by the presentation layer development team cannot be reproduced in the user interface test program, the problem probably lies in the developing presentation layer code.

Overview of Demo Object Model

In the remainder of this chapter, I'll walk you through an implementation of a simple object model that encapsulates a portion of the *NorthWind Traders* database. Implementing this object model is simple enough for you to do as you read this book; however, a completed version of the walkthrough is located in the project *NWind.VBG,* in folder *VB6Adv\Demos\ ObjectModel-\UI.* This walkthrough will illustrate how to implement a top-level object, a simple object, and a collection.

ABOUT PROJECT GROUPS

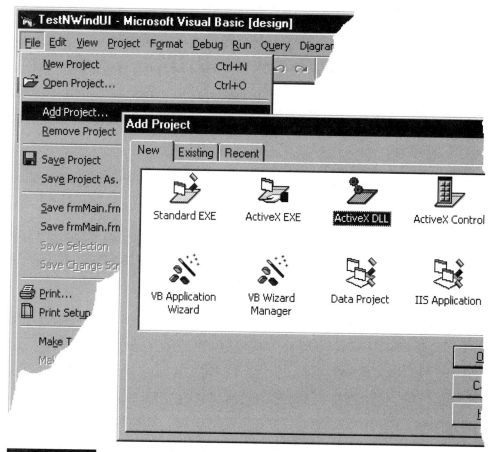

FIGURE 7-1 After creating the user interface project (a Standard EXE), select *Add Project* from the *File* menu and choose *ActiveX DLL* as the project type. This creates a new ActiveX DLL project, and also creates a project group.

Since you cannot run an ActiveX DLL by itself, you'll need a user interface project to test it. The best way to do this is to use project groups. In a nutshell, you'll start by creating a Standard EXE project (for the user interface test project), then you'll add a project of type *ActiveX DLL*. Adding a project to a project creates a project group. Create the user interface project by starting Visual Basic and selecting *Standard EXE* as the project type. Once the user interface project is created, select *Add Project* from the *File* menu and choose *ActiveX DLL* (see Figure 7-1)

You have now created a project group. You can open each project individually, or open them both together by opening the project group. Pay close attention to which project is active – the active project is indicated in the Visual Basic title bar. The project that appears in **bold** in the *Project Explorer Window* is the startup project, and not necessarily the active project.

EXAMPLE: ACTIVEX DLL PROJECT PROPERTIES – GENERAL

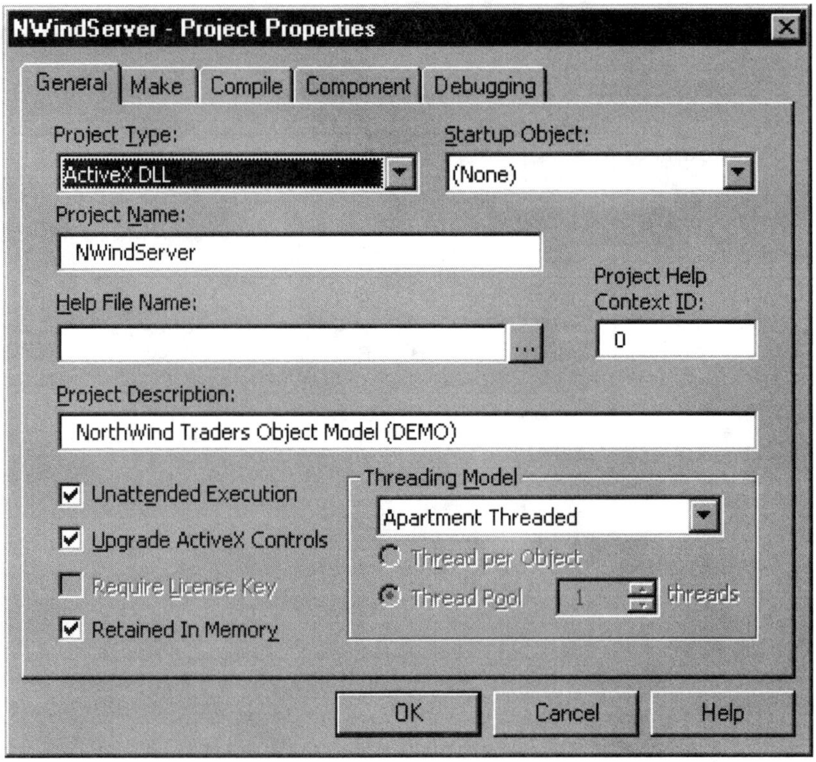

FIGURE 7-2 Project properties are important for ActiveX Component projects, since they affect how your component will be published to the world.

Under the *General* tab of the *Project Properties* dialog for the *ActiveX DLL* project (see Figure 7-2), there are a few important settings you should make. The *Project Name* is important and should be set to something meaningful. This will be used to name your server. Using *NWindServer*, as I did in my example, the objects will be known as *NWindServer.Categories, NWindServer.Category*, and so on.

The *Project Description* will appear in the Visual Basic *References* dialog when you later build and register the ActiveX Component.

Check the *Unattended Execution* checkbox. This prevents you from adding forms to your application. Let the presentation layer do the user interface stuff. If you wish, you can check the *Retained In Memory* checkbox (this is recommended), as I did in my example. This prevents your server from being unloaded when it is not serving objects. The server DLL will instead unload when the client exits.

You should keep the default *Threading Model* of *Apartment-Threaded*. This will identify your component as being safe to be used by multi-threaded clients. In the apartment-threaded model, also known as the single-threaded apartment model, only the thread that created an object can invoke properties and methods on the object. Other instances of objects created by other threads can concurrently execute methods on their objects. Even if the client code uses a different threading model, such as the multi-threaded apartment model, COM will ensure that access to methods is done in a thread-safe manner, serializing calls to objects if necessary using a queue attached to a hidden window created by COM for your server. Avoid the use of global data (public variables declared in standard modules) when using this option. Using the apartment-threaded model is also recommended for components that will be deployed with MTS.

EXAMPLE: ACTIVEX DLL PROJECT PROPERTIES – COMPONENT

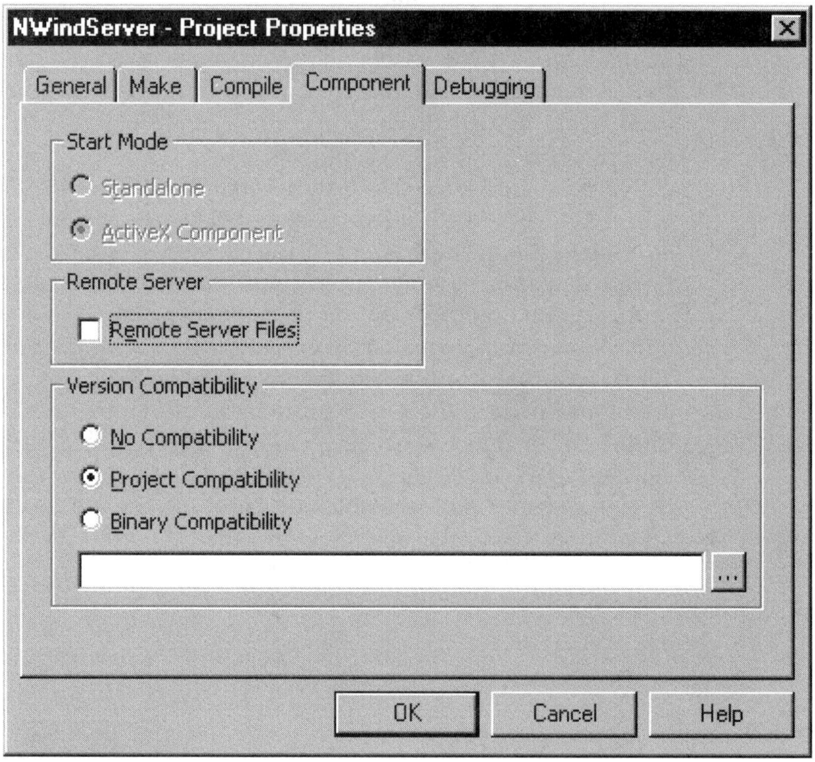

FIGURE 7-3   Leave the default settings under the *Component tab* for now.

Under the *Component* tab of the *Project Properties* dialog, there are no changes to make yet, but I'll discuss these options now and revisit them later (see Figure 7-3). The *Remote Server Files* check box is used for when you want Visual Basic to create a separate type library, or when you need to generate a registry file for distributing ActiveX Components with DCOM. Checking this box is not necessary if you plan to distribute the component locally (with the UI), or remotely using MTS. The *Version Compatibility* option should, for now, be set to *Project Compatibility*. This allows the developer to make any changes to the ActiveX Component. Later, when it is time to build and release the ActiveX Component, you must switch to *Binary Compatibility*. This will cause Visual Basic to display a warning if you make a change that will affect existing client applications (which, remember, are built separately from the ActiveX Component). Refer to Chapter 14 for more information on the version compatibility options.

ACTIVEX DLL PROJECT PROPERTIES – DEBUGGING

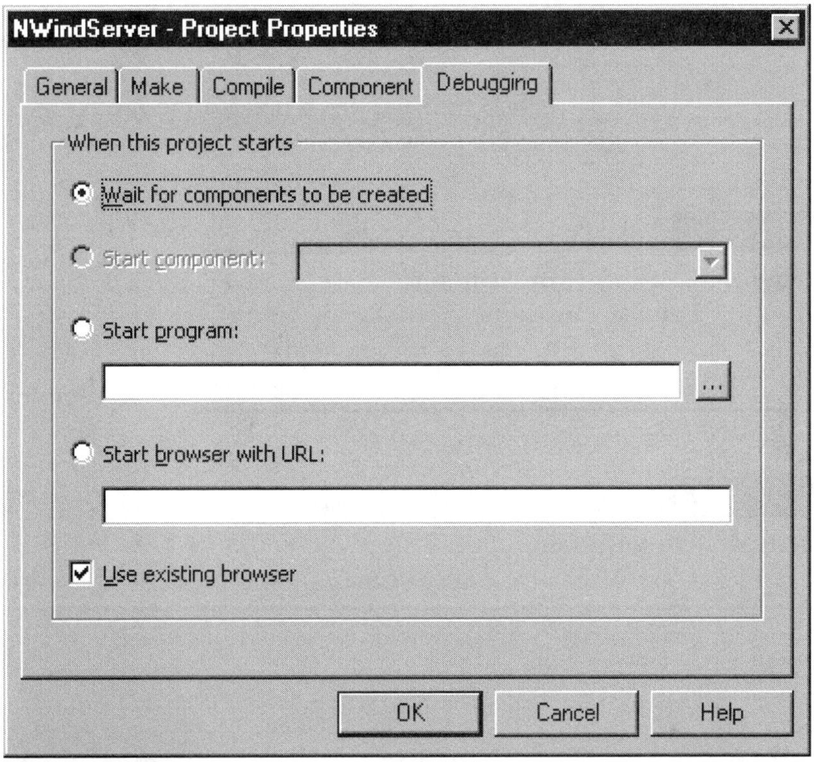

FIGURE 7-4   The *Debugging* tab contains options related to testing and debugging an ActiveX Component.

Under the *Debugging* tab of the *Project Properties* dialog (see Figure 7-4), there are some choices on starting the ActiveX Component. The default selection is *Wait for components to be created*. Using this option, you can set breakpoints in the ActiveX Component and run it under Visual Basic. You can then switch to another application that uses the ActiveX Component and do debugging. You can also select *Start program* and specify a user interface program that you will use for debugging purposes. Finally, you can choose to start the browser and specify a URL. This is useful for debugging components that you are driving from HTML on a Web page.

The settings on this tab are discussed in greater detail in Chapter 14, which focuses on the maintenance of client/server applications, including topics related to troubleshooting software problems in COM servers created with Visual Basic.

Implementing the Category Object

I'll start by implementing a *Category* object that will encapsulate the data contained in a row from the *Categories* table of the *Northwind Traders* database. The *Category* class will have three properties: *ID, Name,* and *Description* (see Table 7-1). The *ID* property will be a read-only property. The class will also have an *Update* method, which updates the related record in the database, changing the *Name*, the *Description*, or *both* (see Table 7-2).

TABLE 7-1	Properties of the Category Object	
Name	**Type**	**Description**
ID	Long	Returns category ID.
Name	String	Returns/sets category name.
Description	String	Returns/sets category description.

TABLE 7-2	Methods of the Category Object
Method	**Description**
Update	Updates record in *Categories* table, changing the record matching the object's ID.

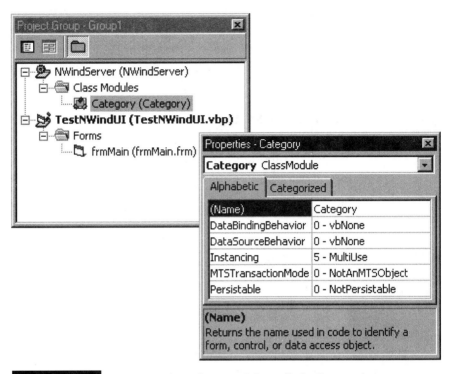

FIGURE 7-5 You get a free class module, called *Class1*, when you start an ActiveX DLL project. You should change the (*Name*) property to *Category*.

In a new ActiveX Component project, Visual Basic gets you started with a class module called *Class1*. You should change the (*Name*) property of this class module to *Category* (see Figure 7-5). This will be the first object created.

In this walkthrough, I will eventually implement a *Categories* collection that will have an *Add* method that can be used to add a *Category* object to the *Categories* collection. Internally, this will insert a new record into the *Categories* table. A client should be able to create *Category* class objects to *Add* them to the *Categories* collection. It is therefore concluded that the *Category* class should have an *Instancing* property of *MultiUse* (this is the default). Ultimately, for example, client code may be written as follows:

```
Dim C As New Category
C.Name = "Books"
C.Description = "Things you Read"
Categories.Add C
```

To create the *Category* class:

1. In the *Project Explorer* window, select the module *Class1*.
2. In the *Properties* window, change the name of the *Class1* module to *Category*.

ADDING THE NAME PROPERTY TO THE CATEGORY CLASS

I'll use *Property Let* and *Property Get* procedures to implement the *Name* property of the *Category* class. As discussed in the previous chapter, this is the preferred technique for implementing properties. You can also implement properties using public variables declared in the class module, but doing so gives you no control over what values can be assigned to the property. In addition, an implementation of properties using public variables does not give you the opportunity to execute side effects related to changes in the property value.

In the *Property Let* procedure, you can trim a value to make sure that it contains no leading or trailing blanks. Add the following code to the *Category* class module to implement the *Name* property.

```
Option Explicit
Private mvarName As String

Public Property Let Name(strName As String)
    mvarName = Trim(strName)
End Property

Public Property Get Name() As String
    Name = mvarName
End Property
```

The Class Builder Utility

The Visual Basic *Class Builder Utility* is an add-in that can perform all the tedious steps involved in creating classes and adding properties, events, and methods to a class. Since the *Class Builder Utility* is an add-in, it is invoked from the *Add-Ins* menu. If the utility is not shown in your *Add-Ins* menu, you must manually add it using the following procedure (note that this procedure only has to be performed once):

1. First, verify that the *Class Builder Utility* is not already included in the *Add-Ins* menu. If it is, you do not need to proceed.
2. From the *Add-Ins* menu, select *Add-In Manager* (see Figure 7-6).
3. Select *VB 6 Class Builder Utility* from the list of *Available Add-Ins.*
4. In the *Load Behavior* frame, check *Loaded/Unloaded* and *Load on Startup.*
5. Click *OK* to dismiss the *Add-In Manager* dialog.
6. Verify that the *Class Builder Utility* appears in the *Add-Ins* menu.

When you use the *Class Builder Utility* to add a property, it will create a private variable to hold the property, and create stock *Property Let* and *Get* procedures that access the private variable.

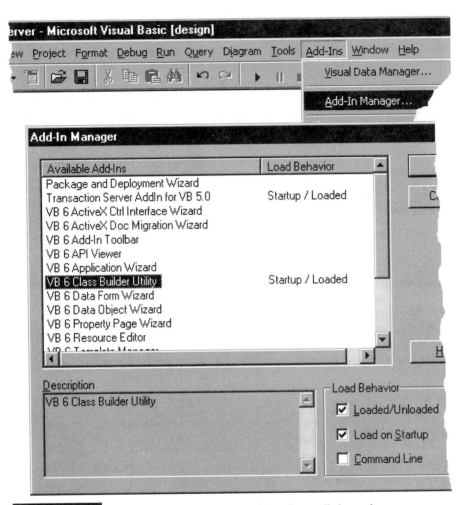

FIGURE 7-6 The *Class Builder Utility* will perform all the tedious steps involved in adding properties, methods, and events to a class.

USING THE CLASS BUILDER UTILITY

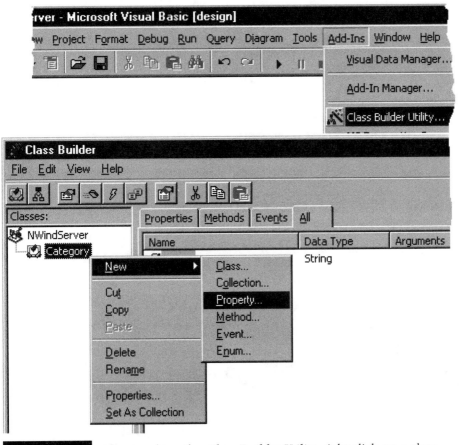

FIGURE 7-7 After invoking the *Class Builder Utility*, right-click on a class and select *New/Property* to add a property to the class.

The *Class Builder Utility* discovers your project's class modules and displays them in its left pane. The right pane shows a list of properties, methods, and events for the selected class (see Figure 7-7). To add a new property, right-click on the target class and select *New/Property*. This will display the *Property Builder* dialog (see Figure 7-8). In the *Property Builder* dialog, you indicate the name and type of the property. You can also indicate whether you want the property implemented as a *Public Property* (the default), *Friend* (more on these later), or *Public Variable* (not recommended). To implement a read-only property, you must manually delete the generated *Property Let* procedure.

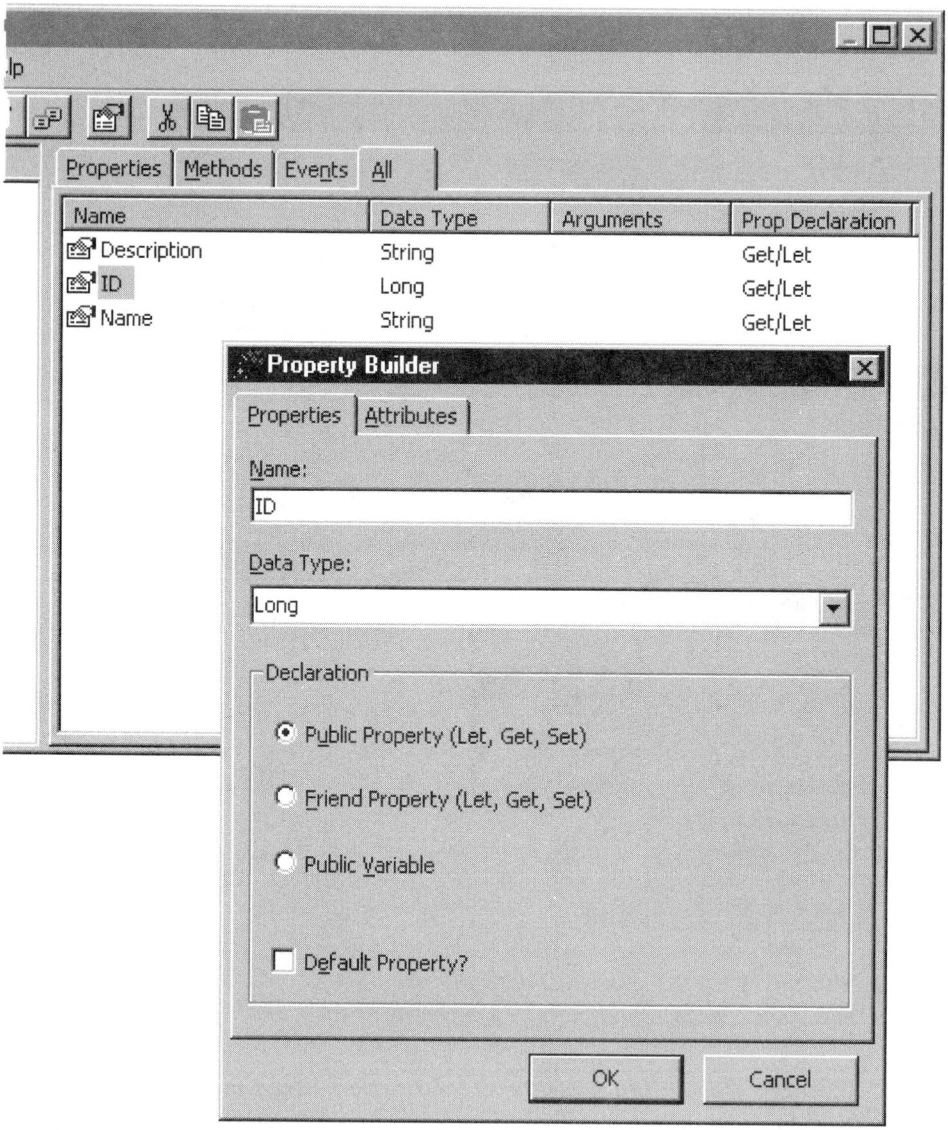

FIGURE 7-8   Using the *Class Builder Utility*, add the *Description* and *ID* properties.

To use the *Class Builder Utility* to add the *Description* and *ID* proper-ties to the *Category* class:

1. In the left pane of the *Class Builder Utility*, right-click on *Category* and select *New/Property*.

2. In the resulting *Property Builder* dialog, enter the name *Description*.

3. Choose *Public Property* for the *Declaration*.

4. Click *OK* to dismiss the *Property Builder* dialog.

5. Repeat the above steps to add the *ID* property, which is of type *Long*.

6. Before exiting the *Class Builder Utility*, select *Update Project* from the *Class Builder Utility's File* menu.

EXPLORING CLASS BUILDER-GENERATED CODE

Shown below is the *Category* class module code after running the *Class Builder Utility*. Code in **bold** was added by the utility.

```
Option Explicit
Private mvarName As String
'local variable(s) to hold property value(s)
Private mvarDescription As String 'local copy
Private mvarID As Long 'local copy
Public Property Let ID(ByVal vData As Long)
'used when assigning value to property, on the
'left side of assignment.
'Syntax: X.ID = 5
    mvarID = vData
End Property

Public Property Get ID() As Long
'used when retrieving value of property, on
'right side of assignment.
'Syntax: Debug.Print X.ID
    ID = mvarID
End Property

    Public Property Let Description(ByVal vData As String)
    'used when assigning value to property, on the
    'left side of assignment.
'Syntax: X.Description = 5
    mvarDescription = vData
End Property

Public Property Get Description() As String
```

```
'used when retrieving value of property, on
'right side of assignment.
'Syntax: Debug.Print X.Description
    Description = mvarDescription
End Property


Public Property Let Name(strName As String)
    mvarName = Trim(strName)
End Property


Public Property Get Name() As String
    Name = mvarName
End Property
```

MODIFYING CLASS BUILDER-GENERATED CODE

The *Class Builder Utility* is a bit excessive in its documentation. You may wish to delete some of the *Class Builder*-generated comments from the code. Also, you must delete any *Property Let* procedures for properties that you want to be read-only. You can also add code to execute any side effects from setting properties, and code to validate property values.

Show below is the result of modifying the *Class Builder*-generated code from the previous activity. Note that I have deleted the *Property Let* procedure for the *ID* property, and have used the *Trim* function to remove leading or trailing blanks from the new value of the *Description* property.

```
Option Explicit

Private mvarName As String
Private mvarDescription As String 'local copy
Private mvarID As Long 'local copy

Public Property Get ID() As Long
    ID = mvarID
End Property


Public Property Let Description(ByVal vData As String)
    mvarDescription = Trim(vData)
End Property


Public Property Get Description() As String
    Description = mvarDescription
End Property


Public Property Let Name(strName As String)
    mvarName = Trim(strName)
```

```
End Property
Public Property Get Name() As String
    Name = mvarName
End Property
```

Friend Procedures

Since there is no longer a *Property Let* procedure to set the *ID* property of the *Category* object, it is necessary to provide some other way of setting the property. I don't want code in the presentation layer to be able to set the *ID* property. This is because the database automatically generates the *CategoryID* field when a new record is added to the *Categories* table. In addition, the field is read-only in the database. However, I do want code in the middleware to be able to set the property. This can be done by creating a *Friend Sub* procedure to set the internal variable that holds the value of the property.

A procedure or function with *Friend* scope can be accessed by code in any module in the project that contains the ActiveX Component. Outside the project, such as in the presentation layer, the procedure or function cannot be accessed. In the following example, I add a *Friend Sub* called *SetID* to the *Category* class module:

```
Option Explicit

Private mvarName As String
Private mvarDescription As String 'local copy
Private mvarID As Long 'local copy

Friend Sub SetID(nID As Long)
    mvarID = nID
End Sub

Public Property Get ID() As Long
    ID = mvarID
End Property
```

Stubbing Methods

Stubbing a property or method is an excellent rapid application development (RAD) technique that enables you to release partially completed middleware to the presentation layer development team. For example, you can stub the implementation of the *Update* method. It cannot be implemented yet, as there is no *Connection* object to get to the *NorthWind Traders* database.

Recall that a method is simply a public sub or function declared in a class module. Following is an example of stubbing the *Update* method. This code can be either added manually or by using the *Class Builder Utility*.

```
Public Sub Update()
    ' Stubbed - Implementation To Be Supplied
End Sub
```

Collections Revisited

If you are not familiar with collections, or the Visual Basic *Collection* class, you should review the previous chapter. In the sections that follow, I will present some advanced concepts related to the design and implementation of collections. The sections presume you are familiar with the concepts related to collections presented in the previous chapter.

Objects that Participate in Collection Implementation

At a minimum, there are typically three classes of objects that participate in the implementation of a collection. First, there is the **item** class. This is the class of object that is contained in the collection. In our example, the item class is the **Category** class. Second, there is the **collection** class itself. This is the class of object that contains zero or more item class objects. In our example, the collection class is the **Categories** class. Finally, there is the **root** or **containing** class. This is the class of object that contains the collection class, which is typically exposed by a property named after the collection class. In my example, the root class is the **NorthWind** class, which will be our top-level object. I will eventually implement a property called *Categories*, which is of type *Categories*, and which returns a *Categories* object.

Types of Collections

Not all collections are the same. Collections can be static or dynamic and can be built early or late. They can also be refreshed each time they are accessed, to provide code in the presentation layer with the most up-to-date data from the underlying database records.

A static collection does not have the *Add* and *Remove* methods. No methods are provided for code in the presentation layer to add or remove items. A *dynamic* collection has *Add* and (optionally) *Remove* methods, to provide code in the presentation layer with the means to add and remove items from the collection. If the collection represents items stored in a database, the *Add* method typically inserts a row into the database, while the *Remove* method typically deletes a record from the database.

Both static and dynamic collections can be built **late**. This is also known as building a collection by procrastination. A late collection is built when the exposing property of the root class is accessed for the first time.

Collections can also be built **early**. Such collections are built when the root class is created, as part of the initialization of the object. These collections are fully populated before code in the presentation layer "hits" the collection. In general, you should avoid early collections. Code in the presentation layer may create the root object without ever hitting the collection, in which case the database is accessed unnecessarily.

Both early and late static and dynamic collections can also be refreshed when accessed. If the underlying data in the database is volatile, this may be the desired implementation. Each time a refreshed collection is accessed by code in the presentation layer, the old collection is discarded and a new collection is built, using the latest information in the database. It requires only a few minor code adjustments to move from one type of collection to another.

In general, you should make your collections *enumerable*, which permits use of the *For Each* loop in Visual Basic. I'll show how this is done shortly. In this example, I will start by implementing the *Categories* collection as a non-refreshed static collection built by procrastination. I will then make small code changes to implement the *Categories* collection as a refreshed static collection. Later, after creating an *Add* method for the *Categories* collection, it will become a refreshed dynamic collection.

The Categories Collection

The *Categories* collection will be an enumerable collection of *Category* class objects. In the first pass at its implementation, there will be no *Add* or *Remove* methods. It will therefore initially be a static collection. The *Categories* collection will have a *Count* property and an *Item* method. It will also have a *Find* method, which returns the *Category* object with the given *Category ID*. Properties of the *Categories* collection are listed in Table 7-3. Methods of the *Categories* collection are listed in Table 7-4.

TABLE 7-3	Properties of the Categories Collection

Property	Type	Description
Count	Long	Returns number of *Category* objects in the collection.

TABLE 7-4	Methods of the Categories Collection

Method	Description
Item (Index As Integer) As Category	Returns Category object in Categories collection at the given index.
Find (ID As Long) As Category	Returns Category object that matches given Category ID from the database.

ADDING THE CATEGORIES COLLECTION CLASS

To create the *Categories* class:

1. Make sure the active project is the *NWindServer* project. You can verify this by checking that *NWindServer* appears in the Visual Basic title bar. If necessary, click on *NWindServer* in the *Project Explorer* window. Remember, the project shown in bold is the startup project, which is not necessarily the active project.

2. From the *Project* menu, select *Add Class Module*. In the resulting dialog, from the *New* tab, select *Class Module* (see Figure 7-9).

3. Set the *Name* property of the new class module to *Properties*.

4. To prevent the creation of *Categories* class objects in the presentation layer, set the *Instancing* property to *PublicNotCreatable*.

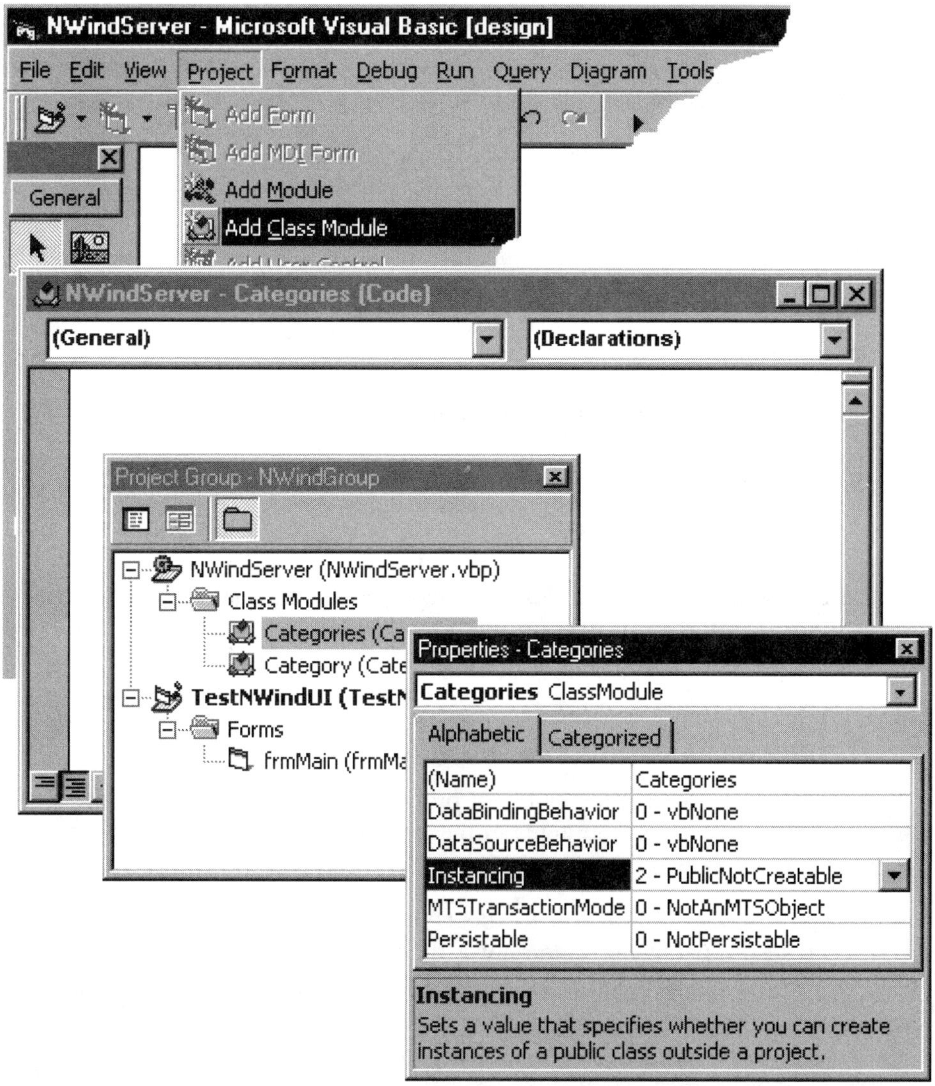

FIGURE 7-9 A new class is added to the project, and renamed *Categories*. The *Instancing* property is set to *PublicNotCreatable*.

IMPLEMENTING THE CATEGORIES COLLECTION CLASS

A collection is usually implemented by using a Visual Basic *Collection* object to hold the items of the collection. Since programmers can insert any object into a Visual Basic *Collection* object, you should give your *Collection* object private scope. You must then implement *Item, Count,* (and possibly) *Add* and *Remove* properties and methods that delegate to the private *Collection* object.

Sample code follows. Remember that we are not yet implementing *Add* and *Remove* methods, as the collection will initially be static.

```
Option Explicit

Private mvarCategories As Collection

Public Property Get Count() As Long
    Count = mvarCategories.Count
End Property

Public Function Item(Index As Integer) As Category
    Set Item = mvarCategories.Item(Index)
End Function
```

Making a Collection Enumerable

When a collection is enumerable, a programmer can use the *For Each* loop to enumerate through the items in the collection. A collection is made enumerable by following this procedure:

1. Add a *Public* function to the collection class called *NewEnum* that takes no parameters and returns the type *IUnknown.*

2. Set the return value of the function to the *_NewEnum* method of your internal collection object. You must use brackets around *_NewEnum* since it is not a valid Visual Basic name.

3. Next, you must explicitly assign a *Dispatch ID* to the *NewEnum* function and make it a hidden method.

4. Set the *Dispatch ID* by selecting *Procedure Attributes* from the *Tools* menu (see Figure 7-10).

5. In the resulting *Procedure Attributes* dialog, select the *NewEnum* procedure.

6. Click the *Advanced* button.

7. Enter −4 for the *Procedure ID.*

8. Check *Hidden* in the *Attributes* frame.

The *NewEnum* function is a standard automation method. Like all standard automation methods, it has a known dispatch ID, which is negative. *NewEnum's* dispatch ID happens to be –4. If an object represents a collection that can be enumerated, it must return a pointer to a new object when its *NewEnum* method is invoked. The object created and returned by *NewEnum* is known as an enumeration object; it must implement the *IEnumVariant* COM interface. The *IEnumVariant* interface has methods for iterating through a collection, such as *Next, Skip, Reset,* and *Clone.*

Since the methods in the *IEnumVariant* interface use data types that are not supported in Visual Basic, you cannot use interface inheritance to implement the interface. However, you can delegate the enumeration to a standard Visual Basic *Collection* object, which is exactly what you are doing when you follow the above procedure.

EXAMPLE: MAKING THE CATEGORIES COLLECTION ENUMERABLE

| **FIGURE 7-10** | An important step in making a collection enumerable is to set its *Procedure ID* (also known as dispatch ID) to –4. You should also hide the member. |

The following code is added to the *Categories* class module. Note that you must also set the *Procedure ID* to –4, as described in the previous section.

```
Public Function NewEnum() As IUnknown
    Set NewEnum = mvarCategories.[_NewEnum]
End Function
```

Initializing a Collection

When a new object of a class is created, the *Class_Initialize* procedure is invoked. This procedure is the appropriate location to place code that initializes the object. For the initialization of the *Categories* collection, I will read all the categories from the database, make *Category* objects out of them, and then add them to the private collection.

Note that you must insert a reference to the *Microsoft ActiveX Data Objects* type library to use the code shown below. Be sure to add this reference to the *ActiveX DLL* project. Note also that you must create the *OLE_DB_NWIND_JET* DSN if you have not already done so. If you have not created this DSN, refer to Chapter 5, which discusses *Database Access with ADO*.

Code to initialize the *Categories* collection is as follows:

```
Private Sub Class_Initialize()
    Dim objRS As New Recordset
    Dim objCat As Category

    Set mvarCategories = New Collection

    objRS.Open "Select * From Categories", _
            "OLE_DB_NWIND_JET", adOpenStatic, _
            adLockReadOnly, adCmdText

    Do While Not objRS.EOF
        Set objCat = New Category
        objCat.SetID objRS!CategoryID
        objCat.Description = objRS!Description
        objCat.Name = objRS!CategoryName
        mvarCategories.Add objCat
        objRS.MoveNext
    Loop

    objRS.Close

End Sub
```

Creating a Top-Level Object

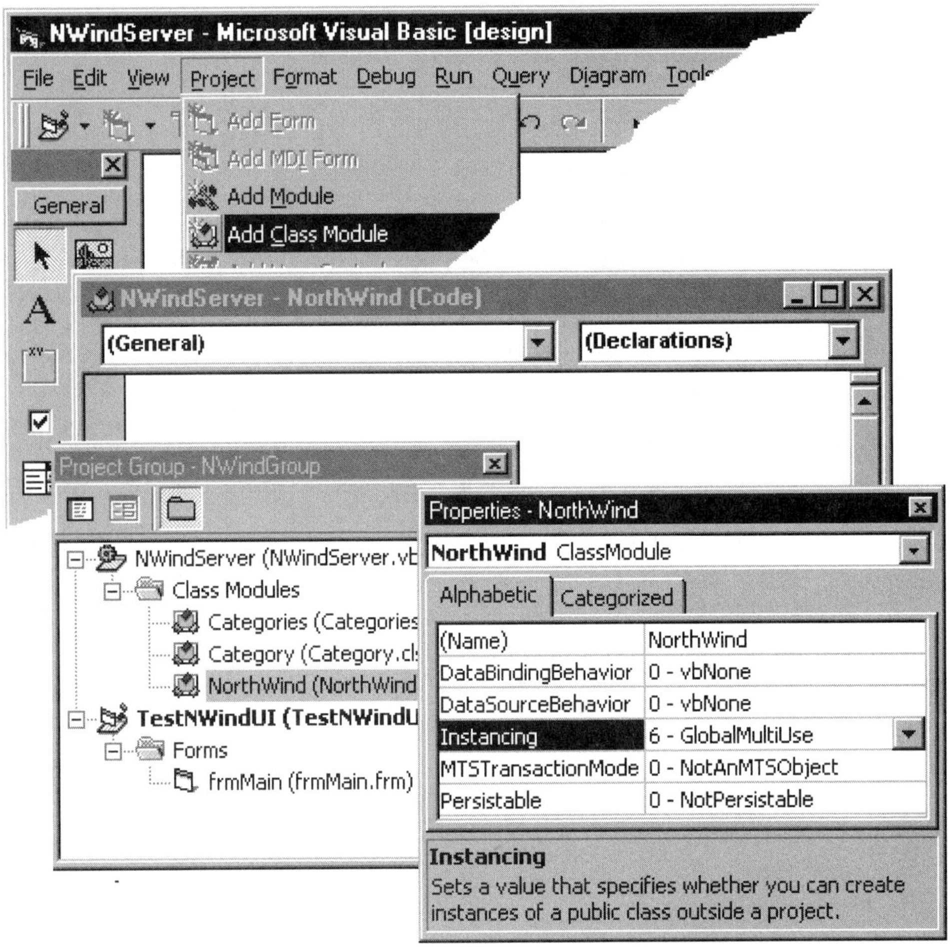

FIGURE 7-11   To create the *NorthWind* top-level object, add a new class module to the ActiveX DLL project, name it *NorthWind*, and set its *Instancing* property to *GlobalMultiUse*.

The properties and methods of a top-level, or root object can be accessed as though they were global variables and global procedures. For example, if the *NorthWind* class is a top-level object and has a property called *Categories*, code in the presentation layer can reference *Categories* as *Categories* instead of using the expression *NorthWind.Categories*.

Top-level objects are also known as global or application objects. To make a class a top-level object, set its *Instancing* property to *GlobalMultiUse*.

To implement the *NorthWind* top-level object, add a new class module to the ActiveX DLL, name the class *NorthWind*, and set its *Instancing* property to *GlobalMultiUse* (see Figure 7-11).

Implementing the NorthWind Categories Property

To implement the *Categories* property of the *NorthWind* class, add a *Property Get* procedure called *Categories* with a return type of *Categories*. If you are not refreshing the collection with each "hit," you must also declare a private variable in the declarations section of the *NorthWind* class module. This private variable must be of type *Categories*. If the collection is to be built early, you should create the collection in the *NorthWind* class's *Class_Initialize*. If the collection is to be built late, you should create the collection in the *Categories Property Get* procedure. If you are not refreshing the collection with each hit, you should check to see if the private variable is *Nothing*. If it is *Nothing*, create the collection. Otherwise, return a reference to the already created collection.

For example, the following code implements the *Categories* collection using late creation without refreshing:

```
Option Explicit

Private mvarCategories As Categories

Public Property Get Categories() As Categories
    If mvarCategories Is Nothing Then
        Set mvarCategories = New Categories
    End If
    Set Categories = mvarCategories
End Property
```

The following code implements the *Categories* collection using late creation with refreshing:

```
Option Explicit

Public Property Get Categories() As Categories
    Set Categories = New Categories
End Property
```

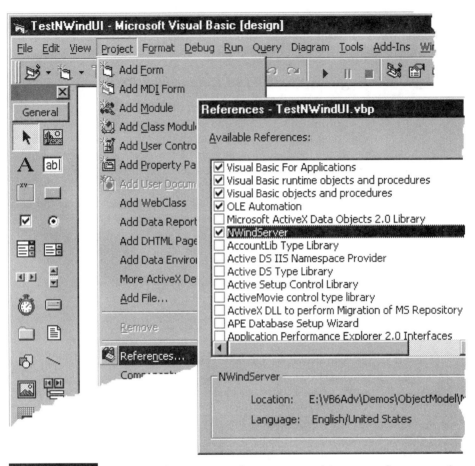

FIGURE 7-12   Switch to the *User Interface Project* and insert a reference to the ActiveX Component.

Setting a Reference to the ActiveX Component

To test the object model, you'll need to switch to the *Test User Interface* project and insert a reference to the object model library (see Figure 7-12). Note that ActiveX Components that are part of a project group show up in the *References* dialog with their project name, and not their description. When you build an ActiveX Component, a DLL is created, and the component's type library is registered using their description you gave in the *Project Properties* dialog.

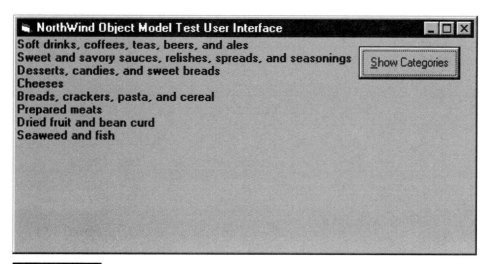

FIGURE 7-13   A simple user interface can be written that displays the descriptions of all the categories in the *Categories* collection.

Implementing a Simple Test User Interface

You can now write a simple user interface test program that lists all the descriptions of the categories in the *Categories* collection (see Figure 7-13). For example, the following code can be added to a command button (*cmdShow*) click event to print the list of categories on the form:

```
Option Explicit

Private Sub cmdShow_Click()
     Dim C As Category
     Me.Cls
     For Each C In Categories
         Me.Print C.Description
     Next
End Sub
```

Using an Enumeration for the Northwind Error Codes

Instead of "hard-coding" error code numbers (and expecting client code to do the same), you can define error codes using an enumeration in your class module. Be sure to make the enumeration public. The best place to define the enumeration is in the declarations section of your top-level object.

For example, the following enumeration may be defined in the declarations section of the *NorthWind* object:

```
Public Enum nwErrors
    nweNoSuchCategory = vbObjectError + 600
    nweCannotAddCategory = vbObjectError + 610
    nweNoSuchProduct = vbObjectError + 620
End Enum
```

Adding the Find Method to the Categories Class

To implement the *Find* method of the *Categories* class, you must create a public function in the *Categories* class module. This method can generate an *SQL Select* statement to find the category with the matching category ID. Sample code follows. Note that if the category cannot be located, the function returns *Nothing* and raises an error.

```
Public Function Find(ID As Long) As Category
    Dim strSQL As String
    Dim strID As String
    Dim objCat As Category
    Dim objRS As New Recordset

    strID = Str(ID)
    strSQL = "Select * From Categories " & _
            " Where CategoryID = " & strID

    objRS.Open strSQL, _
            "OLE_DB_NWIND_JET", adOpenStatic, _
            adLockReadOnly, adCmdText

    If objRS.BOF And objRS.EOF Then
        objRS.Close
        Set Find = Nothing
        Err.Raise nweNoSuchCategory, _
                "NWindServer.Categories", _
                "No category has an ID of " & strID
    Else
        Set objCat = New Category
```

```
        objCat.SetID objRS!CategoryID
        objCat.Description = objRS!Description
        objCat.Name = objRS!CategoryName
    End If

    objRS.Close
    Set Find = objCat


End Function
```

TESTING THE FIND METHOD

Code that tests the *Find* method follows; the sample user interface is shown in Figure 7-14. Note the use of error handling. The code checks for the error raised by the class module. Be sure to set the *Error Trapping* option to *Break on Unhandled Errors*. This option is found on the *General* tab of the *Project Properties* dialog, and is discussed in further detail in Chapter 14, which focuses on maintenance of client/server applications.

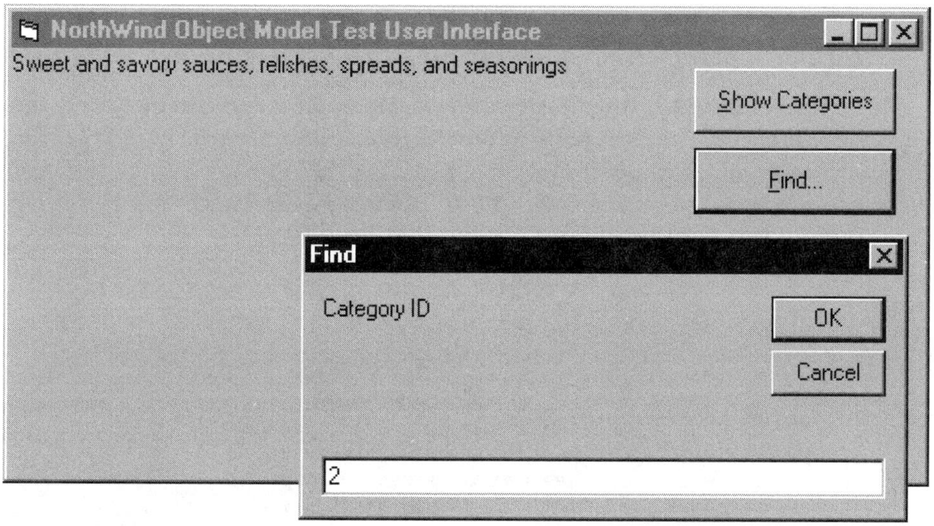

FIGURE 7-14 Code can be added to test the new *Find* method of the *Categories* collection.

```
Private Sub cmdFind_Click()
    Dim nID As Long
    Dim objCat As Category

    On Error GoTo CannotFind

    nID = InputBox("Category ID", "Find")
    Set objCat = Categories.Find(nID)
    Me.Cls
    Me.Print objCat.Description
    Exit Sub

CannotFind:
    If Err.Number = nweNoSuchCategory Then
        MsgBox "Cannot find that category"
    Else
        MsgBox Err.Description, _
               vbOKOnly + vbExclamation, _
               Err.Source
    End If
End Sub
```

Implementing the Add Method of the Categories Collection

The *Add* method of the *Categories* collection can automatically add a new record to the *Categories* table in the *NorthWind Traders* database. Following is a sample implementation:

```
Public Sub Add(ByRef NewCategory As Category)
    Dim objRS As New Recordset

    objRS.Open "Categories", "OLE_DB_NWIND_JET", _
            adOpenStatic, adLockOptimistic, adCmdTable

    objRS.AddNew
    objRS!CategoryName = NewCategory.Name
    objRS!Description = NewCategory.Description
    objRS.Update

    NewCategory.SetID objRS!CategoryID
End Sub
```

TESTING THE ADD METHOD

Following is sample code that tests the *Add* method of the *Categories* collection:

```
Private Sub cmdAdd_Click()
    Dim objCat As New Category
    Dim strName As String
    Dim strDesc As String

    strName = InputBox("Category Name", "Add")
    strDesc = InputBox("Description", "Add")

    objCat.Name = strName
    objCat.Description = strDesc
    categories.Add objCat
End Sub
```

Releasing an ActiveX Component

Once you build, release, and distribute an ActiveX Component, its interfaces become immutable. This means that you cannot do anything that changes public interfaces, such as removing methods or adding parameters to existing methods. Ignoring the rules of immutability will cause existing clients to break, since they are compiled, built, and distributed separately from the client.

Visual Basic has features that allow you to continue to add properties and methods to an existing ActiveX Component, as well as change the implementation of existing properties and methods. To make sure your interfaces remain compatible, follow the steps indicated in the following section once you're ready to build, release, and distribute your server.

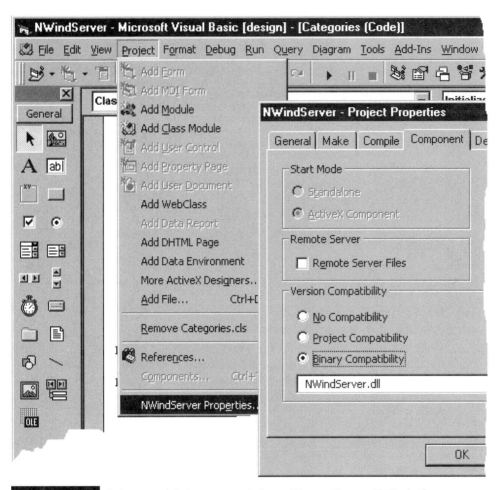

FIGURE 7-15
It is essential that you switch to *Binary Compatibility* before releasing your server.

Switching to Binary Compatibility

The following steps will switch your server to the ***Binary Compatibility*** option. Once you've done this, Visual Basic strongly warns you when you are about to make a change to your server that will break compatibility with existing clients.

1. In the *user interface* project, remove the existing project reference to your ActiveX Component.

2. Switch to the *ActiveX Component* project and select *Make server-name.DLL* to create the ActiveX Component DLL.

3. Still in the *ActiveX Component* project, open the *Project Properties* dialog and switch to the *Component* tab (see Figure 7-15).

4. Select the *Binary Compatibility* option. The box under this option will already be filled in with the name of the DLL you just built.

5. Switch back to the *user interface* project and insert a reference to your component, which will now show up using the project description you gave for the ActiveX Component.

Distributing an ActiveX Component

To distribute an application that uses an ActiveX Component, it is strongly recommended that you use the *Package and Deployment Wizard*. The *Package and Deployment Wizard* is smart enough to build a setup program that is appropriate for an application and its ActiveX Component, but there are a few steps you should take to make it go smoothly.

First, you must create a dependency file for the ActiveX Component. You will do this by using the *Package and Deployment Wizard*. Then, you can create a setup program that distributes both the client and server together. This is done by running the *Package and Deployment Wizard* a second time. The steps are described in the sections that follow.

CREATING A DEPENDENCY FILE FOR THE ACTIVEX COMPONENT

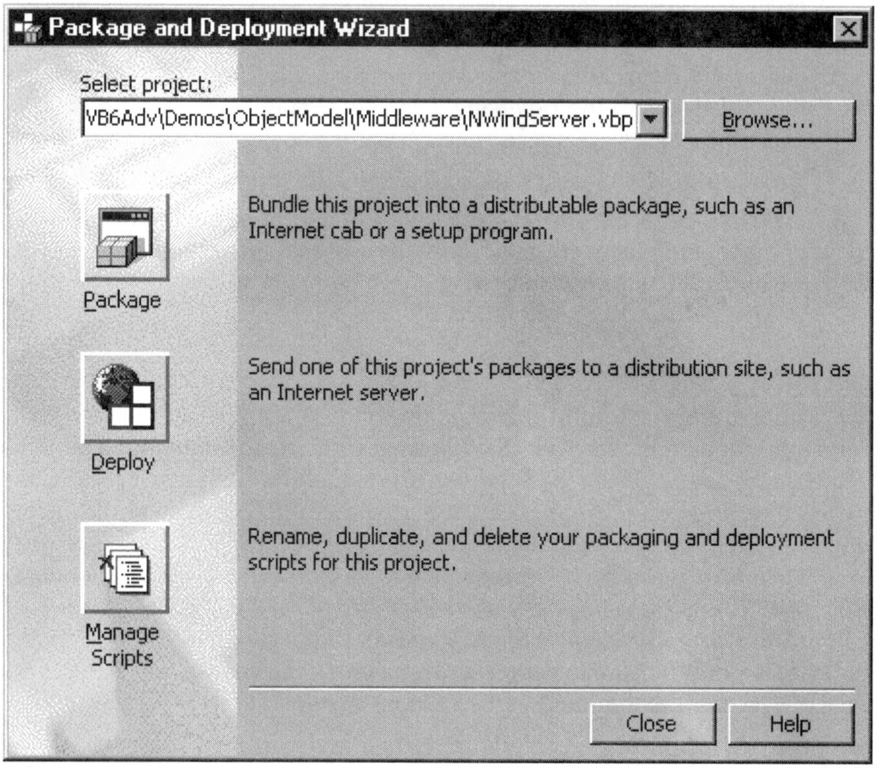

FIGURE 7-16 Start by creating a dependency file for the server. Using the *Package and Deployment Wizard*, select the server project and proceed to the next step.

Before you can create a setup program for a client that uses an ActiveX Component, you must create a dependency file for the ActiveX Component. This is done by using the *Package and Deployment Wizard*. Start the *Package and Deployment Wizard* and select the project containing the ActiveX Component, then click the *Package* button (see Figure 7-16).

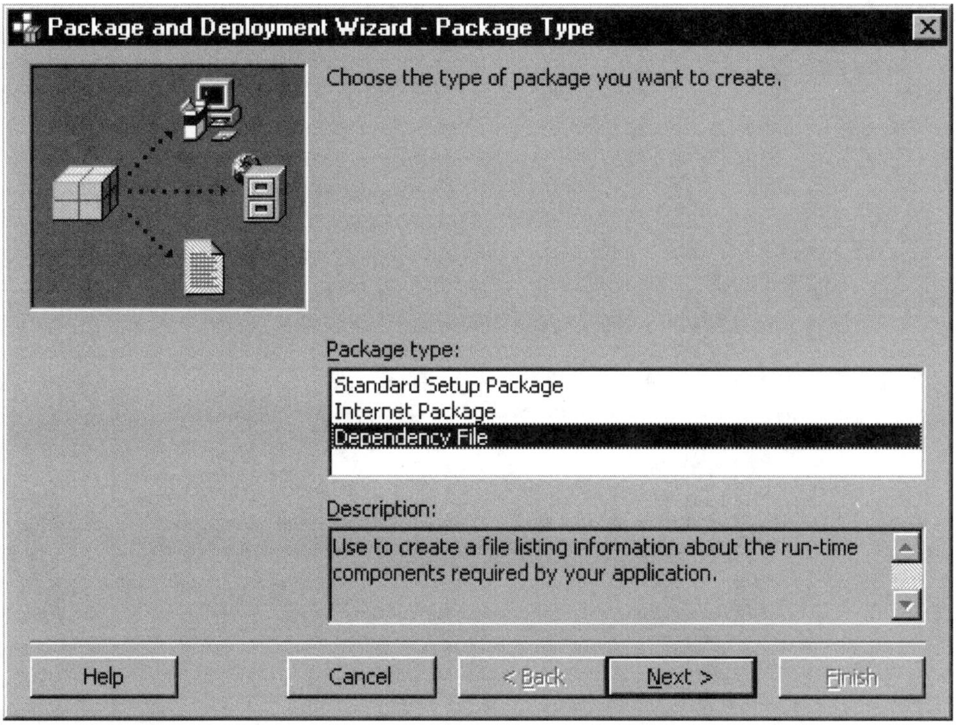

FIGURE 7-17 When prompted for *Package type*, select *Dependency File.*

When you are prompted for the *Package type*, select *Dependency File* (see Figure 7-17).

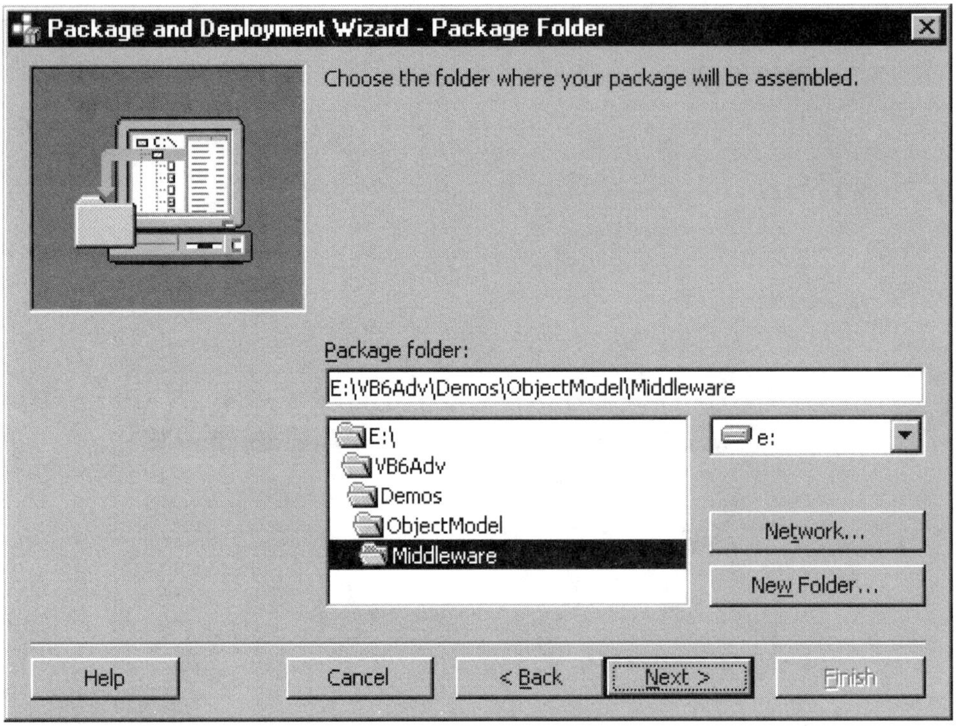

Package and Deployment Wizard - Package Folder

Choose the folder where your package will be assembled.

Package folder:

E:\VB6Adv\Demos\ObjectModel\Middleware

- E:\
- VB6Adv
- Demos
- ObjectModel
- Middleware

e:

Network...

New Folder...

Help   Cancel   < Back   Next >   Finish

FIGURE 7-18 You must place the dependency file in the same folder as the DLL of the server.

When prompted for the *package folder*, select the folder containing the already built DLL of the server (see Figure 7-18). You can now continue to the end of the script of the *Package and Deployment Wizard*.

Creating a Setup Program for the Client and Server

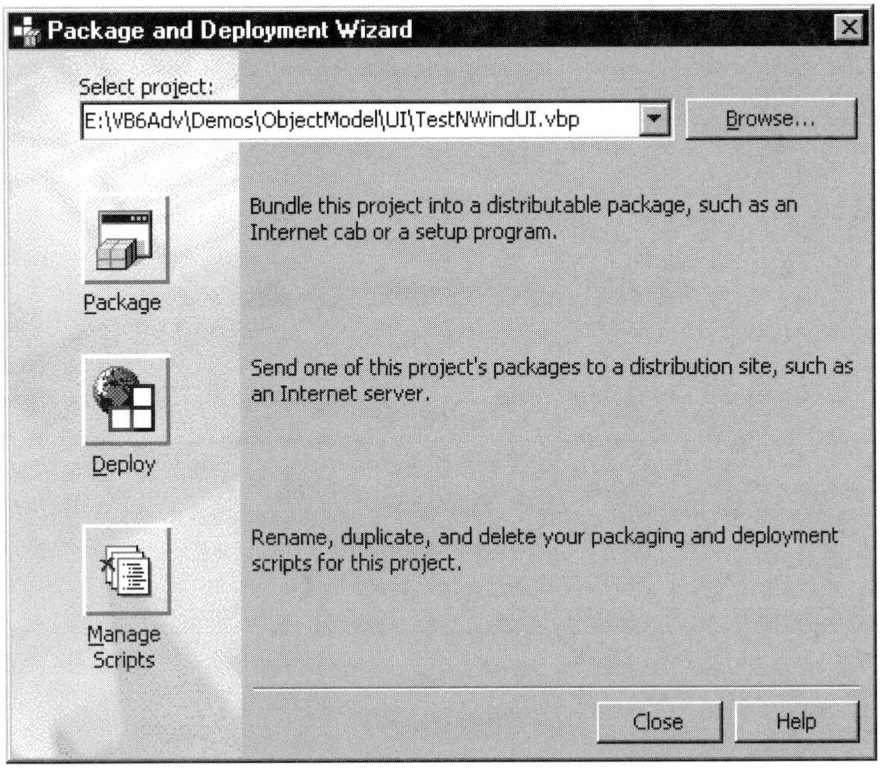

FIGURE 7-19 You can now create a setup program that will distribute the client and server together in one setup program. Back in the *Package and Deployment Wizard*, select the user interface project.

Next, you'll create the setup program for the client and server. Return to the *Package and Deployment Wizard* and select the *client* project (see Figure 7-19).

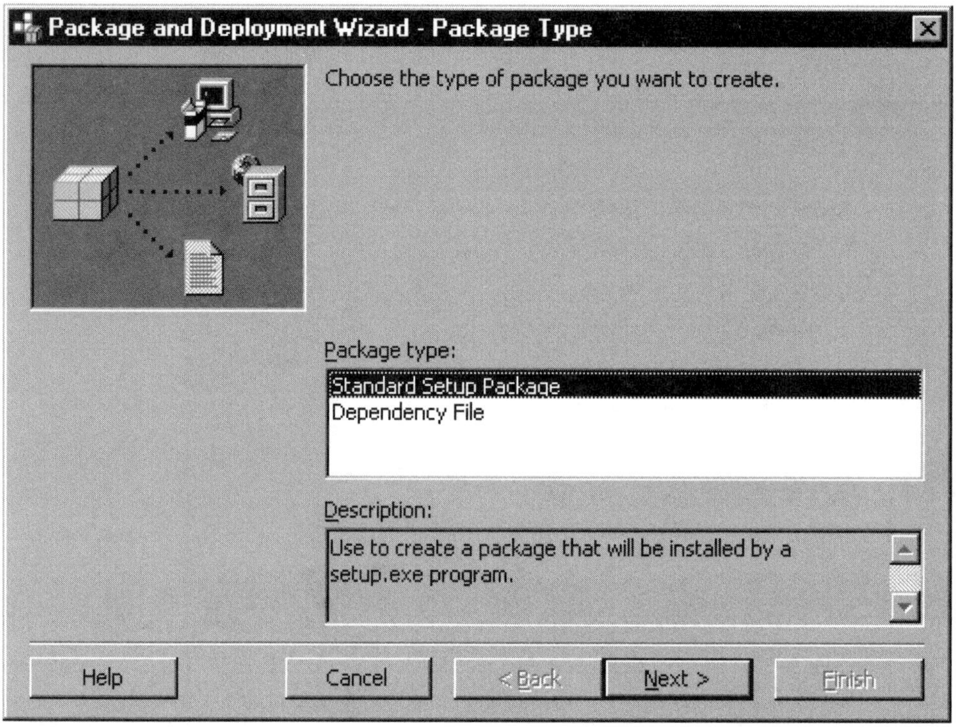

FIGURE 7-20 When prompted for the *Package type*, select *Standard Setup Package.*

Select *Standard Setup Package* for the *Package type* (see Figure 7-20).

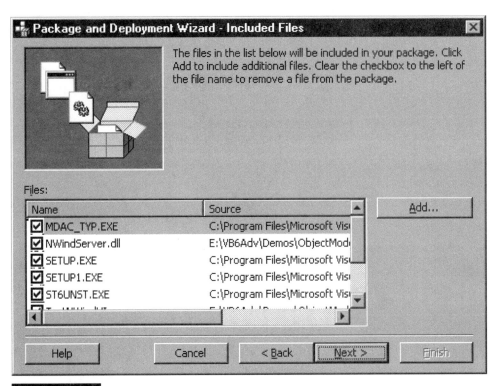

FIGURE 7-21   Note that the *Package and Deployment Wizard* will include the server DLL in the client setup program. You can uncheck it if you wish to create separate setup programs for the client and server.

The *Package and Deployment Wizard* will include the server DLL in the client setup program (see Figure 7-21). If you wish, you can uncheck the server DLL and create a separate setup program for the server.

COM, DCOM, and ActiveX

The **Component Object Model** (**COM**) is the underlying technology that makes most of what Microsoft calls **ActiveX** possible. It is a binary standard that describes how objects can export their interfaces to external programs. As a binary standard, it is language-independent. This means that you can develop a COM component in, say, Visual C++ and control it in, say, Visual Basic – or the other way around! **DCOM** is simply COM, but distributed; it allows clients and servers to be hosted on different computers.

Unless you've lived in a vacuum, you've surely heard of ActiveX. But, if you're like most developers, you probably aren't quite sure what it is. Don't feel bad; the definition of ActiveX is unclear to everyone. This is simply a Microsoft marketing term, rooted in the meaning, "activate the Internet." **ActiveX** is really a loosely defined collection of different Microsoft technologies.

You may have also heard of COM, and may even know that it stands for Component Object Model. COM is a lot easier to define, since it encompasses a specification and low-level routines. COM is the basis for most ActiveX technologies. DCOM is even easier to define, since DCOM **is** COM, but distributed. It allows developers to create client and server applications and transparently distribute them over a network.

By the way, OLE now stands for **object linking and embedding**. This is what OLE originally stood for, but as Microsoft introduced new technologies (OLE Controls, OLE automation), there was a trend to apply the word "OLE" to everything (the word "ActiveX" now has that honor).

What is COM?

Before going into a more technical description of what COM is, I'd like to indicate what COM does—it brings object-oriented and component-based software development to virtually everyone. Object-oriented languages (C++ in particular) have revolutionized software development and enabled developers to reuse objects (code and data encapsulated in a unit) to build new applications. However, C++ objects can only be used by C++ code. This does not really benefit most programmers, since most programmers don't use C++, primarily because of its steep learning curve.

Naturally, one can use DLLs to have languages like Visual Basic access C++ code, but this is not an object-oriented approach. The DLL approach is really just perpetuating procedural programming, passing data to a function. What if you wanted to create an object in C, C++, Visual Basic, Java, or whatever, and allow other developers to use that object from C, C++, Visual Basic, Java, or even within an application such as *Excel* or *Word* or a Web browser? Well, you could use COM. COM is Microsoft's binary specification for what an object is and how it can be used.

With COM, developers tend to talk about components rather than objects, although the two terms are often interchanged. The primary motivation for using the word "component" instead of "object" is to separate the concept of COM from the language of C++.

Used appropriately, COM can solve a number of problems that software developers face. For example, COM encourages the use of components, which are typically specialized to solve a particular problem in a somewhat general way. Using a component-oriented approach to programming extends the fundamental concept of modularity. A component-oriented application tends to be non-monolithic. Applications built without a component-oriented approach tend to be monolithic, loaded with features that not everyone uses, and no doubt full of duplicated code. Component-oriented applications are almost always more flexible. It's easy to add, remove, and enhance features. Using COM, applications can share both data and functionality. By using COM, programmers use a consistent programming model, regardless of whether the client and server pieces are running as the same process, as different processes on the same host, or on different hosts on the network (or even on another operating system).

With COM, programmers can create reusable software components. A **software component** is a piece of reusable software in binary form, as opposed to being in source code form. An application can "plug in" a component and begin using it with little effort. Such components can be developed by an application programmer, by another application programmer (perhaps reused from another project), or by a vendor. Software that is built with this component-oriented approach is often called **componentware**. Components can include such things as user interface objects (buttons, list boxes, etc.). Components can also include functional objects such as spell-checkers, database access objects, image processing components, and others.

However, for componentware to become a reality, there must be some standard for how components are created, initialized, used, and destroyed. This is exactly what COM does; it specifies how these things are done.

COM is Mostly About Interfaces

COM deals primarily with *interfaces*—not user interfaces, but application programming interfaces. In fact, a COM object (also known as a component) is primarily composed of interfaces. An interface is a group of functions. Such functions have a name, possibly some parameters (which are of standard types), and possibly a return value (which is also of some standard type). An interface also has a name. An interface's name refers to a list of functions; that is, the function(s) that make up that interface.

The interfaces that make up a component vary from component to component. You would naturally expect this, since components can do many different things. However, all COM components also have one or more interfaces in common. For example, all COM objects have an interface called *IUnknown* (the "I" stands for interface). The *IUnknown* interface consists of three functions, one of which is the function *QueryInterface*. With *QueryInterface*, an application can discover the interfaces that are supported by the component.

Another standard COM interface enables an application to invoke an object's properties and methods by name. This interface is used, for example, by Visual Basic when an ActiveX Control (a type of COM object) is placed on a form.

COM in Greater Detail

Are you still unsure of what COM is? In the following sections, I'll discuss how COM works in a little more detail. However, it's my opinion that COM will become an increasingly transparent way to program for Windows (and perhaps other operating systems as well). Someday, you'll probably use COM and never even think about it, in much the same way you access files without caring about the intricate details of the underlying file system and device drivers.

COM, which is specified by Microsoft, is a binary object interoperability standard. To help understand what COM does, first think of a program, or a binary collection of code and data, which is simply a block of binary data. If you assume this block is a software component, how can you make use of it in a standard way? Is it possible, in fact, to discover what this component does? If the block follows a standard that insists that it have some standard entry points that can be located at standard offsets from the start of the block, then the host can begin to discover what the block does and begin to use it. COM insists that software components have, at a minimum, pointers to three important functions. These pointers to functions can be obtained in a consistent way, regardless of what the component does. The first function, when called, reveals what the component does. The second function, when called, tells the component that your program is referencing it. The third function, when called, tells the component that your program is finished using that reference. Since the functions are related, it is convenient to group them together. In COM, when we speak of a group of related function pointers, we are talking about an **interface**. In COM, functions are typically referred to as **methods**. Thus, COM objects have interfaces, which are a group of methods (also known as functions).

The IUnknown Interface

In more precise COM terms, the interface discussed in the previous section is called the **IUnknown** interface (see Table 8-1). The *IUnknown* interface contains the three methods discussed previously, which are actually known as **QueryInterface**, **AddRef**, and **Release**. The *IUnknown* interface is the base interface for all other COM interfaces. What this means is, if a COM object implements any other interface, it must derive that interface from *IUnknown*, and implement the *IUnknown* methods in addition to any other methods declared by the interface.

AddRef and *Release* will typically increment or decrement an internal usage count. This way, the object can tell when there are no more references to it, at which time it can free its resources. Since object creation and deletion are language-specific activities, and, since COM is language-independent, the COM object must both create and delete itself. A client of a COM object is responsible for indicating when new references are made to a COM object (by calling *AddRef*), and for indicating when a reference to an object is no longer in use (by calling *Release*). A well-behaved COM object deletes itself, freeing memory and other resources, when its reference count reaches zero. If you use a COM object from Visual Basic, it's Visual Basic that takes care of calling the reference counting functions of the *IUnknown* interface; there is no special code that you have to provide for this purpose. Likewise, COM objects created with Visual Basic provide proper implementations of *IUnknown*.

The other *IUnknown* interface method, **QueryInterface**, returns an **interface pointer**, which is a pointer to another table of functions (methods). An interface is identified by an interface ID (more about this later). If an object does not support a requested interface, *QueryInterface* returns an error (*E_NOINTERFACE*); otherwise, it returns the interface pointer. Once a component user has a pointer to an interface, it can invoke methods in that interface using the table of pointers.

To summarize so far: All COM objects have an interface called **IUnknown**. Using the **QueryInterface** method of the **IUnknown** interface, software can obtain pointers to other routines by requesting an interface pointer (a pointer to a table of functions).

TABLE 8-1	IUnknown Interface Methods

IUnknown Method	**Description**
QueryInterface	Used to determine what the COM object does (e.g., what interfaces it has).
AddRef	Invoked to let the COM object know about a new reference to the object.
Release	Invoked to let the COM object know that a reference is no longer needed.

Other Standard COM Interfaces

The *IUnknown* interface is by no means the only standard COM interface, although it is the minimum interface that a COM object must support. For example, ActiveX Controls and automation servers typically provide an interface known as **IDispatch**. The *IDispatch* interface is used by a COM-using program to invoke a COM object's properties, methods, and events by name. This is how, for example, Visual Basic knows about the properties, methods, and events of an ActiveX Control.

COM objects often rely on other COM objects to get work done. For example, all COM objects must have an accompanying COM object, known as its class factory, that is used to create the COM object. Since COM objects effectively create themselves, creating a COM object on behalf of a client is problematic. COM solves this problem in an elegant way using class factories. When a COM server starts execution, it creates, in a language-specific way, a COM object that implements the *IClassFactory* interface. This interface contains a method called *CreateInstance*, which is used to create new instances of the COM object. COM uses the class factory to create the object for the client.

About Globally Unique Identifiers (GUIDs)

Clearly, objects, including COM objects, must be identified in some unique way. A name is not unique enough. There is nothing preventing two developers, in remote parts of the world, from coincidentally coming up with the same name. A name may be unique locally (that is, on your machine or perhaps within your company), but it cannot be guaranteed to be unique globally. COM objects are identified not by name but by an ID. This ID is partly randomly generated, using the current date and time, a unique ID provided by the computer (for example, a network MAC address), and a random number. The ID is a 16-byte (128-bit) number, and is generated by a low-level routine in the core of the COM API. The odds of two developers coming up with the same ID are extremely slim. A 128-bit number in decimal has 39 digits!

This ID is known as a **Globally Unique Identifier**, or **GUID** (rhymes with squid). If you've ever explored the Windows registry, you've probably seen a few GUIDs. They are identified in hexadecimal to keep the number of digits to a minimum. For example, the following number is a GUID:

```
{B3943EFC-CEC5-178F-AF20-00A0C9034837}
```

GUIDs are used to identify COM objects, interfaces, type libraries, and other items that need to be uniquely identified globally. By the way, it's okay to use the same GUID for two different kinds of things – for example a class may have the same GUID as a type library. Since they are two different things, no confusion arises for the reuse of the GUID.

When a GUID is used to identify a COM object, it is known as a **Class ID**, or **CLSID**. When a GUID identifies an interface, it is called an **Interface ID**, or **IID**. A GUID that identifies a type library is known as a **Library ID**, or **LIBID**. Note that a COM object may consume several GUIDs. It needs one for itself (the CLSID), one for its type library, and one for each and every interface that it has. To be able to use an object's interface, the using object must know both the CLSID of the object and the IID of the interface that it wants to use within the object. These items are kept in the Windows registry, where they may be located by a name, known as the **Programmer ID**, or **ProgID**. Note that the name may not be globally unique, but will be unique on that system. A program that uses a COM object must know about the interface. Not only must it know the IID, but it must also know what the methods are in that interface, as well as the parameters for the methods, and so on. When using Visual Basic to create COM objects, the CLSID and IIDs are generated for you automatically.

What is DCOM?

What is DCOM? The short answer is, DCOM is COM, but distributed. DCOM was introduced in Windows NT 4.0, and is available for Windows 9x (it's available with Visual Studio). DCOM enables a client using an ActiveX Component to be on another system in the network. With DCOM, you can create distributed applications. Your program can consist of a number of components, each running on a different computer. DCOM works by intercepting local calls to a remote object and performing a Remote Procedure Call (RPC), packaging the parameters, and sending them over to the remote object using a process known as marshalling. A similar step returns results back to the caller. All of this happens transparently to the application programmer. In other words, DCOM is COM.

You can install and run servers remotely via DCOM by using the **DCOM-CNFG** utility, although the preferred technique is to remotely deploy servers using Microsoft Transaction Server, which is the approach discussed in this book. You can also deploy clients and servers using DCOM with the Visual Basic *Package and Deployment Wizard* – this is discussed in Chapter 11.

About Interfaces and CoClasses

In the very early days of object-oriented programming, the distinction between an interface and a class was not emphasized nearly as much as it is today. Depending on when you learned about object-oriented programming, you may have been taught that there are two important concepts – class and object (or instance). Now, there is an important distinction between three concepts – interface, class, and object.

An *interface* is a specification for a set of methods (functions). Specifically, an interface is not an implementation of methods! An interface contains no code and no data. An interface describes a semantically related set of functions and fully describes each of the methods – name, return type, order, type, passing mechanism of parameters, and so on. Each interface is unique – being identified by an Interface ID, or IID. Interfaces are defined in a language-neutral manner, and are defined is such a way as to permit their implementation in virtually any programming language.

So, an interface is a specification for functions, and not an implementation of these functions. However, that's exactly what a *class* is – an implementation of one or more interfaces. Since the interface implemented by a class is specified in a language-neutral way, and since the class itself implements the interface in a language-neutral way, a client looking for an implementation of a specific interface does not need to be concerned with how an interface is implemented.

COM calls its classes *CoClasses*. A COM class can be used by any COM-capable language. Programmers of various languages have a certain picture in their minds of what a class is, and COM attempts to distance itself from that concept by using the term "CoClass". A *CoClass* is a class that provides an implementation of one or more interfaces. A class wishing to implement one or more interfaces inherits from the interface (note that this is interface inheritance, not implementation inheritance, as in C++, which supports both). The separation of interface and class makes sense once you think about it. You can provide several implementations of an interface with this approach.

In COM, there are four kinds of interfaces: *standard* (aka COM), *custom, dispatch*, and *dual*. A *standard interface* is provided by the COM specification. Examples include *IUnknown, IClassFactory,* and *IDispatch*. A *custom interface* is an interface specified by any COM developer. There are virtually no restrictions on parameter types in a custom interface, but custom interfaces cannot be used by Visual Basic unless the methods of the interface use only Visual Basic-compatible types. A *dispatch* interface is actually an implementation of the standard *IDispatch* interface, but one through which properties and methods can be invoked by name. Scripting language clients, which are not compiled, must use dispatch interfaces, which can be slow. A *dual* interface can be treated as a dispatch interface or a custom interface, so the advantage is performance while being compatible with scripting languages. You can access a dual interface from any client. COM servers created with Visual Basic will be properly set up to use a dual interface. Both dual and dispatch interfaces are restricted in the data types that can be used as parameters.

Visual Basic will use an *IDispatch* interface if that's all a server provides; however, it will be slower as a significant amount of extra code is executed by both the client and the server to dispatch the client to the correct code in the server. This is the type of interface that *VBScript* and *JavaScript* (as in Active Server Pages) must use. Visual Basic generates dual interfaces for a class, so a scripting client can use its dispatch interface, while a C++ or Visual Basic client can use vtable binding to its interfaces.

Why Create an Interface?

Do you, as a developer of corporate software (and not necessarily commercial software), need to create interfaces? Or do you simply need to develop classes? In COM, you cannot really create a class without also creating an interface – unless you are creating an implementation that consists totally of standard COM interfaces. This is because a client must ask for both an interface, which specifies the set of functions a client expects to be able to call, and a CoClass, which specifies an implementation of the interface. All custom objects implement at least one custom interface (the exception is with classes that implement only *IDispatch* to expose their custom properties and methods; these classes do not implement custom interfaces).

C++ programmers using ATL are much more aware of the separation of interface and class – and know that they must define both an interface and a class that implements the interface, even if there is only one class that will ever implement the interface. However, Visual Basic completely shelters you from this confusing aspect of COM, and creates both a CoClass and a hidden interface when you create a Visual Basic class.

The only way to actually see the interface created by Visual Basic is to view your server's type library – I'll be discussing this shortly. However, the advanced Visual Basic developer must be aware of the fact that there are both classes and interfaces. If not, you will never understand the compatibility features (none, project, and binary compatibility) provided by Visual Basic and you will become frustrated when trying to maintain a COM server. I'll be discussing compatibility in Chapter 14.

Both dispatch and dual interfaces must use automation-compatible types. These types are listed in Table 8-2.

TABLE 8-2	Automation-Compatible Types	
VB Type	**C++ Type**	**Description**
Boolean	boolean	Data item that can have the value TRUE or FALSE.
Byte	unsigned char	8-bit unsigned data item.
Double	double	64-bit IEEE floating-point number.
Single	float	32-bit IEEE floating-point number.
NA	int	Integer whose size is system-dependent. On 32-bit platforms, MIDL treats int as a 32-bit signed integer.
Long	long	32-bit signed integer.
Integer	short	16-bit signed integer.
String	BSTR	Length-prefixed string, as described in the OLE automation topic BSTR.
Currency	CY	8-byte fixed-point number.
Date	DATE	64-bit floating-point fractional number of days since December 30, 1899.
Long	SCODE	Built-in error type that corresponds to *HRESULT*.
Enum	enum	Signed integer whose size is system-dependent.
Object	IDispatch *	Pointer to *IDispatch* interface.
Object	IUnknown *	Pointer to interface that is not derived from *IDispatch*. (Any OLE interface can be represented by its *IUnknown* interface.)

About Type Libraries

A **type library** describes the classes and interfaces provided by a COM server. Type libraries are usually compiled into a TLB file. However, the COM developer can choose to compile type library information (as a resource) into the EXE (for out-of-process servers) or the DLL (for in-process servers). Thus, a type library can be contained in a TLB, EXE, or DLL file. Visual C++ developers (using the ATL Wizard) create their own type libraries. Visual Basic developers do not create their own type libraries. VB automatically compiles type library information into the EXE or DLL. A VB developer can request the creation of a TLB file by selecting the *Remote Server Files* option from the *Component* tab of the *Project Properties* dialog. This option is available for ActiveX EXE, ActiveX DLL, ActiveX Control, and ActiveX Document projects.

Type libraries are described using the Interface Definition Language (IDL). An IDL file has sections that describe the type library itself, the interface(s) defined in the type library, and the class(es) that implement the interfaces. Type libraries, interfaces, and classes are identified both by name (not guaranteed to be unique) and by GUID (guaranteed to be unique). In a type library, an interface defines a set of methods and property put/get routines, which are all really just functions. That is, an interface consists of a set of functions.

A type library defines functions in an interface in greater detail than any mainstream language can (except Ada). For example, a function declared in an interface specifies not only the order, type, and passing mechanism of parameters, but also their direction (in, out, in-out, retval). This is required for producing efficient marshalling code. The IDL that describes a type library is compiled using the MIDL (Microsoft IDL) compiler. Note that Visual Basic and *Visual Developer Studio* automatically perform this step. A Visual Basic developer can extract the IDL for a type library using the *OLE/COM Object Viewer*.

VIEWING A TYPE LIBRARY

Visual C++ developers create their own type libraries (or use the ATL Wizard). Therefore, they will of course have the IDL source code. For a VB developer, or for anyone that does not have access to the IDL for a type library, the type library source code can be generated from the TLB (or EXE/DLL) using the OLE/COM Object Viewer. To use the OLE/COM Object Viewer:

1. Invoke *OLEVIEW.EXE* (included with *Visual Studio*, or can be downloaded from Microsoft). You can invoke this utility from the Microsoft Visual Studio 6.0 Tools group, where it is known as OLE View.
2. From the **File** menu, select **View TypeLib**.
3. Navigate to and select the type library. If you want to view the type library of an in-process COM server developed with Visual Basic, select the server's DLL when prompted for the type library location.

EXAMPLE: VIEWING A TYPE LIBRARY

Assume the following code is contained in a class module named *FinManClass*, in a server project named *FinManServer*.

```
Public X As Integer
Public Function Get3X() As Integer
    Get3X = 3 * X
End Function
```

Upon building the server, you can view its type library with the *OLE/COM Object Viewer*. The IDL will appear as follows (*GUIDs* will vary):

```
interface _FinManClass;

[
  uuid(7822BBCC-DE02-11D1-8F1B-00A0C9216788),
  version(1.0),
  helpstring("FinManServer")
]
library FinManServer
{
    // TLib : OLE Automation :
      {00020430-0000-0000-C000-000000000046}
    importlib("StdOle2.tlb");

    [
      odl,
      uuid(7822BBCA-DE02-11D1-8F1B-00A0C9216788),
      version(1.0),
      hidden,
      dual,
      nonextensible,
      oleautomation
    ]
    interface _FinManClass : IDispatch {
        [id(0x40030000), propget]
            HRESULT _stdcall X([out, retval] short* X);
        [id(0x40030000), propput]
            HRESULT _stdcall X([in] short X);
        [id(0x60030000)]
            HRESULT _stdcall Get3X([out, retval] short* );
    };

    [
      uuid(7822BBCB-DE02-11D1-8F1B-00A0C9216788),
      version(1.0)
    ]
    coclass FinManClass {
        [default] interface _FinManClass;
    };
};
```

Marshalling Code

In COM, **marshalling code** is code that marshals, or packs, parameters for a method call. Marshalling code is used on both sides of a client/server application. From the client side, marshalling packs in and in-out parameters and sends them to the server. On the client side, a call to marshalling code is transparent. The client thinks it's directly invoking the method as if it were a local call. In fact, the interface pointer points to a proxy that contains the marshalling code. On the server side, marshalling code unpacks in and in-out parameters and calls the method locally. The "un-marshalling" code is implemented on the server side by a stub, which is transparent on the server side. Thus, to the server's method, it appears as if it was invoked locally. Marshalling is also used to return values back to the client.

Developers of custom interfaces may write their own marshalling code. In fact, the MIDL compiler generates the marshalling code, which must be built into a DLL. Both dual and dispinterfaces use standard marshalling code supplied by the system. This is possible because there is a limited number of supported types that can be passed across such interfaces, thus making the development of generic code deterministic. Standard (automation) marshalling is provided by OLEAUT32.DLL. The proxy/stub DLL must be present and registered on both the client side and server side. It is registered under HKCR\Interface\{iid}\ProxyStubClsid32. The class ID for *OLEAUT32.DLL* is *{00020424-0000-0000-C0000-000000000046}*.

Marshalling code is not always used. When it is not used, the client has a direct interface pointer to the object. In other words, calls to the server are made via a pointer to a list of function pointers. This is every bit as fast as a direct function call. The only time marshalling code is not used is for in-process server calls between threads with compatible threading models. Put another way, marshalling code is used in all of the following cases:

1. In all calls between a client and any out-of-process server (EXE), local or remote.
2. In all calls between a client and any remote server, EXE or DLL.
3. In calls between threads of a client and a server that have different threading models.
4. In calls between a client thread that resides in a different apartment than the server thread (single-threaded apartment model, aka "Apartment").

It is also possible for a COM server developer to create custom marshalling code. This is an extremely advanced technique that can be used for the development of "smart proxies," which can select between "going remote" and handling a method call locally (perhaps via a cache, etc.).

Self-Registering COM Servers

An out-of-process COM server (ActiveX EXE) should be self-registering. In other words, it should contain code in its *WinMain* to make the appropriate registry entries. Code in *WinMain* should look for the standard switches of */regserver* or */unregserver*. If either switch is missing, *WinMain* should assume a switch of */regserver*. ActiveX EXEs developed with Visual Basic or in Visual C++ (using the *ATL Wizard*) will have properly-generated *WinMains*; that is, they will self-register properly. Since the COM specification says nothing about accepting abbreviated switches, you should never assume it is safe to register an out-of-process server using, for example, */reg* or */r*. Likewise, do not assume you can unregister an out-of-process server using, for example, */unreg* or */u*. Always specify a switch fully and correctly; do not abbreviate or misspell it.

An in-process COM server (ActiveX DLL) can, and should, also be self-registering, but the term is somewhat misleading when applied to this type of server. A DLL cannot run by itself, so it needs a helper utility to get it registered. This helper utility is **regsvr32**, which loads the specified DLL and calls entry points required by self-registered in-process COM servers. If these standard entry points are missing, the server is by definition not a self-registering COM server, and will require manual entry into the registry. The */u* switch is used with *regsvr32* to unregister an in-process COM server. Note that Visual Basic creates in-process COM servers that are self-registering.

The most common error received by developers attempting to register an in-process server with *regsvr32* is **7E** hex – this indicates that *"The specified module could not be found."* If you get this error code, you have probably specified an incorrect path to the DLL – serious COM developers associate the file extension DLL with *regsrv32.EXE*, enabling them to simply double-click on the DLL from the *Explorer* to register it. For a description of how to make this association, see Chapter 1.

If the *7E* error persists even after you verify a correctly specified path-name, it may indicate that the component itself is attempting to load another module as part of its registration; in other words, the component depends on another component or DLL. There is no easy way to troubleshoot this condition. For errors other that *7E* reported by *regsvr32*, use the *Error Lookup Tool* provided with *Visual Studio*. This utility is available from the *Microsoft Visual Studio 6.0 Tools* program group.

I have often been asked why *regsvr32* could not have been designed to be more user-friendly, reporting the exact text of the error message rather than a hexadecimal error code. I can only suggest that the *regsvr32* tool is not a user tool, and was not designed for the casual user. It's an administrator and developer tool – the developers of this type of utility have always assumed that they can waive the user-friendliness requirement.

Windows Registry Entries for COM Servers

I have often been asked about what registry entries are required for COM servers and clients to link up with each other. I've always been suspicious of such questions; is the student suggesting that manual registry entry is appropriate? Of course, curiosity is often the motivation, but more commonly, a developer assumes that knowledge of registry entries may be required if troubleshooting is required. With that in mind, I present in this section and the ones that follow a list of registry entries created by Visual Basic COM servers, starting with out-of-process COM servers.

I have always told students of my developer classes that fearing the registry is counterproductive. Whenever you compile a COM server in Visual Basic, registry entries will be made, and they are permanent (unless, of course, you manually unregister the server). There is really no way to experiment with and learn about the development of COM servers unless you are willing to allow Visual Basic to add entries to your registry.

Having said that, good Windows registry management suggests that there be no "stale" entries in your registry. Performance suffers on a machine with lots of unused registry entries (this degradation is often exaggerated, however). If you are fortunate enough to have a fast machine, the degradation is rarely noticeable. I simply let my registry get larger and larger, especially when I'm developing a new course (or writing a book) and need to develop a lot of small COM servers that illustrate a few key concepts. Although I realize that many readers of this book do not have the same work habits that I do, registry growth is not a problem for me, since I always use the latest operating system and often rebuild the system disks on my machines, especially when starting a new project.

Your registry cannot grow to the point where it consumes all of your disk space. The size of the registry is limited by a setting that can be changed via the *System* icon of the *Control Panel* – select the *Performance* tab and click the *Change* button under *Virtual Memory*. You will receive a warning message if your registry begins to approach this limit. Of course, you can use one of the many registry-cleaning utilities available to trim down the size of the registry if you need to.

Server-Side COM Registry Entries for Local Servers

For an out-of-process COM server (ActiveX EXE) that will be accessed by local client applications, the registry entries in Table 8-3 are used. For local servers developed with Visual Basic or Visual C++ (using the *ATL Wizard*), the appropriate registry entries can be entered by running the server with the */regserver* switch. All registry entries can be removed by running the server with the */unregserver* switch (it is recommended that you do not abbreviate the switch; spell our *unregserver* entirely).

TABLE 8-3	Server-Side Registry Entries for Local Servers

Key Name	**Key Default Value / Subkey Values**
HKCR\prog-id\ *Clsid*	{*object-class-id*}
HKCR\ *CLSID*\ {*object-class-id*}\ *Implemented Categories*\ {40FC6ED5-2438-11CF-A3DB-080036F12502}	Key has no default value; presence of this key indicates that class is an automation object. Used by utilities that browse the registry for COM objects, such as OLEVIEW.EXE.
HKCR\ *CLSID*\{*object-class-id*}\ *LocalServer32*	Pathname of server (EXE)
HKCR\ *CLSID*\{*object-class-id*}\ *ProgID*	prog-ID
HKCR\ *CLSID*\{*object-class-id*}\ *TypeLib*	{*library-id*}
HKCR\ *CLSID*\{*object-class-id*}\ *Version*	1.0
HKCR\ *Interface*\{*object-interface-id*}	Interface-name (VB uses _*class-name*)
HKCR\ *Interface*\{*object-interface-id*}\ *ProxyStubClsid*	{00020424-0000-0000-C0000-000000000046}
HKCR\ *Interface*\{*object-interface-id*}\ *ProxyStubClsid32*	{00020424-0000-0000-C0000-000000000046}
HKCR\ *Interface*\{*object-interface-id*}\ *TypeLib*	{*library-id*} Version=1.0
HKCR\ *TypeLib*\{*library-id*}\ *1.0*	Library description
HKCR\ *TypeLib*\{*library-id*}\ *1.0*\0\ *Win32*	Pathname of type library (TLB, DLL, or EXE)
HKCR\ *TypeLib*\{*library-id*}\ *1.0*\FLAGS	0
HKCR\ *TypeLib*\{*library-id*}\1.0\ *HELPDIR*	Directory path of *Help* file

Note that, with the exception of type library information, which is registered once, each class of object needs its own set of registry entries. Servers that export multiple objects require multiple entries in *HKCR*\ *CLSID* and *HKCR*\ *Interface* (many COM developers use the abbreviation *HKCR* for *HKEY_CLASSES_ROOT,* as I have here). Not all entries are actually required, but all are recommended.

The same set of entries is required server-side for servers that will be accessed from remote clients. In the following section, I will indicate what entries are required client-side to access a remote server.

Client-Side DCOM Registry Entries for Remote Servers

When an out-of-process (ActiveX EXE) server is remote and will be accessed via DCOM, the registry entries in Table 8-4 are used. The Visual Basic Package and Deployment Wizard will create a client-side setup program to automatically create these registry entries. For servers created with Visual C++, or to modify the entries for a VB server, you can use the OLE/COM Object Viewer and/or DCOMCnfg. Of course, you can also use regedit. While it's recommended that you supply all registry entries, not all of the entries shown in the first table are strictly required; required entries appear in Table 8-5.

TABLE 8-4	Client-Side Registry Entries for Remote Servers
Key Name	**Key Default Value / Subkey Values**
HKCR\AppID\{object-class-id}	*RemoteServerName*=server-name
HKCR\prog-id\Clsid	*{object-class-id}*
HKCR\CLSID\{object-class-id}	AppID={*object-class-id*}
HKCR\CLSID\{object-class-id}\ProgID	prog-ID
HKCR\CLSID\{object-class-id}\TypeLib	*{library-id}*
HKCR\CLSID\{object-class-id}\Version	1.0
HKCR\Interface\{object-interface-id}	Interface-name (VB uses _*class-name*)
HKCR\Interface\{object-interface-id}\ProxyStubClsid	{00020424-0000-0000-C0000-000000000046}
HKCR\Interface\{object-interface-id}\ProxyStubClsid32	{00020424-0000-0000-C0000-000000000046}
HKCR\Interface\{object-interface-id}\TypeLib	*{library-id}* Version=1.0
HKCR\TypeLib\{library-id}\1.0	Library description
HKCR\TypeLib\{library-id}\1.0\0\Win32	Pathname of type library (TLB, DLL, or EXE)
HKCR\TypeLib\{library-id}\1.0\FLAGS	0
HKCR\TypeLib\{library-id}\1.0\HELPDIR	Directory path of *Help* file

TABLE 8-5	Required Client-Side Registry Entries for Remote Servers

Key Name	**Key Default Value / Subkey Values**
HKCR\AppID\{object-class-id}	RemoteServerName=server-name
HKCR\prog-id\Clsid	{object-class-id}
HKCR\{object-class-id}	AppID={object-class-id}
HKCR\Interface\{object-interface-id}\ProxyStubClsid32	{00020424-0000-0000-C0000- 000000000046}
HKCR\Interface\{object-interface-id}\TypeLib	{library-id} Version=1.0
HKCR\TypeLib\{library-id}\1.0\0\Win32	Pathname of type library (TLB, DLL, or EXE)

Using a Surrogate for Hosting a Remote In-Process Server

DCOM also supports activation of remote COM objects that are hosted by an in-process server (DLL). To use this feature, however, the remote DLL must have a surrogate EXE to host the DLL. *Windows NT 4.0* (minimum *Service Pack 2*) provides the "stock" surrogate, *DLLHOST.EXE,* for hosting an in-process server that will be accessed via DCOM. To use the stock surrogate, you must add the key *DllSurrogate* under *HKCR\AppID\{object-class-id}* on the server side. The value for this key should be *empty* to specify *DLL-HOST.EXE.* Note that this key is in addition to all other registry values related to the server side. No special key values are required on the client side (other than those that appear as discussed earlier). You can add this key manually on the server, or you can use the *OLE/COM Object Viewer* to do it. To use the *OLE/COM Object Viewer* to set up a DLL surrogate:

1. Invoke the *OLE/COM Object Viewer* (*OLEVIEW.EXE*).
2. Enable expert mode by selecting **Expert Mode** from the **View** menu.
3. Find and select your class under *Automation Objects.*
4. Select the **Implementation** tab, and check the option **Use Surrogate Process**.
5. Switch to the **Registry** tab to verify the changes to the registry.

Threads and Processes

Visual Basic programmers have, until recently, been completely isolated from the issues of processes and threads. *Service Pack 3* of Visual Basic 5, however, introduced apartment model threading. Suddenly, Visual Basic programmers had to be at least aware of what a thread was and how it was distinguished from a process.

A **process** is not much more than a data structure that keeps track of a program in execution. The Windows operating system keeps track of many resources on a process-by-process basis. Such resources include a virtual address space, a working set of physical pages currently visible to the process, handles to files and other system objects, and other resources. Processes do not execute code. That is the job of a thread.

A **thread** is the basic scheduling unit in Windows, and is the basic unit to which the operating system allocates processor time. Processes are always started with one thread, known as the primary thread. The primary thread or any other thread in the process can create additional threads. All threads execute in the context of some process, sharing the same virtual address space of the process. Within a process, all threads have the capability of executing any part of the process's code and accessing any data within the process. Note that this includes code and data that is currently being executed or referenced by another thread within the process.

Windows NT, Windows 2000, and *Windows 9X* support preemptive multitasking. Multiple threads can execute simultaneously, at least apparently so. In actual fact, a multiprocessor computer is required to actually execute multiple threads simultaneously. In a multiprocessor environment, there can be as many executing threads as there are CPUs. On a uniprocessor computer, multiple threads appear to execute simultaneously, each being allocated a time slice. When that time slice expires, the current thread is suspended and another thread is allowed to run.

Preemption is not necessarily something that happens involuntarily to a thread. Threads can voluntarily preempt themselves by executing a Win32 API call that places them into a wait state. Examples include waiting for I/O completion and voluntarily waiting a set amount of time by calling the Win32 *Sleep* function. When a thread executes such a blocking call, there is an opportunity to allow another thread to perform useful work. If a single thread does all work in a process, the application cannot take advantage of this overlapping time. Thus, throughput and concurrency are often improved in multi-threaded applications, even when an application runs on a computer with a single CPU.

Are Multi-Threaded Applications Necessary?

I often joke with my students that threads mean more work. This statement can be interpreted two different ways. First, well-designed multi-threaded applications can make more efficient use of the processor, overlapping wait time with the productive use of otherwise wasted CPU cycles. But developing a multi-threaded application requires more development effort as well. Creating a thread is not trivial, and the required API calls are designed for the C and C++ programmer. Some languages, such as Java and Ada, have inherent threading capabilities – but even in these languages, the use of threads is not trivial. And, once a thread is created, you're not done. Threads must be managed and synchronized. An errant thread can bring down your entire process. A thread that fails to exit will hang your process. Thus, if you treat threads as solutions looking for problems, you will add complexity instead of value to your application.

Having said that, threads are indeed necessary in distributed applications, but primarily for the purpose of serving a greater number of clients. Distributed applications by definition perform network and database I/O. This wait time provides opportunity to begin or continue work on a pending client request. Back in the days when a "distributed application" meant a server application using sockets and TCP/IP communication, it was essential that the server be dynamically multi-threaded. A server typically created a thread that listened for client connections and created a new socket and a new thread to handle a new client connection. Often, these servers limited the number of threads, and thus clients, that could be handled simultaneously, or drew from a "pool" of threads to service client requests. This design model is exactly the basis for components deployed under MTS.

Thus, a remote server should be multi-threaded to service as many concurrent client requests as resources will allow. Fortunately, MTS and/or Visual Basic make it possible for the developer to easily create multi-threaded servers. If you plan to deploy your server under MTS, you must implement the server as an in-process server (ActiveX DLL). If this server is apartment-threaded (covered in the next section), MTS will take care of managing a thread pool. If you have decided not to deploy your remote server under MTS, you can implement it as an out-of-process server (ActiveX EXE) and let Visual Basic manage a thread pool. You can configure DCOM on your own, or use the *Package and Deployment Wizard* to configure DCOM, to enable remote access from clients.

To summarize, in-process COM servers should be thread-capable if used locally from a multi-threaded client – make a thread-safe ActiveX DLL and assume clients may create multiple threads. Don't create threads yourself in an ActiveX DLL. This will enable single and/or multi-threaded clients to use your in-process server locally. Out-of-process COM servers should be multi-threaded to service as many concurrent client requests as possible using a thread pool. Use the features built into Visual Basic to create a thread pool, out-of-process COM server.

Apartment-Model Threading

With **apartment-model threading**, a Visual Basic programmer can create thread-safe COM servers with virtually no effort. This does not mean that you must create threads; in fact, you really should not create threads in Visual Basic, although it is possible under certain circumstances.

If you are creating an in-process server (ActiveX DLL), which is likely and recommended, you must specifically not create threads in Visual Basic – even if you know how to do this. Microsoft strongly recommends that ActiveX DLLs that use the apartment-threading model avoid the creation of threads, and I would concur with that suggestion. By convention, authors of in-process servers expect their client applications to create the threads which, in turn, create and use your objects. So, what you should really do is create COM objects that can be safely used from a multi-threaded client. Later in this section, I'll introduce you to a multi-threaded client application, written in C++, that uses several thread-safe objects created with Visual Basic.

There are several points to keep in mind that are key to your understanding of apartment-model threading. First, the primary motivation for creating threads should be to improve concurrency and increase throughput. If a thread is blocked waiting for code in an object to complete, there should be no reason that another thread cannot safely execute code in the same object. Otherwise, requests from clients become queued up and are forced to execute sequentially. The ideal solution would be to create and assign a separate thread for each object, but this is not necessarily practical. The over-creation of threads would consume too many operating system resources – at some point, no threads would get any work done. A better solution is to create as many threads as needed, up to a point, at which time objects will have to wait for a thread in a "pool" to become available. This is exactly the approach used by MTS, so any solution you may invent would be reinventing the wheel.

Another key point is that objects do not execute code; threads execute code. An object is, after all, implemented by code and data. Many developers speak of an object in "execution," but this is simply a figure of speech. A thread is required to both create and use an object.

Before proceeding with a discussion of apartment-model threading, I should clear up some possible confusion on terminology. In COM, there are actually two different threading models available. The first is known as the single-threaded apartment model, or STA. The second model is known as the multi-threaded apartment model, or MTA. COM does not really consider single-threaded to be a separate threading model – a COM server that is *single-threaded* has only one single-threaded apartment. A COM server can have multiple single-threaded apartments, but only one multi-threaded apartment. If a C++/ATL programmer asks you which threading model you support, and you answer apartment model, there may be a follow-up question – single or multi-threaded apartment?

In Visual Basic, you can choose between a single-threaded or apartment-threaded model. When you select single-threaded, your COM server will have only one single-threaded apartment (STA). When you select apartment model, you COM server (and its client) may have one or more STA.

Visual Basic does not allow you to create a multi-threaded apartment, but this is not bad news. Developers of COM servers that use a multi-threaded apartment (also known as free-threaded) must provide their own synchronization code to ensure thread safety. This means using Win32 synchronization objects such as critical sections, events, semaphores, and mutexes. This, in turn, means using a number of Win32 system services that were never meant to be called by Visual Basic (although it is possible).

In Visual Basic, a COM server's threading options are set in the Properties dialog, specifically on the *General* tab. You may set the threading model for an ActiveX DLL, but not the thread pool options. It's the other way around for an ActiveX EXE – you can set the thread pool options, but not the threading model option.

What is an Apartment?

In real life, of course, an apartment is where someone lives along with his or her "stuff." If you consider the person to be a thread, and that person's stuff as objects, then you have a good analogy of what an apartment is when applied to threading.

When a thread is initialized to use COM, it must indicate what type of threading model it wishes to use. The default is the single-threaded apartment model. When the COM initialization routine is called, an apartment is created and the calling thread is assigned to that apartment. Any objects created by that thread are also assigned to that apartment. An important rule of apartment-model threading is that only the thread that created the object can execute code in the object. This applies to any other objects created by that thread, or any objects created as a side effect of executing code in objects created by that thread. All objects created directly or indirectly by a thread are assigned to that thread's apartment. Other threads that attempt to execute code in objects of another apartment must have their requests queued to the creating thread. The COM runtime environment handles the queuing of the requests.

Of course, more than one person may live in an apartment. It is also the case that more than one thread can be assigned to a single apartment – but only if the server supports the multi-threaded apartment model. In this case, threads in an apartment share objects. Objects created by any thread in an MTA are assigned to the same apartment. Any thread in an MTA can execute code in any object in the same MTA. However, there is no queuing of requests and no type of synchronization provided by COM. It is possible for the same two objects to be in execution at the same time by two different threads. Thus, it is the responsibility of the developer to analyze the code and, using Win32 synchronization objects, prevent simultaneous execution of the non-thread safe sections of code.

By queuing requests for object execution to the creating thread, the STA model makes sure that two different threads cannot execute code in the same object at the same time. Note that this may or may not be necessary to ensure thread safety. Properly written, it is entirely possible that two different threads can execute a method of an object at the same time. But, using the STA model, COM never assumes that any method is safe for simultaneous execution by multiple threads. In fact, two different threads cannot simultaneously execute two different methods of the same object, or even on two different objects at the same time – at least not if both objects are in the same STA. The STA model is a compromise between maximum concurrency and development difficulty. Using the STA model, you will have greater concurrency than a single-threaded server can provide, but probably not as much as a server that uses the multi-threaded apartment model. However, you do not have to write code that uses synchronization objects when you use the STA model.

Thread-Safe Apartments and Global Data

It is possible to develop a COM server that uses apartment threading that will not safely run from a multi-threaded client, but it is actually difficult to do in Visual Basic. You might assume that the main danger is in the use of global data, which should be avoided anyway. But even if your application uses global data, it will most likely be thread-safe in Visual Basic. This is because, in a Visual Basic COM server, global does not always mean global!

In a Visual Basic COM server, each apartment receives its own copy of global data. So, even if your object places some of its instance data in global variables instead of using per-object properties, the global data exists on a per-apartment basis. Setting a global variable (a variable declared as *Public* in a standard module) from one object only affects the objects in that apartment. The same "global" variable set from a thread in a different apartment will receive a different value.

In giving each apartment its own copy of global data, the Visual Basic architects have made it possible to safely use an application designed for a single user in a multi-threaded environment. If an application is designed with the assumption that a single process will use it, it will no doubt work for several processes. It will probably also work for a multi-threaded client, as long as the server does not use global data for the purpose of communicating between objects. Communicating between objects using global data is not reliable when the client is multi-threaded, since each thread has its own apartment and each apartment has its own copy of global data. The apartment-threading model, as implemented by Visual Basic, basically treats each client thread as a separate process. It is as though each thread is a separate and independent user of your application. Objects that are in the same apartment (that is, objects that have been created by the same thread) can share global data. But, if objects are in different apartments (that is, the objects have been created by different threads), they will each have their own copy of global data.

How then, can you share data between objects in such a way that it does not matter in which apartment an object resides? First, you must accept the fact that it cannot be done with global data. In fact, using global data to share information between objects in the same apartment is not a good idea. A C or C++ programmer who creates multi-threaded applications is well aware of the fact that global data is an inappropriate solution to communicating between threads. To synchronize events between threads, a C or C++ programmer on the Win32 platform uses critical sections, events, semaphores, and mutexes. To share data between threads, a C or C++ programmer might use memory-mapped files, *WM_COPYDATA* messages, mailslots, pipes, or other techniques. None of these techniques are easily used from within Visual Basic.

You must approach the problem from a different angle. If you find it necessary to share data between objects, what you have actually discovered is a dependency between the objects. In other words, if one object needs to send information to another object, the objects depend on each other, and must therefore be aware of each other. You must then use the same approach that a client would use to send information to an object – via the invocation of a property or method. Of course, for an object to invoke a property or method on another object, the invoking object must have a reference to the target object. The invoking object can obtain this reference by creating the target object. The reference to the target object can then be stored as a private member variable of the creating object. Since the target object's code is being executed by a thread, which resides in an apartment, any object created by it will reside in the same apartment. What you then have is a hierarchy of dependent objects. If you use this design approach, you will rarely find yourself being forced to use global data to communicate between objects.

Multi-Threaded Out-of-Process COM Severs

Developers of in-process COM servers expect clients to create threads. However, in an out-of-process COM server, it may be desirable to use multiple threads to concurrently service multiple client applications, which themselves may be single-threaded.

Visual Basic allows you to create an out-of-process (ActiveX EXE) COM server that is multi-threaded. You can let Visual Basic automatically create one thread per object, or you can elect to indicate a maximum number of threads that are to be used as a thread pool. If you are creating an out-of-process COM server, it is recommended that you use the thread pool option, but you will need to decide on a maximum number of threads. The best way to arrive at a number is to experiment with a benchmark program. You can use C++ to create a multi-threaded client to test the server, or use Visual

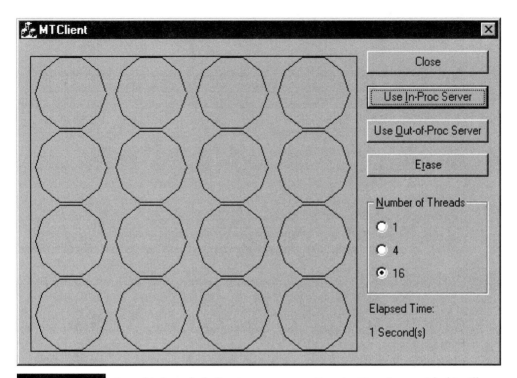

FIGURE 8-1 A multi-threaded client program, written in C++, is provided to illustrate the use of apartment-model/ threading.

Basic to create a single-threaded client and run several copies of this client. At some point, the overhead of creating a large number of threads exceeds the benefits of having a multi-threaded server. Set the thread pool maximum below this number.

You should create a multi-threaded COM server only if you are certain that you will not be deploying your server under MTS. A multi-threaded COM server cannot be deployed under MTS for two reasons. First, it is, by definition, an out-of-process server. MTS will only accept in-process COM servers. Second, MTS servers should not create or terminate threads.

Although I don't recommend creating multi-threaded out-of-process COM servers as part of a distributed application, they do provide academic interest. I'll present an example of an out-of-process COM server later in this section.

Experimenting with Threading Models

In the following sections, I will present a multi-threaded client application, written in C++, which uses objects created by a Visual Basic server (see Figure 8-1). Source code for the client application is provided, but will not be analyzed in this book.

Two versions of a Visual Basic COM server are used by the client application. One version is implemented as an in-process server, while the second version is implemented as an out-of-process COM server. The out-of-process server is currently configured to use a pool of only one thread, but later you will change the server to use a larger pool of threads.

The demonstration requires some setup on your part. You will need to register both the in-process and out-of-process servers. Refer to the section *About Self-Registering COM Servers* for information on how to un-register a server.

To register the servers for the multi-threaded demo:

1. Using *regsvr32*, register the in-process server, *VBDLLServer.DLL*, located in folder *VB6Adv\Demos\Threads\DLLServer*. Refer to Chapter 1 for hints on how to register an in-process server.

2. To register the out-of-process server, run the executable, *VBEXEServer .EXE*, located in folder *VB6Adv\Demos\Threads\EXEServer*. You can do this by double-clicking the filename from *Windows Explorer*.

3. Proceed to the next section to run the demo program.

RUNNING THE MULTI-THREADED DEMONSTRATION PROGRAM

Both servers used by the multi-threaded client implement the same interface that contains logic for computing the endpoints of a circle given the center point, radius, and angle in degrees. The interface exposes three methods, *SetCX, SetCY,* and *GetCirclePoints*. To use either server, a client first calls *SetCX* and *SetCY* to establish the center point of the circle. Then, the client calls *GetCirclePoints*, passing the radius and angle. The *GetCirclePoints* method returns the coordinates via two additional parameters, *X* and *Y*. The interface is purposefully split into these three functions to illustrate how it is nearly impossible to create a non-thread-safe server in Visual Basic. Later in this walkthrough, you will modify the in-process server so that it uses global data to store the circle's center point. With up to sixteen instances of circles, you would think that the use of global data would provide invalid results. However, each thread has its own copy of global data, since each thread resides in its own apartment.

The client application is written in C++, a more appropriate language for the development of multi-threaded programs. It is an MFC dialog-based application that allows you to choose between using the in-process and out-of-process implementations of the server. You may also choose between one, four, and sixteen threads. The client application does not draw perfect circles. Instead, it finds ten points on a circle and draws straight lines between them, therefore drawing decagons.

Both implementations of the server delay $1/10^{th}$ of a second upon calculating an endpoint. This delay is provided both to simulate blocking and to provide some predictability in the duration it takes for the client application to complete. Since the client calls the *GetCirclePoints* method ten times for each circle, each circle takes one second to draw.

You will notice that when the in-process server version is used, it takes about one second to draw all circles, even if sixteen circles are drawn. This is due to the fact that the client creates a thread for each circle. While one thread is blocked for the 1/10th-second delay, another thread can start to get its endpoint. You can visually see the results of using multiple threads; the circles are all drawn at apparently the same time.

When the out-of-process server is used, results clearly show the effect of client requests being queued behind each other. You should expect the elapsed time to be at least one second per circle. It will, in fact, probably be somewhat greater than this predicted time, since the startup time of an out-of-process COM server is greater than that of an in-process COM server. Later, when you modify the server to use a thread pool, you will begin to notice results in the out-of-process server that are close to the results achieved by the in-process server.

You are, of course, encouraged to experiment with this demo program as much as you would like. However, I suggest you first try to stick with the following walkthrough to get the most out of the demo program.

First, observe the difference between server implementations:

1. Make sure that you have registered both COM servers as indicated in the previous section.

2. Run the program *MTClient.EXE* from folder *VB6Adv\Demos\Threads\ MTClient\Release*.

3. Using one thread, click the *Use In-Proc Server* button. The program will draw a circle, and should take about one second to complete. You may observe a startup delay that causes the elapsed time to cross over into taking two seconds – click the *Erase* button, then click the *Use In-Proc Server* button a second time. It will probably take only one second this time. Click the *Erase* button after each time you draw circles.

4. Again using one thread, click the *Use Out-of-Proc Server* button. Results for the out-of-process server should be fairly consistent between uses. This is because the in-process server, once loaded into the process's address space, remains loaded even when no objects are created. This is not true with an out-of-process server, which shuts down when objects no longer exist.

5. Now select four threads and observe the elapsed time when the in-process server is used. It should take about the same amount of time to draw four circles as it took to draw one.

6. Again, using the in-process server, observe the elapsed time for drawing sixteen circles. It takes about the same amount of time to draw sixteen circles as it does to draw one circle.

7. Now draw four circles using the out-of-process server. The resulting

elapsed time will be at least four seconds. Since the current implementation of the out-of-process server uses only one thread to service client requests, it takes about one second to draw each circle.

8. Again, using the out-of-process server, observe the elapsed time for drawing sixteen circles. As you may have predicted, it takes at least sixteen seconds to complete this run.

GLOBAL DATA BEHAVIOR IN APARTMENT-MODEL THREADING

In this section, you will work with the in-process (ActiveX DLL) implementation of the server and observe how each apartment receives its own copy of global data. You will modify the server so that the center point of a circle is located in global data. If each thread were actually using the same copy of this data, only one circle would apparently be drawn – in actual fact, all circles would be located at the same location. However, you will observe no difference in the behavior of the application.

The in-process server implementation is located in the project *VBDLLServer.VBP*, in folder *VB6Adv\Demos\Threads\DLLServer*. The project consists of two modules. One of the modules is a class module that implements the *Trig* object (*Trig.CLS*). The other module is a standard module that contains the global variables *gCX* and *gCY* (*Globals.BAS*). Code in the *SetCX* and *SetCY* methods, located in the *Trig* class module, store the circle's center point both in per-object storage (private variables in the class module) and in the global variables mentioned previously. In the *GetCirclePoints* method, code that uses the global data instead of the per-object data is commented out. In this section, you will modify the *GetCirclePoints* method to use global data instead of per-object data and observe that the server still performs as it did before.

Note that the purpose of this activity is purely academic in nature – I certainly do not encourage the use of global data in COM servers. I want you to observe how even a clearly poorly written program – one that uses global data when it should have used per-object data – can still work properly when apartment-model threading is used in Visual Basic.

The source code for both modules follows, and are in turn followed by instructions for modifying the COM server to use global data. Following is the code contained in the standard module, in which the global data is declared:

```
Public Declare Sub Sleep _
        Lib "kernel32" (ByVal dwMilliseconds As Long)
Public gCX As Double
Public gCY As Double
```

And here is the source code for the class module:

```
Option Explicit

Private m_cx As Double
Private m_cy As Double

Public Sub SetCX(ByVal cx As Double)
    m_cx = cx
    gCX = cx
End Sub
Public Sub SetCY(ByVal cy As Double)
    m_cy = cy
    gCY = cy
End Sub

Public Sub GetCirclePoints(ByVal r As Double, _
                           ByVal t As Double, _
                           ByRef x As Double, _
                           ByRef y As Double)
    Dim nThetaRad As Double
    Dim nCX As Double, nCY As Double

    nThetaRad = (3.141 / 180#) * t
    nCX = m_cx
    nCY = m_cy

    Sleep 100

    '- Uncomment the next two lines to simulate a poorly
    '- written program that uses global data.  The
    '- program will still work because Visual Basic
    '- provides a copy of global data for each apartment.

    'nCX = gCX
    'nCY = gCY

    x = nCX + (Cos(nThetaRad) * r)
    y = nCY + (Sin(nThetaRad) * r)

End Sub
```

To make this modification and observe its effect:

1. Load the project *VBDLLServer.VBP* from folder *VB6Adv\Demos\Threads\DLLServer.*

2. Bring up a *Code Window* for the *Trig* class module.

3. Locate the *GetCirclePoints* method.

4. Find the two lines of code that are commented out. A comment preceding these two lines of code will guide you to the correct location.

5. Uncomment the two lines of code and rebuild the project by selecting *Make VBServer.DLL* from the *File* menu. The server is now using global data to save the circle object's center point.

6. Run the client test program and, using the in-process server, observe the results when one, four, and sixteen circles are drawn. If each object were indeed sharing the same copy of a center point, all circles would be in the same location. Since each apartment has its own global data, the actual results are no different than when the server was using per-object data.

Thread Pools for Out-of-Process Servers

In the next phase of this walkthrough, you will modify the out-of-process server so that it uses a pool of threads to service client requests. Initially, the thread pool will be sufficient to provide a thread for each object when four circles are drawn, but will be insufficient to service sixteen objects.

To enable a thread pool for the out-of-process server:

1. Load the project *VBEXEServer.VBP* from folder *VB6Adv\Demos\Threads\EXEServer.*

2. From the *Project* menu, select *VBExeServer Properties.*

3. In the resulting *Project Properties* dialog, select the *General* tab.

4. Under *Threading Model*, select the *Thread Pool* option and enter *8* for the number of threads (see Figure 8-2).

5. Rebuild the server by selecting *Make VBExeServer.EXE* from the *Project* menu.

6. Run the client test program and observe the elapsed time to draw four circles. It will take less than four seconds to draw these circles, since a thread can be assigned to each object. It will probably still take longer than the in-process implementation of the server, but will take less time than the single-threaded version of the out-of-process implementation.

7. Now observe what happens when you use sixteen threads to access the out-of-process server. All sixteen circles should eventually be drawn, but some must wait for an available thread.

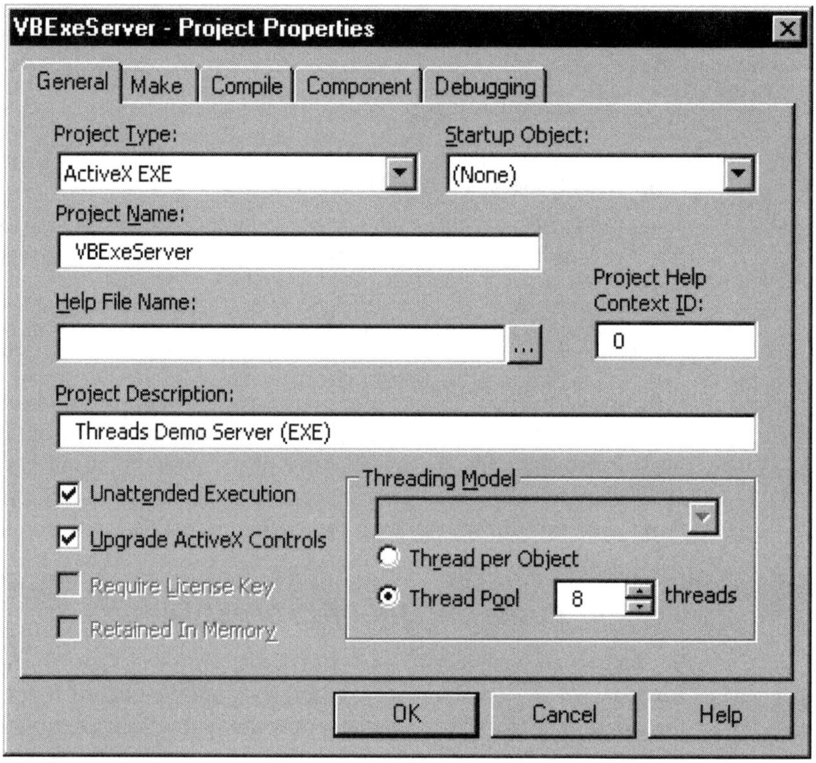

FIGURE 8-2 In an ActiveX EXE, you can assign a pool of threads to service client requests.

Assigning One Thread Per Object

In the final stage of this walkthrough, you will modify the out-of-process implementation of the server so that a separate thread is assigned to each object. The performance of such an implementation will be nearly as good as the in-process implementation. However, assigning one thread per object offers you no control. Several multi-threaded clients may end up causing the creation of dozens or hundreds of threads in your server process. At some point, creating and managing a large number of threads introduces overhead that eliminates the benefits of multi-threading. Use this option only if you are certain that your workload will not introduce an excess of threads.

To assign one thread per object for the out-of-process server:

1. Load the project *VBEXEServer.VBP* from folder *VB6Adv\Demos\ Threads\EXEServer.*

2. From the *Project* menu, select *VBExeServer Properties.*

3. In the resulting *Project Properties* dialog, select the *General* tab.

4. Under *Threading Model*, select the *Thread Per Object* option.

5. Rebuild the server by selecting *Make VBExeServer.EXE* from the *Project* menu. If you receive a *permission denied* error, it may indicate that the server is still running. Make sure you are not still running the client application, and verify that *VBExeServer* is not running by loading the *Task Manager.* Kill the process if necessary.

6. Run the client test program and observe the elapsed time to draw one, four, and sixteen circles. The results should be close to the results observed for the in-process implementation.

Creating ActiveX Controls with Visual Basic

It seems that every one of my advanced Visual Basic students want to know how to create ActiveX Controls. It may well be that you have already decided that it will be necessary for you to create one or more ActiveX Controls for your distributed application, but in practice, this is probably rare. Generally, when one creates an ActiveX Control, it is intended that the control will be used in a dialog-based Win32 client application, such as a Visual Basic or C++/MFC application. A "full-blown" ActiveX Control has a visual appearance and responds to user and program interaction when it appears on a form or dialog window. Strictly speaking, an ActiveX Control is not required in distributed applications, except on the dialog windows of Win32 presentation layer clients. And, for that purpose, there are thousands of third-party ActiveX Controls available; chances are there is already one that will do what you need. Therefore, you will probably not need to develop your own ActiveX Control.

Of course, this conclusion depends on what you mean by the term "ActiveX Control." Microsoft has renamed these entities several times. At various points, these objects have been known as custom controls, VBXs, OLE custom controls, and OCXs, although Microsoft shuns the term "OCX" as applied to an ActiveX Control. Not too long ago, Microsoft renamed OLE custom controls to ActiveX Controls. At the time, it was announced that, to be considered an ActiveX Control, an object must be a COM object that implements, at a minimum, the *IUknown* interface, and is self-registering. An ActiveX Control that meets only these minimum requirements clearly does not do very much. Most corporate software developers in the industry have not really bought into this definition. When one speaks of ActiveX Controls, the image is of a visible control that can be placed on a Visual Basic form, exposes properties and methods, and fires events back to the container in response to user and program interaction. I'll use that stereotype as the basis for the type of object presented in this chapter; that is, an ActiveX Control hosts a custom user interface component.

What is an ActiveX Control?

An ActiveX Control can be hosted in a number of ActiveX Control Containers, including Visual Basic forms, MFC dialogs, and Microsoft's *Internet Explorer* Web browser. However, any COM object that supports the *IDispatch* interface can be hosted and scripted from a Web page. It is not absolutely essential that you package your COM object into an ActiveX Control. Perhaps you are assuming that you need to create ActiveX Controls because some of the client applications in your presentation layer will be ASP-based scripts. If that is the case, I have good news for you – you already know how to create such controls. The COM objects that you created in previous chapters in this book are, by Microsoft's definition, ActiveX Controls. They simply do not have a visible appearance and cannot be directly placed on a dialog window.

An ActiveX Control provides an ideal package for user interface component reusability in other Visual Basic applications. After adding an ActiveX Control to a project, the developer simply sets a few properties, invokes some methods, and responds to events generated by your ActiveX Control. However, like any general, reusable software component, ActiveX Controls are somewhat involved to set up. But with a little extra work, your user interface component can be packaged and distributed as an ActiveX Control, giving other developers the easiest way to reuse your software.

Comparing ActiveX Controls and ActiveX Components

An **ActiveX Control** is an ActiveX entity that is packaged as an OCX. Like the other COM objects discussed in this book, an ActiveX Control exposes properties, methods, and events to developers. However, unlike the other COM objects discussed so far, an ActiveX Control is not hosted in an in-process or out-of-process COM server – or what Visual Basic collectively calls ActiveX Components (note that the name applies to the server hosting the COM objects, and not to the COM objects themselves). An ActiveX Control can be added to the Visual Basic toolbox to give developers the easiest way to reuse your software.

A major difference between an ActiveX Component and an ActiveX Control is that an ActiveX Control must be sited (placed) in a container application. A Visual Basic application serves as an appropriate ActiveX container application, as does an MFC dialog developed with Visual C++.

About the ActiveX Control Demo

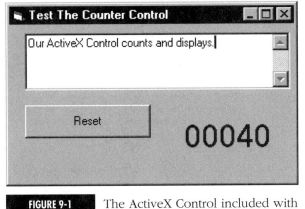

FIGURE 9-1 The ActiveX Control included with this book is called the *Counter Control*.

The software included with this book includes an implementation of an ActiveX Control known as the **Counter Control** (see Figure 9-1). This control has two methods, the **Increment** method increments the count and the **Reset** method resets the count back to zero. As the counter increments, it displays the counter in an "odometer" fashion (with leading zeroes). It starts off in a color set by the user via the **ColorNormal** property. Its **LevelWarn** property, which the user can set, indicates a "warning" level. When the counter reaches the warning level, it changes to the color indicated by the **ColorWarn** property, and raises the **Warn** event. It also has a property called **LevelMax** that indicates a "maximum" level. When the counter reaches the maximum level, it changes to the color indicated by the **ColorMax** property, and raises the **Max** event. Also, at this point, it ignores further **Increment** methods. Finally, there is a read-only property, unavailable at design time, called **CurrentCount**, which gives the current value of the *Counter Control's* count.

Prior to examining the techniques used to build this ActiveX Control, you should run the demo program and try creating a new Visual Basic application that uses the *Counter Control*. To do this, I would encourage you to follow the steps below. Although it is not necessary for you to do so at the moment, you can access the source code for both the ActiveX Control and its client test program by opening the project group *TestGroup.VBG* from folder *VB6Adv\Demos\ActiveXControl*.

1. Register the OCX *MyControl.OCX*, located in folder *VB6Adv\Demos\ ActiveXControl*. Use the *regsvr32* tool, or use the shortcut mentioned in Chapter 1. Note that the technique used to register in-process servers (DLLs) is the same technique used to register ActiveX Controls.

2. Run the program *TestControl.EXE*, located in the same folder as the OCX.

3. Enter text into the text box. With each keystroke, the counter is incremented. When the count reaches 50, the counter's color changes to yellow, and the caption "WARNING!!!" appears.

4. Continue to type into the text box until the counter reaches 100. At that point, the counter will change color to red, and the caption "MAXIMUM REACHED" will appear. The text box will then become locked until you click the *Reset* button.

CREATING A NEW CLIENT TEST PROGRAM

To see how easy it is to use this ActiveX Control from a Visual Basic application, I encourage you to follow the steps below. You will create a new Visual Basic application and add the *Counter Control* to your toolbox (see Figure 9-2). You will then place an instance of the control on your Visual Basic form, and set a few of its properties. Finally, you will add code to the program to drive the control.

1. Create a new Standard EXE project with Visual Basic.

2. From the *Project* menu, select *Components*.

3. In the resulting *Components* dialog, select the *Controls* tab.

4. Scroll down the list of controls until you find the entry *My Counter ActiveX Control*, then check the box next to this entry.

5. Click the OK button to dismiss the *Components* dialog.

6. Note the icon added to your toolbox – it appears as the numbers 1, 2, and 3, with the number 3 just "flipping up" like an odometer. This is the icon for the *Counter Control*. If you let the mouse pointer hover momentarily over this icon, the tooltip *"Counter"* will appear.

7. Double-click the *Counter* icon in the toolbox to add it to your form.

8. Set the *LevelMax* property to *10*, and the *LevelWarn* property to *5*. These properties are simple integer values.

9. Set the *CharSize* property of the *Counter Control* to *2-ccLarge*. This is an example of an enumerated property.

10. Choose a different color for the *ColorNormal* property. Note how Visual Basic displays a palette of color choices, since it is "aware" that the property is a color.

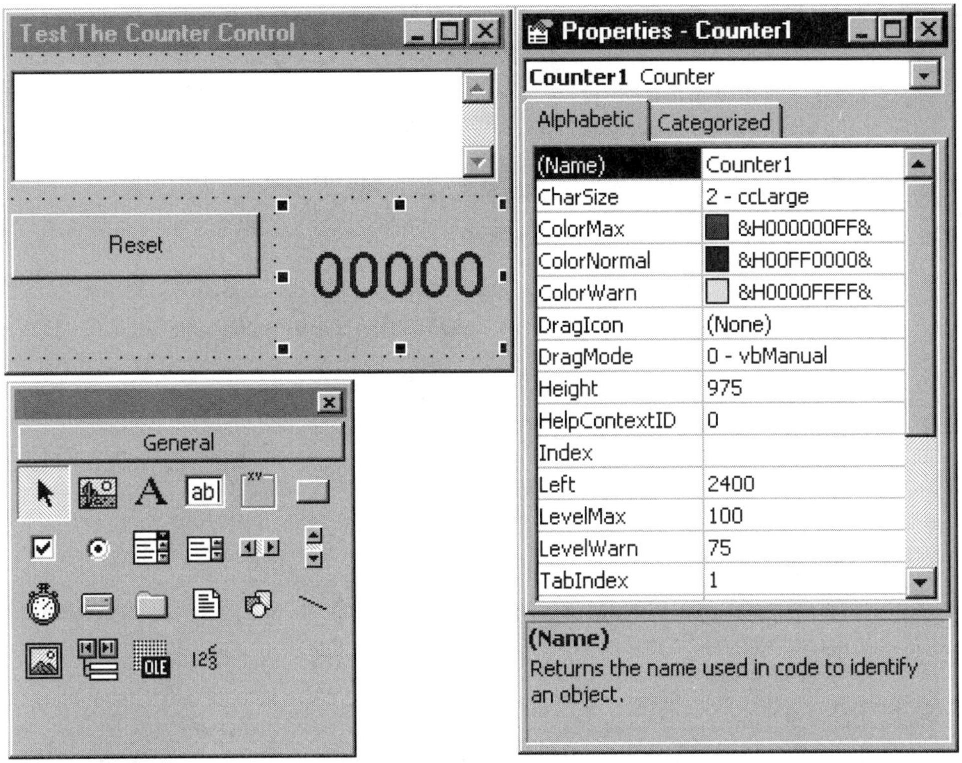

FIGURE 9-2 The *Counter Control* has its own icon in the toolbox, and color properties that show up in the properties window. It also illustrates creating enumerated properties.

11. Add two buttons to your form, labeling one of them *Increment* and the other *Reset*.

12. In the *Increment* button's *Click* event, invoke the *Increment* method on your *Counter Control*, which will be called *Counter1*.

13. In the *Reset* button's *Click* event, invoke the *Reset* method on your *Counter Control*.

14. In the *Code Window*, select *Counter1* from the *Object* list, and select *Warn* from the *Procedure* list. Add code to display a *message box* indicating that the warning level has been reached.

15. Create an event procedure to handle the *Max* event raised by the *Counter Control* – you can simply display as message box indicating that the maximum level has been reached.

16. Run and test your program.

Creating an ActiveX Control

The walkthrough presented in this chapter demonstrates the following techniques related to the creation of an ActiveX Control:

- Creating an ActiveX Control project.
- Creating a Visual Basic project group.
- Setting the default size of an ActiveX Control.
- Using constituent controls to make an ActiveX Control.
- Adding a simple integer property to an ActiveX Control.
- Adding a read-only property that is unavailable at design time.
- Using ambient properties "inherited" from the container application.
- Using standard control property types, in particular, colors.
- Using enumerated properties.
- Adding methods to an ActiveX Control.
- Raising events from an ActiveX Control.
- Assigning a bitmap to be used in the Visual Basic toolbox.
- Compiling, using, and distributing an ActiveX Control.
- Mapping properties to constituent control properties.
- Using the *ActiveX Control Interface Wizard.*
- Adding property pages to an ActiveX Control.

In the remaining sections, I will guide you through the creation of this ActiveX Control. If you follow these steps, you will end up replacing the ActiveX Control distributed with this book. However, you can always re-register the original ActiveX Control if you want to go back to using the original one.

Starting an ActiveX Control Project

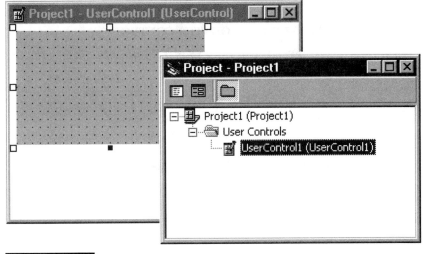

FIGURE 9-3   In an ActiveX Control project, Visual Basic creates one user control for you automatically.

The first step in creating an ActiveX Control is to create an **ActiveX Control project**. When a new ActiveX Control project is created, Visual Basic automatically creates a *User Control* object, giving it a proposed name of *UserControl1* (see Figure 9-3). It is important that you properly set the properties of both the ActiveX Control project and its *User Control* object.

To start a new ActiveX Control project:

1. From the *File* menu, select *New Project*.
2. In the *New Project* dialog, select *ActiveX Control* as the project type.
3. From the *Project* menu, select *Properties*.
4. Verify that the project type is *ActiveX Control*.
5. Verify that the *startup object* is *none*.
6. Set the *project name* to something meaningful. This will be the name of your OCX file.
7. Set the *project description* to something meaningful. This description will show up in the *Components* dialog.
8. Set the *Name* property of the *user control* to something meaningful. This will be how your control is named and will be the *ToolTip* in the Visual Basic *Toolbox*.

9. Resize the control in the designer window. This will be the default size of the control when it is placed on a form.

10. It's a good idea to save the project at this point.

SETTING UP THE COUNTER CONTROL

To get started with the *Counter Control*, access the *Project Properties* dialog (see Figure 9-4) and set the *Project Name* to *MyControls*. When the OCX is built, it will be put into a file by the name of *MyControls.OCX*. Set the *Project Description* to "*The Counter Control ActiveX Control.*" This is how the *Object Browser* will describe your control, and this is what will appear in the Visual Basic *Components* dialog. Set the (*Name*) property of the user control to *Counter*. This will be the class of the control, and will be the *ToolTip* shown in Visual Basic's toolbox window.

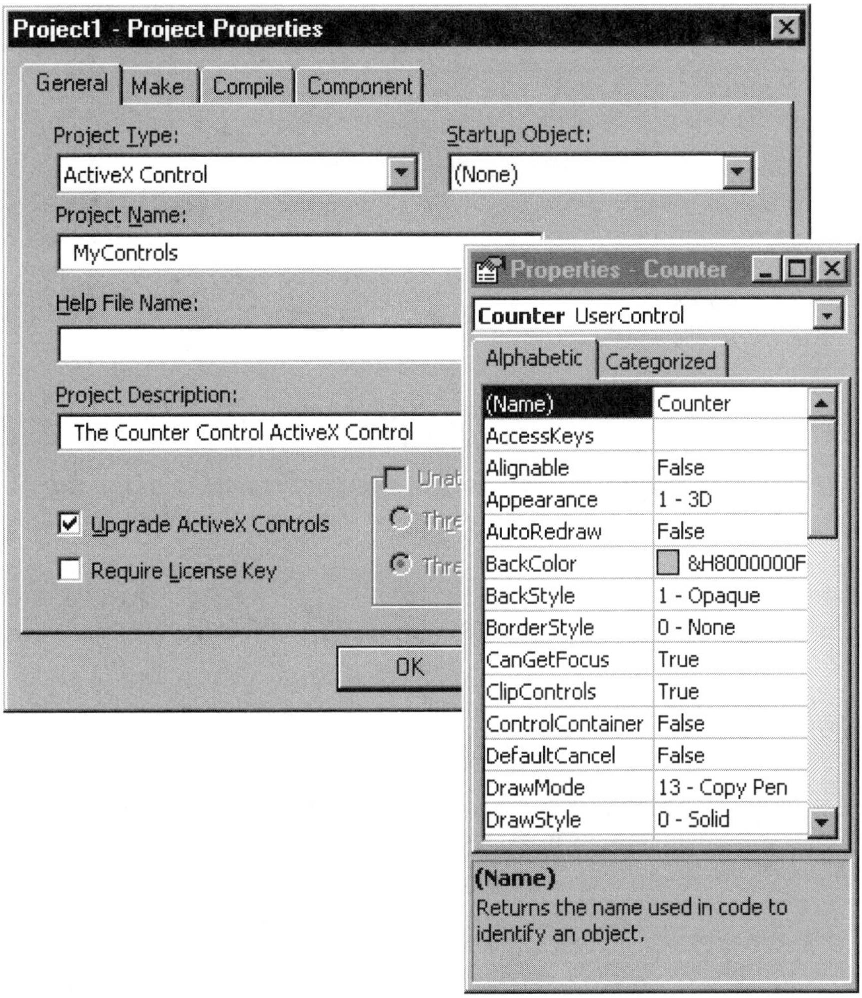

FIGURE 9-4 To create the *Counter Control*, set *Project Properties* as described. Also, set the *(Name)* of the user control to *Counter*.

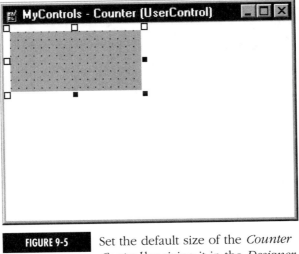

FIGURE 9-5 Set the default size of the *Counter Control* by sizing it in the *Designer Window.*

SETTING THE DEFAULT SIZE OF THE COUNTER CONTROL

The size of the control in the *Active X Control Designer Window* determines the default size of the control when it is placed on a form by a developer (see Figure 9-5). Size the **Counter Control** so that it appears large enough to hold a five-digit number of a font size of 24 – I used a height of 900 twips and a width of 2040 twips. You can change this size many times before finally making an OCX. After performing this step, you should save the project.

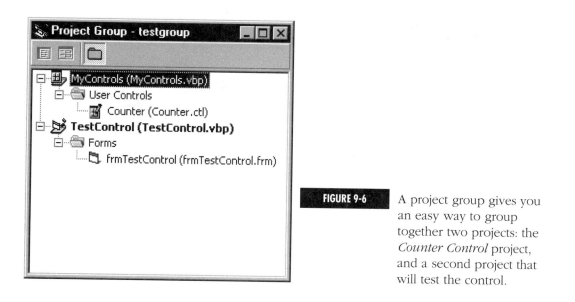

FIGURE 9-6 A project group gives you an easy way to group together two projects: the *Counter Control* project, and a second project that will test the control.

Creating a Project Group

The best way to develop an ActiveX Control is to test it "on-the-fly," and the easiest way to do that is to use a project group (see Figure 9-6). A project group groups together two or more projects. You can still work independently in each project. To create a project group for the *Counter Control,*

1. Add a project by selecting **Add Project** from the **File** menu.
2. Select **Standard EXE** as the project type, and click **OK**. Note that you will see both projects in the *Project Explorer* window.
3. Bring up the properties for the newly added project by selecting **Project1 Properties** from the **Project** menu. Set the *Project Name* to **TestControl**, then click **OK**.
4. In the *Project Explorer* window, right-click on the *TestControl* project and select **Set as Start Up**.
5. Assign the name **frmTestControl** to the form.
6. Save the Project Group by selecting **Save Project Group** from the **File** menu. You will be prompted to save the form, new project, and group.

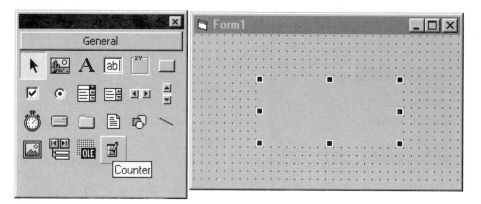

FIGURE 9-7 It certainly won't do much at this point, but it's interesting to try to use your control.

TESTING THE COUNTER CONTROL IN DESIGN MODE

You've really already made an ActiveX Control, but it won't be useful so far. In this phase, you will see what your control looks like in the toolbox, and see the properties automatically given to ActiveX Controls (see Figure 9-7). The control will appear disabled in the *UI* project's toolbox if you have the control open in a *Designer Window.* You cannot use an instance of your control in the user interface project until you have closed the *Designer Window* for the ActiveX Control. To test the control,

1. To place an instance of an ActiveX Control on your form, you must first close the control's *Designer Window.*
2. Find the control's icon in the toolbox by "hovering" over each control until you see *Counter* as the *ToolTip.*
3. Double-click the control's icon to place an instance on the form.
4. Look at the properties given automatically to an ActiveX Control.
5. Double-click on the control on your form to open a code window. Look at the events your control gets automatically. Your control will receive the default name of *Counter1.*

Using a Constituent Control

To save you the trouble of "re-inventing the wheel," you can use existing controls to help make up your ActiveX Control. These controls are referred to as **constituent controls**. To add a constituent control to your ActiveX Control, return to the *Designer Window* for your ActiveX Control, and place the constituent control on the ActiveX Control in the same manner in which you would place a control on a form.

While developers that use your ActiveX Control can see its constituent controls, they cannot by default directly access them. You can, however, expose the properties and methods of your constituent controls by wrapping them in your own properties and methods. This will be the technique illustrated in this book. You can directly expose constituent controls to developers, but this is not recommended.

For your **Counter Control**, you can use a **Label** control, which does a good job of displaying text as a constituent control. The following example assumes you've added a constituent control to your ActiveX Control, a *Label* called *lblInfo*. To expose the *Caption* property, you can write *Property Let* and *Get* procedures as shown below (this step is not necessary for this walkthrough):

```
Public Property Let Caption (newCaption as String)
  lblInfo.Caption = newCaption
End Property

Public Property Get Caption () as String
  Caption = lblInfo.Caption
End Property
```

ADDING A CONSTITUENT LABEL CONTROL TO THE COUNTER CONTROL

For the *Counter Control*, you can use a *Label* control as a constituent control (see Figure 9-8). This *Label* control will be used to display the value of the counter. To add a *Label* control as a constituent control,

1. Open the *Designer Window* for the *Counter Control* (double-click on its entry in the *Project Explorer* window).

2. Double-click the *Label* control icon in the *Toolbox*. Don't be concerned about where the *Label* control sits in the *Counter Control*; you will resize and reposition it at runtime.

3. Set properties of the newly added *Label* control as shown in Table 9-1.

TABLE 9-1	Properties of Constituent Label Control

Label Property	Value
(Name)	*lblCounter*
Autosize	TRUE
ForeColor	BLUE
Caption	00000
Alignment	CENTER

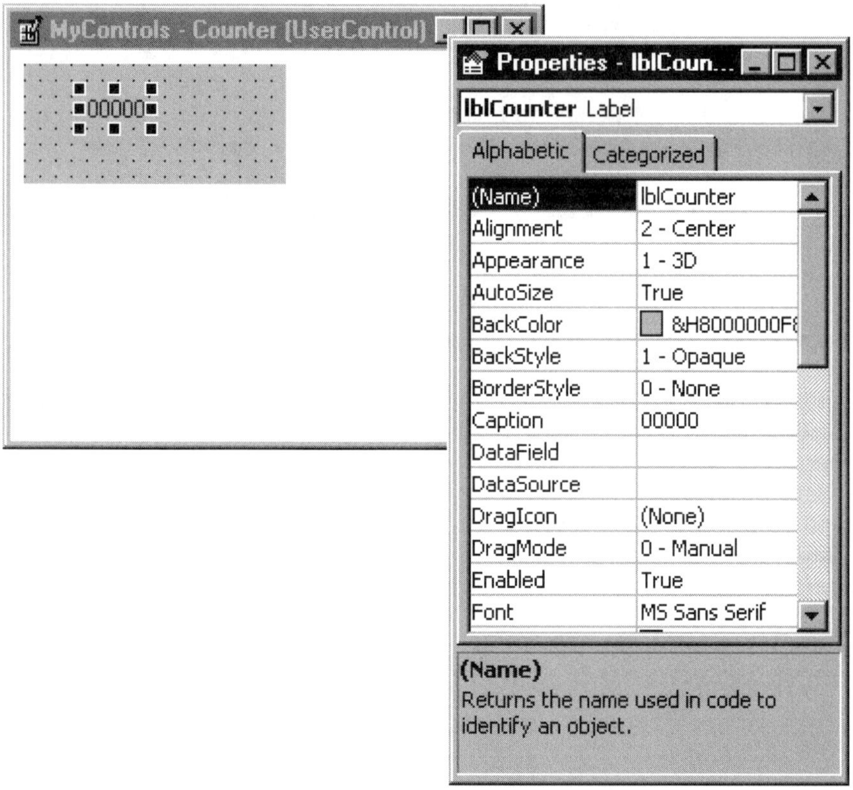

FIGURE 9-8 You'll use a *Label* control to show the value of the counter.

The UserControl Resize Event

Any time an ActiveX Control is resized, including the first time its placed on a form, it receives a **UserControl_Resize** event. If appropriate, you can add code to this event procedure to alter the appearance of your user control. In the *Counter Control*, you can add code to reposition the constituent *Label* control so that it is centered in the *Counter Control* (see Figure 9-9). The following code, for example, will center the *Label* control when the *Counter Control* is resized:

```
Private Sub UserControl_Resize()
     lblCounter.Move (ScaleWidth - lblCounter.Width)/2, _
              (ScaleHeight - lblCounter.Height) / 2
End Sub
```

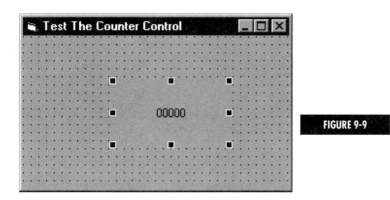

FIGURE 9-9 After adding code to the *Counter Control's Resize* event, the label will automatically position itself in the center of the control.

To test this feature, add the above code to your *Counter Control*, close the *Designer Window* and resize the *Counter Control* in your test form. Note how the label positions itself in the center of the control:

1. Double-click your control in the *Designer Window* (don't double-click the label). This brings up a *Code Window*.
2. Select the event *Resize*.
3. Add code as shown above. The code repositions the label so that it is in the center of the *Counter Control* (you are letting the label's built-in *Autosize* feature resize the label).

Persistent Properties

A **persistent property** is a property whose value is saved by the ActiveX Control container, in this case, a Visual Basic form. Persistent properties are re-initialized from their initial values when the form on which they exist is loaded. In general, properties that are set at design time should be persistent properties.

To implement a persistent property, you must initialize the property in the **InitProperties** event for the control, read the value of the property in the **ReadProperties** event for the control, and write the value of the property in the **WriteProperties** event for the control. All of these tasks are in addition to the task of providing *Property Let* and *Property Get* procedures for the property.

The *InitProperties* event is where you can give the property a default value for when an instance control is created. The code in the *ReadProperties* event also provides a default value. Surprisingly, even the code in the *WriteProperties* event must provide a default value for the property. This is an optimization; Visual Basic will not actually save the property if it is at its default value, thus saving space in the form file.

For a non-persistent property, you will not read or write the property in the *ReadProperties* and *WriteProperties* events. In the *Counter Control*, all properties with the exception of the *CurrentCount* property are persistent.

Reading and Writing Persistent Properties

Persistent properties are read in the **ReadProperties** event, and written in the **WriteProperties** event, both of which are events of the ActiveX Control. Both the *ReadProperties* and *WriteProperties* events pass, as a parameter, an instance of a *PropertyBag* class object, called **PropBag**. Don't be overly concerned about what a *PropertyBag* object is; all you need to know is that is has methods for reading and writing persistent properties.

To write a property to the *PropertyBag* object, invoke the **WriteProperty** method. Its syntax is as follows:

```
PropBag.WriteProperty PropertyName, _
                 PropertyValue, _
                 DefaultValue
```

To read a property from the *PropertyBag* object, invoke the **ReadProperty** method. Its syntax is as follows:

```
PropertyValue = PropBag.ReadProperty (PropertyName, _
                                 DefaultValue)
```

The following example assumes you have a property called **LevelMax**, the value of which is being kept in the private variable **iLevelMax**. The example shows how to read and write the property. Assume the default value of this property is 1000.

```
Private Sub UserControl_ReadProperties _
               (PropBag As PropertyBag)
     LevelMax = PropBag.ReadProperty("LevelMax", 1000)
End Sub

Private Sub UserControl_WriteProperties _
               (PropBag As PropertyBag)
     PropBag.WriteProperty "LevelMax", iLevelMax, 1000
End Sub
```

Property Change Notification

If you are beginning to think that the list of steps for adding a persistent property to an ActiveX Control is growing ridiculously long, here's another! When a property changes, you must notify the container (i.e., Visual Basic). If you do not do this, Visual Basic will fail to synchronize the *Properties* window, and will not know that it needed to write the property's value. The good news is that this is an easy step. Simply use the **PropertyChanged** function, passing the name of the property that changed. This step is typically done in the property's *Property Let* procedure. For example,

```
Public Property Let LevelMax(newLevelMax As Integer)
     iLevelMax = newLevelMax
     PropertyChanged "MaxLevel"
End Property
```

LEVELMAX AND LEVELWARN COUNTER CONTROL PROPERTIES

The first step to adding the **LevelMax** and **LevelWarn** properties is to perform the same steps you learned in adding properties to ActiveX Components. In other words, you must

1. Declare private variables in the declarations section of the control, to hold the actual value of the properties. This step is required because you will not directly expose the properties to the user.

2. Create a **Property Let** procedure for each property. These procedures will simply copy the new value into the appropriate private variable declared above, and notify the container by invoking the **PropertyChanged** procedure.

3. Create a **Property Get** procedure for each property. These procedures will simply return the value from the appropriate private variable declared above.

   For example,

```
Private iLevelMax As Integer
Private iLevelWarn As Integer

Public Property Get LevelMax() As Integer
     LevelMax = iLevelMax
End Property

Public Property Let LevelMax(newLevelMax As Integer)
     iLevelMax = newLevelMax
     PropertyChanged "MaxLevel"
End Property
```

```
Public Property Get LevelWarn() As Integer
     LevelWarn = iLevelWarn
End Property

Public Property Let LevelWarn(newLevelWarn As Integer)
     iLevelWarn = newLevelWarn
     PropertyChanged "MaxLevel"
End Property
```

Since both the *LevelMax* and *LevelWarn* properties are persistent, you have another step to perform. You must add code to the *InitProperties*, *ReadProperties*, and *WriteProperties* events. This is straightforward, and the code is as follows:

```
Private Sub UserControl_InitProperties()
     LevelMax = 1000
     LevelWarn = 800
End Sub

Private Sub UserControl_ReadProperties _
               (PropBag As PropertyBag)
     LevelMax = PropBag.ReadProperty("LevelMax", 1000)
     LevelWarn = PropBag.ReadProperty("LevelWarn", 800)
End Sub

Private Sub UserControl_WriteProperties _
               (PropBag As PropertyBag)
     PropBag.WriteProperty "LevelMax", LevelMax, 1000
     PropBag.WriteProperty "LevelWarn", LevelWarn, 800
End Sub
```

TESTING THE PERSISTENCE OF THE PROPERTIES

You should test your properties to make certain that they persist as expected. The easiest way to do this is to add an instance of your control to a form, then set one of your persistent properties. Close the form and open it again. Examine the property. If it is the same as what you set it to before, you have successfully created a persistent property. Otherwise, review the previous steps and correct your problem.

For example, to test the persistence of the *LevelMax* property,

1. Return to your test form and select the *Counter Control*.

2. In the *Properties* window, change the **LevelMax** property to *100* (see Figure 9-10).

3. Close the form and open it again. If the property is still equal to *100*, you're ready for the next step.

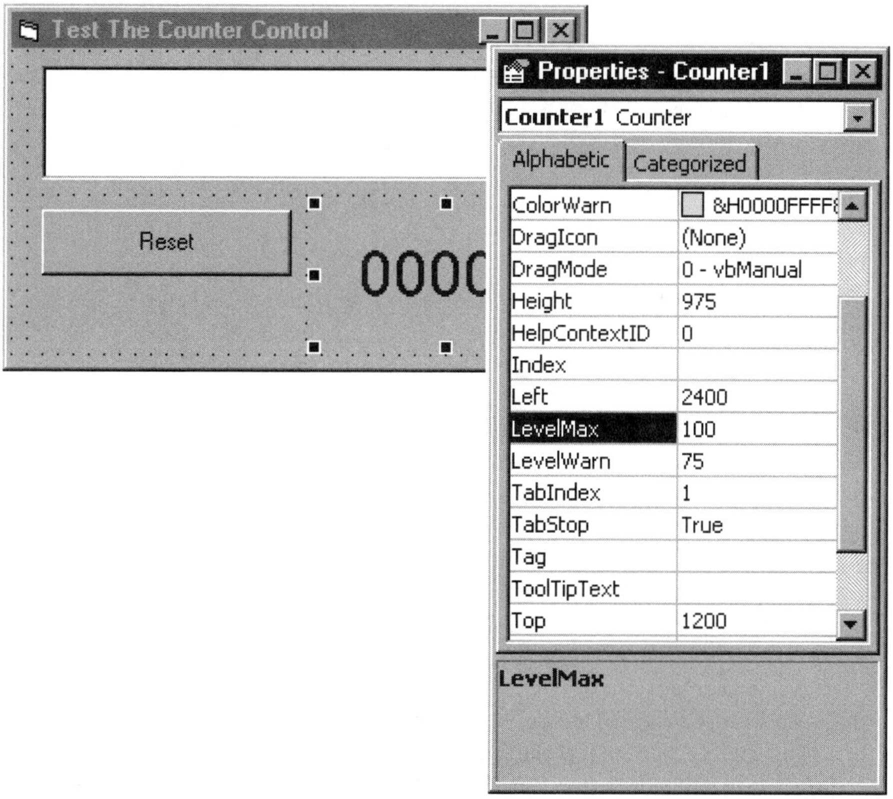

FIGURE 9-10 A persistent property remains at the same value when you close and reopen a form.

Read-Only Properties

To add a read-only property, implement only a ***Property Get*** procedure. You must still initialize the property in the ***InitProperty*** event for the control. Specifically, do not implement a *Property Let* procedure, do not read or write the property in the *ReadProperties* or *WriteProperties* event, and do not notify Visual Basic that the property changed with the *PropertyChanged* procedure. Read-only properties do not show up in the *Properties* window, thus making them available only at runtime.

ADDING THE CURRENTCOUNT PROPERTY

The following code should be added to the ***Counter Control*** to implement a ***CurrentCount*** property, which is initialized to zero when the control is created, and can only be read by the container program:

```
Private iCurrentCount As Integer

Private Sub UserControl_InitProperties()
      iCurrentCount = 0
      LevelMax = 1000
      LevelWarn = 800
End Sub

Public Property Get CurrentCount() As Integer
      CurrentCount = iCurrentCount
End Property
```

Ambient Properties

An **ambient property** is a property that appears to be part of your control, but which is actually supplied by a container. A good example of an ambient property is **BackColor**. By responding to changes in ambient properties, you can make your control more consistent with its container. For example, when the user changes the **BackColor** of a form, you may want to automatically change the background color of your constituent controls (see Figure 9-11). This is, of course, completely optional.

To implement such a feature, you will need to add code to the control's **AmbientChanged** event. This event is sent to the control when one of the container's ambient properties changes. To get the current value of an ambient property, you use the **Ambient** object. This object has properties that match the ambient properties. You will also need to initialize such properties in the **InitProperties** event, and read them in the **ReadProperties** event. You do not need to write them in the **WriteProperties** event, since these properties are actually saved by the container. You can also directly expose ambient properties to make them appear to the developer to be part of your control, but this approach is not recommended. If you did this, you would not be able to respond to the *AmbientChanged* event, and change the background color of the constituent label in response.

For example, to change the constituent *Label* control's background color to the ambient background color,

```
' Set label's background color to ambient
' background color
lblCounter.BackColor = Ambient.BackColor
```

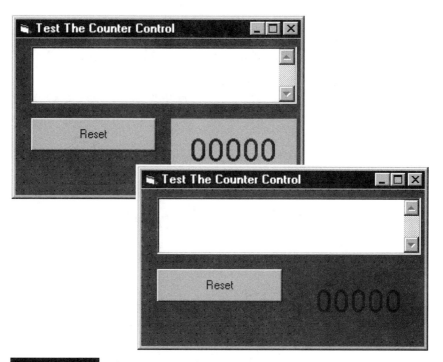

FIGURE 9-11   The control in the background does not respond to changes in the ambient *BackColor* property, while the control in the foreground does.

THE AMBIENTCHANGED EVENT IN THE COUNTER CONTROL

You can enable your *Counter Control* to automatically change its background color, and the background color of the constituent *Label* control, when the form's **BackColor** property changes. You will need to add related code to each of the following event procedures: **InitProperties**, **Ambient-Changed**, and **ReadProperties**. The additional code is shown below.

```
Private Sub UserControl_InitProperties()
        iCurrentCount = 0
        LevelMax = 1000
        LevelWarn = 800
        BackColor = Ambient.BackColor
        lblCounter.BackColor = BackColor
End Sub

Private Sub UserControl_AmbientChanged _
                    (PropertyName As String)
```

```
        BackColor = Ambient.BackColor
        lblCounter.BackColor = BackColor
End Sub

Private Sub UserControl_ReadProperties _
                    (PropBag As PropertyBag)
    LevelMax = PropBag.ReadProperty("LevelMax", 1000)
    LevelWarn = PropBag.ReadProperty("LevelWarn", 800)
    BackColor = Ambient.BackColor
    lblCounter.BackColor = BackColor
End Sub
```

Using Standard Control Property Types

When you indicate to Visual Basic that one of your properties is of a **standard type**, it can handle your property in a manner consistent with other controls. Using standard property types is easy, and adds quite a professional touch to your control.

You will add three color properties to the *Counter Control*: **ColorNormal**, **ColorWarn**, and **ColorMax** (see Figure 9-12). Use the type **OLE_COLOR** as the property type. Visual Basic handles the rest. Other standard property types are defined; see *Help* for more information.

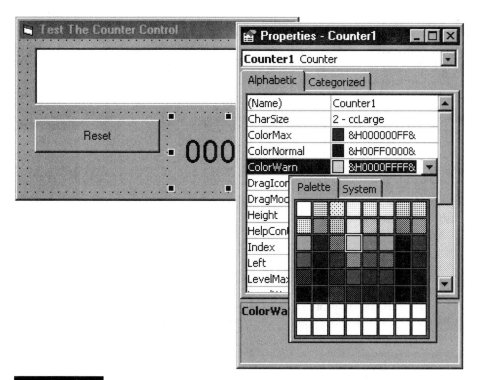

FIGURE 9-12 As a professional touch, you can use standard control property types so that Visual Basic can manage your property in a consistent manner.

ADDING COLOR PROPERTIES TO THE COUNTER CONTROL

You can now add three properties to the *Counter Control*, each of which will be of type *OLE_COLOR* (see Table 9-2). To add these properties, use the same techniques that you used to add the *LevelMax* and *LevelWarn* properties; that is,

1. Declare private variables in the declarations section of the control to hold the values of the properties.

2. Implement both *Property Get* and *Property Let* procedures for each property.

3. Initialize the properties in the *InitProperties* event for the control.

4. Read the properties in the *ReadProperties* event for the control.

5. Write the properties in the *WriteProperties* event for the control.

The only difference, and it's a minor one, is that the type of each property will be *OLE_COLOR*.

TABLE 9-2	Counter Properties of Type OLE_COLOR
Counter Control Property	**Description**
ColorNormal	Color used to display the count when it is below the warning level.
ColorWarn	Color used to display the count when it is between the warning level and maximum level.
ColorMax	Color used to display the count when it reaches the maximum level.

Enumerated Properties

When you want the value of a property to be selected from a list of valid values, the most professional way to implement it is as an enumerated type. Using an enumerated type requires an extra step—defining the enumeration, which is done by defining an enumerated type. When you use an enumeration type as the type of a property, Visual Basic automatically displays a list of valid values at design time when that property is selected in the *Properties* window (see Figure 9-13). Visual Basic also checks at runtime that the developer is setting the property to a legal value.

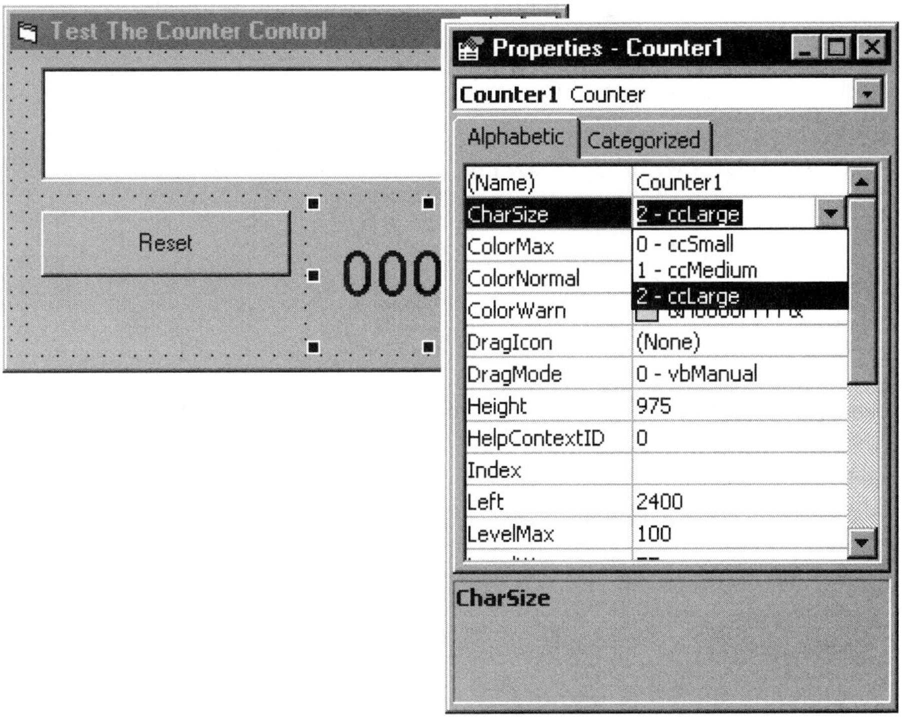

FIGURE 9-13 The *Counter Control's CharSize* property can be set to *Small, Medium,* or *Large,* represented by the numbers *0, 1,* and *2.*

Defining an Enumeration

Enumerations provide a way to define a related set of named constants. For example, Visual Basic has an enumeration called *vbDayOfWeek,* which contains the constants *vbMonday, vbTuesday,* and so on. If you use an enumeration as the type for a property, the choices will appear in a drop-down list in Visual Basic's *Properties* window. The syntax for defining an enumeration is as follows:

```
Public Enum EnumerationTypeName
  constant = value
  constant = value
    .
    .
    .
End Enum
```

Enumerations do not have to be assigned in sequential order, although your *Counter Control* will do that. Just be sure you do not have duplicates. Use the *EnumerationTypeName* as the type for your property.

ADDING THE CHARSIZE PROPERTY TO THE COUNTER CONTROL

Adding the **CharSize** property to the *Counter Control* is exactly like adding the other read/write properties, with one exception – the *CharSize* property is an enumerated type. For example,

```
Public Enum CharSizes
    ccSmall = 0
    ccMedium = 1
    ccLarge = 2
End Enum

Private iCharSize As Integer

Private Sub UserControl_ReadProperties _
                    (PropBag As PropertyBag)
    CharSize = PropBag.ReadProperty("CharSize", ccSmall)
End Sub


Private Sub UserControl_WriteProperties _
                    (PropBag As PropertyBag)
    PropBag.WriteProperty "CharSize", CharSize, ccSmall
End Sub
```

The *Property Let* and *Get* procedures for the *CharSize* property follow. Note the use of the *Select Case* statement in the *Property Let* procedure, which actually changes the font size of the constituent label.

```
Public Property Get CharSize() As CharSizes
    CharSize = iCharSize
End Property

Public Property Let CharSize(newCharSize As CharSizes)
    iCharSize = newCharSize
    PropertyChanged "CharSize"
    Select Case iCharSize
        Case ccSmall
            lblCounter.Font.Size = 8
        Case ccMedium
            lblCounter.Font.Size = 14
```

```
        Case ccLarge
            lblCounter.Font.Size = 24
    End Select
    lblCounter.Move (ScaleWidth - lblCounter.Width) / 2, _
                    (ScaleHeight - lblCounter.Height) / 2
End Property
```

Adding Methods to an ActiveX Control

Methods are added to ActiveX Controls the same way they are added to ActiveX Components – by defining public procedures. Code for the **Increment** and **Reset** methods of the *Counter Control* follows:

```
Public Sub Increment()

    ' Don't increment any more if at max

    If iCurrentCount = iLevelMax Then Exit Sub

    ' Increment, format, display, and change color

    iCurrentCount = iCurrentCount + 1
    lblCounter.Caption = Format(iCurrentCount, "00000")

    If iCurrentCount = iLevelWarn Then
        lblCounter.ForeColor = iColorWarn
    ElseIf iCurrentCount = iLevelMax Then
        lblCounter.ForeColor = iColorMax
    End If

End Sub

Public Sub Reset()
    iCurrentCount = 0
    lblCounter.Caption = "00000"
    lblCounter.ForeColor = iColorNormal
End Sub
```

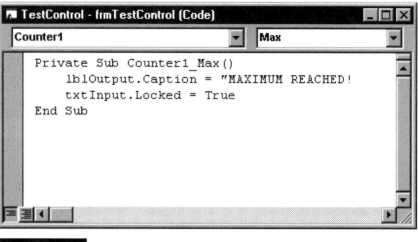

FIGURE 9-14   What good would an ActiveX Control be if it didn't raise events?

Raising Events from an ActiveX Control

Raising an event from an ActiveX Control requires two steps:

1. Declare the event (and, optionally, its parameters). The declarations of the event appear in the declarations section of the ActiveX Control.

2. Raise the event when appropriate (and, optionally, pass parameters to the event handler). This is typically done in a method or *Property Let* procedure.

The syntax for declaring an event is as follows:

```
Public Event eventname [(parameter As type, _
                        parameter As type, …)]
```

The syntax for raising an event is as follows:

```
' Syntax for raising an event:
RaiseEvent eventname [(parameter, parameter, …)]
```

Once you have declared an event in an ActiveX Control, it will be listed in the *Procedure* drop-down list of any form that uses the control (see Figure 9-14).

RAISING EVENTS FROM THE COUNTER CONTROL

You will raise a **Warn** event when the *Counter Control's* **CurrentCount** property reaches its **LevelWarn** property. This event will have no parameters. You will also raise a **Max** event when the *Counter Control's* **CurrentCount** property reaches its **LevelMax** property. This event will not have parameters either. Required code follows:

```
Public Event Warn()
Public Event Max()

Public Sub Increment()

    ' Don't increment any more if at max

    If iCurrentCount = iLevelMax Then Exit Sub

    ' Increment, format, display, and change color

    iCurrentCount = iCurrentCount + 1
    lblCounter.Caption = Format(iCurrentCount, "00000")

    If iCurrentCount = iLevelWarn Then
        lblCounter.ForeColor = iColorWarn
        RaiseEvent Warn
    ElseIf iCurrentCount = iLevelMax Then
        lblCounter.ForeColor = iColorMax
        RaiseEvent Max
    End If

End Sub
```

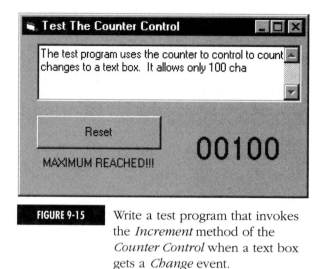

FIGURE 9-15   Write a test program that invokes the *Increment* method of the *Counter Control* when a text box gets a *Change* event.

COMPLETING THE COUNTER CONTROL TEST PROGRAM

To test the *Counter Control*, place a text box, label, and command button on your form along with the *Counter Control* itself (see Figure 9-15). In the text box's *Change* event, invoke the *Increment* method on the *Counter Control*. When the *Warn* event is raised by the *Counter Control*, place the text *"Warning!"* in the *Label* control. When the *Max* event is raised by the *Counter Control*, place the text *"Maximum Reached!"* in the *Label* control. Use the command button to invoke the *Reset* method on the *Counter Control*. For example,

```
Private Sub txtInput_Change()
    Counter1.Increment
End Sub

Private Sub cmdReset_Click()
    lblOutput.Caption = ""
    txtInput.Text = ""
    txtInput.SetFocus
    txtInput.Locked = False
    Counter1.Reset
End Sub

Private Sub Counter1_Max()
    lblOutput.Caption = "MAXIMUM REACHED!!!"
    txtInput.Locked = True
End Sub
```

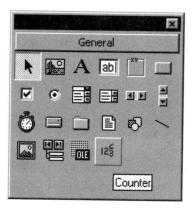

FIGURE 9-16 Assign a bitmap to your ActiveX Control by setting its *Toolbox-Bitmap* property to a bitmap (BMP) file.

```
Private Sub Counter1_Warn()
    lblOutput.Caption = "WARNING!!!"
End Sub
```

Assigning a Toolbox Bitmap

A satisfying final step is to create a bitmap for your control to be used in Visual Basic's toolbox (see Figure 9-16). Visual Basic uses the **ToolboxBitmap** property of your control to determine its appearance in the **Toolbox** window. Toolbox bitmaps are 16 pixels wide by 15 pixels high. Use all of this area; Visual Basic adds borders and 3D adornments. These adornments don't count in the 16x15 area.

Building, Using, and Distributing an ActiveX Control

To build an ActiveX Control, select **Make OCX** from the Visual Basic **File** menu. To use the ActiveX Control that you created in another project, there is a special procedure you must use the first time you add it to a project on your development system, since the OCX is not yet registered.

1. From the **Project** menu, select **Components**.
2. In the *Components* dialog, click the browse button(…).
3. Navigate to and select the OCX you built. Click **OK**.
4. Click **OK** to dismiss the *Components* dialog.

Once you've done the above procedure once on your development system, the control will be registered and can be added like any other ActiveX Control. To distribute the ActiveX Control, use the **Package and Deployment Wizard** to create a setup program.

The ActiveX Control Interface Wizard

Once you know how to manually add properties, events, and methods to your ActiveX Control, you should learn how to use the **ActiveX Control Interface Wizard**. The *ActiveX Control Interface Wizard* completely automates the mundane steps involved in adding properties, events, and methods. For example, with just a few clicks, you can add a property to your control. The wizard will add the *Property Let* and *Get* procedures, declare a module-level variable to hold the property, and provide code to initialize, read, and write the property.

After seeing how to use the *ActiveX Control Interface Wizard*, you may wonder why I didn't show it to you first. The reason is because you really still need to understand the steps, since, in many cases, you'll need to go back and finish the job that the wizard started.

The *ActiveX Control Interface Wizard* is an add-in. If the *ActiveX Control Interface Wizard* does not appear in your *Add-Ins* menu, use the following procedure to add it:

1. From the *Add-Ins* menu, select *Add-In Manager.*
2. Select the entry *ActiveX Control Interface Wizard* (see Figure 9-17).
3. Check the *Loaded/Unload* and *Load on Startup* check boxes.
4. Click the *OK* button.

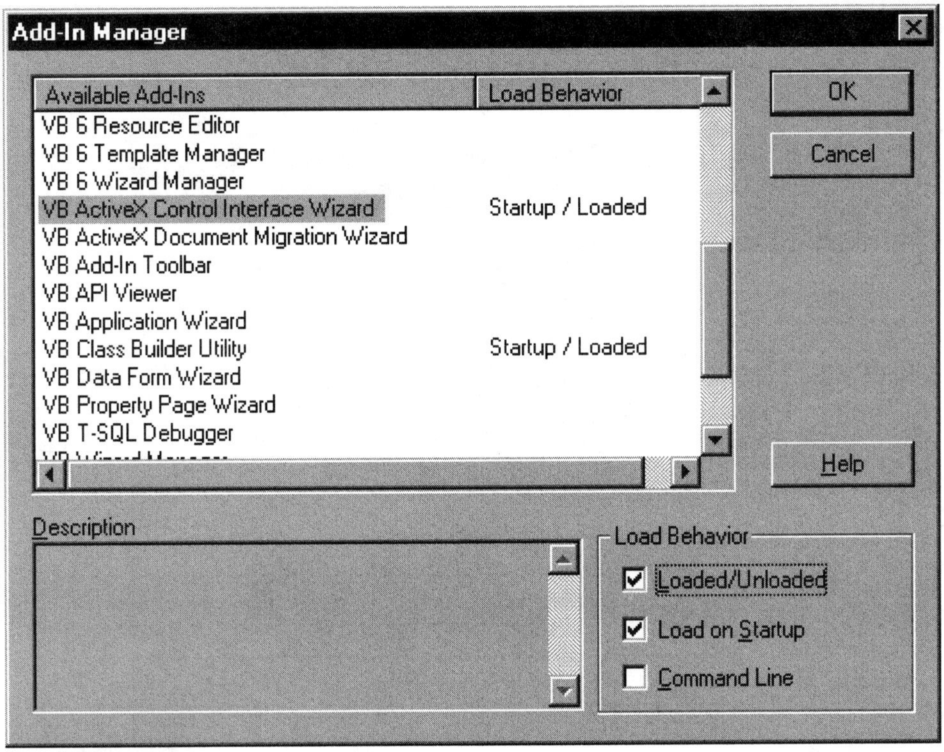

FIGURE 9-17 The *ActiveX Control Interface Wizard* must be added to your *Add-Ins* menu before you can use it.

Using the ActiveX Control Interface Wizard

To start the *ActiveX Interface Control Wizard*, select *ActiveX Control Interface Wizard* from the *Add-Ins* menu. In the first step, you can select from a list of commonly used properties, events, and methods. You can let the wizard completely implement these properties, or you can map them to properties of the constituent control(s). This first step is *not* where you add your own properties, events, or methods. Click *Next* to go on to the next step, where you can add your own properties, events, and methods. For example, you can add **Appearance, BorderStyle**, and **ToolTipText** properties, as shown in Figure 9-18.

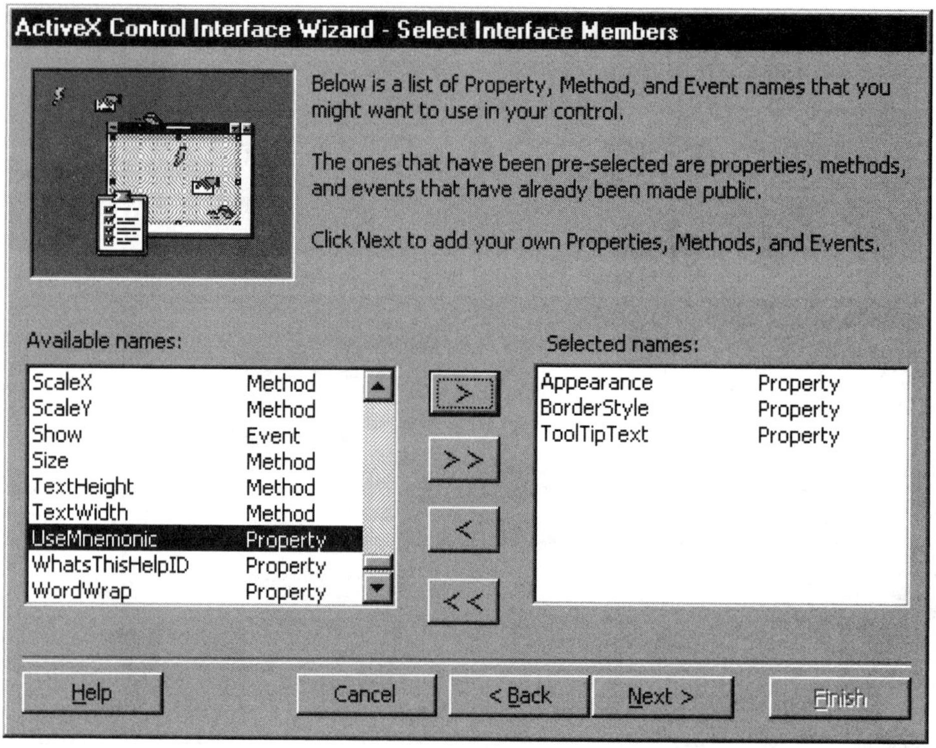

ActiveX Control Interface Wizard - Select Interface Members

Below is a list of Property, Method, and Event names that you might want to use in your control.

The ones that have been pre-selected are properties, methods, and events that have already been made public.

Click Next to add your own Properties, Methods, and Events.

Available names:

ScaleX	Method
ScaleY	Method
Show	Event
Size	Method
TextHeight	Method
TextWidth	Method
UseMnemonic	Property
WhatsThisHelpID	Property
WordWrap	Property

Selected names:

Appearance	Property
BorderStyle	Property
ToolTipText	Property

Help   Cancel   < Back   Next >   Finish

FIGURE 9-18   The first step of the *ActiveX Control Interface Wizard* is to select from a list of common properties, methods, and/or events.

In the next step of the *ActiveX Control Interface Wizard*, you can add new properties, events, and/or methods (see Figure 9-19). You can also edit and/or delete existing properties, events, and/or methods. Be aware that, in general, the wizard provides all necessary code for dealing with the "mechanics" of a property, event, or method. But it does not, of course, know how you want to treat a property, or what you want to do in a method. In most cases, you'll need to go into the wizard-generated code and add your specific processing instructions.

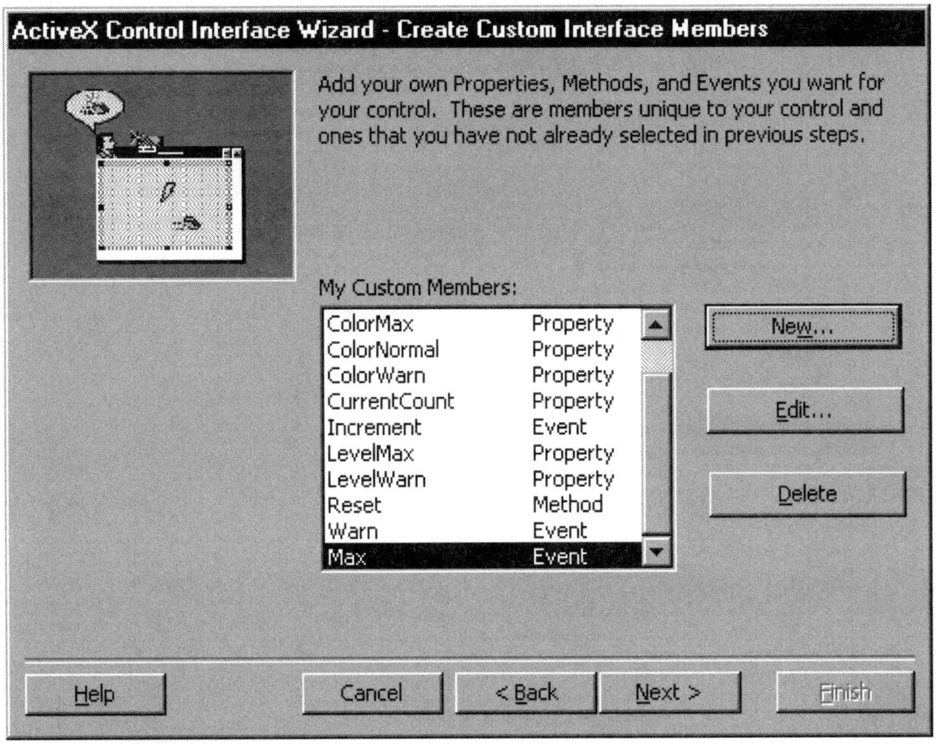

ActiveX Control Interface Wizard - Create Custom Interface Members

Add your own Properties, Methods, and Events you want for your control. These are members unique to your control and ones that you have not already selected in previous steps.

My Custom Members:

ColorMax	Property
ColorNormal	Property
ColorWarn	Property
CurrentCount	Property
Increment	Event
LevelMax	Property
LevelWarn	Property
Reset	Method
Warn	Event
Max	Event

New...
Edit...
Delete

Help   Cancel   < Back   Next >   Finish

FIGURE 9-19   In the next step, you can add new properties and/or edit/delete existing ones.

ADDING A PROPERTY WITH THE ACTIVEX CONTROL WIZARD

To add a *new* property, event, or method, click the **New** button from the *Create Custom Interface Members* step of the *ActiveX Control Interface Wizard.* You'll be prompted for the *Name* of the new member, and you can indicate whether the new member is a *property, method,* or *event.* For example, to add an *AutoReset* property,

1. In the *Create Custom Interface Members* step of the *ActiveX Control Interface Wizard,* select the *New* button.

2. In the resulting *Add Custom Member* dialog box, enter *AutoReset* for the *Name* (see Figure 9-20).

3. For *Type,* select *Property.*

4. Click the *OK* button.

5. Repeat the above steps, adding any other custom properties, events, or methods that you want. When finished, click *Next* to advance the wizard to the next step.

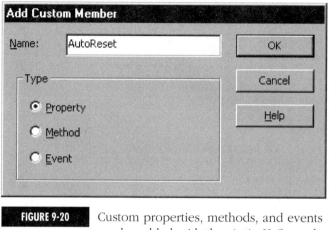

FIGURE 9-20 Custom properties, methods, and events can be added with the *ActiveX Control Interface Wizard*.

MAPPING CONTROL MEMBERS TO CONSTITUENT CONTROLS

The next step of the *ActiveX Control Interface Wizard* provides you with an easy way of mapping selected properties, events, and/or methods of your control to properties, events, and/or methods of any constituent control(s) you may have. For example, you can map the *Appearance* property of your control to the *Appearance* property of the *Label* control (in the case of the *Counter Control*).

For example, two new properties, *Appearance* and *BorderStyle*, can be mapped to the corresponding properties of the constituent *Label* control, as follows:

1. From the *Public Name* list, select the *Appearance* property (see Figure 9-21).
2. In the *Control* drop-down list, select *lblCounter*.
3. The *Member* drop-down list will automatically select *Appearance*, since the label has such a property.
4. Repeat the above steps for the property *BorderStyle*.

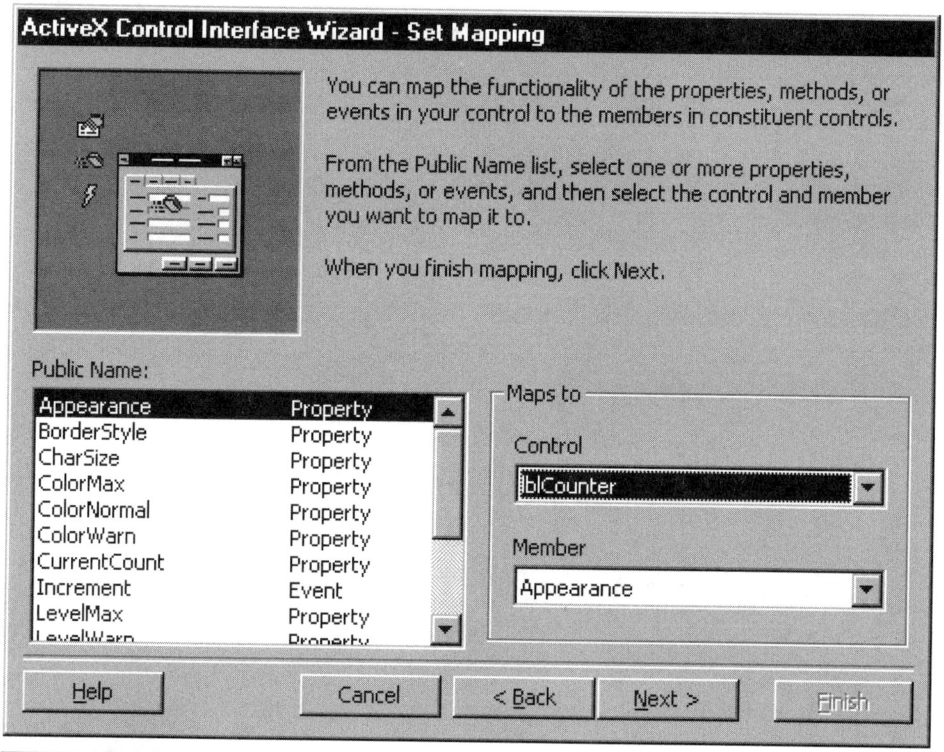

FIGURE 9-21 In the next step of the *ActiveX Control Interface Wizard*, you can map members of your control to properties, events, or methods of your constituent control(s).

SETTING ATTRIBUTES OF UNMAPPED PROPERTIES

In the final step of the *ActiveX Control Interface Wizard*, you provide details about how the unmapped properties, events, and methods are to be implemented (see Figure 9-22). For example, to implement the ***AutoReset*** property:

1. In the *Public Name* list box, select the ***AutoReset*** property.
2. For *Data Type*, select ***Boolean***, and for ***Default Value***, enter *0*.
3. Leave the *Run Time* and *Design Time* choices at ***Read/Write***.
4. Enter a description into the *Description* text box.
5. Repeat the above steps until you've provided information about all the new, unmapped properties you have added. Then, click the *Next* button.

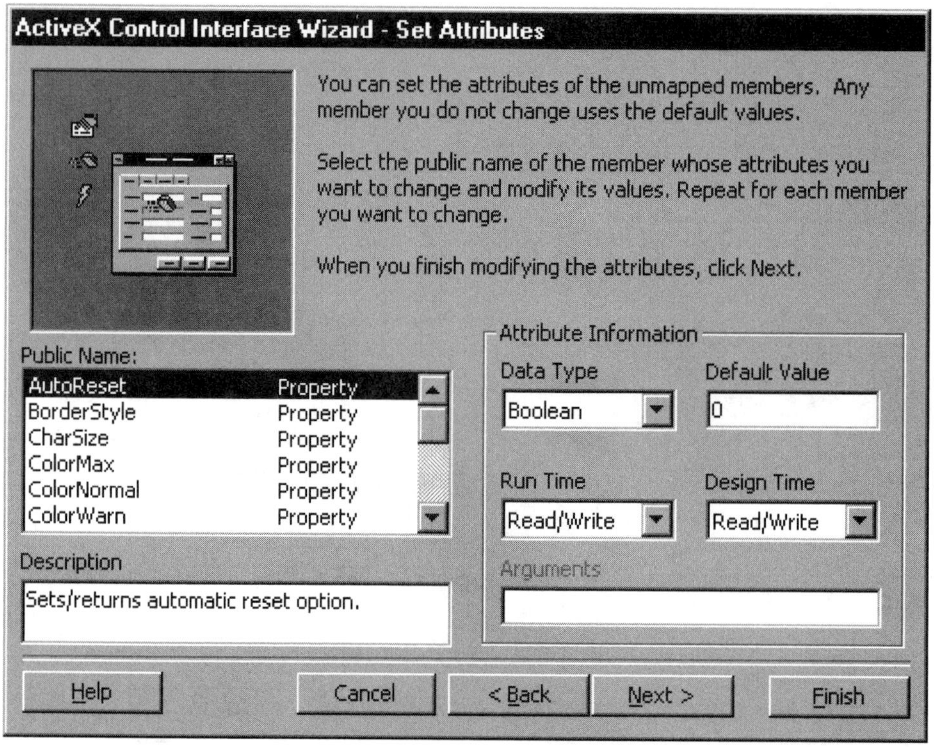

ActiveX Control Interface Wizard - Set Attributes

You can set the attributes of the unmapped members. Any member you do not change uses the default values.

Select the public name of the member whose attributes you want to change and modify its values. Repeat for each member you want to change.

When you finish modifying the attributes, click Next.

Public Name:

AutoReset	Property
BorderStyle	Property
CharSize	Property
ColorMax	Property
ColorNormal	Property
ColorWarn	Property

Description

Sets/returns automatic reset option.

Attribute Information

Data Type
Boolean

Default Value
0

Run Time
Read/Write

Design Time
Read/Write

Arguments

Help   Cancel   < Back   Next >   Finish

FIGURE 9-22   In the final step of the *ActiveX Control Interface Wizard*, you provide information on the data type, default value, accessibility, and description of your unmapped properties, events, or methods.

ACTIVEX CONTROL INTERFACE WIZARD-GENERATED CODE

The *ActiveX Control Interface Wizard* generates all the code to implement the interface to properties, methods, and events. As mentioned, you must add additional code to actually implement specific processing related to the properties, events, and methods added with the *ActiveX Control Interface Wizard*.

For example, when the *AutoReset* property is added with the *ActiveX Control Interface Wizard*, the following modifications were made (shown in **bold**):

```
Option Explicit

Public Event Warn()
Public Event Max()

Public Enum CharSizes
    ccSmall = 0
```

```
        ccMedium = 1
        ccLarge = 2
End Enum

Private iLevelMax As Integer
Private iLevelWarn As Integer
Private iColorNormal As Long
Private iColorWarn As Long
Private iColorMax As Long
Private iCurrentCount As Integer
Private iCharSize As Integer
'Default Property Values:
Const m_def_ToolTipText = ""
Const m_def_AutoReset = 0
'Property Variables:
Dim m_ToolTipText As String
Dim m_AutoReset As Boolean
```

The *ActiveX Control Interface Wizard* also creates both a *Property Let* and a *Property Get* procedure for your properties. For example, the code generated by the wizard related to the **AutoReset** property is as follows:

```
Public Property Get AutoReset() As Boolean
    AutoReset = m_AutoReset
End Property

Public Property Let AutoReset(ByVal New_Val As Boolean)
    m_AutoReset = New_Val
    PropertyChanged "AutoReset"
End Property
```

The *ActiveX Control Interface Wizard* also generates code to initialize the properties it added for you. For example, shown below is the modification to the **InitProperties** procedure related to the **AutoReset** property:

```
Private Sub UserControl_InitProperties()
    iCurrentCount = 0
    LevelMax = 1000
    LevelWarn = 800
    ColorNormal = RGB(0, 0, 255)
    ColorWarn = RGB(255, 255, 0)
    ColorMax = RGB(255, 0, 0)
    CharSize = ccSmall
    BackColor = Ambient.BackColor
    lblCounter.BackColor = BackColor
```

```
        m_ToolTipText = m_def_ToolTipText
        m_AutoReset = m_def_AutoReset
End Sub
```

In addition to the mentioned modifications, the *ActiveX Control Interface Wizard* also adds code to the **ReadProperties** and **WriteProperties** procedures. In other words, the wizard provides all the "plumbing" for your properties, methods, and events.

FINISHING THE IMPLEMENTATION OF THE AUTORESET PROPERTY

It would be nice if the *ActiveX Control Interface Wizard* knew exactly what you wanted to do with the **AutoReset** property. However, it only knows how to set up the interface to the new property. That's why it's called the *ActiveX Control **Interface** Wizard*. You must complete the implementation. Each case is, of course, special, with the exception of some "stock" properties, like *ToolTipText*.

In the case of **AutoReset**, you will invoke the **Reset** method (internally) after firing the **Max** event. The (manually) modified code follows:

```
Public Sub Increment()

    ' Don't increment any more if at max

    If iCurrentCount = iLevelMax Then Exit Sub

    ' Increment, format, display, and change color

    iCurrentCount = iCurrentCount + 1
    lblCounter.Caption = Format(iCurrentCount, "00000")

    If iCurrentCount = iLevelWarn Then
        lblCounter.ForeColor = iColorWarn
        RaiseEvent Warn
    ElseIf iCurrentCount = iLevelMax Then
        lblCounter.ForeColor = iColorMax
        RaiseEvent Max
        If m_AutoReset Then
            Reset
        End If
    End If

End Sub
```

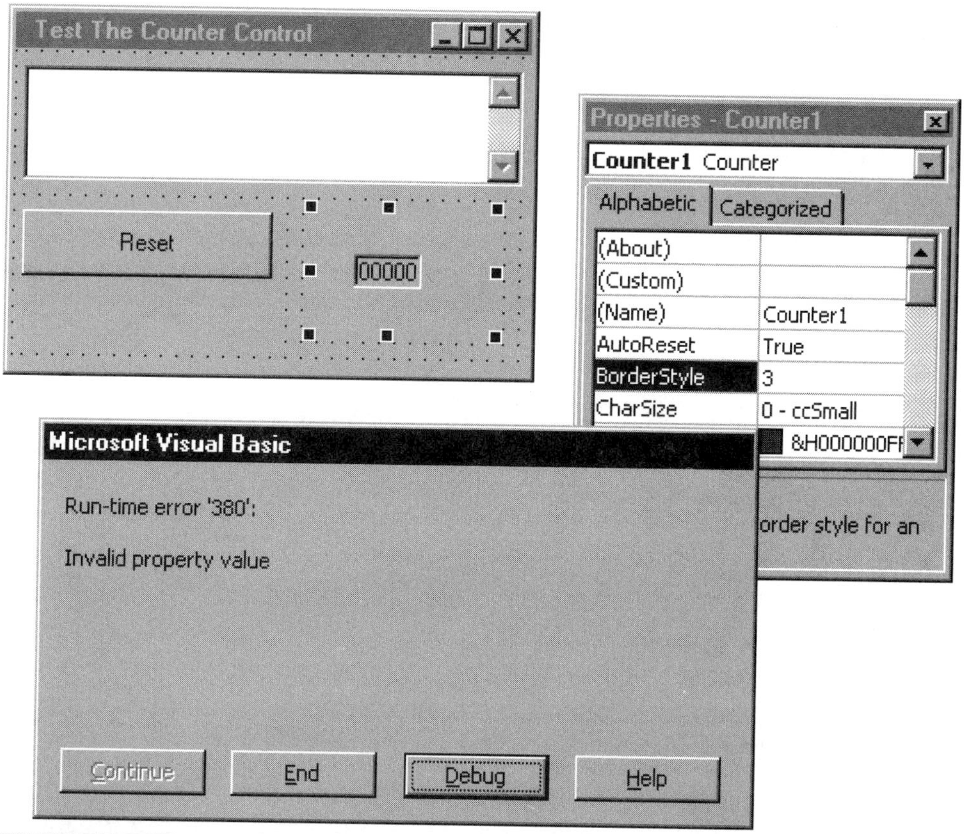

FIGURE 9-23 Looks like you have a bit of a problem with the *BorderStyle* property, unless you can trust all users to set it to either 0 or 1!

A PROBLEM WITH THE BORDERSTYLE PROPERTY

The **BorderStyle** property, which is mapped to the *BorderStyle* property of the constituent *Label* control, has a problem. If it's not set to 0 or 1, code in your ActiveX Control blows up (see Figure 9-23). I'll analyze the problem, then show you how to make your code a bit more robust.

Examine the code below, which is the *Property Let* procedure created by the *ActiveX Control Wizard* for our **BorderStyle** property. Notice that the wizard has declared the property as type **Integer**, which is the same type used by the constituent *Label* control. Notice also that the wizard has not generated any code whatsoever to validate the value.

```
Public Property Let BorderStyle _
               (ByVal New_BorderStyle As Integer)
    lblCounter.BorderStyle = New_BorderStyle
    PropertyChanged "BorderStyle"
End Property
```

The best solution to correct the *BorderStyle* problem is to create a new enumeration for the two possible values of the *BorderStyle* property (*0—None, 1—Fixed Single*). Then, you'll change the type used by the *BorderStyle* property from *Integer* to your new enumeration. The enumeration can be defined in the control's declarations section, as follows:

```
Public Enum BSConstants
    bsNone = 0
    bsFixedSingle = 1
End Enum
```

You must then modify the *Property Let* and *Get* procedures for the *BorderStyle* property of the *Counter Control,* changing the *Integer* type to *BSConstants*, as follows:

```
Public Property Get BorderStyle() As BSConstants
    BorderStyle = lblCounter.BorderStyle
End Property
```

```
Public Property Let BorderStyle _
        (ByVal New_BorderStyle As BSConstants)
    lblCounter.BorderStyle = New_BorderStyle
    PropertyChanged "BorderStyle"
End Property
```

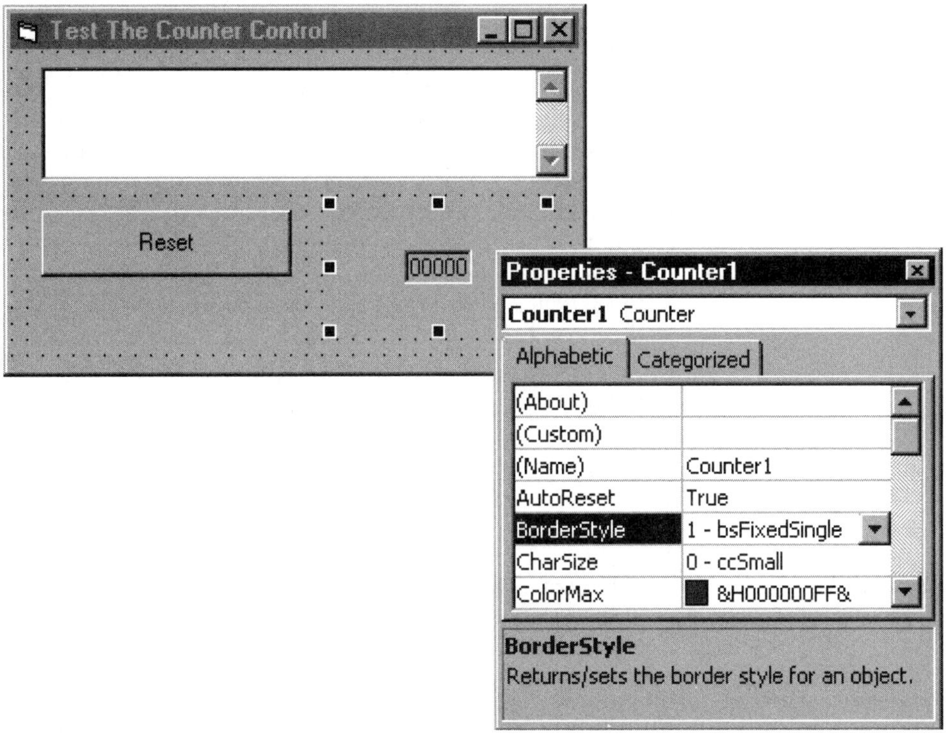

FIGURE 9-24 The *BorderStyle* property is much more well-behaved now.

Once you have made these modifications, the *Counter Control* will display a list of choices for the *BorderStyle* property, as shown in Figure 9-24. Now, the **BorderStyle** property can only be set to 0 or 1. Plus, you have an enumeration that shows up in the *Properties* window. This is much more professional. This exercise also helps to illustrate why it's important to understand the inner workings of ActiveX Controls. Simply using the *ActiveX Control Interface Wizard* is not enough; you have to know when and where to go in and make your modifications.

ActiveX Control Finishing Touches

Assuming your ActiveX Control does something useful and is robust and reliable, there is little else left to do other than what has already been discussed. However, a professional ActiveX Control often has a few finishing touches that can make a very favorable impression on its user. For example, the thoughtful developer of an ActiveX Control will provide descriptions of properties that Visual Basic will display in the *Properties* window. An ActiveX Control may also have a default property, as does the text box control (the *Text* property). Finally, ActiveX Controls, especially ones with a lot of properties, or with a complex set of properties, often provide property pages to a developer, enabling dialog-based selection of property values and options. In the closing sections of this chapter, I'll describe how you can add these professional touches to your ActiveX Control.

Describing Your Properties, Events, and Methods

To give your controls an even more "polished" and professional look, you should provide descriptions of all your properties, methods, and events. The description appears at the bottom of the *Properties* window when your property is selected, as shown in Figure 9-25. Descriptions for methods and events (as well as properties) appear in the **Object Browser**. You can also provide a category for each property, by selecting the category from the *Property Category* drop-down list. To assign a description and/or category to a property of a control:

1. Make sure the *ActiveX Control* project is selected.
2. From the **Tools** menu, select **Procedure Attributes** and click **Advanced**.
3. Select the property, event, or method from the **Name** drop-down list.
4. Enter a description in the **Description** text box.
5. If a property is selected, you can select a category from the **Property Category** drop-down list.

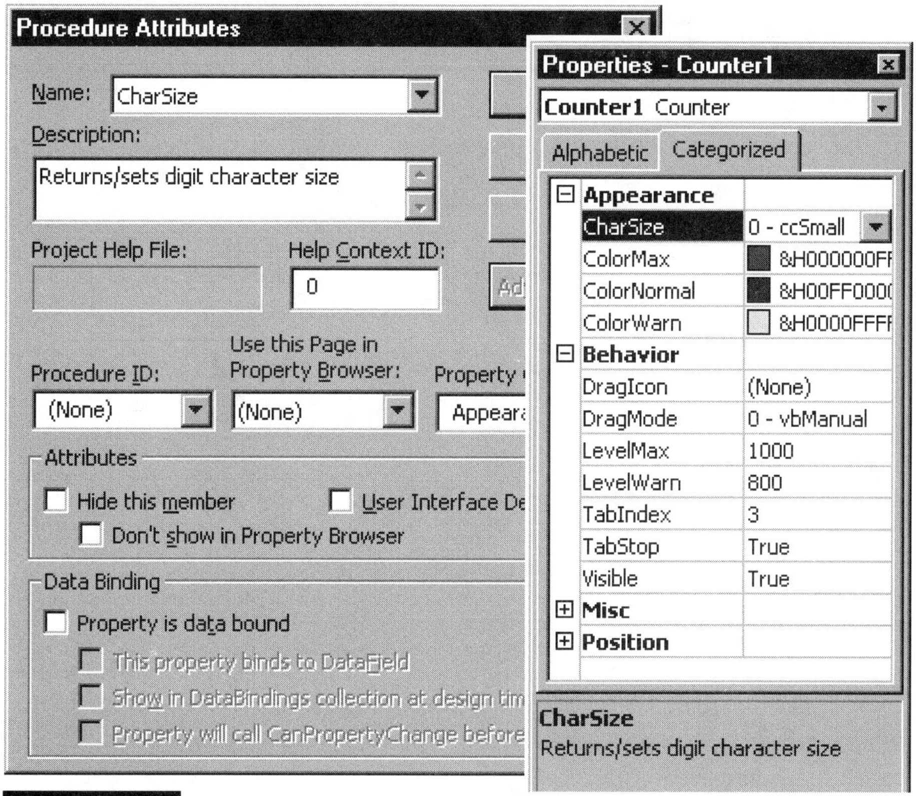

FIGURE 9-25 You can provide descriptions for your properties, events, and methods by using the *Procedure Attributes* dialog. You can also provide a category for your properties.

Providing a Default Value for Your ActiveX Control

Controls should have a default value, which is the property used when an instance of the control is referenced without a property. For example, the *CurrentCount* property might be an appropriate default value for the *Counter Control* (see Figure 9-26). If you do this, the following two statements would be identical:

```
n = Counter1.CurrentCount
n = Counter1
```

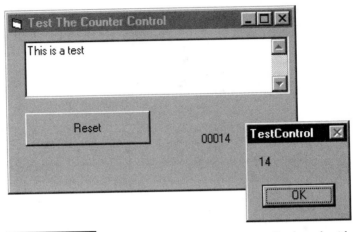

FIGURE 9-26 The above message box was displayed with the statement *MsgBox Counter1*. Since the control's default *value* is *CurrentCount*, the *CurrentCount* property is displayed.

To assign a property as the default value of your control,

1. Make sure the *ActiveX Control* project is selected.

2. From the **Tools** menu, select **Procedure Attributes** and click **Advanced**.

3. Select the property that is to be the default value.

4. From the **Procedure ID** drop-down list, select *(Default)*.

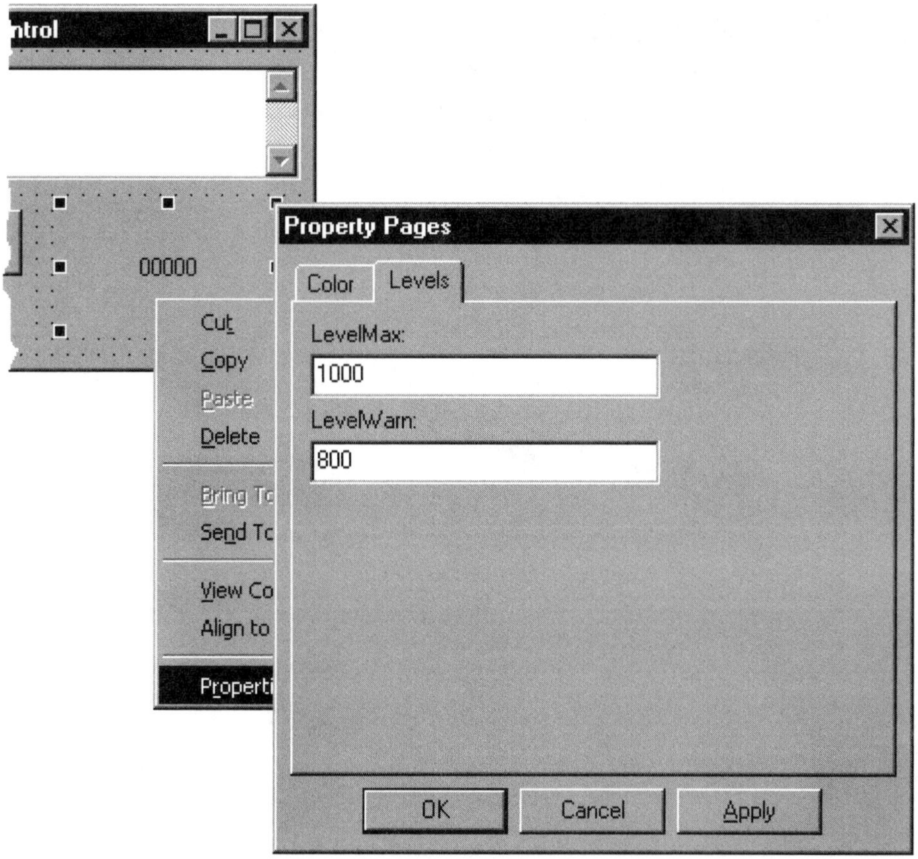

FIGURE 9-27   Property pages can make it easier for developers to assign properties to your control, since they can be arranged by function.

Property Pages

Property pages make it easier for developers to assign properties to your control, by providing a dialog window with controls that enable the developer to select and enter values for the control's properties (see Figure 9-27). They also make it possible for your control to be inserted into containers that can hold ActiveX Controls, but don't have *"Properties* windows." The easiest way to add property pages is to use the **Property Page Wizard**, discussed in the following section.

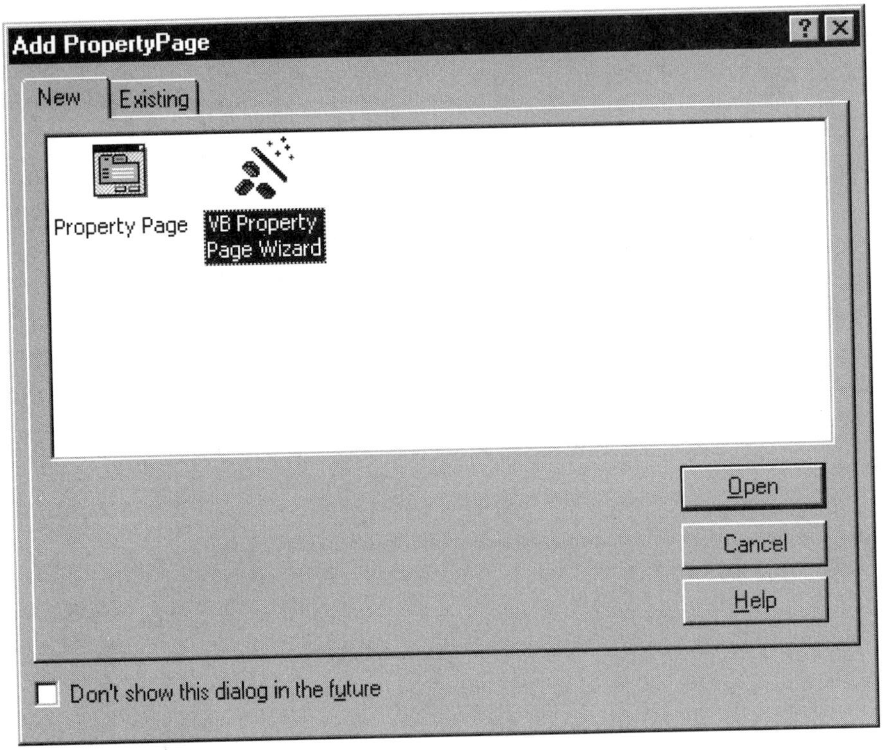

FIGURE 9-28   Start the *Property Page Wizard* by selecting *Add Property Page* from the *Project* menu. In the resulting dialog box, select *VB Property Page Wizard*.

Using the Property Page Wizard

The Visual Basic *Property Page Wizard* will do all the work required for adding property pages to your control. To start the *Property Page Wizard*:

1. From the *Project* menu, select *Add Property Page*.
2. Double-click on the *VB Property Page Wizard* icon (see Figure 9-28).

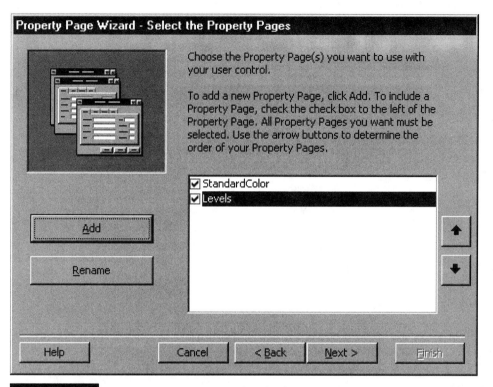

FIGURE 9-29 Property pages are created in the first step of the *Property Page Wizard.*

The *Property Page Wizard* adds a property page for any properties defined as *OLE_COLOR*. You can add additional pages as follows:

1. In the *Select the Property Pages* step of the *Property Page Wizard*, click the *Add* button.

2. You will be prompted for the name of a new property page. In my example, I entered *Levels* (see Figure 9-29).

3. You can continue to add additional pages. When you are finished, click the *Next* button.

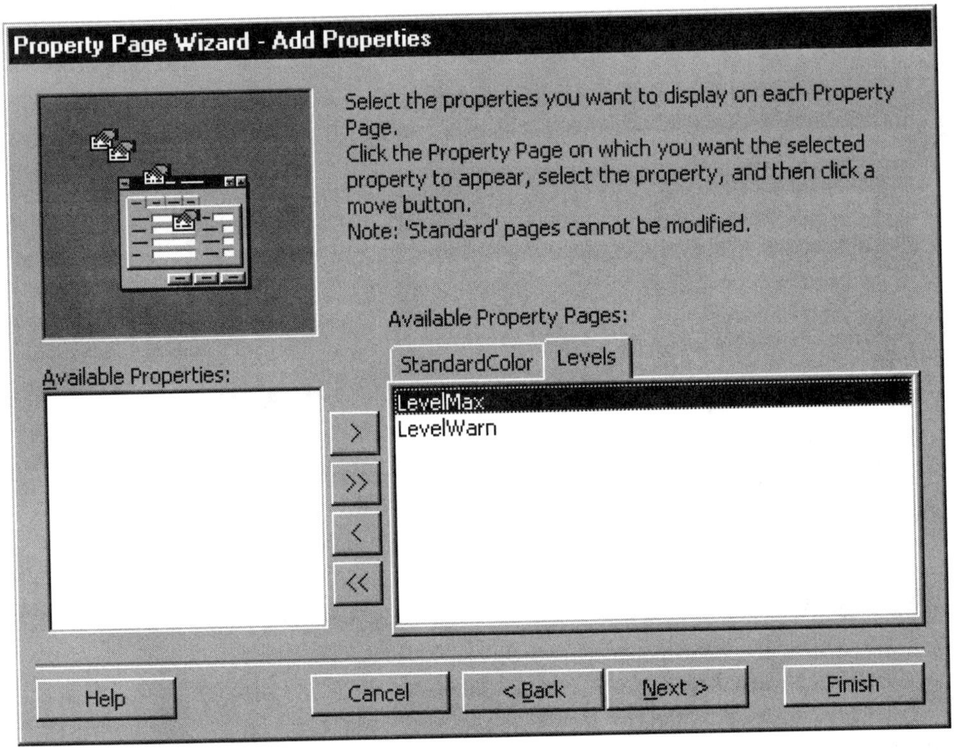

Property Page Wizard - Add Properties

Select the properties you want to display on each Property Page.
Click the Property Page on which you want the selected property to appear, select the property, and then click a move button.
Note: 'Standard' pages cannot be modified.

Available Property Pages:

StandardColor | Levels

LevelMax
LevelWarn

Available Properties:

>
>>
<
<<

Help | Cancel | < Back | Next > | Finish

FIGURE 9-30 For each property page, move the desired properties from the *Available Properties* list over to the list under the selected property page tab.

The final step is to add the desired properties to each property page.

1. Select a property page using one of the tabs under *Available Property Pages* (see Figure 9-30).

2. Move the desired properties from the *Available Properties* list to the property page by using one of the move buttons.

3. Repeat for each property page, then click **_Finish_**.

Using ActiveX Controls with the Internet

Displaying an ActiveX Control on a Web browser such as *Internet Explorer* is easy to do. No additional programming is required for the ActiveX Control, although you will need to provide scripting code in HTML.

A sample HTML source file follows. Notice the use of the HTML *OBJECT* tag. You'll need to substitute the *Class ID* with your control's Class ID, which can be obtained from the Windows registry. Under the key *HKEY _CLASSES_ROOT*, look for an entry named *project_name.control_name*. For example, the *Counter Control*, which is contained in the Visual Basic project *MyControls*, will be listed in the registry under the key *MyControls.Counter*. If you registered the *Counter Control* that is distributed with this book, you can view the HTML shown below with *Internet Explorer*. The file *COUNTER.HTM* is located in folder *VB6Adv\Demos\ActiveXControl*.

To use ActiveX Controls on a Web page, it is suggested that you use an Internet development tool, such as *Microsoft Visual InterDev 6.0*.

```
<HTML>
<TITLE>Testing My Counter Control</TITLE>
<OBJECT
    ID="Counter1"
    CLASSID="clsid:6B9B874D-B8C4-11D0-9002-D140C15BF82F"
    BORDER="0"
    WIDTH="108"
    HEIGHT="55">
    <PARAM NAME="CharSize" value="2">
    <PARAM NAME="LevelWarn" value="10">
    <PARAM NAME="LevelMax" value="20">
</OBJECT>

<INPUT TYPE="button" name="B1" value="Button">

<SCRIPT LANGUAGE="VBScript">
Sub B1_OnClick
    Counter1.Increment
End Sub

Sub Counter1_Warn
    MsgBox "Warning!"
End Sub
</SCRIPT>

</BODY>
</HTML>
```

Automation Fundamentals

When a Windows application is useful to an end-user, it is often useful to another developer as well. Such applications can be especially useful to a power user who, lacking the skills or perhaps the time to create a brand-new application, must make use of existing applications to create an apparently new application. If the developer of this useful Windows application was thoughtful enough, he or she would have created an automation interface, which would enable another program to start the application, and remain in control of the application even after it started. This is what *automation* is all about – enabling a standalone application to be capable of being driven by another application.

About Automation

With automation, you can access the objects of another application, and this can be quite powerful (and abstract!). For example, you can access the *CheckSpelling* method of *Excel's Application* object to add a spell-checking feature to your Visual Basic application, and doing so will take less than 20 lines of code.

Today, there is clearly a great emphasis toward code reuse. You have seen how objects can be packaged in ActiveX Components (COM servers), which amounts to code reuse at the component level. What I have not yet discussed, but will discuss in this chapter, is how code can be reused at the application level. In this chapter, you will see how to add an automation interface to your applications. As an illustration of the benefits of adding an automation interface to an application, I will get you started on using the automation interfaces of both the *Microsoft Excel* and *Microsoft Internet Explorer* applications.

As an historical note, you should know that automation has been around for some time now, and does not really generate much in the way of excitement among developers any longer. But I believe automation is the forgotten interface – because once developers have placed layer upon layer, finally resulting in a presentation layer Win32 client application, there's no place else to go. What this means is that all your components in the layers below the presentation layer are reusable – but your applications are not. Considering the fact that code in your presentation layer often provides the sequencing and orchestration of the objects in the middle tiers, there's a lot of opportunity for code reuse. So, you should definitely consider providing an automation interface on top of your Win32 presentation layer applications.

Automation Overview

Some applications support automation as a means of communication. Such applications are known as **automation servers**. Applications that support automation expose their objects to other applications. Applications that control automation servers are known as **automation controllers.** Writing an automation controller is the emphasis of the first part of this chapter. The second part of this chapter covers the creation of automation servers in Visual Basic.

To access another application's objects, you must use object variables. An **object variable** is a variable that contains a reference to an object, as opposed to ordinary variables that hold values. An object variable can be declared literally as **Object**, but this is inefficient as it uses a dynamic binding technique that requires the method or property name to be looked up every time it is invoked. Instead, you should declare the variable using the automation server's class name. This will result in your program using the most efficient binding mechanism supported by the automation server. To use the server's class name as the type, you must set a reference to the automation server's type library. The syntax used to specify an automation server's class is *ServerName.ClassName*. You can omit *ServerName* if *ClassName* is not ambiguous. For more information on using objects from a Visual Basic application, see Chapter 2.

Each application that supports automation has a different list of supported objects. You must consult the application's documentation to find the list of objects. For example, *Excel* exports a global object called ***Application***, which would be refenced as *Excel.Application* in your program.

For example, to declare an object variable to control an *Excel* application object,

```
' Late binding:
Private objExcel As Object


' Early binding:
Private objExcel As Excel.Application
```

Referencing an Automation Server's Type Library

Before you can begin to use an automation server's objects, you should insert a reference to its type library. While not strictly required, this provides the following advantages:

1. You can declare the object variables using the server's class name instead of *Object*, which results in more efficient binding.
2. You can use the Visual Basic keyword ***New*** instead of the ***CreateObject*** function (although you may want to use the *CreateObject* function anyway).
3. Visual Basic can do compile-time syntax checking on the methods and properties you invoke on the object, provided you declare it as *class name* instead of *Object*.

To insert a reference to an automation server's type library,

1. Select ***References*** from the Visual Basic ***Project*** menu.
2. Scroll the list of references until you find the one(s) you need.
3. Check the box next to the description of the automation server's type library. If you cannot find it, it may not be registered. You can click the browse button(…) and navigate to the type library (**TLB** file).
4. Click the **OK** button to dismiss the dialog.

Creating an Automation Server Object

The **CreateObject** function starts an automation server and establishes an object reference to the automation server object. The **New** keyword in Visual Basic effectively does the same thing – the difference between the two is discussed in Chapter 2. You must use the **Set** statement in conjunction with the *CreateObject* function and the *New* keyword.

When an object exposed by an automation server is created, the automation server is started. This is the same application that starts when the application is started from the command line or from the *Start* button – in other words, when started in standalone mode. However, automation servers, by default, do not show their main window when created through automation. Automation servers often provide a property, typically called **Visible**, which controls the visibility of the application's main window. Both *Microsoft Excel* and *Microsoft Internet Explorer*, two automation servers I'll be discussing in this chapter, behave this way. When a user starts either application, they are presented with a main window containing the application's user interface. But when started by a program via automation, neither application displays its main window unless and until its *Visible* property is set to *TRUE*. This is also how I will implement a demonstration automation server in the second half of this chapter.

By the way, the most frequent question I'm asked regarding automation is whether or not it is necessary for an automation server to be installed on the same machine as the client. Typically, the student is wondering whether or not an automation server can be remotely deployed using DCOM – the answer to this question is yes. You can use DCOM to remotely access an automation server. But the server must be available somewhere. For example, if you don't have *Microsoft Excel* installed on your machine, you will not be able to run the following demo. The second demo cannot be run on your machine unless you have installed *Microsoft Internet Explorer*. There is often a misconception when one first uses automation that code from the automation server is somehow compiled into the automation controller, which can then be distributed without the automation server – this is absolutely not true. It is necessary for the automation server to be present and correctly installed on the same machine as the automation controller – or, if not, it must be installed remotely (using DCOM) and client-side registry entries must be present to enable the automation controller to locate the remote server. DCOM (the Distributed Component Object Model) is the subject of the next chapter.

Creating an Excel Automation Server

To start *Microsoft Excel* as an automation server using early binding, insert a reference to the *Microsoft Excel* type library, and use the following statements:

```
Dim ExcelObject As Excel.Application
Set ExcelObject = CreateObject ("Excel.Application")
```

Properties and Methods of an Automation Server

The properties and methods of an automation server vary depending upon the application. You must consult an application's documentation for details. Some examples of the properties and methods of *Excel's Application* object appear in Table 10-1. This is clearly not a complete table, but is enough for me to illustrate how easy it is for you to create an automation controller in Visual Basic.

TABLE 10-1	Important Properties and Methods of the Excel Automation Server	
Property/Method	**Use**	**Example**
Workbooks	Accesses the *Workbooks* collection.	
ActiveWorkbook	Accesses the active workbook.	
Add	Adds a workbook or worksheet.	*ExcelObject.Workbooks.Add*
Cells	Accesses a particular cell in the active worksheet.	*ExcelObject.Cells(1,1).Value = txtInput.Text*
Saved	Set to TRUE to "trick" Excel into "thinking" it has saved a workbook.	*ExcelObject.ActiveWorkbook.Saved = True*
CheckSpelling	Checks the spelling of a word or cell, and optionally provides correct spelling suggestions in a dialog box.	*ExcelObject.Cells(1,1).CheckSpelling "", True,True*
Quit	Terminates *Excel.*	*ExcelObject.Quit*

A Spell-Checker in a VB Application

To see an example of how an automation controller written in Visual Basic uses *Microsoft Excel's* automation interface, run the application *Chkspell.EXE,* located in folder *VB6Adv\Demos\AutomationClient\ChkSpell.* Enter some text into the text box, being certain to misspell some words! Click the *Start Excel* button, then click the *Check Spelling* button.

If you have any misspelled words, you should see a *Spelling* dialog, which is actually displayed by *Microsoft Excel.* The demo is not perfect – the dialog may initially appear behind the application's window – but it does serve as an interesting academic illustration.

The program works by starting Microsoft Excel through *automation.* When the *Check Spelling* button is clicked, the contents of the text box are sent to a cell in the *Excel* application. The code then invokes the *CheckSpelling* method on this cell; this is what displays the modal dialog that indicates your spelling errors (see Figure 10-1). When the *CheckSpelling* method completes, the user has attended to each misspelled word, and control returns to the Visual Basic application, which copies the contents of the cell back to the text box.

The code is as follows:

```
Option Explicit
Private ExcelObject As Object

Sub cmdStartExcel_Click ()
    Set ExcelObject = CreateObject("Excel.Application")
    ExcelObject.Workbooks.Add
End Sub

Sub cmdCheckSpelling_Click ()
    ExcelObject.Cells(1, 1).Value = txtInput.Text
    ExcelObject.Cells(1, 1).CheckSpelling "", True, True
    txtInput.Text = ExcelObject.Cells(1, 1).Value
End Sub

Sub Form_Unload (Cancel As Integer)
    If Not (ExcelObject Is Nothing) Then
        ExcelObject.ActiveWorkbook.Saved = True
        ExcelObject.Quit
    End If
End Sub
```

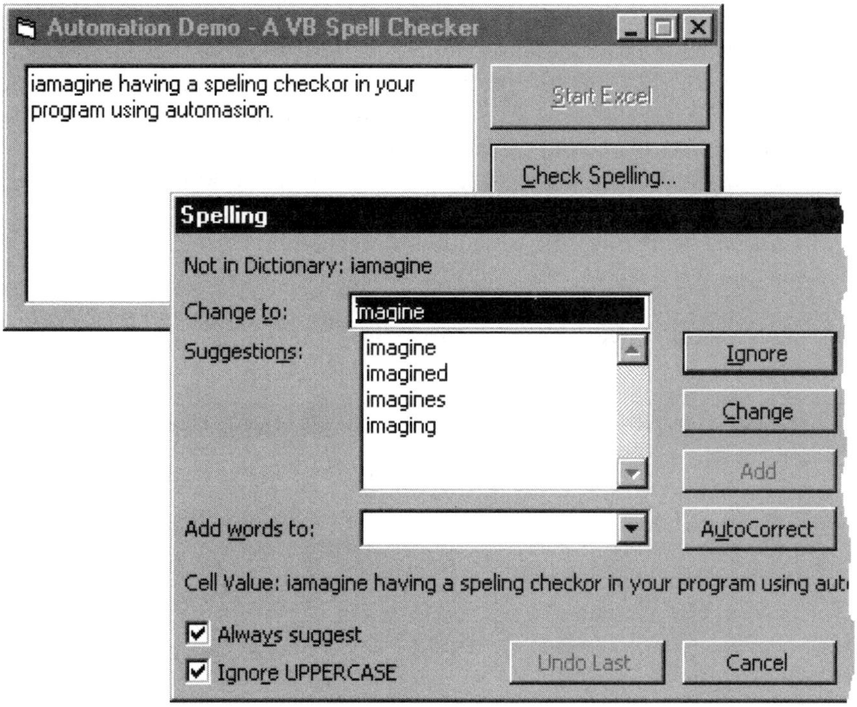

FIGURE 10-1 It takes less than 20 lines of code to get a spell-checker in Visual Basic using the *CheckSpelling* method of the *Excel Application* Object.

Automation and Microsoft Internet Explorer

If *Microsoft Internet Explorer* were a food, it would have to be lasagna. In developing *Internet Explorer*, Microsoft has done an excellent job of illustrating how an application, using COM, can be developed using reusable layers. At the foundation of these layers is a COM object that knows how to implement all that is required of a Web browser, except for the visible side of a Web browser. On top of this layer is an ActiveX Control that knows how to display the visible appearance of a Web browser, but does not provide a user interface. On top of that layer is an application, *Microsoft Internet Explorer*, which knows how to put all the layers below it together, and provide the necessary user interface. And it does not stop there – *Internet Explorer* has an automation interface! *Microsoft Internet Explorer's* automation interface can be used to drive *Internet Explorer* from an *automation controller*, written in Visual Basic, C++, or any other COM-capable programming language.

To use *Internet Explorer's* automation interface, first add a reference to **Microsoft Internet Controls**. *Internet Explorer's* type library exports the

InternetExplorer object – creating a new instance of this object starts *Internet Explorer*. To handle events generated by *Internet Explorer*, be sure to declare the object variable with the keyword ***WithEvents*** . The application starts invisibly (like *Excel* does). Set the ***Visible*** property to ***TRUE*** if you want the user to see the *Internet Explorer* window.

For example, the following Visual Basic program starts *Internet Explorer* when the *GO* button is clicked. It furthermore directs *Internet Explorer* to navigate to a URL contained in the text box *txtURL:*

```
Option Explicit
Dim WithEvents IE As InternetExplorer

Private Sub cmdGo_Click()

    If IE Is Nothing Then
        Set IE = New InternetExplorer
    End If

    IE.Navigate txtURL.Text
    IE.Visible = True

End Sub
```

INTERNET EXPLORER'S PROPERTIES, EVENTS, AND METHODS

Internet Explorer's automation interface exposes a number of properties, methods, and events, some of which are documented in the Table 10-2. *Internet Explorer's* user interface is built on top of the Microsoft Web Browser ActiveX Control, discussed in Chapter 18. As you will see, the properties, methods, and events exposed by *Internet Explorer's* automation interface are basically the same as those exported by the ActiveX Control.

TABLE 10-2	Important Properties, Events, and Methods of Internet Explorer

Type	**Name**	**Description**
Event	*NavigateComplete*	Fires when a new hyperlink is being navigated to. Passes URL as string parameter.
Event	*DownloadBegin*	Fires when the downloading of a page has started.
Event	*DownloadComplete*	Fires when the downloading of a page is complete.
Event	*ProgressChange*	Fires during download progress. Passes *Progress* and *ProgressMax* as long integers. Useful for updating a *Progress Indicator* control.
Event	*TitleChange*	Fires when document title changes, passes title as text string.
Property	*Busy*	Queries to see if something is still in progress.
Property	*LocationName*	Gets the UI-friendly name of the URL currently being viewed.
Property	*LocationURL*	Gets the full URL of the page currently being viewed.
Property	*Visible*	Shows/hides *Internet Explorer's* window.
Method	*GoBack*	Navigates to the previous item in the history list.
Method	*GoForward*	Navigates to the next item in the history list.
Method	*GoHome*	Navigates to the home/start page.
Method	*GoSearch*	Navigates to the search page.
Method	*Navigate*	Navigates to the given URL or file.
Method	*Quit*	Causes *Internet Explorer* to exit.

INTERNET EXPLORER AUTOMATION INTERFACE DEMO PROGRAM

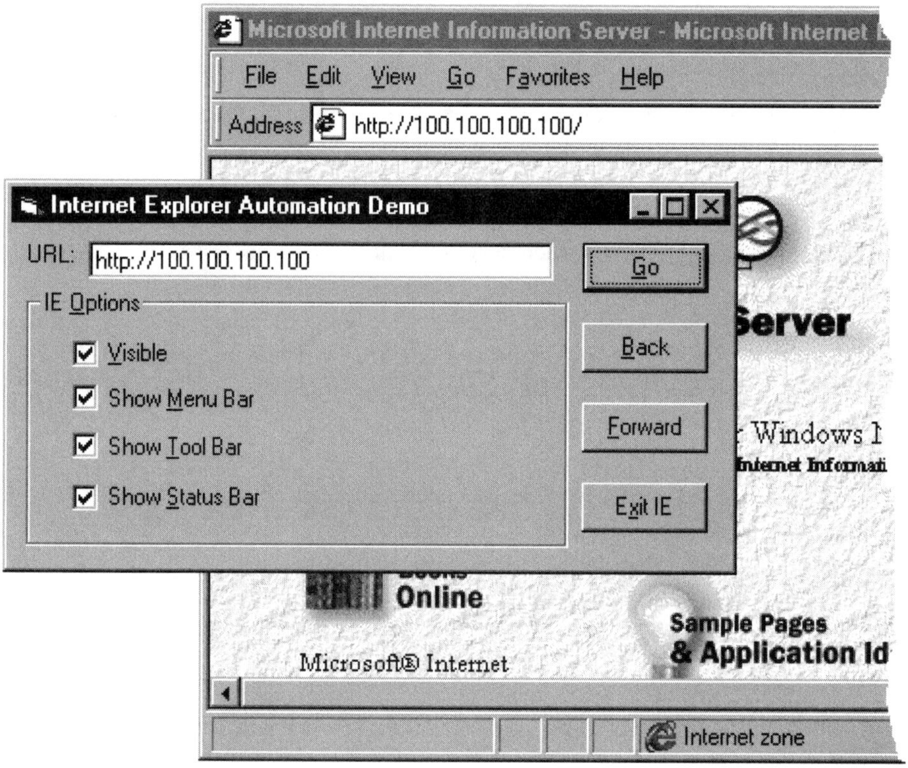

FIGURE 10-2 The second automation demo controls *Internet Explorer* through its automation interface.

To explore the sample application, run *IEAutomate.EXE* from folder *VB6Adv\Demos\AutomationClient\IEAutomate*. You will also find the Visual Basic project, *IEAutomate.VBP*, in this folder. The demo program uses *Internet Explorer's* automation interface to drive the *Internet Explorer* application (see Figure 10-2). Note that, to run the demo, you'll need access to the Internet, or you can access a local page on your intranet.

Here's the code from the demo program:

```
Option Explicit
Dim IE As InternetExplorer

Private Sub chkMenuBar_Click()
```

```
    IE.MenuBar = chkMenuBar.Value
End Sub

Private Sub chkStatusBar_Click()
    IE.StatusBar = chkStatusBar.Value
End Sub

Private Sub chkToolBar_Click()
    IE.ToolBar = chkToolBar.Value
End Sub

Private Sub chkVisible_Click()
    IE.Visible = chkVisible.Value
End Sub

Private Sub cmdBack_Click()
    IE.GoBack
End Sub

Private Sub cmdForward_Click()
    IE.GoForward
End Sub

Private Sub cmdGo_Click()
    If IE Is Nothing Then
        Set IE = New InternetExplorer
    End If
    IE.Navigate txtURL.Text
    IE.Visible = True
End Sub

Private Sub cmdIEExit_Click()
    IE.Quit
    Set IE = Nothing
End Sub

Private Sub txtURL_Change()
    cmdGo.Enabled = (txtURL.Text <> "")
End Sub
```

Creating an Automation Server in Visual Basic

An **automation server** is an application that can be run either standalone, or can be started and driven by another application. To develop an automation server in Visual Basic, use a project type of ActiveX EXE, also known as an out-of-process COM server. Unlike the other types of COM servers I have discussed in this book, an automation server is not marked for unattended execution. An automation server is an out-of-process COM server that can, of course, display forms, dialogs, and message boxes. COM servers that host COM objects in the middle tiers of a distributed application do not display forms, dialogs, or message boxes, and as such, are marked for unattended execution. For more information on the unattended execution feature, refer to Chapter 7.

Automation Server Startup Behavior

To create a well-behaved automation server that exhibits behavior similar to the automation servers I've presented in this chapter (*Microsoft Excel* and *Microsoft Internet Explorer*), your application cannot assume that a main window should be displayed. It is essential that your application's startup object is **Sub Main**, and specifically is not a form, as it would be in a typical Standard EXE project.

In the procedure *Sub Main* (which you must of course write), your code must check the startup mode of the application. If your application was started in standalone mode, it loads and shows your main form. If, however, the application was started via automation, it neither loads nor shows your main form. The startup mode can be determined by reading the **StartMode** property of the **App** object. This property has two possible values, represented by the constants **vbSModeStandalone** and **VbSModeAutomation**. A *StartMode* property value of *vbSModeStandalone* indicates that the application was started in standalone mode, while the value *vbSModeAutomation* indicates that the application was started through automation.

You must also implement at least one public class module. This class module will provide the properties, methods, and event sources for your automation interface (to learn how to add class modules to an application, see Chapter 7). For example, it is in this class module that you will implement the **Visible** property, which, when set to *TRUE*, will show your main form and, when set to *FALSE*, will hide your main form. I'm actually oversimplifying this a bit here – in reality, you will need to show/hide all your currently invisible/visible windows. Also, I should point out that it is perfectly acceptable to use two methods, **Show** and **Hide**, to show and hide your main window – this is the way *Microsoft Word's* automation interface works. However, most automation interfaces use the *Visible* property, so this is the approach I would recommend.

The *Initialize* method of this class module should create your main form, but specifically should not show it. Remember, you will show/hide the main form in the *Property Let* procedure for your *Visible* property. The *Terminate* method of this class module should unload your main form (again, this really applies to all the windows that are displayed by your application). It is recommended that you do not simply load the main form; instead, create a new instance of the form. A form is, after all, a kind of class module – although not a public one. You should create an instance of your main form by using the *Set* and *New* keywords. This will enable proper behavior of your automation server when used by multiple clients; using the *Load* statement actually loads what is called the design time instance of your form. I will be providing specific code examples related to this activity shortly.

The class module that provides your automation server's interface acts as a thin wrapper around your user interface. Methods and properties implemented in this interface should logically match the operations provided by the application when it is run standalone. It is not unusual for an automation server developer to provide an elaborate and hierarchical object model that wraps the application's user interface – in fact, *Microsoft Excel* does exactly that.

Single- and Multi-Use Automation Servers

You must decide how you want your application to behave when multiple automation controllers access it, and here you have a choice. You can elect to start a new instance of the application each time it is created by an application. This is how, for example, *Excel* behaves. Alternatively, you may decide to have each client access the same instance of the application – in other words, only the first client ends up starting your application, while other clients end up referencing the already running instance. This is how *Microsoft Word* behaves when it is accessed via automation. It is slightly more difficult to implement an automation server whose instance is shared between clients. I recommend developing automation servers that start fresh with each new client invocation.

If you decide to start a new instance of the application each time it is created by concurrently running automation controllers, you must set the *Instancing* property of your class module to *MultiUse*. If you want all concurrent automation controllers to access a common instance of your application, set the class module's *Instancing* property to *SingleUse*. For more information on the *Instancing* property, refer to Chapter 7.

Adding an Automation Interface to an Existing Application

The best way to learn how to create an automation interface is to add one to an existing application, thus converting it from a Standard EXE to an automation server, which is an ActiveX EXE type of project. This is a topic with merit in and of itself – you may have an existing application for which you want to add an automation interface. Adding an automation interface to an existing application requires that you carry out the steps as described in the previous section, and additionally do a bit of retro-fitting to enable the application to be controlled via automation. In the following sections, I will guide you through the steps of adding an automation interface to an existing application, using a program provided with this book.

AN EXAMPLE USING AN EXISTING APPLICATION

To illustrate how to add an automation interface to an existing application, I'll use a very simple existing application as a starting point – this program is the solution to a lab I often use when teaching fundamentals of Visual Basic. The program illustrates the use of graphics methods in Visual Basic. When you click in the indicated box (which is a *Picture Box* control), a box is drawn, centered at the mouse coordinates (see Figure 10-3). Scroll bars allow the user to set the color, and a text box allows the user to enter the size, in twips, of the box. An *Erase* button, when clicked, erases the drawing area.

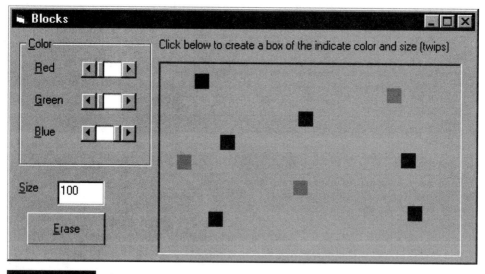

 The sample Standard EXE draws blocks wherever you click.

First, run the standalone version of the program:

1. From folder *VB6Adv\Demos\AutomationServer\StandardEXE*, run program *BlocksEXE.EXE*.
2. Click anywhere in the indicated area to draw a box.
3. Adjust color settings by modifying the settings in the *Red, Green,* and/or *Blue* scroll bars. Click in the drawing area to create a few more blocks.
4. Change the size by entering a number in the *Size* text box – try a number like *200* or *300*. Click in the drawing area to create a few more blocks.
5. Click the *Erase* button to clear the drawing area, and draw some more blocks.
6. Exit the program.

Source code for this very simple application is as follows:

```
Private Sub picDrawing_MouseDown(Button As Integer, _
                                 Shift As Integer, _
                                 X As Single, Y As Single)
    Dim Color As Long
    Dim Size As Integer

    Size = txtSize.Text

    Color = RGB(hsbRed.Value, hsbGreen.Value, hsbBlue.Value)
    picDrawing.Line (X - Size, Y - Size) - _
                    (X + Size, Y + Size), _
                    Color, BF
End Sub

Private Sub cmdErase_Click()
    picDrawing.Cls
End Sub
```

USING AN AUTOMATION CONTROLLER TO DRIVE THE PROGRAM

A second version of the demo program, which fully implements an automation interface, is provided with this book (see Figure 10-4). Also provided is a fully developed automation controller. I encourage you to run these applications – instructions are provided below. Later, I will guide you through the steps I took to convert the first version of the application to an automation server.

To run the automation controller program,

1. Register the automation server program, *Blocks.EXE*, located in folder *VB6Adv\Demos\AutmationServer\Server*. Simply double-click on the EXE from *Windows Explorer* or invoke it from the *Run* dialog, accessible from the Windows Start button. This will also start the program in standalone mode – simply exit the program after it starts.

2. Run program *TestAutoServer.EXE* from folder *VB6Adv\Demos\ AutomationServer\Client*.

3. Click the *Start Automation Server* button. This starts the application, but you will not see its window.

4. Click the *Show/Hide Window* button. You will then see the application's main window. Clicking the button a second time will hide it.

5. Click the *Draw Random Block* button. You will see a block appear in a random location of the drawing area of the *Blocks* application.

6. Experiment with the other buttons provided by the automation controller's interface; for example, try clicking the *Set Random Color, Set Random Size,* and *Erase Blocks* buttons.

7. Exiting the automation controller application will cause the server to exit as well.

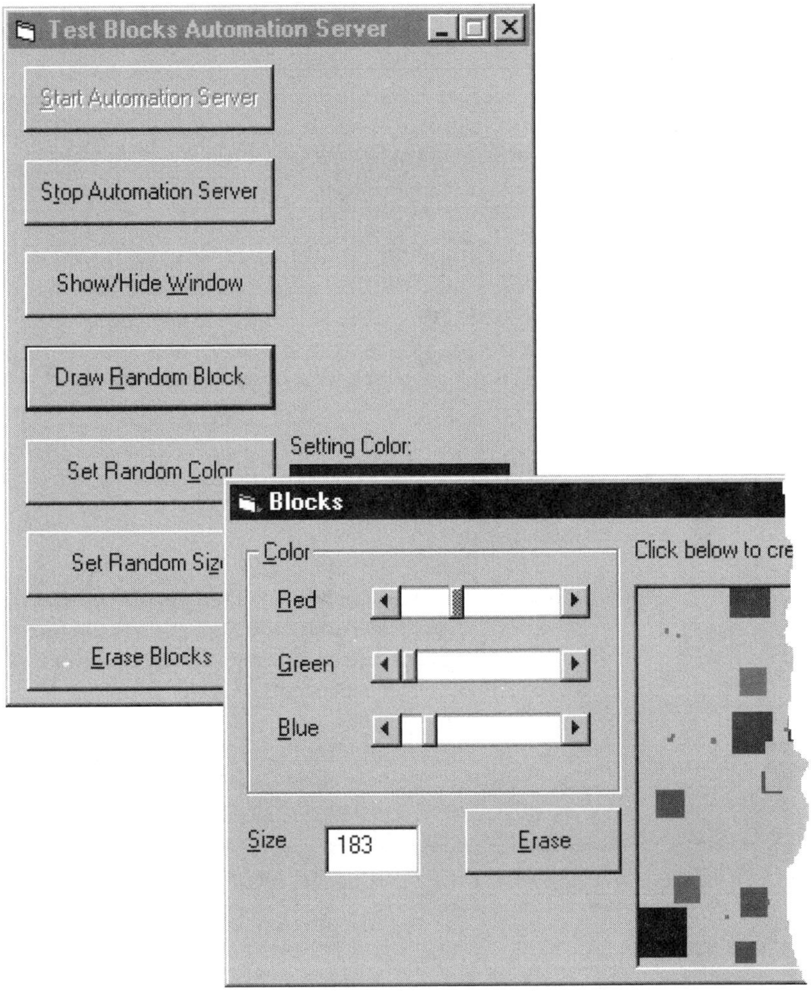

FIGURE 10-4 A second version of the application implements an automation interface.

ADDING A STANDARD MODULE WITH A SUB MAIN

The first step in adding an automation interface to an existing Visual Basic application is to add a *Standard Module* and, in this module, implement a *Sub Main*. In this module, you should declare a *private* object variable, using your *main form name* as its type. In the *Sub Main*, you should check the startup mode of the application. If the startup mode indicates that the application was started in standalone mode, create an instance of the main form and invoke the *Show* method on it, specifying *vbModeless* as the *Modal* parameter of the *Show* method. If the startup mode is not standalone, it must be in automation mode, in which case, your code does nothing else.

An example of this module, which was taken from the automation server version of the application included with this book, follows:

```
Option Explicit
Private objMainForm As frmMain

Private Sub Main()

    '- Display the form only if the application has
    '- started in standalone mode.  If not, there is
    '- only one other possibility - it has been
    '- started through automation.

    If App.StartMode = vbSModeStandalone Then
        Set objMainForm = New frmMain
        objMainForm.Show vbModeless
    End If

End Sub
```

CHANGING PROJECT ATTRIBUTES

The next step in adding an automation interface to an existing Visual Basic application is to change the project type from *Standard EXE* to *ActiveX EXE*, as shown in Figure 10-5. You can do this by accessing the *General* tab of the *Project Properties* dialog. Access the *Project Properties* dialog by selecting *Properties* from the *Project* menu. From the same dialog, change the *Startup Object* to *Sub Main*.

Finally, within the same dialog, provide a meaningful *Project Description*, since the text you place here is the description that developers will see in Visual Basic's *References* dialog. In the sample server included with this course, the description *Blocks Automation Server Demo* was used.

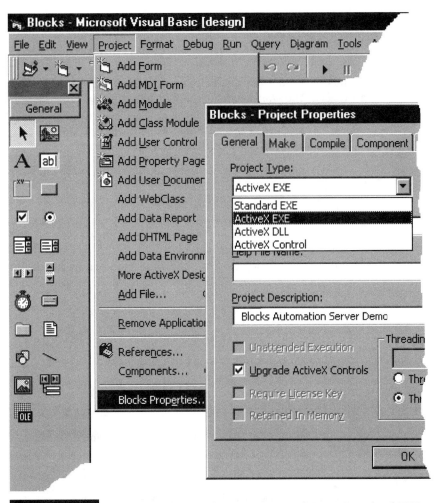

FIGURE 10-5 You must change the project type from a *Standard EXE* project to an *ActiveX EXE* project.

PROVIDING A SINGLE-USE CLASS MODULE

Next, you should add a class module to the project and set this class module's *Instancing* property to *SingleUse*. This setting will result in a new instance of the application for each concurrent automation controller. If you prefer to have each automation controller access the same instance of the running application, set the *Instancing* property to *MultiUse*.

The name you select for this class module is important, since this is how other developers will declare the object variables that reference your automation server. By convention, many automation server developers use the class name *Application* to represent their automation server. This is the name I used in the accompanying demo program.

In the declarations section of this class module, declare a private object variable using your application's main form name as the object type. In the class module's *Initialize* method, create, but do not show, an instance of this form object. The *Terminate* method of the class module should *Unload* the form object. Sample code for performing these activities appears in the next section.

IMPLEMENTING A VISIBLE PROPERTY

Your single-use class module should implement a *Visible* property that, when set to *TRUE*, shows your form object. Use *vbModeless* as the *Modal* parameter to the *Show* method. When the property is set to *FALSE*, invoke the *Hide* method on the form object.

The property is implemented using *Property Let* and *Get* procedures with a private member variable holding the properties value. Sample code, which also illustrates the code that should appear in your class module's *Initialize* and *Terminate* methods, follows. Refer to Chapter 7 for more information on adding properties to a class module.

```
Option Explicit

'- Private member variables that hold values
'- of the properties

Private m_fVisible As Boolean

'- Private variable that holds reference to main form

Private m_objMainForm As frmMain

'- Initialize/terminate methods

Private Sub Class_Initialize()

    '- Create, but do not show, the main form

    Set m_objMainForm = New frmMain

    '- Initialize private member variables that
    '- hold property values

    m_fVisible = False

End Sub
```

```
Private Sub Class_Terminate()
    '- Unload the main form
    Unload m_objMainForm
End Sub

'- Public property let/get procedures

Public Property Let Visible(fVisible As Boolean)
    m_fVisible = fVisible
    If m_fVisible Then
        m_objMainForm.Show vbModeless
    Else
        m_objMainForm.Hide
    End If
End Property

Public Property Get Visible() As Boolean
    Visible = m_fVisible
End Property
```

WRAPPING APPLICATION FUNCTIONALITY

In addition to the essential and ubiquitous *Visible* property, you will want to wrap your application's functionality with properties and methods implemented in the class module. Each automation server's set of properties and methods will naturally vary. You should design properties and methods that are meaningful and for which there is an association with the activities performed by an interactive user of the application. Depending on the complexity of the application, and how much "surface area" you want to give to the objects hosted by your automation server, it may be necessary to use a hierarchical object model, as *Microsoft Excel* does.

The sample application presented in this chapter, while simple, provides a good example for analysis. The program, used interactively, allows the user to draw boxes wherever the mouse button is clicked. The user can also select a color and size, and can erase the drawing area. Since a good automation server provides an interface that provides equivalent functionality to an automation controller, you will want to expose this functionality through the automation interface.

It is often necessary to introduce additional functionality to the automation interface that is not available, or which is implicitly available to the interactive user. For example, if I expect an automation controller to be able to draw boxes in the picture box, I must provide some way for the controller to know how big the box is. Thus, I have introduced two properties – *MaxWidth* and *MaxHeight* – that an automation controller can read to discover the limits of the drawing area. An interactive user, of course, sees the drawing area and knows where he or she can or cannot click to draw a box.

In mapping the interactive user's capability of setting a box's size and color, properties are ideal candidates. An interactive user's capability of drawing and erasing boxes can be mapped to methods. In my implementation, I have provided the *Size* and *Color* properties, and the *Draw* and *Erase* methods.

To add an automation interface to an existing application, it is often necessary to make some modifications to the existing user interface code. The degree of modification can vary from minor to severe, depending on how tightly the user interface logic is coupled with the application logic. A major consideration is how the user interface requires the user to carry out an action. For example, menu selections and button clicks are easy to map to methods in your class module. User interface gestures such as drag-and-drop, mouse movement tracking, and mouse down events are more difficult to map to an automation interface. In the case of the *Blocks* application, it will be easy to map the *Clear* function to the *Erase* button, but the action taken by the interactive user to draw a block – by pressing the left mouse button over the picture box control – will be more difficult.

An analysis of the application reveals that the application logic for drawing a block is directly and fully enclosed in the picture box control's *MouseDown* event. A quick fix would be to modify the scope of the *MouseDown* event procedure to *Public,* and invoke the event procedure from the class module. While this approach would work, it is inelegant. Calling the *MouseDown* event procedure requires passing more than just a pair of coordinates – the procedure's argument list also includes *Key* state and *Mouse Button* state parameters. Therefore the approach taken was to separate the user interface logic from the application logic by providing a public general procedure to draw the box. The *MouseDown* event procedure is then modified to call this new general procedure. The *Draw* method of the *Application* class module calls the same general procedure as the *MouseDown* event procedure. Related code from the automation server's main form follows:

```
Public Sub DrawBox(ByVal x As Single, ByVal y As Single)
    Dim Color As Long
    Dim Size As Integer

    Size = txtSize.Text

    Color = RGB(hsbRed.Value, hsbGreen.Value, hsbBlue.Value)
    picDrawing.Line (x - Size, y - Size) - _
                    (x + Size, y + Size), _
                    Color, BF
End Sub
```

```
Private Sub picDrawing_MouseDown(Button As Integer, _
                                 Shift As Integer, _
                                 x As Single, y As Single)
    DrawBox x, y
End Sub
```

The implementations of the *Draw* and *Erase* methods, as well as the *Size* and *Color* properties follow – this code appears in the *Application* class module. Note the technique that is used to reference the controls on the main form – use the syntax *form_name.control_name.property_name* to access a property of a control on a form, and use the syntax *form_name.control_name.method_name* to access a control's method. It's essential that the actions invoked via an automation interface update the controls of the application's main window. This is what the user will expect, and it provides positive feedback that the interface has responded to a method or property invocation. For example, setting the *Size* property from the automation interface updates the text box used by an interactive user to set the box size. Changing a color by setting the *Color* property updates the application's scroll bars. In addition to providing the visual feedback mentioned previously, this technique has an added benefit – in carrying out requests that originate from the automation controller by interacting with the controls on the form, the existing user interface logic takes care of the rest, resulting in the reuse of application logic.

```
Public Property Get MaxWidth() As Integer
    MaxWidth = m_objMainForm.picDrawing.ScaleWidth
End Property

Public Property Get MaxHeight() As Integer
    MaxHeight = m_objMainForm.picDrawing.ScaleHeight
End Property

Public Property Let Size(nSize As Integer)
    m_objMainForm.txtSize.Text = Str(nSize)
End Property

Public Property Get Size() As Integer
    Size = Val(m_objMainForm.txtSize.Text)
End Property

Public Property Let Color(rgbNewColor As Long)
    Dim nRed As Integer
    Dim nGreen As Integer
    Dim nBlue As Integer
```

```
    nRed = rgbNewColor And &HFF
    nGreen = (rgbNewColor / (2 ^ 8)) And &HFF
    nBlue = (rgbNewColor / (2 ^ 16)) And &HFF

    m_objMainForm.hsbRed.Value = nRed
    m_objMainForm.hsbGreen.Value = nGreen
    m_objMainForm.hsbBlue.Value = nBlue

End Property

Public Property Get Color() As Long
    Color = RGB(m_objMainForm.hsbRed.Value, _
                m_objMainForm.hsbGreen.Value, _
                m_objMainForm.hsbBlue.Value)
End Property

Public Sub Draw(ByVal nX As Integer, ByVal nY As Integer)
    m_objMainForm.DrawBox nX, nY
End Sub

Public Sub Clear()
    m_objMainForm.cmdErase.Value = True
End Sub
```

DCOM
Step-by-Step

Building objects that meet COM standards, as you have seen, enables any COM-capable programming language to use your objects. The benefits are reusability, reduced complexity through modularity, and isolation of implementation details to the component. Tactical benefits of using COM include enabling a project manager to use a divide-and-conquer approach to development, placing developers on teams according to their skill sets. Another important benefit is flexibility of deployment. A COM component used by a client can be hosted in a COM server that resides on a remote computer – this is because any COM component is ready to use DCOM, the Distributed Component Object Model.

About DCOM

In this chapter, you'll see how to use DCOM to communicate remotely between an ActiveX Component and a client. As you'll see, there are no extra programming steps required for using DCOM instead of COM. However, using DCOM presents several challenges in the way of setup and installation. You will also need to carefully consider revision control, since changes to interfaces may break existing clients if you're not careful.

Since MTS arrived on the scene, the importance of understanding how to deploy objects remotely using DCOM has lost some significance. Just as it is not essential for a Visual Basic developer to have an in-depth understanding of COM to build COM objects, it is entirely possible to use DCOM via the services provided by MTS – and not understand a thing that occurs under the hood. However, the serious component developer needs to understand some fundamental concepts of COM; the Visual Basic developer who has read Chapter 8 will have more than a necessary fundamental understanding of COM. Likewise, the serious distributed application developer will need to have a fundamental understanding of DCOM. And, it certainly wouldn't hurt to know how to manually deploy a remote client/server configuration. If you follow along with the walkthrough presented in this chapter, you will have done precisely that.

There is another consideration to a developer's understanding of DCOM. While using MTS provides an easier environment for the remote deployment of objects using DCOM, all but the most trivial of COM objects must be written to run under the MTS executive. If you have decided that you do not want to instrument your objects to run under the MTS executive, yet you want to remotely deploy the objects, you will have to use DCOM on your own. As you will see in this chapter, the steps involved are not difficult. Part of the problem, however, is that there are more than a few of these simple steps. One mistake made during the execution of these steps will result in a failure that may be difficult to troubleshoot. I have included some guidelines for troubleshooting DCOM problems at the end of this chapter; however, there is no substitute for taking your time and being careful.

Services Provided by DCOM

As a whole, DCOM provides an application programmer with the necessary services to facilitate communication between a client application and a remote server application. In essence, this is no different than the services provided by the *WinSock* interface (see Chapter 4) and other communications services provided by the Win32 API – such as named pipes. The difference between DCOM and these other remote process communications methods is that DCOM is virtually transparent to both the client and server applications.

Prior to the availability of DCOM, a developer creating a client/server application on Windows needed to be familiar with some type of network programming technique. As mentioned, sockets and named pipes provide a developer with a solution for sending cross-system messages from one application to another. However, a programmer using such solutions needs to be familiar with the necessary system calls and must instrument an application for using them; this requires the developer to learn yet another API. Sockets, named pipes, network DDE, and other process-to-process communications techniques all have their advantages and disadvantages; any one of them offers a viable solution to developing distributed applications. None of them, however, are equivalent to each other in terms of their APIs – each technique requires the programmer to learn how to use a different set of system functions.

Programmers who have created distributed applications using sockets or named pipes are aware that differences in data representation between machines can cause problems. For example, a 16-bit integer on one machine may be stored with the high byte followed by the low byte, while on another machine it is the other way around. If all machines participating in the distributed application have, for example, Intel architecture, differences in data representation is not a problem. But if your application needs to communicate with a process running on a VAX, Alpha, or Motorola architecture, for example, problems related to differences in data representation will arise when you attempt to send binary data across the network.

OSF/DCE and Remote Procedure Calls (RPCs)

If a programmer is required to learn a communications API and focus on differences in data representation, the complexity of creating distributed applications increases significantly. These and other issues were addressed about a decade ago by the Open Software Foundation (OSF), which defined an operating system- and architecture-independent environment for distributed application development. This environment, known as the Distributed Computing Environment, or OSF/DCE, is the basis for Microsoft's Distributed Component Object Model.

At the heart of OSF/DCE, and thus at the heart of DCOM, is the Remote Procedure Call (RPC) mechanism, known as DCE RPC. The brilliance of DCE RPC lies in its simplicity from an application developer's perspective. It is based on the presumption that all programmers, while perhaps unfamiliar with the specific APIs of various process-to-process communications mechanisms, are familiar at least with the concept of a procedure call. All programmers have created a function or procedure that is called from within their program. However, programmers calling a procedure have typically operated under the assumption that the called procedure exists within the executing process's address space. A remote procedure actually executes in the context of a different process, perhaps executing on a different machine on the network.

When a developer using DCE RPC calls a remote procedure, the code actually executes a proxy function that, externally, appears identical to the actual procedure. The proxy appears identical to the actual procedure because the proxy procedure's parameter list and return type are identical to that of the real procedure – in other words, the proxy has the same signature as the actual procedure. The purpose of the proxy procedure is to marshal (package into a block for transmission) the input parameters and send them to the remote server. All issues related to communicating with the server, including locating the server's host, establishing a connection, sending the parameters, and waiting for a reply, are handled by code contained in the proxy. Code for the proxy is actually generated by development tools envisioned by the OSF – including the IDL (Interface Definition Language) compiler – and linked into the client's application. The developer of the client application calls the proxy as though it were a local version of a fully implemented procedure.

The server process contains a similar version of the remote procedure, known as a stub. The role of the server stub is to unmarshal the input parameters and send them to the actual implementation of the remote procedure, which it calls locally. Output parameters and function results are marshaled back to the client proxy, which unmarshals them and returns them back to the remote caller.

The DCE RPC mechanism, therefore, works by intercepting calls from the client and sending them to the server. This is entirely consistent with how COM works, which must often intercept object method calls to marshal arguments to out-of-process servers and provide synchronization between apartments. The same mechanism makes it possible for COM to intercept object method calls and insert additional code to handle the low-level details of network connections and protocols, enabling you to focus on details related to the development of your application.

Using the DCE RPC mechanism, Microsoft's DCOM extends COM to enable clients to use objects that are hosted on different machines in your network. All of the features of DCOM automatically become available to a developer using COM. DCOM is a seamless evolution of COM, enabling a developer to leverage knowledge of COM and take existing COM objects to a new level. No additional code is required in either a client or the server application to use DCOM. The programming tools provided within *Visual Studio*, including Visual Basic, create COM objects that can either be hosted locally or remotely – the additional tasks required to distribute an object are administrative in nature. In other words, additional programming is not required, but additional setup is. In the remaining sections of this chapter, I will guide you through the steps required to set up a client and server for remote communications using DCOM.

Before Getting Started with DCOM

I'll warn you that working with DCOM can be frustrating – this is why I called this chapter *DCOM Step-by-Step*. I suggest you follow the guidelines and procedures presented in this chapter very carefully. There are shortcuts, but unless you have deployed several distributed applications using DCOM, you cannot yet assume that you know where these shortcuts are.

Also, if you want to experiment with DCOM, be aware you'll probably leave "stale" entries in your registry; in fact, you may leave many stale entries, depending on the level of playing that you do. Refer to Chapter 8 for information on unregistering COM servers.

I can offer another piece of advice – do not actually distribute your application until it's ready! Test it locally (on the same system) as much as possible. Distributed applications are, by their nature, more complex in terms of installation and version control than their standalone counterparts. Don't complicate them further by releasing software that's not ready. If you discover bugs in your server after it's been deployed with DCOM, they can of course be fixed without breaking compatibility with installed clients. Servers can withstand some modification without requiring a reconfiguration or reinstallation of the clients. Exactly how much modification can a server withstand without breaking compatibility with existing installed clients? If you don't know, don't distribute the application until you fully understand how to maintain interface and object compatibility. The topic of client/server compatibility is introduced briefly in this chapter, and is covered in greater detail in Chapter 14.

I will assume that you are running the demonstrations included with this book using *Windows 2000* or *Windows NT 4.0 Service Pack 4*. But if you have not at least installed Windows NT 4.0 Service Pack 2, the DCOM example will not run properly. To run DCOM under *Windows 9x*, you need *DCOM For Windows 9x* (available with Visual Studio 98).

A DCOM Walkthrough

In the following sections, you will create a COM object hosted in an out-of-process COM server (ActiveX EXE) along with a client test program. After testing the client/server application locally, you will deploy the client on a remote machine, from which it will access the remote server. The application you will create is a very simple one – it is deliberately simple to keep the focus on DCOM. Of course, you will need two machines connected via a network to follow along with the walkthrough.

You will use the *Package and Deployment Wizard* to create the client setup program that will enable the remote client to communicate with your server. The setup program generated by the *Package and Deployment Wizard* will create the necessary registry entries on the client – these registry entries are all that are required to enable the remote client to communicate with the server. While these registry entries can of course be manually entered into the registry, it is not the recommended approach. Refer to Chapter 8 for a description of the necessary client-side registry entries.

Setting up a DCOM Server Project

A DCOM server project requires only a few differences in setup. The easiest type of server to deploy with DCOM is an out-of-process COM server (ActiveX EXE). Although an in-process COM server (ActiveX DLL) can be deployed remotely using a DLL surrogate, its installation cannot be easily automated with the *Package and Deployment Wizard.* In the latter part of this chapter, I will describe how to deploy an in-process COM server remotely using a DLL surrogate.

Setting up an out-of-process COM server for deployment with DCOM starts with creating a new ActiveX EXE project and properly setting project properties. This is illustrated in the next few sections.

GETTING STARTED: CREATE A LOCAL CLIENT/SERVER APPLICATION

The first step to creating a successful DCOM application is to create a successful COM application. To get started, create a simple ActiveX Component that exports perhaps one or two properties and methods, and maybe an event or two. Once you've created the server, you can create a simple test client. Test the client and server locally, on your development system. After you've successfully tested the application locally, you can prepare to distribute the application.

To get started with DCOM, create a new ActiveX EXE project (see Figure 11-1).

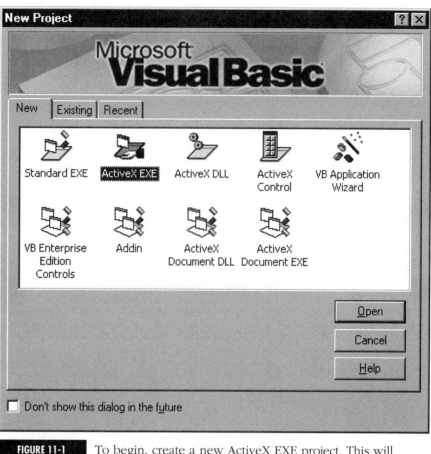

FIGURE 11-1 To begin, create a new ActiveX EXE project. This will become your server.

PROJECT PROPERTIES: GENERAL TAB

Prior to writing a single line of code in your DCOM server, important project properties must be established. You should start with the *General* tab of the *Project Properties* dialog and verify that the *Project Type* is *ActiveX EXE*. Set the *Project Name* to the name you want the server to be called, and provide a meaningful description in the *Project Description* text box. Finally, check the *Unattended Execution* box – this prevents you from adding forms and other user interface objects, which don't belong in a remote server.

In a production version of a DCOM server, you will probably want to increase the size of the server's thread pool. In theory, the more threads in the thread pool, the more concurrent client requests your server can handle, thus increasing server throughput. In practice, increased throughput is only achieved by overlapping the time the server spends waiting for a blocking operation,

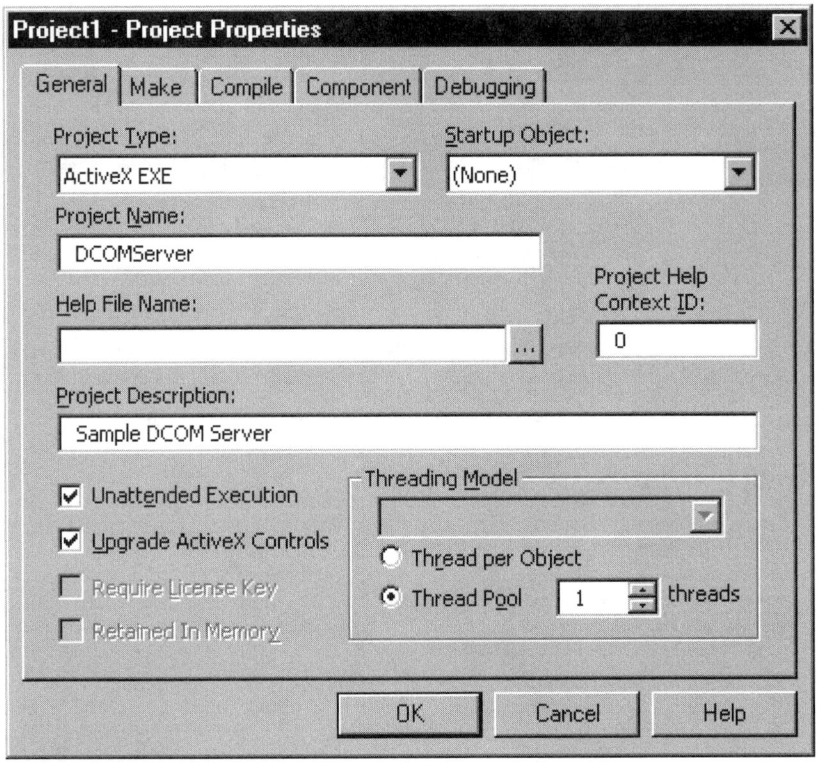

FIGURE 11-2 The *General* tab of the *Project Properties* dialog includes some properties that are important to the proper use of DCOM.

such as an I/O request, with the productive use of otherwise wasted CPU cycles. Apparent throughput may be increased as an effect of time slicing between threads, a service provided by the operating system. In any case, the thread pool attributes of a COM server can easily be changed at a later time without affecting compatibility between the server and installed clients. For more information on threads and threading models, refer to Chapter 8.

To set related *Project Properties* on the *General Tab (see* Figure 11-2*),*

1. Give the server a name by typing it into the *Project Name* text box of the *Project Properties* dialog, under the *General* tab.

2. In the same dialog, provide a description in *Project Description.*

3. Check the *Unattended Execution* box.

PROJECT PROPERTIES: MAKE TAB

Settings on the *Make* tab of the *Project Properties* dialog are also important, although not as important as they were in Visual Basic 5.0. In particular, the settings in the *Version Number* frame have significance. It is recommended that you check the box *Auto Increment*, or at least be prepared to manually increment the server's version number each time you build the server. Checking the *Auto Increment* option causes Visual Basic to automatically increment the version number whenever you build your project.

Previously (in VB5), this step was required to prevent "false installs" on the target machine. If the version number of the application being installed was less than or equal to the version number of the application already installed, the SETUP.EXE program generated by the old *Setup Wizard* would not install the application – and not tell you that it didn't install it. This behavior has changed in the setup program created by the *Package and Deployment Wizard* in VB6, but it's still recommended that you check the *Auto Increment* check box or, as mentioned, manually increase the version number whenever you build the server.

Under the *Make* tab of the *Project Properties* dialog, (see Figure 11-3), check the *Auto Increment* box, which you'll find grouped with the *Version Number* controls.

| FIGURE 11-3 | The settings on the *Make* tab are not as critical as they were in Visual Basic 5, but you should still be aware of the effect they have on your server. |

PROJECT PROPERTIES: COMPONENT TAB

There are three important settings under the *Component* tab of the *Project Properties* dialog box (see Figure 11-4). First, make sure the *Start Mode* option is set to *ActiveX Component*. This allows you to run the server under the Visual Basic development environment; if you don't check this option, your server will exit immediately when you run it under Visual Basic. Second, check the *Remote Server Files* box. This causes Visual Basic to generate *VBR* (Visual Basic registry) and *TLB* (type library) files whenever you build the server. You'll need both when you reach a later step, building a setup program for distributing the client. Finally, select the *Project Compatibility* option. Later, you will change this setting to *Binary Compatibility*. I'll explain what this setting accomplishes in a later section of this chapter; Binary Compatibility is described in greater detail in Chapter 14.

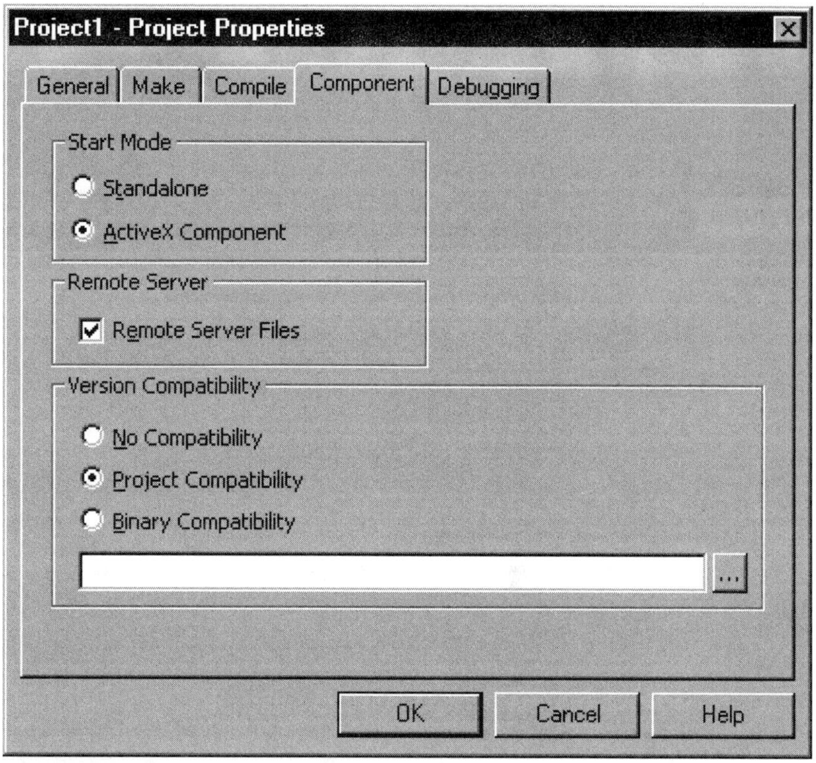

FIGURE 11-4   It is necessary to generate some extra files when you build a DCOM server. Checking the *Remote Sever Files* box enables the generation of these required files.

To set related *Project Properties* on the *Component* tab,

1. On the *Component* tab of the *Project Properties* dialog, set *Start Mode* to *ActiveX Component*.
2. Check the Remote Server Files box.
3. Select the Project Compatibility option.

Implementing and Building the Server

With the properties of the server project properly set, you're ready to implement and build the server. As mentioned, you will create a very simple server. It will export a single class called **DCOMClass**. The *DCOMClass* class will have only one property, an integer property called **ObjectCount**, which will be a read-only property implemented with a *Property Get* procedure. There will be one method, called **Reverse**, which, given a string, will return the reversed version of that string. There will be one event, called **Loopback**, which will be raised when the *Reverse* method is invoked. It will pass a single *String* parameter, which will be the value passed to the *Reverse* method.

✳ Recall that global data declared in a module is shared between instances of the class. Therefore, in this implementation, you will declare the number of objects as a Public variable in a module. Also recall that the *Class_Initialize* event occurs each time a new instance of a class is created. Therefore, this is the best place to increment the number of objects. The *Class_Terminate* event occurs each time an instance of a class is deleted. This is the best place to decrement the number of objects.

In summary, you will have two modules in the server project—a class module for the *DCOMClass* class and a standard module for a global variable (number of objects). Add a standard module to the project and give it the name **Globals**. In the declarations section, a public variable of type *Integer*, called *gnObjectCount,* should be declared. For example,

```
Option Explicit
Public gnObjectCount As Integer
```

Since you've created an ActiveX EXE project, you already have a blank class module. Furthermore, the **Instancing** property of the class will be correctly set to **5 – MultiUse**. The **Name** of the class should be set to **DCOMClass**. Add the **ObjectCount** property, and implement it as a *Property Get* procedure. Add a **Reverse** method, which takes a string parameter and returns the reversed string. Declare an event called **Loopback**, which is raised when the *Reverse* method is called. Finally, add code to handle the class *Initialize* and *Terminate* events—the code should increment/decrement the global object count. The code from the class module follows:

```
Option Explicit
Event LoopBack(strString As String)

Private Sub Class_Initialize()
    gnObjectCount = gnObjectCount + 1
End Sub

Private Sub Class_Terminate()
```

```
        gnObjectCount = gnObjectCount - 1
End Sub

Public Property Get ObjectCount() As Integer
        ObjectCount = gnObjectCount
End Property

Public Function Reverse(strString As String) As String
        RaiseEvent LoopBack(strString)
        Reverse = StrReverse(strString)
End Function
```

Once you've implemented the server, you can build it. Building the server creates the EXE file, and also creates the VBR and TLB files. The VBR file will be used in a later step, specifically, when you distribute the client. The TLB file is the server's type library file, which describes the server's classes and the properties, events, and methods contained in each class.

After building the server, you can close the server project and start creating the client project. Or, if you prefer, you can run the server under Visual Basic while you start Visual Basic again to develop and test the client.

Implementing a Test Client Program: User Interface

The next step is to implement, build, and then test a simple client application to access the server. Even when you begin development on a production version of your server, it is strongly recommended that you create and run the client test application on the same system as the new server; that is, on your development machine. Since you will be creating a setup application for this client program, it is recommended that you set the *Auto Increment* option, as you did for the server.

Your test client will be a Standard EXE project that displays a form with a few controls. To create this from scratch, use Figure 11-5 as a guide for creating the necessary controls.

1. Start a new *Standard EXE* project for the client test program.
2. Under the *Make* tab of the *Project Properties* dialog, check *Auto Increment* for the version number.
3. Create the controls for the user interface of your simple client test program.

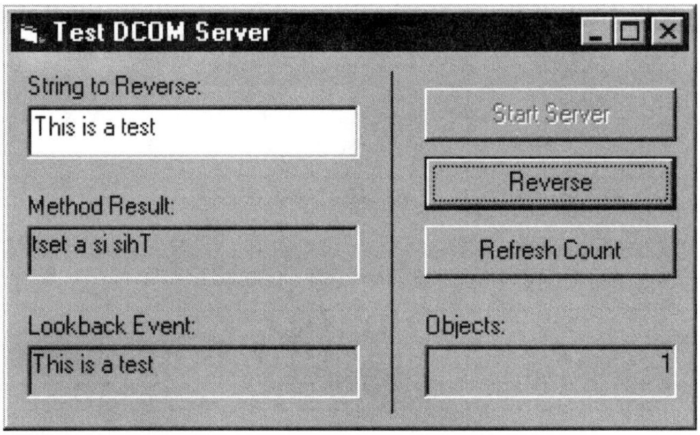

FIGURE 11-5 The user interface of a simple client test program.

IMPLEMENTING A TEST CLIENT PROGRAM: THE CODE SIDE

Next, insert a reference to the type library of your server (see Figure 11-6). You can then declare and use objects exported by the server. Then, add code to your client demo program to test the server. Code from the implemented sample follows:

```
Option Explicit
Private WithEvents objServer As DCOMServer.DCOMClass

Private Sub cmdStart_Click()
    Screen.MousePointer = vbHourglass
    Set objServer = New DCOMServer.DCOMClass
    lblObjects.Caption = objServer.ObjectCount
    cmdReverse.Enabled = True
    cmdRefresh.Enabled = True
    cmdReverse.Default = True
    txtString.SetFocus
    Screen.MousePointer = 0
End Sub

Private Sub cmdRefresh_Click()
    lblObjects.Caption = objServer.ObjectCount
End Sub

Private Sub cmdReverse_Click()
    Dim strstring As String
    strstring = txtString.Text
    lblMethodResult.Caption = objServer.Reverse(strstring)
```

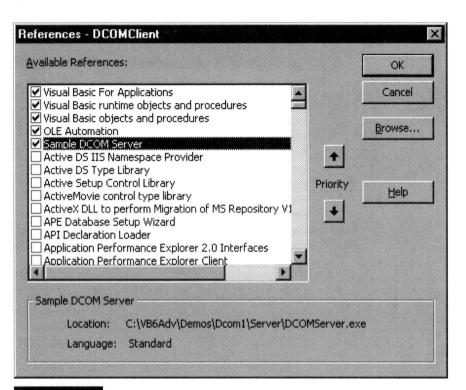

FIGURE 11-6   Your client test program requires a reference to the DCOM server's type library.

```
End Sub

Private Sub objServer_LoopBack(strstring As String)
    lblLoopback.Caption = strstring
End Sub
```

BUILDING AND TESTING THE CLIENT APPLICATION

Next, build and execute the client application on the same system as your server. You can run the client test application from Visual Basic to verify the operation of the server. However, at some point before distributing the client to a remote machine, you should also test the client application outside of the Visual Basic development environment, running the EXE file from the *Start* menu (*Start/Run*).

If your client won't run on the local machine at this point, it cannot possibly have anything to do with DCOM. Up to now, you've done nothing other than create a simple out-of-process COM server (ActiveX EXE). Refer to Chapters 6, 7, and 8 for fundamentals of class modules, ActiveX Components, and COM if you have trouble identifying the source of any problems you may be experiencing at this point.

To summarize, at this point you should

1. Build the client program.
2. Run the client's EXE from outside Visual Basic.
3. Test the client code and its interaction with the server.

Distributing the Application

Before distributing the application, there are some important steps to take, back in the server project—specifically, you need to get serious about compatibility between client and server. By default, Visual Basic selects *Project Compatibility*, which means that new class, interface, and library IDs may be generated with every build of the server. Project compatibility is really only valid for testing. When you're releasing software, you should switch to *Binary Compatibility* (see Figure 11-7). This is especially important in a distributed application. Selecting *Binary Compatibility* makes sure you don't make incompatible changes to your server. Binary compatibility is discussed in further detail in Chapter 14.

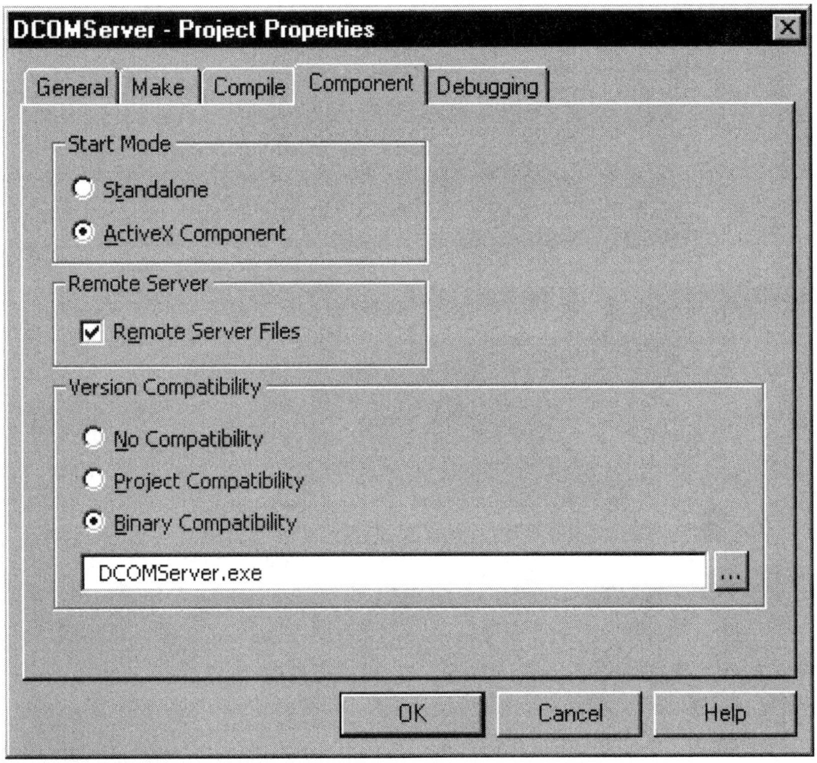

FIGURE 11-7   Switch the server's *Version Compatibility* option to *Binary Compatibility* before you distribute a client application.

To summarize, you should now

1. Return to the *server* project and bring up the *Project Properties* dialog.
2. Under the *Components* tab, check *Binary Compatibility*.
3. Rebuild the server.
4. Save the project again.

The key to successful deployment of a distributed application using DCOM is to use an appropriate setup generation tool. In Visual Basic, this means the **Package and Deployment Wizard**. Although you can install a server and a client manually, there is little motivation for doing so.

The first step will be to create a dependency file for the server. The *Package and Deployment Wizard* will use this file when it creates a setup program for the client application. If you keep the server on the same machine as the one you developed it on, you don't need to create a setup program for the server. To install the server on another machine (which is typical), you'll run the *Package and Deployment Wizard* on the server a second time to create a full setup program for the server.

In this walkthrough, you will leave the server installed on the machine on which it was developed. Therefore, the next step will be to create a setup program for the client application. It's recommended that you place the client setup files in a shared directory on the server, where they can be accessed from client machines. Then, you'll run the client setup program on each machine that you want the client application to run on.

CREATING A DEPENDENCY FILE FOR THE SERVER

A **dependency file** lists the runtime components that must be distributed with your application. If your application requires a component, as is the case when a client application uses a server, the *Package and Deployment Wizard* must know the dependencies of the server application as well. It is therefore necessary to generate a dependency file from your server before creating a setup program for the client application (see Figure 11-8). The generation of a server's dependency file is accomplished by using the *Package and Deployment Wizard*, as described in the following steps:

1. Start the *Package and Deployment Wizard*.
2. Select the *Server Project* and click the *Package* button.
3. Select *Dependency File* as the *Package Type*.
4. Click *Next* to go on to the next step.
5. When prompted for the *Package Folder* location, select the same folder as the server's project file (see Figure 11-9).
6. Click *Next* to go on to the next step.
7. Answer *No* when asked about *Remote Automation* support.
8. Click *Next* on the *Included Files Screen*.
9. Click *Next* on the *Cab Information Screen*.
10. Click *Next* on the *Install Locations Screen*.
11. Click *Finish* on the *Finished Screen*.
12. You have now created the required *Dependency File*.

FIGURE 11-8	Select *Dependency File* for the package type to build the dependency file required by the client setup program.

CREATING A SETUP PROGRAM FOR THE CLIENT

Next, you'll create a setup program for the client, using the *Package and Deployment Wizard* again. In a later step of the *Package and Deployment Wizard*, you'll modify the reference to the server so that it will be accessed remotely instead of locally.

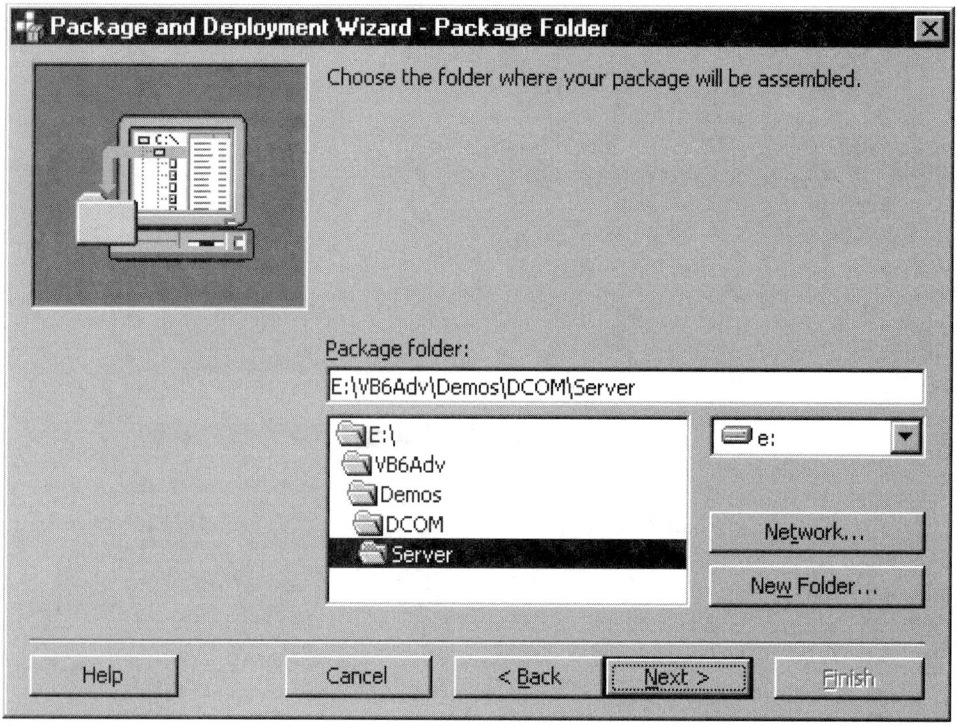

FIGURE 11-9 Place the server's dependency file in the same folder as the server's project file.

To begin creating a setup program for the client,

1. Start the *Package and Deployment Wizard* again, and select the *client* project.
2. Click the *Package* button.
3. Select *Standard Setup Package* for the *Package Type* (see Figure 11-10).
4. Select a folder that will be accessible over the network.

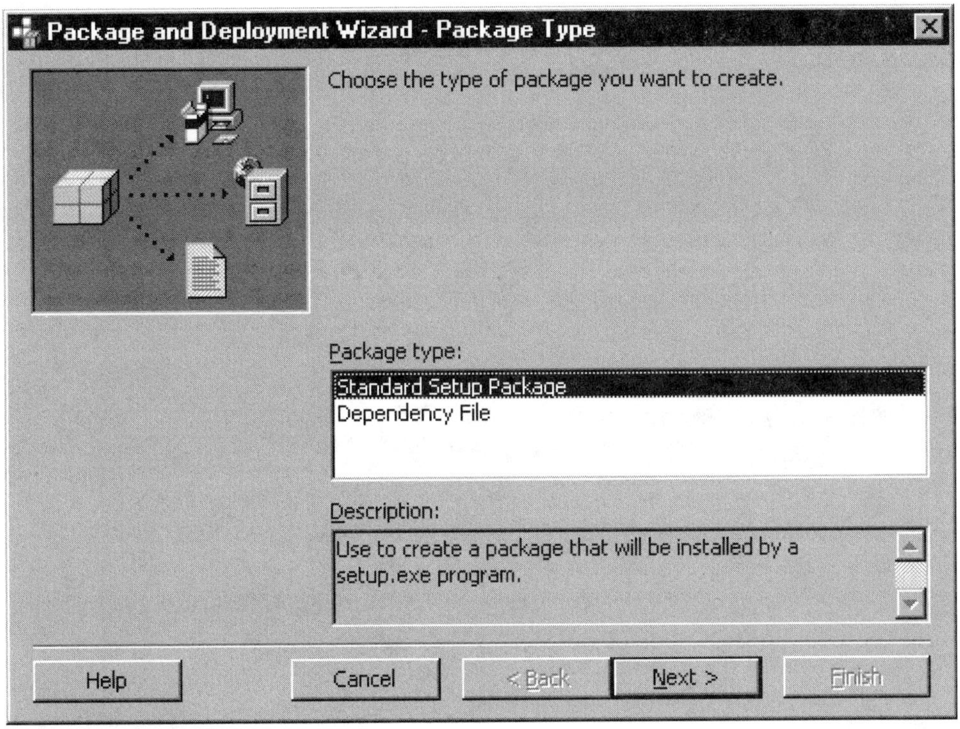

Package and Deployment Wizard - Package Type

Choose the type of package you want to create.

Package type:

| Standard Setup Package |
| Dependency File |

Description:

Use to create a package that will be installed by a
setup.exe program.

| Help | Cancel | < Back | Next > | Finish |

FIGURE 11-10   To create a setup program for the client application, specify *Standard Setup Package* for the package type.

To enable remote access to a server, you must manually add the server's VBR file to the list of files included with the client setup program. In the *Included Files* screen of the *Package and Deployment Wizard*, you must click the *Add* button and select the server's VBR file. Remember that the VBR file is generated by Visual Basic only if you select the *Remote Server Files* option.

To enable remote access to the server and add its VBR file to the client setup program:

1. In the *Included Files* screen, uncheck the server's *EXE* file.

2. Click the *Add* button, and in the resulting dialog, select *VBR* as the *File Type* (see Figure 11-11).

3. Navigate to and select the server's *VBR* file. You will find it in the server's project folder, provided you remembered to check the *Remote Server Files* option in the server's *Project Properties* dialog.

4. Click *Next*.

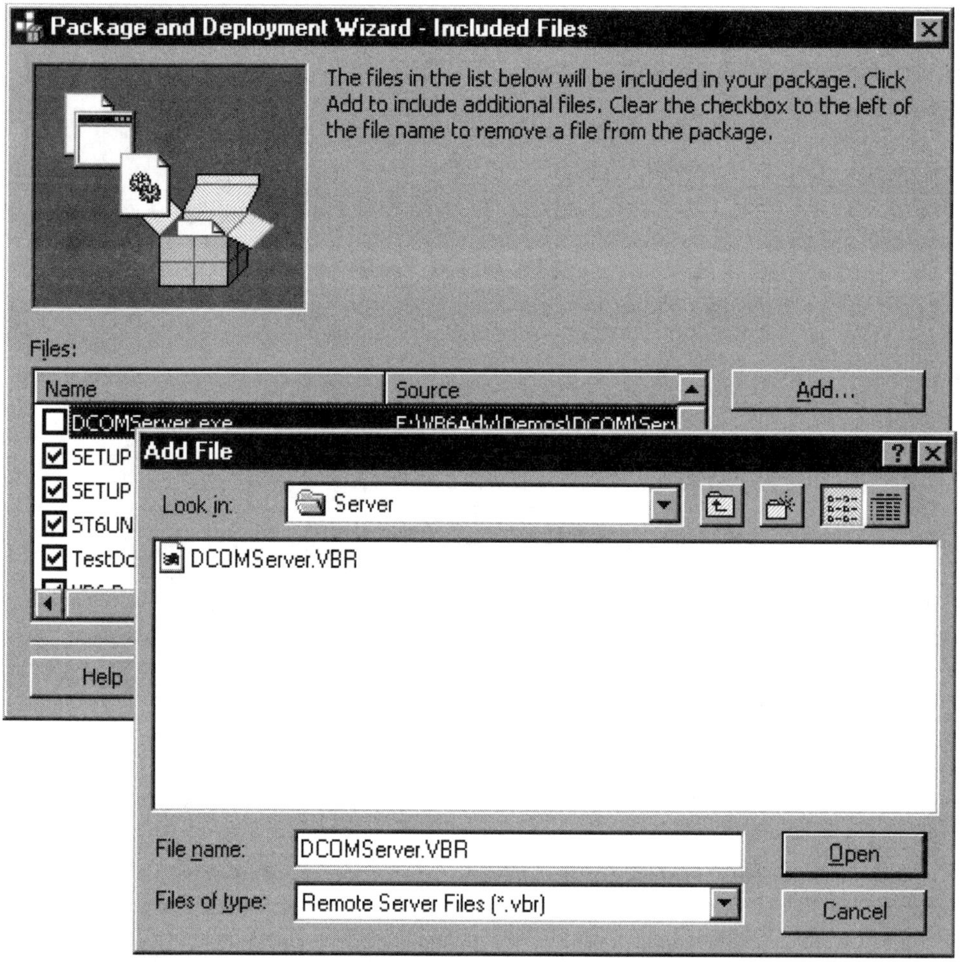

FIGURE 11-11 In the *Included Files* step of the *Package and Deployment Wizard*, add the server's *VBR* file to the list of files included with the client setup program.

The final step related to building a setup program for a remote client is to provide the network address or node name of the machine hosting the server. You will provide this information in the *Remote Servers* screen of the *Package and Deployment Wizard*, which appears only if you added a VBR file to the list of included files for a client setup program.

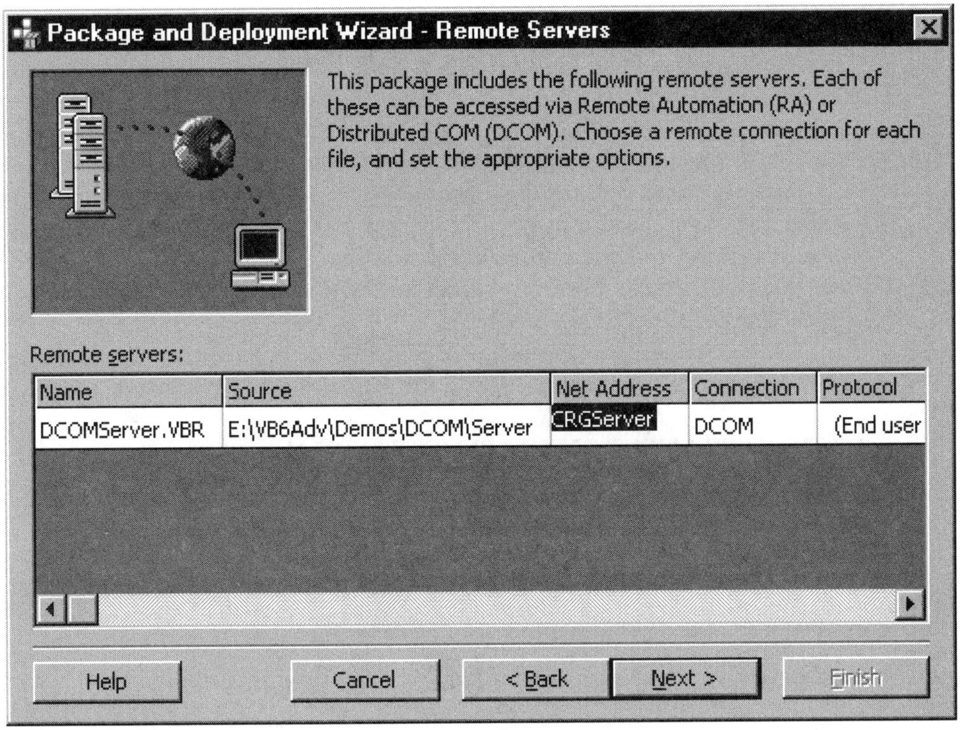

FIGURE 11-12   When you include a VBR file in a client setup program, the *Package and Deployment Wizard* allows you to specify to location of the remote server.

To provide a network address or node name of the machine hosting the server:

1. In the *Remote Servers* screen, enter the *Network Address* of the server (see Figure 11-12).

2. Click *Next*.

3. Select *Single cab* in the *Cab Options* screen and click *Next*.

4. Click *Next* on the *Installation Title* screen.

5. Accept the default *Start Menu Items* by clicking *Next*.

6. Accept the default *Install Locations* by clicking *Next*.

7. Accept the default *Shared Files* options by clicking *Next*.

8. Click *Finish* on the last screen.

INSTALLING THE SERVER AND THE CLIENT

Next, the server should be installed. This is done by executing the *Setup.EXE* program created by the *Package and Deployment Wizard. Do this only on the server machine!* After installing the server, install the client application by running the *Setup.EXE* program created for the client. *Do this only on the client machine(s)!*

Note that this walkthrough assumes that you are leaving the server installed on your development machine – obviously not something that is typically done in practice. Normally, you will use the *Package and Deployment Wizard* to create a setup program for the server, and execute this setup program on the target server machine.

To continue this walkthrough, install the client on a remote machine using the setup program you generated with the *Package and Deployment Wizard.*

TESTING THE CLIENT ON THE REMOTE SYSTEM

At this point, you can run the client on the remote system. Since you installed the program with the *Package and Deployment Wizard*, there will be an entry for it in the *Programs* group. One error you may get is *80070721*, or *Error 70 (Permission Denied)*, which indicates a security problem. The fix for this problem is discussed in the following section.

Permission Errors

Error number *80070721* or *70* is commonly seen when attempting to start a server from a remote client. It indicates a security problem. To fix the problem, run the **dcomcnfg** program, which ships with Windows NT 4.0 and Windows 2000. Simply click on the *Start* button, choose *Run*, enter *dcomcnfg*, and click *OK*. Configure your server to run under the identity of the interactive user, as described below. Note that you may also need to set other permissions as well. Permissions for accessing and launching a server from a remote client can be set from the *dcomcnfg* program.

To fix permission errors received by the client application,

1. Run the **dcomcnfg** program by selecting *Start*, then *Run*. Enter *dcomcnfg* and click *OK*.
2. Under the *Applications* tab, select your server.
3. Under the *Identity* tab, select the option *The Interactive User*.
4. Click *OK*.
5. Test the client on the remote system again.

Important Web Resources Related to DCOM

For additional help and troubleshooting information, see *http::www.microsoft-.com/oledev*. This Web page has all the latest information on DCOM, as well as other ActiveX/OLE information. You'll also find a link to the archives of the DCOM mailing list. If you're having a problem getting DCOM to work, chances are someone else has as well, and has posted a message and received a reply on how to fix the problem. You can also subscribe to the DCOM mailing list – you'll find instructions on how to do this on the Web page. Be aware, however, that you'll get lots of mail if you subscribe to this list.

Using CreateObject to Specify the Server Location

If your server's location changes from time to time, or if you otherwise do not know where your server will be located, you can specify the server in the **CreateObject** function. Its syntax is as follows:

```
Dim objName As ClassName
Set objName = CreateObject ("Library.ClassName", _
                            "NetworkServer")
```

For example, the following code will start the server created in this chapter on host *CRGServer:*

```
Dim objServer As DCOMServer.DCOMClass
Set objServer = CreateObject ("DCOMServer.DCOMClass", _
                              "CRGServer")
```

[handwritten: only do this for this]

[handwritten: WRONG!!]

[handwritten: Package & Deployment wizard can do this]

Note that if you use this approach, you should provide a custom setup program so that the user can specify the server location during installation. Optionally, you can provide a configuration dialog to let the user select the network server. You can save this information in the registry using the *SaveSetting* statement. For more information on saving application settings in the Windows registry, see Chapter 3.

A common misconception is that using *CreateObject* results in Visual Basic using the inefficient dispatch binding method, instead of vtable binding. This is not true. Visual Basic uses dispatch binding if your declare your object **As Object** instead of **As ClassName**. If you declare your object *As ClassName* instead of *As Object*, Visual Basic uses vtable binding (not dispatch binding), regardless of whether or not you use *New* or *CreateObject* to create the object. For more information on late and early binding, refer to Chapter 2.

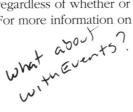

[handwritten: what about with Events?]

Using DCOM to Remotely Access an ActiveX DLL

An ActiveX EXE can run in its own process, but an ActiveX DLL cannot. An ActiveX DLL can be executed remotely using DCOM, but you must set up a DLL surrogate. With Windows NT and Windows 2000, there is a "stock" DLL surrogate called *DLLHOST.EXE.* Setting up an ActiveX DLL to run remotely requires a couple of extra registry entries. The easiest way to set up these registry entries is to use the *OLE/COM Object Viewer.* To use the *OLE/COM Object Viewer,* start the *OLE View* program from the *Visual Studio Tools* group.

To set up an ActiveX DLL to be hosted by a DCOM surrogate, follow the same procedure for setting up an ActiveX EXE, as presented in this chapter. Once you have installed the client and server, perform the following steps on the server before attempting to test the client:

1. Start the *OLE/COM Object Viewer.*
2. From the *View* menu, turn on *Expert Mode.*
3. In the left pane, under the *Object Classes* node, find and expand the *All Objects* node.
4. Scroll down until you find your object's Prog ID (example: *Training Server.Schedule*). Select the object by clicking on it (see Figure 11-13).
5. In the right pane, select the *Implementation* tab.
6. Check the *Use Surrogate Process* check box.
7. As there is no *OK* button, you must move off the tab to apply the changes. Just click on the *Registry* tab and then click back on the *Implementation* tab to apply and confirm the change.
8. Repeat the above four steps for each class of object in your server.

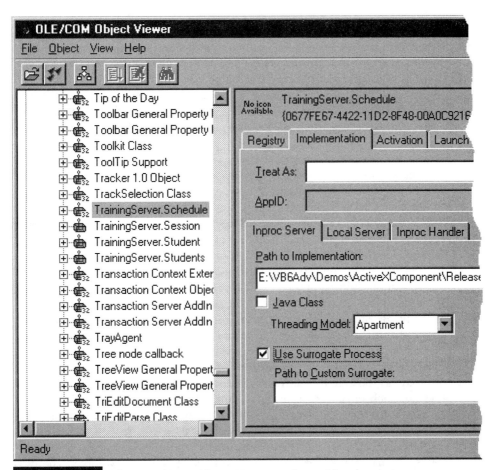

FIGURE 11-13 The *OLE/COM Object Viewer* tool provides the easiest way to enable a DLL surrogate for remoting an in-process COM server (ActiveX DLL).

Troubleshooting DCOM Problems

If you make sure to test your DCOM server with a local client application, and you are careful in performing the related steps of the *Package and Deployment Wizard*, you should not have any trouble remotely accessing your DCOM server. Should you have problems, there are two invaluable tools that can assist in troubleshooting – the *Error Lookup Utility* and the Windows NT or Windows 2000 *Event Viewer*.

Using the Error Lookup Utility

If your client application fails in attempting to start the remote DCOM server, the first step is to obtain the error code. If you are not trapping errors, you should see a message box or error dialog, as shown in Figure 11-14. If you are trapping errors and cannot see an error dialog, temporarily disable your error trapping code or, if you are running the program from within Visual Basic, select the *Break on All Errors* option from the *Project Properties* dialog, and run the program again. For more information on this and other error trapping options, refer to Chapter 14.

Programs that report errors *429* and *430* do not provide sufficient information for troubleshooting. These errors simply indicate either that the object could not be created or did not support the requested interface. If you receive either of these errors, double-check or repeat your steps – it is also recommended that you check the event log, as described in the following section. Both errors generally indicate installation problems, often with the registry. You may also want to try rebuilding your client (not the server) and repeating the operation. If you receive errors *429* or *430* after rebuilding and re-deploying your server, you probably have a problem with compatibility. Be sure to use the *Binary Compatibility* option, described earlier in this chapter and in Chapter 14, before deploying any type of COM server, especially one you are remotely accessing with DCOM.

If the hex value of the error you receive is in the format *8004XXXX*, you may not be able to use the *Error Lookup* utility, but you can give it a try anyway. Such errors are application-defined errors and are not likely to be known by the *Error Lookup* utility. If you receive such an error, try using the *Event Viewer*, as described in the following section.

In all other cases, the *Error Lookup* utility can often provide you with exactly the information you require for troubleshooting your DCOM server. The program is distributed with the *Visual Studio 6.0* suite of tools and should be listed as *Error Lookup* in the *Microsoft Visual Studio 6.0 Tools* program group. If you cannot find the program via the *Start* button, try to find the file ERRLOOK.EXE.

Once you've started the *Error Lookup* utility, enter the error code, in hex, in the text box provided, then click the *Look Up* button. Again referring to Figure 11-14 as an example, you can see how I determined the problem in my example – the error message indicates that the *RPC server is unavailable*. Indeed, at the time I ran this demo, my server, *CRG*, was down.

Note that you must often ignore the text of the error message displayed by Visual Basic, which often uses a generic message for many of the same classes of errors. For example, Visual Basic displayed an error message of *Automation error* in this case, but that is not what error *800706BA* indicates. In addition to the *Automation error* message, Visual Basic often displays the overly generic *ActiveX Component Cannot Create Object* error. It is quite impossible to troubleshoot DCOM problems using only these error descriptions.

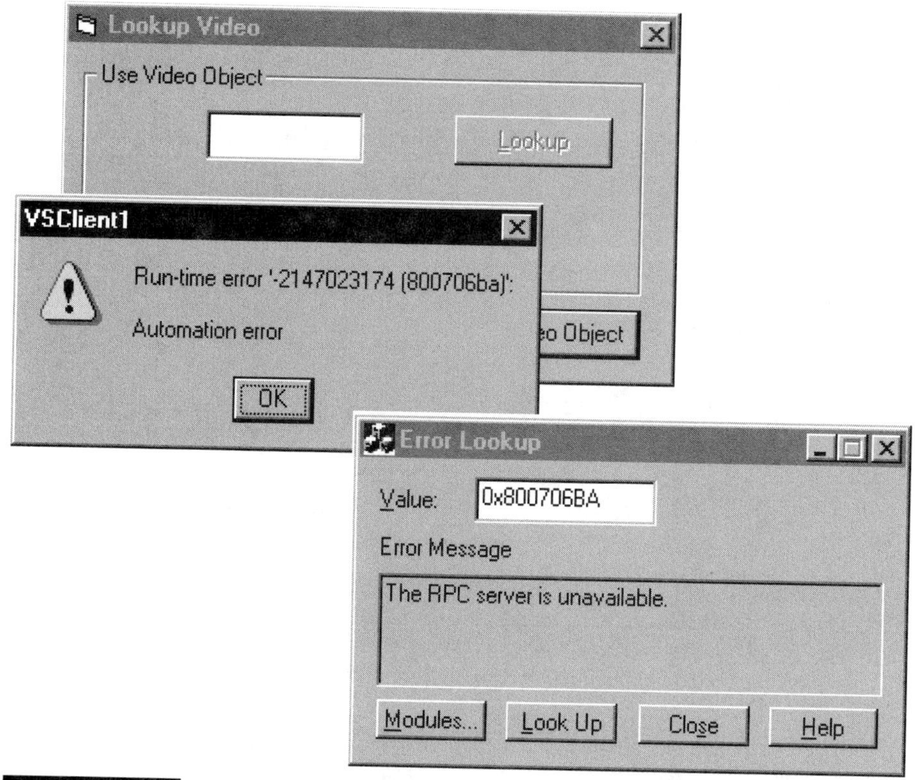

FIGURE 11-14 The *Error Lookup* utility can provide valuable information for DCOM server troubleshooting.

Using the Event Viewer

Most errors related to DCOM are written to the Windows NT and Windows 2000 event log, which can be viewed by the *Event Viewer* administrative tool. It is worthwhile to check the event logs of both the client and the server machines, starting first with the clients.

As you can see from Figure 11-15, the same problem described in the previous section resulted in an extremely clear message being written to the event log. The message indicates that *DCOM was unable to communicate with the computer CRG using any of the configured protocols*. It is not always this simple, and in fact you may see a message that simply lists the error code encountered by the client or server. If this is the case, go back and use the *Error Lookup* utility to look up the error message associated with the error code reported in the event log.

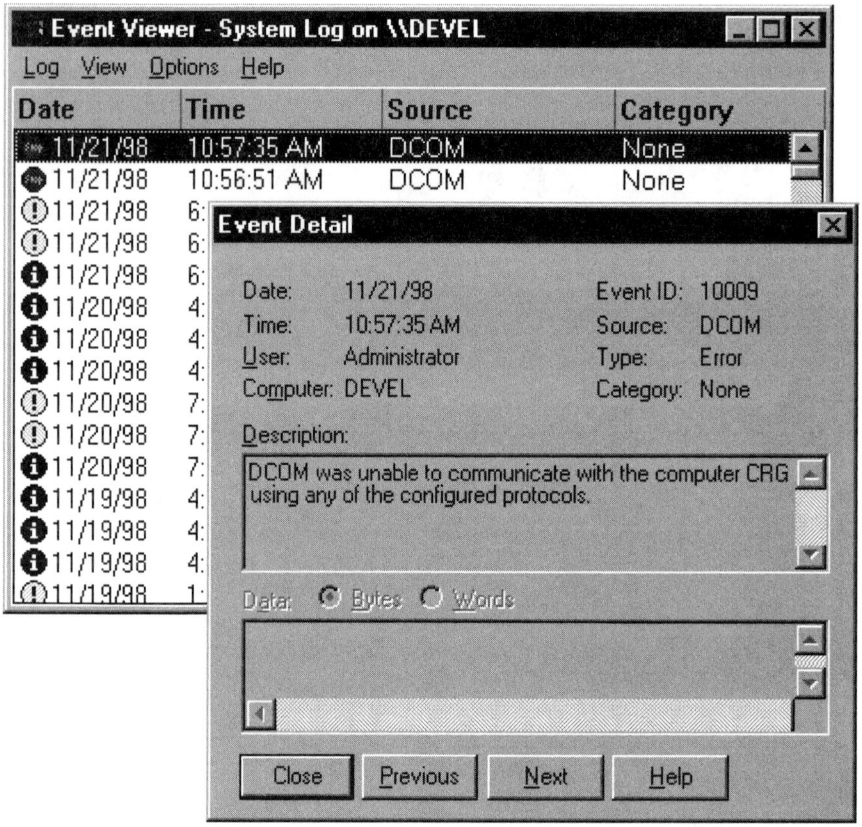

FIGURE 11-15   The *Event Viewer* is another valuable source of information for troubleshooting DCOM servers. Check both the client and server machines for DCOM messages in the event log.

Introducing Microsoft Transaction Server

Using Microsoft Transaction Server will greatly simplify the management and monitoring of your distributed components. Plus, MTS provides a more scalable environment for deploying your components, since it can activate them "just in time" to reduce server-side resource requirements. MTS also manages transactions for you, even across components and on different databases, using the Distributed Transaction Coordinator, and has support for database connection pooling.

About MTS

Microsoft Transaction Server is an environment that makes it easier to develop and deploy high performance, scalable, and robust enterprise, Internet, and intranet applications. MTS defines an application programming model for developing distributed, component-based applications, and provides a run-time environment for deploying and managing these applications.

The MTS Runtime Environment

In addition to a graphical interface for system administration and component management (the by now well-known "spinning balls"), MTS includes a runtime environment that MTS components use to communicate with MTS. The MTS runtime environment provides services for distributed transactions, automatic management of processes and threads, object instance management, and a distributed security service to control object invocation and use. MTS works with any application development tool capable of producing an ActiveX Component as a DLL. This includes Visual Basic, Visual C++, and Visual J++, among others.

MTS works with database management systems, which MTS generically lumps together under the title of resource managers. A ***resource manager*** manages persistent data on behalf of a client. A special kind of resource manager is a ***transactional resource manager***, which manages a resource capable of rolling back its work. This obviously includes *SQL Server, Oracle,* and other database management systems, but also includes *Microsoft Message Queue,* which is a transactional resource manager. If an MTS component stores a message in *Microsoft Message Queue* and then later requests a rollback, the message is "unsent."

About the MTS Explorer Utility

The *MTS Explorer* utility is a *Microsoft Management Console* snap-in that provides a user interface for deploying, monitoring, and managing MTS components. The utility presents an *Explorer*-style interface with two panes. The left pane displays a hierarchical tree of items, such as computers, packages, components, and interfaces. The right pane displays a list view showing details of items selected from the left pane (see Figure 12-1).

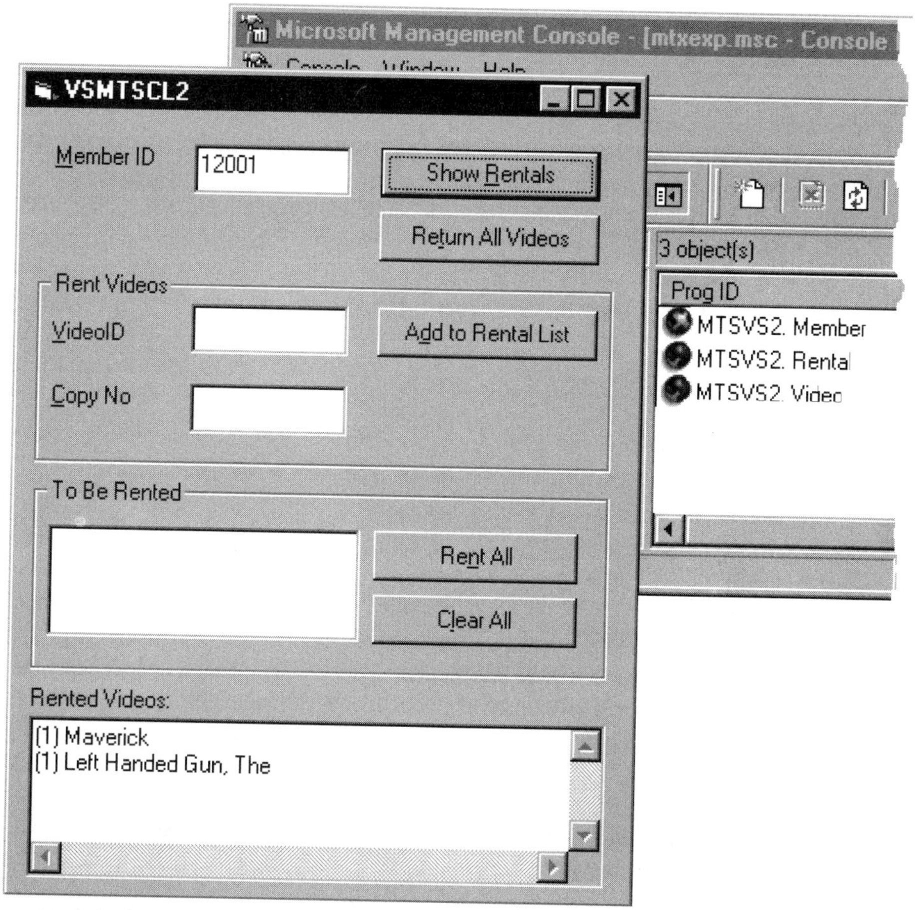

FIGURE 12-1 The *MTS Explorer*, shown here behind a client application that is using MTS components, enables you to configure, deploy, and monitor MTS components.

MTS Packages and Components

An MTS package is installed on a computer, and hosts components. A package defines a process boundary; all components installed within a package run under a single, multi-threaded process. Since a package is assigned an identity (Windows NT/2000 user account) under which the process executes, it also defines a trust boundary. And, since any thread in a process can bring down the entire process and all its threads, an MTS package also defines a fault boundary. However, even if your component triggers a fatal error condition, a new instance of the packages-hosting process is created the next time a client creates one of your MTS components.

An MTS component is a COM object. They are not called objects, however, since this is an overloaded word. C++, Visual Basic, and Java programmers all have different conceptions of what an object is. It is interesting to note the extent to which our industry attempts to avoid the use of certain overloaded terms, all in the interest of avoiding confusion. For example, the term "server" is also overloaded. The term can be used to describe a program that provides software services to a client application, but it can also be used to describe hardware – as in the computer that has your database on it – that's also called the server. Therefore, in Visual Basic, a COM server is called an ActiveX Component! But, an ActiveX Component is a server that hosts one or more COM objects, which can be deployed as MTS components. So, in the interest of avoiding confusion by avoiding overloaded terms, our industry often creates confusion. This is simply something that goes with the territory, and you'll have to live with it.

ABOUT MTSDEMO1

The first MTS demo program included with this book will introduce you to creating an MTS package, loading a component into the package, and activating and monitoring the MTS package. If you follow the walkthrough, you will then modify the MTS component to use just-in-time activation and re-install the MTS component into MTS. The ActiveX DLL that you will deploy under MTS contains only one COM object, the *MTSDemo1.Video* object. This object, a simple demonstration object that does not participate in the "final" version of the *Mom-n-Pop Video Store* demo, implements one method, *LookupVideo*, which returns the title of a video given its video ID. The object is a stateless object, meaning that it does not hold any state, or context, between client invocations. This means that the object can be deleted as soon as a method has completed, and later re-created when a client invokes another method. To install the demo, you will create an MTS package, then deploy the ActiveX Component into MTS.

Prior to running this demo, you must have the necessary software installed as described in Chapter 1. You must have also created the *SQLVideoStore* DSN, also described in Chapter 1.

Creating an MTS Package

One or more MTS components, which in turn come from COM objects hosted in an in-process COM server, are placed into MTS packages. To create a new package to be used by the first MTS demo program,

1. Start the *Microsoft Transaction Server Explorer* utility, available from the *Windows NT 4.0 Option Pack* program group.

2. In the left pane of the *MTS Explorer* utility, expand *Microsoft Transaction Server*, then *Computers*, then *My Computer*, then *Packages Installed*.

3. Click on *Packages Installed* with the left mouse button. Then, right-click on *Packages Installed* and select *New*, then *Package* (see Figure 12-2).

4. Click the *Create an empty package* button in the resulting *Package Wizard* dialog. On the following dialog, enter the name *MTSDemo1* for the name of the new package, then click *Next*.

5. On the *Set Package Identity* dialog, keep the default setting of *interactive user* and click *Finish*.

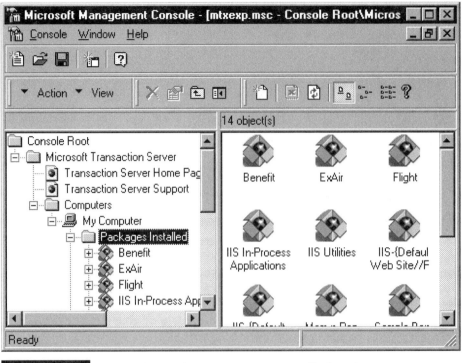

FIGURE 12-2 Using *MTS Explorer*, you can see installed packages.

Installing an MTS Component into a Package

The next step is to insert components into the newly created, empty MTS package. To install the *Video* component for the first MTS demo,

1. Under *Packages Installed*, expand the package *MTSDemo1*.

2. Using the left mouse button, click on *Components* under *MTSDemo1*. Then, right-click on *Components* and select *New*, then *Component* (see Figure 12-3).

3. In the resulting *Component Wizard* dialog, click the *Install new components* button.

4. In the resulting *Install Components* dialog, click the *Add Files* button. In the resulting *Select files to install* dialog, navigate to and select the *DLL* that implements the first MTS demo. The DLL is called *MTSDemo1.DLL*, and can be found in folder *VB6Adv\Demos\MTSDemos\MTSDemo1\Middleware*. Once this DLL has been selected, the *Components found* list on the *Install Components* dialog will list the component *Video*.

5. Click *Finish* to dismiss the *Install Components* dialog.

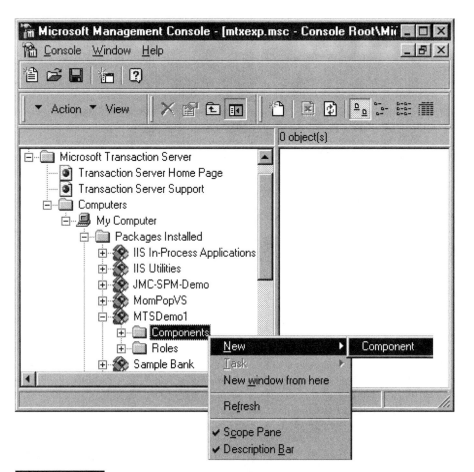

FIGURE 12-3 Once a package is created, you install components into the package.

Running and Monitoring MTS Components

To run an MTS component, the object must be created by a client application. The client application creates the object the same way it creates any COM object, either by using the *New* keyword, or by calling the *CreateObject* function. You can monitor the components in an MTS package by selecting *status view* while the *Components* item is selected.

To test the components you just installed,

1. Run program *MTSClient1.EXE* from folder *VB6Adv\Demos\MTSDemos\MTSDemo1\UI.*

2. Enter a *Video ID* into the text box. Recall that video IDs range from *52000* to *52030* (see Figure 12-4).

3. Click the *Look Up* button. The title of the video will appear in the *Title* box.

4. The first video you look up will take longer than subsequent ones, due to a startup delay. To verify this, try looking up a second video.

If you have any problems running the demo, make certain that you have deployed the *Mom-n-Pop Video Store* demo program as described in Chapter 1, and that your *SQL Server* database is available.

When you click the *Look Up* button in the user interface test program, you should see the ball spin next to the object *MTSDemo1.Video* in the *MTS Explorer* utility. The spinning ball indicates that the object is in the activated state. When an object is in the activated state, the object exists on the server and is actually taking up memory there. However, once you look up a video by its ID, this object is actually idle. Note that the *MTS Explorer* utility does not display anything that indicates the object is idle; this is something that only you know, as the developer of the component. It is the responsibility of the MTS component developer to add code that indicates to the *MTS Executive* when an object is about to go into an idle state and can be deleted.

Idle objects consume resources on the server, and this can affect the scalability of the application. One or two, or perhaps even dozens of idle objects may not affect server performance, but hundreds or certainly thousands may. Since the object is a stateless object (as you will see later when its code is examined), MTS could actually delete this object, and re-create it later should the client application invoke another method. This is known as just-in-time activation, and you will soon modify the demo program to indicate to MTS that the *Video* object is stateless and can be deactivated.

You will probably notice a delay when you run the user interface test program for the first time. This is a startup delay that is suffered by the first application to start an MTS component in a package. By default, MTS keeps the hosting process running for three minutes when there are no longer any references to objects in the package. Subsequent applications using the component do not experience this startup delay. You can verify this by exiting the user interface test program and running it again, repeating the previous instructions.

MTS keeps the hosting process running for performance reasons, but this can be a double-edged sword for developers. If you need to modify the server and rebuild it, you must be certain that the hosting process has shut down before you rebuild the DLL containing the components. Otherwise, you will receive a *Permission Denied* error from Visual Basic when you attempt to rebuild the DLL. In the following section, you will forcefully shut down the hosting process so that you can modify and rebuild the COM server.

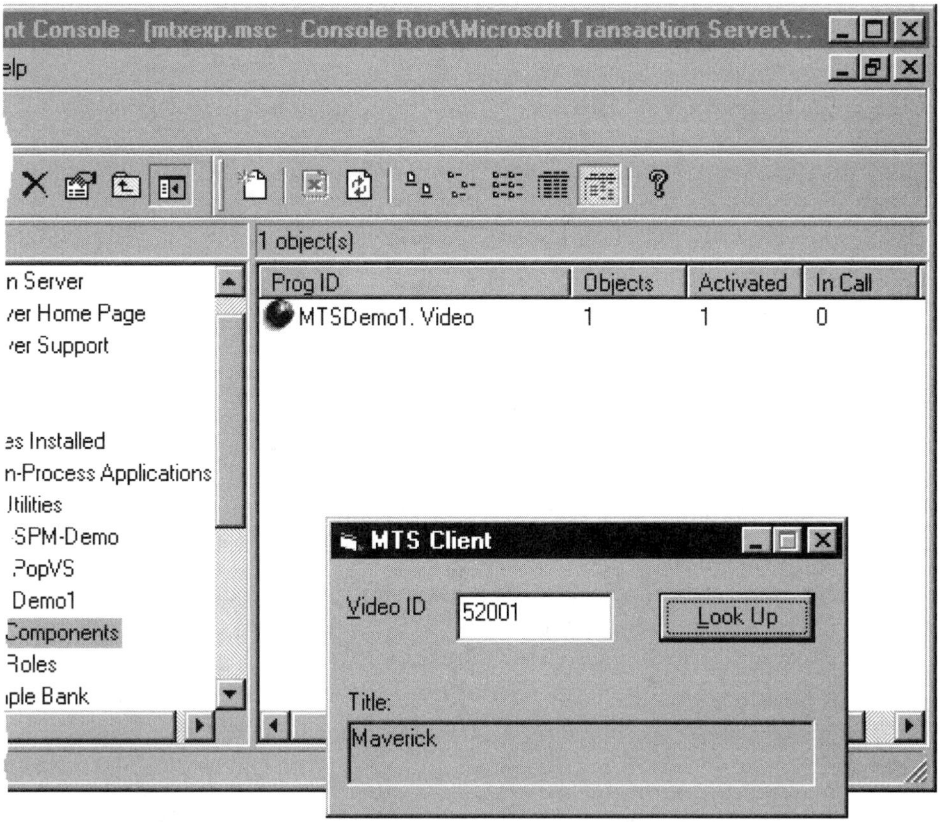
nt Console - [mtxexp.msc - Console Root\Microsoft Transaction Server\...
elp
1 object(s)
n Server
ver Home Page
ver Support
es Installed
n-Process Applications
Jtilities
SPM-Demo
PopVS
Demo1
Components
Roles
ple Bank
Prog ID
Objects
Activated
In Call
MTSDemo1. Video
1
1
0
MTS Client
Video ID
52001
Look Up
Title:
Maverick

FIGURE 12-4 The status view shows how many of each object exist, are activated, and are in-call.

Enabling Just-in-Time Activation

With just-in-time activation, a stateless MTS object can be deleted by the *MTS Executive* upon completion of a method. Note that the *MTS Executive* will delete the object even though the client application continues to hold a reference to the object. When and if the client invokes another method on the object, MTS will create a new instance of the object to service the request, after which that object will be deleted as well.

Later in this chapter, you will learn more about just-in-time activation and how to communicate with the *MTS Executive* to indicate that your object can be deleted. For now, you should follow the steps below (all of which are explained in detail later), to observe the effects of just-in-time activation:

1. Prior to modifying the *MTSDemo1.Video* object, you must shut down the hosting process. This is done by selecting your package with the left mouse button, then right-clicking on the package. On the resulting Context menu, select *Shut down.*

2. Open project *VB6Adv\Demos\MTSDemos\MTSDemo1\Middleware\MTSDemo1.VBP.*

3. Bring up the *Code* window for the class module *Video* and locate the *LookupVideo* method source code.

4. In the *LookupVideo* method, locate the line of code, near the end of the method, that is commented out and contains the notation *uncomment this line for JIT activation.* Uncomment this line of code.

5. Save the project and rebuild the DLL.

6. Return back to the *MTS Explorer* utility. Select your package with the left mouse button. Then, right-click on your package and select *Refresh.* This re-registers the component with MTS.

7. Run the client test program as before and observe the *objects* column and *activated* column in the *status view* for your components (see Figure 12-5).

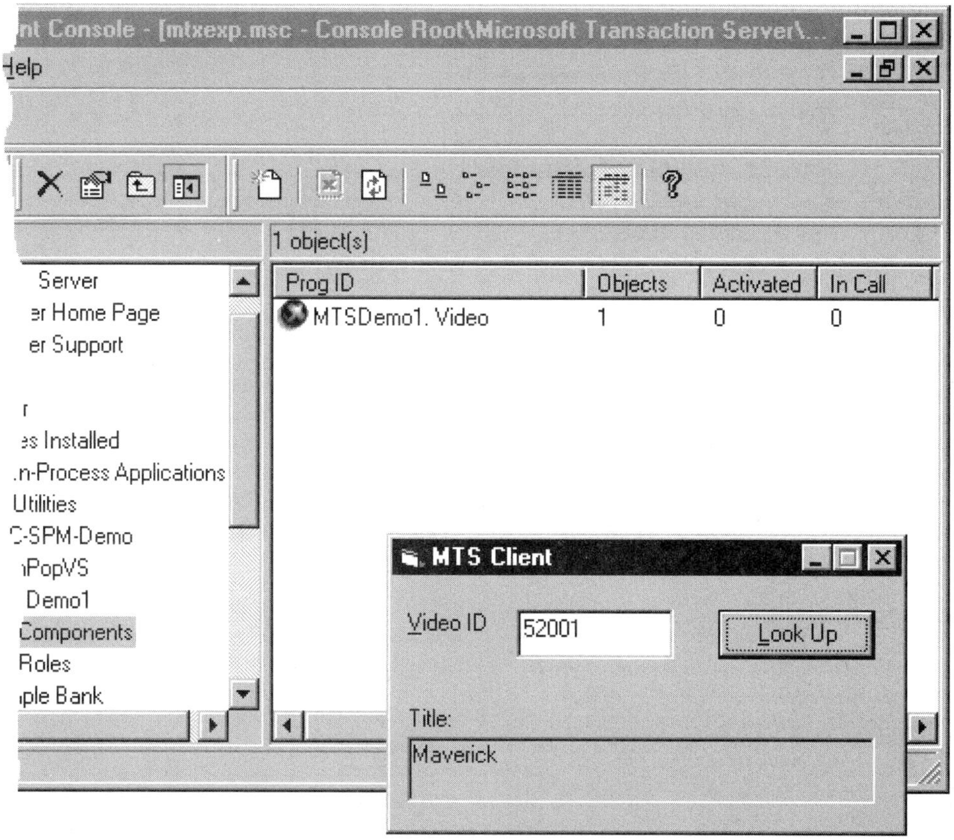

FIGURE 12-5 When you enable just-in-time activation, you will notice that the *Video* object does not remain in the activated state.

```
Option Explicit

Public Function LookupTitle(ByVal nID As Long, _
                            ByRef strTitle As String) _
              As Long

    Dim cn As New Connection
    Dim rs As Recordset
    Dim strSQL As String
    Dim ctx As ObjectContext

    Set ctx = GetObjectContext

    strSQL = "Select Title From Videos " & _
```

```
                        " Where VideoID = " & Str(nID)

    cn.Open "SQLVideoStore"
    Set rs = cn.Execute(strSQL, , adCmdText)

    If rs.BOF And rs.EOF Then
        ctx.SetAbort
        LookupTitle = -1
        Exit Function
    End If

    strTitle = rs.Fields("Title").Value

    rs.Close
    cn.Close

    If Not ctx Is Nothing Then
        ' ctx.SetComplete    '** Uncomment this line
    End If

    LookupTitle = 0

End Function
```

The MTS API

There is an API (Application Programming Interface) that programmers use in MTS components to communicate with the *MTS Executive*. Unlike the ODBC API, for example, the MTS API is not a procedural API, but an API implemented with a pair of COM interfaces, *IObjectContext* and *IObject-Control*. The *IObjectContext* interface is implemented by objects created by the *MTS Executive*, while the *IObjectControl* interface is actually an outgoing interface that can be implemented by an MTS client. Of the two, the *IObjectContext* interface is more widely used. It is only necessary for an MTS component to use the MTS API; client code uses ordinary COM services to create and use components that run under MTS. In Visual Basic, this means that you can use either the *New* keyword or the *CreateObject* function to create MTS components. There are, however, restrictions to service-side object creation; these restrictions are covered later in this chapter.

About the ObjectContext Object

The most widely used methods implemented by the *ObjectContext* object are related to object lifetime management and transaction control, but there are also important security-related methods. Using the methods of the *ObjectControl* object, an MTS component can declare that its work is complete and that an object can be deleted, even though a base client may continue to hold a reference to the object. This is known as just-in-time activation and is an important feature that is used to improve the scalability of an application. Methods of the *ObjectControl* object are also invoked to indicate whether or not the current transaction should be committed or rolled back. There is another important method related to the creation of additional MTS components from within an already created MTS component. Again, these methods are almost always used server-side, and never used client-side – unless the MTS component is also a client of another MTS component.

While the methods of the *IObjectContext* interface are invoked from an existing object created by the *MTS Executive*, *IObjectControl* provides an interface that MTS objects can implement to receive notification of important MTS events. Your object can declare that it implements the *IObjectControl* interface (known in Visual Basic as *ObjectControl*), in which case you are obligated to provide three methods in your class – *Activate, Deactivate,* and *CanBePooled*. Your *Activate* method is invoked by MTS when your object is about to be activated, while your *Deactivate* method is invoked by MTS when your object is about to be deactivated. Upon deactivation, MTS will invoke your *CanBePooled* method, in which you return a Boolean value indicating whether or not your MTS component can be returned to a pool of objects instead of being deleted. At this time, it is recommended that MTS components written in Visual Basic return *FALSE* from this method (object pooling, as of MTS 2.0, has not been implemented).

Resource Dispensers

An MTS component can also be developed to use a resource dispenser, such as the ODBC resource dispenser. A **resource dispenser** is a service that manages non-persistent shared state on behalf of the application components within a process. The ODBC resource dispenser automatically pools and allocates database connections for MTS components that use standard ODBC interfaces (including via ADO and RDO). Another example of a resource dispenser is the *Shared Property Manager*, covered later in this chapter.

EXAMPLE: USING THE ODBC RESOURCE DISPENSER

Using the *ODBC Resource Dispenser* is automatic when you use the ODBC API, either directly or indirectly through RDO or ADO. Shown below is a fragment of code that uses the *ODBC Resource Dispenser*. Note that it simply uses an *ADO Connection* object to connect to the database.

```
Public Function LookupTitle(ByVal nID As Long, _
                            ByRef strTitle As String) _
          As Long

    Dim cn As New Connection
    On Error GoTo CannotLookup

    strSQL = "Select Title From Videos " & _
          " Where VideoID = " & Str(nID)

    cn.Open "SQLVideoStore"
    Set rs = cn.Execute(strSQL, , adCmdText)
          .
          .
          .
    cn.Close


End Function
```

Using the ObjectContext Object

Examine virtually any method of an object developed to run under MTS and you'll notice that the code nearly always immediately invokes a function called *GetObjectContext*, storing the result in a variable declared *As ObjectContext*. The code is obtaining a reference to its object context, itself an object created by the *MTS Executive*. It is through invocations of methods on this object that an MTS component communicates with the *MTS Executive*. Methods of the *ObjectContext* object are listed in Table 12-1.

Every object created by the *MTS Executive* has an associated object context. In general, multiple instances of the same class of object each have their own object context. MTS internally uses this object to keep track of the state of an object as it executes as part of an activity. It contains information such as the identity of the base client, and the current transaction state, if any. It also provides methods that are invoked by MTS components to communicate with the *MTS Executive*.

It is through method calls to the *ObjectContext* object that a component indicates that its work is complete (*SetComplete* and *SetAbort*). There are also methods that components invoke to indicate their "vote" for transaction outcome (*SetComplete*, *SetAbort*, *EnableCommit*, and *DisableCommit*), there are methods related to security (*IsSecurityEnabled*, *IsCalledInRole*, and *Security*), and there are methods for creating other MTS components (*CreateInstance*). Prior to using the *GetObjectContext* function and invoking any methods of the *ObjectContext* object, you must include a reference to the MTS type library.

TABLE 12-1	Methods of the ObjectContext Object
Method	**Description**
CreateInstance	Instantiates another MTS object by using the current object's context.
SetAbort	Declares that the transaction within which the current object is executing must ultimately be aborted. Also indicates that the object has completed its work and that it should be deactivated upon returning from the current call.
SetComplete	Declares that the current object has completed its work and can be deactivated upon returning from the currently executing method.
DisableCommit	Declares that the current object's transactional updates can't be committed in their current form.
EnableCommit	Declares that the current object's work is not necessarily done, but that its transactional updates could be committed in their current form.
IsInTransaction	Indicates whether the current object is executing within a transaction.
IsCallerInRole	Indicates whether an object's direct caller from outside the server process is in a specified role (either individually or as part of a group).
IsSecurityEnabled	Indicates whether or not security is enabled for the current object. At this time, security is only disabled when the object is running in the client's process.

The following code uses the **ObjectContext** object to declare when its job is done (either successfully or not). In addition to providing transaction control, using the *ObjectContext* object to report component completion also enables just-in-time activation for the component.

```
Public Function LookupTitle(ByVal nID As Long, _
                            ByRef strTitle As String) _
                            As Long

    Dim cn As New Connection
    Dim rs As Recordset
    Dim strSQL As String

    Dim ctx As ObjectContext
    Set ctx = GetObjectContext

    strSQL = "Select Title From Videos " & _
             " Where VideoID = " & Str(nID)

    cn.Open "SQLVideoStore"
    Set rs = cn.Execute(strSQL, , adCmdText)

    If rs.BOF And rs.EOF Then
        ctx.SetAbort
        LookupTitle = -1
        Exit Function
    End If

    strTitle = rs.Fields("Title").Value

    rs.Close
    cn.Close

    ctx.SetComplete
    LookupTitle = 0

End Function
```

Note that the above code shows a method *(LookupVideo)* of an MTS component (Video). MTS components often have several methods, and an MTS package often hosts one or more MTS components.

MTS Component Restrictions

In theory, any COM object that is hosted in an in-process COM server (ActiveX DLL) can be deployed under MTS. However, this is not recommended. Even though MTS components are COM objects, they do run under the *MTS Executive* and, as such, have additional requirements beyond those of ordinary COM objects. This is due to the fact that the *MTS Executive* provides services that COM alone does not provide.

The most important restriction for a COM object that is to be run under MTS is related to the passing of object references, which must be passed safely and with the knowledge of MTS. An MTS component cannot, therefore, simply pass a reference to itself, to another component, or back from itself. If you must pass a reference to an object created by the *MTS Executive*, you must use the global function *SafeRef* to make a copy of the reference.

Another important restriction involves the creation of new MTS components by an object created by the *MTS Executive*. Creation of such objects should not be done by using the *New* keyword if the object being created is part of the same project as the creating object (note that this is typically the case with MTS components, which are often deployed into a single MTS package that comes from a single ActiveX DLL project). Instead, MTS components should use either the *CreateObject* function or the *CreateInstance* method of the *ObjectContext* object to create objects. The *CreateObject* function is used when you do not want the new object to inherit the creating object's transaction context. This case, however, is unusual. Typically an MTS component creates other objects to have those new objects participate in the same activity and under the same transaction context as the creator. Thus, the typical way objects are created by MTS components is with the *CreateInstance* method of the *ObjectContext* object. Note that this method requires the Prog ID of the object as a string. In Visual Basic, the format of this string is *ProjectName.ClassName*. An example of an MTS component that creates another MTS component is provided in Chapter 13.

Transactions in MTS

Work performed within a database (or any transactional resource) should be done within the context of a transaction. It has often been said that transactions must pass the *ACID* test, meaning atomicity, consistency, isolation, and durability. Transactions make work performed by a component atomic, ensuring that either all the work is made durable (committed) or none of it is (rolled back). A transaction transforms a database from one consistent state to another consistent state. Transactions run in isolation, protected from other, concurrent transactions. And, once committed, work performed by a transaction is durable, surviving network, software, and server failures.

In the days of procedural programming, writing modular database code was always problematic. Unfortunately, object-oriented programming has not done much to improve things. The problem one often faces involves developing a procedure that needs to perform a database update. If an update needs to take place within the context of a transaction, it is always an issue as to whether or not the procedure should start the transaction, or if a caller of the procedure should start the transaction. If the procedure starts the transaction, a problem is raised – what if a particular calling procedure also needs to perform a database update, and further, what if it is necessary for its work to take place within the context of the same transaction? This type of situation is commonplace, and not elegantly solved. If the first procedure starts a transaction and calls a second procedure that also starts a transaction, what you have are nested transactions. The nested transaction's outcome is independent of the outer transaction. Therefore, code often must check to see if it is already in a transaction and if so, not start another one – unless of course it wants to be a nested transaction. You can see how complicated things might become.

MTS solves this problem in an elegant and interesting way – by insisting that you not start transactions at all! Instead, an MTS developer declares components to be transactional, and also provides a transaction attribute. When client software outside MTS (known as a base client) invokes a method on an MTS component, it is said to be initiating an activity. In MTS, an activity is a set of one or more MTS components that are executing on behalf of a base client. Note that an activity can consist of more than one object, as in the case where an MTS component creates another MTS component while performing its work.

If the MTS component invoked by the base client has a transaction attribute indicating that it requires a transaction, MTS starts that transaction on behalf of the component. If this component, in turn, uses another MTS component, that component's transaction attributes are checked as well. If that component requires a transaction or has a transaction attribute of supports transactions, MTS will not start another transaction. Instead, work performed by the second object will take place under the context of the original transaction. If, on the other hand, the second component has a transaction attribute indicating that it requires a new transaction, MTS starts a new, nested transaction. Transaction attributes are discussed in further detail later in this chapter. Practical examples and a case study of using transaction attributes are provided in Chapter 13.

Transaction outcome is determined by MTS components, but not via an explicit commit or rollback call. Instead, transactional MTS components use the *SetComplete, SetAbort, EnableCommit,* and/or *DisableCommit* methods of the *ObjectContext* interface. These methods are described in the following section.

It is interesting to note how much database programming has changed. It used to be that database programmers were told to obtain a database connection at the beginning of a program, and hold onto it for the life of the program. The reason being, database connections are expensive to obtain. However, this solution does not scale very well – database connections are an expensive server-side resource. Programmers have also always been told to explicitly start and commit or rollback transactions. Now, using MTS, we wait until the last minute to obtain a database connection, and never explicitly begin, commit, or rollback transactions. These are things that, in the "old days," would have made a database program inefficient and unreliable. Now, it's significantly easier on the developer, who no longer must worry about these details.

MTS Components and Transaction Outcome

MTS developers often speak of how MTS components "vote" on transaction outcome – that is, whether or not a transaction should be committed or rolled back. However, this is a bit misleading since it takes only one rollback vote to roll back a transaction. An MTS component indicates its opinion by invoking one of four methods in the *IObjectContext* interface, available from the *ObjectContext* object. Which method you use depends on two conditions – whether or not the component is stateless or stateful, and whether or not your component is voting for a commit or rollback. Stateful and stateless objects are discussed in more detail in a later section.

If your component is stateless, and you want your component to vote for committing the current transaction, your component should invoke the *SetComplete* method. Stateless components vote for a rollback by invoking the *SetAbort* method. Both methods also indicate that an object has completed its work and can be deleted, even though a base client still holds a reference to it. Later, when the same base client invokes another method on the same object, MTS creates a new object. Since the object is stateless, the client never notices that the method actually executes on a different object.

MTS components that have persistent properties or that reference global data are, by definition, stateful, and must use a different pair of methods to indicate their vote for transaction outcome. A stateful MTS component invokes *EnableCommit* to vote for a commit, and invokes *DisableCommit* to vote for a rollback. This pair of methods differs from *SetComplete* and *SetAbort* in that they do not request deletion of the object by the *MTS Executive*. Methods related to transaction outcome are listed in Table 12-2.

Internally, all four methods simply set internal flags in the object's context. The flags are not evaluated until the object's method completes; therefore, the last call to *SetComplete, SetAbort, EnableCommit,* or *DisableCommit* in a component's method is the one that counts.

TABLE 12-2	ObjectContext Methods Related to Transaction Outcome
Method	**Description**
SetComplete	Indicates that the object has successfully completed its work for the transaction. The object is deactivated upon return from the method that first entered the context.
SetAbort	Indicates that the object's work can never be committed. The object is deactivated upon return from the method that first entered the context.
EnableCommit	Indicates that the object's work isn't necessarily done, but that its transactional updates can be committed in their current form.
DisableCommit	Indicates that the object's transactional updates can't be committed in their current form.

Transaction Attributes of an MTS Component

All MTS components have a transaction attribute that indicates whether or not the component requires a transaction or supports a transaction. This attribute can be set using the *MTS Explorer* utility, or by setting the *MTSTransaction-Mode* property of a class module developed with Visual Basic. If set within Visual Basic, the attribute is only read when the component is installed with the *MTS Explorer* utility. If the attribute is changed, you must rebuild, then refresh, your MTS component.

There are four different transaction attributes in MTS, but most MTS components are declared as either *Supports a transaction* or *Requires a transaction*. Note that this attribute is applied on a per component basis; there is no way to declare on a method-by-method basis which methods of an object require a transaction and which do not. Therefore, be sure to design the objects in your data services layer appropriately. If some methods of a component require a transaction while others do not, consider moving some of the methods to another object.

If any of the methods of a component perform work on the database that must take place within the context of a transaction, that component's transaction attribute should be set to *requires a transaction*. When a base client invokes a method on such an object, MTS automatically starts a transaction. If this component, in turn, invokes a method on another MTS object that *Requires a transaction* or *Supports transactions*, work performed by the second object takes place within the context of the same transaction.

If a component's methods do not have to execute within the context of a transaction, its transaction attributes should be set to *Supports transaction*. If a base client invokes a method on such an object, MTS does not start a transaction. Such objects only execute within the context of a transaction when invoked by an MTS object that is already executing within the context of a transaction. As mentioned, in this case, these objects will execute under the same transaction as the invoking object's transaction.

An object with a transaction attribute of *Requires a new transaction* will execute under a new, nested transaction under certain circumstances. If a method of such an object is invoked directly by a base client, MTS starts a transaction. Note that this case is the same as if the object's transaction attribute was *Requires a transaction*. But, if a method in the object is invoked by another MTS component that is already executing within a transaction, MTS starts a new, independent transaction.

The final transaction attribute, *Does not support transactions*, indicates that the object does not participate in "voting" for transaction outcome. This is the default value, and is intended for components that are not developed specifically for MTS. Such components may be legacy objects that explicitly control their own transactions or do not use transactions at all. Transaction attributes are summarized in Table 12-3.

Some of the constants for the Visual Basic *MTSTransactionMode* property, mentioned earlier in this section, have no obvious correspondence to the settings described by the *MTS Explorer* utility. The constant, *NoTransactions,* is the same as the MTS transaction attribute *Does not support transactions*. The constant *UsesTransaction* is the same as *Supports transactions*. The other two constants, *RequiresTransaction* and *RequiresNewTransaction*, have obvious counterparts to the *MTS Explorer* transaction attribute descriptions.

| TABLE 12-3 | MTS Transaction Attributes |

Transaction Attribute	**Description**
Requires a transaction	Indicates that the component's objects must execute within the scope of a transaction. New objects inherit the transaction from the context of the client. If the client doesn't have a transaction, MTS automatically creates a new transaction for the object.
Requires a new transaction	Indicates that the component's objects must execute within their own transactions. MTS automatically creates a new transaction for the object, regardless of whether its client has a transaction.
Supports transactions	Indicates that the component's objects can execute within the scope of their client's transactions.
Does not support transactions	Indicates that the component's objects shouldn't run within the scope of transactions, or controls its own transactions.

Stateful and Stateless MTS Objects

It is a common misconception that MTS objects must be stateless. MTS components can maintain state across multiple method and property invocations with a given client. If they do, they are said to be stateful MTS components. It is simply not recommended that they do this, as prolific use of stateful objects can compromise the scalability of an application. Expecting the server to maintain states for hundreds or thousands of objects is unreasonable. However, it is also unreasonable to expect that all client applications will be well-behaved and delete objects when they are no longer needed or expected to be idle for a long period of time. Therefore, it is the responsibility of the MTS component developer to design MTS components to be stateless, and to let the *MTS Executive* know when the component's work is done and the component can be deleted.

Implementing a stateless component is not difficult. It simply means avoiding the implementation of properties and also avoiding the use of global data. Instead, you implement only methods and require that these methods be passed all the parameters they require to perform a particular function. It may not be elegant, but that's how it's done.

When an MTS component is stateless, it means the object does not hold any intermediate state from one client call to the next. Note that this applies to almost any property you can imagine, with the exception of very simple, typically constant, read-only properties. This is why most MTS components only expose methods and no properties. It is also why many methods of MTS components have more parameters that one typically sees with objects in general. It is a major mind-set shift for many developers to buy into the concept of stateless objects. But it does work, and the concept provides an excellent technology for vastly improving the scalability of an application. Using stateless objects, which are created, used, then deleted over and over again, is not as severe a performance hit as you might think. If you are doubtful of this, create a few stateless prototype objects and observe their performance in their "natural" use – invoked from a script in an Active Server Page, for example. With all the other activity involved in such a benchmark – opening a URL, sending HTTP responses to the browser, and so on, you are not likely to notice the additional overhead of object deletion and re-creation. The exception is components that take a long time to initialize. With such components, you have the option of making them stateful. Remember that MTS can host stateful components, although it is recommended that your components be stateless.

When the stateless objects involved in an MTS activity report their completion to the *MTS Executive*, via either *SetComplete* or *SetAbort*, the *MTS Executive* can deactivate the objects and reclaim any resources, including memory and database connections, used by the components. The deletion of objects takes place upon completion of an activity, that is, when the outermost component's method call completes, and not immediately upon calling the *SetComplete* or *SetAbort* methods. This is possible because the *MTS Executive* actually invokes your component on behalf of the base client. Remember that the calls to *SetComplete* and *SetAbort* actually set internal flags; these flags are not evaluated until your component's outermost method returns to the *MTS Executive*.

Stateless objects increase the scalability of an application. Stateful objects, which invoke either *EnableCommit* or *DisableCommit*, hold onto their resources even while idle. This has the opposite effect, decreasing the scalability of the application.

Some experts have suggested that an MTS component can be both stateful and stateless. However, not all experts agree with this suggestion. In theory, it is possible for an MTS component to hold its state across some method calls while ultimately calling *SetComplete* when some designated "final" method is invoked. For example, a complex transaction may be implemented across, say, three method calls, which must be invoked in sequence by the client. The first two methods call neither *SetComplete* nor *SetAbort*. The final method in the sequence, as the theory goes, calls *SetComplete*. While this sounds good in theory, it is not a good idea to sit on the fence – either design your object to be stateless or stateful. If you design it to be both, you must document which methods are final and cause the object to lose state, and you are thus expecting client developers to read and understand your documentation. Of course, many developers will not read or understand your documentation, and you may be plagued by reports of so-called bugs in your component. Besides, the whole concept of stateful versus stateless components should be implemented in a way that is transparent to client-side developers. They may not actually want to hear that the components they are creating get deleted without their knowledge.

While I don't recommend making an MTS component both stateful and stateless, I do want to reiterate that MTS can host both stateful and stateless components. In fact, both stateful and stateless components can coexist in the same MTS package. Such a solution may be ideal for your application.

Just-in-Time Activation

Client code, which can be unaware of whether or not your component is stateless, typically creates one of your MTS components, and may continue to hold a reference to it during the client application's lifetime. In reality, the actual object is being repeatedly activated and deactivated many times while the client holds onto a reference to what it thinks is a persistent object. The ability for an MTS component to do this is known as *just-in-time activation*. To the client, it appears that a single instance of the object exists from the time it's created to when it's deleted. In actual fact, the work performed by what the client thinks is a single object may have been performed by several different instances of the object.

MTS objects are deactivated upon completion of a method if, in the course of executing that method, they invoke either *SetComplete* or *SetAbort*, or when client code releases its final reference to the object. Since MTS uses the normal COM reference counting mechanism to request that the object delete itself, all MTS objects must be well-behaved COM objects and implement normal reference-counting. Visual Basic objects are well-behaved COM objects and implement normal reference-counting logic. However, since MTS is responsible for invoking the *IUnknown* methods *AddRef* and *Release* on your component, nothing must be done by either your code or the client's code to interfere with the *MTS Executive's* responsibilities in invoking these reference-counting methods. Since MTS basically intercepts all calls by the client via the *ObjectContext* object, there is nothing a client can do to interfere with the *MTS Executive's* reference-counting responsibilities. But you, as the developer of the MTS component, can. Be sure to use the *SafeRef* function whenever you make an internal copy of a reference to your own object, as in storing the reference in a temporary variable, or when you pass it as a parameter, or when you pass a copy of a reference back to the client. Remember that the *MTS Executive* wraps your object in an *ObjectContext* object, so there are really two objects involved. You want to be sure that the proper object's reference count is maintained. Using *SafeRef* to copy your MTS component's reference is the only safe way to ensure proper object reference-counting. The effect of violating this restriction is so severe that most MTS developers avoid such coding situations all together. Just remember to be very careful with object references when implementing MTS components.

Implementing ObjectControl

It may be necessary, in some situations, for you to release resources and perhaps reacquire them during the deactivation and reactivation of your stateless component. If so, your component can implement the *Object-Control* interface and receive notification of activation and deactivation. If your object implements *ObjectControl*, and is not already activated, the *MTS Executive* calls your *Activate* method prior to executing any of its methods. This method can be used to initialize your object and/or to acquire required resources. The *Deactivate* method of MTS objects that implement *Object-Control* is invoked when the object is about to be deactivated. You can use this method to release resources acquired by the object. Methods of *ObjectControl* are summarized in Table 12-4.

Implementing *ObjectControl* obligates you to implement the *CanBe-Pooled* method in addition to the *Activate* and *Deactivate* methods. This method is invoked by the *MTS Executive* to discover whether or not your object must be deleted upon deactivation, or if it can be returned to a pool of objects awaiting reactivation. At the time of this writing, object pooling in MTS has not been implemented – it is recommended that Visual Basic MTS components return *FALSE* from this method.

TABLE 12-4	Methods of ObjectControl

IObjectControl Method	Description
Activate ()	Invoked by MTS when your object is activated.
Deactivate ()	Invoked by MTS when your object is deactivated.
CanBePooled() As Boolean	Invoked by MTS when your object is deactivated, for you to indicate if your object can be pooled.

EXAMPLE: IMPLEMENTING OBJECTCONTROL

The *MTSVS2* demo program, located in folder \ *VB6adv\Demos\MTS Demos \MTSDemo2\Middleware*, implements the *ObjectControl* interface (see code fragment below). When activated, the code loads the *ObjectContext* object into a module-level variable, and when deactivated, sets this variable to *Nothing*. This is not necessarily recommended code—it is simply an example. Do not feel that you are obligated to implement *ObjectControl;* there is no need, for example, to implement it in the *Mom-n-Pop Video Store* data services layer.

```
Option Explicit
Implements ObjectControl

Private gCtx As ObjectContext

'**********************************************************
'* Implementation of Methods in ObjectControl Interface *
'**********************************************************

Private Sub ObjectControl_Activate()
    Set gCtx = GetObjectContext
End Sub

Private Sub ObjectControl_Deactivate()
    Set gCtx = Nothing
End Sub

Private Function ObjectControl_CanBePooled() As Boolean
    ObjectControl_CanBePooled = False
End Function
```

MTS Transaction Support Demo

The second MTS demo illustrates transaction support in MTS. You will first install the demo package and observe the behavior of its components using the default transaction attribute of *Does not support transactions*. You will rent a copy of one video to a customer, then attempt to rent to a second customer a list of videos, one of which is the video already rented to the first customer. Without the proper transaction attribute setting for the MTS components involved in the activity, some of the videos are rented to the customer, while others are not – this is not proper transactional behavior, which is, of course, an all or nothing thing. You will then set the transaction attributes properly, and run the demo a second time.

You will need to install the demo DLL into an MTS package before running the demo. Use the instructions presented previously in this chapter. It does not matter what you call the MTS package. The demo uses the *Mom-n-Pop Video Store* database, but it is not the implementation of the final version of the 3-tier version of the *Mom-n-Pop Video Store* application (the final version of the data services layer of the demo application is analyzed in Chapter 13). The demo has an associated user interface project for testing the MTS components. The DLL is located in folder *VB6Adv\Demos\MTSDemos\MTSDemo2\ Middleware,* while the user interface test program, *VSMTSCL2.EXE,* is located in folder *VB6Adv\Demos\MTSDemos\MTSDemo2\UI.*

The MTS project implements three objects: **Video, Member**, and **Rental**. The *Video* object is used to look up video information in the database. It has three methods: *GetTotalCopies, IsRented,* and *LookupTitle.* The *Member* object is used to look up member information from the database. It has only one method, *LookupName.* The **Rentals** object is used for rental and return transactions. It has four methods: *Rent, RentedList, ReturnAll,* and *ValidateVideo.* This is the object I'll examine in the following sections.

EXAMPLE: THE RENTAL OBJECT

The **Rental** object in the demo MTS project handles renting and returning videos, and provides validation routines that check that a video ID and copy number are valid. It can also check to see if a video is rented (see *Rental Methods* below for a list of methods).

To rent a video, or list of videos, the presentation layer must put the list of videos in a two-dimensional variant array. The first column is the *Video ID* and the second column is the *Copy Number.* This complexity is due to the fact that the *Rental* object, like all the objects in this MTS demo, is stateless. You must pass all the information required for the object to perform a transaction. Methods of stateless objects often require a large number of parameters, or, as in this case, a complex array of parameters. This is why it is a good idea to wrap access to the data services layer with the business objects layer (or object model). As the object model is typically deployed with a Win32 presentation layer application on the client side, its objects can be stateful.

All methods of the *Rental* object return a *Long* value that is an error code. An error code of zero indicates success. Returning an error code from the data services layer is preferred over raising exceptions. The *MTS Executive* does not permit exceptions to propagate outside the hosting process.

To summarize, the methods of the *Rental* object are as follows:

```
Public Function Rent(nMemberID As Long, _
                vVideoList As Variant) As Long

Public Function RentedList(ByVal nMemberID As Long, _
                ByRef vVideoList As Variant) _
           As Long

Public Function ReturnAll(ByVal nMemberID As Long) As Long

Private Function ValidateVideo(nVideoID As Long, _
                nCopyNo) As Long
```

EXAMPLE: THE RENT METHOD OF THE RENTAL OBJECT

The *Rent* method of the *Rental* object is shown in the following listing. Note that this method, like all the methods in the data services layer, connects to the database at the start of the method, and disconnects at the end of the method. While this may sound inefficient, connection pooling actually makes it very efficient. Also note that the *Rental* object invokes *SetComplete* when it has completed its task normally. If an error is encountered, the *Rental* object invokes *SetAbort.* You'll see the distinction shortly.

```
Public Function Rent(nMemberID As Long, _
                vVideoList As Variant) As Long

   On Error GoTo CannotRent

   ' Get a database connection.

   Dim M As New Member
   Dim nStatus As Long
   Dim strTemp As String
   Dim cn As New Connection
   Dim objCtx As ObjectContext

   Set objCtx = GetObjectContext
```

```
cn.Open "SQLVideoStore"

' See if member exists.

nStatus = M.LookupName(nMemberID, strTemp)

' If we cannot find this member, abort the txn.

If nStatus <> 0 Then
    Rent = -1
    If Not gCtx Is Nothing Then
        objCtx.SetAbort
    End If
    Exit Function
End If

' Insert rental record for each video.  As we
' do this, check to see if video exists and is
' not already rented.
'
' Note that this demo assumes 3 night rental.

Dim dtRented As Date
Dim dtDue As Date
Dim i As Integer
Dim nVideoID As Long
Dim nCopyNo As Integer
Dim strSQL As String

dtRented = Date
dtDue = dtRented + 3

For i = 0 To UBound(vVideoList, 2)

    ' Get video id and copy number from
    ' variant array.

    nVideoID = vVideoList(0, i)
    nCopyNo = vVideoList(1, i)

    ' Make sure video ID and copy number are valid.

    nStatus = ValidateVideo(nVideoID, nCopyNo)
    If nStatus <> 0 Then
        Rent = nStatus
        If Not gCtx Is Nothing Then
```

```
            objCtx.SetAbort
        End If
        Exit Function
    End If

    ' Build an SQL string to insert into the
    ' Rentals table.

    strSQL = "Insert Into Rentals Values (" & _
            Str(nVideoID) & ", " & _
            Str(nCopyNo) & ", " & _
            Str(nMemberID) & ", " & _
            "'" & Format(dtRented, "Short Date") & _
            "', " & _
            "'" & Format(dtDue, "Short Date") & "')"

    ' Execute the SQL Insert statement.

    cn.Execute strSQL, , adCmdText

Next

' Successful completion.

cn.Close
Rent = 0

If Not gCtx Is Nothing Then
    objCtx.SetComplete
End If

Exit Function

CannotRent:
If Not gCtx Is Nothing Then
    objCtx.SetAbort
End If
Rent = -6
End Function
```

RUNNING MTSDEMO2

The first run through the demo program will illustrate a problem. If you provide a list of videos to rent that includes a video that is already rented, the *Rental* object will abort. However, any videos up to the already rented one are rented to the customer. Any videos following the already rented video are not rented. In Figure 12-6, the second video (*Maverick*, copy number 1) is already rented. The member will rent *Airplane,* but not *Tales From The Hood.* You can reproduce this problem by following the instructions below.

1. After installing the *MTSDEMO2* components, run the client test utility, *VSMTSCL2.EXE.*

2. Enter *12001* for the *Member ID.*

3. For *VideoID*, enter *52001*, and for *Copy No*, enter *1.* Click the *Add to Rental List* button.

4. Click the *Rent All* button, then click the *Show Rentals* button to verify that copy number *1* of video *52001* has been rented to member *12001*. Do not exit the program yet.

5. Enter *12002* for the *Member ID.*

6. For *VideoID*, enter *52005*, and for *Copy No*, enter *1.* Click the *Add to Rental List* button.

7. For *VideoID,* enter *52001*, and for *Copy No*, enter *1.* Click the *Add to Rental List* button. Note that this is the copy you already rented to member *12001.*

8. For *VideoID*, enter *52006*, and for *Copy No*, enter *1.* Click the *Add to Rental List* button, then click the *Rent All* button.

9. An error message is displayed, indicating that one of the videos on the rental list is already rented to another member. Click *OK* to dismiss this error message.

10. Click the *Show Rentals* button. You will notice that the first video on the list, *52005*, is rented to the member. The second video, which was already rented, is not rented to the member, but neither is the third video, which is available for rental. The *Renal* object aborted upon reaching the error, but should have performed a complete rollback.

11. Using the test user interface program, return all the videos rented by both members *12001* and *12002* to clear the rental state for the next run through the demo.

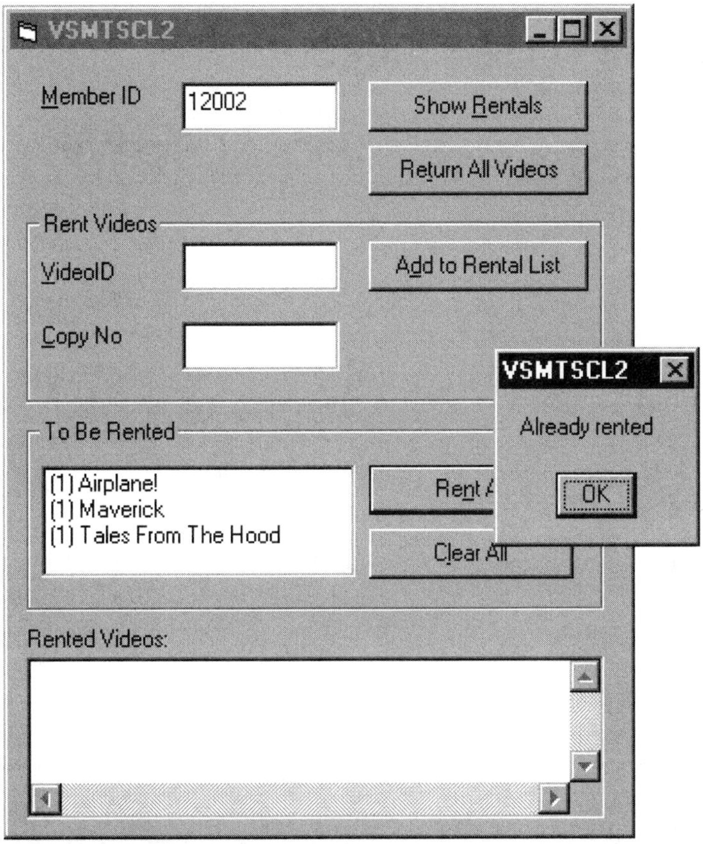

FIGURE 12-6   If one of the videos in the list is already rented, the *Rental* object aborts. However, any videos prior to the one that's already rented are rented to the member. Any videos following the rented video are not rented – the state is indeterminate!

SETTING TRANSACTION ATTRIBUTES ON THE RENTAL OBJECT

To specify that MTS should run the methods of the *Rental* object under a transaction, you should set the *Transaction support* attribute of the *Rental* object to *Requires a transaction.* You can do this by following the instructions below. Once this attribute is set, the *MTS Executive* will automatically start a transaction when one of the *Rental* object's methods is invoked.

The *Transaction support* attributes of the *Member* and *Video* objects should be set to *Supports transactions,* again following the instructions below. This attribute indicates that the objects wish to participate in voting for transaction outcome, but only when they are invoked from MTS components that are already executing within the context of a transaction.

Note that the *Transaction support* attributes of a component can also be set from the *MTSTransactionMode* property of the Visual Basic class module that implements the MTS component.

To set the MTS transaction attributes for the *MTSDEMO2* components,

1. Shut down the MTS package you created that contains the *MTSDEMO2* components.

2. Select the *Rental* component from the list of *MTSDEMO2* components. Right-click on the component and select *Properties*.

3. In the resulting *Properties* dialog, select the *Transaction* tab (see Figure 12-7).

4. Select the attribute *Requires a transaction*, then click *OK* to dismiss the *Properties* dialog.

5. Repeat steps 2-4 for the *Video* and *Member* object, but for each of these objects, select the *Supports transactions* attribute.

6. Run the client test program again, as described in the section *Running MTSDEMO2*. Verify that no videos are rented to the second client. MTS has automatically rolled back the transaction.

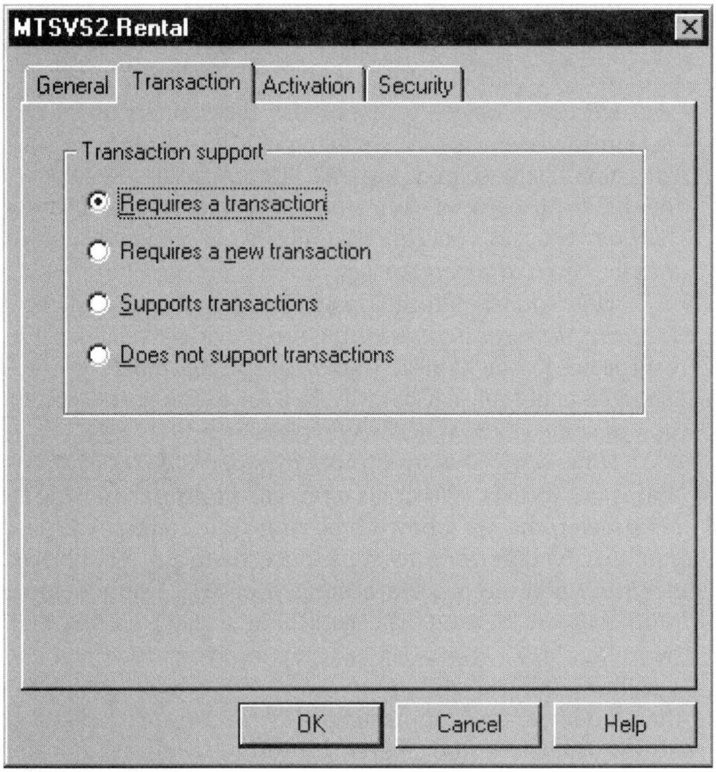

FIGURE 12-7 The *Rental* object's *Transaction support* attribute is set to *Requires a transaction.*

The MTS Shared Property Manager

Since it's not safe to share data among objects using global variables, MTS provides a resource manager known as the *Shared Property Manager.* The *Shared Property Manager* allows you to share global state within a server process by exposing properties and methods via three objects: *SharedPropertyGroupManager, SharedPropertyGroup,* and *SharedProperty.*

To use the *SharedPropertyGroupManager* object, you must first set a reference to the *Shared Property Manager* type library. Also before using the *SharedPropertyGroupManager,* you must create an instance of a *SharedPropertyGroupManager* object. Microsoft recommends using either the *CreateObject* function or the *CreateInstance* method of the *ObjectContext* object, although **New** works fine as well.

After creating the *SharedPropertyGroupManager* object, you can invoke its *CreatePropertyGroup* method to create a *SharedPropertyGroup* object. It's easy to tell if you've created the group, or if the group is already created; this information can be useful if you need to execute code to initialize the shared property. Once a *SharedPropertyGroup* object is created, use the *CreateProperty* method of the *SharedPropertyGroup* object to create a *SharedProperty* object. You can also determine if the property is created or has already been created, enabling your application to perform one-time initialization of the shared property, if appropriate. Finally, you can set or read the *Value* property of your *SharedProperty* object. The *Value* property is a *Variant* type, so you can basically place whatever type of data you want into the *SharedProperty* object.

This sounds like a lot of steps, and indeed it is. But, the *Shared Property Manager* is responsible for providing reliable, thread-safe access to your shared data. Considering what the *Shared Property Manager* does, its interface is not all that hard to use. An example follows after further discussion of some of the functions involved.

How long will shared properties persist? The short answer to this question is not forever. When no more clients are referencing the objects in your MTS server, the MTX process hosting your components can shut down (you can specify how long to wait, once there are no objects, before shutting down). When the process hosting your MTS components exits, your shared properties are deleted. The next time a client creates one of your components, the MTX process starts again, and your code will end up creating and initializing the property group again. If you want a value to persist for longer than the lifetime of the hosting *MTS Executive* process, save the information in the database – the *Shared Property Manager* is not appropriate for this type of persistent data.

The CreatePropertyGroup Method

Parameters for the *CreatePropertyGroup* method are listed in Table 12-5. Following is the syntax and description of parameters for the *SharedPropertyGroupManager* object's *CreatePropertyGroup* method. (Note: The syntax assumes that *objPGM* is your *SharedPropertyGroupManager* object.)

```
Dim objPG As SharedPropertyGroup
Set objPG = objPGM.CreatePropertyGroup (Name, IsoMode, _
                                RelMode, Exists)
```

The first time you invoke the *CreatePropertyGroup* method, its *Exists* parameter returns with a value of *FALSE*. You can use this value to determine whether or not you need to perform any sort of custom initialization.

TABLE 12-5	Parameters of the CreatePropertyGroup Method

Parameter	Description
Name	Name of the shared property group to create or return (if already created).
IsoMode	Specifies the isolation level for the properties in the shared property group. The default value of **LockSetGet** prevents simultaneous access to the same property (locking one property at a time), while the **LockMethod** constant locks all properties at once when a property in the group is accessed.
RelMode	Specifies the release mode for the properties in the shared property group. To keep the shared data around for the life of the *MTS Executive* process, you should specify the **Process** constant for this parameter.
Exists	This parameter is returned as **TRUE** if the shared property group has already been created; **FALSE** otherwise.

Thread-Safe References to Shared Properties

It is possible to write thread-safe code that references the properties in your shared property group, but you must indicate the appropriate isolation mode in your call to the *CreatePropertyGroup* method. The safest setting is *LockMethod*. This locks the entire property group from any access while a method is using any property from the group. A less safe setting is *LockSetGet*, which locks the property during each read or write to the property.

Use the *LockMethod* setting when you must perform a non-atomic update to the property. For example, if you must read the property, then update it, then write it back, that is a non-atomic reference, and you must use *LockMethod*. You can use *LockSetGet* if your references are atomic.

It is your responsibility to set the proper isolation mode option. Neither option will cause your code to fail, but you may get unexpected results due to race conditions or other synchronization anomalies. If you have non-atomic updates to a property with an isolation mode of *LockSetGet*, you cannot guard against another thread using the shared property value while it is being updated and in an inconsistent state. On the other hand, if you use *LockMethod* when the references are atomic, you will sacrifice concurrency, causing some threads to wait unnecessarily.

Shared Property Manager Demo

The demo *VB6Adv\Demos\MTSDemos\MTSDemo3\Server\SPDemo.VBP* (see Figure 12-8) is a simple example of using the *Shared Property Manager*. A component, called *SPCounter*, has a property called *Count*, which is initialized to one (1) and incremented each time the property is invoked. After installing the components into a package, run several copies of the client to see how each client's objects are sharing the same "global" data. The *Mom-*

n-Pop Video Store application also makes use of the *Shared Property Manager*, as described in the following chapter.

There are two client demo programs for this server. The first version shows the current count every time you click a button (the server increments the count after each reference). The second client test program accesses the count in a loop. The server simulates blocking by sleeping for 100 milliseconds to allow other threads to execute while one thread is in the middle of executing the method. If you run two or more copies of the second client demo program, you will begin to notice delays as the clients wait for the thread(s) ahead of them.

The demo can be made far more interesting if you experiment with the isolation mode. The server program properly uses an isolation mode of *LockMethod*, since it performs a non-atomic update of the property, in fact simulating a lengthy operation by calling the *Win32 Sleep* function. If you run two copies of the second client demo program, neither program ever gets the same number. You can verify this by checking that one of the client's final numbers is 200 (each client invokes the *Count* method 100 times). Try modifying the server code to use the *LockGetSet* isolation mode. You will see clear evidence that the two clients often get the same number, and the highest number reached by either client will be unpredictable.

```
Option Explicit
Private Declare Sub Sleep Lib "kernel32" _
        (ByVal dwMilliseconds As Long)

Public Property Get Count() As Integer

    '- Returns a count.  Increments the count every time
    '- the property is referenced (starts at 1).  Uses the
    '- MTS Shared Property Manager.

    Dim objCtx As ObjectContext
    Dim objSPM As SharedPropertyGroupManager
    Dim objSPMGroup As SharedPropertyGroup
    Dim objSProp As SharedProperty
    Dim bExists As Boolean
    Dim nTemp As Integer

    '- Get MTS object context.

    Set objCtx = GetObjectContext

    '- Create property group or get reference
    '- to existing one.
```

```
Set objSPM = New SharedPropertyGroupManager
Set objSPMGroup = objSPM.CreatePropertyGroup _
                    ("SPDemoProps", _
                    LockMethod, _
                    Process, _
                    bExists)

'- Create property or get reference
'- to existing one.

Set objSProp = objSPMGroup.CreateProperty("Count", _
                                          bExists)

'- If property was created, initialize it.  Otherwise,
'- increment it.

If Not bExists Then
    objSProp.Value = 1
Else

    '- To simulate executing a blocking call
    '- while we hold the property value, grab
    '- the value, sleep for 1/10th second, then
    '- update and write the property.

    nTemp = objSProp.Value + 1
    Sleep 100
    objSProp.Value = nTemp

End If

'- Return value of property.

Count = objSProp.Value
objCtx.SetComplete

End Property
```

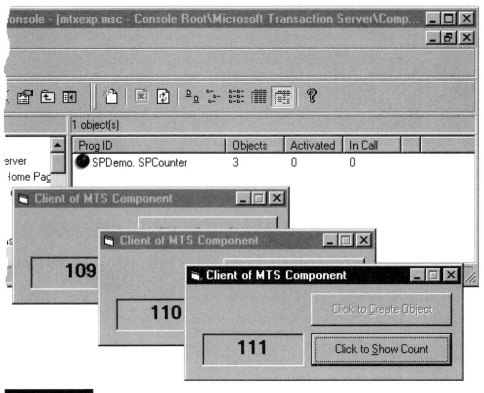

FIGURE 12-8   The third MTS demo illustrates the use of the *Shared Property Manager.*

Deploying MTS Servers

Once you've successfully developed, tested, and debugged your MTS server, you will probably want to move it from your development system over to the production server. Then, you will want to provide some way for client machines to get the necessary entries in their registries that will enable remote access to the production server. MTS, through the *MTS Explorer Utility*, provides a simple way of doing just that.

In a nutshell, you export the package on your development system, import the package on the production system, and then export the package on the production system. The last step creates a client setup program. Each client machine must execute the client setup program that was created when the package was exported on the production server. Note that the client setup program makes the necessary registry entries on the client machine to enable client applications to access the remote server. The client setup program created by MTS does not set up the client program itself. You must separately create a setup program for the client application. Note that you can customize a setup program to perform both steps on the client machine. To deploy an MTS server and set up the required client-side registry entries,

1. In the *MTS Explorer* utility, select the package that hosts your components.
2. Right-click on the package and select **Export**.
3. Navigate to and select a location for the PAK file that can be accessed on the network.
4. Move to the production server machine. On this machine, start the *MTS Explorer* utility and create a new package.
5. When prompted, select **Import Existing Package** and select the package you exported previously.
6. On the same machine (server), right-click on the new package and select **Export**.
7. Navigate to and select a location for the PAK file that can be accessed on the network. Note that this step also creates a **Client** folder that will contain an EXE that clients can execute to update their registries and copy the necessary support files for remote access to your server.
8. On each client machine, execute the *EXE* in the *Client* folder created from the above step.

Security and MTS

In a production system using MTS components, you must be at least minimally concerned about security. Most applications using MTS will be using databases, and even it the components simply read from the database, the confidentiality of your data should not be compromised. In addition, it is central to N-tier client/server application philosophies that remote clients create processes and/or remotely execute code on your server. Even if you cannot possibly imagine someone being capable of compromising your system security using your MTS components, there are some minimum considerations. Years ago, when I taught seminars on system security, I would tell students that, as a good rule of thumb, you should assume a high sophistication level for potential adversaries – in fact, you should assume they are smarter than you are. In other words, if there is a way to compromise system security or confidentiality, an adversary will discover it. In addition, security is often placed in systems to protect the casual user from accidentally performing operations that are harmful to the system. In this case, I would suggest that you assume a low sophistication level for the casual user. In other words, assume they are inexperienced enough that they might actually do something that you consider ridiculous.

In developing a 3-tier client/server application using MTS, there are, coincidentally, three levels of security that can be applied. These levels range from a coarse to fine granularity, and include package identity, declarative security, and programmatic security.

About MTSDEMO4 – The MTS Security Demo

The fourth MTS demo and corresponding walkthrough illustrate every possible use of the features of MTS security. If you follow along with the walkthrough, you will install an MTS component that has been enabled for programmatic security – you will be able to execute one of the methods of the component, but not the other. You will then create an MTS role and add your account to this role, which will enable you to run the second method of the component. Finally, you will observe the use of advanced security measures, which enable an MTS client to discover the identity of the immediate and base clients using the component.

To get started with the demo, deploy the server *SecDemoServer.DLL*, located in folder *VB6Adv\Demos\MTSDemos\MTSDemo4\Server*. Refer back to the instructions accompanying the description of the first MTS demo. It does not matter what you call the package – use defaults for the package identity when you install it. In the first step, you will change the package identity anyway.

MTS Package Identity—Your First Line of Defense

Recall that when a component from an MTS package is first created, a process is created that runs the *MTS Executive* and hosts your components. You can specify under which NT/2000 user account your package should run, and this is your first line of defense. This account is first provided when installing the package for the first time, and can later be changed via the *Identities* tab of the package's *Properties* dialog.

It is typical to select the interactive user for a package's identity during development. However, this literally indicates that the hosting process will run under whatever NT/2000 account is logged on as the interactive user at the time the hosting process is created. If the interactive user is the *Administrator* or some other highly privileged account, your MTS process is running with a full set of privileges and entitlements. Of course, the actions performed by the MTS process are limited by the code that you develop. However, if there is a hole in your code that is discovered by an adversary, you don't want to have to explain why your components were running under the *Administrator* account.

You will achieve the greatest peace of mind knowing that the hosting MTS process is running under an account that has barely enough privileges and access rights to perform the actions required by your components. This is why your first line of defense must be to assign an appropriate NT user account to the package's identity. The *SecDemoServer* used for this demo only reads the system time, so it can run under the *Guest* account, assuming you have such an account on your system, and it is enabled. Follow the instructions below to change the identity of your package.

1. Using the *MTS Explorer* utility, select the package you used to deploy *SecDemoServer*. Right-click on the package and select *Properties*.

2. In the resulting *Properties* dialog, select the *Identity* tab (see Figure 12-9).

3. Check the option *This user*, then click the *Browse* button.

4. In the resulting *Set Package Identity* dialog, select the *Guest* account, if available. If not, select another suitable account, or create one if necessary. Be sure the account you select is enabled; by default, Windows NT does not enable the *Guest* account. Once you've selected an account, click the *OK* button to dismiss the *Set Package Identity* dialog.

5. Back in the *Properties* dialog, enter the password of the account, then click *OK* to dismiss the *Properties* dialog.

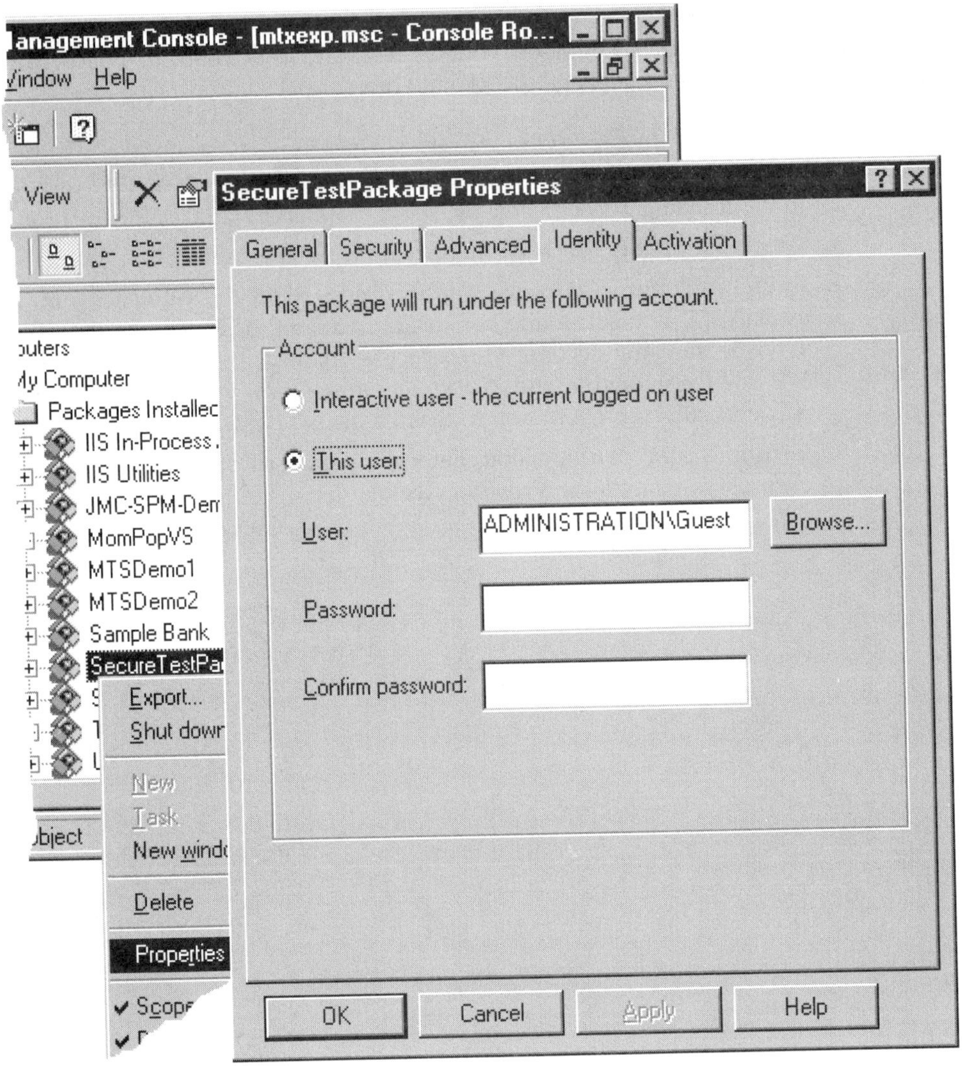

FIGURE 12-9 The package *Identity* specifies under which NT account your MTS components will run. This is your first line of defense.

Declarative Security – Your Second Line of Defense

Using MTS declarative security does not require instrumentation of your component – it is simply an administrative task that results in the limitation of the use of components in your package to users assigned to MTS roles. With declarative security, an MTS administrator, and not necessarily a programmer, can secure the use of MTS Components.

With programmatic security, discussed in a later section, a programmer includes code in the component to check the role membership of the base client prior to executing a method or a critical section of code in a method. Both declarative and programmatic security require the creation of MTS roles, so knowing how to do this is prerequisite to using either or both security measures.

There is an interesting side effect of using programmatic security that will be discussed in detail in a later section, but which needs an explanation at this time. If an MTS component has been instrumented to check role membership, the role must be defined or the related role-checking method raises an exception. To see this effect, run the accompanying client program as follows:

1. Run the client demo program *SecureTest.EXE* from folder *VB6Adv\ Demos\MTSDemos\MTSDemo4\Client.*

2. Click the *Make Object* button.

3. Click the *Show Server Time* button. This method is secured with programmatic security, expecting the caller to be in the role of *Manager.* Since the role is currently not defined, the client application reports an error returned from the server.

Defining an MTS Role

As mentioned, both declarative and programmatic security in MTS rely on role membership of the base client. Prior to using either type of security, an MTS role must be defined. An **MTS role** is simply a string that describes the responsibility or job description of the user executing the methods of an MTS component. Examples of MTS roles might include *Manager, Clerk, Librarian,* and others. Once a role is created, you associate an NT user account or account group with the role.

In the following stage of running the security demo, you will create two MTS roles, but will not yet assign the roles to any user, including yourself. You will see slightly different behavior when running the client test application. You will be able to run the client program and access the *GetInfo* method (the information returned by this method is explained in a later section), but you will still not be able to access the method that returns the server time. However, this time the error will indicate that you are not authorized to execute the method – contrast this error condition with the previous one, in which the server reported that the MTS role of *Manager* was not defined.

To create the *Manager* and *Clerk* roles,

1. Shut down the MTS package by selecting the package, right-clicking on the package name, and selecting *Shut Down*. It is essential to shut down an MTS package before modifying the list of roles or role memberships.

2. Expand your package so that you can see the item *Roles* under the package. Right-click on *Roles* and select *New*, then *Role* (see Figure 12-10).

3. In the *New Role* dialog, enter *Manager* as the name of the new role, then click *OK*.

3. Repeat the above two steps, adding a role called *Clerk*.

5. Repeat the previous demo. When you click the *Show Server Time* button, an error message is displayed, indicating that you are not authorized to execute the method. Now that the *Manager* role exists, the server no longer receives an error when checking your role membership. However, you are not yet assigned to the role, so you cannot execute the method.

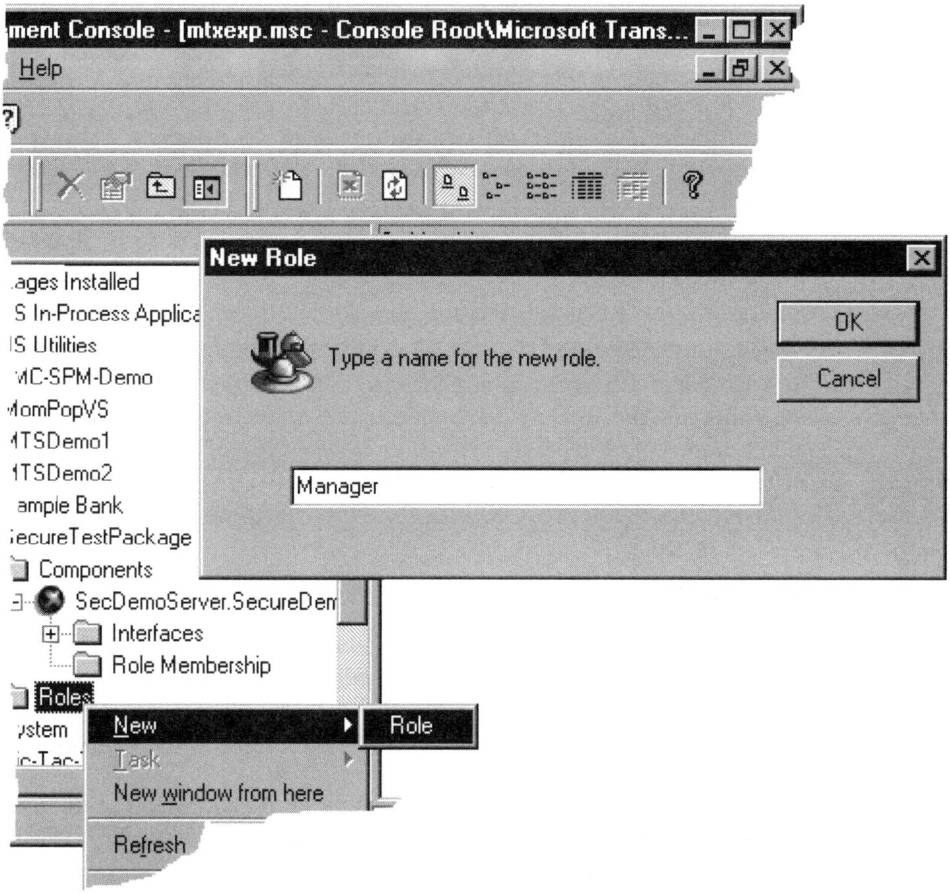

FIGURE 12-10 In the next part of the walk-through, you create two MTS roles, *Manager* and *Clerk.*

Enabling Package Authentication for Declarative Security

Now that you have two MTS roles defined, you can experiment with declarative security. In the next step, you will limit access to the MTS component to accounts associated with either the *Clerk* or *Manager* role. Later, you will experiment with programmatic security, observing that, while *Clerks* and *Managers* can access some of the methods of the component, only a *Manager* can access the system time method. The MTS component has not been instrumented to consider the *Clerk* role; no code exists in the component to check for a *Clerk*. In fact, using *Clerk* as a role is just a suggestion – you can use any role names you wish when assigning declarative security.

To properly use declarative security, it is necessary to associate NT user accounts and/or account groups with the role. You must also enable package authentication to protect your components. It is interesting to perform the latter step first and observe what happens when you attempt to access any of the methods of components running with Package Authentication enabled. You can do this as follows:

1. Shut down the package as described in the previous step of this walk-through.

2. In the *MTS Explorer* utility, select the package you used to deploy the demo. Right-click on the package and select *Properties.*

3. On the *Properties* dialog, select the *Security* tab. Check the option *Enable authorization checking.* Then click *OK* to dismiss the *Properties* dialog.

4. Run the client test program and click the *Make Object* button. Try clicking either the *Get Security Info* button or the *Show Server Time* button. In either case, you receive a *Permission Denied* error. This is evidence of declarative security; the component is not involved in granting or denying your application permission to use the methods of its components.

Assigning NT User Accounts to MTS Roles

In the next step of this walkthrough, you will use declarative security to grant access to the component to both *Clerks* and *Managers.* You will then assign your user account to the *Clerk* role to verify that you can at least access the *Get Security Info* method of the component. Finally, you will assign yourself to the role of *Manager* and verify that you can then access the *Show Server Time* method of the component. Remember that the method that returns the server time is protected with programmatic security; I will be discussing this in detail in the next section.

To add your account to the *Clerk* and *Manager* roles,

1. Shut down your package as you have been doing prior to any step that modifies the security attributes of your MTS components.

2. In the *MTS Explorer* utility, select the package you used to deploy the demo. Expand the package so that you can see the item *Roles,* then expand the item *Roles* so that you can see the items *Clerk* and *Manager.*

3. Expand *Clerk* (under *Roles*) so that you can see the item *Users.* Select *Users,* then right-click on *Users* and select *New,* then *User* (see Figure 12-11).

4. In the resulting *Add Users and Groups to Role* dialog, click the *Show Users* button. Then, locate your user account and double-click on it to add your account to the role. Click the *OK* button to dismiss the dialog.

5. Now you must indicate which roles are authorized, via declarative security, to access the components in your package. Expand your package so you can see the *Components* item.

6. Expand the *Components* item so that you can see the name of the component, which should be *SecDemoServer.SecureDemo.* Expand *SecDemoServer.SecureDemo* so that you can see the items *Interfaces* and *Role Membership.*

7. Select *Role Membership,* right-click on *Role Membership,* and select *New,* then *Role.*

8. In the resulting *Select Roles* dialog, you should see both the *Clerk* and the *Manager* role listed. Select both roles (use *shift-click* to make multiple selections), then click *OK* to dismiss the *Select Role Membership* dialog.

9. Run the client test program again. This time, you can access the *Get Security Info* method, but not the *Show Server Time* method. In a way, you are back where you started when you first installed the package, but with one major exception – only *Clerks* and *Managers* can execute the *Get Security Info* method.

10. Now you can add yourself to the *Manager* role and verify that you can access the *Show Server Time* method. Remember to shut down your package before proceeding to the next step.

11. Repeating Steps 2 - 4, add your account to the *Manager* role.

12. Run the client test program again and verify that you can access all methods of the server.

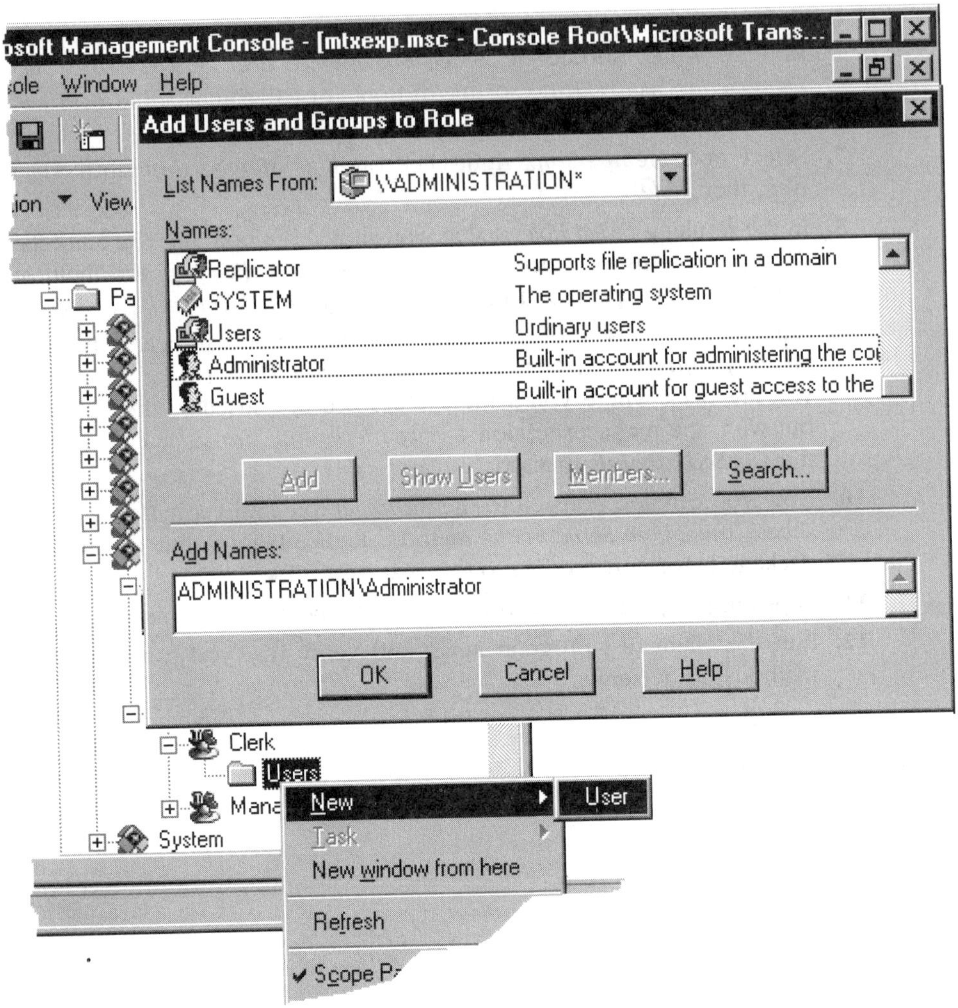

FIGURE 12-11   Add your account to both the *Clerk* and the *Manager* roles.

How Programmatic Security Works

Using programmatic security in MTS, your components can be written to protect certain methods, or certain critical sections of code for certain methods, from unauthorized access. In the case of the demo component, which provides two methods, one method is unrestricted, while the other allows only access from users in the *Manager* role. You can also use programmatic security to limit access to features implemented by a section of code in a method, or you can program logic that triggers programmatic security under certain conditions.

For example, the *Mom-n-Pop Video Store* middleware could provide a method that forgives all late charges for a customer. Consider what may happen if a longtime member of the video store explains that unforeseen circumstances prevented the prompt return of rented videos. A *Manager* should be able, at his or her discretion, to cancel late charges for a customer. A *ForgiveLateCharges* method could use MTS programmatic security to verify that the caller is associated with the role *Manager* before executing. In this case, no part of the method executes if the caller is not in the proper role. This is equivalent to a manager in a retail environment inserting a key in a point-of-sale terminal to override the store's credit limit. Naturally, you can provide your own code to password-protect such methods, but why reinvent the wheel? Using the NT security services is far more reliable.

As another example, the video store may have a business rule that states that no member shall be able to rent new videos if they have outstanding late videos, unless overridden by a manager. In this case, the method of the data services layer object that implements the transaction that rents videos may conditionally check if the caller is in the *Manager* role before renting new videos to a customer that has not yet returned late videos. In this case, part of the method executes regardless of what role the caller is in, provided the mentioned condition is not true.

MTS programmatic security relies on a programmer calling the *ObjectContext* methods, **IsSecurityEnabled** and **IsCallerInRole.** Additionally, a program can use advanced security techniques to verify the identity of the base client, using the *SecurityProperty* object of the *ObjectContext* object. In the following section, I will introduce you to using the *IsCallerInRole* function and illustrate how it is used in the demonstration component. Later, I'll describe the use of the *SecurityProperty* object, which can be used to verify the identity of the remote base client.

Determining if Security is Enabled

Prior to using the *IsCallerInRole* method to verify whether or not a caller's user account is associated with a particular role, it is recommended that you call the **IsSecurityEnabled** method to verify that security is enabled. If security is not enabled, the *IsCallerInRole* method behaves unpredictably. Security is always enabled for server packages, which is the default type of package. A **server package** runs in its own process, while a **library package** runs in the same process as the client. I have not discussed library packages in this book, nor do I intend to, as the typical type of package used for N-tier client/server applications is a server package.

If you deploy your package as a server package, security will always be enabled. Thus, it is not strictly required that your component use the *IsSecurityEnabled* method prior to calling *IsSecurityEnabled.* However, Microsoft recommends that you do, so my component does.

Using the IsCallerInRole Method

The *IsCallerInRole* method of the *ObjectContext* object is a very simple method that returns a Boolean value indicating whether or not the caller is a member of a role. The role is passed as a string and is the single parameter of the method. So, it's easy to use this method, but there is a catch. If the role you pass as the parameter to *IsCallerInRole* is undefined, the method does not, as you might expect, return FALSE. Instead, it raises error number *8004E00C*, which is defined by the constant **mtsErrCtxRoleNotFound**. To make your code as robust as possible, you must use an error handler that traps this exception. The method will also raise an error if security is not enabled, as in when the package has been deployed as a library package. In this case, the error is *8004E00D*, for which the constant **mtsErrCtxNo-Security** is defined. Other than the possibility of *IsCallerInRole* raising one of these two errors, using the method is straightforward as illustrated below:

```
Option Explicit

'- Error constants returned by the methods -'
'- of this object                          -'

Public Enum SecDemoServerConstants
    secNotInMTS = -1
    secSecurityDisabled = -2
    secNoManagerRole = -3
    secNotAuthorized = -4
End Enum

Public Function SecureTime(ByRef dtNow As Date) As Integer
    Dim objCtx As ObjectContext

    '- Get the ObjectContext object.  Note that this
    '- demo can ONLY be run under MTS.

    Set objCtx = GetObjectContext
    If objCtx Is Nothing Then
        SecureTime = secNotInMTS
        Exit Function
    End If

    '- Make sure security is enabled.

    If Not objCtx.IsSecurityEnabled Then
        SecureTime = secSecurityDisabled
        Exit Function
    End If
```

```
'- Make sure caller is in Manager role. Note that
'- we must protect the following code with an error
'- handler, since the IsCallerInRole method raises
'- an error if the role is not defined, rather than
'- simply returning FALSE.

On Error GoTo CannotGetTime

If Not objCtx.IsCallerInRole("Manager") Then
    SecureTime = secNotAuthorized
    Exit Function
End If

'- Return time, since caller is in correct role.

dtNow = Now
SecureTime = 0
Exit Function

CannotGetTime:
    If Err.Number = mtsErrCtxRoleNotFound Then
        SecureTime = secNoManagerRole
    Else
        Err.Raise Err.Number, Err.Source, Err.Description
    End If
End Function
```

Obtaining the Identity of the Client

In certain applications with advanced security requirements, it may be necessary to obtain the identity of the base client that is remotely using the component. Your application may, for example, wish to verify that the client's account is one of a list of valid accounts, or that the client is making a request from a proper host. Such information can be obtained using the *SecurityProperty* object, which in turn is accessed by invoking the *Security* method of the *ObjectContext* object.

The *SecurityProperty* object has four methods, which can be used to obtain the identity of the base client and/or the identity of the component that created the component. In the security demo that I have been presenting, the values of these properties are displayed in the client test program under the headings *Direct Caller, Direct Creator, Original Caller,* and *Original Creator.* The values come from, respectively, the *SecurityProperty* object methods *GetDirectCallerName, GetDirectCreatorName, GetOriginal-CallerName,* and *GetOriginalCreatorName.* Clearly, these methods form a pair of two related methods, one pair returning the direct creator and caller, and the other pair returning the original creator and caller.

The direct caller/creator identifies the process immediately involved in the activity prior to the execution of the method invoking the *SecurityProperty* methods, while the original caller/creator identifies the base client process. In the walkthrough presented in this chapter, these processes are the same; this is directly due to the fact that only one MTS component and only one MTS package is involved – a typical case.

If the components in your data services layer are complex, you may decide to split components across packages. There are other motivations for splitting components across package boundaries, as each package defines a process, security, and fault isolation boundary. However, stacking components up in this manner may provide a determined adversary with additional opportunities for compromising security via spoofing and masquerading. While the immediate client, in other words, may be trusted, it may be necessary for you to validate the identity of the "ultimate," base client.

The following code illustrates how to obtain the identity both the direct and original callers and creators:

```
Public Function GetInfo(ByRef strDirectCaller As String, _
                ByRef strDirectCreator As String, _
                ByRef strOriginalCaller As String, _
                ByRef strOriginalCreator As String) _
            As Integer

    Dim objCtx As ObjectContext
    Dim objSec As SecurityProperty

    On Error GoTo CannotGetInfo

    '- Start by clearing out the return parameters.

    strDirectCaller = ""
    strDirectCreator = ""
    strOriginalCaller = ""
    strOriginalCreator = ""

    '- Get the ObjectContext object.  Note that this
    '- demo can ONLY be run under MTS.

    Set objCtx = GetObjectContext
    If objCtx Is Nothing Then
        GetInfo = secNotInMTS
        Exit Function
    End If
```

```
'- Return info from SecurityProperty object.

Set objSec = objCtx.Security
strDirectCaller = objSec.GetDirectCallerName
strDirectCreator = objSec.GetDirectCreatorName
strOriginalCaller = objSec.GetOriginalCallerName
strOriginalCreator = objSec.GetOriginalCreatorName

GetInfo = 0
Exit Function

CannotGetInfo:
    GetInfo = -3
    strDirectCaller = Err.Description
End Function
```

Implementing the Data Services Layer with MTS

In the previous chapter, I introduced you to Microsoft Transaction Server and provided you with examples, some more practical than others, of components deployed under the MTS environment. This chapter takes a completely practical approach by examining the code in the data services layer of the *Mom-n-Pop Video Store* 3-tier client/server application. After reviewing the requirements and recommendations for creating MTS components, I'll show you how the components of the *Mom-n-Pop data services layer* were implemented and designed to be stateless.

Requirements for MTS Components

All MTS components must be hosted in an in-process COM server. In Visual Basic, this means an ActiveX DLL. All MTS components must be well-behaved COM objects, implementing the required COM interfaces and properly maintaining a reference count. If you use Visual Basic to create your MTS component, it will be a well-behaved COM object and will properly maintain reference-counting.

You should minimally use apartment-model threading. Visual Basic permits you to specify the single-threaded threading model, but there is no motivation for using the single-threaded model. Along the lines of threads, your MTS component must not create, manage, or terminate threads. Although this is not typically done in Visual Basic, which provides no direct native techniques for creating threads, it is possible in Visual Basic if you use the Win32 API. This is strongly discouraged.

Finally, it is recommended that you design your objects to be stateless. Although MTS will, in theory, allow you to deploy any well-behaved COM object, one of the primary motivations for using MTS is for taking advantage of its just-in-time activation features. An object that must hold state between method calls is not stateless, and consumes server-side resources even while in an idle state.

MTS Components Implement Business Rules

It is strongly recommended that your MTS components implement your business rules, with perhaps the exception of volatile or frequently changing business rules. Seasonal or promotional rules of your business may be implemented in such a way as to facilitate ease of change. Such changeable business activities are often promoted through the use of Internet front-ends (browser-based clients), and can perhaps be better maintained directly in Active Server Page scripts. For example, if the *Mom-n-Pop Video Store* wished to promote on-line registration of new members by offering a free nights' rental of a video, a developer may desire to make arrangements to implement the supporting code in ASP script. For regular business activity, however, you must view the data services layer, in which you deploy MTS components, as the foundation of your business rules. This strategy extends to the N-tier model, in which you perhaps use an object model to wrap the methods of your stateless data services layer components. From a logical perspective, the object model may apparently implement the business rules, but unless you are developing a 2-tier application, the object model should not actually implement the business rules. Again, view your object model as a thin layer of object-oriented code over your MTS components. Remember, not all your presentation layer applications (clients) can access the stateful objects of your object model. Scripting languages executing in an Active Server Page and native Visual Basic code executing in an Internet IIS application must use the stateless objects in your data services layer. Developing Active Server Page applications is covered in Chapter 15. The development of Internet IIS applications is covered in Chapter 16.

Implementing business logic in the data services layer ensures that all clients, regardless of how they enter into the tiers of the application, access a common set of business rules implemented by a common set of components.

The Role of Stored Procedures

In a 3-tier architecture that implements a data services layer, reliance on stored procedures is not as strong as it is in the 2-tier model, although this statement will raise some eyebrows. Many programmers, lacking experience in database design and tuning, accept the word of the database designer that stored procedures are the absolute fastest way to access and update data, and that they are, in fact, "way faster." In actual fact, the most significant performance gain from stored procedures comes from the fact that the data is processed where it resides. If a remote client application brings back a large amount of data, then processes it into the data it requires, it involves network round-trips, an open database connection, and state management by the database server. Data processed and consolidated locally is significantly faster than data processed remotely, regardless of how the data is processed – either by a stored procedure or by an MTS component written in a high-level language. If you can get a database designer to admit to this fact, it will be pointed out to you that a stored procedure has also been precompiled and is often cached for future use. There is no doubt that this results in a performance gain, but this gain is not as significant as performance gains from local data processing. Besides, the same can be said for ADO command objects – using them results in precompiled, cached (in your program) procedures that access the database. Data services layer components are really glorified stored procedures – you can develop them in a COM-compatible language such as Visual Basic, which offers a far richer programming environment than the SQL language. Having said that, I'm not suggesting that you do away with stored procedures. They simply do not have to be extremely complex, and they do not have to contain all the logic for implementing your business rules. Data services layer objects, however, *must* contain all the logic for implementing your business rules.

Be Business-Focused

You must be business-focused when designing your MTS components. Resist the temptation to abstract away important tasks identified with your business activities. For example, it is significant that, in the *Mom-n-Pop Video Store,* a member enters the store, browses for videos, picks out a few videos to rent, and approaches the clerk to complete the transaction. If your design is too abstract, you may decide that the *Video* object has a *Rent* method – but you will have great difficulty in designing such an object to be stateless and run under MTS, primarily since a member may rent a list of videos and, as part of the same transaction, return some videos and pay late charges. Don't be afraid to model the business as the business. Some designers fear that concentrating on such apparently minor details will result in an inelegant abstraction. However, this is key to a successful implementation of a multitier architecture. Abstract, elegant, stateful objects have a place – in the object model that wraps the components of the data services layer. They don't belong in the data services layer, which tends to contain objects that are more concrete and directly business-oriented.

Each Layer Adds Value

One of the funniest skits I remember seeing on *Saturday Night Live* occurred when virtual reality was the flavor of the month. A spoof of a commercial touted the brand new *"Virtual Reality Book."* When you donned the special glasses, you could see and read pages from a virtual book. An icon displayed in the corner of your field of vision allowed you to actually turn the pages as though you were actually reading a real book. The virtual book promoted in the commercial did not place you into the scenes of the book, contained no 3-D animations, and in fact, displayed only text. Naturally, the point was, why not just get a real book and read it? What value did the virtual book add to a real book?

Trust me, it was funnier if you saw it. But it's not funny when a developer applies the same silliness to a multi-tiered application. Students have often asked me if it is "correct" to define an "object" for each table in a database and provide properties that map to the fields of the table. While you will no doubt end up doing this for some of your tables, it is not the status quo. Why should I have to go through your objects to get to the tables? Why don't I just go to the tables? What value does your object add if it is simply a direct encapsulation of your table? Just like the virtual book, which added no value to the real book, having an object in the object model that directly encapsulates a data services layer object, that directly encapsulates a stored procedure, that directly encapsulates a table, adds no value to the application. All it adds is unnecessary complexity.

In the *Mom-n-Pop Video Store* object model, the *LateCharges* collection of the *Member* object is a good example of adding value with each layer. The *Late Charges* collection contains properties that identify the title of the video rented by the member, when the video was rented, when it was supposed to be returned, when and if it was returned, and what the late fee is. Note that this information comes from multiple database tables in the database. The *LateCharges* collection object uses a method of a data services layer object that performs a set of complex queries on the database, the results of which are returned as a recordset. When the recordset is returned to the object model, the *LateCharges* collection object creates and populates a collection of *LateCharge* objects. The title, due date, and late fee of a given late charge are then available to Win32 presentation layer clients as properties of the *LateCharge* object. The Win32 client never sees a database table or recordset, and is therefore completely isolated from the database tier. Thus, late charge handling in the *Mom-n-Pop Video Store* application is an example of both adding value with each layer, and of implementing the business rules in the data services layer, to provide a common foundation and provide responsibility isolation to each layer.

Mom-n-Pop MTS Components

The *Mom-n-Pop* data services layer is made up of four components. One of these components, the *DateSimulator* component, exists only for simulating the date, and would probably not appear in a released version of the data services layer. The other components are the *VideoData, MemberData,* and *PointOfSale* objects. Each of these objects is discussed briefly in Table 13-1, and further in the sections that follow.

In general, when data needs to be returned from a *Mom-n-Pop* MTS component, it is returned in the form of a disassociated recordset. In general, when list data needs to be sent to a *Mom-n-Pop* MTS component, it is sent in the form of a variant array. For example, the *PointOfSale* object requires an array of videos to be rented.

TABLE 13-1	Mom-n-Pop MTS Components
Object	**Description**
VideoData	Provides an interface to the data services layer for obtaining information about a video.
MemberData	Provides an interface to the data services layer for obtaining information about a member of the video store.
PointOfSale	Provides an interface to the data services layer for performing the point-of-sale transactions for a member.

The MemberData MTS Component

The *MemberData* MTS component includes methods to look up a member by ID or by last name. It also includes methods to find out what videos a member has rented and which ones, if any, are late. Finally, it includes a method to update a member's record in the database. Note that the *FindByID* and *Search* methods return a recordset to the business layer. Methods of the *MemberData* component are summarized in Table 13-2.

Note the *Update* method. Your first reaction is bound to be "that's a lot of parameters!" This, however, is typical for MTS components that are stateless. You must pass all the required information to accomplish a given business task to a method of a stateless object.

What if you must change the parameters? For example, if a field is added, removed, or changed, you would need to change the *Update* method. The best approach is to find a way of changing the object without changing existing methods. Since this is not always possible, you may have to break compatibility and manually edit every client application that accesses the object. The fewer clients that access a stateless object, the better. This is yet another motivation for providing a thin layer of object-oriented stateful objects (the object model) over the data services layer.

| TABLE 13-2 | Methods of the MemberData Component |

Method	Description
FindByID (*nMemberID* As Long) As Recordset	Looks up a member by ID, returning a disassociated recordset containing the result.
Search (*strLastName* As String) As Recordset	Looks up all members with last names containing the string passed as a parameter, returning a disassociated recordset containing the results.
Sub Update(*nMemberID* As Long, *strLastName* As String, *strFirstName* As String, *strAddress1* As String, *strAddress2* As String, *strCity* As String, *strState* As String, *strZip* As String, *strPhone* As String)	Updates the member record with the matching member ID.
GetRentedVideos (*nMemberID* As Long) As Recordset	Returns list of videos rented by indicated member, passing back results as a disassociated recordset.
GetLateVideos (*nMemberID* As Long, *dtTodaysDate* As Date) As Recordset	Returns list of late videos rented by indicated member, passing back results as a disassociated recordset.

The VideoData MTS Component

The *VideoData* MTS component includes methods to obtain information about videos in the database, and a method to return a video (used to return a video from the desk). Methods of the *VideoData* object are summarized in Table 13-3.

TABLE 13-3	Methods of the VideoData Component
Method	**Description**
FindByID (*nVideoID* As Long) As Recordset	Looks up a video by ID, returning the result as a disassociated recordset.
GetAvailability (*nVideoID* As Long, *nCopiesRented* As Integer, *dtNextDue* As Date, *dtToday* As Date)	Returns number of copies rented, and the earliest date due for the video indicated by the *nVideoID* parameter.
GetCategories () As Recordset	Returns list of categories as a disassociated recordset.
GetCopiesAvailable (*nVideoID* As Long) As Integer	Returns number of copies available for a given video. An optimized version, *GetAvailability*, should be used when you also want the next due date of a video.
GetIsRented (*nVideoID* As Long, *nCopyNo* As Integer) As Boolean	Returns TRUE if the indicated copy of the indicated video is already rented.
GetLateFee () As Currency	Returns the video store's late charge.
GetNextDateDue (*nVideoID* As Long, *dtToday* As Date) As Date	Returns next due date of indicated video. An optimized version, *GetAvailability*, should be used when you also want the number of copies available for a video.
GetRentedCopies (*nVideoID* As Long) As Recordset	Returns a list of copies of indicated video that are rented to members. Information is returned in the form of a disassociated recordset.
ReturnVideo (*nVideoID* As Long, *nCopyNo* As Integer, *dtReturnDate* As Date)	Returns a rented video. Videos can also be returned via he *PointOfSale* object. This version can be used to return a video from the video store's return desk.
Search (*strTitle* As String) As Recordset	Returns a list of videos containing the indicated string in their title. Results are returned in the form of a disassociated recordset.
Public Sub Update(*nVideoID* As Long, *nCategoryID* As Integer, *strTitle* As String, *nYear* As Integer, *strCast* As String, *strDirector* As String, *strDescription* As String, *nRating* As Integer).	Updates video record with matching ID

The PointOfSale MTS Component

The *PointOfSale* MTS component implements only one method, *RingUp-Member*. It is the most complex method, both to call and to implement. The *RingUpMember* method must be passed all the necessary information about the transaction occurring at the point-of-sale. This means a list of all videos the member is both renting and returning, as well as the amount collected from the member. This amount must match the amount computed by the object, or the transaction fails. Other scenarios that cause the component to fail (and request rollback of the transaction) include an invalid member ID, an invalid video ID, an invalid copy number, or an already-rented copy of a video appearing in the list of candidate video rentals.

The *RingUpMember* method returns an error code indicating the success or failure of the method (see Table 13-4). Constant error codes (see Table 13-5) are created by a public enumeration using the techniques discussed in Chapters 6 and 7. I will guide you through a rental transaction—from client, to object model, to data services layer—later in this chapter.

TABLE 13-4	Methods of the PointOfSale Component

Method	Description
Public Function *RingUpMember* (*nMemberID* As Long, *vRentalPicks* As Variant, *vReturnPicks* As Variant, *nAmtCollected* As Currency, *dtToday As Date*) As Integer	Performs primary point-of-sale transaction for the video store, renting and returning videos, and collecting the amount due. Also updates the database to reflect rented and returned videos, and adjusted late charges.

TABLE 13-5	RingUpMember Error Constants

Error Constant	Value	Description
posNoError	0	No error occurred.
posErrIncorrectBalance	1	Computed balance due does not match amount collected from customer.
posErrVideoRented	2	One of the videos is already rented.
posErrUnknownError	100	Some other error occurred.

Case Study: Using the Shared Property Manager

The *Mom-n-Pop Video Store* data services layer makes use of the *Shared Property Manager*, introduced in the previous chapter. The *VideoData* component uses the *Shared Property Manager* to save the late fee for the video store. The value is often referenced by code both in the object model and in the data services layer, but does not generally change. Storing it as a property using the *Shared Property Manager* saves database accesses. Related code follows:

```
Public Function GetLateFee() As Currency

    '- Get late fee from database and return to caller.

    Dim objContext As ObjectContext
    Set objContext = GetObjectContext()

    '- Use the Shared Property Manager to save this value
    '- so that we don't have to keep going to the database
    '- to get it.

    Dim objSPM As SharedPropertyGroupManager
    Dim objSPMGroup As SharedPropertyGroup
    Dim objLateFeeProp As SharedProperty
    Dim bExists As Boolean

    Set objSPM = New SharedPropertyGroupManager
    Set objSPMGroup = objSPM.CreatePropertyGroup _
                      ("MomPopSharedProps", _
                       LockSetGet, _
                       Process, _
                       bExists)

    Set objLateFeeProp = objSPMGroup.CreateProperty _
                      ("LateFee", bExists)

    '- If property was created, look up late fee
    '- in the database.  Otherwise, return value.

    If Not bExists Then

        '- Find late fee from database.

        Dim RS As New Recordset
        Dim nLateFee As Currency

        RS.Open "Select Fee From LateFee", _
```

```
                    gstrConnectString, _
                    adOpenStatic, _
                    adLockReadOnly, _
                    adCmdText

        nLateFee = RS.Fields("Fee").Value
        RS.Close

        '- Write late fee to shared property.

        objLateFeeProp.Value = nLateFee

    Else

        '- Return late fee from shared property.

        nLateFee = objLateFeeProp.Value

    End If

    '- Done.

    If Not objContext Is Nothing Then
        objContext.SetComplete
    End If

    GetLateFee = nLateFee

End Function
```

Object Interaction Scenario – Finding a Member by ID

The diagram shown in Figure 13-1 is a **sequence diagram** (often used in object-oriented design), which shows the interaction between objects given a scenario. In this case, the diagram illustrates what happens when the following code is executed from a client in the presentation layer:

```
Dim objMember As Member
Set objMember = FindMemberByID (12001)
```

Descriptions of each step appear in the following paragraphs. I will also trace through the code involved in renting videos to a member. The following steps correspond to the sequence diagram:

1. Code in the presentation layer invokes *FindMemberByID*. This is a method of the global object *VideoStore*, so it looks like a global function.

2. The *VideoStore* object creates a *MemberData* object, which is an MTS component.

3. A *MemberData* object is returned to the *VideoStore* object.

4. The *FindByID* method is invoked on the *MemberData* object.

5. The *FindByID* method creates an SQL *Select* statement to create a recordset containing fields that describe the member. The query is submitted to the database through ADO.

6. ADO returns a *Recordset* object to the *MemberData* object.

7. The *MemberData* object returns a disassociated recordset to the *VideoStore* object.

8. The *VideoStore* object creates a *Member* object.

9. A *Member* object is returned to the *VideoStore* object.

10. Using the fields in the returned disassociated recordset, the *VideoStore* object sets properties of the newly created *Member* object.

11. The *Member* object is returned to the presentation layer.

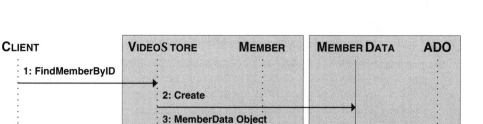

CLIENT	VIDEOSTORE	MEMBER	MEMBERDATA	ADO

1: FindMemberByID

2: Create

3: MemberData Object

4: FindByID

5: SELECT

6: Recordset

7: Recordset (Disassociated)

8: Create

9: Member Object

10: Set Properties

11: Member Object

OBJECT MODEL   **MTS**

FIGURE 13-1   Object interaction scenario for looking up a member by member ID.

Case Study: Performing a Rental Transaction

To perform the primary transaction of the video store, ultimately the *RingUpMember* method of the *PointOfSale* MTS component must be executed. From the Win32 client program (*MPV3UI.EXE*), this is made somewhat easier since this UI program uses the middle tier object model. The steps that must occur if using the object model are as follows:

1. A *Member* object must be created for the member that is renting videos.
2. Each candidate rental must be added to the *NewRentals* collection of the *Member* object.
3. Each video to be returned must be added to the *Returns* collection of the *Member* object.
4. The balance must be computed, which includes both charges for new rentals and any outstanding late charges from the member. In the object model, this amount can be computed by invoking the *ComputeBalance* method of the *Member* object. Note that this method does not commit

any changes to the database, although objects from the data services layer are involved in this computation.

5. Finally, the *RingUp* method is invoked on the *Member* object, passing the amount collected. This method, in turn, invokes the *RingUpMember* method of the *PointOfSale* MTS component.

CREATING A MEMBER OBJECT

To get a *Member* object that represents the member renting videos, the user interface uses the *FindMemberByID* method of the *VideoStore* object. Since the *VideoStore* object is a top-level object, the UI code does not need to explicitly reference the object. Instead, *FindMemberByID* appears as a global function.

To create a *Member* object, code in the Win32 user interface client application uses the following code, which appears directly in the user interface program:

```
Private Sub FindMember()
    Screen.MousePointer = vbHourglass
    On Error GoTo CannotFindMember
    Set objMember = FindMemberByID(nMemberid)
    txtMemberName.Text = objMember.LastName & ", " & _
                         objMember.FirstName
    Screen.MousePointer = 0
    Exit Sub

CannotFindMember:
    Screen.MousePointer = 0
    If Err.Number = vseNoSuchMember Then
        MsgBox "No such member", vbExclamation, _
               "Video Store"
        Set objMember = Nothing
        Exit Sub
    Else
        Err.Raise Err.Number
    End If
End Sub
```

The *FindMemberByID* method of the *VideoStore* object (invoked above by the Win32 client) uses the *MemberData* object of the data services layer to locate information about the member. The *MemberData* object returns a disassociated recordset containing the member's information. The *Member* object copies fields from this recordset into properties of the *Member* object. Note that the *FindMemberByID* method creates a *MemberData* object as soon as it is needed, then keeps the same instance for the life of the program. This is the recommended approach to managing the lifetime of a data services layer object. MTS, remember, handles the just-in-time activation and reactivation of the object.

Continuing with the trace of the rental transaction, the previously listed code, which appears in the presentation layer, invokes the following code, which is defined in the object model, specifically in the *VideoStore* class module:

```
Public Function FindMemberByID(ByVal nMemberID As Long) _
                        As Member

    '- Find and return member with this member id,
    '- using object in Data Services layer.

    If gobjMemberData Is Nothing Then
        Set gobjMemberData = New MPV3DAT.MemberData
    End If

    Dim RS As Recordset
    Set RS = gobjMemberData.FindByID(nMemberID)

    If RS.EOF And RS.BOF Then
        RS.Close
        Set FindMemberByID = Nothing
        Err.Raise vseNoSuchMember, "Members", _
                "Member does not exist"
    End If

    '- Copy Member's information into object and return.

    Dim M As New Member
    CopyMemberRsToMemberObj M, RS
    RS.Close

    Set FindMemberByID = M

End Function
```

Note that the code shown above, which is contained in the object model, uses a *MemberData* object *(gobjMemberData)*. The *MemberData* object, located in the data services layer, creates an SQL *Select* statement to locate the indicated member when its *FindByID* method is invoked. This recordset is passed back to the object model as a disassociated recordset. When this recordset is returned to the presentation layer (in the above listed code), a general procedure, *CopyMemberRsTo-MemberObj*, copies fields of the recordset to an instance of a *Member* object, a stateful object defined in the object model. This procedure will be analyzed shortly.

Following is the *FindByID* method of the *MemberData* object, defined in the data services layer:

```
Public Function FindByID(ByVal nMemberID As Long) _
                          As Recordset

    '- Find member with this ID

    Dim objContext As ObjectContext
    Set objContext = GetObjectContext()

    Dim RS As New Recordset
    Dim strSQL As String

    strSQL = "Select * From Members Where MemberID = " _
            & Str(nMemberID)

    '- Make a recordset that we can pass up
    '- to the Object Model or ASP UI layer

    RS.CursorLocation = adUseClient
    RS.Open strSQL, _
            gstrConnectString, _
            adOpenStatic, _
            adLockReadOnly, _
            adCmdText

    '- Done

    If Not objContext Is Nothing Then
        objContext.SetComplete
    End If

    Set FindByID = RS
    Set RS = Nothing

End Function
```

Continuing the trace of a rental transaction, the above listed code returns back to the *VideoStore* class module in the object model, where fields of the recordset returned by the *MemberData* object are copied to properties of a *Member* object. A helper function, ***CopyMemberRsToMemberObj***, is used for this purpose, as follows:

```
Public Sub CopyMemberRsToMemberObj(M As Member, _
                            ByVal RS As Recordset)

    '* Copies fields from a recordset created from the
    '* members table to a member object

    M.SetID RS.Fields("MemberID").Value
    M.FirstName = RS.Fields("FirstName").Value
    M.LastName = RS.Fields("LastName").Value
    M.Address1 = RS.Fields("Address1").Value
    M.Address2 = RS.Fields("Address2").Value & ""
    M.City = RS.Fields("City").Value
    M.State = RS.Fields("State").Value
    M.Zip = RS.Fields("Zip").Value
    M.Phone = RS.Fields("Phone").Value

End Sub
```

ADDING TO THE NEWRENTALS COLLECTION

As the client application user adds to the list of videos to be rented by the member, code in the presentation layer adds a *Pick* object to the *NewRentals* collection of the *Member* object. The presentation layer code uses a helper function, *AddNewTitle*, to insert the candidate rental into the member's *NewRentals* collection. Recall that *NewRentals* is actually a property that provides access to a *Picks* object, which is a collection of *Pick* objects.

The general procedure, *AddNewTitle*, defined in the Win32 client application, is as follows:

```
Private Sub AddNewTitle()
    ' Add candidate rental to member's new rental pick list
    Dim nCopyNo As Integer

    nCopyNo = txtCopyNo.Text

    objMember.NewRentals.Add objVideo, nCopyNo

    ' Add candidate rental to list view

    Dim L As ListItem

    Set L = lvNewRentals.ListItems.Add(, , Str(objVideo.ID))
    L.SubItems(1) = txtCopyNo.Text
    L.SubItems(2) = objVideo.Title
    L.SubItems(3) = Format(objVideo.Price, "0.00")

    fTxnInProgress = True

End Sub
```

In the object model, the *Add* method of the *Picks* collection (invoked via the expression *objMember.NewRentals.Add*) creates a new *Pick* object and adds it to an internal collection. Note that *state* (in this case, a list of new rentals) is held in the object model and not in the data services layer. The data services layer is not involved as candidate rentals are added to the *NewRentals* collection of a *Member* object. Similar code is used to add videos to the *Returns* collection of the *Member* object.

Following is the *Add* method of the *Picks* collection, which is defined in the object model and is invoked by code in the Win32 client:

```
Public Sub Add(PickObject As Object, CopyNo As Integer)

    '- Cache away the price and title of video.

    Dim nID As Long
    Dim nPrice As Currency
    Dim strTitle As String

    If TypeOf PickObject Is Video Then
        Dim V As Video
        Set V = PickObject
        nID = V.ID
        nPrice = V.Price
        strTitle = V.Title
    Else
        Dim RV As RentedVideo
        Set RV = PickObject
        nID = RV.VideoID
        nPrice = 0
        strTitle = RV.Title
    End If

    '- Create a new Pick object, set its properties,
    '- and add it to the Picks collection.

    Dim objNewPick As New Pick
    objNewPick.SetVideoID nID
    objNewPick.SetCopyNo CopyNo
    objNewPick.SetPrice nPrice
    objNewPick.SetTitle strTitle

    mcolPicks.Add objNewPick

End Sub
```

COMPUTING THE BALANCE FOR THE TRANSACTION

When the user clicks the *Finish* button in the user interface, the balance for the transaction is computed. The balance is computed using the *ComputeBalance* method of the *Member* object. This method returns a *Details* object, which contains *Detail* items. The *Member, Details,* and *Detail* objects are all defined in the object model. *Detail* items can be displayed back to the point-of-sale operator to confirm the details of a transaction before committing. Only related code from the presentation layer is shown below; some code is omitted for clarity:

```
Private Sub cmdFinish_Click()
        .
        .
        .
    '- Compute balance and create Point-of-Sale form
    '- to finalize transaction

    Dim objDetails As Details
    Dim objDetail As Detail
    Dim lvDetails As ListView
    Dim L As ListItem
    Dim nTotal As Currency

    objMember.ComputeBalance objDetails

    '- Move each detail to a ListView item

    Load frmPOS
    Set lvDetails = frmPOS.lvDetails

    For Each objDetail In objDetails
        Set L = lvDetails.ListItems.Add(, , _
                            Str(objDetail.ItemID))
        L.SubItems(1) = objDetail.Code
        L.SubItems(2) = objDetail.Description
        L.SubItems(3) = Format(objDetail.Amount, _
                            "Currency")
    Next

    nTotal = objDetails.Total
    frmPOS.lblBalanceDue = Format(nTotal, "Currency")
    frmPOS.lblAmountTendered = Format(nTotal, "Currency")
        .
        .
        .
End Sub
```

When the *ComputeBalance* method of the *Member* object is invoked, all necessary information for renting the new videos has been cached away in properties of the *Pick* objects in the *NewRentals* collection. However, to calculate the late charges due a member, the *ComputeBalance* method references the *LateCharges* collection, which needs to access code in the data services layer.

Following is the *ComputeBalance* method of the *Member* object, which is defined in the object model:

```
Public Function ComputeBalance _
      (ByRef objDetails As Details) As Currency

   Dim nTotal As Currency
   Dim objDetail As Detail
   Dim strDesc As String
   Dim objPick As Pick

   Set objDetails = New Details

   For Each objPick In Me.NewRentals
      Set objDetail = New Detail
      objDetail.SetItemID objPick.VideoID
      objDetail.SetCode "N"
      objDetail.SetDescription "RENT: " & objPick.Title
      objDetail.SetAmount objPick.Price
      objDetails.Add objDetail
      nTotal = nTotal + objPick.Price
   Next

   '- Now compute late charges

   Dim LC As LateCharge

   For Each LC In Me.LateCharges
      Set objDetail = New Detail
      objDetail.SetItemID LC.VideoID
      objDetail.SetCode "L"
      objDetail.SetDescription "LATE: " & LC.Title
      objDetail.SetAmount LC.Charge
      objDetails.Add objDetail
      nTotal = nTotal + LC.Charge
   Next

   '- Return total as function result

   ComputeBalance = nTotal

End Function
```

COMPUTING LATE CHARGES

When the *LateCharges* collection of the *Member* object is referenced, a new collection of *LateCharge* objects is created. The late charges are obtained in the object model by invoking the *GetLateVideos* method of the *MemberData* object, which is a data services layer object. The data is returned from the data services layer as a disassociated recordset.

The *LateCharges* collection is exposed via the *LateCharges* property of the *Member* object. The collection is not built until the *LateCharges* property is accessed. Following is the *Property Get* procedure for the *LateCharges* property of the *Member* object, which is defined in the object model:

```
Public Property Get LateCharges() As LateCharges

    Dim RS As New Recordset
    Dim LC As LateCharge

    Set mvarLateCharges = New LateCharges

    '- Using an object in the Data Services Layer, get a
    '- recordset that consists of Late Charges.

    Set RS = gobjMemberData.GetLateVideos _
                    (Me.ID, _
                     GetTodaysDate)
    RS.Open

    '- Add each late charge record to the LateCharges
    '- collection.

    Dim nDaysLate As Integer
    Dim nLateCharge As Currency

    Do While Not RS.EOF
        Set LC = New LateCharge
        CopyLateChargeRsToLateChargeObj LC, RS
        ComputeLateCharge GetTodaysDate, LC.DateDue, _
                        nDaysLate, nLateCharge
        LC.SetWasReturned (Not IsNull(RS!DateReturned))
        mvarLateCharges.Add LC
        RS.MoveNext
    Loop

    RS.Close

    '- Return this collection.
```

```
Set LateCharges = mvarLateCharges
```

End Property

The above object model code uses the *MemberData* object in the data services layer, which performs a query to return the late charges due a customer. The results are returned by the *MemberData* object's *GetLateVideos* method as a disassociated recordset. Since late charges include both returned and not yet returned videos, a union query is performed that uses both the *LateCharges* and *Rentals* tables.

Note that the *GetLateVideos* method needs to create a *VideoData* object to get the late fee for the video store. This information is available from the *GetLateFee* method of the *VideoData* object. Since the *VideoData* object is an MTS component, the *MemberData* object must use the *CreateInstance* method of the *ObjectContext* object to create the component.

Following is the *GetLateVideos* method of the *MemberData* object, defined in the data services layer:

```
Public Function GetLateVideos(ByVal nMemberID As Long, _
                              ByVal dtTodaysDate As Date) _
                 As Recordset

    Dim objContext As ObjectContext
    Set objContext = GetObjectContext()

    Dim RS As New Recordset
    Dim strSQL As String
    Dim nLateFee As Currency
    Dim objVideoData As VideoData

    '- Get the Late Fee.

    Set objVideoData = objContext.CreateInstance _
                          ("MPV3DAT.VideoData")

    nLateFee = objVideoData.GetLateFee
    Set objVideoData = Nothing

    '- Build first Select statement.

    strSQL = "Select LateCharges.VideoID, MemberID," & _
        "        CopyNo, DateRented, DateDue," & _
        "        DateReturned, DaysLate, Charge, Title" & _
        "   From LateCharges, Videos" & _
        "  Where LateCharges.VideoID = Videos.VideoID" & _
        "    And LateCharges.MemberID = " & Str(nMemberID)
```

```
'- Add the second Select statement, which creates a
'- query of videos not yet returned by which are late.

strSQL = strSQL & _
    "Union " & _
    "Select Rentals.VideoID, MemberID, " & _
    " CopyNo, DateRented, DateDue, NULL, " & _
    " DateDiff(day,DateDue,'" & dtTodaysDate & "'), " & _
    " DateDiff(day,DateDue,'" & dtTodaysDate & "') * " & _
        Str(nLateFee) & ", " & _
    "    Title " & _
    "  From Rentals, Videos " & _
    " Where Rentals.VideoID = Videos.VideoID " & _
    "   And Rentals.MemberID = " & Str(nMemberID) & _
    "   And DateDue < '" & _
            Format(dtTodaysDate, "Short Date") & "'"

'- Execute the SQL Select statement.

RS.CursorLocation = adUseClient
RS.Open strSQL, _
        gstrConnectString, _
        adOpenStatic, _
        adLockReadOnly, _
        adCmdText

'- Done. -'

If Not objContext Is Nothing Then
    objContext.SetComplete
End If

RS.Close
Set GetLateVideos = RS
Set RS = Nothing


End Function
```

FINALIZING THE TRANSACTION

Once the details and balance of the transaction have been computed and presented, the user clicks the *OK* button on the *Point of Sale* form to finalize the transaction. This causes code in the presentation layer to execute the *RingUp* method of the *Member* object. The *Member* object's *RingUp* method, in turn, invokes the *RingUpMember* method of the *PointOfSale* object, which is a data services layer object. To invoke this method, the *Pick* objects in the *NewRentals* collection must be converted to a two-dimensional variant array so that they can all be passed as a single parameter to the *PointOfSale* object.

Following is the *RingUp* method of the *Member* object, which is defined in the object model:

```
Public Sub RingUp(ByVal nTotalCollected As Currency)

    '- Build the array of videos to be returned.  This must
    '- be a two-dimensional variant array containing a list
    '- of Video IDs and Copy Numbers.

    Dim i As Integer
    Dim nReturns As Integer
    nReturns = Me.Returns.Count

    ReDim vReturnPicks(nReturns, 2) As Variant

    For i = 1 To nReturns
        vReturnPicks(i, 0) = Me.Returns.Item(i).VideoID
        vReturnPicks(i, 1) = Me.Returns.Item(i).CopyNo
    Next

    '- Now build the array of videos to be returned.  This
    '- array has the same format as the previous one.

    Dim nRentals As Integer
    nRentals = Me.NewRentals.Count

    ReDim vRentalPicks(nRentals, 2) As Variant

    For i = 1 To nRentals
        vRentalPicks(i, 0) = Me.NewRentals.Item(i).VideoID
        vRentalPicks(i, 1) = Me.NewRentals.Item(i).CopyNo
    Next

    '- Now ringup this transaction using a PointOfSale
    '- object, which is defined in the Data Services
    '- Layer.
```

```
      Dim nErrCode As Integer

      If gobjPointOfSale Is Nothing Then
          Set gobjPointOfSale = New MPV3DAT.PointOfSale
      End If

      nErrCode = gobjPointOfSale.RingUpMember _
                          (Me.ID, _
                           vRentalPicks, _
                           vReturnPicks, _
                           nTotalCollected, _
                           GetTodaysDate)

      '- Check return code for success.

      If nErrCode <> posNoError Then
          If nErrCode = posErrIncorrectBalance Then
              Err.Raise vseIncorrectAmount, _
                      "VideoStore.Member", _
                      "Transaction balance is incorrect"
          ElseIf nErrCode = posErrVideoRented Then
              Err.Raise vseAlreadyRented, _
                      "VideoStore.Member", _
                      "One or more videos already rented"
          Else
              Err.Raise vseUnknownError, _
                      "VideoStore.Member", _
                      "Unknown Data Services Layer Error"
          End If
      End If

End Sub
```

Finally, the *RingUp* method of the *PointOfSale* object, which is a data services layer object, executes. This code actually records the transaction in the database. This method is lengthy and uses helper functions to accomplish many of the tasks. The helper functions are not shown in this book; you can load the project to view all related code if you wish.

Following is the *RingUpMember* method of the *PointOfSale* object, defined in the data services layer:

```
Public Function RingUpMember _
              (ByVal nMemberID As Long, _
               ByVal vRentalPicks As Variant, _
               ByVal vReturnPicks As Variant, _
```

```
                    ByVal nAmtCollected As Currency, _
                    ByVal dtToday As Date) As Integer

'- Establish an error handler, then create a VideoData
'- object, and a MemberData object, both of which are
'- used by this object.  Since these objects must be
'- managed by MTS, we use ObjectContext.CreateInstance
'- to create them.

Dim objContext As ObjectContext
Set objContext = GetObjectContext()

On Error GoTo CannotRingUp

If Not objContext Is Nothing Then
    Set objVideoData = objContext.CreateInstance _
                                ("MPV3DAT.VideoData")
    Set objMemberData = objContext.CreateInstance _
                                ("MPV3DAT.MemberData")
Else
    Set objVideoData = New VideoData
    Set objMemberData = New MemberData
End If

'- Open connection to database.  If we are not running
'- under MTS, we start our own transaction.

Set objConnection = New Connection
objConnection.Open gstrConnectString

If objContext Is Nothing Then objConnection.BeginTrans

'- Return all the videos in the Return Picks array,
'- then compute late charges.

Dim nLateCharges As Currency
ReturnAllVideos nMemberID, vReturnPicks, dtToday
nLateCharges = GetLateCharges(nMemberID, dtToday)

'- Rent all the videos in the Rental Picks array, then
'- make sure the balance collected matches the total
'- amount due.

Dim nTotal As Currency
Dim nRentalCharges As Currency
nRentalCharges = RentAllVideos(nMemberID, _
```

```
                                            vRentalPicks, _
                                            dtToday)

        nTotal = nLateCharges + nRentalCharges

        If nTotal <> nAmtCollected Then

            '- Since amount collected does not match amount
            '- due, we cannot complete the transaction.  If
            '- we are not running under MTS, we abort our
            '- own transaction.
            '- Otherwise, we call SetAbort.

            RingUpMember = posErrIncorrectBalance

            If Not objContext Is Nothing Then
                objContext.SetAbort
            Else
                objConnection.RollbackTrans
                objConnection.Close
                Set objConnection = Nothing
            End If

            Exit Function

        End If

        '- Remove all late charges from the LateCharges
        '- table for this member, since they have been
        '- paid.  Also, for any late videos not yet
        '- returned, change their due dates to today, since
        '- late fees to date for these videos have also
        '- been paid.

        RemoveLateCharges nMemberID
        AdjustDueDates nMemberID, dtToday

        '- Done.  Disconnect from database and release
        '- VideoData and MemberData objects.  If we are
        '- running under MTS, tell MTS that our work
        '- completed successfully, otherwise we commit
        '- our own transaction.

        If Not objContext Is Nothing Then
            objContext.SetComplete
        Else
```

```
         objConnection.CommitTrans
         objConnection.Close
         Set objConnection = Nothing
      End If

      Set objVideoData = Nothing
      Set objMemberData = Nothing

      RingUpMember = posNoError        ' 0=Success Code
      Exit Function

CannotRingUp:

      '- Error raised.  If running under MTS, tell MTS that
      '- our work completed unsuccessfully.  Otherwise, we
      '- abort our own transaction.

      If Not objContext Is Nothing Then
          objContext.SetAbort
      Else
          objConnection.RollbackTrans
          objConnection.Close
          Set objConnection = Nothing
      End If

      Set objMemberData = Nothing
      Set objVideoData = Nothing

      If Err.Number = vbObjectError + 3604 Then
          RingUpMember = posErrVideoRented
      Else
          Err.Raise Err.Number, Err.Source, Err.Description
      End If

End Function
```

Maintenance of N-Tier Client/Server Applications

In many respects, maintenance of multi-tiered client/server applications is easier than the maintenance of monolithic desktop applications, since there is typically a central location for the installation of the middleware. When the middleware is updated on the server, all installed clients will automatically start using the new middleware. However, in other respects, maintenance of multi-tiered client/server applications is more challenging for the same reasons it is easier! In particular, since the tiers of a multi-tiered application are compiled and built separately, it is essential that interface compatibility be maintained. In this chapter, you will look carefully at the tools and technologies provided by Visual Basic and COM that help you maintain interface compatibility. You will also examine techniques used to troubleshoot problems in the middleware using the Visual Basic debugger.

Also in this chapter, I'll introduce you to the new *Visual Studio Analyzer* tool, which can be useful for locating bottlenecks in an N-tier client/server application.

Modifying a COM Server

At some point, it will become necessary for you to make changes to an installed COM server (ActiveX Component). Naturally, bugs will need to be fixed, and new features will need to be added. Before you make changes to an installed server with an installed client base, you must be aware of the types of changes that can be made, and how to make them.

Compatible and Incompatible Changes

There are certain changes that you must never make to an installed server. Remember, when the server is changed, you potentially affect existing, installed clients. Whether or not these existing clients are obsoleted depends on the type of changes made. Changes to the server fall into two broad categories: compatible changes and incompatible changes. A **compatible** change to the server allows existing clients to use the new server without having to change or reinstall the client. An **incompatible** change to the server prohibits existing clients from using the new server. In this case, you'll have to uninstall the old client(s) and rebuild and reinstall new clients.

Broadly speaking, most bug fixes fall into the category of compatible changes, provided the fix involves only the implementation of one or more methods and not the interfaces of these methods. For example, if you discover that a method has an error in logic, you can change that logic and maintain compatibility with existing client applications, provided no changes are made in the parameters of the method. On the other hand, if you discover that one of the parameters of a method should have been, for example, a double instead of an integer, such a change would make existing clients incompatible with the new server.

In general, you can add new properties, methods, and events to a server and remain compatible with existing clients, although many hard-core COM developers disagree, stating that such modifications break the interface immutability rules of COM. The disagreement is largely between C++/ATL and Visual Basic COM developers. A C++/ATL developer can add new procedures to a COM interface, provided new ones appear at the end of the vtable (the table of pointers to interface functions) and new dispatch IDs (if a dispatch interface is provided) are generated. If the new method is inserted into the middle of the vtable, and/or the new method uses the same dispatch ID as a previously released method, the new interface will be incompatible with existing clients. Visual Basic will automatically place new interface methods at the end of its generated vtable and will create new dispatch IDs for new methods, retaining the old ones. It is a lot easier for a C++/ATL developer to make a mistake while attempting to maintain compatibility.

Creating New Interfaces

Most C++/ATL developers are aware of how to maintain compatibility with old clients when adding new features to an existing COM server. However, even with this knowledge in hand, many C++/ATL developers insist it is fragile to add new features using this approach. While an existing client application, which is already compiled, cannot access the new features of a server, it's the flip side that raises an issue. Problems arise when an old version of the server is incorrectly installed on a machine on which new clients have been installed. Such client applications, when accessing the new functions of a server, will jump past the ends of their vtables, probably resulting in a memory violation. The solution to the problem is to develop a new interface for the new server, and use interface inheritance to maintain compatibility with existing clients. Typically, the new interface is given a unique number – for example, you may have an interface called *IVideo*, and call the new interface *IVideo2*. The new server implements the old interface, while providing an implementation of the new interface. Existing clients ask for the old interface, while newly developed clients accessing the new features of the server ask for the new interface. Since the old server does not implement the new interface, new clients cannot accidentally access an old server. If such a situation arises, COM will report an error to the client at the time of object creation – the error will indicate that the object does not support the requested interface.

In evaluating both sides of the argument for adding new functionality to a server, you must place the issues in context. Developers of commercial software, in which there may be a large existing client base, must take the matter more seriously than a typical developer of corporate software. Depending on the level of administrative control you have over the deployment, maintenance, and version control of software, the possibility of having an old version of a server incorrectly installed on a machine may be small. It is simply a matter of using caution when upgrading servers. On the other hand, many developers of corporate software have a large base of client application developers who use COM servers developed in-house; such developers may have little or no control over the installation and supervision of server upgrades. If you fall into this category, you may want to consider avoiding adding new functionality to an existing server. Instead, use interface inheritance to create a new interface that contains the new features while maintaining compatibility with existing clients. Be aware, however, that implementing such a solution is tedious and time-consuming. If you don't have to use this solution, my recommendation would be to avoid it – simply add new features to your Visual Basic COM server and make sure that an old server is never installed on the same machine as a new client.

A key phrase to use here is "binary compatibility." Without binary compatibility, each and every change to the server may result in new library, class, and interface IDs being generated. Options other than *Binary Compatibility* are really only intended for use during the initial development of the server and its clients. If you must make an incompatible change and do not want to "break" existing clients, it is recommended that you do so in a new copy of the server, giving the new server a completely new name. Note that if you make compatible changes to the server, existing clients cannot use the new features of the server, unless you rebuild those clients.

Levels of Version Compatibility

There are three levels of version compatibility. Version-identical compatibility indicates that the interfaces are all the same. That is, the server has all the same public classes, and all these classes have the same properties, methods, and events. Note that code internal to the procedures may have changed, as in a bug fix, for example, but this still means version-identical. Version-compatible compatibility means that objects, properties, methods, and/or events have been added to the server, but existing objects still retain the old properties, methods, and events. Existing clients can use the new server—although not its new features. Version-incompatible means that the interface to at least one property, method, or event that existed in the old server has been changed, or has been completely removed or renamed. Existing client applications that have references to the component cannot use the new version.

Version-Identical Interfaces

Clearly, there is a possibility of discovering a bug in a server at some point following installation, and existing clients are using it. Consider the COM server presented in Chapter 11. If you had a bug in, for example, the *Property Let* procedure for the property *Echo*, you could go into the code and fix the bug. After recompiling the new server, you would end up with a version-identical interface. It's considered version-identical because you did not add any properties, methods, or events, or change the interface to any existing ones. In other words, internal changes to server code typically result in a version-identical interface. As another example, you may "tweak" a property procedure or method to improve performance. Again, if you don't change the interface, you'll have a version-identical interface.

If, however, you decide to add a parameter to an existing method, you would be changing the interface, and therefore would not have a version-identical interface – this would be an example of a version-incompatible interface. As another example, if you were to add a completely new method or property, then you would again be changing the interface, and you would not have a version-identical interface – but, since you added a property or method, this would be considered a version-compatible interface.

Note that you should still update the version number of your server when making version-identical changes (use automatic version incrementing). This ensures that the setup programs for applications that use your component will replace old versions during setup.

Version-Compatible Interfaces

If you were to add a new class to your server, this would be an example of creating a version-compatible interface. It's considered version-compatible because existing clients would be unaffected by the addition of the new class. They would, of course, continue to use the existing classes that were there before you added the new class.

As another example, you can add new properties, methods, and events to existing classes, and still have what's considered a version-compatible interface. Existing clients continue to use only the properties, methods, and events that existed before you made the additions. Again, always increment the version number of the COM server when it is rebuilt – it's recommended that you use automatic version incrementing.

Version-Incompatible Interfaces

Lastly, there are version-incompatible interfaces. A version-incompatible interface results when you make changes to the server that make it impossible for the existing clients to use the new server. Consider, for example, changing a method so that it requires an additional parameter. Existing clients would not, of course, be passing that additional parameter. If existing clients were to be able to invoke this method, without passing the additional parameter, the results on your server would be unpredictable, probably resulting in a severe failure.

Clearly, you want to avoid version-incompatible interfaces. If you are using binary compatibility, Visual Basic will warn you if you make an incompatible change. If you ignore these warnings and proceed, you will have broken existing clients. In this case, you'll have to rebuild the existing clients, create a new setup program for the newly rebuilt clients, uninstall the old clients from each system, and run the new setup program on each system to install the newly rebuilt clients. If you don't follow this procedure after having made an incompatible change to the server, existing clients will no longer be able to use the server. They will get an error when attempting to start the server.

Every large project, unless it has gone through very careful planning, will probably have to suffer through one or two of these version-incompatible changes. Once you've had to go through one, it's doubtful that you'll want to go through it again.

The following types of changes will break compatibility with existing clients:

1. Changing the project name.
2. Changing the name of an existing public class.
3. Removing a public class module.
4. Changing a public class to a private class.
5. Deleting a public variable from a public class module.
6. Deleting a public procedure (method) from a public class module.
7. Deleting a property procedure from a public class module.
8. Changing the data type of a public variable (property) in a public class module.
9. Changing the data type of a public function (method) in a public class module.
10. Changing the data type of a property procedure in a public class module.
11. Changing the name of a parameter in a method or property procedure in a public class module.
12. Changing the type of a parameter in a method or property procedure in a public class module.
13. Changing the order of parameters in a method or property procedure in a public class module.
14. Changing the number of parameters in a method or property procedure in a public class module.

The rules for determining whether or not a change will result in an incompatible change do not consider whether or not existing clients have actually used the property, method, or event you are changing. For example, assume that you have a method in a server that an existing client does not currently use, and you remove that method. The question is, is the existing client able to use the new server? After all, it wasn't using the method that was changed! The answer is that it's an incompatible change. Visual Basic does not attempt to analyze an existing client to see if it might be affected by the change. In short, if you make any of the changes listed above, the new server is incompatible and existing clients won't be able to use it, even if careful analysis reveals that they would not actually have been affected by the change.

Version Compatibility Options

On the *Component* tab of the *Project Properties* dialog, you will find a set of options for version compatibility. These choices are *No Compatibility, Project Compatibility*, and *Binary Compatibility*. The first two options, *No Compatibility* and *Project Compatibility*, can be set at any time. The *Binary Compatibility* option can only be set after you have built the server at least once, and requires that you select the existing EXE or DLL of your server as a reference for a compatible ActiveX Component (COM server). The setting actually has no effect until the next time you rebuild the server.

The version compatibility options were introduced in Visual Basic 5.0 and have caused a great deal of confusion among Visual Basic developers since then. Part of the confusion arises from the fact that the features provided by this option are complex by nature. Another source of confusion stems from the fact that bugs related to the implementation of this feature have plagued Microsoft – fixes to the *Binary Compatibility* option were present in every service pack released for Visual Basic 5.0. Finally, even when binary compatibility *did* work, how it behaved was confusing enough for Microsoft to have changed its behavior in Visual Basic 6.0 – again adding to the confusion surrounding this option. And, problems with the new implementation presented themselves no sooner than the release of Visual Basic 6.0 – so, to observe the behavior of the option as described in this book, be sure that you have installed the latest service pack of Visual Basic 6.0.

Using Project Compatibility

The *Project Compatibility* setting is the default version compatibility option, and should be the one a developer uses during the development of an ActiveX Component. The setting is especially ideal when a client test application is part of the same project group as the ActiveX Component. With project compatibility, the same library, class, and interfaces IDs are used each time you make a version-compatible change to the server. If you use a project reference to your server in a client that is part of the same project group as your server, the client application is recompiled against the new server, even if a version-incompatible change is made to the server.

When a version-incompatible change is made to the server, as when, for example, a method's parameters change, using the *Project Compatibility* option results in Visual Basic creating a new interface ID for the object that supports the method. The object's class ID and the server's library ID will remain the same in this case. Visual Basic does not retain the old interface ID in the registry, nor does the new version of the server implement the old interface. Thus, making a version-incompatible change to the server will cause already compiled clients to fail during the creation of any object with a changed interface. A Visual Basic client will receive error number 430 in this case, indicating that the object does not support the requested interface. However, since the library has the same ID, client projects will not have a missing library reference, as is the case when the *No Compatibility* option is used – this option is discussed in a later section.

When the *Project Compatibility* option is used, you are not warned when you are about to build a new version of a COM server for which you have made a version-incompatible change. Remember that it is typical for a developer to make a number of changes to a COM server's interfaces during development. You would not want to have to dismiss a warning dialog every time you compiled a version of your server as it is being developed. You must understand that, by selecting the *Project Compatibility* option for version compatibility, you are, in effect, stating that you are still developing the server, and are not yet concerned about retaining compatibility with existing clients. Once the interfaces of your server have stabilized, you will normally build a version of your server with the *Binary Compatibility* option.

Using Binary Compatibility

Once the interfaces of your COM server have stabilized, it is recommended that you immediately switch the version compatibility option to *Binary Compatibility* and rebuild the server. This setting requires that you select an already compiled EXE or DLL as a benchmark that Visual Basic uses to verify that future modifications to your server are version-compatible.

When an ActiveX Component project uses binary compatibility, the server can be compiled as many times as desired – each time the server is compiled, it retains the same library, class, and interface IDs as were used in the benchmark ActiveX Component. If, however, you attempt to compile the server after having made a version-incompatible change, Visual Basic presents a warning dialog, as shown in Figure 14-1.

Although you have three alternatives when you are presented with this dialog, it is my opinion that you should take steps to ensure you never see this dialog in the first place. Certainly the dialog should never come as a surprise. If it is discovered that a version-incompatible change will need to be made, the development team should meet and discuss options. In this meeting, you should discuss alternatives to making the change and assess the impact the change will have on the installed client application base. If a separate team of developers is responsible for client application development, include these developers in the discussion as well. Your options include retiring the old server and creating a new, renamed version of a new server, as well as providing a new version of the server that implements the old interface. However, depending upon the reach of impact, it is often easier to manually break compatibility with old clients prior to making the version-incompatible change. In this case, you will change the server's version compatibility option to *No Compatibility* and rebuild the server. Once this step is performed, existing clients will no longer be able to access the server. You can then switch the version compatibility option to *Project Compatibility* and make the necessary changes to the server while you test the new features with newly compiled (and perhaps newly edited) client applications. When you are satisfied with the changes, you should then switch the version compatibility option back to *Binary Compatibility.* Note that using this approach causes you to return, in effect, back to doing development. In essence, this is exactly what you are doing – certainly if you are changing interfaces, then you must have discovered, although late in the game, a flaw in the original interface design.

If the dialog shown in Figure 14-1 appears, catching you off-guard, there is only one valid option – click the *Cancel* button, which cancels building the server. Undo all changes related to making the version-incompatible change(s), and regroup. Proceeding with either the *Break Compatibility* or *Preserve Compatibility* option may end up with undesirable effects.

To deal with the issue from this dialog, you have two choices – you may break or preserve compatibility. If you choose to **break** compatibility, new interface IDs are generated for the interfaces that have changed. Class and library IDs are preserved. Existing clients that attempt to create objects whose methods have changed will receive error *430* – indicating that the object does not support the requested interface. Note that this is the same behavior as project compatibility.

If you choose to **preserve** compatibility, Visual Basic retains the class, library, and interface IDs used by the benchmark ActiveX Component. Using this option sounds enticing, since existing client applications will still be able to both create objects and obtain interface pointers to those objects, even for interfaces that have changed. The problem, however, is that the new interface pointers will be invalid and incompatible with how the client is compiled. An existing client may, for example, call a method and pass the incorrect number or type of parameters, resulting in a crash either client-side or server-side. Use the *Preserve Compatibility* option only if you are sure that no existing clients are using the new version of the method, or will otherwise be unaffected by the change. Again, this setting is risky and its use is not recommended.

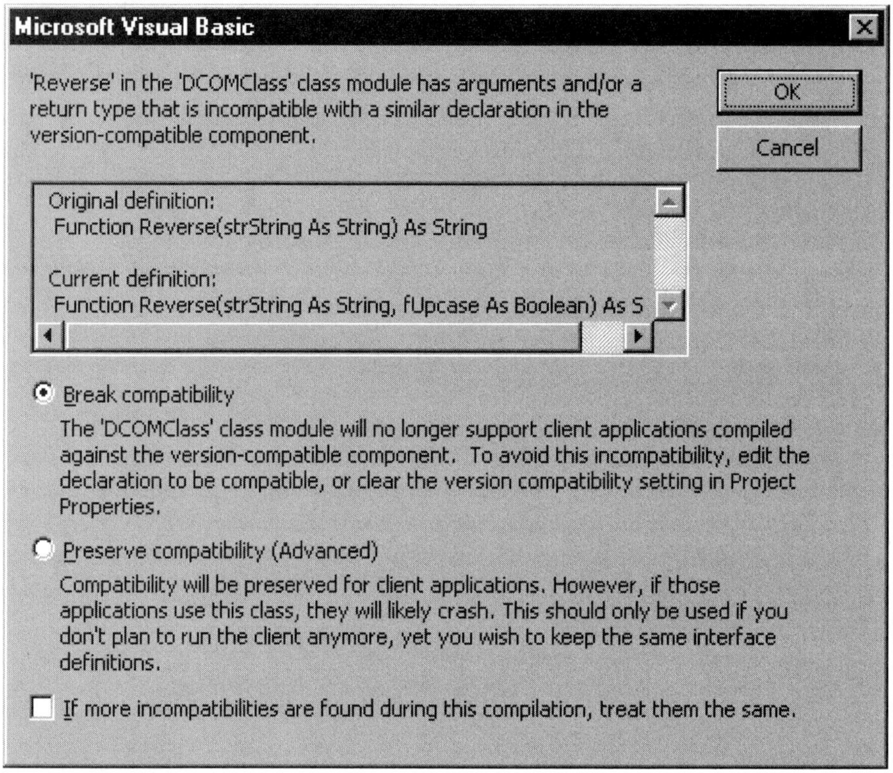

Microsoft Visual Basic   ☒

'Reverse' in the 'DCOMClass' class module has arguments and/or a   ┌─────────┐
return type that is incompatible with a similar declaration in the   │   OK   │
version-compatible component.   └─────────┘
                                                                        ┌─────────┐
                                                                        │ Cancel │
                                                                        └─────────┘

┌──┐
│ Original definition: ▲ │
│ Function Reverse(strString As String) As String   │ │
│   │ │
│ Current definition: │ │
│ Function Reverse(strString As String, fUpcase As Boolean) As S ▼ │
│ ◄ │   ►   │
└──┘

◉ Break compatibility

   The 'DCOMClass' class module will no longer support client applications compiled
   against the version-compatible component. To avoid this incompatibility, edit the
   declaration to be compatible, or clear the version compatibility setting in Project
   Properties.

○ Preserve compatibility (Advanced)

   Compatibility will be preserved for client applications. However, if those
   applications use this class, they will likely crash. This should only be used if you
   don't plan to run the client anymore, yet you wish to keep the same interface
   definitions.

☐ If more incompatibilities are found during this compilation, treat them the same.

FIGURE 14-1   This dialog is presented when you make a version-incompatible change with the binary compatibility set.

Using No Compatibility

When a server is recompiled with the *No Compatibility* option setting for version compatibility, Visual Basic generates new library, class, and interfaces IDs. In all existing client applications, you will see a missing reference to a server's type library. Additionally, existing clients will not be able to create objects hosted by the COM server – they will receive error number *429*, indicating that the object cannot be created.

This setting should be used when you are about to make one or more version-incompatible changes to a server. Properly used, this setting plays an important role in the orderly creation and deployment of a server with one or more new interfaces that are incompatible with existing clients. I recommend building a server with this setting prior to making any version-incompatible changes to the server. After building the server once with this setting, you should change the version compatibility setting to *Project Compatibility*. You can then make as many changes as necessary to the server, knowing that old clients cannot access the new server. Naturally, you must rebuild, and probably edit, existing client applications. Once the new changes have stabilized, change the server's version compatibility setting back to *Binary Compatibility*, and hope that you do not have to go through the exercise again.

When a server's type library receives a new ID, existing client application projects will receive a missing reference to the type library. If you are making version-incompatible changes to a server, this is normal and to be expected. To handle the situation, load the client application project and remove the reference to the old type library using the *References* dialog, available from the *Project* menu. After removing the missing reference, dismiss the *References* dialog by clicking the *OK* button. Then, return to the *References* dialog and select your server's type library. Once you have done this, try to rebuild the client application. If the client application uses any methods whose parameters have changed, the Visual Basic compiler will give you an error. You can edit and correct these method invocations as necessary. Again, be sure that you have returned the server's version compatibility option to *Binary Compatibility* before retrofitting a client to use the new server.

Example: Making a Compatible Change to the Server

As an example of a change that will result in a version-identical interface, assume you wish to concatenate the string *"ECHO"* to the front of the string sent to the *Loopback* event created in the chapter on DCOM. Since the change is made internally and does not affect the interface, the interface is identical to the previous version of the server. If you rebuild the software on the same system on which the server is installed, no further steps are necessary. However, if the server is installed on more than one system, you'll have to make a new *Setup* program and reinstall the server (this is recommended anyway).

Following is an example of the modified code, which results in a version identical-interface:

```
Public Function Reverse(strString As String) As String
    RaiseEvent LoopBack("ECHO: " & strString)
    Reverse = StrReverse(strString)
End Function
```

Example: Making an Incompatible Change to the Server

If, on the other hand, you wanted to add a new parameter to the *Loopback* event, your new server would have a version-incompatible interface. For example, if you added a parameter for the time to the *Loopback* event, then all clients would have to have changes made to their source code to accept the new parameter.

For example, the following version-incompatible changes would need to be made to the server:

```
Option Explicit
Event Loopback(msg As String, t As Date)

Public Function Reverse(strString As String) As String
    RaiseEvent LoopBack(strString, Now)
    Reverse = StrReverse(strString)
End Function
```

Once the above changes are made, existing client applications are no longer compatible with the server's new interface. The following changes would be required to the client's *Loopback* event handler:

```
Private Sub Server_Loopback(msg As String, t As Date)
    txtEcho.Text = Format(t) & ": " & msg
End Sub
```

Using "Implements" to Maintain Server Compatibility

An advanced approach to maintaining server compatibility is to use *Implements* to get interface inheritance. With this approach, your server can implement an interface provided by, for example, version 1 of your class. Later, instead of changing the interface, you can add a new interface, using code common to version 1 if necessary. Using this approach is tedious and should only be applied if you want to prevent new clients from accessing old servers. If you have control over the deployment and version control of clients and servers, you may find it easier to break compatibility with old clients, creating new interface IDs for the modified interfaces, as discussed in the sections that describe the *Project Compatibility* and *Binary Compatibility options*.

Debugging ActiveX Components

The Visual Basic debugger makes it easy to debug COM servers (ActiveX Components). If you suspect there is a bug in your COM server, you can run it under the Visual Basic development environment, setting breakpoints in areas where you suspect the problem may lie. When an ActiveX Component is run under Visual Basic, it waits until a client application creates one of its objects. You can then run a compiled version of the client, or run the client application under a second instance of Visual Basic running on your development machine. You must then reproduce the steps that revealed the bug in the client application; if you have correctly set one or more breakpoints in related code in your server, your server application will reach a breakpoint. You can then examine the variables and step through code in your server to discover the problem.

Debugging Tips

While this all sounds very easy, there are a few pointers to keep in mind. First, if your ActiveX Component is an out-of-process server (ActiveX EXE), make certain that an instance of the server is not already running before running the server under the Visual Basic debugger. Errors in the server can sometimes leave an instance of the server application running on your machine. You can use the *Task Manager* to see if an instance of the server is already running – be sure to check the *processes* list and not the *applications* list. Entries in the *Task Manager's application* list have main windows; your COM server will not show up there. If you find an instance of your server already running, select it and click the *End Process* button to terminate it. Since it is also possible, with an errant server, to have the ActiveX EXE running multiple times, make sure there are no other instances of the server running before starting it under the Visual Basic debugger.

Another consideration is related to timing. If a breakpoint is set in a method of an object implemented in a server, the client application may time out while waiting for the server to send back results. Generally, you can proceed to debug the current method even though the client is timing out. However, if control returns back to the client, as will happen when you exit the method, the client will abort and no further debugging will be possible. If this happens, restart the server application, setting the breakpoint a bit further along in the execution path. Eventually, you will center in on the problem.

When a breakpoint is reached in the server application, you cannot return to the client application. If you attempt to do so, you may receive an error dialog indicating that the *action cannot be completed because a component request is pending*. You may have seen this dialog before; it includes a *Switch To* button that allows you to switch to the server application hosting the busy object. If you receive this dialog unexpectedly, it is probably because your server is sitting at a breakpoint – return to the server application and click the *Resume* button to get it past the breakpoint.

Finally, you must be aware that, to run MTS components using the Visual Basic debugger, you must either be running Windows 2000 (originally known as Windows NT 5.0), or if using Windows NT 4.0, you must have Service Pack 4 installed. As long as either of these conditions are met, running MTS components under the Visual Basic debugger is easy, but is subject to the same limitations discussed in the previous paragraphs. That is, timing may be a problem and you cannot switch back to the client application when your server is stopped at a breakpoint. Also, you must make sure that the *MTS Executive* is not already running your server – shut down the server process in MTS before running it under the Visual Basic debugger. MTS is discussed in Chapters 12 and 13.

Troubleshooting Walkthrough

In the following sections, you will discover and correct a bug that exists in the 2-tier version of the *Mom-n-Pop Video Store*. To build your confidence in troubleshooting and rebuilding COM servers, it is strongly recommended that you follow along with this walkthrough.

Walkthrough: Troubleshooting ActiveX Components

There's at least one known bug in the 2-tier version of the *Mom-n-Pop Video Store* application. It has been left there purposely so that you can use it as a learning exercise (it's fixed in the 3-tier version). If you try to rent the same copy of the same video to a member, the program will abort with an error, since the program attempts to insert a duplicate key into the *Rentals* table. To troubleshoot the problem, you'll load the *MPV2BUS* project into Visual Basic and run it from the Visual Basic development environment. Then, you can use the Visual Basic debugger to troubleshoot the problem.

First, run the released version of the 2-tier *Mom-n-Pop Video Store* user interface (refer to Chapter 1 for information on deploying and running this application). Access the *Rent Videos* dialog, and select a valid member ID. Next, select the same currently available copy of the same video twice, adding each to the list of videos to rent. When you click the *Finish* button, a final confirmation dialog appears – click *OK* on this dialog. This will cause the program to abort with an error that indicates the program attempted to store a record with a duplicate key (see Figure 14-2).

The bug occurs because the user interface application verifies that copies added to a member's new rentals list are available. The user interface makes sure that an already rented copy of a video is not added to this list. However, the copy that you enter twice is not rented – and there is no check to make sure that the same copy is not entered twice in the *New Rentals* list. Note, how-

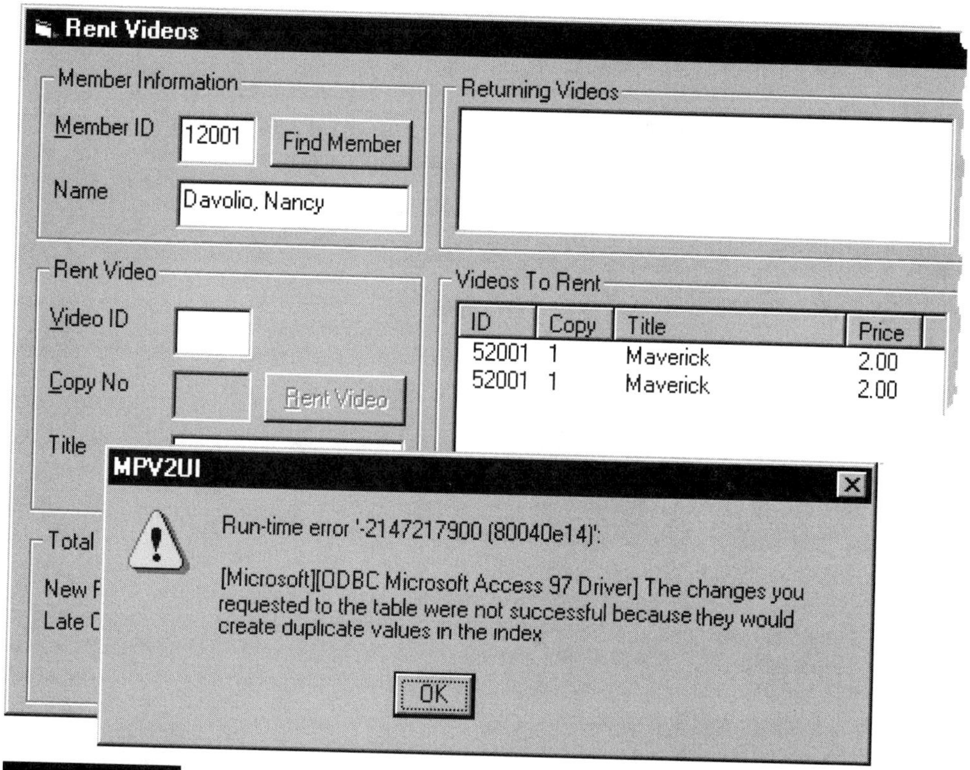

FIGURE 14-2 There is a bug in the 2-tier version of the *Mom-n-Pop Video Store* application. It has been left there as a learning exercise.

ever, that the condition is eventually caught. But when the condition is caught, it results in a fatal error that causes the user interface application to abort.

Rather than check for duplicate entries in the *New Rentals* table, the solution will be to trap the error raised by the database and convert the error to an exception that is already trapped in the user interface – the *video already rented* error. Before you can make such a modification, however, you must locate the source of the error, so that it can be trapped and converted. That's exactly what you will do in this walkthrough, which will also demonstrate the differences in behavior for error trapping options, and will provide you with practice in building a new version of a server that maintains version compatibility. In other words, after correcting the problem, you will not need to rebuild the client application.

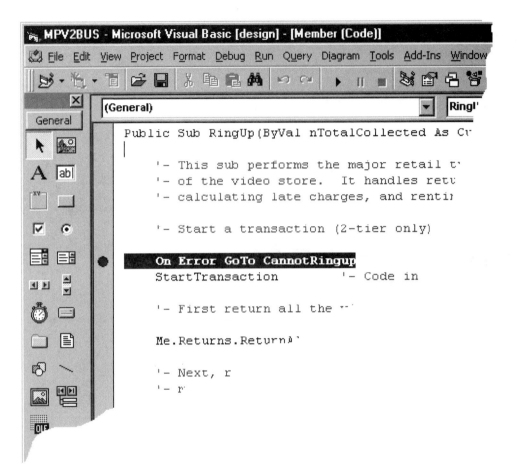

```
MPV2BUS - Microsoft Visual Basic [design] - [Member (Code)]

File  Edit  View  Project  Format  Debug  Run  Query  Diagram  Tools  Add-Ins  Window

(General)                                                          Ring|'

Public Sub RingUp(ByVal nTotalCollected As Cu
|

    '- This sub performs the major retail t'
    '- of the video store.  It handles retu
    '- calculating late charges, and rentin

    '- Start a transaction (2-tier only)

    On Error GoTo CannotRingup
    StartTransaction          '- Code in

    '- First return all the ''

    Me.Returns.Return|''

    '- Next, r
    '- r
```

FIGURE 14-3
If you are familiar with the application, you will probably have a good idea of where the problem is. In this case, you can set a breakpoint in the ActiveX Component before running it in Visual Basic.

Setting Breakpoints in an ActiveX Component

If you have an idea where a problem is, you can set a breakpoint in the ActiveX Component before running it (see Figure 14-3). When you recreate the problem using the user interface, your breakpoint will be reached. You can then step through the program, examining and modifying variables as needed. In this case, assume you don't know where the problem is, and let the debugger show you where the exception is being raised. In other words, for this walkthrough, you won't set a breakpoint yet; you'll just run the ActiveX Component as described in the following section.

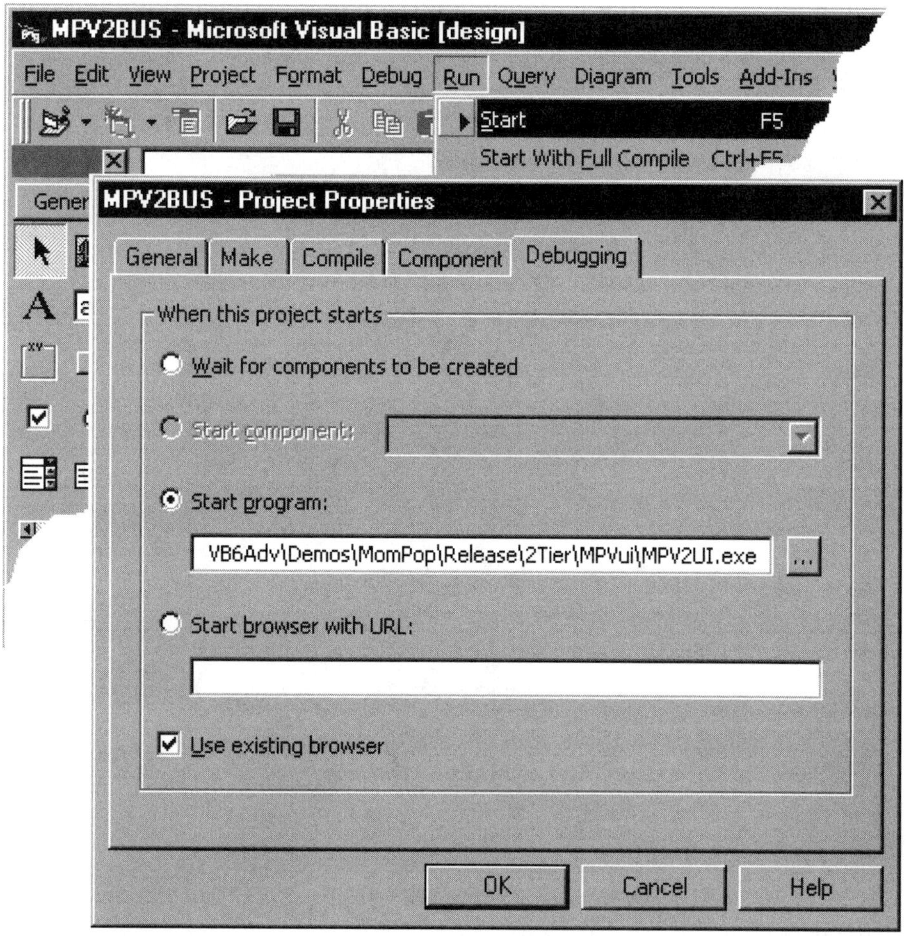

FIGURE 14-4 The first time you run an ActiveX Component from Visual Basic, you will be presented with the *Debugging* tab. You can then specify a program that Visual Basic will start automatically.

Running an ActiveX Component from Visual Basic

The **Debugging** tab of the **Project Properties** dialog includes an option that allows you to specify a program to automatically start when you run the ActiveX Component from Visual Basic. This tab is automatically displayed the first time you run an ActiveX Component. It is helpful to specify the user interface executable as the program to start.

To continue the walkthrough, load the *MPV2BUS* project and access the *Project Properties* dialog, selecting the *Debugging* tab. Select *Start program* and enter the location of the user interface program *MPV2UI.exe* (see Figure 14-4).

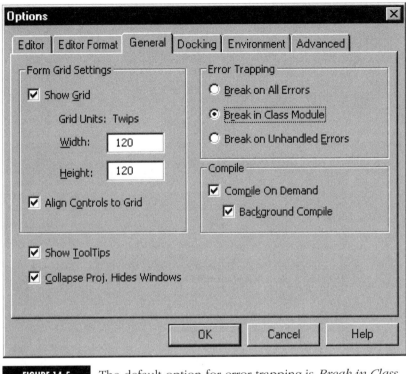

FIGURE 14-5 The default option for error trapping is *Break in Class Module*. As you'll see, this default setting will not help you identify where a particular problem is occurring.

You can run the ActiveX Component at this point, but first proceed to the next section to set error trapping options.

Error Trapping Options – Break in Class Module

To troubleshoot a raised error, you may have to alter the **Error Trapping** setting. This option is available from the *General* tab of the *Options* dialog, available from the *Tools* menu (see Figure 14-5). If you use the default setting of **Break in Class Module**, the program will enter break mode when an error is raised in the class module. However, if you are using error trapping with the *On Error* statement, the breakpoint may not actually be at the exact line of code that is causing the error.

The *Break In Class Module* option causes Visual Basic to enter break mode where an error is raised. In this case, you are taken to a line of code that uses **Err.Raise** to re-raise an unexpected error (see Figure 14-6). For example, the figure is showing that a problem is occurring in the *RingUp* method of the *Member* object, but, using this *Error Trapping* option, you

```
 MPV2BUS - Member (Code)

(General)                                    ▼    RingUp

         ' -        that have been returned.
         ' -
         ' -  Microsoft Visual Basic
         ' -
              Run-time error '-2147217900 (80040e14)':
         Re
         Ad   [Microsoft][ODBC Microsoft Access 97 Driver] The changes you
              requested to the table were not successful because they would create
              duplicate values in the index, primary key, or relationship.  Change the
         ' -  data in the field or fields that contain duplicate data, remove the
              index, or redefine the index to permit duplicate entries and try again.

         C(

         E:     Continue         End         Debug         Help


CannotRingup:
     RollbackTransaction        '- Code in DBGLOBALS.BAS
⇨ |  Err.Raise Err.Number, Err.Source, Err.Description
End Sub


Private Sub Class_Initialize()
     ' Create new collections for renting/returning video
     Set mvarNewRentals = New Picks
```

FIGURE 14-6   When you reproduce the error and click the *Debug* button on the error dialog, you enter break mode at a line of code that uses the *Err.Raise* statement to re-raise an unexpected error. This does not tell you where the error is.

cannot see the exact line of code that is causing the error. The reason is that the *RingUp* method of the *Member* object sets up an error handler. In the error handler, it rolls back the transaction and re-raises the error to abort the program. Here, you should really check for a *duplicate key* error and re-raise a custom error that indicates that a video is already rented (the user interface already handles that error). Before fixing the code, I would encourage you to experiment with a few more error trapping options by continuing to follow this walkthrough over the next few sections. Ideally, you want to find the *Error Trapping* option that will cause the program to enter break mode exactly at the line of code that has the problem.

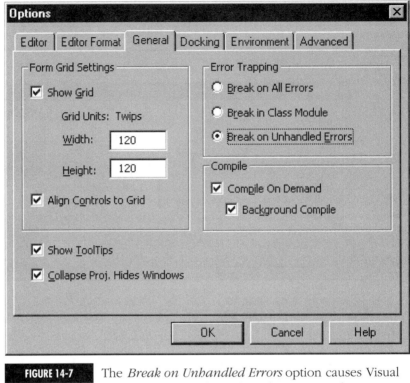

FIGURE 14-7   The *Break on Unhandled Errors* option causes Visual Basic to enter break mode only on errors that occur on statements not covered by an *On Error* statement.

Error Trapping Options – Break on Unhandled Errors

Next, you'll look at the **Break on Unhandled Errors** option (see Figure 14-7). This option instructs Visual Basic to enter break mode only on errors that occur on statements not covered by an *On Error* statement.

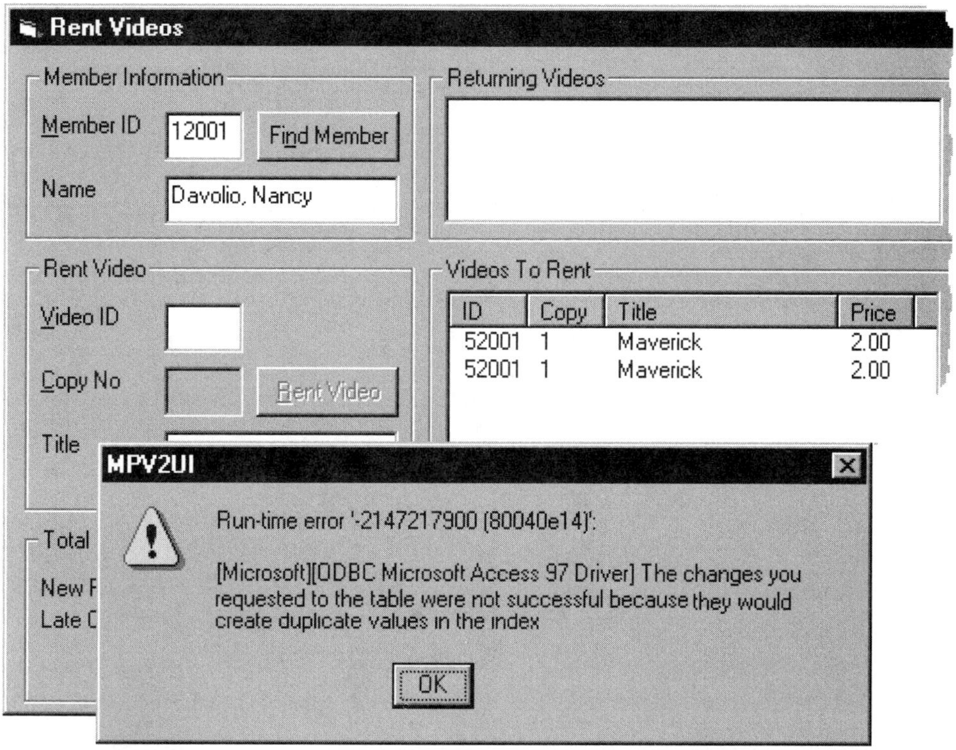

FIGURE 14-8 When you use the *Break on Unhandled Errors* option, the user interface program aborts without the ActiveX Component hitting any breakpoints at all!

The *Break on Unhandled Errors* choice is inappropriate in this case as well. Since the method in question has an error handler, any errors that occur in the method will be considered "handled." The program will abort without trapping at any statement, as shown in Figure 14-8.

Note that this setting is actually the preferred setting under normal circumstances. However, when there is a bug in your error-handling code, or when your error handler incorrectly dismisses an unexpected error, the setting may not be appropriate. Sometimes, error handlers themselves can be the source of the problem, as may be the case with this component.

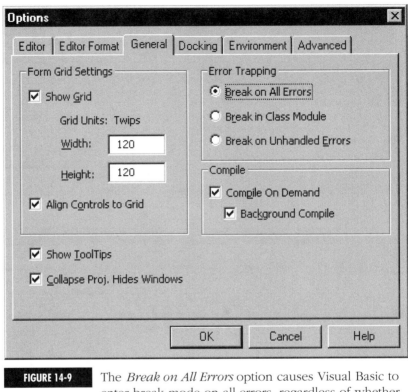

FIGURE 14-9 The *Break on All Errors* option causes Visual Basic to enter break mode on all errors, regardless of whether or not they occur on statements that are covered by an error handler.

Error Trapping Options – Break on All Errors

To see where an error is being raised when it occurs on a statement covered by an error handler, you must use the *Break on All Errors* error trapping option (see Figure 14-9). As you'll see, this option takes you directly to the line of code that is causing the error.

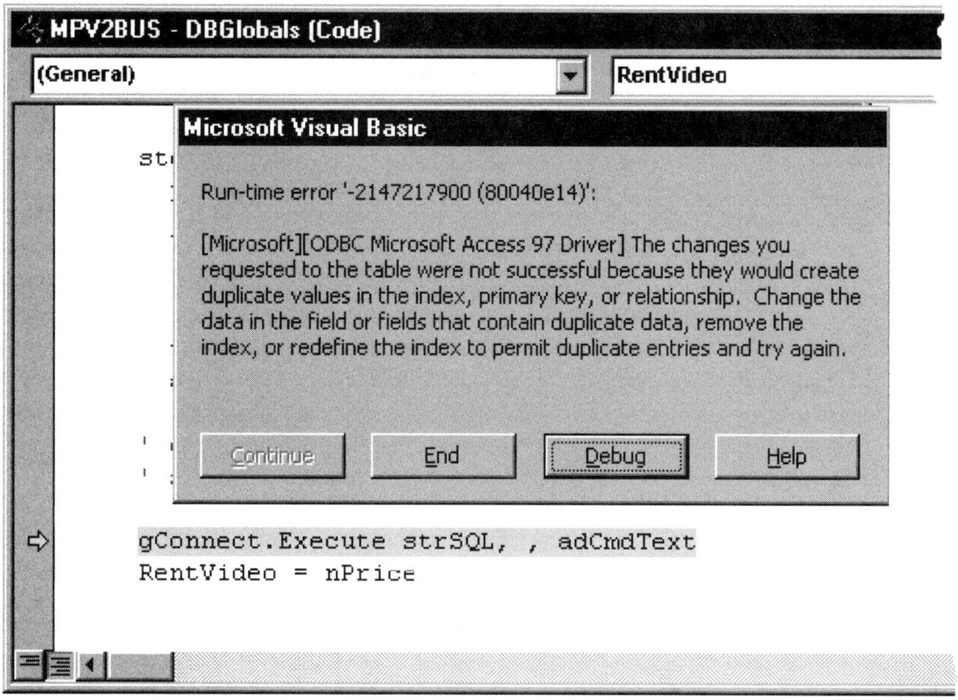

FIGURE 14-10 Here is the actual statement that is causing the error.

The *Break on All Errors* option causes Visual Basic to enter break mode on any statement that causes an error, even if the statement is covered by an *On Error* statement. In this case, you see the *Execute* method invoked on an ADO *Connection* object (see Figure 14-10). This is the statement that is responsible for attempting to add a duplicate primary key to the *Rentals* table.

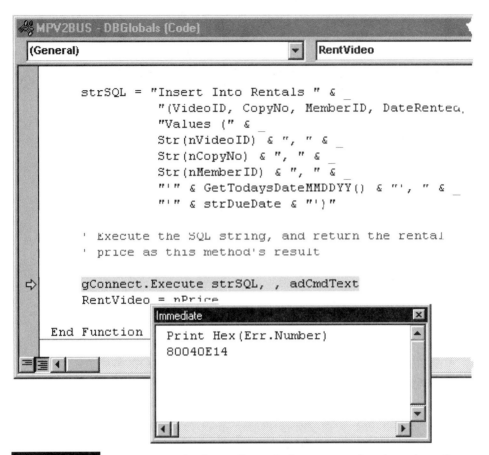

```
strSQL = "Insert Into Rentals " & _
         "(VideoID, CopyNo, MemberID, DateRented, _
         "Values (" & _
         Str(nVideoID) & ", " & _
         Str(nCopyNo) & ", " & _
         Str(nMemberID) & ", " & _
         "'" & GetTodaysDateMMDDYY() & "', " & _
         "'" & strDueDate & "')"

' Execute the SQL string, and return the rental
' price as this method's result

gConnect.Execute strSQL, , adCmdText
RentVideo = nPrice
```

```
End Function
```

```
Immediate
Print Hex(Err.Number)
80040E14
```

FIGURE 14-11 You can use the *Immediate* window to examine the value of *Err.Number.*

Examining the error number reveals the hex value *80040E14* (see Figure 14-11). You should know that the hex value *80040000* is also the constant **vbObjectError**. For your information, this is actually the COM constant *FAC_ITF*, which indicates that an error occurred on a custom interface facility. In this case, the custom interface happens to be ADO (we simply know that because the statement in question is invoking a method on an ADO object). The hex value *E14* is decimal 3604. This error, according to the ADO documentation, is the *duplicate key* error.

Fixing the Problem

In the error handler for the *RingUp* method of the *Member* class, you should check for error *3604*, and raise a custom error that indicates when a video is already rented. You can then rebuild the program. Since this is a version-compatible change, we will not break compatibility with the existing client applications. Verify this by applying the change shown in the following listing, then rebuild the server. Run the client application again to verify that a custom error message is displayed. The client application should no longer abort.

The following modifications are made to the *RingUp* method of the *Member* class in the project *MPV2BUS*:

```
Public Sub RingUp(ByVal nTotalCollected As Currency)

    On Error GoTo CannotRingup
    StartTransaction          '- Code in DBGLOBALS.BAS

    '- First return all the videos

    Me.Returns.ReturnAll Me.ID

    '- Next, rent all the videos selected in this
    '- member's NewRentals collection (type is class Picks)

    Dim nTotal As Currency
    nTotal = Me.NewRentals.RentAll(Me.ID)

            .
            .
            .

    '- Done, commit transaction

    CommitTransaction              '- Code in DBGLOBALS.BAS

    Exit Sub

CannotRingup:
    RollbackTransaction       '- Code in DBGLOBALS.BAS
    If Err.Number = vbObjectError + 3604 Then
        Err.Raise vseAlreadyRented, "Member", _
                "Video is already rented"
    Else
        Err.Raise Err.Number, Err.Source, Err.Description
    End If
End Sub
```

Introducing Microsoft Visual Studio Analyzer

Microsoft Visual Studio Analyzer is a new tool distributed with the *Enterprise* edition of *Visual Studio 6.0*. It has the potential for being an extremely useful utility for locating bottlenecks in a distributed application. However, as you will see, the amount information collected from *Visual Analyzer* can potentially be immense. Furthermore, the events logged by *Visual Analyzer* may not be meaningful to you unless you are familiar with COM internals. It is possible to instrument your application so that custom events are written along with already defined COM, ASP, and MTS events. Doing so will provide you with familiar "footholds" that can be related back to tasks in your application. However, it is not specifically required to instrument your application. All you have to do, as you will see in the following sections, is run your program while you record to an event log with *Visual Analyzer*.

About Visual Studio Analyzer Event Logs

An **event log** in a *Visual Studio Analyzer* project records events for COM, ADO, ASP, MTS, *SQL Server,* and other components that have been pre-instrumented into these facilities by Microsoft. In addition to the selective inclusion of components, events can be filtered before being written to the event log.

While an event log is being recorded, all you have to do to collect information on your application is run and exercise it. After running the application, you will stop recording to the event log and view it for analysis.

It's amazingly easy to record these events to a *Visual Studio Analyzer* event log. The hard part lies in the interpretation of the results. To get you started, I'll show you how you can use the *Visual Studio Analyzer Project Wizard* to create an event log that records every possible event generated by every possible component.

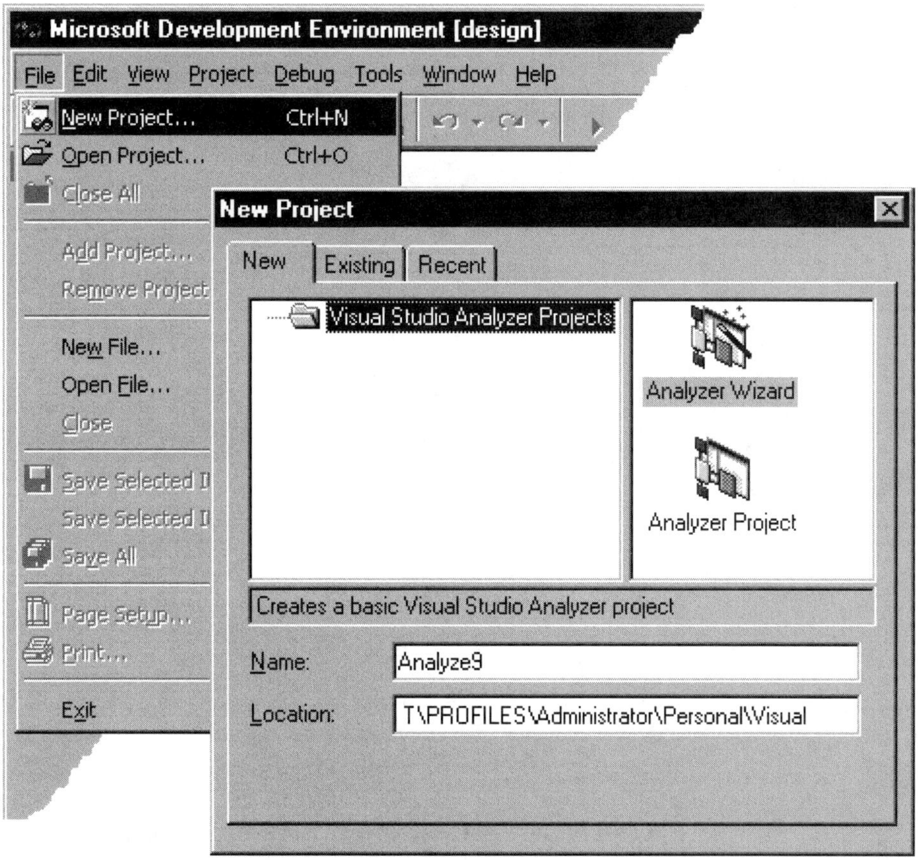

Microsoft Development Environment [design]

File   Edit   View   Project   Debug   Tools   Window   Help

New Project...   Ctrl+N

Open Project...   Ctrl+O

Close All

Add Project...

Remove Project

New File...

Open File...

Close

Save Selected I

Save Selected I

Save All

Page Setup...

Print...

Exit

New Project

New | Existing | Recent

Visual Studio Analyzer Projects

Analyzer Wizard

Analyzer Project

Creates a basic Visual Studio Analyzer project

Name: Analyze9

Location: T\PROFILES\Administrator\Personal\Visual

FIGURE 14-12   Start by creating an *Analyzer Wizard* project.

Using the Visual Studio Analyzer Project Wizard

First, start *Visual Analyzer* by selecting *Visual Studio Analyzer* from the *Microsoft Visual Studio 6.0 Enterprise Tools* program group. You will be presented with a *New Project* dialog, from which you should select *Analyzer Wizard*. If you don't see a *New Project* dialog, select *New* from the *Project* menu, as illustrated in Figure 14-12.

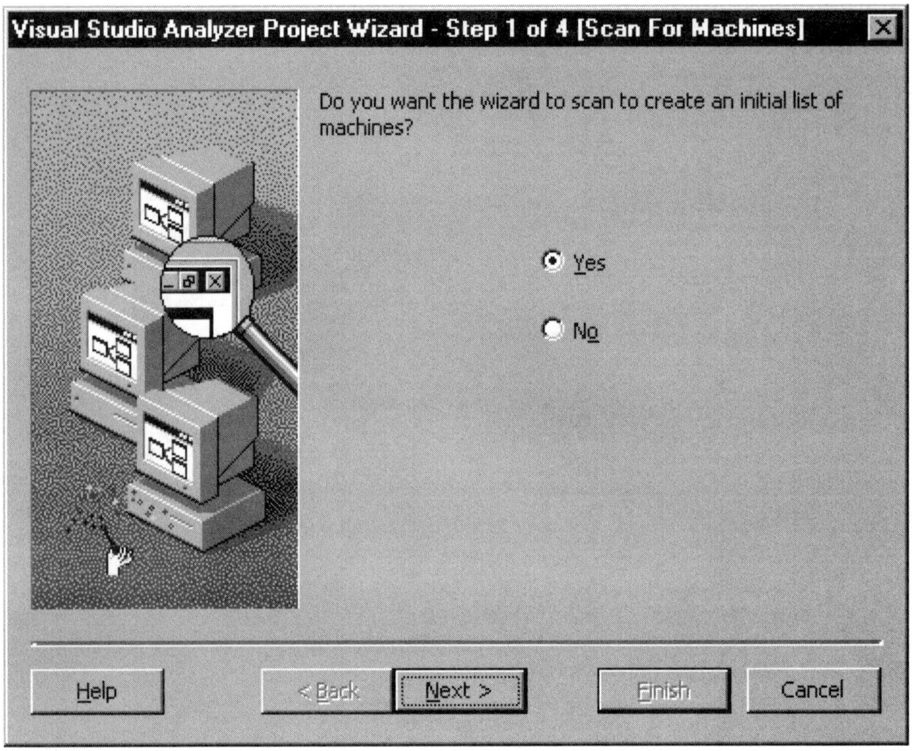

FIGURE 14-13 You can request the wizard to scan for a list of available machines on your network.

In the first step of the *Visual Studio Analyzer Project Wizard*, you can request that the wizard scan for an initial list of machines from which data will be collected (see Figure 14-13). You can than refine this list in the next step of the wizard. If you are using the *Visual Studio Analyzer* for the first time, I suggest you select *No* and click the *Next* button.

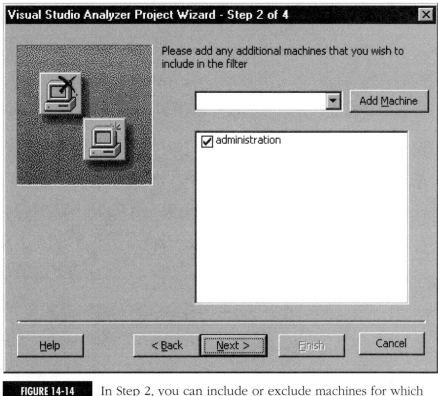

FIGURE 14-14 In Step 2, you can include or exclude machines for which data will be collected.

In the second step of the *Visual Studio Analyzer Project Wizard,* you can add and remove machines to be included in data collection (see Figure 14-14). To keep "noise" out of the event log, you should select only machines that will actually participate in the benchmark. For a quick demonstration of the *Visual Studio Analyzer's* features, select only your machine and click the *Next* button.

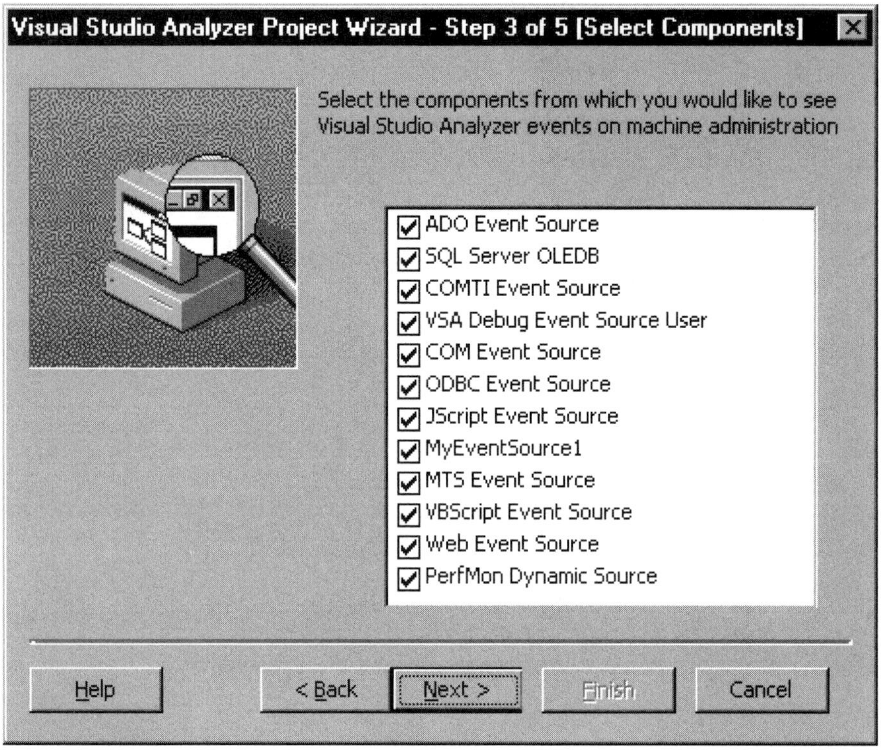

FIGURE 14-15 In Step 3, you can include or exclude components for which events will be collected.

In Step 3 of the *Visual Studio Analyzer Project Wizard*, you can include or exclude the components for which you will gather data (see Figure 14-15). Each component is capable of generating several events; these can be selectively filtered in the following step. By default, the wizard selects all components; leave this setting alone for now and click the *Next* button.

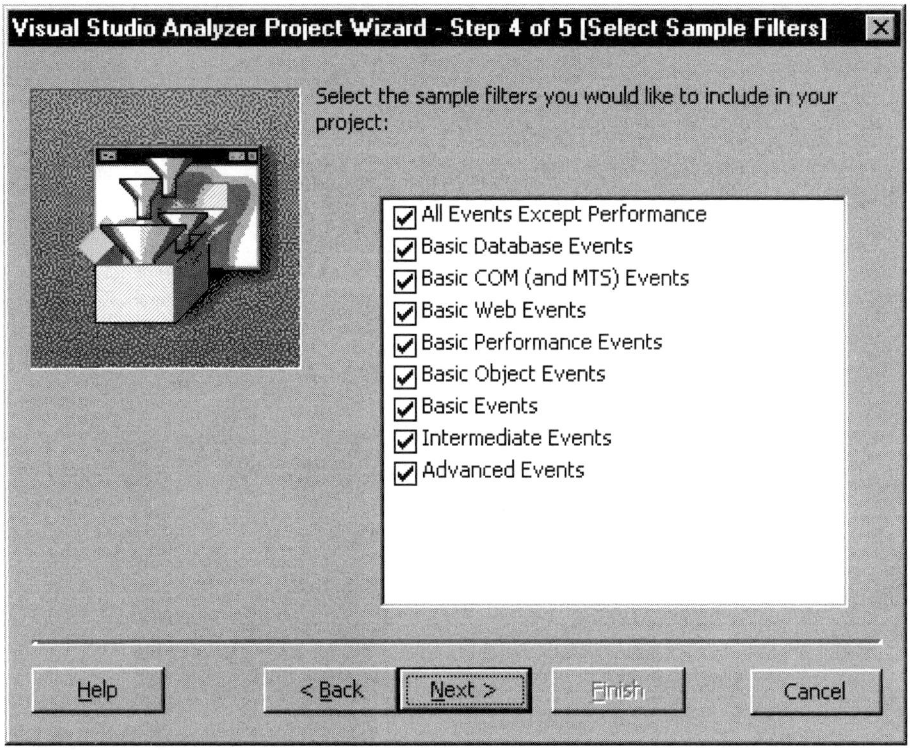

FIGURE 14-16 In Step 4, you can include or exclude filters that further refine which events will be recorded.

In Step 4 of the *Visual Studio Analyzer Project Wizard,* you can include or exclude event filters. The wizard will, by default, propose all sample filters provided by the *Visual Studio Analyzer* (see Figure 14-16). As an interesting demonstration of the type of data that can be collected by the *Visual Studio Analyzer,* you should accept the proposed filters by clicking the *Next* button.

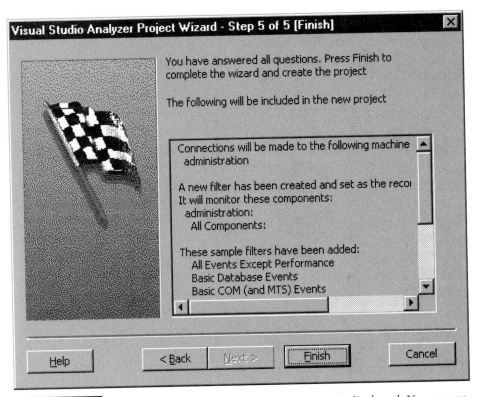

FIGURE 14-17   In the final step of the wizard, a summary is displayed. You can go back and modify your options before clicking the *Finish* button.

In the final step of the *Visual Studio Analyzer Project Wizard* (see Figure 14-17), a summary report is displayed. If you wish, you may click the *Back* button and modify your steps. Again, for an interesting demonstration of the *Visual Studio Analyzer,* click the *Finish* button.

Once you click the *Finish* button, there is literally nothing to do to begin recording. You already are recording. At this point, you can run the 3-tier version of the *Mom-n-Pop Video Store* application, or if you prefer, you can run your own application. You must of course exercise the program somewhat. When you have completed that activity, proceed to the next section for instructions on viewing the recorded events.

Viewing an Analyzer Event Log

Once you have run the application for which you are collecting data, you must return to the *Visual Studio Analyzer* and stop recording. You can stop recording to the event log in a number of ways. For one, you can click the *Record Events* button, which, when recording, actually stops event recording. An alternative way to stop recording is to right-click on the event log name in the *Project Explorer* window and select *Record Events*. You can find your event log in the *Project Explorer* window, under the project name, which should have been given a proposed name of *AnalyzeN*, where *N* is some unique number. Under this entry is an entry titled *Event Logs* – your event log is under this entry.

Once you have stopped recording to the event log, you can analyze it by double-clicking on the event log name. You will be presented with a number of events, as illustrated in Figure 14-18.

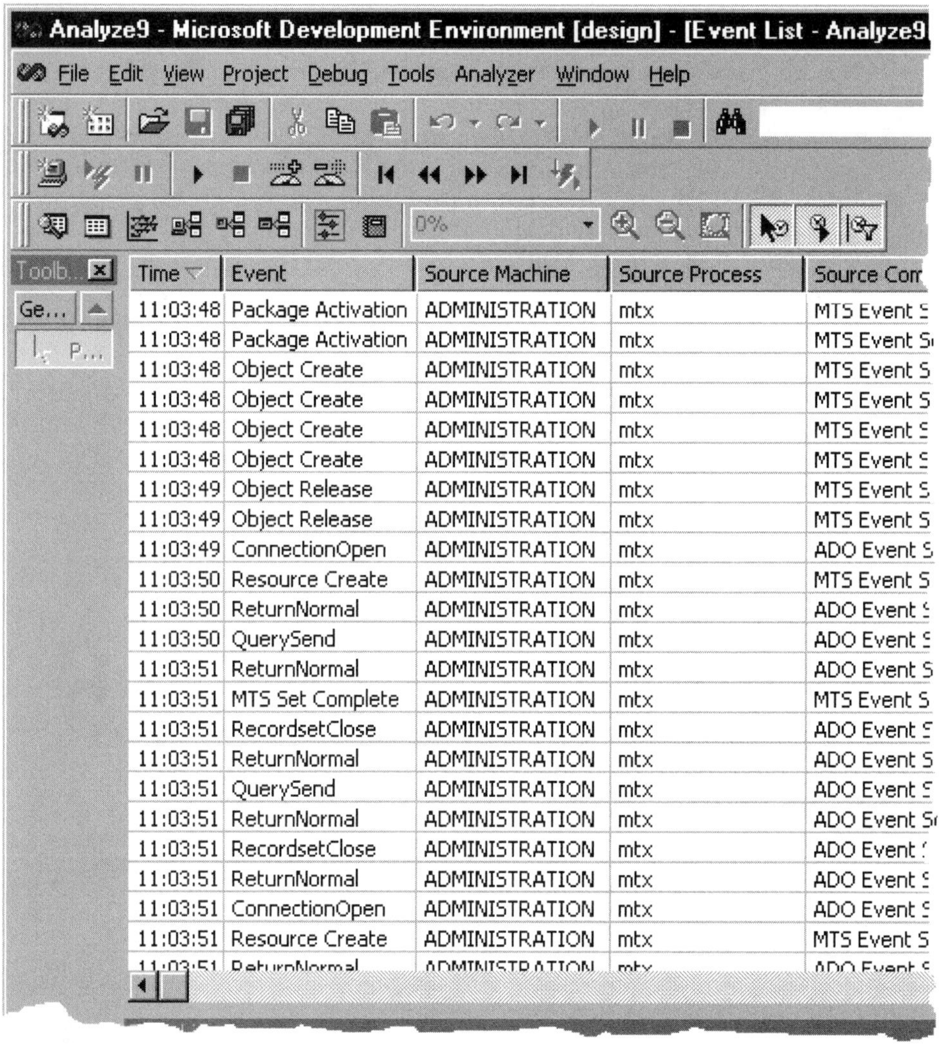

FIGURE 14-18 In its normal view, the event list can be intimidating in the amount of data it presents. You can record custom events from your program to help you locate familiar tasks performed by your program.

By right-clicking on the event log name and selecting *Chart,* you can view the events in a chart format, as illustrated in Figure 14-19. When viewed in a chart format, events that take longer to complete can be seen more readily.

Whether or not the *Visual Studio Analyzer* can help you locate bottle-necks in your application depends on your ability to interpret its results and relate them back to the tasks of your application. If you keep the benchmark

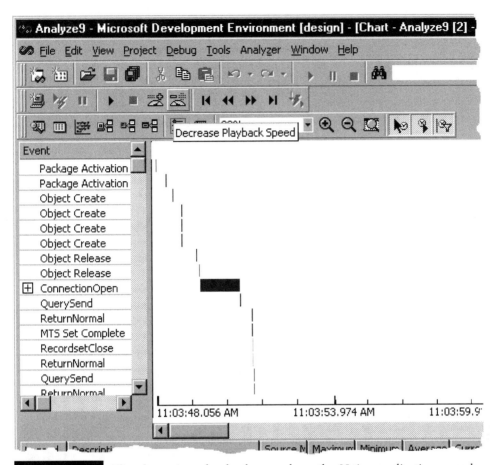

FIGURE 14-19 The chart view clearly shows where the N-tier application spends most of its time. In the above example, the lengthiest operation is clearly when a connection is opened on the database.

small and narrow in scope, this should be easier than if you attempt to test and record every feature of your application at once.

As I mentioned earlier, you can also instrument your application so that it writes custom events to the *Visual Studio Analyzer* event log. While this is possible in Visual Basic, it is by no means trivial. I will leave you to the voluminous *Visual Studio Analyzer Help* file for information on how this is done.

Creating an Internet Interface with Active Server Pages

You can create browser-neutral dynamic Web content by using Active Server Pages (ASP), which are Web pages that specify script that runs on the Web server. Code in an ASP page generates HTML to send to the browser. In an ASP page, you can also have HTML text. Applications written with ASP provide the Internet front-end of an Enterprise application. Such ASP applications typically access the stateless, scalable objects running under MTS, defined in the data services layer of your Enterprise application.

About Active Server Pages

Active Server Pages (ASP) is a server-side scripting environment used by Web developers to create dynamic and interactive Web server applications. ASP combines HTML with server-side and, optionally, client-side scripting languages such as VBScript and JScript (ECMA Script).

ASP scripts run when the browser opens a page with the ASP file extension. When this happens, the Web server merges static HTML included in the ASP page with dynamically generated HTML from server-side script in the ASP page. The Web server does all the work, not the browser, which generally receives only HTML. Although browser compatibility is an issue even when using just HTML, you have more issues of compatibility when executing client-side scripts. You may, if you wish, execute client-side scripts, but you must be even more careful about browser compatibility. ASP source code cannot be viewed by the end-user, since the results of the script are sent to the client's browser. If the client attempts to view the source of the page, it will see only the generated HTML.

The Mom-n-Pop Web Site Demo

The *Mom-n-Pop Video Store* demo Web site uses only a few HTML tags. The result is a Web site with a very modest appearance. In fact, using HTML tables is about as fancy as the Web site gets. There are two reasons for this approach. First, the goal is to illustrate what is required to use ASP and how your Web pages can tie into the data services layer of your enterprise application. Too many bells and whistles in the HTML would make it seem more complicated than it actually is. Second, it is not a goal of this book to teach HTML. I assume that you either already know HTML, or will learn it eventually from another source.

To run the *Mom-n-Pop Video Store* Web site demo, you must have *IIS 4.0* or later installed on your server. Copy folder *MomPop*, which is located under folder *VB6Adv\Demos\MomPop\WebSite*, to your *WWW Root* site, usually located on *InetPub\wwwroot*. You must also have already installed at least the data services layer of the *Mom-n-Pop Video Store* demo enterprise application. Refer to Chapter 1 for instructions on deploying the *Mom-n-Pop Video Store* application. To start the demo, point your browser to the *default.html* page under the *MomPop* Web site.

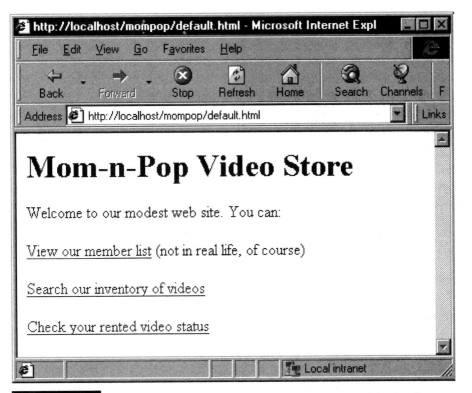

FIGURE 15-1 The home page is not an Active Server Page. It is simply an HTML page that consists of text and hyperlinks.

THE MOM-N-POP HOME PAGE

To start, point your browser to the ***default.html*** page of the *Mom-n-Pop* Web site. The URL is *http://localhost/mompop/default.html*. The page consists of hyperlinks to the other Web pages (see Figure 15-1). The *default.html* page is not an ASP page. It simply consists of text and links to the other pages of the *Mom-n-Pop* Web site. From the home page, take the link *View our member list.*

FIGURE 15-2   *The Member List* page is an Active Server Page that accesses a data services layer object to list all the members of the video store.

MOM-N-POP MEMBER LIST WEB PAGE

The *Member List* page (see Figure 15-2) is an ASP page. It uses an object in the data services layer to get a list of all the members in the video store. Naturally, this information would not be presented to a client in real life, but this page is one of the simplest pages in the demo. This page also illustrates how to process a disassociated recordset, which is returned by the object in the data services layer. Disassociated recordsets are discussed later in this chapter, as well as in Chapters 12 and 13.

MOM-N-POP VIDEO TITLE SEARCH PAGE

The *Video Inventory Search* (see Figure 15-3) page is not an ASP page. The page consists of input controls that submit a request to the server. When the *Submit* button is pressed, the form's *action* tag specifies that the browser will load the file *ShowVideos.ASP*, which is an ASP page. The HTML for the *Video Inventory Search* page is as follows:

FIGURE 15-3   The *Video Inventory Search* page is not an ASP page. It consists of input controls to submit a query to the server.

```
<html>
<body>
<H3>Search our Video Inventory</H3>
<P>
Enter part of the Video's title below.

<FORM METHOD="GET" ACTION="ShowVideos.asp">
<P>
Title to Search:
<INPUT TYPE="text" NAME="VideoTitle">
<INPUT TYPE="submit" NAME="btnEnter" VALUE="Enter">
</FORM>

</body>
</html>
```

The page displayed as a result of visiting the *Lookup Video* page is an *ASP* page.

MOM-N-POP VIDEO SEARCH RESULTS PAGE

Clicking the *Enter* button on the *Look Up Video* page submits a request to the server. As a result, an ASP page is executed on the server, which generates the HTML to display the videos with a title matching the string entered by the client (see Figure 15-4).

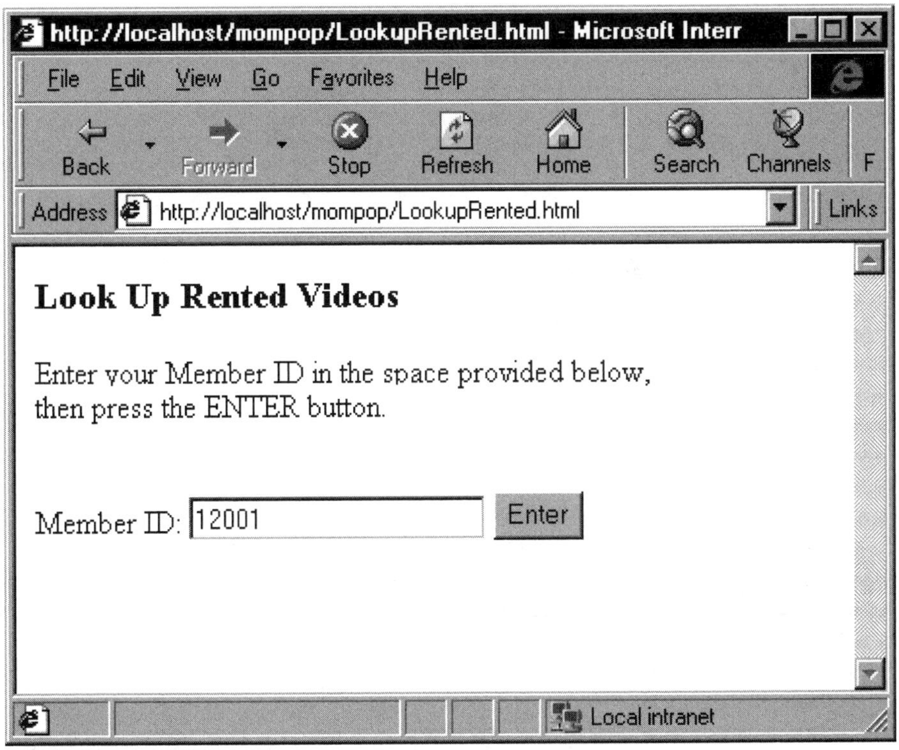

FIGURE 15-5   The page to look up videos rented by a member is not an ASP page. It uses HTML to accept the user's input and submit it to a page that is an ASP page.

MOM-N-POP MEMBER STATUS PAGE

The *Look Up Rented Videos* page (see Figure 15-5) allows a member to view the status of the videos they have rented. This page is not an ASP page. It contains client-side *VBScript* as an example of how to mix client-side with server-side script. More on this later.

The *Look Up Rented Videos* page illustrates the use of client-side script with ASP. If a non-numeric member ID is entered, a message box is displayed (see Figure 15-6). This validation is performed client-side by a script included on the page, and written in *VBScript*. The HTML source code for accomplishing this is as follows:

```
<html>
<body>
<H3>Look Up Rented Videos</H3>
<P>
Enter your Member ID in the space provided below,
then press the ENTER button.

<FORM METHOD="GET" NAME="MyForm" ACTION="ShowRented.asp">
<P>
Member ID:
<INPUT TYPE="text" NAME="MemberID">
<INPUT TYPE="button" NAME="btnEnter" VALUE="Enter">
</FORM>
<SCRIPT LANGUAGE="VBScript">
<!—
Sub btnEnter_OnClick
  Dim TheForm
  Set TheForm = Document.MyForm
  If IsNumeric(TheForm.MemberID.Value) Then
    TheForm.submit
  Else
    Msgbox "That is not a valid Member ID."
  End if
End Sub
//—>
</SCRIPT>
</body>
</html>
```

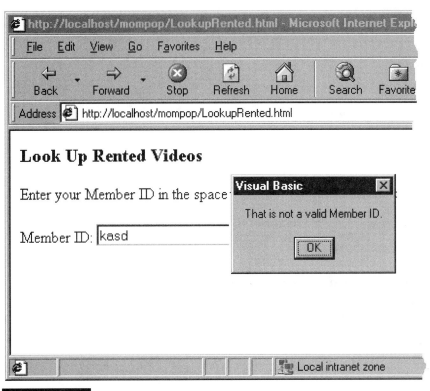

FIGURE 15-6 The *Look Up Rented Videos* page also illustrates that it is possible to execute client-side script if you wish. The value entered in the *Member ID* text box must be numeric.

MOM-N-POP MEMBER STATUS RESULTS PAGE

When the client submits the *Look Up Rented Videos* page, an ASP page is executed, which returns the results to the client (see Figure 15-7).

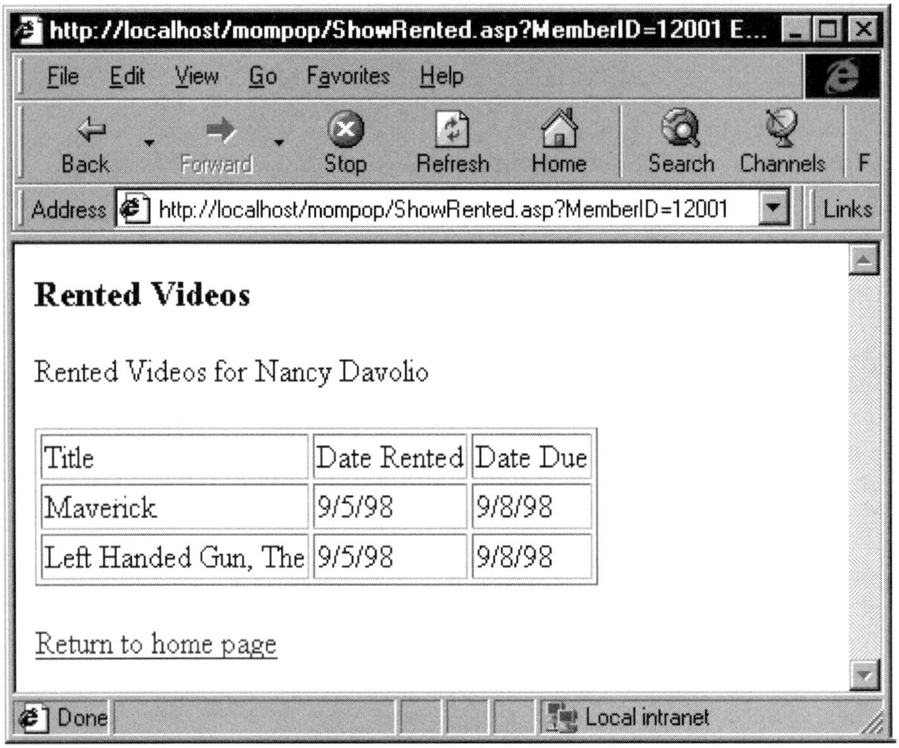

FIGURE 15-7   The page that is returned as a result of using the *Look Up Rented Videos* page is an ASP page. It contains the most complex logic of all the pages in the demo suite.

VIEWING SERVER-GENERATED HTML FROM AN ASP PAGE

You can use the *Rented Video Results* page, which is an ASP page, to see how ASP pages work. If the client selects **Source** from the **View** menu in the browser, they will see only the HTML generated by the ASP page, and not the ASP source (see Figure 15-8).

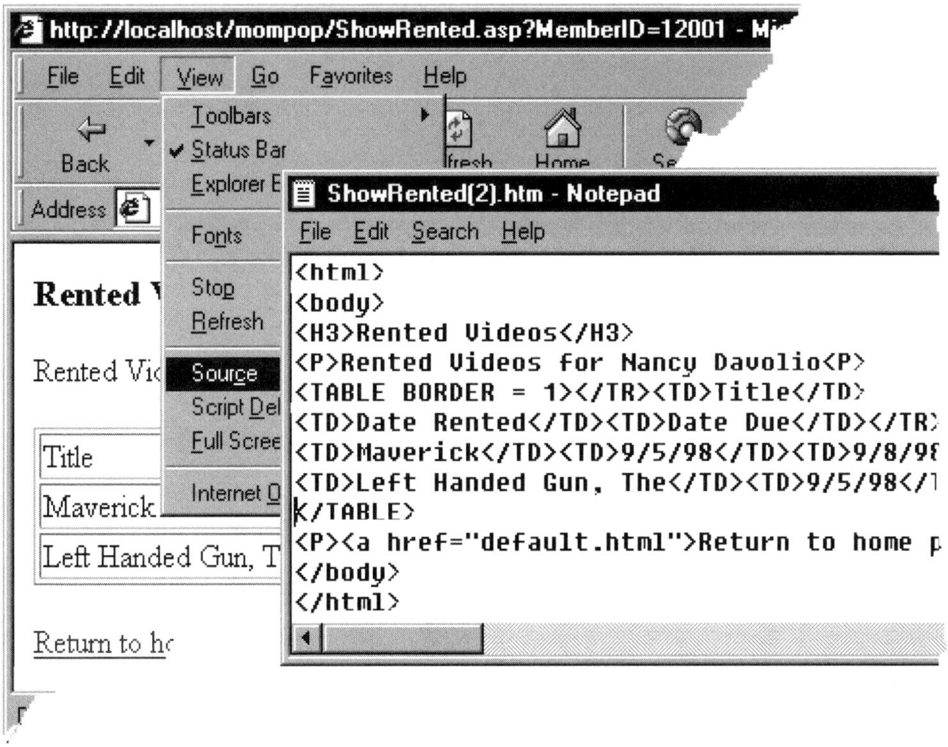

FIGURE 15-8 If the client selects *View/Source*, notice that all that is returned is "raw" HTML.

Creating Active Server Pages

Active Server Pages are text files with the extension ASP. They may contain text, HTML tags, and ASP script commands. To create an ASP file, give any HTML file the file extension of ASP instead of HTM or HTML.

The ASP file must reside in a directory on your Web site. This directory must have *Script* or *Execute* permission. Do not convert all your HTML files into ASP files. ASP files require extra processing, so if a page uses only standard HTML, give the file an extension of either HTML or HTM. Both HTM and ASP files can reside in the same directory.

ASP files can be created with any text editor. However, using a combination of *Microsoft Visual InterDev* and *Microsoft Front Page* provides the most productive environment. The *Mom-n-Pop* Web site pages are very simple, and were created with *Notepad*. An overused joke in our industry, in fact, is that the most popular tool for creating Web pages is *"Visual Notepad."*

Adding Script Commands to ASP Pages

An **ASP script** is a set of commands that cause the Web server to perform an action. Scripts are distinct from normal HTML text in that they are surrounded by the delimiters <% and %>. ASP scripts execute on the server. To execute scripts on the client, the <SCRIPT> tag is used. A simple example, which displays the current server's time, follows. The string *"= Now"* is surrounded by the ASP script delimiters, <% and %>.

```
<HTML>
<BODY>
The server's current system time is <%= Now %>.
</BODY>
</HTML>
```

The ASP Built-In Objects

ASP scripts can use built-in ASP objects to perform tasks such as gathering information from a browser request, storing information about a user, and so on. This section briefly describes some of the built-in objects included with ASP.

- The **Application** object is used to share information between all users of a Web application.
- The **Request** object is used to obtain information posted with an HTTP request and provides methods to upload information to the server.
- The **Response** object is used to send information to the browser, such as script-generated HTML. It can also be used to set cookie values.
- The **Server** object provides access to methods on the server, including the **CreateObject** method, which is used to create ActiveX Components on the server.
- The **Session** object is used to store information needed by the user on a session. Values stored via methods of the *Session* object persist while a user accesses the pages of your application.

Declaring and Using Variables in ASP Scripts

Variables are declared in *VBScript* using the *Dim* keyword. Variables declared inside a procedure have local scope. Such variables are created and destroyed upon entry to and exit from the procedure. Variables declared outside a procedure have global scope. Such variables can be accessed by script that appears anywhere on the ASP page.

If you need to access a variable from any page, the variable must be given either application or session scope. Variables with application scope can be accessed by any user of the Web application. To give a variable application scope, store it in the **Application** object. For example,

```
<%
Application("Greeting") = "Welcome to Mom-n-Pop's Video Store"
Request.Write Application("Greeting")
%>
```

Variables with session scope are available by individual users of the application as they use the ASP pages. Each user will have a separate copy of the variable. To give a variable session scope, store it in the *Session* object. For example,

```
<%
Session("MemberID") = 12001
Request.Write Session("MemberID")
%>
```

Sending Content to the Browser

In an ASP page, any text that appears outside the ASP script delimiters is sent directly to the browser. Inside ASP script, you use the *Write* method of the *Response* object to dynamically send HTML to the browser. For example,

```
<H1>Sent Directly as HTML</H1>
<% Response.Write "This is received by the browser as well" %>
```

HTML Forms and the Request Object

HTML forms are the most common method used to gather information from the user. An HTML form can consist of simple controls such as text boxes and buttons. HTML forms can have an ACTION that indicates which URL to go to when the form is submitted from the browser. This URL may specify an ASP page. For example,

```
<html>
<body>
<H3>Search our Video Inventory</H3>
<P>
Enter part of the Video's title below.

<FORM METHOD="GET" ACTION="ShowVideos.asp">
<P>
Title to Search:
<INPUT TYPE="text" NAME="VideoTitle">
<INPUT TYPE="submit" NAME="btnEnter" VALUE="Enter">
</FORM>
```

```
</body>
</html>
```

The target ASP page uses the **QueryString** collection of the **Response** object to read the submitted value. Note that the value passed to the *QueryString* collection is the same as the *NAME* given to the input control.

```
<% Response.Write "Search for video title = " & _
                Request.QueryString("VideoTitle") %>
```

Creating Objects in ASP Script

You can create objects, including data services layer objects, in ASP script using the *CreateObject* method of the *ASP Server* object. Data services layer objects are preferred over business objects (those in your object model), because they are stateless. If you use business objects from ASP script, your application will not be as scalable, since business objects, by their nature, hold state. Since potentially thousands of users may access your application simultaneously when it is placed on the Web, scalability becomes more of an issue with ASP scripts. Use stateless objects running under MTS from ASP scripts. For more information on MTS and stateless objects, refer to Chapters 12 and 13.

You must specify the programmer ID (ProgID) of an object as the parameter for the *CreateObject* method. The sample code below creates two objects. One object is a recordset object, which is used to process results of a query. The other object is a data services layer object. Once an object is created, you can invoke methods and read/set properties of the object.

```
<%
Dim objRS
Dim objMemData
Set objRS = Server.CreateObject("ADODB.Recordset")
Set objMemData = Server.CreateObject("MPV3DAT.MemberData")
Set objRS = objMemData.Search ("%")
             •
             •
             •
%>
```

Processing Recordsets in ASP Scripts

You can return recordsets from a method of an object in the data services layer. Such recordsets are known as disassociated recordsets because the client has no associated connection to the database. To return a disassociated recordset from the data services layer, be sure to

1. Specify the ***adUseClient*** option for the recordset's ***CursorLocation*** property (recommended).
2. Create a static recordset.

A fragment of sample code from the data services layer follows. This example is examined in greater detail in the sections that follow. For a complete example of how objects in a distributed application work together, refer to Chapter 13.

```
RS.CursorLocation = adUseClient
RS.Open strSQL, _
        gstrConnectString, _
        adOpenStatic, _
        adLockReadOnly, _
        adCmdText
```

EXAMPLE: THE MEMBERDATA MTS COMPONENT

Following is the *GetRentedVideos* method of the *MemberData* object, which is a data services layer object running as an MTS component. The method returns a disassociated recordset.

```
Public Function GetRentedVideos(ByVal nMemberID As Long) _
            As Recordset

    '- Find all the videos rented by this member.
    '- This method uses a stored procedure (RentedVideos).

    Dim objContext As ObjectContext
    Set objContext = GetObjectContext()

    Dim RS As New Recordset
    Dim objCommand As New Command
    Dim P As Parameter

    Set P = objCommand.CreateParameter("nMemberID", _
                                adInteger, _
                                adParamInput)
```

```
objCommand.Parameters.Append P

objCommand.CommandText = "RentedVideos"
objCommand.CommandType = adCmdStoredProc
objCommand.Prepared = False
objCommand.ActiveConnection = gstrConnectString

objCommand.Parameters(0).Value = nMemberID

RS.CursorLocation = adUseClient
RS.Open objCommand, , adOpenStatic, adLockReadOnly

'- Done. -'

If Not objContext Is Nothing Then
    objContext.SetComplete
End If

Set GetRentedVideos = RS
Set RS = Nothing

End Function
```

EXAMPLE: USING THE GETRENTEDVIDEOS METHOD FROM ASP

Following is the source code for the ASP *ShowRented.ASP*, which uses the
MemberData object's **GetRentedVideos** method to display rented videos to
a member over the Web. Note that the code uses the method shown in the
previous section. The resulting data is returned as a disassociated record set.

```
<html>
<body>
<H3>Rented Videos</H3>
<%
Dim nMemberID
Dim objMember
Dim objRS

nMemberID = Request.QueryString("MemberID")

Set objRS = Server.CreateObject("ADODB.Recordset")
Set objMember = Server.CreateObject("MPV3DAT.MemberData")
Set objRS = objMember.FindByID(nMemberID)
```

```
If objRS.BOF And objRS.EOF Then
    Response.Write "That is an invalid member id."
Else
    Response.Write "<P>"
    Response.Write "Rented Videos for " & _
                    objRS("FirstName") & " " & _
                    objRS("LastName")
    Response.Write "<P>"
    objRS.Close
    Set objRS = objMember.GetRentedVideos (nMemberID)

    If objRS.BOF And objRS.EOF Then
        Response.Write "You have not rented any videos."
    Else
        Response.Write "<TABLE BORDER = 1></TR>"
        Response.Write "<TD>Title</TD>"
        Response.Write "<TD>Date Rented</TD>"
        Response.Write "<TD>Date Due</TD>"
        Do While Not objRS.EOF
            Response.Write "</TR>"
            Response.Write "<TD>" & objRS("Title") & "</TD>"
            Response.Write "<TD>" & objRS("DateRented")
            Response.Write "</TD>"
            Response.Write "<TD>" & objRS("DateDue") & "</TD>"
            objRS.MoveNext
        Loop
    End If
    Response.Write "</TABLE>"
End If

objRS.Close
Set objRS = Nothing
Set objMember = Nothing
%>
<P><a href="default.html">Return to home page</a><P>
</body>
</html>
```

Internet IIS Applications

Pieter Mondriaan produced the painting *Composition in Red, Yellow, and Blue* in the 1900's when artists were exploring new ways of representing our world in an abstract manner. Unlike other abstract paintings created by his predecessors, in this painting he shirks anything suggestive of the material world. I like the painting because it seems so complete, with every aspect of the painting complementing itself. Vertical and horizontal lines divide the composition into an amorphic grid that separates squares of different colors and sizes. Everything in the painting seems so basic, with its white background, primary colors, and geometric shapes. Yet, it doesn't feel austere, and even with the hard edge stratification of the colors, the placement of the squares looks cozy and comfortable. The painting has an underlying complexity in juxtaposition with explicit simplicity, but it can be appreciated even without this insight. It looks like a painting that anyone, upon first impression, would think they could create, but I don't think it is. Certainly, I could not produce such a painting.

If you ran the demo from the previous chapter, which presented a Web site for the *Mom-n-Pop Video Store*, you know by now that I am not capable of creating interesting Web pages either. This is because I was not born with graphic and artistic skills. I'm a programmer, and programming is what I like. I know of several very talented graphic artists that can easily put my Web site demos to shame. Which brings me to the reason I like IIS applications, new in Visual Basic 6.0, so much.

About Internet IIS Applications

A Visual Basic **IIS application** is a compiled COM server that is capable of both sending HTML to a browser and responding to events generated from a Web user's interaction with an HTML page. This may sound like client-side, browser-limited technology, but it is not. An IIS application runs server-side and can easily be written to be browser-neutral. In many respects, an IIS application is like an ASP application; however, you develop an IIS application using native Visual Basic code, not a subset of Visual Basic (i.e., *VBScript*). Additionally, the HTML pages of an IIS application are separate from the code driving the application. This separation has tremendous tactical advantages. As a programmer, I can focus on providing the business logic that will drive the Web application. As a program manager, I can find a qualified graphic artist to create the HTML for me. The programmer's code ties it all together, providing the business logic and choreographing the sequence of Web pages visited by the user.

IIS applications use HTML instead of Visual Basic forms to present a user interface. But, they use compiled Visual Basic code to process requests and respond to events originating from the browser. IIS applications reside on the server. They receive requests from a browser, run code associated with the requests, and return responses, as HTML, to the browser. IIS applications, unlike ASP scripts, use the full set of Visual Basic statements. Instead of using *VBScript* to process requests and send responses, you use standard, compiled Visual Basic code using the Visual Basic programming environment. A Web designer can create the HTML templates, and your Visual Basic code can add additional elements to the HTML template. In other words, your code is not embedded in an HTML document.

The Mom-n-Pop Internet IIS Demo

The *Mom-n-Pop* Internet IIS demo (see Figure 16-1) is no fancier from the outside than the ASP demo you viewed in the previous chapter. But there is a major difference in that the IIS application's HTML is completely separate from any and all application logic.

The easiest way to run the demo is to load it into Visual Basic and run it from there. The demo project is *MomPopIIS.VBP*, located in folder *VB6Adv\Demos\MomPop\WebSite\MomPopIIS*. After loading the project, run it and answer *Yes* when asked by Visual Basic if it is okay to run out-of-process components. To install the application so that it can be accessed from your browser, or any browser on your intranet, build the project from Visual Basic. You can then access the application using the URL *http://youhostname/mompopiis/momPopIIS.ASP*.

http://localhost/MomPopIIS/MomPopIIS.ASP?WCI=LookupVide

| File | Edit | View | Go | Favorites | Help |

Back   Forward   Stop   Refresh   Home   Search   Fa

Address http://localhost/MomPopIIS/MomPopIIS.ASP?WCI=LookupVideo&

Video Title Search Results

Search results for string = The

Return to Mom-n-Pop Home Page

Video ID	Title	Year	Director
52014	Associate, The	1996	Donald Petrie
52023	Killing Street, The	1984	R. Joffe
52002	Left Handed Gun, The	1958	A. Penn
52021	Postman, The	1988	J. Stelling
52024	Rumble In The Bronx	1996	S. Tong
52015	Scarlet Letter, The	1995	R. Joffe
52006	Tales From The Hood	1995	R. Cundieff
52013	Twilight Zone The Movie	1983	S. Spielberg
52026	Welcome To The Dollhouse	1996	T. Solondz

Local intranet zone

FIGURE 16-1   The Web page above was generated from a Visual Basic IIS application.

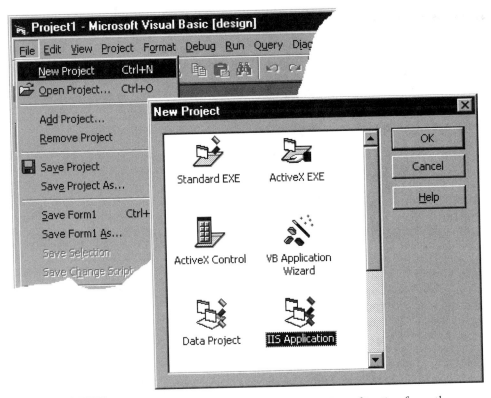

FIGURE 16-2 To start a new IIS application, select *IIS Application* from the *New Project* dialog.

Creating an IIS Application

In IIS applications, there are many similarities to applications that use only ASP scripts and data services layer objects. Like ASP script applications, you have access to the Active Server Pages object model. You use *Request, Response,* and other ASP objects to process requests and send responses.

You can start a new IIS application by selecting **IIS Application** from the *New Project* dialog (see Figure 16-2). In a new IIS application, a **WebClass** object with a proposed name of *WebClass1* is automatically added to your project. A **WebClass** is an object that resides on the server and responds to browser input. A *WebClass* is designed in a *Webclass Designer* window. In its lifetime, a *WebClass* is associated with only one client. Typically, an IIS application will have only one *WebClass*. There are some motivations for creating additional *WebClass* objects (see *Help* for more information).

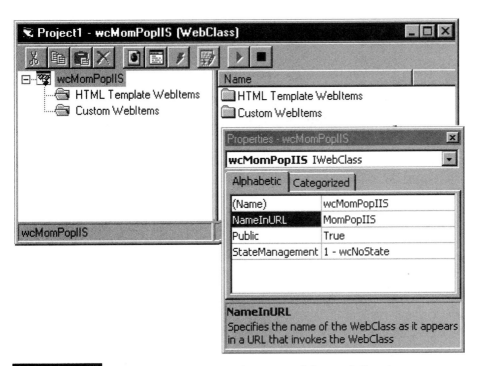

FIGURE 16-3   In the demo program, the name of the *WebClass* is set to *wcMomPopIIS*, and the *NameInURL* property is set to *MomPopIIS*. All other properties are kept at their defaults.

A *WebClass* object contains one or more *WebItems*. A **WebItem** is typically an HTML template, but you can also create custom *WebItems*. The *Mom-n-Pop* IIS demo uses only HTML templates as *WebItems*.

Properties of WebClass Objects

A **WebClass** object has a name; the conventional prefix is **wc**. The **NameInURL** property is the name that will be used in URL references to the WebClass. The **StateManagement** property indicates whether or not the *WebClass* object stays alive between browser requests; the default value of *1 – wcNoState* causes the *WebClass* object to be destroyed and recreated between requests. The **Public** property must be set to **TRUE** for the IIS application to run. Properties of *WebClass* objects are accessed in the *Properties* window (see Figure 16-3).

You must save your project after setting the above properties. You cannot add HTML templates to an IIS application until it is saved at least once.

Adding HTML Templates to a WebClass

HTML templates enable an IIS application to send HTML pages to the browser. To add an HTML template, right-click on the *WebClass* object and select *Add HTML Template* (see Figure 16-4). You can (and should) name the HTML template after the HTML page. You should not retain the Visual Basic proposed name (*Template1, Template2,* etc.), since this would make your code less readable.

When an HTML template is added to an IIS application, it is scanned for HTML tags that are capable of sending requests to the browser. Such tags include forms and hyperlinks. Be sure to use the **POST** method for any forms defined in your HTML templates. An IIS application cannot process forms that use the **GET** method.

The HTML file added to your project is copied to your Visual Basic project directory (in fact, this is why you must save the project first). The copy of the HTML file becomes the source for the HTML template once it is added to your project. If you need to change the HTML, you must change the copy in your project directory.

HTML templates can be removed from a *WebClass*. To remove an HTML template, right-click on the template and select *Delete.* You can also edit an HTML template from the Visual Basic development environment. To edit an HTML template, right-click on the HTML template and select *Edit HTML Template.* By default, Visual Basic invokes *Notepad* as the editor, but you can select another HTML editor (for example, *Microsoft Front Page*) from the *Advanced* tab of the *Project Properties* dialog.

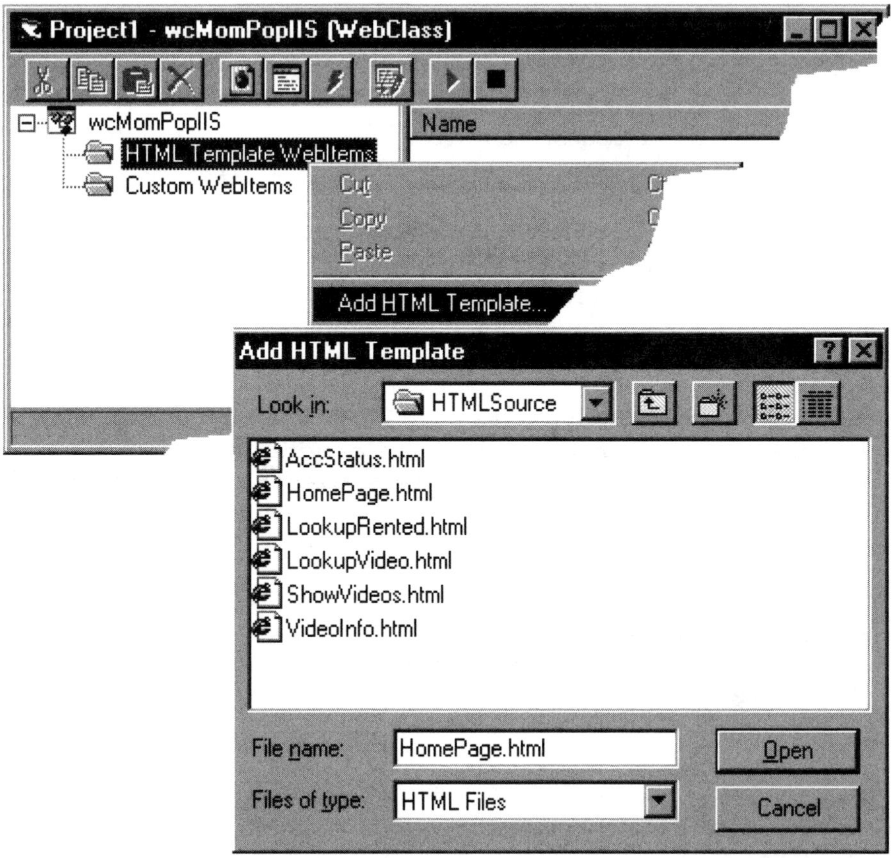

FIGURE 16-4 After saving your project, you can add HTML templates to your *WebClass*. Right-click on your *WebClass* object and select *Add HTML Template*.

EXAMPLE: HTML TEMPLATES ADDED TO THE DEMO PROGRAM

Shown below are some of the HTML templates added to the demo program. There are other templates in the demo project in addition to these two; these HTML templates make up the first examples we'll examine from the demo. In Figure 16-5, you can see how the *WebClass Designer* window is updated after adding these templates.

The first template to examine is the one for the *Home Page:*

```
<html><body>
<h1>Mom-n-Pop Video</h1>
<P>Welcome to our modest web site.
<P><I>Powered by Visual Basic IIS Project</I></P></body>
```

Following is the HTML template for the *Lookup Rented Videos* page. Note that the HTML contains no script; native Visual Basic code for driving the Internet application resides in the *WebClass.*

```
<html>
<body>
<H3>Look Up Rented Videos</H3>
<P>Enter your Member ID in the space provided below, then
press the ENTER button.

<FORM METHOD="post" NAME="FormGetMemberID">
<P>
Member ID:
<INPUT NAME="MemberID" >
<INPUT TYPE="submit" NAME="btnEnter" VALUE="Enter">
</FORM></P>
</body>
</html>
```

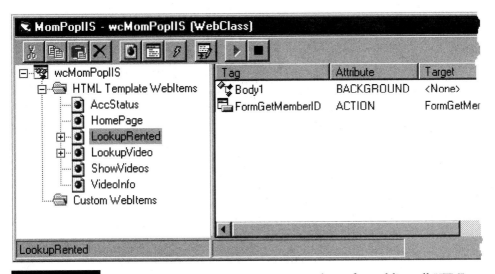

FIGURE 16-5 Results of the *WebClass Designer* window after adding all HTML templates to the *WebClass*.

WebClass Events

There are six events that can be sent to your *WebClass* object. The events that occur to a *WebClass* object are similar to the events that occur to a Visual Basic form. The first of these, the ***Initialize*** event, is fired when a *WebClass* object is created. This happens when a client accesses the Active Server Page that hosts your IIS application. The *Initialize* event is always the first event to occur to a *WebClass*. However, it occurs every time your *WebClass* receives an HTTP request if your *WebClass* does not retain state (that is, the *StateManagement* property is set to *wcNoState*).

The next event that occurs to a *WebClass* is the ***BeginRequest*** event. This event is fired each time the *WebClass* receives a request from the browser, including the first time (in which case, the event occurs after the *Initialize* event).

The ***Start*** event occurs only after the first *BeginRequest* event. This is an important event, as it is typically used to send an initial response to the browser. Usually, this involves setting the initial *WebItem* for the application; that is, the first HTML page of the IIS application. More on this event shortly.

The ***EndRequest*** event occurs after the request has been processed and the application has returned a response to the browser.

The ***Terminate*** event occurs just before the *WebClass* object is destroyed. This occurs after the completion of every request if the *StateManagement* property of the *WebClass* is set to *wcNoState*.

The best analogy you can make to form events is the analogy between a form's ***Load*** and ***Unload*** events and a *WebClass* object's *BeginRequest* and *EndRequest* events.

EXAMPLE: THE WEBCLASS START EVENT

In a *WebClass* object's *Start* event, IIS applications typically point the client's browser to the first HTML page in the IIS application. Remember that an HTML page in an IIS application is considered a *WebItem;* specifically, it is an *HTML Template WebItem.* To point the browser to a particular *WebItem* (HTML page), you set the *WebClass* object's **NextItem** property to the *WebItem* that corresponds to the HTML page. This activates the *WebItem.*

In the following example below, the *Start* event for the *wcMomPopIIS WebClass* object sets the first page to the *HomePage WebItem* object.

```
Private Sub WebClass_Start()
    '- When this Web app starts, the first page
    '- is the HomePage WebItem.
    Set NextItem = HomePage
End Sub
```

Types of WebItem Events

A **WebItem** (e.g., HTML template) can generate events. There are three kinds of events that *WebItems* in a *WebClass* can generate. I will illustrate examples of all of the following event types in the analysis of the accompanying demo program.

- A **standard event** is a predefined event that will appear in the *Code Editor* window's *Procedure* drop-down list. Examples include the *Respond* and *ProcessTag* events.
- A **template event** is an event that must be connected to be treated as an event. Once connected, a Template Event will appear in the *Code Editor* window's *Procedure* drop-down list. Examples include hyper-links and forms.
- A **custom event** is added by the developer. Custom events can be added dynamically or at design time using custom *WebItems.*

The rules for when a particular event is fired are somewhat complex. Gaining an understanding of these rules is one of the greatest challenges you face as an IIS application developer. Examples from the demo program should help clarify the following rules:

1. If a request specifies an event, and there is an event procedure for that event, that event is fired and the corresponding event procedure is invoked.
2. If a request specifies an event, and there is not an event procedure for that event, the *UserEvent* event is fired.
3. If there is no event specified in the request, the *Respond* event for the template is fired.

Standard WebItem Events

All *WebItems*, including *HTML Template WebItems*, have three standard events that appear in the *Code Editor* window's *Procedure* drop-down list. The **Respond** event is fired when an HTML template is activated by a user request or by the activation of the template from your code. The **ProcessTag** event is fired so that your application can replace tags in the HTML template. More on this event later. The **UserEvent** is fired for events that are added at runtime. More on this later.

Of the above events, the *Respond* event is the most commonly used. The *Respond* event is fired when a *WebItem* is first activated. This can happen from either the client side or the server side. A *WebItem* is activated from the server side when the *NextItem* property of the *WebClass* object is set.

Writing an HTML Template

In the processing of an HTTP request, you can write an HTML template to the browser by invoking the **WriteTemplate** method of the *HTML Template WebItem*. This is typically done in the *WebItem's* **Respond** event. You can write additional HTML after and/or before writing the template. This is done by invoking the **Write** method on the **Response** object, which is an ASP object.

To write an HTML hyperlink to a *WebItem* within your *WebClass*, use the **URLFor** function. This function returns the URL from a corresponding *WebItem* object. For example,

```
Private Sub HomePage_Respond()

    '- Since there is no specific event for HomePage,
    '- the Respond event will run when the HomePage
    '- WebItem is navigated to.

    '- This procedure outputs links to the other
    '- pages, using the URLFor function to find the
    '- URL given the WebItem.

    HomePage.WriteTemplate
    With Response
        .Write "<HTML><BODY>"
        .Write "<A HREF=""" & URLFor(LookupVideo) & """>"
        .Write "Search our video inventory</A>"
        .Write "<P>"
        .Write "<A HREF=""" & URLFor(LookupRented) & """>"
        .Write "Look up your account status</A>"
        .Write "</BODY></HTML>"
    End With

End Sub
```

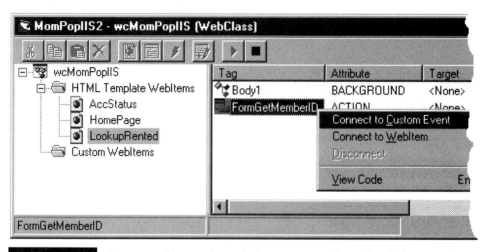

FIGURE 16-6 Connect a form or hyperlink to an event by right-clicking on the tag and selecting *Connect to Custom Event.*

Connecting a Template WebItem Event

Hyperlinks and forms can act as event sources if they are connected as events. For example, the *LookupRented WebItem* has a form called *FormGetMemberID,* which specifies the *Post* method (the source for this HTML pages appears a few pages back). You can connect an event that will be fired when the form is submitted to the form. The event procedure, once connected, will be called *LookupRented_FormGetMemberID.*

In this event procedure, you can navigate the browser to another *WebItem.* In the demo program, the **AccStatus** *WebItem* is set as the value of the *NextItem* property. This will fire the *AccStatus_Respond* event. To connect a form or hyperlink to an event, use the following procedure (see Figure 16-6):

1. Select the *WebItem* in the left pane of the *WebClass Designer* window.

2. In the right pane, right-click on the tag and select *Connect to Custom Event.*

After connecting the event, you can select it from the *Procedure* drop-down list in the *Code Editor* window, and write code for the event. The following code, for example, navigates the client's browser to the *Account Status WebItem* when the *LookupRented* form is submitted:

```
Private Sub LookupRented_FormGetMemberID()
    Set NextItem = AccStatus
End Sub
```

Accessing Posted Data and Generating an HTML Page

To access data posted from a form, use the ***Request*** object's ***Form*** collection. This is the same technique used in Active Server Page script. A lengthy code example illustrating this technique follows this paragraph. Note that the code is in pure Visual Basic and not in *VBScript* – this is the major attraction of IIS applications. See Figure 16-7 for an example of the HTML generated by the following code when viewed in a browser.

```
Private Sub AccStatus_Respond()
    Dim RS As Recordset
    Dim objMember As MemberData
    Dim nID As Long
    Dim strDateRented As String
    Dim strDateDue As String

    ' Validate member id

    If Not IsNumeric(Request.Form("MemberID")) Then
        OutputReturnToLookupRented
        Exit Sub
    End If

    ' Lookup member by id

    nID = Request.Form("MemberID")

    Set objMember = New MemberData
    Set RS = objMember.FindByID(nID)

    If RS.BOF And RS.EOF Then
        RS.Close
        OutputReturnToLookupRented
        Exit Sub
    End If

    ' Display member information

    AccStatus.WriteTemplate

    With Response
        .Write "<HTML><BODY>"
        .Write "<P>" & RS("FirstName") & _
            " " & RS("LastName")
        RS.Close
```

```vb
        ' Get and display rented videos, if any

        Set RS = objMember.GetRentedVideos(nID)

        If RS.BOF And RS.EOF Then
            .Write "<P>No videos rented."
        Else
            .Write "<TABLE BORDER=1><TR>"
            .Write "<TR><TD>Title</TD>"
            .Write "<TD>Date Rented</TD>"
            .Write "<TD>Date Due</TD></TR>"
            Do While Not RS.EOF
                strDateRented = Format(RS("DateRented"), _
                                    "Short Date")
                strDateDue = Format(RS("DateDue"), _
                                    "Short Date")
                .Write "<TR><TD>" & RS("title") & "</TD>"
                .Write "<TD>" & strDateRented & "</TD>"
                .Write "<TD>" & strDateDue & "</TD></TR>"
                RS.MoveNext
            Loop
        End If

    End With

    '- Save state with the URLData property

    URLData = Str(nID)

    With Response
        .Write "<A HREF=""" & URLFor(CurrentAddress) & """>"
        .Write "Show my current address info</A>"
        .Write "</BODY></HTML>"
    End With

    RS.Close
    Set RS = Nothing
    Set objMember = Nothing

End Sub
```

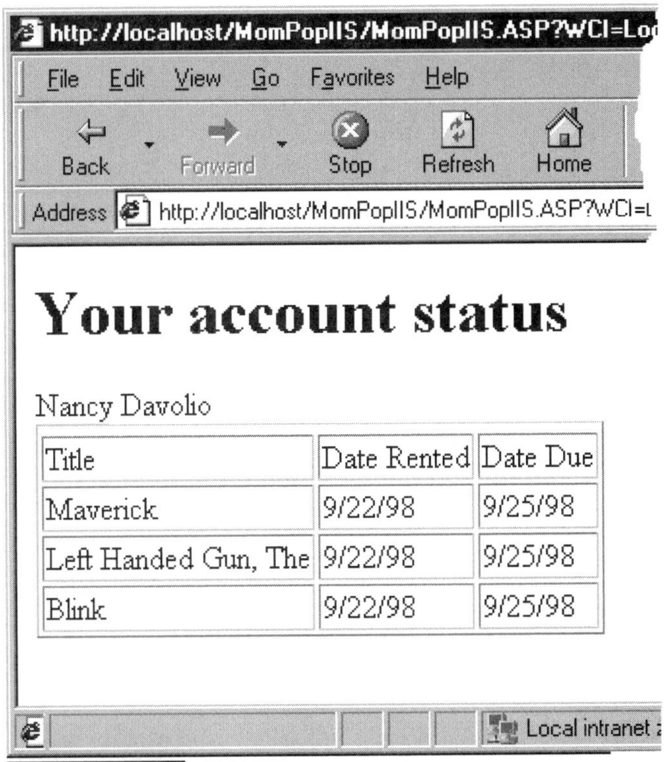

FIGURE 16-7 Shown above is the generated HTML from the code example presented previously.

HTML Tag Replacement

If desired, you can use special tags in your HTML templates that can be replaced at runtime by your IIS application. Tags that indicate replacement are enclosed in angle brackets like any other HTML tag, but are identified by a prefix The default prefix is **WC@**, but you can define any prefix you want by setting the **TagPrefix** property of the *WebItem* that contains the tags to be replaced.

In the *ShowVideos* page (see Figure 16-8), the string following the caption *"Search results for string ="* is a tag that is replaced at runtime by the IIS application. In the following sections, I'll illustrate how this is done.

Video ID	Title	Year	Director
52014	Associate, The	1996	Donald Petrie
52023	Killing Street, The	1984	R. Joffe
52002	Left Handed Gun, The	1958	A. Penn
52021	Postman, The	1988	J. Stelling
52024	Rumble In The Bronx	1996	S. Tong
52015	Scarlet Letter, The	1995	R. Joffe
52006	Tales From The Hood	1995	R. Cundieff
52013	Twilight Zone The Movie	1983	S. Spielberg
52026	Welcome To The Dollhouse	1996	T. Solondz

FIGURE 16-8 Following the text ***Search results for string =,*** the HTML has a replacement tag that, at runtime, is replaced with the search string entered by the user.

RUNTIME TAG REPLACEMENT

When an HTML template that includes replacement tags is sent to the browser (typically as a result of invoking the *WriteTemplate* method on the *WebItem*), the **ProcessTag** event is invoked on the *WebItem*. You are passed one **TagName** at a time to this event procedure; the *ProcessTag* event is called once for each tag in the HTML template.

Your code should look at the *TagName* parameter, and return the replacement string in the **TagContents** parameter. Setting the **SendTags** parameter to **FALSE** indicates that only the tag contents should be sent to the browser, not the tags themselves. You would typically set *SendTags* to **FALSE** (this is the default value if you don't assign it a value). You can actually send another replacement tag, generated by the *ProcessTag* event, to recurse through tag replacement. In this case, set the *SendTags* parameter to **TRUE**, and set the *WebItem's* **ReScanReplacements** property to **TRUE**.

A simple example of tag replacement follows:

```
Private Sub ShowVideos_ProcessTag(ByVal TagName As String, _
                                  TagContents As String, _
                                  SendTags As Boolean)


    '- Simple example of tag replacement.  See HTML
    '- for WebItem ShowVideos to see the tag.

    Dim strSearchString As String
    strSearchString = Request.Form("VideoTitle")
    If TagName = "WC@SearchString" Then
        TagContents = strSearchString
    End If

End Sub
```

The HTML containing the tag to be replaced is as follows:

```
<html>
<body>
<H3>Video Title Search Results</H3>
<P>Search results for string = <WC@SEARCHSTRING>
xxx</WC@SEARCHSTRING></P>
</body>
</html>
```

Dynamic Creation of WebItem Events

You can dynamically create hyperlinks that fire custom events to provide custom event handling. The *ShowVideos* page (see Figure 16-9), which displays the result of a query for video title, illustrates this technique. The generated table includes, for each video ID, a hyperlink to more information about that video. The hyperlink is to the *VideoInfo* HTML page. The approach to using this technique is discussed in the following sections.

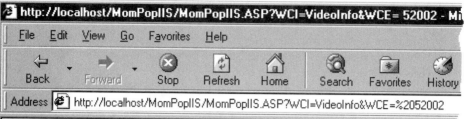

About this video

Left Handed Gun, The

1958

Directed by: A. Penn

Western follows the exploits of Billy the Kid from the Lincoln County cattle wa
death at the hands of Pat Garret

Starring.

Paul Newman
John Dehner
James Best
Hurd Hatfield

Return to Mom-n-Pop Home Page

FIGURE 16-9 The above illustration is a page generated from the
VideoInfo HTML template, which uses custom events.

The *Mom-n-Pop* IIS application uses this technique to generate a Web
page that describes a video in inventory. The effect is that there is apparently a Web page for each and every video in the store. In actual fact, there are
no such Web pages; each Web page is dynamically generated from the IIS
application. To view this feature, from the *ShowVideos* HTML page, which
lists the results of a query for title, you can click on one of the links to get
more information about a video. The links are created dynamically, and connected to user-defined events that are connected at runtime.

CUSTOM WEBITEM EVENTS

Using the **_URLFor_** method, you can fire custom events from the browser. The first parameter to the _URLFor_ method indicates the _WebItem_ that is associated with the URL, while the second parameter is a string that indicates a custom event name. When the user selects the hyperlink, the **_UserEvent_** event is sent to the _WebItem_. The name of the event is passed as the parameter to the event procedure.

The _ShowVideos_ page uses this technique, creating a custom _WebItem_ event for each generated link in the table of videos matching a query. The _ShowVideos_Respond_ event generates the required HTML for the _ShowVideos_ page, including the hyperlinks that contain the dynamically generated custom events. The code is shown below:

```
Private Sub ShowVideos_Respond()

    '- Respond event for ShowVideos WebItem.  This page
    '- has some tags on it, so when the template for the
    '- WebItem is written, it will trigger the
    '- ProcessTags event.

    Dim RS As Recordset
    Dim V As New VideoData
    Dim strSearch As String

    '- Write the template.  This will trigger the
    '- ProcessTags event.

    ShowVideos.WriteTemplate

    '- Get the VideoTitle posted to the form.  It comes
    '- from an INPUT control named VideoTitle.  We can
    '- get this information from the Form collection of
    '- the Request object.

    strSearch = Request.Form("VideoTitle")

    '- Using an object in the Data Services Layer,
    '- get the list of videos, as a recordset.

    Set RS = V.Search(strSearch)

    '- If no videos match, display a message and a
    '- link to allow the user to go back and enter
    '- new search criteria.
```

```
If RS.BOF And RS.EOF Then
    RS.Close
    With Response
        .Write "<HTML><BODY>"
        .Write "Sorry, no videos match that query"
        .Write "<A HREF=""" & URLFor(LookupVideo)
        .Write """>"
        .Write "Enter another search string</A><P>"
        OutputHomePageLink
        .Write "</BODY></HTML>"
        Exit Sub
    End With
End If

'- Write a table of matching videos.  We will create
'- a link for each Video ID using a custom event.
'- When the user clicks this link, a page is created
'- that describes the video.

With Response
    .Write "<HTML><BODY>"
    .Write "<TABLE BORDER=1>"
    .Write "<TR><TD>Video ID</TD>"
    .Write "<TD>Title</TD>"
    .Write "<TD>Year</TD>"
    .Write "<TD>Director</TD></TR>"
End With

Do While Not RS.EOF
    With Response
        .Write "<TR><TD>"
        .Write "<A HREF="""
        .Write URLFor(VideoInfo, Str(RS("VideoID")))
        .Write """>"
        .Write RS("VideoID") & "</A></TD>"
        .Write "<TD>" & RS("Title") & "</TD>"
        .Write "<TD>" & RS("Year") & "</TD>"
        .Write "<TD>" & RS("Director") & "</TD>"
        .Write "</TR>"
    End With
    RS.MoveNext
Loop

'- Done

RS.Close
```

```
Response.Write "<HTML><BODY>"
OutputHomePageLink
Response.Write "</BODY></HTML>"

Set RS = Nothing
Set V = Nothing
```

End Sub

HANDLING USEREVENT EVENTS

All user events are sent to a single **UserEvent** procedure for the correspond-ing *WebItem*. The *UserEvent* event procedure is passed a string parameter, **EventName**, which contains the name of the event as specified in the **URLFor** method. It is often necessary to use a **Select Case** statement to pro-vide appropriate processing for the particular *User Event* that was raised.

In the demo program's case, the name of the event is actually a string representation of the video ID that the user clicked. Therefore, the program converts the *EventName* parameter to a number, and uses an object in the data services layer to look up information on the selected video. The code follows:

```
Private Sub VideoInfo_UserEvent(ByVal EventName As String)

    '- This event is triggered when the user clicks
    '- on a generated link in the table of videos.

    Dim V As New VideoData
    Dim nVideoID As Long
    Dim RS As Recordset
    Dim strCastList As String
    Dim strCastMember As String
    Dim nPos As Integer

    VideoInfo.WriteTemplate

    nVideoID = EventName
    Set RS = V.FindByID(nVideoID)

    With Response

        .Write "<HTML><BODY>"
        .Write "<H2>" & RS("Title") & "</H2>"
        .Write "<H3>" & RS("Year") & "</H3>"
        .Write "<H4>Directed by: " & RS("Director")
```

```
                    .Write "</H4>"
                    .Write "<P>"
                    .Write RS("Description")
                    .Write "<P>Starring:<P>"

                    '- Cast is cr-lf delimited string of actors.
                    '- Use the VB Replace function to replace cr-lf
                    '- with the <BR> tag.

                    strCastList = Replace(RS("Cast"), vbCrLf, "<BR>")
                    .Write strCastList & "<P>"

            End With

            OutputHomePageLink
            Response.Write "</BODY></HTML>"

            RS.Close
            Set RS = Nothing
            Set V = Nothing

        End Sub
```

Saving State in IIS Applications

Internet applications tend to be stateless, meaning that between requests and responses between the browser and server, information is not maintained. However, if you want your IIS application to retain state between requests, there are a number of approaches you can take.

Before taking any approach to maintain state between requests, you should know that saving state in an Internet application affects its scalability. Normally, a *WebClass* object is destroyed when a response to a request completes; another *WebClass* object is created when another request is made. If the *WebClass* object needs to hold state, you have to make sure it is not destroyed between a request/response cycle. This can be done by setting the *WebClass's* **StateManagement** property to *2 – wcRetainInstance*. If you set the *WebClass* object's *StateManagement* property to *wcRetainInstance*, the *WebClass* object is not destroyed until the Internet application terminates. Therefore, variables declared in the declarations section of your *WebClass* module will retain their values. You can force the deletion of a *WebClass* object by invoking the **ReleaseInstance** method.

You can also store state in any other objects used by your IIS application, provided you retain references to each object. This is done by either setting the *WebClass* object's *StateManagement* property to *wcRetainInstance,* or by storing the object reference in the ASP **Session** object. You can also store values in general (not just object references) in the *Session* object to maintain state between requests. Storing state in the *Session* object does not require you to keep the *WebClass* alive between requests.

Storing State Client-Side

Instead of storing state on the server, you can store state on the client. State can be stored client-side using either cookies or the **URLData** property of the *WebClass.* Of the two choices, using cookies is the least preferred, since the client can disable the browser from receiving cookies. The more reliable approach is to use the **URLData** property of the *WebClass* object.

When you set the *URLData* property to a string, that string is subsequently sent as part of the URL to any *WebItem* within the *WebClass.* The data is actually stored with the HTML in the client's browser. Since the client's browser is storing the state information, the size of your state information is limited. Do not expect to be able to store more than about 2 Kilobytes of data using this technique.

To store state client-side using the *URLData* property, simply set the *URLData* property to a string that you can later parse to extract the state data. To retrieve state stored client-side using the *URLData* property, simply read back the *URLData* property, parsing out the state data if required.

For example, the demo for this chapter stores the member ID in the *URLData* property when the member's account status is accessed (*WebItem AccStatus*). On this page is a link to show the member's current address information. When that page is accessed, the state data is retrieved.

EXAMPLE: STORING STATE CLIENT-SIDE

The following code uses the *URLData* property to store state in a URL that is handed back to the browser. The saved information is the member's ID.

```
Private Sub AccStatus_Respond()
    Dim RS As Recordset
    Dim objMember As MemberData
    Dim nID As Long
    Dim strDateRented As String
    Dim strDateDue As String

    ' Validate member id

    If Not IsNumeric(Request.Form("MemberID")) Then
        OutputReturnToLookupRented
        Exit Sub
    End If

    ' Look up member by id

    nID = Request.Form("MemberID")

    Set objMember = New MemberData
    Set RS = objMember.FindByID(nID)

            .
            .
            .

    '- Save state with the URLData property

    URLData = Str(nID)

    With Response
        .Write "<A HREF=""" & URLFor(CurrentAddress) & """>"
        .Write "Show my current address info</A>"
        .Write "</BODY></HTML>"
    End With

    RS.Close
    Set RS = Nothing
    Set objMember = Nothing

End Sub
```

EXAMPLE: RETRIEVING STATE STORED CLIENT-SIDE

The following code retrieves the member ID by reading back the *URLData* property. The member ID was stored in the *URLData* property when the user responded to the *Lookup Account Status* page.

```
Private Sub CurrentAddress_Respond()
    Dim nID As Integer
    Dim RS As Recordset
    Dim objMember As New MemberData

    '- Make sure there is data in URLData

    If URLData = "" Then
        Set NextItem = LookupRented
        Exit Sub
    End If

    '- Write template, then get member id

    CurrentAddress.WriteTemplate

    nID = Val(URLData)
    Set RS = objMember.FindByID(nID)
    RS.Open

    If RS.BOF And RS.EOF Then
        Set NextItem = LookupRented
        Exit Sub
    End If

    With Response
        .Write RS!FirstName & " " & RS!LastName & "<BR>"
        .Write RS!Address1 & "<BR>"
        .Write RS!City & "<BR>"
    End With

    OutputHomePageLink

    RS.Close
    Set RS = Nothing
    Set objMember = Nothing

End Sub
```

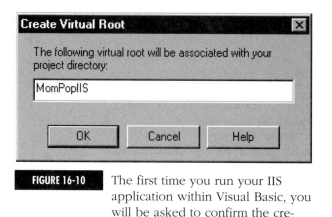

| FIGURE 16-10 | The first time you run your IIS application within Visual Basic, you will be asked to confirm the creation of a virtual root.

Testing, Debugging, and Building an IIS Application

Since you will typically develop your IIS application outside your Web server's home directory, it is necessary for Visual Basic to create a virtual root for your application. A **virtual root** is a directory that appears as a subdirectory of your Web server's home directory, but which is actually outside your Web server's home directory. When you run an IIS application for the first time within Visual Basic, you are prompted to create a virtual root (see Figure 16-10).

You can set breakpoints and examine and modify variables within the Visual Basic debugger. In other words, you debug an IIS Application like any other Visual Basic program.

To build an IIS application, select **Make** from the **Project** menu. Note that this is the same method you use to build any other type of Visual Basic application. When an IIS application is built, a DLL is created along with an ASP file that hosts the application and creates its runtime component. This ASP file also serves as the starting page for your application.

Deploying an IIS Application

If you have developed the IIS application on the server on which it is to be deployed, you don't have to take any additional steps to deploy the application. To deploy the application on another machine, use the ***Package and Deployment Wizard*** to package and deploy the IIS application:

1. Build the application by selecting ***Make*** from the ***Project*** menu.
2. Using the *Package and Deployment Wizard*, build a **CAB** file that contains the required files for your application.
3. Using the *Package and Deployment Wizard*, deploy the application to the target Web server.

Alternatively, you can manually copy the required files, but you must manually create a virtual root and register your IIS application's DLL.

ActiveX Documents

Once you understand what they are, you'll probably agree that using ActiveX Documents is the one of best ways to build and deploy a client-side intranet application. An **ActiveX Document** is a program that has the semantics of a document – it looks like a document, but acts like a program! ActiveX Documents can be hosted in an ActiveX Document Container application; *Internet Explorer* is such an application. The best news about ActiveX Documents is that they are almost identical to Visual Basic forms – which means you don't have to learn HTML or a scripting language to create intranet applications.

About ActiveX Documents

ActiveX Documents may be responsible for blurring the distinction between a traditional (static) document, and an application. ActiveX Documents are complete applications with the semantics of traditional documents. Instead of the user "running a program," the user opens a document or accesses a hyperlink, which, behind the scenes, starts the *ActiveX Document Component* that "controls" the document.

ActiveX Document Containers are programs that have the necessary interfaces to contain, or host, an ActiveX Document within their native user interface. **ActiveX Document Components** are programs that can open documents within an ActiveX Document Container.

Viewing an ActiveX Document with Internet Explorer

Currently, the only widely used ActiveX Document Containers are *Microsoft Internet Explorer* and *Microsoft Binder*. There are, however, lots of ActiveX Documents. For example, *Microsoft Word* documents are ActiveX Documents. What this means is that *Microsoft Word* is perfectly comfortable displaying a view of its data in *Internet Explorer's* interactive environment (see Figure 17-1). Remember that *Internet Explorer* is an ActiveX Document Container.

Microsoft Word will also display its own user interface objects, such as its menus, toolbars, and status bars in the Internet Explorer's user interface. This is because the ActiveX Document and its container negotiate for user interface "space."

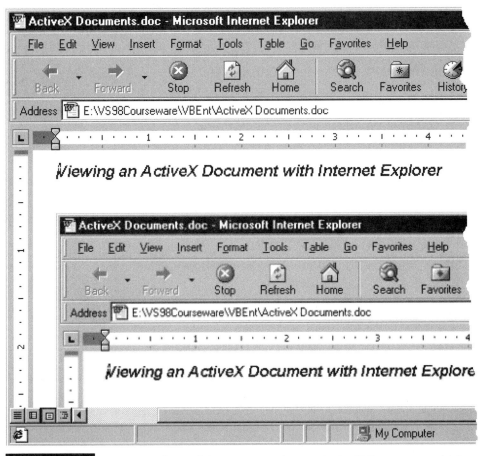

FIGURE 17-1 A *Microsoft Word* document is also an ActiveX Document, which can be viewed by an ActiveX Document Container, such as *Internet Explorer*.

Why Use ActiveX Documents?

Imagine using only one application to open, view, and update any document, regardless of content. Furthermore, imagine that that single application can be written once, and future applications will roll right into it, since the document provides a standard interface that the container expects to find. The technology has far-reaching applications, especially for the Internet. However, it is expected that the type of functionality provided by ActiveX Documents will be of special interest to developers at corporations who need to publish documents on their intranet.

One of the main advantages of using ActiveX Documents is that the data can be viewed in its native format (without being converted, for example, to HTML). There are other advantages to using ActiveX Documents, including:

1. If you know Visual Basic, there is little else you need to learn, other than how to create ActiveX Documents (which is easy to learn). You don't need to learn HTML.

2. You can use the Visual Basic development environment, which you are already familiar with. You don't need to learn another development environment.

3. You can create Visual Basic applications that are easily and widely available, via the *Internet Explorer.*

4. The ActiveX Document executes on the client, containing all the necessary code to deliver the results of complex calculations.

5. ActiveX Documents can access *Hyperlink* objects, which makes them capable of causing a container to move to new Web pages, making navigation easy for the user.

Creating an ActiveX Document Application

Visual Basic offers two types of ActiveX Document projects. Your choice is to either create an ActiveX Document DLL or an ActiveX Document EXE. The major difference is that ActiveX Document EXEs can have a standalone user interface, while ActiveX Document DLLs cannot – they rely on an *ActiveX Document Container* application to load them.

In the first sections of this chapter, I will walk you through the creation of a simple ActiveX Document DLL. The application calculates the wind chill factor given temperature and wind speed. This would be a very simple Visual Basic application, requiring the developer to know only how to create simple controls and write simple event procedures. As you'll see, it's also a way to provide an easy introduction to ActiveX Documents. If you prefer, you may load and run a completed version of this walkthrough. The project is *MyDocument.VBP,* located in folder *VB6Adv\Demos\ActiveXDoc.* Later in this chapter, I will illustrate a sample *Mom-n-Pop Video Store* client application that is built using ActiveX Document technology.

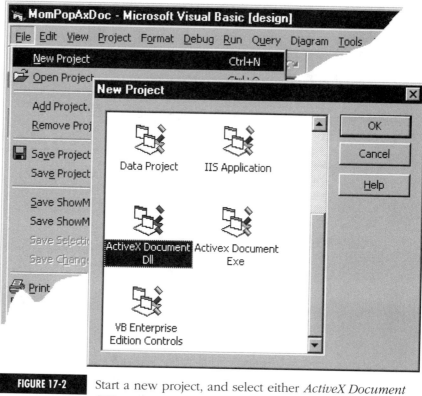

FIGURE 17-2 Start a new project, and select either *ActiveX Document DLL* or *ActiveX Document EXE* as the project type.

Starting a New ActiveX Document Project

To start a new ActiveX Document project, start Visual Basic and select either *ActiveX Document DLL* or *ActiveX Document EXE* as the project type (see Figure 17-2). An ActiveX Document built as an EXE can have a standalone interface, while an ActiveX Document built as a DLL cannot. To follow along with the *Wind Chill* walkthrough, select an *ActiveX Document DLL.*

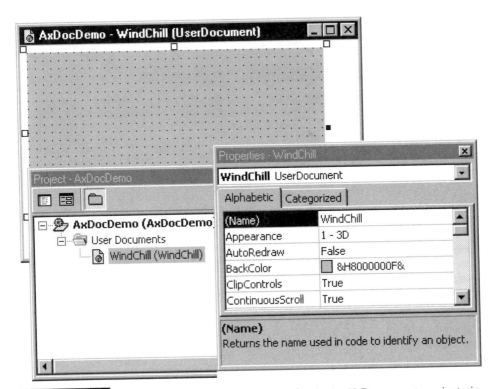

FIGURE 17-3 The development environment for ActiveX Document projects is nearly identical to the environment used to design forms.

Using the ActiveX Document Designer

When an ActiveX Document project is created, you'll get a single *User-Document* object. Visual Basic gives this document a proposed name of *UserDocument1*. ActiveX Documents are designed in an *ActiveX Document Designer* window, which you will find to be quite similar to the *Form Designer*. To activate the *ActiveX Document Designer*, double-click on *User-Document1* in the *Project Explorer Window* (see Figure 17-3).

You should set the **Name** property of the ActiveX Document to a meaningful name. When your project is built, Visual Basic will create a file named after your document, adding an extension of .VBD. This VBD file is your ActiveX Document and is what is accessed by *Internet Explorer*.

Like a standard Visual Basic application with multiple forms, an ActiveX Document project may have multiple *UserDocument* objects, each of which would be like separate Web pages in the ActiveX Document application.

LAYING OUT CONTROLS ON THE USER DOCUMENT OBJECT

Once you start the *ActiveX Document Designer*, you'll probably notice that it has much in common with ordinary Visual Basic applications. You design your ActiveX Document in the same way you design a standard Visual Basic form. You can add controls, set properties, invoke methods, and respond to events in the same way you do when you create an ordinary Visual Basic application.

Figure 17-4 shows the layout of an ActiveX Document that will calculate the wind chill factor. A command button called *cmdCalculate* obtains the temperature from *txtTemperature*, and the wind speed from *txtWindSpeed*. After calculating the wind chill factor, the results are displayed in the label *lblResult*. The required code is as follows:

```
Option Explicit

Private Sub cmdCalculate_Click()
    Dim fTemp As Single
    Dim fSpeed As Single
    Dim fWindChill As Single

    If Not IsNumeric(txtTemperature.Text) Then
        MsgBox "Please enter a valid temperature"
        txtTemperature.SetFocus
        Exit Sub
    End If

    If Not IsNumeric(txtWindSpeed.Text) Then
        MsgBox "Please enter a valid wind speed"
        txtWindSpeed.SetFocus
        Exit Sub
    End If

    fTemp = txtTemperature.Text
    fSpeed = txtWindSpeed.Text

    fWindChill = ((10.45 + (6.686 * Sqr(fSpeed)) - _
                 (0.447 * fSpeed)) _
                 / 22.034 * (fTemp - 91.4)) + 91.4

    lblResult.Caption = "At a wind speed of " _
                 & Format(fSpeed, "##0.00") _
                 & " and a temperature of " _
                 & Format(fTemp, "##0.00") _
                 & " the wind chill factor is " _
                 & Format(fWindChill, "##0.00")

End Sub
```

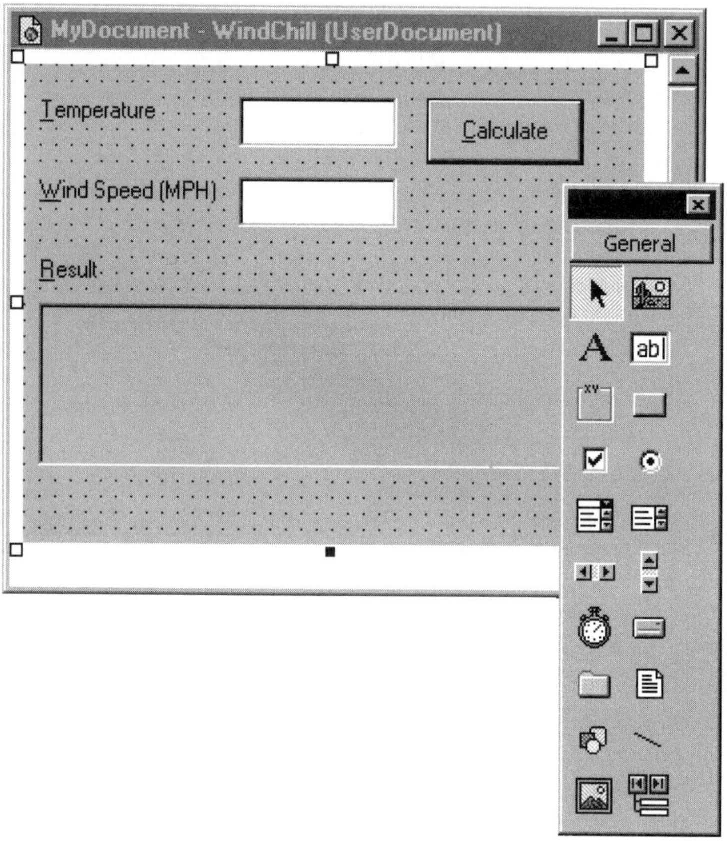

FIGURE 17-4 The *UserDocument* object can be configured with controls just like a Visual Basic form.

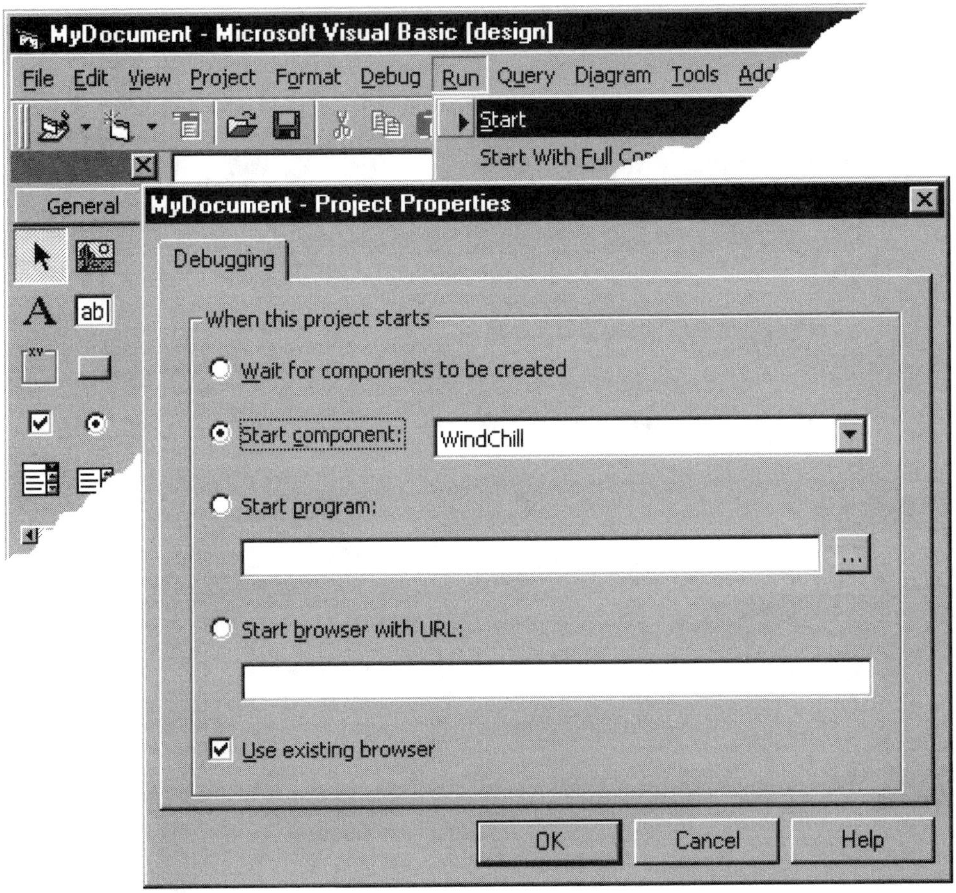

MyDocument - Microsoft Visual Basic [design]

File Edit View Project Format Debug Run Query Diagram Tools Add

▶ Start
Start With Full Co...

General

MyDocument - Project Properties

Debugging

When this project starts

○ Wait for components to be created

● Start component: WindChill ▼

○ Start program:
_____ ...

○ Start browser with URL:
_____

☑ Use existing browser

OK   Cancel   Help

FIGURE 17-5   The first time you run your ActiveX Document project, Visual Basic displays the *Debugging* dialog.

Running Your ActiveX Document from Visual Basic

To run and debug your ActiveX Document from Visual Basic, click the *Start* button or select *Start* from the *Run* menu. You may set breakpoints, if desired, before running the application. The first time you run your ActiveX Component from Visual Basic, the *Debugging* dialog will be displayed (see Figure 17-5). You can indicate which component (that is, ActiveX Document) to start. After clicking the *OK* button, *Internet Explorer* is activated, displaying your ActiveX Document (see Figure 17-6).

When you exit *Internet Explorer*, you'll notice that your ActiveX Document remains in *Run* mode. This is normal. You must click the *End* button to stop the application, even after you exit *Internet Explorer*. If you attempt to end your ActiveX Document application while *Internet Explorer* is

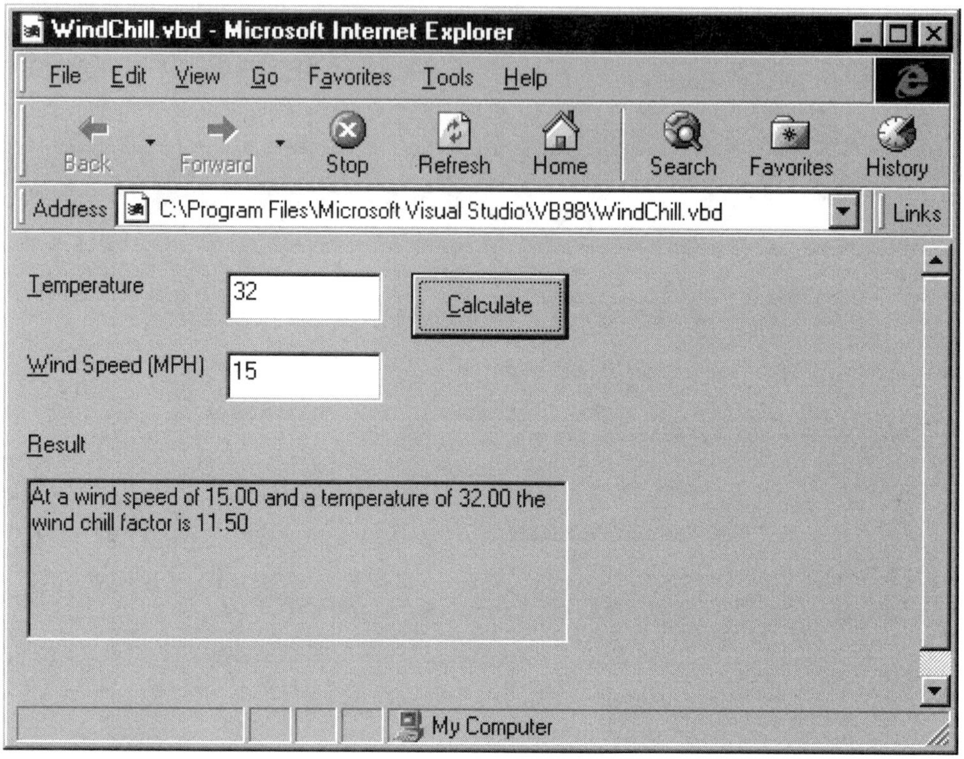

FIGURE 17-6   Your program appears in the client window area of *Internet Explorer.*

still running, Visual Basic will display a warning dialog, giving you a chance to confirm whether or not you want to terminate the application while *Internet Explorer* is still running. Terminating the ActiveX Document while *Internet Explorer* is viewing it will usually cause an error in *Internet Explorer.*

Even while running the ActiveX Document application under Visual Basic, the application must be viewed with *Internet Explorer.* After building the application, you can simply open the Visual Basic-generated VBD file from *Internet Explorer.* This will cause *Internet Explorer* to launch the DLL associated with the ActiveX Document, provided the ActiveX Document application is properly installed and registered on your system. Ideally, you should create an Internet/intranet download setup program so clients can install the ActiveX Document application on their systems. You can provide a URL that links a client to the setup program. I'll illustrate how this is done once I've presented a second ActiveX Document example from the *Mom-n-Pop Video Store.*

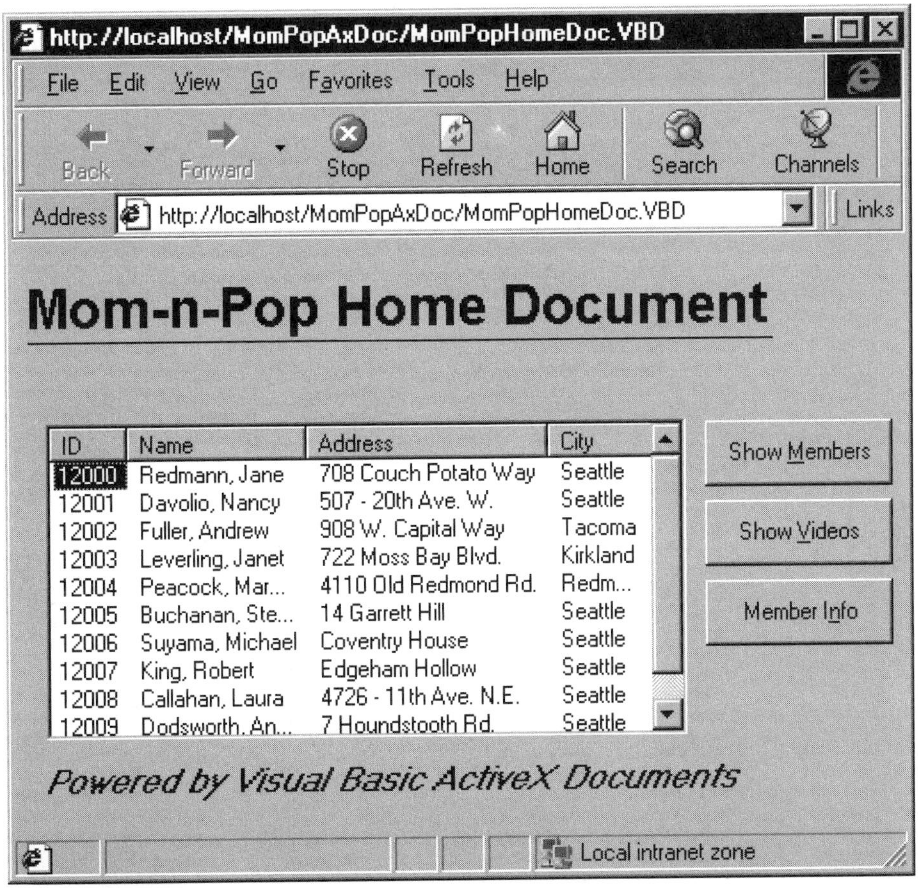
http://localhost/MomPopAxDoc/MomPopHomeDoc.VBD
File Edit View Go Favorites Tools Help
Back Forward Stop Refresh Home Search Channels
Address http://localhost/MomPopAxDoc/MomPopHomeDoc.VBD
Links
Mom-n-Pop Home Document
ID Name Address City
12000 Redmann, Jane 708 Couch Potato Way Seattle
12001 Davolio, Nancy 507 - 20th Ave. W. Seattle
12002 Fuller, Andrew 908 W. Capital Way Tacoma
12003 Leverling, Janet 722 Moss Bay Blvd. Kirkland
12004 Peacock, Mar... 4110 Old Redmond Rd. Redm...
12005 Buchanan, Ste... 14 Garrett Hill Seattle
12006 Suyama, Michael Coventry House Seattle
12007 King, Robert Edgeham Hollow Seattle
12008 Callahan, Laura 4726 - 11th Ave. N.E. Seattle
12009 Dodsworth, An... 7 Houndstooth Rd. Seattle
Show Members
Show Videos
Member Info
Powered by Visual Basic ActiveX Documents
Local intranet zone

FIGURE 17-7 The *Mom-n-Pop Video Store* ActiveX Document Application is a client-side, *Internet Explorer*-based application that implements a subset of the *Video Store* interface.

Mom-n-Pop Video Store ActiveX Document Application

The *Mom-n-Pop Video Store* ActiveX Document application (see Figure 17-7) illustrates how it is possible to use additional ActiveX Controls and control middleware objects from an ActiveX Document. The application also illustrates the use of multiple *UserDocument* objects in an ActiveX Document application.

You can run the application from Visual Basic by loading project *MomPopAxDoc.VBP,* located in folder *VB6Adv\Demos\MomPop\WebSite\MomPopAxDoc*.

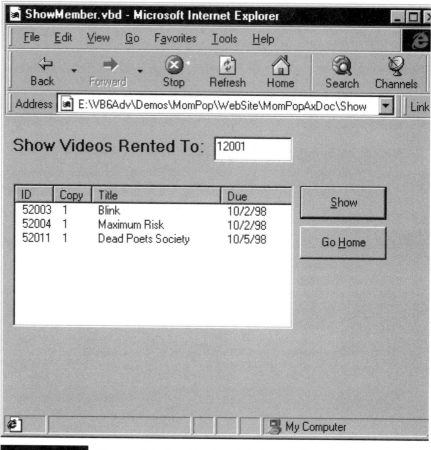

FIGURE 17-8   If you click the *Member Info* button from the first user document, you'll be directed to another user document.

The second user document object of the *Mom-n-Pop* ActiveX Document application shows videos rented to a particular member (see Figure 17-8). Moving from document to document in an ActiveX Document application is similar in concept to loading and showing forms in a Visual Basic application, but it is not done the same way. To move to another user document, you must use the **NavigateTo Method** of the *UserDocument's* **Hyperlink** object. This is the next topic.

Using the Hyperlink Object's NavigateTo Method

To move from document to document in an ActiveX Document application, you do not load and show forms. Instead, you must use the **NavigateTo** method of the *UserDocument's* **Hyperlink** object. *Internet Explorer* will jump to the URL requested in the parameter to the *NavigateTo* method. Note that this does not necessarily have to be another ActiveX Document. It can be an HTML page, an ASP page, or any other URL that *Internet Explorer* is capable of navigating to. The *Mom-n-Pop* ActiveX Document application uses only user documents; navigating between documents is accomplished with the following code:

```
Private Sub cmdMemberInfo_Click()
    UserDocument.Hyperlink.NavigateTo _
         App.Path & "\ShowMember.VBD"
End Sub

Private Sub cmdHome_Click()
    UserDocument.Hyperlink.NavigateTo _
         App.Path & "\MomPopHomeDoc.VBD"
End Sub
```

In addition to the *NavigateTo* method, the *Hyperlink* object has **GoBack** and **GoForward** methods. These are simple methods that accept no parameters. However, you must add error handling code, since the methods will raise errors if there is no history in the requested direction.

The ActiveX Document Migration Wizard

Many already-developed Visual Basic applications may benefit from conversion to ActiveX Document applications. The **ActiveX Document Migration Wizard** is provided to help with such conversion efforts.

Adding in the Migration Wizard

Before using the *ActiveX Document Migration Wizard*, it must be added to the Visual Basic *Add-Ins* menu. Refer to Figure 17-9 and the following instructions to add the wizard to Visual Basic:

1. First, check to see if the *ActiveX Document Migration Wizard* is already in your *Add-Ins* menu. If it is, you don't need to proceed.
2. From the *Add-Ins* menu, select *Add-In Manager.*
3. From the *Available Add-Ins* list, select *VB6 ActiveX Doc Migration Wizard.*
4. In the *Load Behavior* frame, check both the *Loaded/Unloaded* and *Load on Startup* check boxes.
5. Click *OK* to dismiss the *Add-In Manager* dialog.

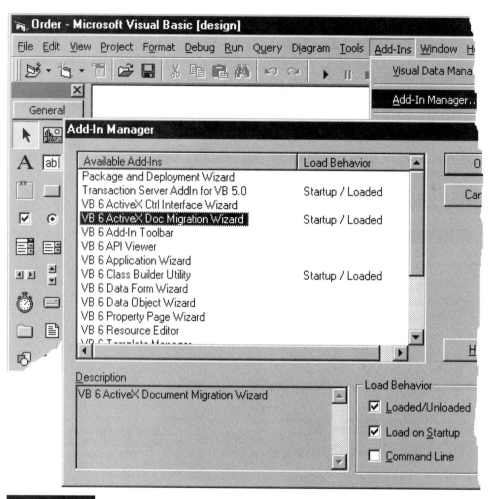

FIGURE 17-9 The *ActiveX Document Migration Wizard* will migrate an existing Standard EXE project's forms into ActiveX Documents.

Using the ActiveX Document Migration Wizard

The *ActiveX Document Migration Wizard* converts selected forms to user documents. It also converts your project type to either an ActiveX Document DLL or EXE. To retain the original version of your project, along with a new implementation as an ActiveX Document, make a copy of the project before converting it to an ActiveX Document application.

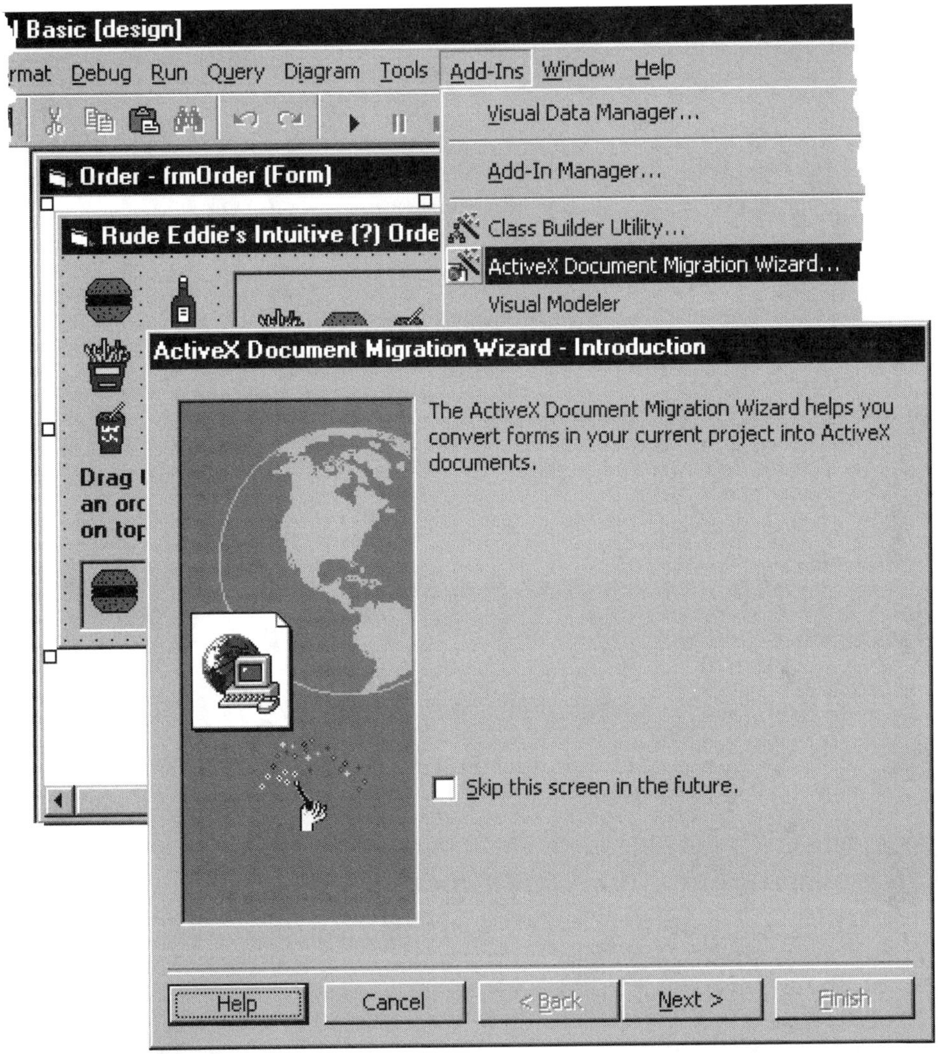

FIGURE 17-10   As an example of using the *ActiveX Document Migration Wizard*, you can convert the clipboard/drag-and-drop demo introduced in Chapter 3.

In the next section, I'll illustrate how to convert the clipboard/drag-and-drop demo program from Chapter 3 to an ActiveX Document application. To get started, load project *Order.VBP* from folder *VB6Adv\Demos\ Clipboard* and invoke the *ActiveX Document Migration Wizard* from the *Add-Ins* menu (see Figure 17-10)

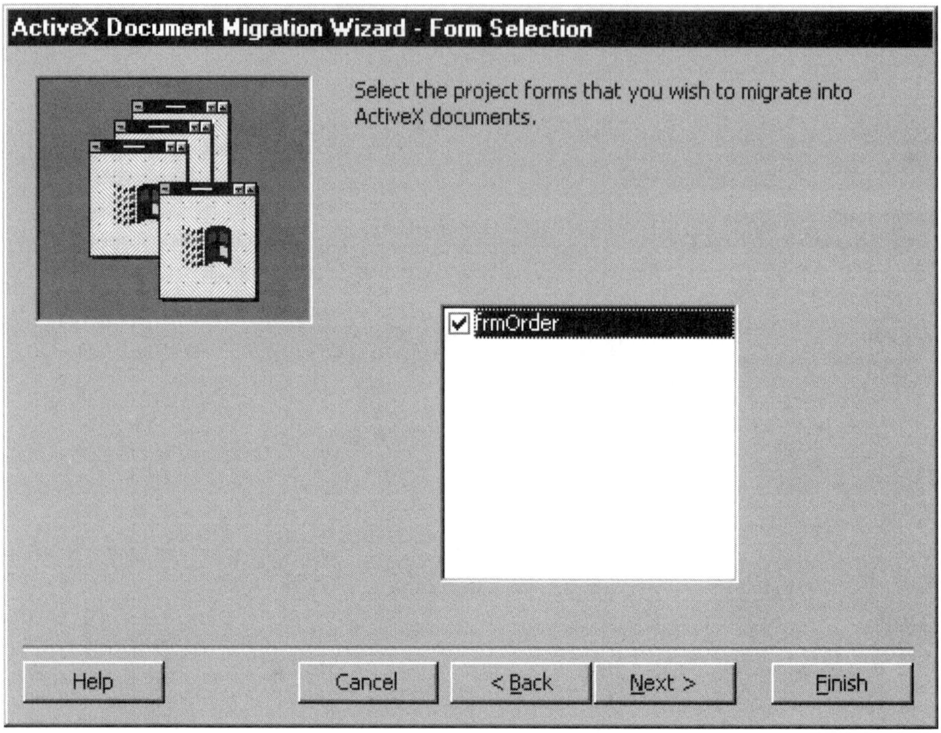

ActiveX Document Migration Wizard - Form Selection

Select the project forms that you wish to migrate into ActiveX documents.

☑ frmOrder

| Help | | Cancel | < Back | Next > | | Finish |

FIGURE 17-11 In the first screen of the wizard, you select the forms you wish to convert to ActiveX Documents.

EXAMPLE: USING THE ACTIVEX DOCUMENT MIGRATION WIZARD

On the first screen of the wizard, select the forms that you want to convert to ActiveX Documents. The clipboard demo has only one form, *frmOrder*. Select it (see Figure 17-11), then click the *Next* button.

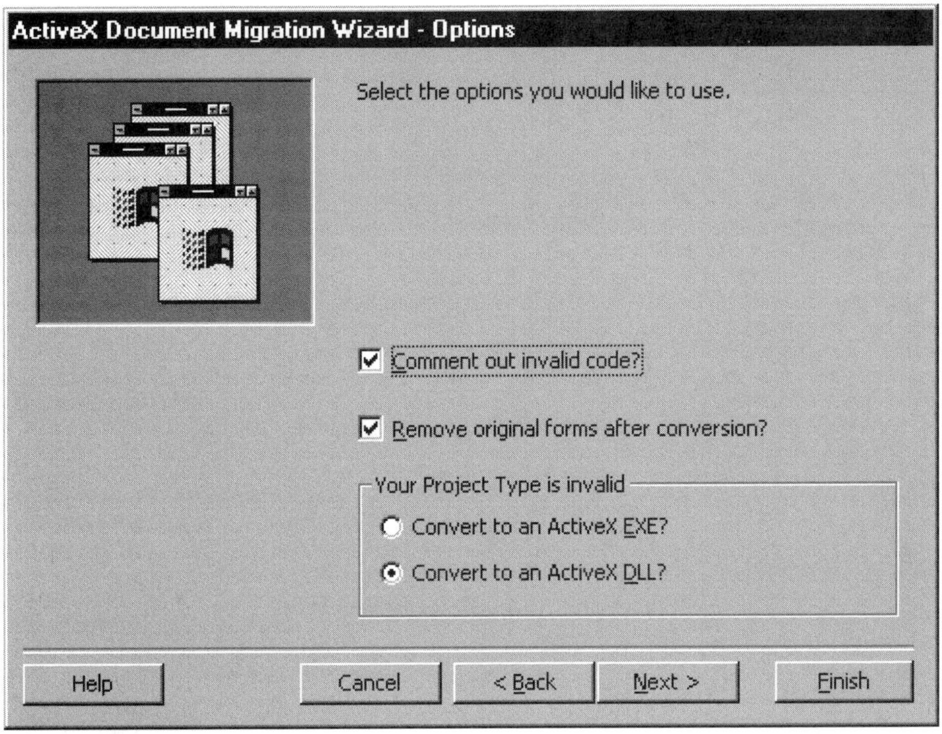

ActiveX Document Migration Wizard - Options

Select the options you would like to use.

☑ Comment out invalid code?

☑ Remove original forms after conversion?

┌─ Your Project Type is invalid ──────────
│ ○ Convert to an ActiveX EXE?
│ ◉ Convert to an ActiveX DLL?
└──────────────────────────────────────

| Help | | Cancel | < Back | Next > | | Finish |

FIGURE 17-12 On the next screen, you indicate which type of ActiveX Document project you want. You also indicate what you want to do to the original forms, and what you want done with invalid code.

On the next screen, you indicate how you want the wizard to handle invalid code. Invalid code includes using the *End* statement, as well as the *Load* and *Unload* statements, and, in general, any code dealing with forms. You must also indicate whether you want an ActiveX EXE or ActiveX DLL project.

You can choose to comment out invalid code, in which case you may need to go back and edit code that is invalid in an ActiveX Document project. You can also choose to remove the original forms once they are converted to user documents. For the purposes of this walkthrough, you should select both options, and choose *ActiveX DLL* as the project type (see Figure 17-12).

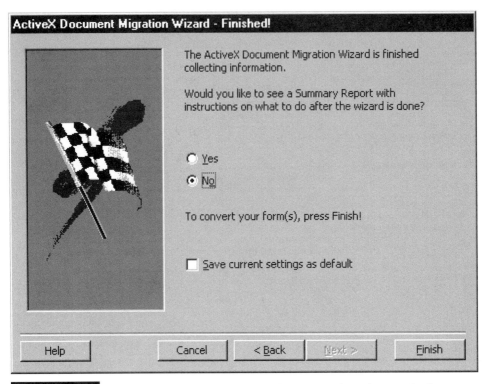

FIGURE 17-13 In the last screen of the wizard, you simply indicate whether or not you want to see a summary report.

On the last screen, you are asked if you wish to see a summary report. As the summary report contains useful information regarding what you must do to complete your project, it is recommended that you view this report. In this walkthrough, however, you can choose not to view the summary report (see Figure 17-13).

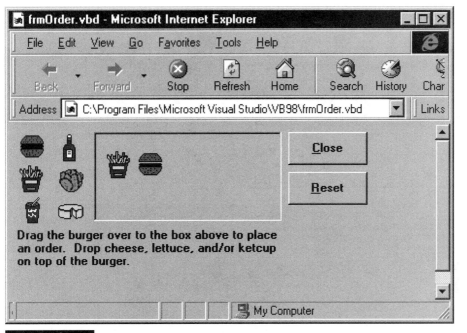

 FIGURE 17-14   Now the drag-and-drop/clipboard program runs inside *Internet Explorer.*

Once the last step has completed, you can test your program. You will probably need to change all code related to managing the forms in your old application, using the ***NavigateTo*** method of the ***Hyperlink*** object instead. Since the Standard EXE project used in this example has no other forms and uses no code that is invalid for an ActiveX Document project, you can run the program when the migration wizard completes its final step (see Figure 17-14).

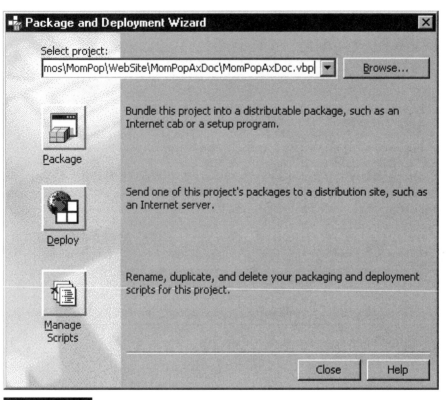

FIGURE 17-15 Use the *Package and Deployment Wizard* to create an Internet download setup for your ActiveX Document.

Distributing an ActiveX Document Application

The easiest way to distribute your ActiveX Document application is to use the *Package and Deployment Wizard*. The *Package and Deployment Wizard* will create an Internet download setup that includes the creation of the HTML required to download the ActiveX Document. In the first step of the *Package and Deployment Wizard*, select your ActiveX Document project (see Figure 17-15).

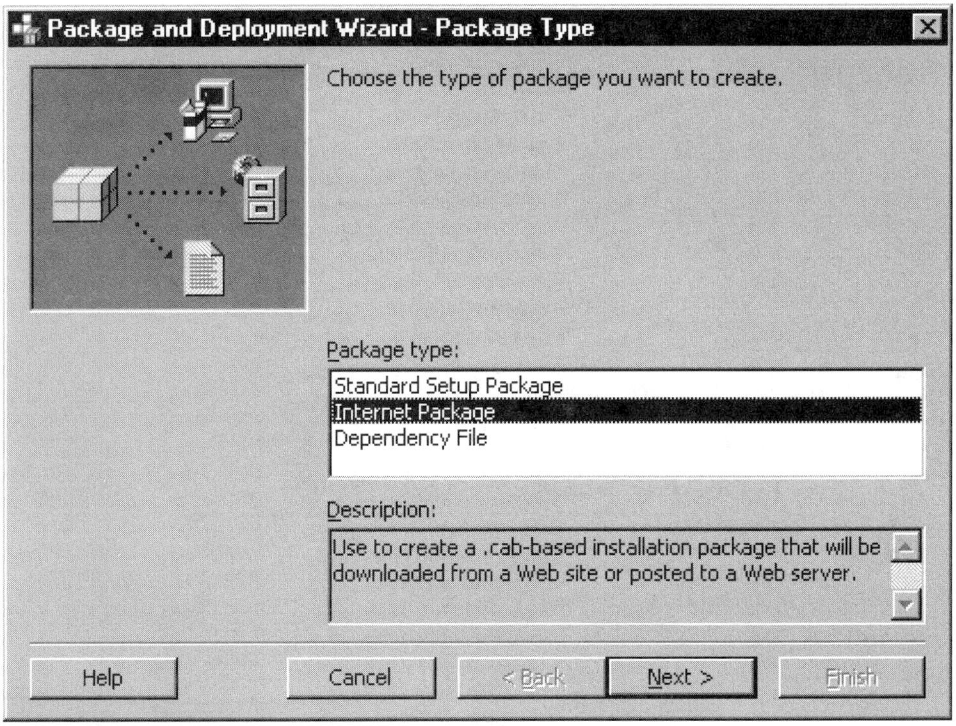

FIGURE 17-16 In the next step of the *Package and Deployment Wizard*, indicate that you want to create an *Internet Package*.

After selecting your ActiveX Document project, the *Package and Deployment Wizard* will ask you to choose the type of package that you want to create (see Figure 17-16). You should select **Internet Package** to create an Internet download setup. This creates a cab-based installation package that can be downloaded from a Web site.

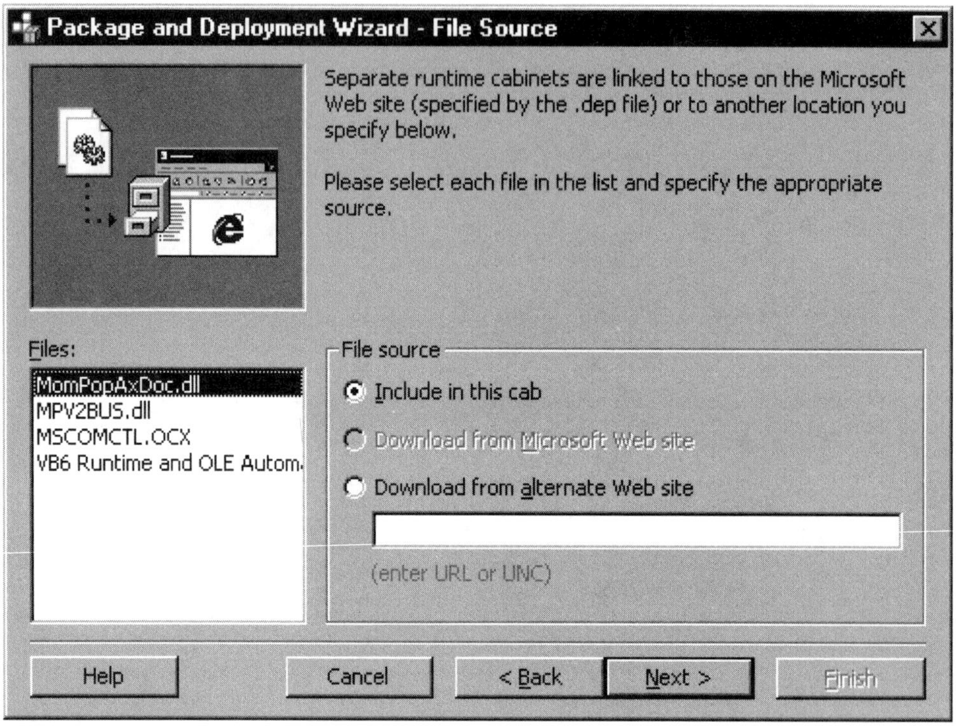

FIGURE 17-17 Using ActiveX Documents requires certain runtime components that will exist on systems that have *Visual Basic* installed.

ActiveX Document use requires a set of "runtime components," or DLLs. These components will be available on systems that have *Visual Basic* installed. Other systems must download these files before using an ActiveX Document.

The *Package and Deployment Wizard* generates code in the setup program to download these runtime components if they are missing. You can use Microsoft's Web site, or specify your own URL where these components can be found (see Figure 17-17). Alternatively, you can choose to include the files in the cab generated by the *Package and Deployment Wizard*, in which case they are statically included in the cab you are creating and are sourced from your own machine. This is the default option. Note that each file requires a choice independently. You can choose to have some files included in the cab you are creating, while others are downloaded from the Microsoft Web site, while still others are downloaded from an alternate Web site.

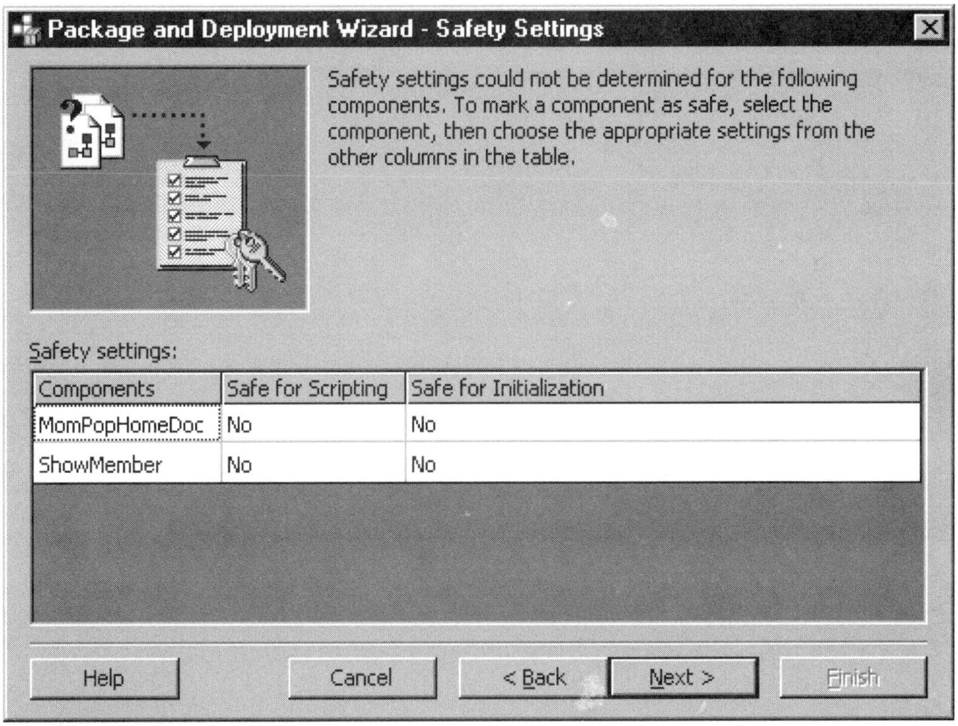

FIGURE 17-18 In the above-illustrated *Package and Deployment Wizard* step, you can assure the user that your code is safe for *initialization* and *scripting*.

To assure the end-user that your code is safe, mark each component as *Safe for Initialization* and *Safe for Scripting* (see Figure 17-18). This is a "promise" to the end-user that your component will not be responsible for harmful effects on the target system. Naturally, this does nothing to actually make your code safe. Basically, you are indicating that you have tested the code, and to your knowledge it is safe to download.

Upon completion of this, the final step, the *Package and Deployment Wizard* will create an HTML document that will contain the necessary code to download and activate your ActiveX Document. Once you've provided a link to this HTML from an intranet page, you will have provided a way for clients to download and activate the application. If you later modify the application, be sure to increment its version number and rebuild an Internet download setup with the *Package and Deployment Wizard*. Each time your user points their browser to the generated HTML, any new versions of the application are downloaded to the client's computer.

EIGHTEEN

The Internet Transfer and Web Browser Controls

Moving up a level from the *WinSock* control discussed in Chapter 4, you may find use for the *Microsoft Internet Transfer* control and/or *Web Browser* control. The **Internet Transfer control** provides programmatic access to HTML and other popular Internet protocols, including FTP. The **Web Browser control** goes much further, allowing you to embed an HTML browser in your application.

The Microsoft Internet Transfer Control

The *Microsoft Internet Transfer control* provides an application with easy access to the most widely used protocols on the Internet, including the Hypertext Transfer Protocol (HTTP) and the File Transfer Protocol (FTP). Using the HTTP protocol, you can connect to World Wide Web servers to retrieve HTML documents. With the FTP protocol, you can log on to FTP servers to download and upload files. The **UserName** and **Password** properties of the *Internet Transfer* control allow you to log on to private servers that require authentication.

The *Internet Transfer* control is not a Web browser tool. As its name implies, it is used solely to transfer data using the HTTP or FTP protocol. HTML is text. It must be formatted to display it graphically. This is one of the tasks that a Web browser does, and such functionality can be included in your application if you use the *Web Browser* control, covered later in this chapter. Use the *Internet Transfer* control for transferring data over the *Internet* or intranet. It is especially useful for automating FTP transfers.

Using the Internet Transfer Control

To begin using the *Microsoft Internet Transfer control* in an application, you must add the component *Microsoft Internet Controls* to your application. The *Microsoft Internet Transfer control* gives your program the ability to retrieve data using the HTTP, Secure HTTP, and FTP protocols. Generally, the Uniform Resource Locator (URL) determines the type of protocol used. For example, the URL *http://www.microsoft.com* requests the HTTP protocol. As another example, the URL *ftp://ftp.microsoft.com* requests the FTP protocol.

Data transmission starts when you invoke the **OpenURL** method of the *Internet Transfer* control. The method returns the data as a return value. For example,

```
Text1.Text = Inet1.OpenURL ("http://www.microsoft.com")
```

After opening the URL, you can read the **Protocol** property of the *Internet Transfer* control to determine what the protocol is (this property can also be set before invoking *OpenURL*). Protocol property constants are listed in Table 18-1. Be aware that transferring via HTTP brings back HTML, which is text. There's a big difference between viewing HTML as text and viewing it in a Web browser, which formats the HTML graphically. To view HTML graphically, use either the *Web browser* control or use automation with *Internet Explorer.* The use of the *Web browser* control is covered later in this chapter; see Chapter 10 for information on how to use automation to control *Internet Explorer.* You'll probably find the *Internet Transfer* control more

TABLE 18-1	Protocol Property Constants	
Protocol Property Value	**Constant**	**Indicates**
0	*icUnknown*	Unknown protocol.
1	*icDefault*	Default protocol.
2	*icFTP*	File Transfer Protocol (FTP).
3	*icGopher*	Gopher protocol.
4	*icHTTP*	Hypertext Transfer Protocol (HTTP).
5	*icHTTPS*	Secure HTTP.

appropriate for automating FTP file transfers. For example, you may want to transfer information in a file to a server (or vice-versa) on a regular basis (hourly, nightly, etc.). You can easily do this with a Visual Basic program that uses the *Internet Transfer* control to automate the FTP transfer. You can also get the contents of the HTTP header, if that interests you, by invoking the **GetHeader** method of the *Internet Transfer* control. This method returns the HTTP header, which is in text format.

Using the HTTP Protocol with the Internet Transfer Control

To transfer HTML text using the HTTP protocol and *Internet Transfer* control, invoke the **OpenURL** method, specifying the URL as the method's parameter. The *OpenURL* method returns the HTML as text. You can also retrieve the HTTP header, using **GetHeader**.

The *InetXFER* demo program (see Figure 18-1), located in folder *VB6Adv\Demos\InetXfer*, demonstrates displaying the raw HTTP protocol information from a Web page. The same demo program illustrates transferring files using the FTP protocol from the *Internet Transfer* control. The code to open a URL and display both the returned HTTP protocol information and header is as follows:

```
Private Sub cmdGo_Click()
    On Error GoTo goerror

    txtDocument.Text = Inet1.OpenURL(txtURL.Text)
    txtHeader.Text = Inet1.GetHeader
    Exit Sub

goerror:
    MsgBox Err.Description
End Sub
```

| **FIGURE 18-1** | The demo program can be used to view HTML and HTTP headers, as well as test FTP commands. |

FTP and the Internet Transfer Control

The ***File Transfer Protocol*** (FTP) is used to transfer files from one host to another on a network. FTP is useful for transferring files between different operating systems, such as between UNIX and Windows. There is a very large base of public FTP sites. To transfer data to or from an FTP site, you can use the *FTP.EXE* program that comes with Windows.

Another alternative is to use your Web browser. HTTP can also be used to transfer files from a remote computer to yours. However, HTTP cannot transfer a file to a remote system from yours. Only FTP can do that. You may find an FTP site that contains information that is updated on a regular basis. Using the *Internet Transfer* control, you can create a Visual Basic application that automates the retrieval of a file using the FTP protocol. To use FTP, you execute FTP commands, such as the ***Get*** command, which is used to copy a file from the remote host to your system. There is also, for example, a ***Dir*** command (lists the contents of a folder), and a ***CD*** command (change directory). FTP commands are listed in Table 18-2.

Some FTP sites allow anonymous access, while others require a username and password. The *Internet Transfer* control has a ***Username*** property and a ***Password*** property for this purpose. By default, the *Internet Transfer* control uses a username of *anonymous* and a password of your *email address*, which is the traditional way an anonymous user uses FTP.

When using the *Internet Transfer* control, you execute FTP commands by invoking the ***Execute*** method, which takes both the URL and the FTP command as string parameters. The *Execute* method returns immediately, before finishing the transfer. Your program does not stall waiting for the command to be executed. To determine when the command completes, you need to create a handler for the ***StateChanged*** event. The event procedure is passed a single parameter, ***State***. When this value is ***icResponse-Completed,*** you know the command has finished executing. Some FTP commands, such as ***Dir***, return data back to you, which can be retrieved using the ***GetChunk*** method of the *Internet Transfer* control. This method takes a single parameter, the number of bytes you want to retrieve from the response. Use *0* to indicate all data. For example,

```
Private Sub cmdDirectory_Click()
    Inet1.Execute "ftp://ftp.uci.com", "Dir"
End Sub


Private Sub cmdGetFile_Click()
   Inet1.Execute "ftp://ftp.uci.com", _
                "Get readme.txt C:\readme.txt"
End Sub


Private Sub Inet1_StateChanged (ByVal State As Integer)

    ' See if state is "response complete."
    ' If so, execute GetChunk.  This returns the
    ' directory list and stores it in the text box.
    ' GetChunk has no effect, but is safe to execute,
    ' when the Get command completes.

    If State = icResponseCompleted Then
       txtDir.Text = Inet1.GetChunk(0)
    End If

End Sub
```

TABLE 18-2	FTP Commands

FTP Command	Description
CD directory	Changes to specified directory.
CDUP	Goes up a level in the directory.
CLOSE	Closes the FTP connection.
DELETE file	Deletes specified file.
DIR [name] LS [name]	Searches the directory for the specified file. If no file is specified, the command asks for a full list of files in the current directory. The remote host determines the format for wildcards. You must use *GetChunk* to retrieve the list of files.
GET srcfile destfile RECV srcfile destfile	Retrieves remote file, srcfile, and copies to local file, destfile.
MKDIR dirname	Creates the specified directory.
PUT srcfile destfile SEND srcfile destfile	Copies local file, srcfile, to remote file, destfile.
PWD	Prints working directory. Uses *GetChunk* to retrieve the string of the current working directory.
RENAME file1 file2	Renames *file1* to *file2*.
RMDIR fidname	Removes specified directory.

The Web Browser Control

You can add features of a Web browser by using the *Microsoft Web Browser* control. The *Web Browser* control is actually an integral part of *Microsoft Internet Explorer* and is installed along with it. With the *Web Browser* control, you can provide all the features of a Web browser, which are embedded in your application.

The *Web Browser* control has properties and methods for displaying HTML pages (formatted graphically, just like the *Internet Explorer*), and for navigating around Web sites. However, visually, the *Web Browser* control is not much more than a picture box. You'll have to add buttons, menus, and/or toolbars to your application to provide users with a way of control the Web browser. An alternative to using the *Web Browser* control is to "drive" the *Internet Explorer* application using automation. This technique is presented in Chapter 10. Using the *Web Browser* control, you can develop your own user interface for a Web browser, or use it to control the seamless movement between local and Web content. The main distinction is that the *Web Browser* control has no user interface elements to control it. Use the *Web Browser* control when you want to provide features of a browser in an embedded format; that is, presented from within your application. Since the *Web Browser* control does not include menus, toolbars, or other user interface elements, these may need to be added. But don't get too carried away and invent an entirely new Web browser—if this is what you're trying to do, it may be more appropriate to use the automation interface of *Internet Explorer.*

Getting Started with the Web Browser Control

The *Web Browser* control is installed when you install *Internet Explorer,* and is implemented in the file *SHDOCVW.DLL.* To add a *Web Browser* control to your form, insert the component *Microsoft Internet Controls.* Important properties, events, and methods are listed in Table 18-3 to help you get started.

TABLE 18-3   Properties, Methods, and Events of the WebBrowser Control

Type	Name	Description
Event	NavigateComplete	Fires when a new hyperlink is being navigated to. Passes URL as string parameter.
Event	DownloadBegin	Fires when the downloading of a page has started.
Event	DownloadComplete	Fires when the downloading of a page is complete.
Event	ProgressChange	Fires during download progress. Passes *Progress* and *ProgressMax* as long integers. Useful for updating a *Progress Indicator* control.
Event	TitleChange	Fires when document title changes; passes title as text string.
Property	Busy	Queries to see if something is still in progress.
Property	LocationName	Gets the UI-friendly name of the URL currently being viewed.
Property	LocationURL	Gets the full URL of the page currently being viewed.
Method	GoBack	Navigates to the previous item in the history list.
Method	GoForward	Navigates tot he next item in the history list.
Method	GoHome	Navigates to the home/start page.
Method	GoSearch	Navigates to the search page.
Method	Navigate	Navigates to the given URL or file.

EXAMPLE: USING THE WEB BROWSER CONTROL

The sample application, *Browser.VBP*, located in folder *VB6Adv\Demos\Browser*, is shown running in Figure 18-2. A partial listing of code from that demo follows:

```
Private Sub cmdGo_Click()
    WebBrowser1.Navigate txtURL.Text
End Sub

Private Sub cmdReload_Click()
    WebBrowser1.Refresh
End Sub

Private Sub cmdStop_Click()
    WebBrowser1.Stop
End Sub

Private Sub WebBrowser1_BeforeNavigate _
        (ByVal URL As String, _
         ByVal Flags As Long, _
         ByVal TargetFrameName As String, _
             PostData As Variant, _
         ByVal Headers As String, _
             Cancel As Boolean)
    txtURL.Text = URL
End Sub

Private Sub WebBrowser1_StatusTextChange _
        (ByVal Text As String)
    lblStatus = "Status: " & Text
End Sub
```

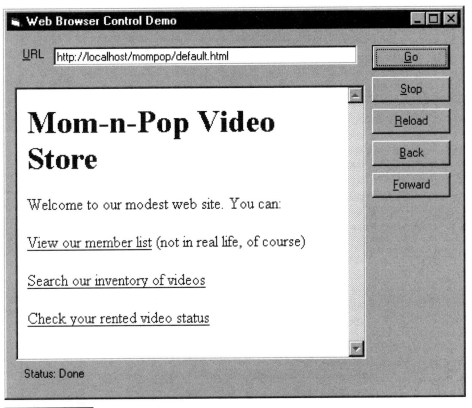

FIGURE 18-2 The demo application uses the *Web Browser* control to illustrate how to embed Web browsing capabilities into a Visual Basic application.

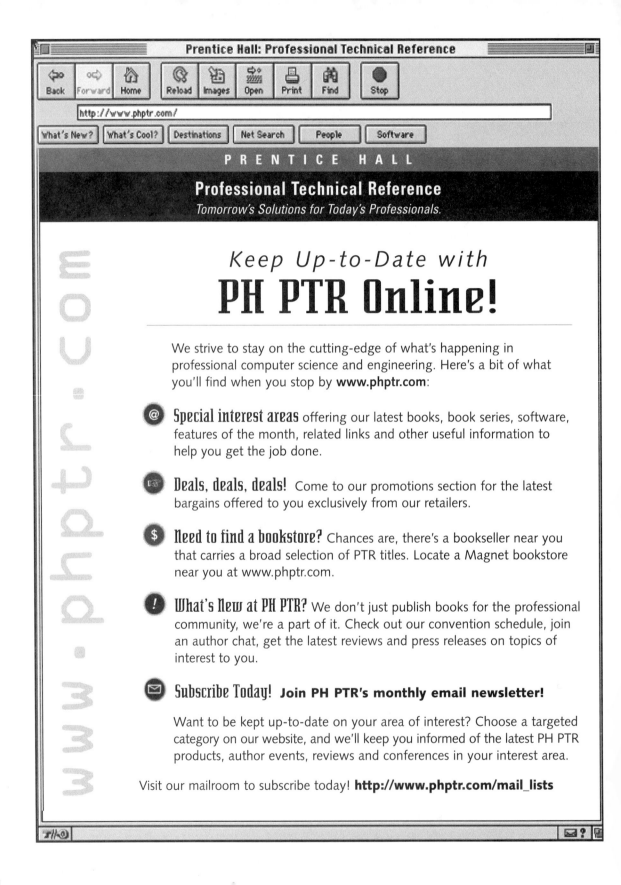

LICENSE AGREEMENT AND LIMITED WARRANTY

READ THE FOLLOWING TERMS AND CONDITIONS CAREFULLY BEFORE OPENING THIS DISK PACKAGE. THIS LEGAL DOCUMENT IS AN AGREEMENT BETWEEN YOU AND PRENTICE-HALL, INC. (THE "COMPANY"). BY OPENING THIS SEALED DISK PACKAGE, YOU ARE AGREEING TO BE BOUND BY THESE TERMS AND CONDITIONS. IF YOU DO NOT AGREE WITH THESE TERMS AND CONDITIONS, DO NOT OPEN THE DISK PACKAGE. PROMPTLY RETURN THE UNOPENED DISK PACKAGE AND ALL ACCOMPANYING ITEMS TO THE PLACE YOU OBTAINED THEM FOR A FULL REFUND OF ANY SUMS YOU HAVE PAID.

1. **GRANT OF LICENSE:** In consideration of your payment of the license fee, which is part of the price you paid for this product, and your agreement to abide by the terms and conditions of this Agreement, the Company grants to you a nonexclusive right to use and display the copy of the enclosed software program (hereinafter the "SOFTWARE") on a single computer (i.e., with a single CPU) at a single location so long as you comply with the terms of this Agreement. The Company reserves all rights not expressly granted to you under this Agreement.

2. **OWNERSHIP OF SOFTWARE:** You own only the magnetic or physical media (the enclosed disks) on which the SOFTWARE is recorded or fixed, but the Company retains all the rights, title, and ownership to the SOFTWARE recorded on the original disk copy(ies) and all subsequent copies of the SOFTWARE, regardless of the form or media on which the original or other copies may exist. This license is not a sale of the original SOFTWARE or any copy to you.

3. **COPY RESTRICTIONS:** This SOFTWARE and the accompanying printed materials and user manual (the "Documentation") are the subject of copyright. You may not copy the Documentation or the SOFTWARE, except that you may make a single copy of the SOFTWARE for backup or archival purposes only. You may be held legally responsible for any copying or copyright infringement which is caused or encouraged by your failure to abide by the terms of this restriction.

4. **USE RESTRICTIONS:** You may not network the SOFTWARE or otherwise use it on more than one computer or computer terminal at the same time. You may physically transfer the SOFTWARE from one computer to another provided that the SOFTWARE is used on only one computer at a time. You may not distribute copies of the SOFTWARE or Documentation to others. You may not reverse engineer, disassemble, decompile, modify, adapt, translate, or create derivative works based on the SOFTWARE or the Documentation without the prior written consent of the Company.

5. **TRANSFER RESTRICTIONS:** The enclosed SOFTWARE is licensed only to you and may not be transferred to any one else without the prior written consent of the Company. Any unauthorized transfer of the SOFTWARE shall result in the immediate termination of this Agreement.

6. **TERMINATION:** This license is effective until terminated. This license will terminate automatically without notice from the Company and become null and void if you fail to comply with any provisions or limitations of this license. Upon termination, you shall destroy the Documentation and all copies of the SOFTWARE. All provisions of this Agreement as to warranties, limitation of liability, remedies or damages, and our ownership rights shall survive termination.

7. **MISCELLANEOUS:** This Agreement shall be construed in accordance with the laws of the United States of America and the State of New York and shall benefit the Company, its affiliates, and assignees.

8. **LIMITED WARRANTY AND DISCLAIMER OF WARRANTY:** The Company warrants that the SOFTWARE, when properly used in accordance with the Documentation, will operate in substantial conformity with the description of the SOFTWARE set forth in the Documentation. The Company does not warrant that the SOFTWARE will meet your requirements or that the operation of the SOFTWARE will be uninterrupted or error-free. The Company warrants that the media on which the SOFTWARE is delivered shall be free from defects in materials and workmanship under normal use for a period of thirty (30) days from the date of your purchase. Your only remedy and the Company's only obligation under these limited warranties is, at the Company's option, return of the warranted item for a refund of any amounts paid by you or replacement of the item. Any replacement of SOFTWARE or media under the warranties shall not extend the original warranty period. The limited warranty set forth above shall not apply to any SOFTWARE which the Company determines in good faith has been subject to misuse, neglect, improper installation, repair, alteration, or damage by you. EXCEPT FOR THE EXPRESSED WARRANTIES SET FORTH ABOVE, THE COMPANY DISCLAIMS ALL WARRANTIES, EXPRESS OR IMPLIED, INCLUDING WITHOUT LIMITATION, THE IMPLIED WARRANTIES OF MERCHANTABILITY AND FITNESS FOR A PARTICULAR PURPOSE. EXCEPT FOR THE EXPRESS WARRANTY SET FORTH ABOVE, THE COMPANY DOES NOT WARRANT, GUARANTEE, OR MAKE ANY REPRESENTATION REGARDING THE USE OR THE RESULTS OF THE USE OF THE SOFTWARE IN TERMS OF ITS CORRECTNESS, ACCURACY, RELIABILITY, CURRENTNESS, OR OTHERWISE.

IN NO EVENT, SHALL THE COMPANY OR ITS EMPLOYEES, AGENTS, SUPPLIERS, OR CONTRACTORS BE LIABLE FOR ANY INCIDENTAL, INDIRECT, SPECIAL, OR CONSEQUENTIAL DAMAGES ARISING OUT OF OR IN CONNECTION WITH THE LICENSE GRANTED UNDER THIS AGREEMENT, OR FOR LOSS OF USE, LOSS OF DATA, LOSS OF INCOME OR PROFIT, OR OTHER LOSSES, SUSTAINED AS A RESULT OF INJURY TO ANY PERSON, OR LOSS OF OR DAMAGE TO PROPERTY, OR CLAIMS OF THIRD PARTIES, EVEN IF THE COMPANY OR AN AUTHORIZED REPRESENTATIVE OF THE COMPANY HAS BEEN ADVISED OF THE POSSIBILITY OF SUCH DAMAGES. IN NO EVENT SHALL LIABILITY OF THE COMPANY FOR DAMAGES WITH RESPECT TO THE SOFTWARE EXCEED THE AMOUNTS ACTUALLY PAID BY YOU, IF ANY, FOR THE SOFTWARE.

SOME JURISDICTIONS DO NOT ALLOW THE LIMITATION OF IMPLIED WARRANTIES OR LIABILITY FOR INCIDENTAL, INDIRECT, SPECIAL, OR CONSEQUENTIAL DAMAGES, SO THE ABOVE LIMITATIONS MAY NOT ALWAYS APPLY. THE WARRANTIES IN THIS AGREEMENT GIVE YOU SPECIFIC LEGAL RIGHTS AND YOU MAY ALSO HAVE OTHER RIGHTS WHICH VARY IN ACCORDANCE WITH LOCAL LAW.

ACKNOWLEDGMENT

YOU ACKNOWLEDGE THAT YOU HAVE READ THIS AGREEMENT, UNDERSTAND IT, AND AGREE TO BE BOUND BY ITS TERMS AND CONDITIONS. YOU ALSO AGREE THAT THIS AGREEMENT IS THE COMPLETE AND EXCLUSIVE STATEMENT OF THE AGREEMENT BETWEEN YOU AND THE COMPANY AND SUPERSEDES ALL PROPOSALS OR PRIOR AGREEMENTS, ORAL, OR WRITTEN, AND ANY OTHER COMMUNICATIONS BETWEEN YOU AND THE COMPANY OR ANY REPRESENTATIVE OF THE COMPANY RELATING TO THE SUBJECT MATTER OF THIS AGREEMENT.

Should you have any questions concerning this Agreement or if you wish to contact the Company for any reason, please contact in writing at the address below.

Robin Short
Prentice Hall PTR
One Lake Street, Upper Saddle River, New Jersey 07458

About the CD-ROM

Overview

The accompanying CD-ROM contains the complete source code for all examples appearing in this book, as well as a README.TXT file, which contains the latest information regarding the contents of the CD-ROM. All examples are packaged into Microsoft Visual Basic 6.0 project files, with the exception of one sample program that is written using Microsoft Visual C++ 6.0. The required DLLs for running the C++ sample program are also contained on the CD-ROM, so having Visual C++ installed on your computer is not required. Review the file README.TXT for additional information.

System Description

Many of the sample programs included on the CD-ROM will run under Microsoft Windows 95/98 with the Professional Edition of Microsoft Visual Basic 6.0. This includes the 2-tier version of the Mom-n-Pop Video Store sample program. However, the 3-tier version of the Mom-n-Pop Video Store sample program requires, in addition to Microsoft Visual Basic 6.0, Windows NT 4.0 (Server or Workstation, Service Pack 4 recommended), MTS 1.0 or later (2.0 or later recommended), and SQL Server 6.5 or later (samples have been successfully tested with SQL Server 7.0). In order to run the Web demonstration programs, you will also need Microsoft IIS. Note that, with the exception of Windows NT and SQL Server, all the required software components are included in the Enterprise Edition of Microsoft Visual Basic 6.0.

How to use the CD-ROM

If you wish, you may copy the folder VB6ADV from the CD-ROM to your hard drive. If you use this procedure, the source code for all the examples will be copied to your hard drive. This will require less than 15 MB of disk space. Alternatively, you may copy individual examples as you wish to review and experiment with them. Although it is not specifically required, it is recommended that you preserve the same relative directory structure on your hard drive as on the CD-ROM. Many of the examples are ready to run. However, some examples, in particular the n-tier versions of the Mom-n-Pop Video Store, require significant setup. You can find instructions for setting up these examples in the text.

Operating Systems

Most of the demonstration programs will run under Windows 95/98. However, the 3-tier sample program requires Windows NT 4.0 Workstation or Server, and MTS. Windows NT Service Pack 3 is required; Service Pack 4 is recommended.

For More Information

The author will post errata and frequently asked questions on his Web page, http://www.jmalco.com. Any errors will be posted to http://www.jmalco.com/vberrata.htm. You will be able to find a list of frequently asked questions at http://www.jmalco.com/faq.htm. To report problems or ask a question, please send email to vbook@jmalco.com. Also, be sure to read the text of this book and the README.TXT file on the CD-ROM for information about the sample programs.

Technical Support

Prentice Hall does not offer technical support for the software on the CD-ROM. However, if there is a problem with the CD, you may obtain a replacement copy by sending an email describing your problem to:

discexchange@phptr.com